P9-DMQ-652

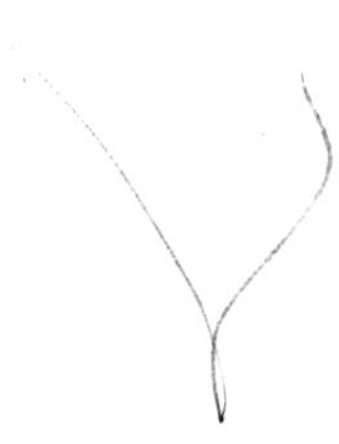

# RENAISSANCE

ANDREW GRAHAM-DIXON

# RENAISSANCE

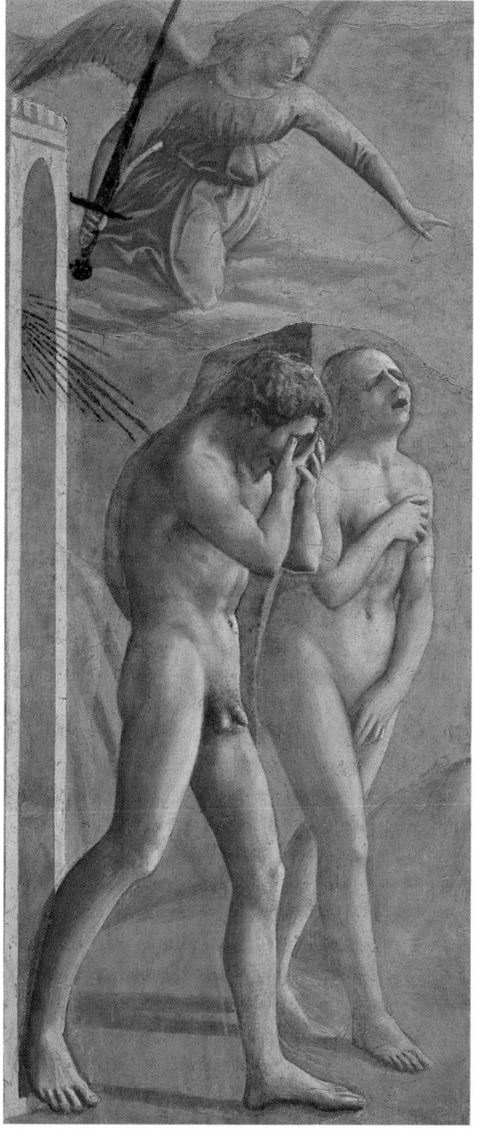

1 MASACCIO *Expulsion from Paradise* mid-1420s



UNIVERSITY OF CALIFORNIA PRESS
BERKELEY LOS ANGELES

*For Sabine, my wife,*
*and for Isabelle Mary, my friend,*
*both of whom I met at the beginning,*
*in Florence, and who are with me still;*
*and for my mother and father,*
*who sent me on this journey*
*in the first place.*

This book is published to accompany the television series
*Renaissance*, produced by the BBC in 1999
Executive Producer: Nicholas Rossiter
Series Producer: Jamie Muir
Producers: John Bush, Jamie Muir,
Roger Parsons, Tim Robinson, Paul Tickell

University of California Press
Berkeley and Los Angeles, California
Published by arrangement with BBC Worldwide Ltd



ISBN 0-520-22375-6



Commissioning Editor: Sheila Ableman
Project Editor: Lara Speicher
Copy Editor: Ruth Thackeray
Designer: Linda Blakemore
Picture Researcher: Bella Henman

Set in Bembo by BBC Books
Printed and bound in France by Imprimerie Pollina s.a.
Colour separations by Radstock Reproductions Ltd, Midsomer Norton
Jacket printed by Imprimerie Pollina s.a.

9 8 7 6 5 4 3 2 1

# CONTENTS

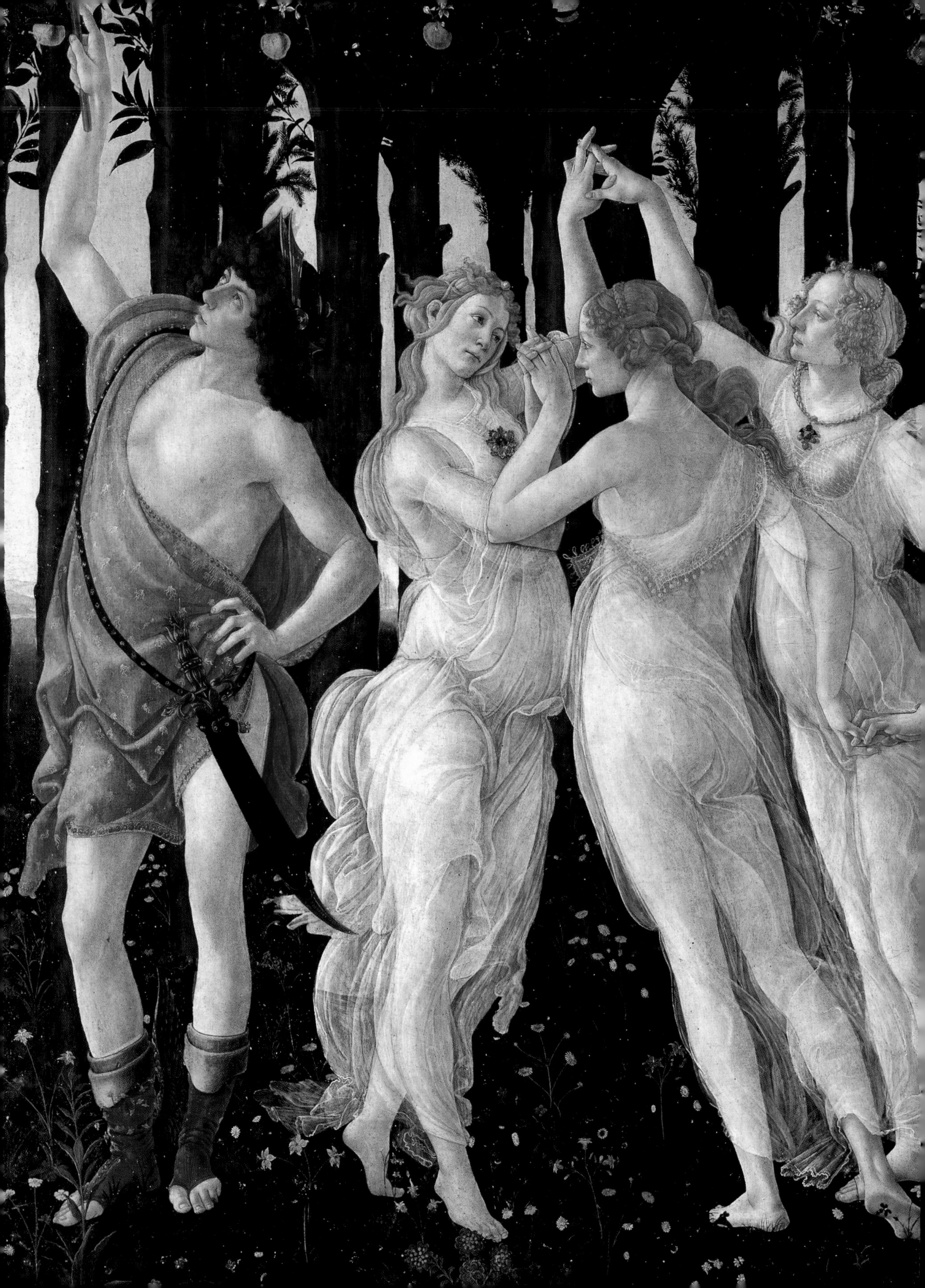

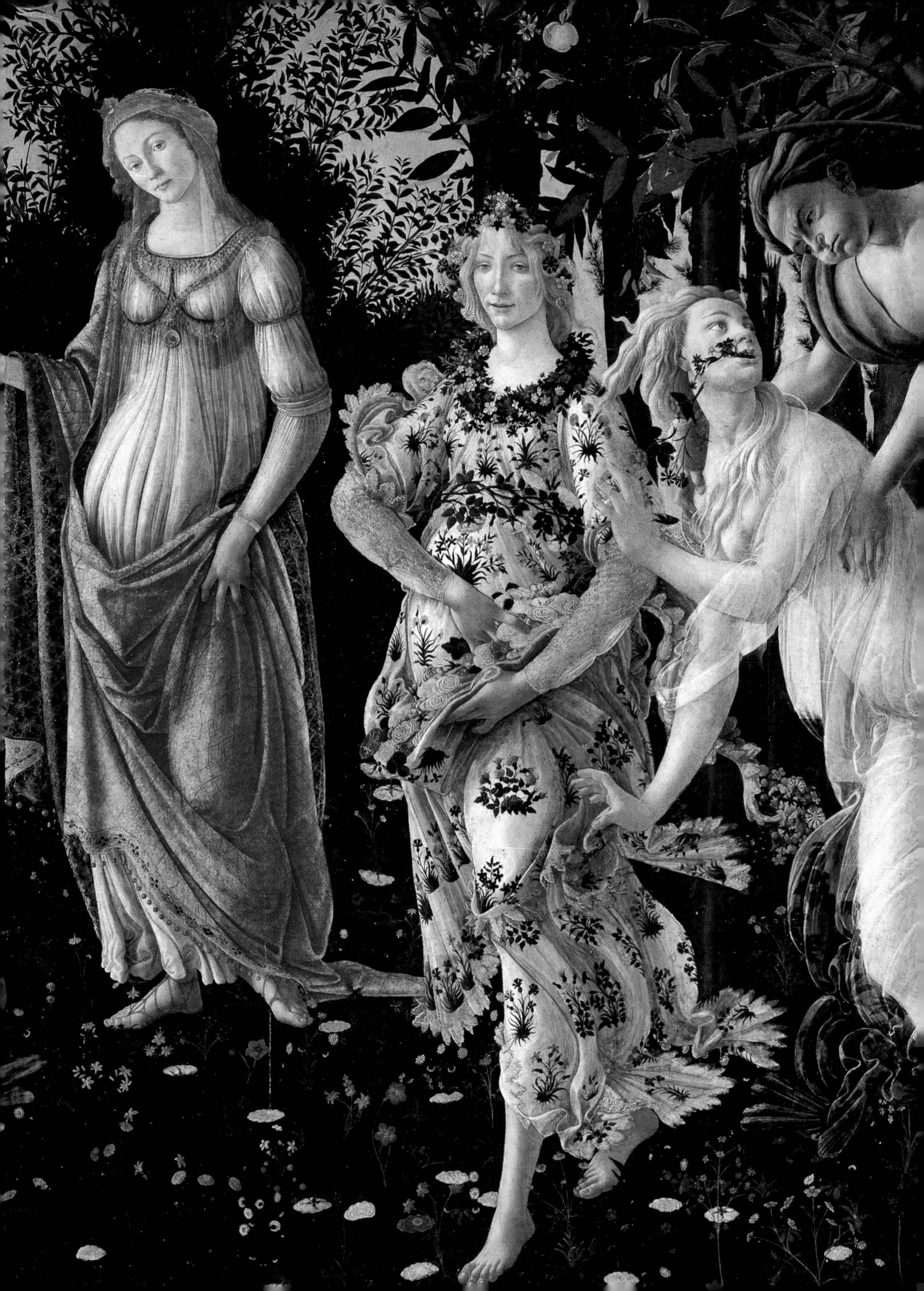

# FOREWORD

Like its predecessor, *A History of British Art*, this book was commissioned by the British Broadcasting Corporation, and a six-part television series has been produced out of its six chapters. Although certain textbook views of the Renaissance come under discussion in the pages that follow I have not, myself, set out to write a textbook. What follows is a collection of six essays or explorations, arranged in more or less chronological order. In their collage-like way they are an attempt to synthesize a vast subject into some kind of coherent narrative.

In each chapter I concentrate on a different aspect of Renaissance civilization. Chapter One is about its mixed origins and essentially impure character. Chapter Two is about the contribution of fifteenth-century Florence and its artists to the development of Western thought and art. Chapter Three is an investigation of the genesis of the idea of genius, as well as a meditation on the challenges which that emerging idea posed to artists and society. Chapter Four explores the relationship between the Renaissance and the Reformation, often (wrongly, in my view) treated as separate phenomena. Chapter Five is an examination of Venice, the most unusual and, perhaps, the quintessential Renaissance city. In Chapter Six I attempt to give a few answers to the question of how the Renaissance came to an end, if indeed it did, and I speculate on some aspects of its legacy. I have been guided throughout by my own enthusiasms and instincts.

Throughout the book I view the Renaissance primarily, but not exclusively, through the prism of its art and architecture. I think this approach – which is hardly novel – is justified by the nature of the subject. It was through the medium of art that Renaissance man expressed himself most vividly and, perhaps, most profoundly. Close contemplation of Renaissance art and architecture naturally forces the mind outwards, to address issues larger than those of aesthetics or artistic technique alone. In discussing, say, Giotto, I have found myself talking about Francis of Assisi and the revolution in piety which he and other mendicant friars helped to bring about; in discussing Mantegna I have found myself talking about Machiavelli, and his disenchanted view of politics. The consideration of particular works of art has frequently led me to a broader consideration of those forces - intellectual, moral, social, political - which helped to shape the world in which we live.

Like *A History of British Art* - although perhaps in a slightly gentler, less polemical way – this book attempts to present a series of arguments about the past and why we should be interested in it. Those arguments have been structured to coincide with itineraries. Each chapter is a journey as well as an essay, so that almost everything I have to say is said with a particular location, or object, in mind. This structure has been determined, to a certain extent, by the nature of television, which requires that for every thought there needs also be a visible (filmable) scene or subject. While some authors might feel this an onerous restriction, I have found it a useful discipline. I find it helpful to have to tether my thoughts to things.

I have incurred numerous debts in the course of writing this book. My colleagues and friends at the BBC have worked with tireless dedication to help me to develop and realize the picture of the Renaissance which it presents. Paul Tickell, who directed the corresponding programmes in the television series, played a highly significant part in developing and reorientating the arguments presented in Chapters One and Three. John 'Jacob Burckhardt'

2 (PREVIOUS PAGES) SANDRO BOTTICELLI *Primavera* (detail) *c.* 1482

Bush forced me to clarify my ideas about Florence. I hope I clarified them enough. Tim Robinson and Roger Parsons, who directed the fourth and sixth programmes in the series, also helped me to develop the corresponding chapters. Emma Laybourne, who was also the researcher-in-chief on *A History of British Art*, helped to supply many yawning gaps in my knowledge and contributed a multitude of ideas. Francis Whately synthesized an enormous mass of material on papal Rome and early sixteenth-century Northern Europe. Victoria Page researched Chapter Five with exemplary efficiency, clarity and enthusiasm.

Nicholas Rossiter, my Executive Producer, has been hugely helpful and usefully iconoclastic. Rosemarie Bradford has wielded the whip with a smile and worked harder than anyone should. Many thanks also to Kim Evans. It was a pleasure to work once more with Luke Cardiff, the principal cameraman on *Renaissance* and his team, who opened my eyes to much that I had overlooked: Mike Sarah, Louie 'Carpet Channel' Caulfield, Godfrey 'Sit on My Boat' Evans. Thanks too to Rudy 'Film Star' Montagnani and to Spike Geilinger, Chris Hartley and their teams. *Mille grazie* to Rosemary Plumb, Pat Liani Weston, Francesca Boesch and Carol Snook, for finding so many lost keys, rousing so many sacristans, and cutting through so much red tape.

Special thanks too to Jamie Muir, Series Producer and director of Programme Five, who has been my chief running mate in the marathon of getting this book and the accompanying television series written. I don't know anyone else who could have done the job that he did – let alone with such good humour and such exemplary humanity.

This book has benefited greatly from conversations which I, and fellow members of the production team, have had with the following: Iain Buchanan, David Buckton, Peter Burke, Bruce Boucher, Francesco Buranelli, Lorne Campbell, Joanna Cannon, Georgia Clarke, Richard Cocke, Charles Cooper, Robin Cormack, Jill Dunkerton, Gabrielli Finaldi, Craig Harbison, Bridget Heal, Sandy Heslop, Paul Hills, Martin Holman, Charles Hope, Deborah Howard, Maurice Howard, Peter Humfrey, Sachiko Kusukawa, John Lowden, Elizabeth McGrath, Nicholas Penny, Catherine Reynolds, Patricia Rubin, Ruth Rubinstein, Antje Schmitt, Christine Shaw, Paul Taylor, Simon Thurley, Thomas Tuohy, Amanda Vickery, Evelyn Welch, John White. Thanks to all the above. Especial thanks, too, are due to Alison Cole, Derek Southall and Msgr Timothy Verdon, who in the course of three short conversations transformed my view of the early Renaissance.

At BBC Books, I would like to thank Sheila Ableman, Lara Speicher and Ruth Thackeray. The book would have been much the poorer without their editorial contributions. Many thanks too to Linda Blakemore and Pene Parker. I also owe a great debt to David Ekserdjian, who, in his capacity as Banana-skin Remover in Chief, helped to purge my original manuscript of a multitude of errors. Notwithstanding all his efforts, a certain number of mistakes have been allowed to remain in the text, as a gesture of goodwill to those specialist art historians who may resent a journalist such as myself stepping on to their territory. Those mistakes will, I trust, be revealed when the book is reviewed.

Lastly, I must thank my family, but above all my wife Sabine, my best and chief editor, for spending so many hours reading and re-reading my manuscript, editing, cutting, restructuring, rethinking. Now that the darkness has been dispelled, I think we could all do with a bit of a *Rinascita* too.

*Andrew Graham-Dixon, July 1999*

CHAPTER ONE

# IN SEARCH OF ORIGINS

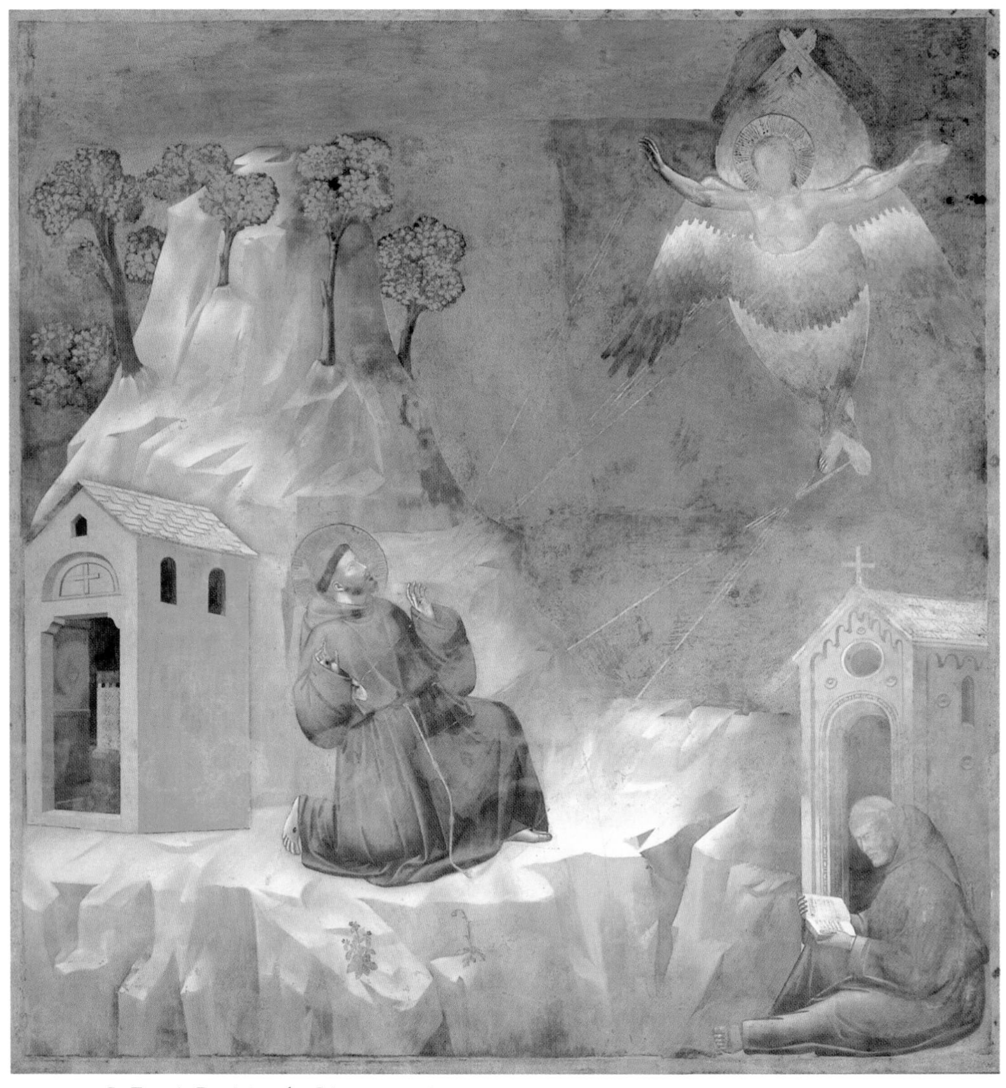

3 GIOTTO *St Francis Receiving the Stigmata* 1296–7

It is obvious that some term, descriptive of the change which began to pass over Europe, has to be adopted. That of Renaissance, Rinascimento or Renascence is sufficient for the purpose, though we have to guard against the tyranny of what is after all a metaphor. We must not suffer it to lead us into rhetoric about the deadness and the darkness of the middle ages...

Entry on 'The Renaissance', *Encyclopaedia Britannica,* Thirteenth edition, 1926

His religion was feeling; the preaching in which he revealed it worked through feeling; his relation to men and nature was conditioned by feeling. His life was a great Dithyrambus on feeling. Therein lay the explanation of his powerful influence.

HENRY THODE, *Francis of Assisi and the Beginning of the Art of the Renaissance in Italy*, 1885

## THE ROMAN ROAD

It was in Italy, surrounded by the ruins of the ancient world, that men first dreamed of reviving the spirit of classical antiquity. Spurred by the melancholy conviction that their own era was a Dark Age, they sought enlightenment in the grandeur of once mighty Greece and Rome. They hunted out ancient texts and unearthed the tangible remains of the long-lost past. They brought the language of classical architecture back into use, emulated the sculpture of the antique world and attempted to revive what they imagined the lost traditions of classical painting to have been. 'Renaissance', or *Rinascita*, in Italian, was the word coined to express their thrilling fantasy of a rebirth, of a return to the first bright dawn of civilization.

That, more or less, is the version of the Renaissance that I was taught at school. Like many of the things that one is taught at school, it is not wrong, but neither is it the full picture. Part of the problem lies in the very power of the word 'Renaissance' – which, in its rousing simplicity, offers rather too much encouragement to those who would oversimplify the past. During the course of half a millennium and more, this potent metaphor of renewal has gained widespread acceptance as a term of neutral historical description. It is now not uncommon to find an entire period, stretching from the fourteenth century to the start of the seventeenth, referred to, *en bloc*, as 'The Renaissance'. Thus has a colourful figure of speech been thrown over some three centuries of European history. Like many blanket terms it conceals much truth, mingled deceptively with certain errors and false preconcpetions.

The original textbook account of the subject was written, during the middle years of the sixteenth century, by Giorgio Vasari (1511–74). In his pioneering history of the fine arts, *The Lives of the Artists*, Vasari set out to describe what he called 'the rise of the arts to perfection, their decline and their restoration or rather renaissance'.[1] In his hands, certain myths about Renaissance civilization were also polished to a kind of perfection.

Vasari's book, while long and full of entertaining circumstantial detail, was in its broad outlines impressively clearcut. Long ago there had been the first, golden age of the ancients, a time when, in Greece and Rome, a multitude of great works of painting, sculpture and architecture had been created. This was succeeded by a period of iconoclastic destruction and loss, the chief engine of which was 'the fervent zeal of the new Christian religion'. This benighted era lasted for many centuries until, around 1300, in Tuscany, art was rescued by a group of enlightened individuals who went back to the models of antiquity and to a more naturalistic portrayal of the world. Giotto, pupil of Cimabue, was the first of such men. Then came the generation of Florentines led by Donatello. Finally, art was brought to perfection by 'the divine' Michelangelo – Vasari's own mentor.

Vasari's view of the patterns of historical and art historical development is still extraordinarily influential. But it should be treated with caution. His picture of the Renaissance – as a return to the pure, Greco-Roman source of higher civilization, a fresh start after more than a millennium of barbarism – is misleading in certain respects. One of its chief flaws lies in the fact that it distorts the role played by Christianity in the development of art. In stressing the dangers to art of certain types of Christian enthusiasm, Vasari failed to acknowledge adequately the other side of the coin: the positive, galvanic part played by the church in the history of art down the centuries.

Vasari's view of history also rested on a misconception of the relationship between the self-consciously new age of the Renaissance and the period which preceded it – the Dark Age, as he saw it, being a time of more or less undifferentiated ignorance and stasis, lit only by a few sparks of isolated individual genius. But in many ways it makes more sense to think of the Renaissance as a culmination rather than a rebuttal of certain medieval tendencies. It is impossible to appreciate the energies which animate a painting such as Masaccio's *Expulsion from Paradise* [1] – with its ugly, agonized, expressive figures – or a sculpture such as Donatello's *St John the Baptist* [132] – a figure of the prophet pulsating with inner mental energies – if one has been led to think of those masterpieces purely in terms of a classically inspired rejection of the medieval past. How 'medieval', indeed, such acknowledged masterpieces of 'Renaissance' art can seem.

Vasari was by no means mistaken in all his views. A profound upheaval in human sensibilities, with Italy at its epicentre, did indeed take place between the thirteenth and sixteenth centuries. It led, among other things, to the re-establishment of a classical vocabulary of architecture and to the revitalization of realistic representation in sculpture and painting. But that upheaval was not simply the product of an all-Italian love affair with antiquity. Many different cultures, together with dreams other than that of classical revival, pure and simple, played their part in it. There was more to the world of the Renaissance than *Rinascita* alone.

If no attempt is made to understand the mixed origins of Renaissance civilization, then the richness and much of the beauty of its art will remain unappreciated and misunderstood. The way back to those origins is no straight Roman road leading directly to the classical past, but a more winding and circuitous route. All roads do not lead to Rome. This one begins (and ends) in Venice.

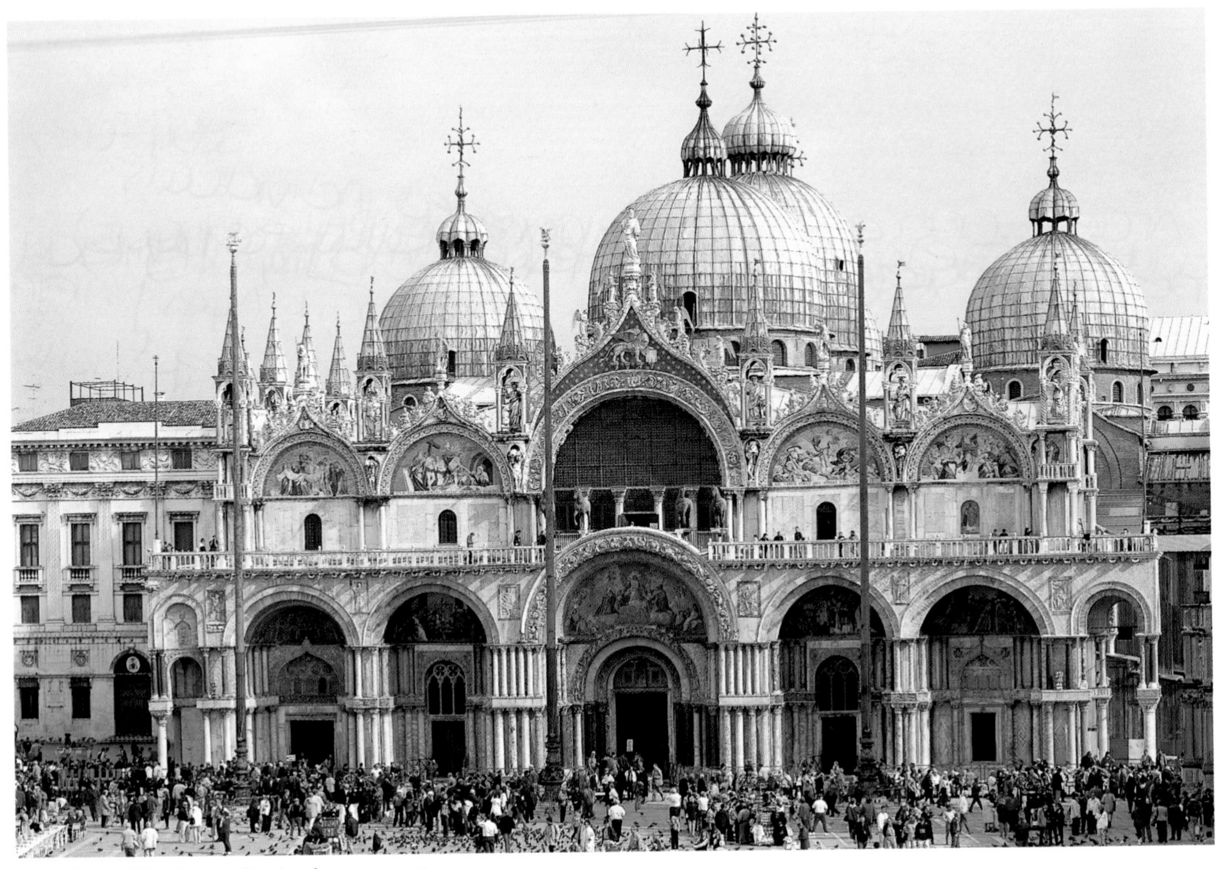

4 Basilica of San Marco, Venice, begun *c.* 1063

## ART BLEEDS

One of the most impressive monuments to the art and faith of the pre-Renaissance world is the onion-domed basilica of San Marco, in Venice [4]. Built in the late eleventh century, it was created in large measure by master craftsmen from the Byzantine Empire, in the Near East. Much restored, it remains a fundamentally Eastern church, a Hagia Sophia on the fringes of the Adriatic. It is a testament to the closeness of the contacts between Eastern and Western branches of Christianity during the time of its making. Byzantine craftsmen were highly sought after in Venice, and here they created an interior of blazing splendour.

On the inside, San Marco seems more organic than planned, a kind of cave or grotto dedicated to the overwhelming of the senses. Look down and vision loses itself in the intricacies of its patterned floor. Look up and the eye is intoxicated by the dim burnished gold of countless mosaic tesserae, figuring host upon host of impressive but hieratic saints and angels.

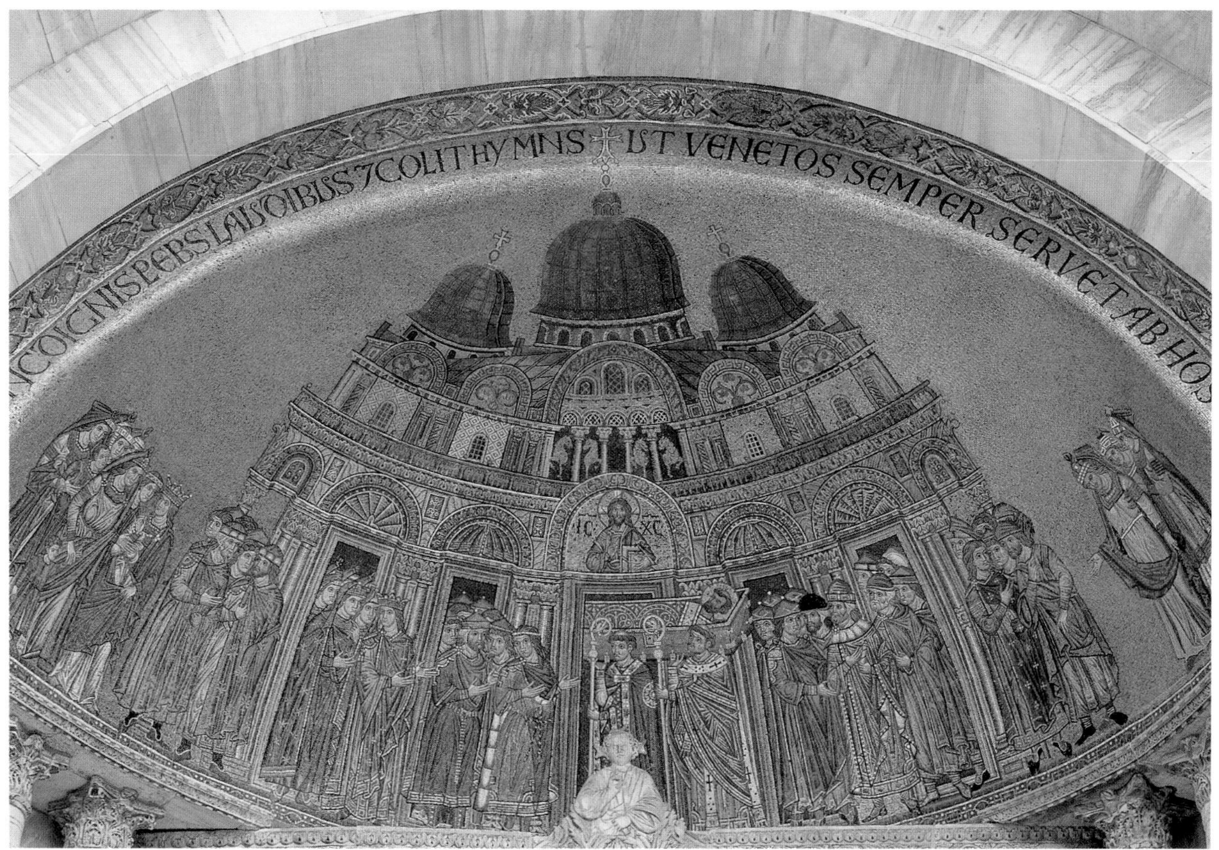


5 *Translation of the Relics of St Mark* showing *Christ Pantocrator*, basilica, San Marco, Venice *c.* 1270

The basilica expresses a theology focused, essentially, on the transcendent otherness of God – and not on the brief interval when, in the figure of the mortal Christ, he took on human form. The images of God and his saints in San Marco were created in order to conjure up the awe-inspiring and mysterious nature of heaven itself. Here, relatively little emphasis was placed on the human dimension of the Christian story. Christ was represented triumphant, as Christ Pantocrator [5], all-powerful and dauntless, the master of human destiny. Mosaic was valued for its glittering, otherworldly qualities, and considered the most appropriate medium for the depiction of sacred mysteries, precisely because it created images so far removed from representations of mundane reality. The gold of Byzantium may have derived, ultimately, from the gold of ancient Egypt, where Greco-Byzantine painters had lived and worked from ancient times. The hieratic golden transformation of the figure in Byzantine mosaics and paintings (where much gold leaf is used, in a technique known as chrysography) perhaps carries with it distant memories of the stiff and solemn gold-embossed mummies of the pharaohs.

By no means all of the art created in Italy during the course of the eleventh and twelfth centuries was as splendid as that created for the interior of San Marco. But nearly all of it did observe the same fundamentally non-naturalistic set of conventions.[2] During the thirteenth century, however, a dramatic change came over art on the Italian peninsula. Instead of depicting Christ the king, artists began to depict Christ the man, bloodied and suffering. Painting and sculpture were altered for ever. It was at this moment that the true foundation stone of Renaissance art was laid. A single charismatic individual was largely responsible for bringing Christ down to earth, and for effecting this change – not an artist, but a man sometimes referred to by his followers as *alter Christus*, 'another Christ'. He was St Francis of Assisi.

At the end of the twelfth century, when St Francis was born, Italy was in the throes of a social transformation. In the late Middle Ages the Italian peninsula was the scene of a sudden expansion in banking, trade and the textile industry. This brought with it the reconstruction of great cities, the start of a genuinely bourgeois culture and the premonitory signs of the break-up of feudal society. The process has been called the Medieval Industrial Revolution. It brought extreme wealth to some and it also altered the fabric of human experience.

During this period the first systematic recovery of urban life since the days of the Roman Empire took place. The textile industry required a considerable workforce to maintain profitable production, and cities on a large scale sprang up to serve it. This urban expansion also brought about a social crisis. Tens of thousands of impoverished rural labourers flooded towards the cities – one of the largest of which was Florence, its textile production and dyeing works served by the river Arno – where the slave wages on offer in the new industry were preferable to the complete uncertainty of life lived on the land.

There was, at the start of this process, nowhere for this horde of people to live in the old medieval rabbit warrens of streets that made up the towns of the time. Initially, they made vast rudimentary encampments outside the city walls. There was no existing mechanism for the care – and, perhaps just as important to those who employed them, the control – of such a mass of people. The church was ill equipped to minister to their needs and found itself unable to cope. It was this spiritual and social void that the mendicant friars, notably St Francis and other charismatic preachers such as his contemporary St Dominic, set out to fill. They took Christ's message to the new urban poor, huddled in their shanty towns around the city gates, as well as to the newly rich within the city walls. The friars represented a new breed of aggressive, ascetic, itinerant holy man, who went out into the world to reclaim it for God rather than retiring into enclosed monasteries to do his work.

Largely under the impetus of the Dominicans and Franciscans, during the early thirteenth century there was a church-building boom to cater for the new urban congregations. The most famous Franciscan church – the richest, the most splendidly decorated, the most frequently visited and the most hallowed – is the basilica of San Francesco, built after the saint's death in his home town of Assisi. It is also, however, the least characteristic of the great Franciscan foundations, being a shrine to an individual rather than a building designed to save and serve the masses. A much stronger sense of what St Francis and Franciscanism were truly about is conveyed by such Franciscan churches as Santa Croce in Florence [6]. These were working churches. They are big but not especially finely worked, with thin walls and simple wooden roofs. They had to be large, to accommodate the masses who came to hear the friars preach; and because their sermons had to be audible, the acoustics had to be good. Since hundreds of such buildings were needed to meet the social emergency of the time, they also had to be relatively inexpensive and quick to build. Nowadays the interior of Santa Croce is lined with splendid marble monuments to illustrious Florentines, but originally the effect would have been much plainer, all the decoration having once consisted of paintings carried out in the cheap and fast-worked medium of fresco, or coloured plaster. The traces of such work still survive in fragments around the edges of the tombs, but the best place to appreciate the original effect of the decoration is in the apse, where the original frescos remain intact, albeit faded – a world of vivid images designed to communicate the stories of the Christian faith to a congregation many of whose members could neither read nor write.

The Franciscan churches were always built on the edge of town, the better to minister to those living, in their makeshift dwellings, on the margins of the city. This can be difficult to appreciate now that the cities they once bordered have expanded to contain them. But the original relationship of church to city has been accidentally preserved in Pistoia, where the church of San Francesco is abutted by the main bus station, a large square inhabited, at night, by a population of modern transients. In Florence the links are preserved in the very architecture of Santa Croce's surroundings: the line of houses facing the church, punctured by narrow winding streets, was once the boundary of the town.

The frenzy of Franciscan church-building may be traced directly back to the events of St Francis's short life, which entered legend, thanks to his disciples, almost as soon as he had died. He was born around 1181, the son of a wealthy cloth

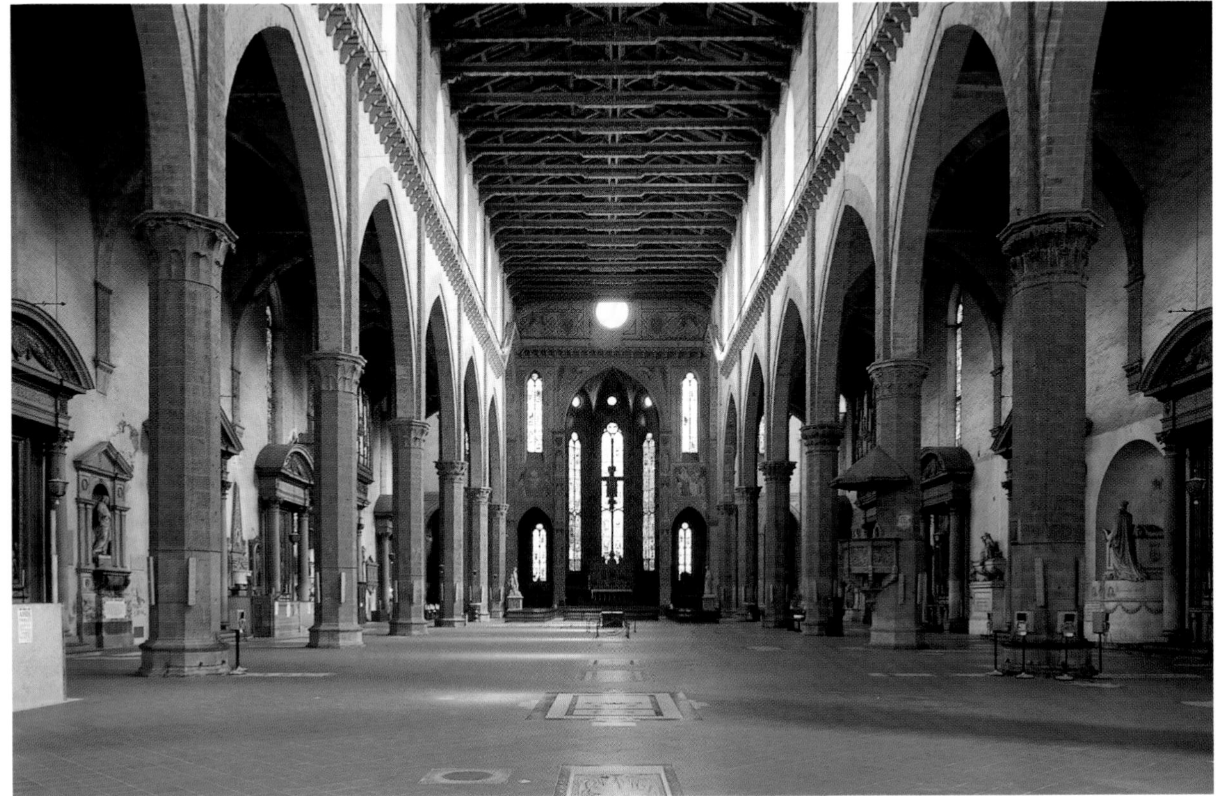

6 Interior of Santa Croce, Florence, begun 1294

merchant, but before he reached his mid-twenties he had renounced all worldly goods in order (as he put it) 'to wed Lady Poverty'. One day in 1205 he had a vision in the ruined church of San Damiano just outside Assisi. Standing in this small dark cell of a church, before a plain wooden panel painting of *Christ Triumphant upon the Cross* [8],[3] Francis experienced a vision. The figure of Christ seemed to speak to him: 'Don't you see that my house is falling down? Go and build it up again.'[4] Out of that one, small, tumbledown church, where Christ had seemed to speak, would come a host of other churches. Out of that one speaking image there would come a great flood of other images, covering the great wall spaces of Franciscan architecture.

At first, Francis acted literally on the instructions of the speaking image and began to repair ruined churches, using money derived from the sale of bales of his father's cloth. He was summoned by the Bishop of Assisi and reprimanded for damaging his father's livelihood. Francis's response was to renounce worldly goods

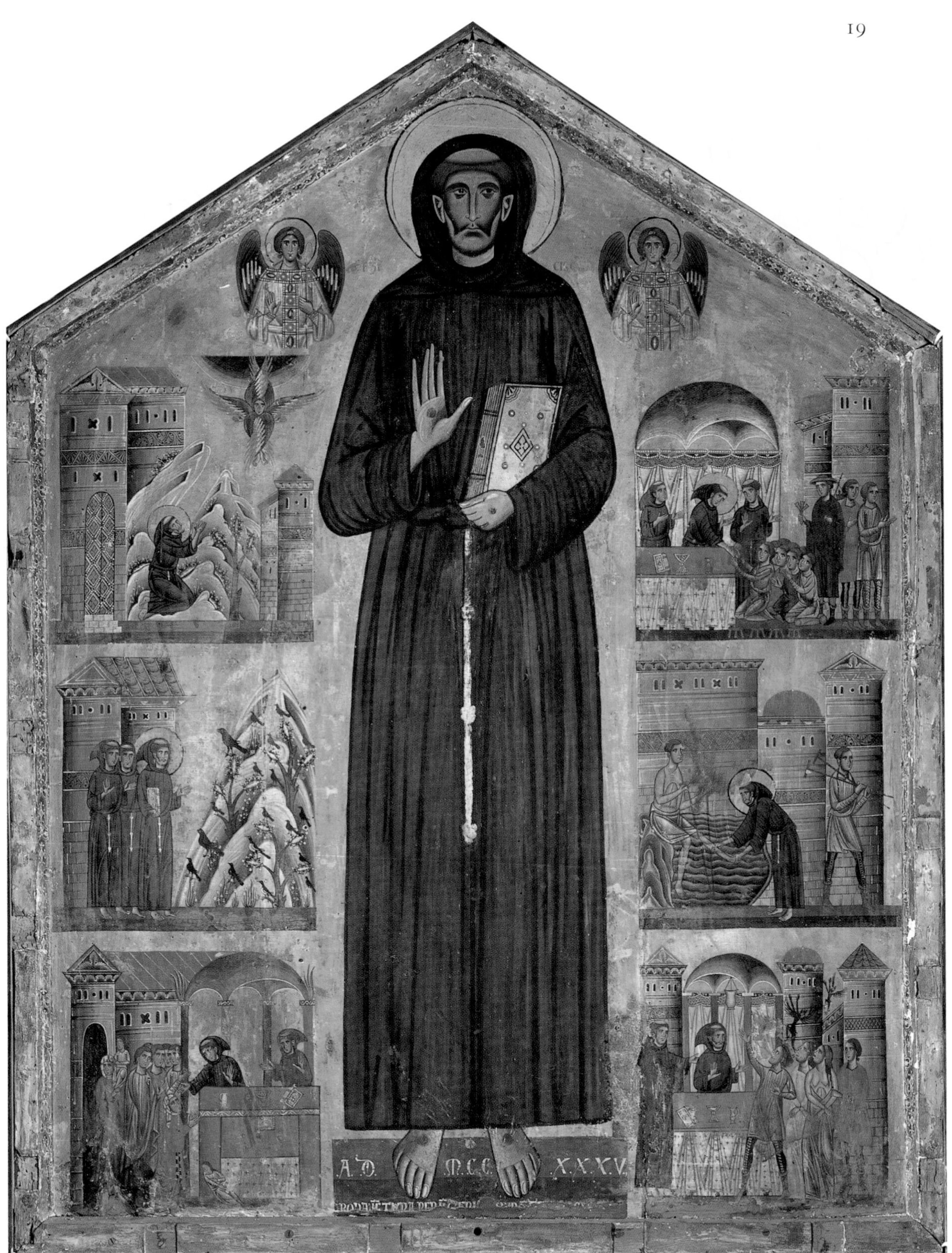


7 BONAVENTURA BERLINGHIERI *St Francis and Scenes from His Life* 1235

and his earthly father. He modelled his life, from then on, on that of the Saviour, becoming a travelling preacher. He and those who followed him adhered to strict ideals of poverty and humility, emulating Christ and his apostles.

Thomas of Celano, in the first biography of Francis, begun in 1228 (just two years after the saint's death), recalled the effect which the experience before the crucifix in San Damiano had on him: 'he found himself other than he had been when he entered … he became almost deranged … he felt that the change he had undergone was beyond expression.'[5] It is significant that Francis's first revelation should have been prompted by the sight of a work of art. He felt that images could bring men closer to God, and much of his preaching was fervently visual – acted out as well as spoken. He himself was an artist, a performer, whose existence was consecrated to the imitation of Christ in startingly vivid terms. His sermons were delivered in the plain and unadorned speech of ordinary men and punctuated by *coups de théâtre* designed to provoke a kind of visionary sympathy with the sufferings of Christ – a visceral, not merely intellectual, appreciation of the extent of God's self-sacrificing love for man. One day in the main city square of Assisi he gave a sermon on Christ's suffering to the assembled townspeople, at the end of which he asked them to remain where they were. He then went into the church of San Rufino and took off his habit, ordering one of his followers, Brother Pietro, 'to drag him naked in front of the people, with the cord he had round his neck. He commanded another friar to take a bowl filled with ash, climb onto the platform from which he had been preaching, and from there to throw and pour it onto his head.'[6]

Francis's theatricality was closely linked to his desire for a felt rather than a reasoned faith. In 1223 he was spending Christmas in a monastery near the village of Greccio, in Umbria, when he told another of his followers, Brother John Velitta: 'This Christmas I would really like to bring home to the people of Greccio what the birth of Christ at Bethlehem was like. They ought to see how poor he was, lying there on straw, with the ox and the ass beside him.'[7] Francis devised a vivid sculptural assemblage, a three-dimensional mock-up of the scene of the Nativity. He ordered a crib to be made, and had models of Joseph and Mary and the Christ child, fashioned in as lifelike a manner as possible, placed within it. On Christmas night the local people were invited to worship and they came bringing torches. Francis sang the Christmas gospel and spoke to the people of the birth of Christ and the gift of the grace of God. Those who were there noticed that every time he said the name of Jesus he seemed to fall into a trance. Every time he said the word Bethlehem he bleated like a lamb.

Francis's teaching was rooted in pathos, so he emphasized Christ at his most vulnerable, focusing on the Nativity and the Passion, baby Jesus and Christ on the Cross – an emphasis which would be followed by the Catholic church and its artists for centuries. The most extreme instance of Francis's passionate identification with Christ's suffering on the Cross is the story of his reception of the stigmata – the moment when, according to his followers, the bleeding wounds of Crucifixion were burnt into his hands and feet by a Christ-like figure who appeared to him in a vision [3].

This particular episode goes to the heart of St Francis's electrifying brand of piety. He received the stigmata when he was alone, fasting and meditating in the wilderness. But although he mortified the flesh and denied his own body, St Francis also, paradoxically, put the body, suffering and agonized though it was, centre stage. The intense physicality of so much Western art, its morbidity and its eros, may be traced in some degree back to his example.

During and immediately after the saint's own lifetime, the new piety spread by his followers worked its way into the character of art throughout the Italian peninsula. His intense identification with Christ, and with the human dimensions of the Christian story, led directly to a new and insistent physicality in Italian art. Within their own sphere of activity, painters were encouraged to do what Francis had done. They were to move their audiences, to make scripture visible and apprehensible. Francis, receiving the stigmata, had bled. Now art bled too.

The impact of the Franciscan movement on painting in Italy in the thirteenth century was most immediately and graphically apparent in pictures of Christ on the Cross. One way of seeing and thinking about the Saviour was displaced by another. Earlier Italian depictions of Christ on the Cross, such as the one in San Damiano before which Francis underwent his mystical experience, are based on the traditional triumphant images of the Italo-Byzantine style, *Christus Triumphans*, which showed a Christ who has transcended his human suffering and looks out calmly from the Cross with his head held high. During the early decades of the thirteenth century, under the influence of the new spirituality promoted by the Franciscan and other mendicant orders, this vision of Christ fell out of favour. Painters began, instead, to paint a more mortal Christ, *Christus Patiens*, a Christ suffering in torment on the Cross – just as Francis had conjured him up in his sermons and theatrical performances.

There is a naturalistic imperative built into the very nature of the Franciscan sensibility, which demands sympathy with the mortal pains of Christ. To compare the *Christus Triumphans* [8] that St Francis saw with Coppo di Marcovaldo's deeply

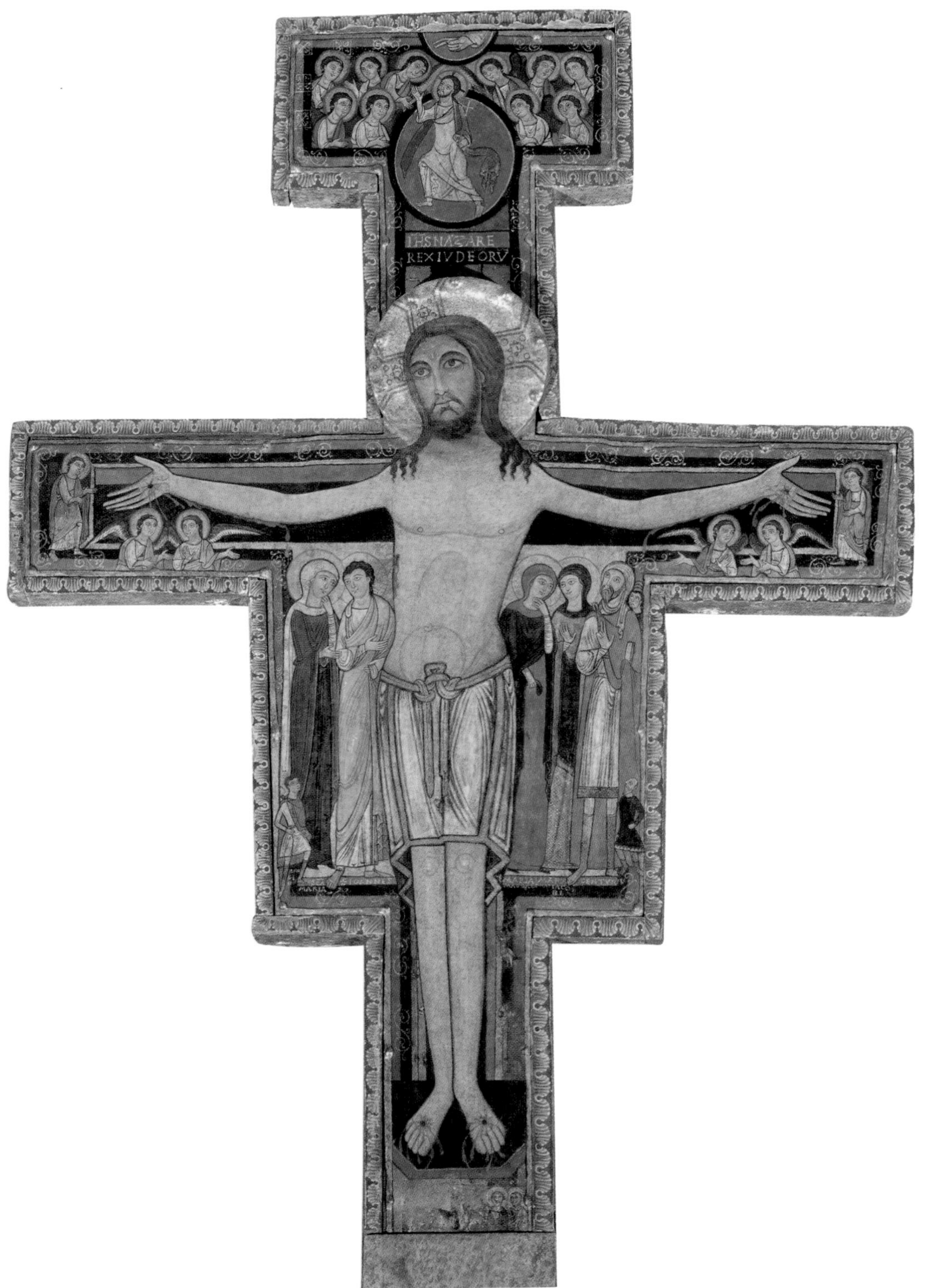


8 ARTIST UNKNOWN *Christus Triumphans (Christ Triumphant upon the Cross)*, late 12th century

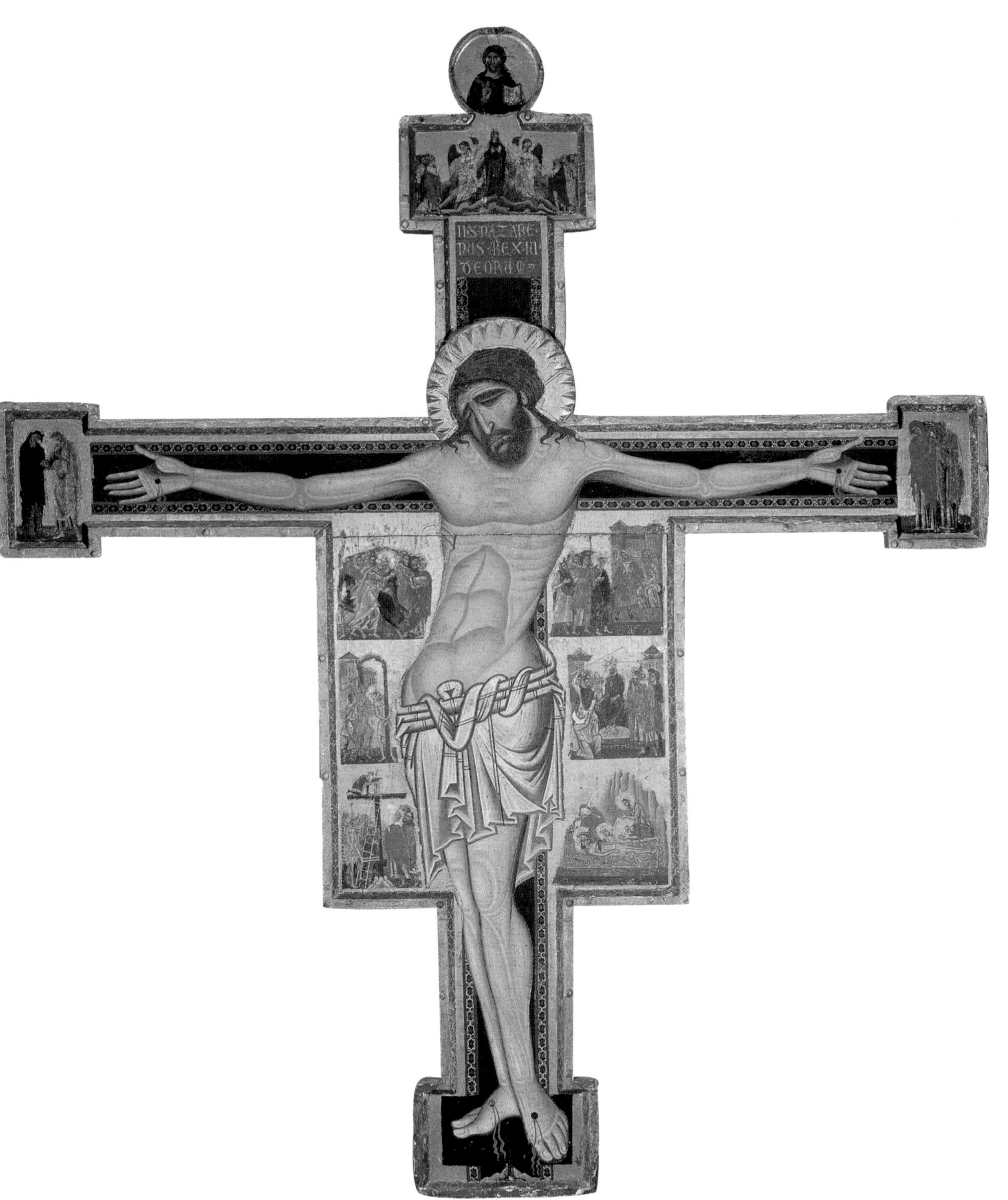

9 COPPO DI MARCOVALDO *Christus Patiens (Christ Suffering on the Cross) c.* 1250–55

emotional *Christus Patiens* [9] of some fifty years later is to measure the gap between the religious sensibilities of one era and another – to see the difference between art before and after Francis. The bland, calm, complacently all-powerful Christ of the earlier painting has given way to another, more disturbing and engaging figure. Coppo's Christ is racked by pain and sorrow, his arms awkwardly outstretched, his tendons straining against his own weight, his body sagging and twisted to the left. His beard is flecked with sweat and his dark eyes are filled with an appalling pain. This was the face of the new art.

'Heed all these things as though you were present',[8] advised the author of the *Meditations on the Life of Christ*, the most influential thirteenth-century Franciscan tract, written at about the time when Coppo di Marcovaldo painted his Crucifixion. Coppo's work of art was itself an attempt to enable the ordinary person to make precisely that leap of the imagination – to place himself or herself at the foot of the Cross, in Golgotha, and to weep over the death of the God who became a man. On either side of Christ's agonized body there is a series of small but harrowing vignettes from his last days, including *The Betrayal*, *The Flagellation* and a touching if imperfectly preserved *Lamentation*, in which Mary presses her cheek to the cheek of her dead son as he lies on the ground, as if hoping to revive his cold body with the warmth of her own. The Franciscan faith did not only revolutionize the image of Christ; it also gave an entirely new status and urgency to narrative art. Emphasis was placed, in particular, on the Passion of Christ, on his humiliation and isolation and suffering in the days leading up to his death.

The extreme nature of this shift in religious priorities should not be underestimated. It is not only the 'historical background' to the civilization of the Renaissance, as textbooks often express the matter, but a fundamental part of it. The rise of Franciscanism marked a sea-change in attitudes, and in that sea-change may be found the origins of many of the most distinctive impulses of Renaissance art. The notion that an enhanced realism, an enhanced psychological penetration or an enhanced persuasiveness might be desirable in art – all these Renaissance articles of faith can demonstrably be shown to have been prefigured in the imperatives of Franciscan piety. Franciscanism was a credo which unleashed the imagination of artists, because it encouraged a certain independence of vision, an independence which has become deeply ingrained in the Western art tradition itself. It is sometimes thought that the Christian religion and the ambition for a Renaissance were forces pulling against one another. As the role of Franciscan ideas in accelerating artistic change demonstrates, religion was one of the great driving forces behind Renaissance art – not the brakes, so to speak, but the motor.

## FLESH AND STONE

Francis's emphasis on the body penitential, the body bleeding and in pain, had just as powerful an effect on sculpture as on painting, and it led artists in thirteenth-century Italy to look at the art of the past with a different eye. Roman sculpture acquired a new significance for the sculptors of the thirteenth century. They looked at such art not with the archaeological fascination of later, more self-consciously 'Renaissance' artists and humanists but in more practical terms and with a more straightforward voracity. Roman sculpture, which pitted real bodies one against another, contained many useful hints and suggestions for sculptors imbued with the new Franciscan set of priorities. It became a kind of treasure house of suggestions, both physical and emotional. Looking at the relics of antiquity, artists saw a world of possibilities for their own work: bodies sensual, bodies beautiful, bodies writhing, all ripe for transposition into the stories of the Christian faith.

Early in the second half of the thirteenth century Nicola Pisano carved an elaborate marble pulpit for the Baptistery in Pisa. It is the first and most compact example of what has been called thirteenth-century classicism – a composite work of sculpture in which figures clearly modelled on those in ancient Roman art enact scenes from biblical legend. The Virgin in Nicola's *Adoration of the Magi* [10], heavy and statuesque, with her straight Roman nose and impassive eyes, looks like a Juno who has mysteriously wandered into the wrong story. The three kings, with their neatly trimmed beards and swept-back wavy hair, are also derived from ancient Roman sarcophagi – many of which still line the walls of the Campo Santo, a set of medieval cloisters built on the site of a Roman graveyard, less than 100 metres from the Baptistery in the centre of Pisa. Another and in some ways yet more striking instance of Nicola's classicism is to be found in the form of his *Daniel*, who supports one of the corners of the pulpit on his shoulders. Modelled on an ancient statue of Hercules, he is one of the earliest heroic nude figures in Italian art, and thus may be said to have inaugurated a tradition which would culminate in the gigantic *David* of Michelangelo.

There is none the less a slightly awkward, inexpressive quality to some of the scenes on Nicola Pisano's pulpit, as if he had not quite managed to digest his influences when he created it. There is a new weight and solidity to these bodies, carved in relief, but they do not always relate dynamically to one another and the overall effect is occasionally flat. The pulpit is like a play written in a foreign language – a language which, the playwright senses, contains infinite possibilities, but in which he himself cannot quite attain eloquence. But the ambition behind it

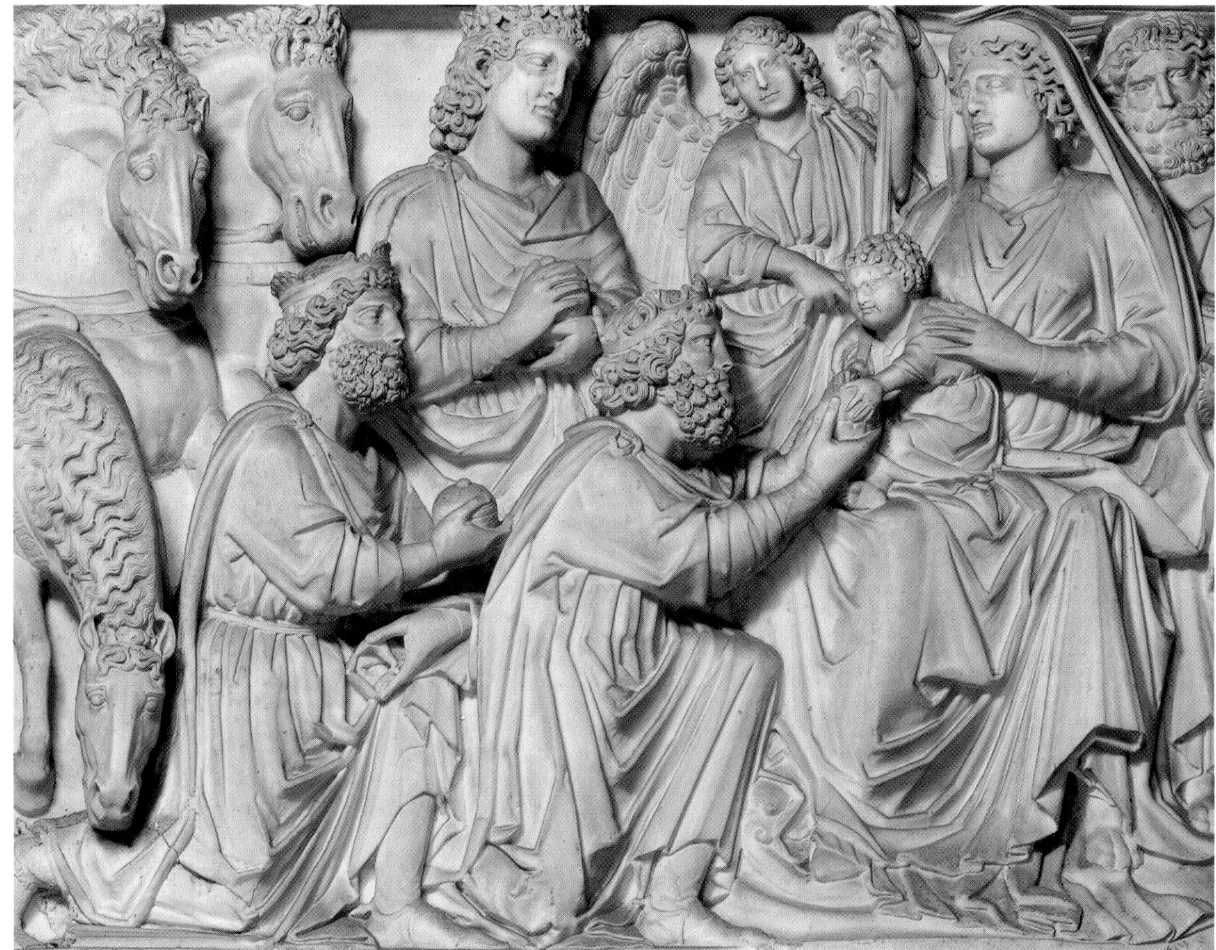

10 NICOLA PISANO *Adoration of the Magi*, detail from the pulpit, Baptistery, Pisa 1259–60

is unmistakable – to find a way of making an art more naturalistic, more physically credible, more direct and more dramatic. That ambition would be more fully realized by Nicola's son, Giovanni Pisano, in *his* masterpiece – the pulpit which he carved some forty years later, during the early years of the fourteenth century, for Pisa Cathedral.

Giovanni Pisano's pulpit, like his father's in the neighbouring Baptistery, is also supported by a number of nude and heroic figures, each of which displays a strong consciousness of the forms and the emotional possibilities latent in Roman art. Giovanni looked not only to Rome for inspiration, but also to recent developments in Northern art, which had undergone its own naturalistic revolutions in

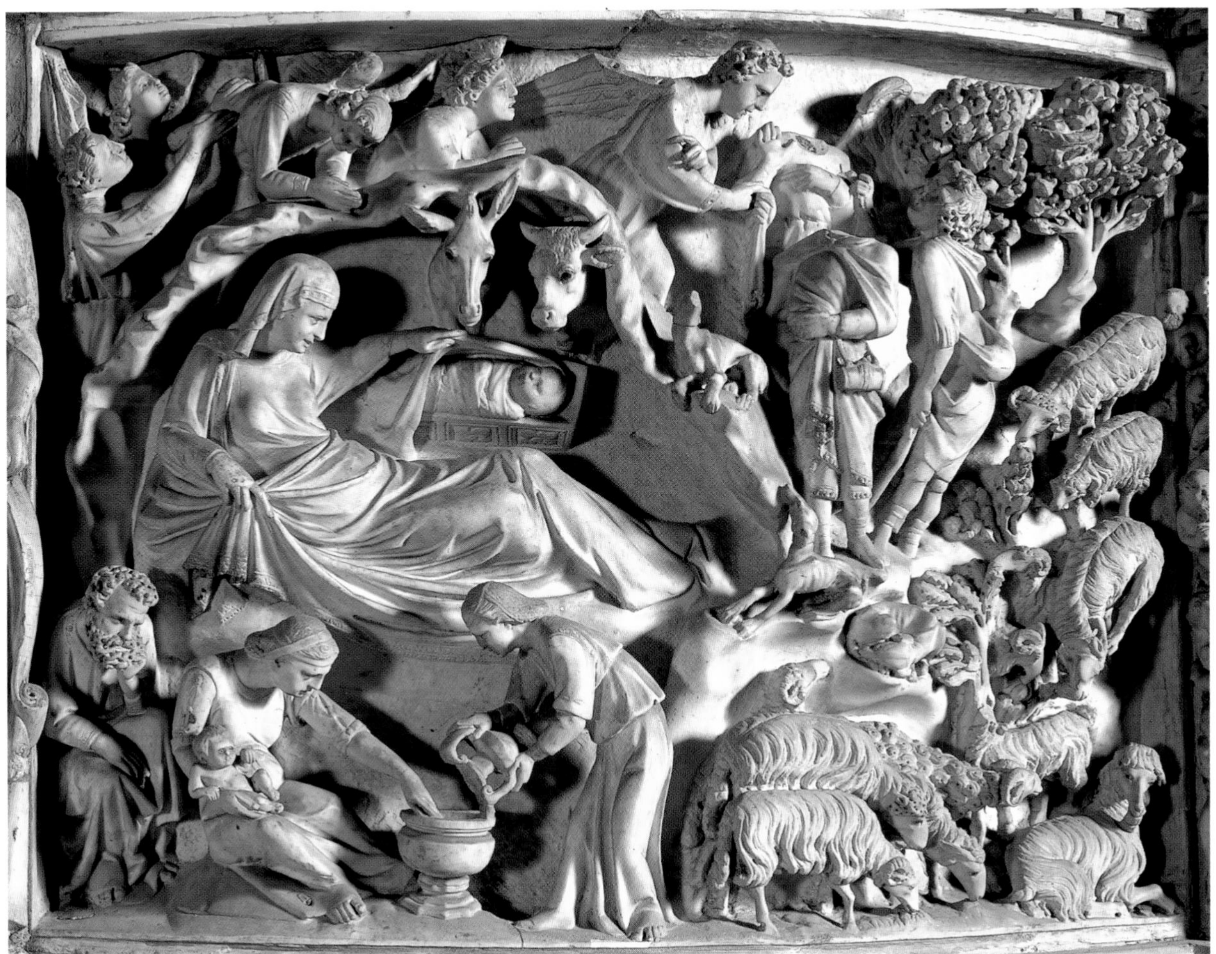

11 GIOVANNI PISANO *The Nativity*, detail from the pulpit, Pisa Cathedral 1302–10

the thirteenth century. He may have known and been inspired by the vigorous, highly realized sculpture of the great French Gothic cathedrals as well as by the sarcophagi in the Campo Santo. He must also have been influenced by the agonized physiques in thirteenth-century paintings of the Crucifixion. Such influences all converged to one end in his work – a dramatic heightening of actuality and feeling. The body antique and the body ascetic have merged into one.

It was Giovanni Pisano, more than any other artist, who brought Italian sculpture to life in the age of affective piety. The reliefs on the Pisa Cathedral pulpit are among the most original narrative works of European sculpture. *The Nativity* [11] recalls Francis's determination 'to bring home to the people of Greccio what the birth of Christ at Bethlehem was like.' That is precisely what Giovanni showed the people. He also showed them Mary's tender joy in her swaddled child, and the baby's own sleepy vulnerability. The infant Christ appears twice within the panel, once sleeping, once being washed; and in the second vignette, where the baby sits supported within the crook of the midwife's arm, Giovanni brilliantly captured the creased, solemn, comical, dopey, myopic, heavy-headed essence of a newborn child. The landscape in which the artist set his scene has been imagined with startling fullness and clarity, a compendium of visual detail with sheep grazing, shepherds standing and a dozing dog curled up into a ball. Giovanni revels in the plenitude of the Creation, showing a joy in the making of his fictive world which both embodies and communicates the joyfulness of his biblical theme. All here seems fresh and new, touched with grace; this is a world charged with the vital impulse. Giovanni's style itself has an organic character in this relief. The art historian John White has compared it to a vine heavy with fruit.[9] The determination to place a scene within a landscape as fully realized as this was new in Italian art, and here too Francis may have played a role. His ecstatic joy in nature, expressed most vividly in the *Canticle of the Sun*, encouraged artists to pay a different quality of attention to the visible world.

Giovanni Pisano was not lacking in a tragic sense. *The Crucifixion* on his great pulpit is a depiction of the three crosses on Calvary with the good and bad thieves flanking Christ above a milling crowd of onlookers. Mary faints as Roman soldiers break the legs of the thieves. The apostles reach up towards the horribly suffering figure of the dying Christ, whose skin is stretched to the thinnest of membranes over the cage of his chest and whose bony arms have been almost pulled from their sockets by the tugging weight of his torso. The scene is crowded with figures, each of whom – with the exception of the single, unpleasantly meticulous centurion piercing Jesus's side with a now-broken spear – expresses a different version of the same compassion or despair.

Another of the most memorable reflections of the new religious and artistic sensibility during the century after Francis's death was Lorenzo Maitani's series of marble reliefs which decorate the pilasters on the façade of Orvieto Cathedral. Begun around 1310 – just as Giovanni Pisano was finishing his great pulpit for Pisa Cathedral – and completed in 1330, the reliefs represent stories from the Old and New Testaments. Like his Pisan predecessors Maitani was fruitfully aware of the example of ancient Roman art. His decision to do away with conventional frames and to tell his stories in continuous, flowing bands of imagery is strikingly reminiscent of Trajan's Column in Rome and it lends his work a foliate quality, making

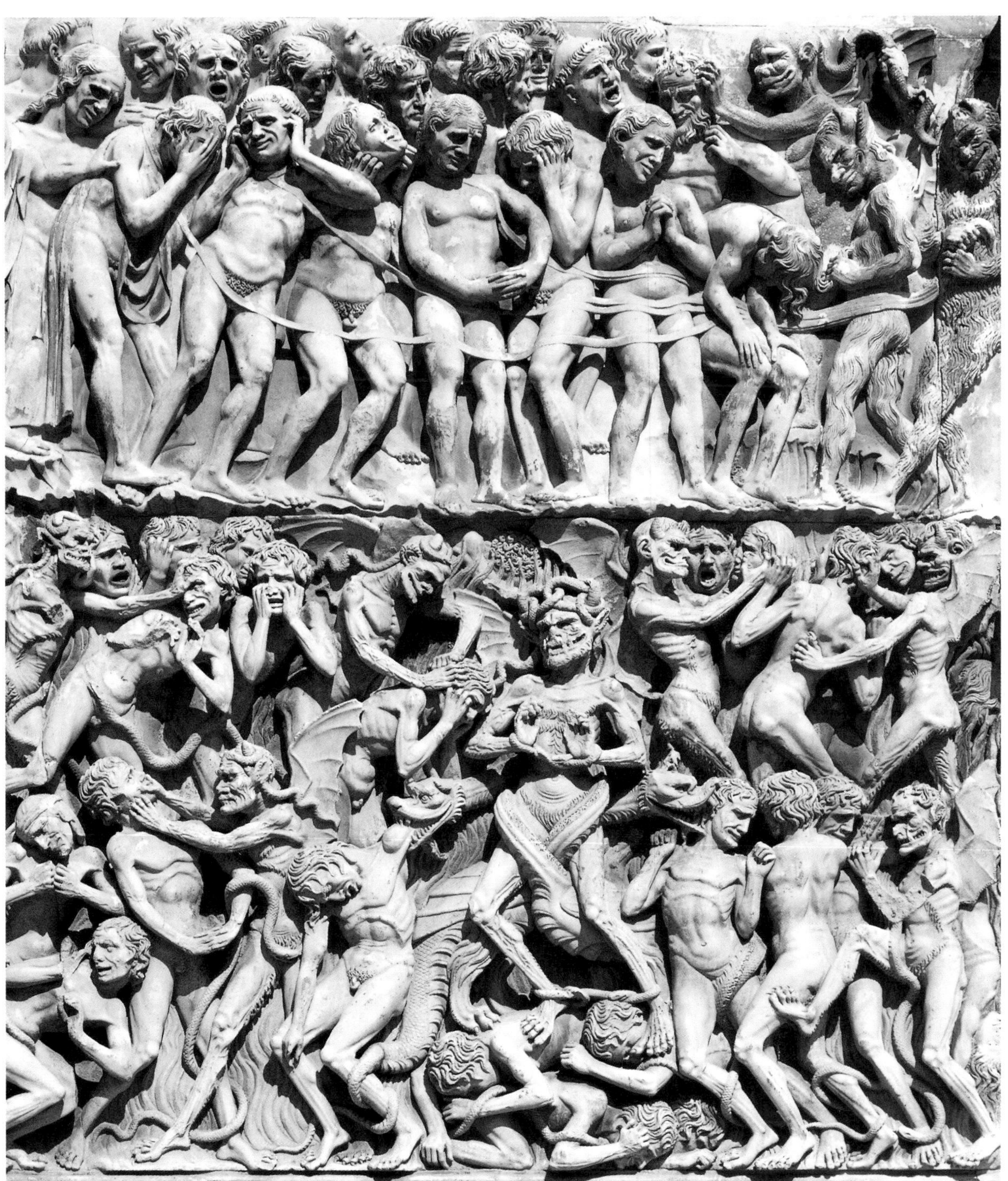

12 LORENZO MAITANI *The Last Judgement* (detail), façade, Orvieto Cathedral *c.* 1310–30

each of the pilasters a tree, sprouting images. The most memorable scene at Orvieto is that of hell in the relief depicting *The Last Judgement* [12]. Amidst much weeping and wailing and gnashing of teeth, the damned writhe and strain against the demons and snakes that have come to torture them; one of them has been part-swallowed by a dragon-like creature. The scene impressed Michelangelo deeply. This figure, slumped in abjection and horror, was adapted (reversed) for that of Christ in one of the last and greatest of Michelangelo's works: the late, pathetic, unfinished *Pietà* in the Museo dell'Opera del Duomo in Florence.[10]

## GIOTTO AND EMPATHY

Nicola and Giovanni Pisano had a great influence not just on Italian sculptors but also on Italian painters, and especially on Giotto, who is often regarded as one of the founders of Western painting. Giotto's finest surviving works, a series of early fourteenth-century frescos in the Arena Chapel, in Padua, brought Italian narrative painting to a new pitch of expression. The paintings in the Arena Chapel – so-called because it was built on the former site of the Roman arena in Padua – were commissioned from Giotto by Enrico Scrovegni, the wealthy son of a usurer. Scrovegni seems to have intended the chapel as an expiation of the sins of his father, whom Dante thought wicked enough to place in his *Inferno*. Giotto's masterpiece, painted between approximately 1302 and 1312, was more than a skilful plea for a rich man's soul. It was a grand, lucid summation of narrative developments in the fresco tradition that had developed and accelerated during the previous hundred years. Painting was still in the throes of change at the turn of the fourteenth century, but from this flux Giotto created a monument.

Although the Arena Chapel was a private commission, carried out for an unusually rich and prescient patron, it was shaped by the priorities of Franciscan piety just as surely as any of the ecclesiastical buildings of the mendicant expansion (Enrico Scrovegni had close contacts with the Franciscan order). A barrel-vaulted stone rectangle, the chapel consisted of nothing except walls to be painted, necessarily pierced by a couple of windows. Giotto projected his imagination on to every wall. Walking into the building is an overwhelming experience, like stepping into a cinema and finding that fifty films are being shown simultaneously.

The walls are painted with scenes from *The Life of the Virgin*, scenes from *The Life of Christ* and *The Last Judgement*. Giotto's narrative and pictorial sense was strongly influenced by the miracle plays of his time, which were themselves

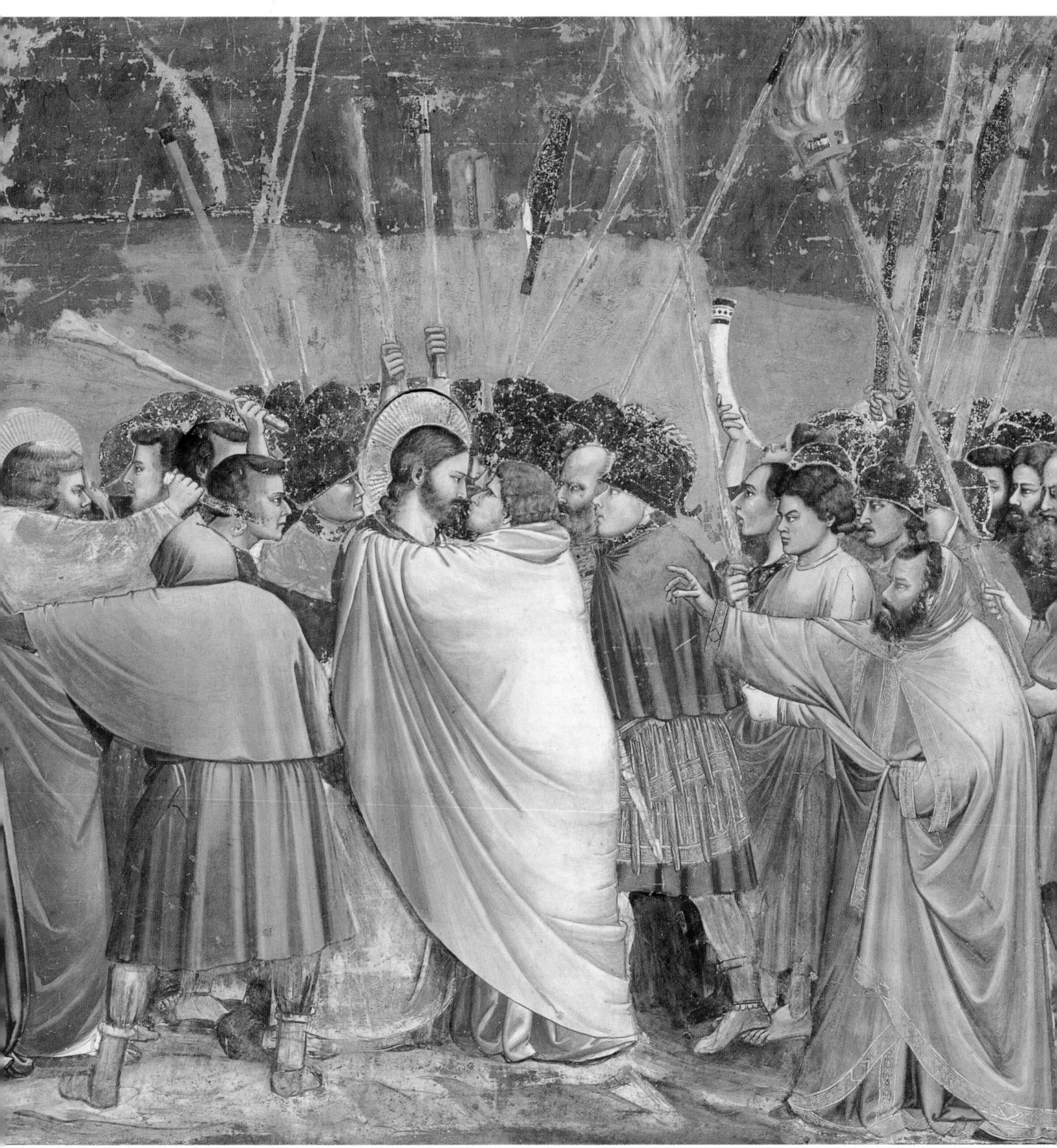

13 GIOTTO *The Betrayal of Christ* (detail) *c.* 1303–6

strongly influenced by the Franciscan approach to the communication of scripture. He treated the space almost as if he were a playwright working in two dimensions. He reduced the complex narratives of apocryphal texts to strong and simple patterns of action.[11]

One of the earliest scenes from *The Life of the Virgin* is a convoluted tale in which Mary's father Joachim seeks shelter among his shepherds because, having been rebuked by the high priest for his childlessness, he dare not go home in such shame. Giotto reduced this story to a single dramatic scene in which two men, living rough in the middle of nowhere, are suddenly confronted by their employer, asking for a bed for the night. Joachim stands, head bowed, while his shepherds hesitate. One glances at the other, his face furrowed by doubt, to see if his own embarrassment is shared. That glance, shot furtively sideways, is something which only Giotto, among thirteenth- and early fourteenth-century painters, could have invented.

Giotto simplified and reduced the elements of art in order to get to the centre of the emotions and meanings of the stories which he was given to depict. In a later scene from *The Life of the Virgin* Joachim embraces his wife Anne before the gate to Jerusalem. Everything in the structure of the picture – a careful piece of asymmetry, in which the husband and wife are placed to the left of the arch that frames a group of witnesses to their joy – concentrates attention on the hug that is its reason for being. The figures of Joachim and Anne, gently inclined towards one another, *absorbed* in one another, are full of a tenderness which is all the more convincing for being so self-contained. Two draped columnar figures have become one. The fall of their robes, the touching of their faces, the linking of their arms and bodies, all are united in a pattern of love.

While Giotto's sense of drama was nourished by the sacred theatre and the sermons of his time, his sense of form was influenced by contemporary sculpture. It is reasonable to suppose that he was familiar with the pulpits of Nicola and Giovanni Pisano. The figures in Giotto's art are full of life but they have been conceived as if they have a sculptural mass. Many of them have the Roman solidity, the slow solemn bulk of the figures in Nicola Pisano's work. The sculptural *gravitas* of Giotto's figures sets them apart from mundane existence, gives them a weight and a consequence that underlines the significance of the story being told. In the scene of *The Flight into Egypt*, Mary, riding her donkey side-saddle with the Christ child in her lap, has been given the grandeur of an equestrian statue.

It has been well said that painters can be divided into two classes, those who make man light and those who make him heavy. Giotto belongs to the second category. He has a formidable sense of gravity. His figures are statuesque, weighty presences, more solid-seeming than the world they occupy, which is rendered in a deliberately schematic way. Giotto's landscape is a bare place in which few trees grow, a staged backdrop of mountains that look like icebergs. Likewise the buildings in which Giotto's action takes place are not ornate but stereotypical. They are necessary settings – a portico, a gate, a manger – which have been made deliberately nondescript in character.

Giotto made no attempt to adjust the scale of the figures to the scale of the architecture. Such a concession to merely mimetic ends would necessarily have diminished the figures in his art and that would have been unthinkable. The double scale, which remained a convention of Italian painting until the fifteenth century, has often, quite wrongly, been regarded as a quaint and naive device. But it simply gave visible form to the priorities of Giotto's painting. (Its replacement during the fifteenth century by the convention of mathematically calculated linear perspective may be counted a loss as well as a gain.) Nothing, in Giotto, must detract from the narrative, so nothing inessential intrudes into his works.

Story is all, in this space, but narrative events are invariably tinged by a sense of ritual. Characters always seem aware of the momentousness of the actions in which they are engaged and this is part of what lends them their grave and solemn air. The apostles gathered around Christ in *The Last Supper* and *The Washing of Feet* have been made to seem powerfully if quietly conscious of the sacramental nature of that which they are witnessing. Even Giotto's traitorous Judas – his embrace of Christ is a dreadful, clinging, unreciprocated gesture which parodies that of Joachim and Anne – seems to know the enormity of what he has done. *The Betrayal of Christ* [13] is a vile act formalized, given a kind of stateliness by the artist. It is an obscene rite.

Giotto's dramaturgical focus was unwavering, but unlike many of the more nakedly emotive painters preceding him he had the ability to communicate with a nuance of expression or gesture. He showed artists the power of understatement. When he came to the climax of the cycle of *The Life of Christ* he depicted neither the Christ triumphant of the pre-Franciscan tradition nor the Christ in agony favoured by the painters of late thirteenth-century Italy. Instead he simply painted Christ dead on the Cross, thin and white and hanging. It is a scene of aftermath to which all present respond with mingled pain and dignity. The Magdalene touches the blood oozing from Christ's feet and begins to shudder, trying still to hold in her tears. The Virgin Mary, fainting, her face impassive as she slips from consciousness, is supported by Mary and John the Evangelist.

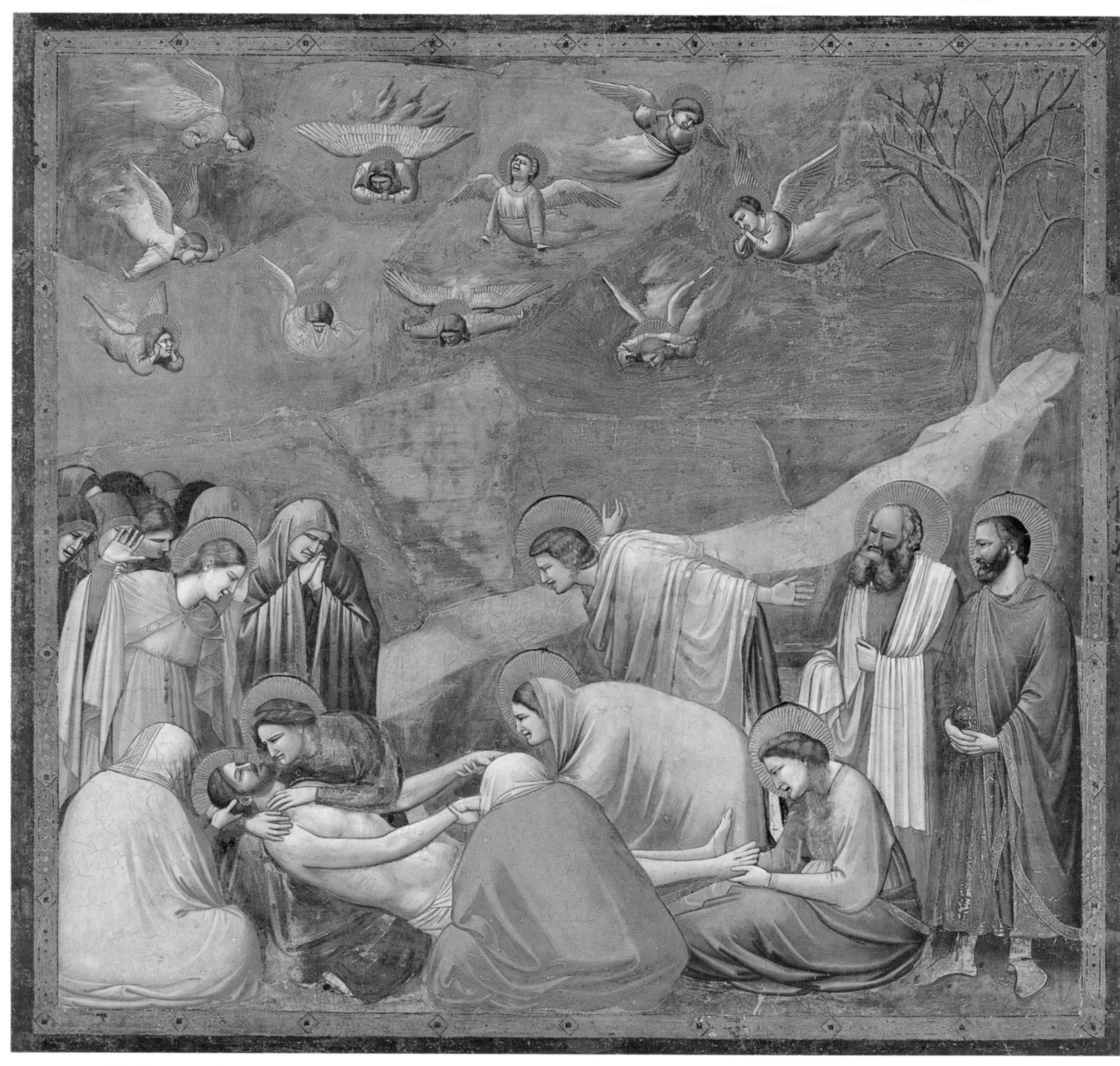

14 GIOTTO *The Lamentation* c. 1303–6

Even when he came to paint *The Lamentation* [14], the yet more sorrowful aftermath of this aftermath, and the true emotional climax of the entire sequence of frescos, Giotto showed restraint. The grieving figures are not in paroxysms of sorrow. They have not lost control of themselves. The angels above seem to be in greater agonies. Christ, who once was upright, now lies stretched out on the ground. The tragedy is here expressed, with the utmost formal simplicity, as a shift in axis. A vertical has become a horizontal. The outrage of Christ's murder seems all the more dreadful when painted by Giotto because his figures generally seem so upright that to see one any other way is extremely unsettling.

The mourners gathered around Christ seem full, almost to overflowing, with an inner life. Giotto's mastery of expression, here, plays against the statuesque qualities of his figures. Seeing them show such emotion is shocking. It is as if one were to see a statue cry, tears coursing down a stone face. In painting their grief, Giotto went beyond grief alone. He encapsulated man's capacity for fellow feeling. By making this dreadful sorrow into a *process*, Giotto invited – is still inviting – us to participate and show our own fellow feeling.

The grief of his figures seems inextricably bound up with a quality of spiritual contemplation. By giving them this quality, making them at once actors in a scene and meditators upon it, Giotto has bridged the gap between art and the world. We too, the congregation before the picture, are invited to become witnesses to Christ's death, to see and to feel its dreadfulness. It is as if his figures are responding to the scene on our behalf – are showing us the way to respond to the death of Christ. There is a kind of openness about their faces, not exactly a blankness but an Everyman quality. They could be everyone, and by extension everyone could be them. Because Giotto's art insists on including us it is still as harrowing as when it was first painted.

## THE EASTERN ORIGINS OF WESTERN ART

Giotto's place in art history has been subject to certain misunderstandings. For Vasari, Giotto was the artist who decisively turned painting away from the primitive influence of the Byzantine East and set it moving in a new direction. But the origins of Renaissance art are not to be found in a presumed conflict between styles during which the 'advanced' West defeated the 'primitive' East. It is preferable to think of the Renaissance, not as a battle for supremacy, but as a tapestry formed from many threads. The beauty of its art lies, more often than not, in the weave.

Vasari credited Giotto with the final annihilation of the *maniera greca* – shorthand for the 'Greek' or Byzantine style which held sway during the twelfth century and much of the thirteenth – and with the re-establishment of a pure naturalistic style akin to that of ancient Roman art. It became a commonplace to argue, punningly, that Giotto had thus 'translated' art from Greek into Latin. It is on this argument that Giotto's reputation as the father of Western painting rests. Yet Vasari's reasons for arguing as he did were not entirely commendable. He was a fiercely patriotic Tuscan, and his desire to place Giotto, a fellow Tuscan, on his pedestal of pre-eminence was doubtless coloured by this. Vasari was also motivated by a desire to put Italian art and artists on the map – even if it meant redrawing, or erasing, the rest of the world. If Italian art could be shown to have moved forward by turning away from the Byzantine *maniera greca*, then it stood to reason that the whole Byzantine Empire and all that it stood for – culturally, religiously, artistically – could safely be dismissed as a superseded form of civilization.

It suited Vasari to argue this, because he was living in the aftermath of an irrevocable split between Western and Eastern Christianity. The Council of Florence, the Byzantine church's last, desperate attempt to seek succour in its struggle with the Ottoman Empire, had collapsed more than a century before he wrote *The Lives of the Artists*. His lifetime coincided with a moment when 'Western' civilization first came to think of itself as just that, and when, not surprisingly, it wanted to affirm its superiority over the East.

But the 'translation' theory of the birth of Western painting does not quite work. No matter how great an artist Giotto is reckoned to have been – and he was indeed a very great artist – he should not be regarded as the father of Western painting. It is not sensible to attempt to issue any one individual with that particular certificate of paternity. It is also important to recognize that the Byzantine East, far from being a purely retrograde force, played a vital formative role in the early development of Renaissance art. Rather than being unchanging and remote – as it is often portrayed in textbook histories of art – Byzantine art was a dynamic force, capable of renewing and transforming itself.

The truth is that Byzantine artists preceded their Italian counterparts in effecting a naturalistic, empathetic revolution in pictures of Jesus Christ and the Christian story. During the twelfth century artists working in various regions of the Byzantine Empire began to focus on the Passion and the pain of Christ. They developed what has become known as 'the volume style' of depicting the human figure, which gave a new immediacy and corporeality to the depicted form. Byzantine artists themselves turned away from the *maniera greca* and recovered some of the Greco-Roman naturalism that lay at the origins of their own tradition – for Byzantium was itself the last culture to have direct links with the classical cultures, the inheritor of the schools of painting and sculpture represented by Apelles and Phidias.

All of these innovations were accomplished, not in the medium of mosaic so commonly associated with Byzantine art, but in wall paintings. The most striking surviving examples are to be found not at the heart of the Byzantine Empire, in

Constantinople, but at its Slavic fringes, in what are now Serbia, Croatia and Macedonia.

The monastery church of St Pantaleimon, in Nerezi in modern Macedonia, contains a particularly vibrant and affecting sequence of such frescos. The name of the artist who created them is unknown, but he almost certainly learnt his craft in Constantinople. Whoever he was, he was a master of dramatic painting. *The Raising of Lazarus* is a scene of concentrated astonishment. We see the dead man resurrected, still in his winding sheet. He seems in a trance, as if stunned by the death from which he has been released. A crowd of amazed witnesses in the painting watches as we do, thus drawing us into the scene.

The angular, awkward figure of Christ being taken down from the Cross is as affecting as that in any Italian thirteenth- or fourteenth-century *Deposition*. His elongated body, racked with *rigor mortis*, seems to invite our empathetic contemplation. The image which completes the narrative of Christ's Passion in this small and not terribly well-known church is an unashamedly passionate *Lamentation* [15]. It is an outburst of pictorial feeling, a scene of mourning in which Mary cradles the dead Jesus between her legs as if he has just been born – a fusion of life and death in a single, unforgettable image – while the apostles bend in misery and devotion, kissing their Lord's hands and feet. It is as full of feeling as Giotto's painting of the same subject in the Arena Chapel, although the Byzantine version is more tempestuous. Like trees in a storm, the mourners around the dead body of Christ have been bent nearly double by anguish.

The artist responsible for the body of the fresco cycle at Nerezi – others seem to have assisted him in places, but the chief scenes are evidently the work of a single hand and eye – had to make do with whatever materials were available on the remote Macedonian mountainside on which St Pantaleimon stands. Tests have shown that he used goat's milk and pigments taken from local plants when he created his colours. The style of his paintings is bold and summary, tremendously free but imbued with a powerful sense of both three-dimensional and emotional reality. In the figures of the individual saints painted around the sides of the church, the line of continuity from ancient Greece and Rome to Byzantine painting is clear. This is perhaps not a case of the rediscovery of antiquity, but, rather, of the survival in Byzantine art of methods taught in the painters' workshops of the classical world. The figure of *St Valentine* has all the immediacy of a Roman tomb portrait. The same might be said of *St John the Baptist* [16], but this figure, daunting and intense, seems yet more animated. He seems to look forward as well as back – towards Donatello's fierce and impassioned art.

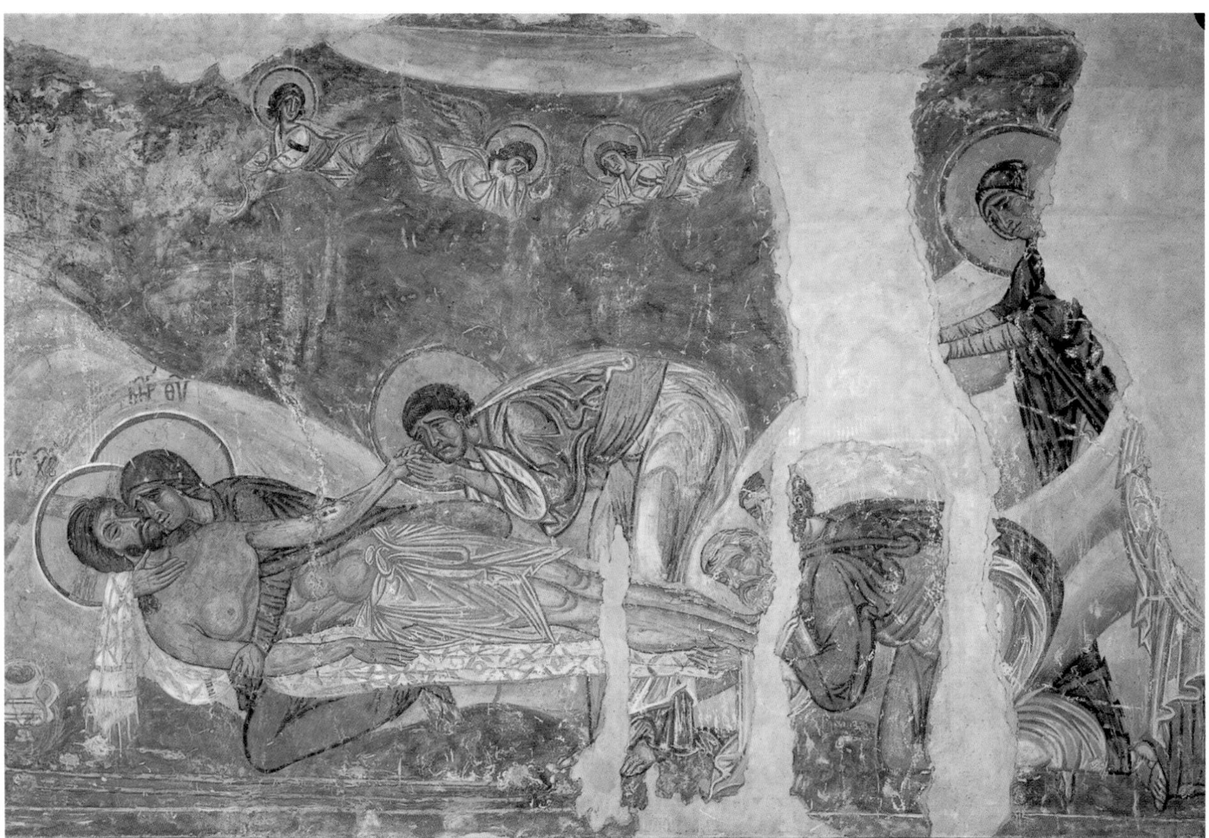


15 ARTIST UNKNOWN *The Lamentation* (detail), St Pantaleimon, Nerezi, Macedonia *c.* 1164

These works are an object lesson for all who have chosen to regard the Byzantine tradition as a retrograde, obstructive force in the history of early Renaissance art. The paintings at Nerezi date from 1164, which means that they predate Giotto's Arena Chapel frescos by a century and a half. They are not only masterpieces. They deserve to stand at the head of any account of the history of 'Western' painting.

It is highly unlikely, indeed almost inconceivable, that Giotto, or Nicola and Giovanni Pisano, or any of the other pioneering figures of the early Italian Renaissance knew the paintings at Nerezi. But during the twelfth, thirteenth and fourteenth centuries there was a constant traffic of people, art and ideas between Byzantium and the West. Travelling friars would have been aware of a large range of Byzantine art and artefacts. They could not have failed to recognize the potential of such art to complement the evangelistic and emotive preaching techniques

16 ARTIST UNKNOWN *St John the Baptist*, St Pantaleimon, Nerezi, Macedonia *c.* 1164

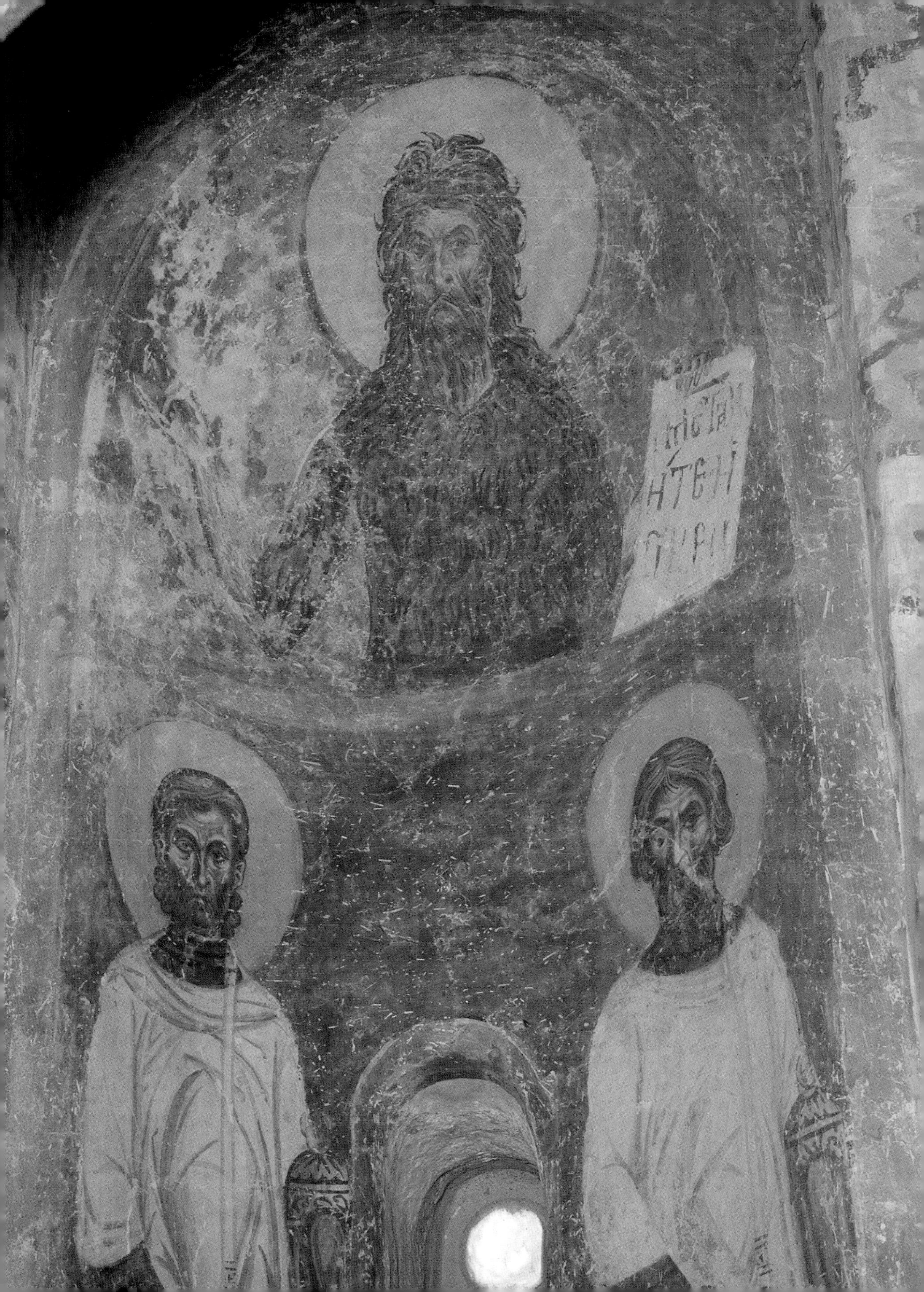

developed by men such as St Francis and St Dominic. The works of Italian artists from the early thirteenth century onwards show the unmistakable influence of the new Byzantine art.

It is a fitting irony that Vasari's adopted home town, Florence, should itself contain one of the great monuments to this cross-fertilization of artistic styles and ideas – a work of art which amounts to a compelling contradiction of Vasari's often repeated notion that the example of Byzantium somehow held Western artists back. The mosaic cycle on the ceiling of the city's beautiful Romanesque octagonal Baptistery [17] was carried out between the mid-thirteenth and mid-fourteenth centuries by a number of artists whose identities remain unknown. Here, in this compendium of universal history, from Creation to Last Judgement, the new naturalism popularized by Nicola and Giovanni Pisano and by Giotto seems to coexist with the ancient, iconic power of mosaic to conjure the transcendent God. At its heart is the image of Christ Pantocrator. A huge and daunting figure, with his great staring eyes of judgement and his hands outspread – one blessing palm outwards, one condemning palm turned away – he is the very image of awe-inspiring divinity.

Yet in the concentric circles of narrative imagery that surround this great figure are scenes exemplifying the new immediacy of Italian art in the age after Francis. These include sparse but dramatic scenes of *Adam and Eve*, their *Creation* and *Fall*. *Cain Murdering Abel* is captured with admirable economy of action. Next there are huge, heaving scenes of crowds and congestion that seem to harbour an extreme pessimism. The advent of humanity is seen as a curse on the world, like a plague of pests or vermin. Hell is as vivid as hell has ever been, in art. Thanks to the bright colours and reflective surfaces of mosaic, the multi-hued monsters have a shiny, reptilian quality. The most horrible of them has crammed half a man, head first, into its mouth. The victim's legs have yet to be consumed and they dangle from the creature's lips like two strands of spaghetti, waiting to be sucked into its fetid maw.

Dante, who was brought up in Florence, was certainly impressed by the scale and grandeur of the Baptistery's mosaic decoration. There is reason to believe that *The Divine Comedy* – and especially *Inferno*, where the poet describes the damned and their torments – was shaped to some degree by this vision of human history.

> Babel of tongues, the horrid language of despair,
> Outcries of suffering, accents of ire,
> Voices deep and hoarse and sounds of hands were there
> Making a tumult which turns in a gyre.[12]

Yet the overall effect of the ceiling is, perhaps, more musical than poetic. The eye is swept along by changes of visual pace – the slow, measured depiction of heaven giving way to the fast, action-crammed imagery of hell – like the variations and resolution of a musical theme. It is a work of art which constantly changes with the light, the gold of the mosaic tiles dimming and then brightening with the passage of the sun outside. The gold gives the image an aura, in the literal sense of that word. It brings it to life.

It would be wrong to think of the image of transcendence embodied at the heart of the Baptistery ceiling, in the figure of that great Christ Pantocrator, as a mere hangover from Byzantium. The embers of this old, deeply spiritual tradition of expression have continued to glow at the heart of Western art – not in mosaic, perhaps, which was an art form that would be less and less practised during the Renaissance and after, but in painting. When much later artists wanted to conjure a sense of the transcendent – when they wanted to paint the world as if it were an epiphany of divine presence – it was to the golden dream of Byzantine and Italo-Byzantine art that they returned. Yellow, the colour of the sun, became, for these later artists, the true primary, the most cosmically significant of all the colours.

Turner's Venetian sunsets, visions of nature filled with intimations of the infinite, are Byzantine explosions of colour. Vincent Van Gogh painted God into his own Provençal landscapes in the shape of a sun which is perhaps yet more explicitly another version of the Byzantine dome: in such late works as *The Sower* the touches of his paint are even applied to look like the separate tesserae which piece together to form a mosaic.

The links between the West and the Byzantine East are manifold. Yet despite the work of generations of Byzantine scholars, and despite the polemical anger with which the ill-fated Robert Byron argued for the importance of Byzantine art to the West – in *The Origins of Western Painting*, published shortly before his death, in 1942, under German U-boat attack – we continue to live in the shadow of old prejudices against Byzantium. Byzantine art and 'Western' art are treated, museologically, as separate entities. There are, for example, no Byzantine paintings in the National Gallery in London. In 1860, when quizzed about its holdings of Byzantine art, Sir Antonio Panizzi, the director of the British Museum, admitted that most of these were 'stowed away in the basement'; futhermore, he added that he did not 'think it any great loss that they are not better placed than they are'.[13] Attitudes may have changed since then but they have not changed enough.

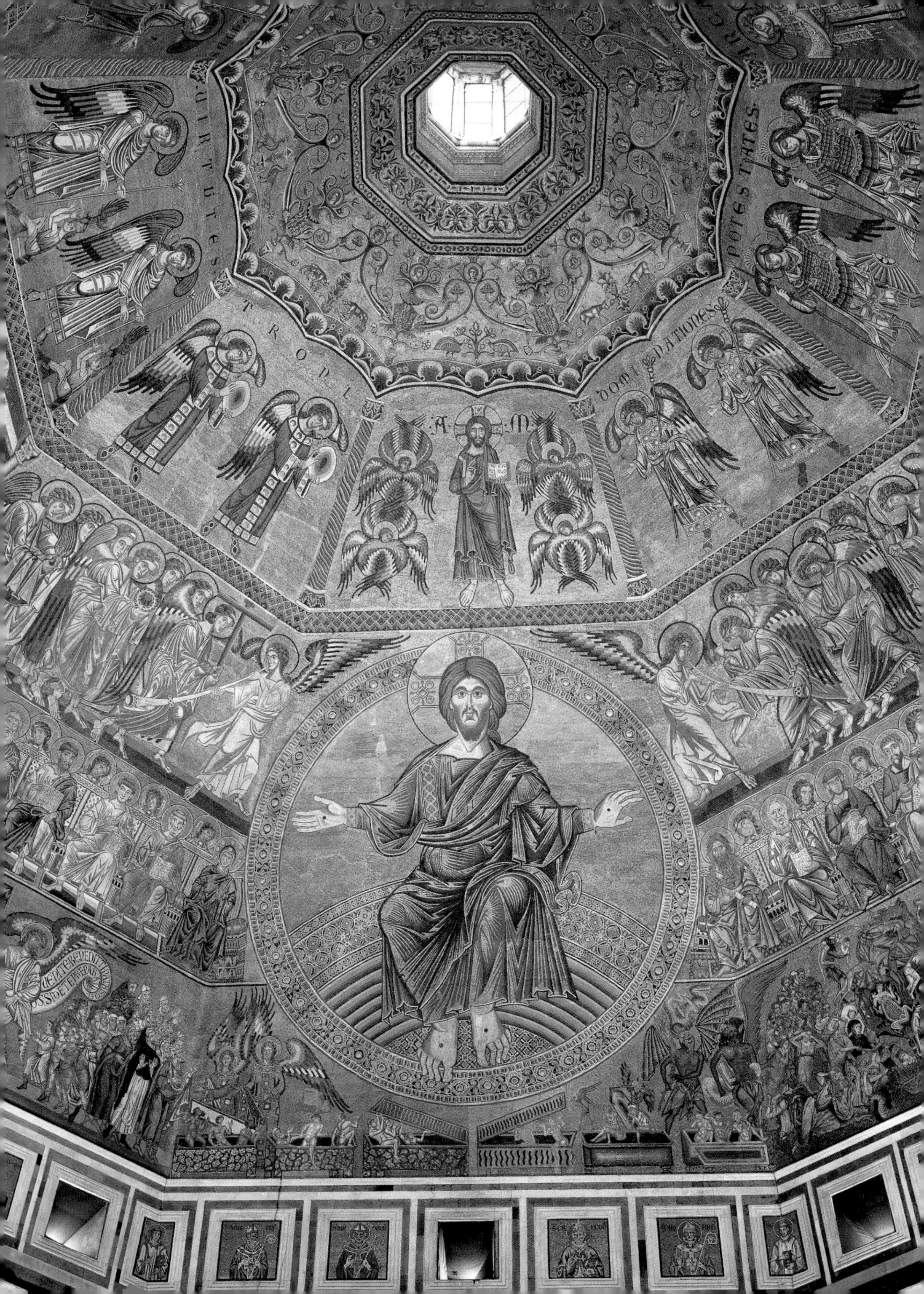
VIRTUTES
POTESTATES
TRONI
DOMINATIONES

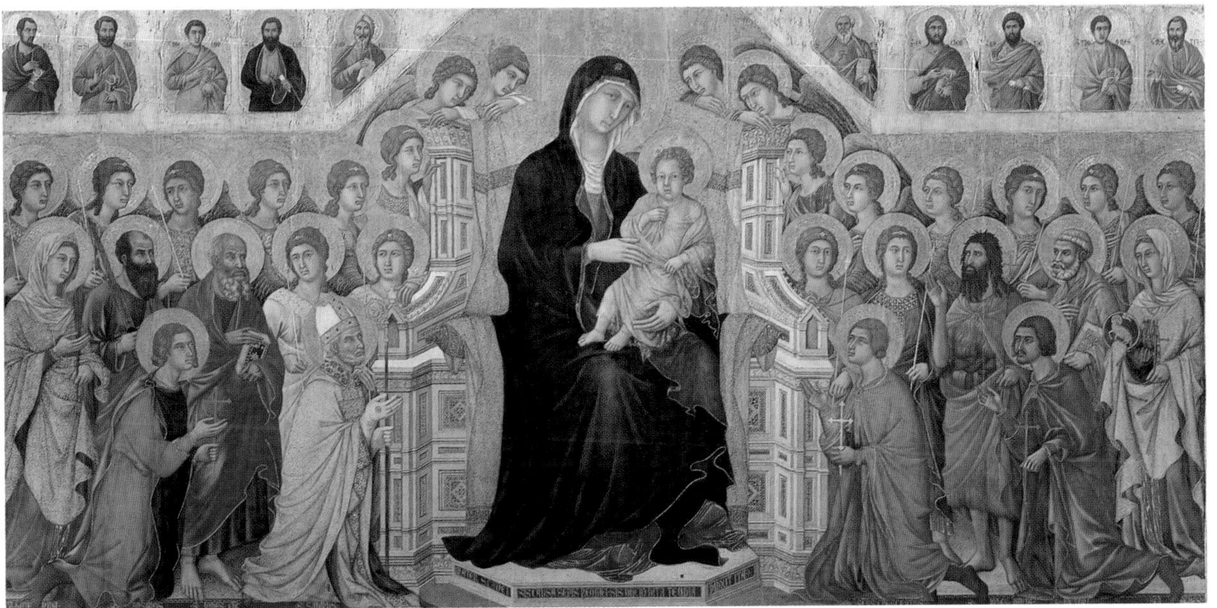

18 DUCCIO *The Virgin and Child Enthroned*, central front panel, *Maestà* 1308–11

## DUCCIO

The late thirteenth and early fourteenth centuries represent a fascinating time during which two visual languages, the naturalistic and the transcendent, so to speak, could enrich and complement one another. During this period the people of Siena, Florence's Tuscan neighbour, embarked on a programme of embellishing their cathedral. Its beautiful walls of black-and-white-striped stone ruled out the creation of a fresco cycle, but the Sienese were determined to furnish their city with a work to rival those created elsewhere. The artist Duccio was contracted to paint an altarpiece of unprecedented size and complexity. This work, the *Maestà* (Italian for 'majesty'), was to be his greatest achievement.

On its completion in 1311, after several years of work, contemporary accounts record that the altarpiece 'was carried to the Duomo, the shops were locked up and the Bishop ordered a great and devout company of priests and brothers with a solemn procession, accompanied by the Signori of the Nine and all the officials of the Commune, and all the populace and the most worthy were in order next to the said panel with lights lit in their hands, and then behind were women and children with much devotion; and they accompanied it right to the Duomo making procession around the Campo, as was the custom, sounding out all the

17 [OPPOSITE] ARTISTS UNKNOWN Ceiling, Baptistery, Florence *c.* 1225–1325

bells in glory out of devotion for such a noble panel as this.'[14] The cortège was accompanied by the sound of trumpets and bagpipes.

In the late eighteenth century the *Maestà* was mutilated and more than a dozen of the predella panels were lost altogether. A further fifteen, ripped from their original context and sold on, have found their way to various eminent and evidently unashamed museums around the world. The rest of Duccio's work, skilfully restored and carefully conserved, is now to be seen behind glass in the Museo dell'Opera del Duomo in Siena.

The main front panel of the painting, which is still in Siena, depicts *The Virgin and Child Enthroned* [18]. They are shown seated on a marble throne decorated with that intricate form of inlay known as Cosmati work, surrounded by angels and a congregation of Siena's patron saints. Devotion to the Virgin is almost as old as Christianity itself, but the cult of Mary had been intensified in Italy during the thirteenth century by the mendicant orders. Their emphasis on Christ the babe in arms and Christ the suffering man also meant a new sympathy for, and identification with, his loving mother.

The heaven which she occupies is an extraordinary creation, almost woven rather than painted. Duccio has conceived his paradise as a richly figured weave threaded through with exotic beauty. The artist shared many Byzantine artists' love of surface pattern but his sense of design was enriched, also, by other sources. A boom in textile imports into Italy in his day had opened up new worlds of decorative possibility. The Sienese were familiar with exotic fabrics from the Far and the Near East, from China and the Ottoman Empire. Moorish geometrical patterns could be seen on cloth imported from Spain, while Chinese patterned silks had been introduced via Venice by traders in the late thirteenth century. New effects, such as damascening and satin weave, were evoked by Duccio in passages of paint worked, with extreme delicacy, with gold leaf.

There is an oriental quality, too, to some of the sinuous figures which crowd the panel. It is as if Duccio's attraction to Chinese, Persian and Islamic decorative motifs infused his whole imagination. Yet suspended within this shimmering fabric of an image, with the iconic Virgin and Child at its centre, the faces of the saints have a powerful actuality. Their immediacy as painted beings is perhaps all the more unavoidable and impressive for being contained so tightly within a pictorial scheme. St Catherine, with her solemn, oval face, full of feeling and sensitivity, may stand for all of them. Haloed golden courtiers, they are none the less intensely present, a crowd of the real in a space that is ideal.

Duccio decorated the back of his altarpiece with many much smaller narrative scenes. The sequence begins with Christ's *Entry into Jerusalem*, a scene of civic excitement which shows how attentive to bustling life the artist could be. Christ rides his donkey up a red cobbled road towards the gates of what is evidently a Tuscan hill town. Duccio surrounds him with a crowd of onlookers, putting in much that Giotto left out. A group in Giotto is always a chorus but Duccio has painted a crowd. The result is a different kind of actuality, less like sacred theatre and more like bustling life. Just within the walls of the town, some boys are climbing trees to cut palms and get a view of what all the fuss is about. Below the winding road there are some shoots of long, unkempt grass growing next to a pink wall. The artist marks Christ off from this mundane world by running a border of gold along the edge of his blue cloak. This bright, shivering line sets him apart from that which surrounds him in all the panels of the Passion. The result is a transfiguration, a golden arabesque suggesting a spiritual force field around Christ.

One of the finest of the dispersed panels from the predella is *The Transfiguration* [19] in the National Gallery in London. At the bottom of this picture Saints Peter, John and James seem to be reeling in a sort of dance of amazement. Above them the prophets Moses and Elijah bear symmetrical witness to the great miracle. Elijah is on tiptoe with a scroll unfurling from his hands. At the centre of all this choreography, standing on a small eminence of rock – sufficiently convincing as geology and highly effective as design – is the figure of Christ. He is at once hieratic and human. He has dark hair and an olive complexion; his wrists and hands are slim. There is a forbidding expression on his face. His clothes have been highlighted in gold in the old Italo-Byzantine technique of chrysography, an effect which removes him somewhat from the world occupied by the other figures in the painting. He has been transfigured, by Duccio, into pattern – although there is still enough of man about him to make us feel that the transfiguration is taking place as we look.

The apparent modesty of this small painting is deceptive, for it contains within it much of Duccio's subtle and inclusive genius. He has combined different registers or distances of representation within a single image, contrasting the immediate, disarrayed humanity of the apostles in the foreground with the solemn removed stasis of Christ. The different elements within the artist's style are not in antagonism with one another, but in harmony. The naturalistic and non-naturalistic impulses in his painting combine to expressive effect. Each would be less without the other. Stylistic ambiguity is not the chink in Duccio's armour. It is his strength, his essence. Duccio renders one style unto God and another unto man. Divinity is communicated by design.

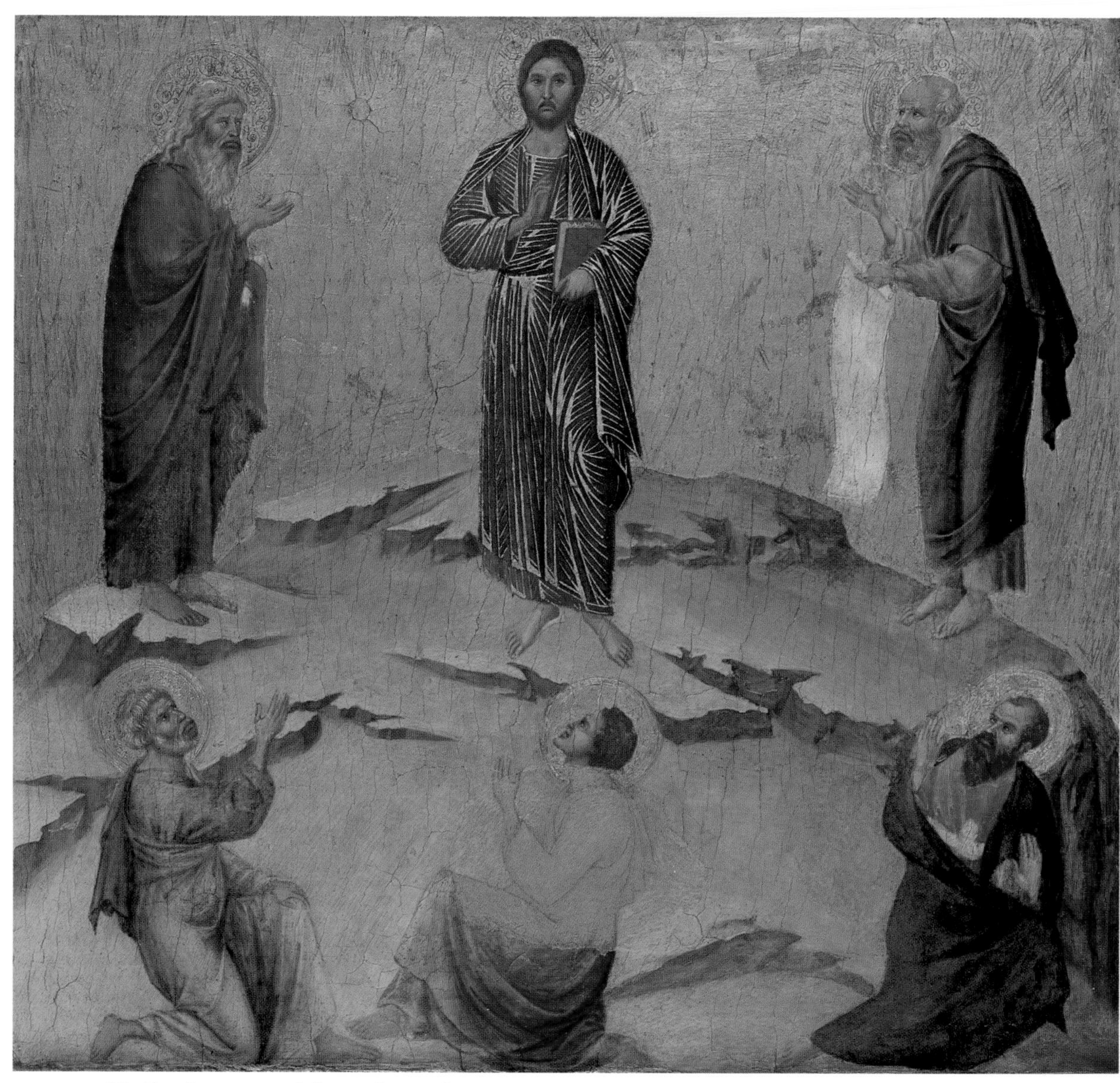

19 DUCCIO *The Transfiguration*, predella panel, *Maestà* 1308–11

The vault of Duccio's heaven is gold, and the landscape in which he places his actors is fluid. No one ever stands quite firm on its shifting ground. This suits the artist's interpretation of the character of Christ in the story. He is inherently edgy and uncomfortable and is suited – from the viewpoint of tragic expression – by a world in which he cannot settle. He is slender and wistful and not terribly authoritative in many of the scenes on the back predella of the *Maestà*. A saddened victim of atrocities, he never seems at home. As the sequence dedicated to telling the story of the Passion unfolds, he becomes progressively more alone. In scene after scene, Duccio emphasizes his isolation. All three of St Peter's denials of Christ are depicted, which is unusual in painting of the time. It is almost as if Duccio is playing different variations on the theme of betrayal, although there is nothing heartless, nothing merely playful, about the process. The result is simultaneously pathetic and decorative. Duccio takes an immense pleasure in patterning and repetition, and it is through these repetitions that the story builds to its climax.

In the scene of *The Crucifixion*, according to long-established tradition, the assembled crowd is divided into a good half and an evil half. Here, once again, Duccio adapted his style according to his meaning. The wicked soldiers and Jews on Christ's left (sinister) side are depicted in a style that might almost be that of some unusually gifted folk artist; yet on his right a great subtlety of line and delicacy of expression is reserved for the apostles and Mary. While Giotto's figures are like living statues, Duccio's Christ is painted as if he were an ivory figurine. The scenes following Christ's Resurrection reflect the deepening religious mystery of the story in a style that becomes more fugitive and incorporeal. All that is solid seems on the point of melting into thin air. The figures, especially that of the risen Christ, seem like flames – emanations of pure spirit. They seem to evoke mystical experience: the ecstatic suspension of the body between heaven and earth.

## NORTHERN EUROPE

The civilization of the Renaissance cannot be purified to a single strain or distilled to a single tendency – and the impetus behind it cannot be restricted to that of the Italian humanists, even though they were the ones who gave it its name. The Renaissance had roots reaching back in time and spreading geographically out not only towards the East but also to the North.

The patterns of influence connecting the art and architecture of Southern and Northern Europe in the thirteenth, fourteenth and fifteenth centuries are impossible to reconstruct with perfect precision. But the interwoven, international character of early Renaissance art is beyond doubt, and the importance of the North in helping to form it is beyond question.

The spread of the Franciscan movement in Italy was paralleled by similar changes in the devotional climate in more northerly parts of Europe. Social conditions in the most thriving cities of the Burgundian Empire – which stretched from Ghent in modern-day Belgium to Dijon in modern-day France – mirrored those in Italy. At the heart of that empire lay Bruges which, with its network of canals to facilitate the import of wool, was often referred to as the Venice of the North. It was also another Florence, for here, triggered by the burgeoning wool trade, there was a boom in banking and commerce. The Bladelin House, in the centre of the old town, testifies to the close links that were established between Florence and Bruges. Once the house of Pieter Bladelin, one of the richest men in the city, it became a Medici bank in the early fifteenth century. The Medici coat of arms still decorates the courtyard and main reception rooms of the building, which is now a convent.

The booming economies of such Northern towns as Ghent and Bruges had led to the development of a wealthy and vocal urban population, substantial sections of which felt inadequately served by the inflexible hierarchies of the established church. Fringe religious communities developed, not only in the Low Countries but also in the Rhineland and across central Europe, which tended to emphasize a more personal piety. Groups of pious men and women organized themselves into groups devoted to the apostolic life. In Bruges, a Beguinage was established in 1245 – a community of lay sisters who, without taking vows, followed a devout life and helped to care for the sick and the poor. Their enclave still survives in the city, although their houses and mission have been taken over by Carmelite nuns. Another such community, of priests and laymen, known as the Brothers of the Common Life, aimed, like Francis and his followers, to live in austere imitation of Christ. *The Imitation of Christ*, a book of devotional exercises written by Thomas à Kempis, probably between 1415 and 1424, is a faithful and suitably ascetic statement of the ideals which animated the New Devotion.

It was in the context of such currents of spirituality that the new and increasingly naturalistic art of the great German and French cathedrals developed – at Bamberg, at Amiens, at Reims, at Chartres – during the thirteenth century and after. Such works may have had an influence on Italian sculptors, including Giovanni Pisano, and the passionate piety and heightened emotions of his work may, in turn, have influenced the greatest sculptor to work in the Duchy of Burgundy at the end of the fourteenth century, Claus Sluter. Only the base of Sluter's Well of Moses, created for the Chartreuse of Champmol in Dijon, now survives. But the grand and nearly life-size prophets which remain in place – meditating, with suitably grave expressions, on the death of Christ – have a brooding air of tragedy about them. No more than a decade separates these works and the early Florentine masterpieces of Donatello, and purely in terms of their physical and emotional intensity they are worthy of the comparison. The fragmentary *Corpus of Christ* [20] from the Well of Moses (now in the Musée Archéologique in

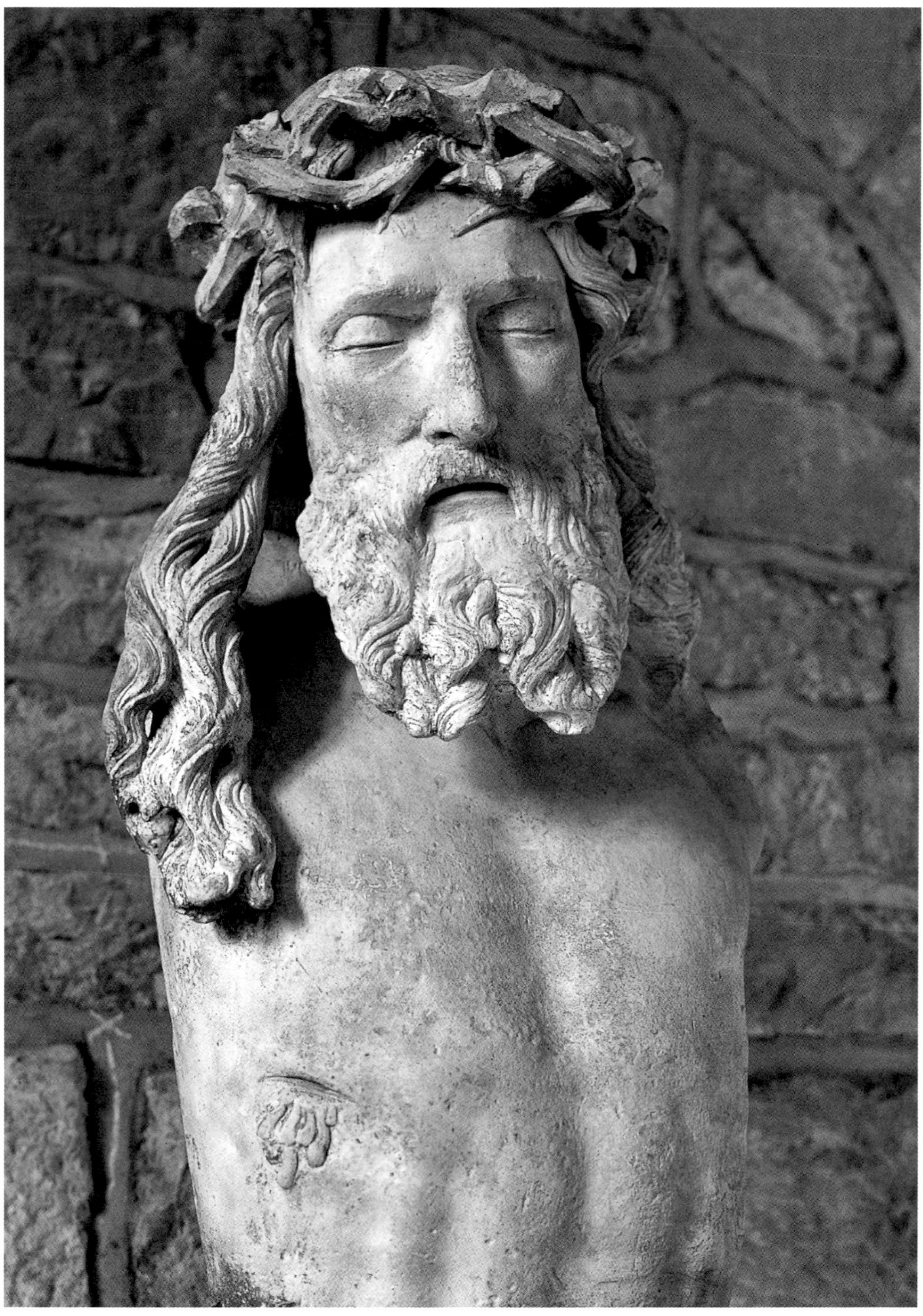

20 CLAUS SLUTER *Corpus of Christ*, Well of Moses, begun *c.* 1396

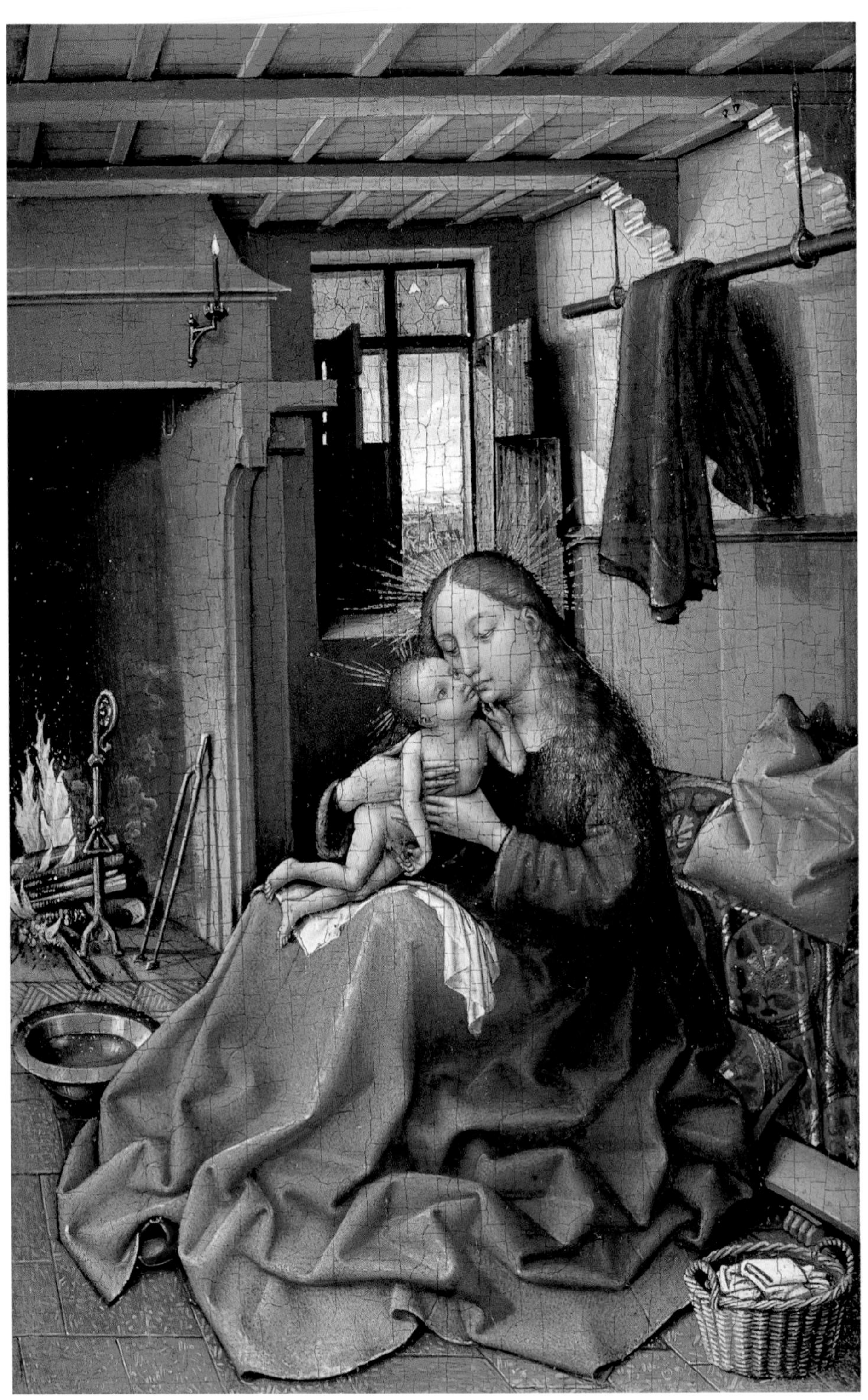

21 JACQUES DARET [ATTRIBUTED] *Virgin and Child in an Interior c.* 1435

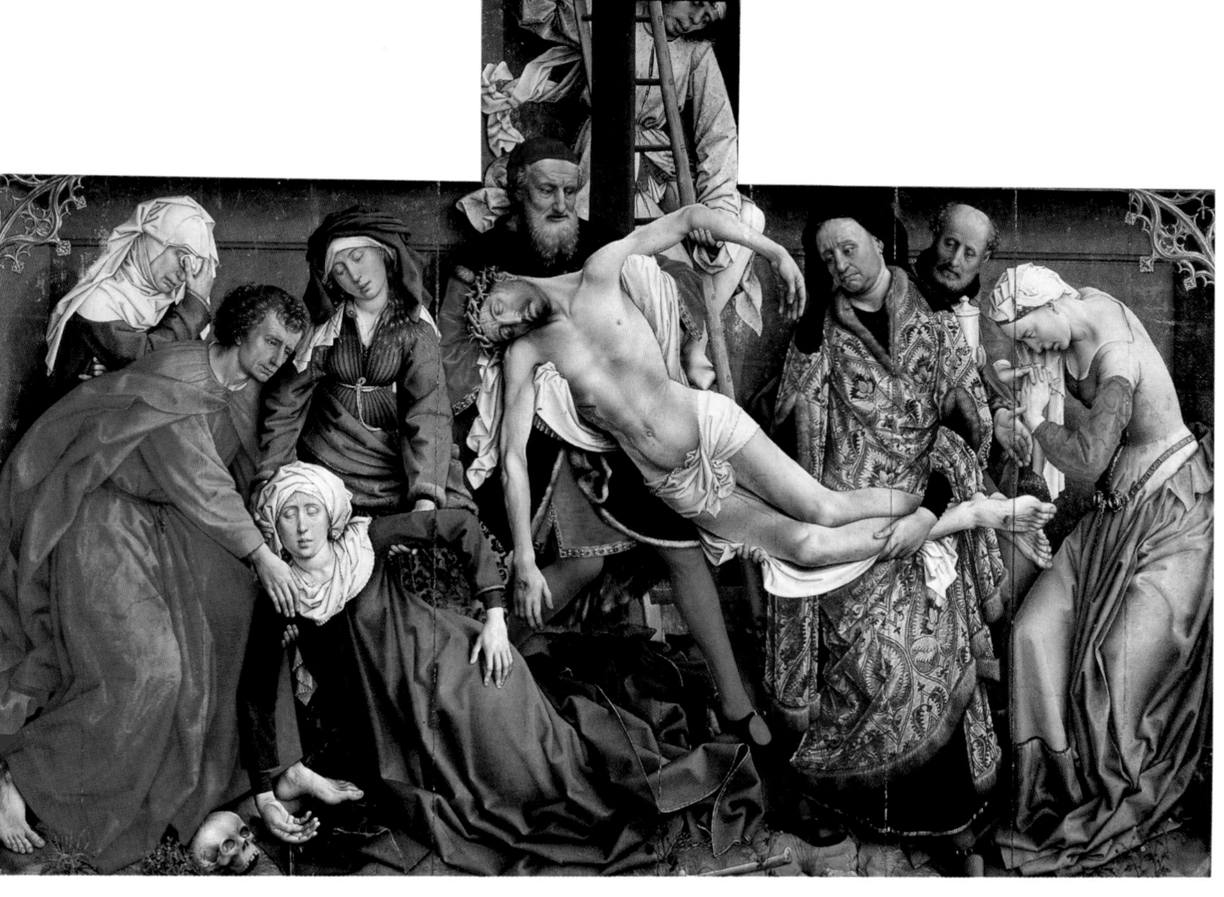

22 ROGIER VAN DER WEYDEN *The Deposition c.* 1435

Dijon), is perhaps the most impressive relic of Sluter's work. Crowned with thorns, suffering, eyes closed and withdrawn, this is powerfully pathetic Northern variation on the theme of Christ in agony.

During the early years of the fifteenth century Northern artists made their greatest contribution to the development of European painting, achieving an often disturbing naturalism in the relatively untried medium of oil paint. The small devotional paintings of the Netherlandish painters of this time mark an exquisite and homely culmination of the pan-European impulse to make the sacred seem real. Their talent was for domestication more than dramatization. The tiny *Virgin and Child in an Interior* [21], formerly thought to be by Robert Campin and now attributed to Jacques Daret, places Mary and the infant Jesus in a small, low-ceilinged room in a house somewhere in the Low Countries. It is bathtime. The mother prepares to place her small and slightly skinny baby in a copper basin of water which she has been warming by the fire that burns in the grate beside her. There is a towel on the rail above her and a basket full of fresh nappies to one side. Through the window at the back right of the scene the rooftops of a Northern trading town – possibly Bruges – may be made out.

The sense of the real in fifteenth-century Northern European painting is so intense that it becomes uncanny. The liquidity and brilliance of colours suspended in oil lends a particular lustre to details such as the copper ewer and the lights reflected in it. A dappled patch of light conveys the passage of sunshine on to a wall through the small panes of a thickly glazed window with astonishing virtuosity. Such effects would come as a revelation even to the Italians, who had done so much to achieve their own effects of naturalism in the different media of egg tempera and fresco. No wonder, perhaps, that the early Netherlandish artists should have acquired a reputation as necromancers and alchemists. Their illusions are enchantments.

The objects in Daret's interior seem haloed (and hallowed), as if the sacredness of the Virgin and Child has somehow irradiated their environment. Things have the quality of visions. A candle hung on a wall, a basket of linen, a plumped cushion, a length of hanging cloth – these items acquire the mysterious vividness and portentousness of things seen in dreams. This can partly be accounted for iconographically, for the objects in the painting do have symbolic religious associations. The ewer and basin are objects used by the priest in the celebration of Mass; the lit candle and crackling fire are ancient symbols of illumination; the basket of linen may even recall the basket in which Moses was set adrift upon the water. But these objects are more than prompts to dry symbolical exegesis. There is something about the way in which they have been depicted – their isolation and presentation like precious things to be held in the palm of the hand; the way light lies on them like a form of emphasis, shining with a more than natural radiance – that makes them seem out of the ordinary. They have been subjected to the transforming and never entirely explicable alchemy of painting.

Rogier van der Weyden, who like Daret was apprenticed to Robert Campin in his youth, had a more extreme and demonstrative religious imagination than his master. He painted slender, white-faced Virgins and emaciated Christs in crisp drapery. But the rooms in which these figures appear, and the surrounding landscapes, are not often observed with Campin's minute attention to detail. Van der

Weyden focused on the body and on the passion of the Christian story. His works offer a yet closer parallel, in Northern European art, to the intensity of Italian art under the impetus of Franciscan and Dominican imperatives of piety.

In his startling *Seven Sacraments*, now in the Koninklijk Museum voor Schone Kunsten in Antwerp, van der Weyden brought the dying Christ straight to the centre of contemporary fifteenth-century life. The painting is not a depiction of Christ on the Cross so much as a re-enactment of the Crucifixion in the nave of a Northern Gothic cathedral. It is as if the image of Christ normally seen above the high altar has not only come to life, but been thrust to the very front of the church, to tower above the congregation. The past has been projected into the present. Around the edges of the Crucifixion, in the two side aisles of the painted cathedral, time unfolds in a different way. Here the seven sacraments are shown being administered, from birth to marriage to the last rites. A single life is being measured out in the rituals of the church, event after event, from birth to death. But the overriding context for this worldly passage of time remains the eternity of salvation promised by Christ's sacrifice. The peculiar perspective of the painting reinforces this in a subtle and imaginative way. Looking at the picture, we realize that our point of view is actually in mid-air. It is as if we are levitating, like the angels with their fluttering banderoles who hover around the picture like butterflies; as if we are rising up, like the soul of the dead man as it leaves his body, into heaven.

Van der Weyden's masterpiece, the huge and harrowing *Deposition* [22], now to be found in the Prado in Madrid, combines the new and almost photographic realism of the Netherlandish tradition with what seems to have been a deliberate archaism in the treatment of pictorial depth. The pallid, floppy body of the dead Christ and nine attendant mourners, including the swooning Mary, all painted near life-size, have been squeezed into the narrowest of spaces, somewhat like a wooden box, from which they threaten to fall forward at the very feet of the spectator. Golgotha, the place of the skull, has been abbreviated to a single skull and bone on a patch of stony ground which is the incongruous floor to this tiny, shallow room with walls of tan-coloured wood. It is as if the painter deliberately turned his back on the sophisticated spatial illusionism of Northern fifteenth-century painting and reasserted the older, more emphatic distortions of scale found in painting in the thirteenth and fourteenth centuries. (The strangeness of the picture can probably be explained, in part, by the artist's desire to imitate the effects of polychrome sculpture.) But there is a terrible pathos to the scene and looking at the picture feels almost like a form of trespass – like crowding round a hospital bed just after someone has died.

## MUNDUS ALTER

In a town that floats on water nothing seems quite familiar. Petrarch called Venice *mundus alter*, 'another world'. The place is still apt to seem dauntingly strange and exotic, peculiarly unlike a Western city to those with fixed ideas about what the West is and how it came into being. Elements of Greece and Rome coincide, here, with memories of Byzantium and Islam, Spain and Africa and beyond. Venice is in many ways a confusing place, a collage of cultures, but its confusion is salutary, carrying with it a lesson about the dangers of simplifying the relationships that have shaped our world – and the foolishness of assuming that the lines of separation currently drawn across the globe have always, immutably, been there.

In the styles of Venetian architecture, on the façades of all the city's palaces as they elegantly crumble inch by inch into the lagoon, may be read, albeit obscurely, the patterns of addition and erasure and mingling by which civilizations are truly made. It is tempting to believe that in the history of ornament such as this the truest history of man's ideas and affections might lie.

Venice's unique and precarious situation has led even some of the city's most devoted admirers to regard it as a sport, a wonderful freak. But that which makes Venice unique is also that which should lead us to understand it not as the exception but as the very pattern of post-antique civilization in the West – the model of its growth and change and development.

The inhabitants of Venice, who came to think of the sea before them as their home and the terra firma behind them as a threat, have always regarded themselves as unlike those living on the mainland. (This may explain why the British, who also live surrounded by water, cut off from continental Europe, have always felt such fellow feeling for the city and its people.) The Venetians were forced by their original predicament to seek out contact with others. The compulsion became a habit which remained with them through all the long period – it lasted almost until the end of the eighteenth century, when Napoleon conquered the city – during which Venice retained its independence. From the moment of its foundation it was a mongrel city, formed from immigrancy, and its place names are an A–Z of the peoples who have, cohabiting, played their part in forming it. The Fondaco dei Tedeschi, the Warehouse of the Germans, coexists with the streets of the Spaniards, the Jews and the Moors.

It took Venice some time to produce an artist whom art historians have universally agreed to call a fully fledged 'Renaissance' artist. Despite their self-evident genius, the works of Giovanni Bellini (*c.* 1430–1516), like the city in which

23 GIOVANNI BELLINI *Madonna and Child with Saints*, San Zaccaria, Venice 1505

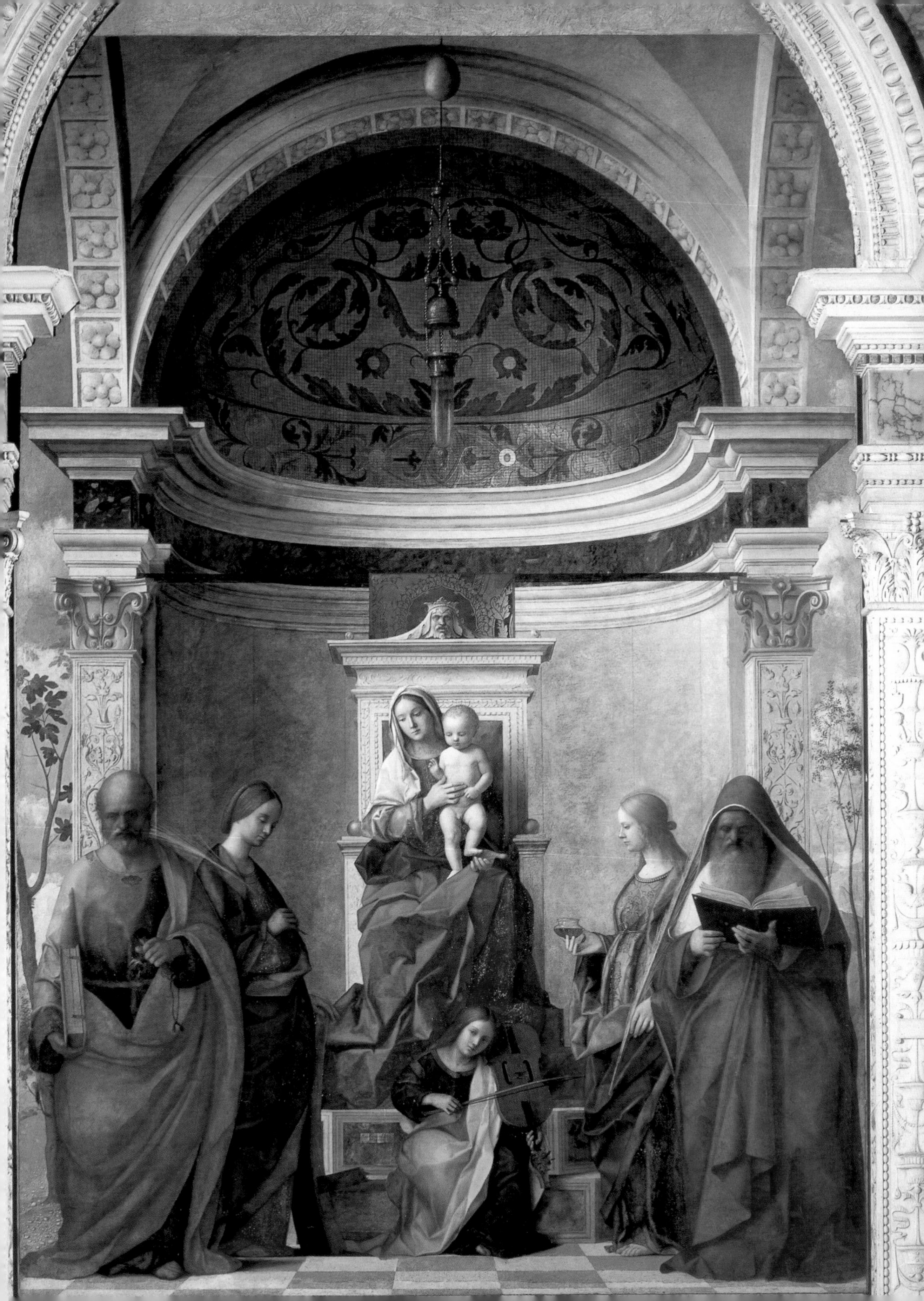

they were produced, remain among the most elusive achievements of the Renaissance. He is one of the hardest artists to pin down, to restrict to a given achievement, because he seems to take so much from such a bewilderingly disparate range of sources. Yet if one regards Renaissance culture as *essentially* mixed, the fruit of many histories and impulses, rather than as an engine of pure progress, then perhaps Bellini's work is its truest archetype.

Bellini's art was shaped by the character of Venice as a city of trade and exchange, a city through which ideas and styles travelled as constantly as people and goods. He was in touch with Renaissance ideas about Greece and Rome and the rebirth of the ancient world in modern-day Italy. He understood the power and the beauty of Byzantine art, many examples of which were to be found in Venice. He was familiar with Northern oil painting, held in high regard in Venice, and much collected there. From the pictorial elements of such works – from their solemnity, their piety, their naturalism and atmospheric effects – Bellini created his own language of painting, capable of immense expressive subtlety and of communicating a remarkable range of feelings.

Among the most northerly of his paintings, in its sharp minuteness of effect, is his *St Francis in Ecstasy* in the Frick Collection in New York. This impressive panel was painted in the mid-1470s. The saint stands before his small cell carved out of rock. Living alone with the book and skull on the lectern behind him, he is ascetic yet rich, blessed by visions. The landscape setting Bellini devised for him – stark rocks which are yet overgrown with lush greenery and which abut a beautiful, fertile, settled valley – restates the idea of poverty which is another form of wealth. The saint holds out his hands to receive the rays of the sun, a kind of naturalized version of receiving the stigmata. A donkey stands nearby, mute witness to the miracle. Bellini was one of the first Italian artists to understand the potential of oils, and this painting shows his capacity to use the medium to impart freshness and lustre. He set out to make the landscape seen in art seem itself like a vision, touched with the radiance of one of those days when it seems as though God is indeed in his heaven and all is right with the world. The light that plays over the landscape in which Francis finds himself is hard and clear, like the light after heavy rain (rainclouds are blowing away in the distance over the hills).

Bellini's highly achieved naturalism always seems to coexist with a dissatisfaction with the capacities of naturalism alone, and many of his devices are designed not to realize so much as subtly to abstract – to indicate, rather as Duccio does, although within the context of a different pictorial language, the gap that separates the sacred from the mundane. Many of his most cherished and affecting pictures are treatments of the theme of the Virgin and Child and in several Bellini frankly resorts to Byzantine archetypes. The so-called *Madonna greca* (in the Pinacoteca di Brera, Milan), is a particularly beautiful and solemn example of the genre. The stony-faced maiden clasping her sad little son with such pained solicitude seems to contain within her an almost unbearable sorrow. Yet she remains, as her son does, utterly removed from us: an icon of grief.

No Venetian author could ever have written, as the Florentines Vasari and Ghiberti did, of the sterility and ugliness of the *maniera greca*; and it is an inherent part of Bellini's genius that no matter how clearly he understood the power and appeal of the new Southern and Northern forms of pictorial naturalism, neither did he ever cease being haunted by the more mystical Byzantine modes of expression. His art, it might be said, exists in the gap between fixed styles.

Among the richest of all Bellini's works are his late altarpieces. In the San Zaccaria altarpiece [23], painted in 1505, four saints stand beside the enthroned Virgin and Child. Bellini's mastery of the techniques of oil painting is so absolute, in this work, that he plays with the medium's illusionistic possibilities even to the extent of painting out of focus. The saints have been placed almost too close to us, so they are slightly blurred, while the Virgin and Child are sharp and clear. The Madonna and Jesus are plainly the centre of attention, even though they are not in the line of vision of the saints, who are contemplating them with their inner eye. By exploring depth of field Bellini has also explored depths of consciousness. This type of picture is generally known as a *sacra conversazione*, or sacred conversation, but *sacra meditazione* would be a better description.

The painted architecture in which the scene is set, with its finely chiselled, classical pilasters, is a reminder that this is a 'Renaissance' painting in the literal sense of that word – a picture which attempts to recover the lost beauties of antiquity. Yet much more than that alone is taking place in this picture. The vulnerable body of the infant Christ, held up with infinite tenderness, is a sign of the continuing legacy of Franciscanism. The pensive saints, serious and substantial and statuesque, ultimately recall the art of Giotto. The vivid play of colour in the draperies of the figures recalls that of Duccio and the Sienese traditions of painting.

Many different histories of art and religion are written into the surface of Bellini's painting. There is even a trace of San Marco here. The mosaic semi-dome above the Virgin and Child, each tessera lovingly painted, is like a trace memory of the splendours of Byzantium, shadowy but not quite forgotten. All is held perfectly in balance. Like the unheard melody played by the angel at the base of the Virgin's throne, like the Renaissance itself, Bellini's painting is a harmony of many parts.

CHAPTER TWO

# THE PURE RADIANCE OF THE PAST

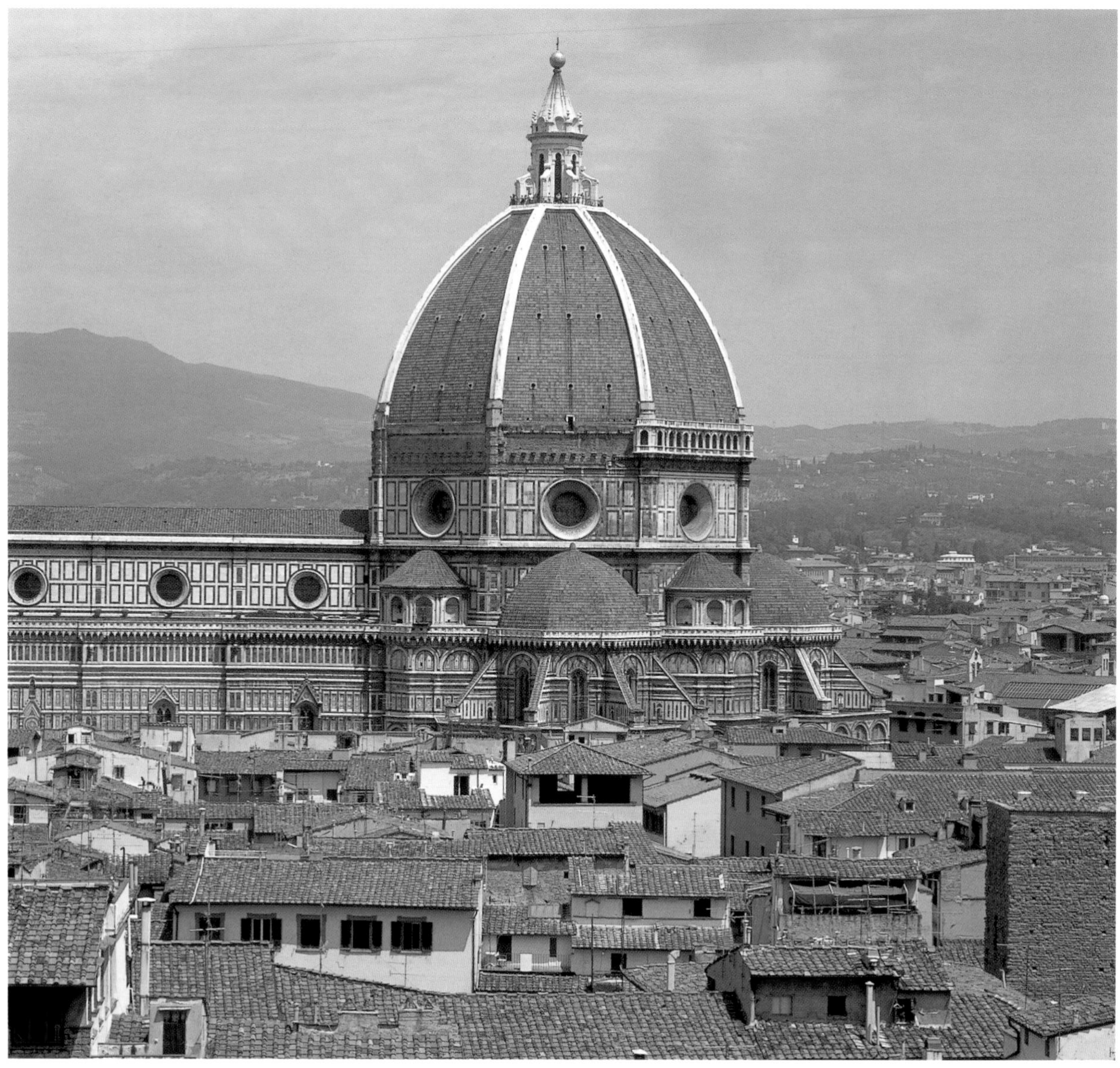

24 FILIPPO BRUNELLESCHI Dome, Florence Cathedral 1420–36

I used to marvel and at the same time to grieve
that so many excellent and superior arts and sciences from our
most vigorous antique past could seem lacking and almost wholly lost.
We know from remaining works and through references to them that
they were once widespread. Painters, sculptors, architects, musicians,
geometricians, rhetoricians, seers and similar noble and amazing
intellects are very rarely found today and there are few to praise them.
Thus I believed, as many said, that Nature, the mistress of things,
had grown old and tired. She no longer produced either geniuses
or giants which in her more youthful and more glorious days
she had produced so marvellously and abundantly.

Since then, I have been brought back here to Florence …
into this our city, adorned above all others. I have come to
understand that in many men, but especially in you, Filippo
[Brunelleschi], and in our close friend Donato [Donatello]
the sculptor, and in others like Nencio [Ghiberti] …
and Masaccio, there is a genius for every praiseworthy thing.

LEON BATTISTA ALBERTI, *On Painting*, 1434

## 'THE WORKSHOP OF THE MODERN EUROPEAN SPIRIT'

While playing the small-time crook Harry Lime in *The Third Man*, Orson Welles improvised a brief but memorably forthright speech on the nature and history of Western civilization: 'In Italy for thirty years under the Borgias, they had warfare, terror, murder, bloodshed – they produced Michelangelo, Leonardo da Vinci and the Renaissance. In Switzerland they had brotherly love, 500 years of democracy and peace – and what did they produce? The cuckoo clock.'[1]

Harry Lime, an unreliable man in most respects, was also an unreliable historian. He was wrong on two counts. The cuckoo clock, according to those whose business it is to know about such things, was invented by a German horologist living in the Black Forest; and the Swiss have been by no means as intellectually inert as he suggested. Indeed, Harry Lime's own ideas about the achievements of Michelangelo, Leonardo and the Italian Renaissance would have been very different if it had not been for a book which was written in Switzerland.

The man responsible for that book – the most influential work written on the subject during the last two centuries – was a Professor of History at Basel University called Jacob Burckhardt (1818–97). In 1860 he published *The Civilization of the Renaissance in Italy*. Together with Vasari's *Lives of the Artists*, it forms the Bible of Renaissance studies, Burckhardt being, so to speak, the New Testament to Vasari's Old.

While his contemporary Charles Darwin went in search of man's biological origins, Burckhardt went in quest of man's cultural and intellectual origins. He found them, or so he thought, in Renaissance Italy. He believed that the men of the Italian Renaissance shook off the yoke of ancient religious superstitions and began to manifest the first signs of what he termed 'the modern European spirit'. Burckhardt summed up what he meant by that large and sweeping claim, near the beginning of the second part of *The Civilization of the Renaissance in Italy*, in what remains a frequently quoted passage:

> In the Middle Ages both sides of human consciousness – that which was turned within as that which was turned without – lay dreaming or half-awake beneath a common veil. The veil was woven of faith, illusion and childish prepossession, through which the world and history were seen clad in strange hues. Man was conscious of himself only as a member of

> a race, people, party, family or corporation – only through some general category. In Italy this veil first melted into air; an *objective* treatment and consideration of the state and of all the things of this world became possible. The *subjective* side at the same time asserted itself with corresponding emphasis; man became a spiritual *individual* and recognized himself as such.[2]

Thus the age of faith gave way to the age of reason and modern man was born.

Not only did Burckhardt frame what remains one of the grandest and clearest expositions of what the Renaissance was, and why it mattered; he also left a clear trail for those who would follow in his footsteps and decide for themselves whether his large claims were actually true. Burckhardt's advice was simple. If you want to understand the Renaissance, go to Florence. Once there, muse on its past, study the sculpture and painting and architecture which was produced there, and you will understand why the city was 'the most important workshop of the Italian, and indeed of the modern European spirit'.[3]

Burckhardt was one of a long line of people to have sung the praises of Renaissance Florence, including Vasari. But when he wrote his book the city had fallen somewhat out of fashion. He put Florence back on the map. Ever since he published *The Civilization of the Renaissance in Italy*, a visit there has become, in many people's minds, one of life's essential experiences: not a mere journey, but a rite; a necessary pilgrimage to that sacred place identified as the cradle, not only of the Renaissance, but of modern Western civilization.

## THE FIFTH ELEMENT

Florence today is a relatively modest town but at the start of the fifteenth century it was one of the largest and most prosperous cities in Europe. Its population had been reduced by the Black Death but in 1400 it still stood at around 70,000 – considerably more than that of Paris or London. Unlike most other city states on the Italian peninsula, Florence remained a republic, although it was always a politically volatile place, in turns riven and driven by the fierce competitive tendencies of its people.

Florence's wealth, rooted in the textile trade and in banking, had been accumulated gradually over more than two centuries. Through the twin channels of trade and commerce, the city reached out to shape the rest of Europe. When the crowned heads of Europe wished to wage war on one another, it was to Florentine moneylenders that they turned. The city's coin, the florin, was the only truly international currency. Because of Florence's commercial power and the extent of the city's influence, Tuscan, the native Florentine dialect, became the most commonly spoken language in all of Italy (modern Italian is directly derived from it). In 1300 Pope Boniface VIII joked that there must be five elements, not four, because 'wherever you find Earth, Water, Air and Fire you also find Florentines'.[4]

To prosper in this thriving, mercantile society – a fundamentally urban world quite unlike much of the rest of Europe, dominated as it was by the landed nobility and the clergy – certain very particular skills were required. Numeracy was vital. So too was a high degree of literacy, and various associated abilities including a mastery of Latin, which was the official language of statecraft and diplomacy.

The fourteenth century, during which the type of Italian city state epitomized by the Florentine Republic had grown and prospered, had seen the gradual evolution of a new approach to education tailored to the needs of those living and working in such a society. The fundamental innovation of the men who formulated this new approach was a changed syllabus which gave particular emphasis to five academic subjects: grammar, rhetoric, poetry, history and moral philosophy. The teachers who offered these subjects took their inspiration from the Roman orator and politician Marcus Tullius Cicero, and based their syllabus on his description of the course of studies most appropriate for the education of a free-born Roman male citizen. They did so, in part, because they believed that the social conditions of the Roman Republic in the first century BC, when Cicero had written, were duplicated in the city republics of fourteenth-century Italy.[5]

The new teachers called their course of studies the *studia humanitatis* – a term borrowed, like their syllabus, from Cicero – and they in turn became known by the nickname given to them by their students: *humanisti*, or humanists. This might seem no more than a footnote to the history of secondary education, but 'humanism', an educational and literary movement geared to the training of lawyers, merchants, bankers, orators and statesmen, was to have an immeasurable impact on the fabric of society. Nowhere would its effects be more keenly experienced than in Florence.

## 'THE PURE RADIANCE OF THE PAST'

By the middle of the fourteenth century the *studia humanitatis* – an education, so to speak, in persuasiveness, which focused on Latin authors primarily as models of fine rhetoric and sound argument – had been infused with a strain of idealism.

The key figure in this development was the scholar and poet Petrarch. Born in Arezzo in 1304, he eventually settled at the papal court of Avignon. He had a strong belief in the ethical value of literature, in the power of the word to influence human thought and action. He saw in the authors of ancient Rome, above all in Cicero, whom he called 'the great genius of antiquity', powerful moral examples for the present. Petrarch did more than any other humanist to change attitudes to the classical past. His followers became increasingly interested in ancient poets, orators and historians, not simply as examples of style, but in their own right, as figures worthy of study and even a form of devotion.

One consequence of this was an explosion of information about the classical world. The humanists searched the monastic libraries of Europe and Byzantium for works by the ancient writers whom they most admired. In the process they discovered much that had been lost and to a great extent established the modern canon of Latin and Greek texts. But, most important of all, they began to read classical authors in a new way. It was this, rather than the physical location of previously lost texts, which constituted the heart of the 'rediscovery' of antiquity.

Humanism was never (as is sometimes assumed) a philosophical stance comparable, say, to logical positivism or existentialism. It was a new approach to the literature of the past. But it did have certain philosophical implications, in that the intellectual priorities of the humanists predisposed them to certain ways of thinking. Classical writers had been well known to scholars of the eleventh, twelfth and thirteenth centuries, but they had been treated as 'authorities' and their works split up into '*sententiae*', or individual factual statements about specific issues. These discrete remarks, detached from the texts of which they originally formed part, were then treated as matter for debate by scholastic theologians – with the result that hardly an author was ever read for himself, but was instead experienced piecemeal, his opinions subsumed within a scheme not of his own making. The humanists, however, came to believe that every opinion was to be read in its proper context. They placed great importance on the need to go back to the full, original text of every author's work. As a result, the writers of the past were given back their individuality and, with it, their vitality.

Petrarch's sympathetic engagement with the ancient authors impressed upon him how inalienably different they were from his own contemporaries. Armed with this insight, he taught his contemporaries to see the gap which separated their world from that of classical antiquity. His most original contribution to the thought of his time was the concept of historical discontinuity. The notion that history is made up of distinct periods or eras, each of which has its own individual characteristics, was both new and extremely powerful. The polemical conclusions which Petrarch drew from this idea altered his world for ever.

He argued that Western civilization had fallen into darkness with the crumbling of the Roman Empire. It was at that point, he argued, that the classical world had become disjunct with the world that succeeded it. From the notion of a past that had been lost, a world that had receded into dead history, he elaborated a dream of rebirth – a fantasy of bringing that classical world back, once more, to life. He argued that with the humanist revival of classical scholarship, the light of true civilization had begun to shine again. But this was only the beginning. 'After the darkness has been dispelled, our grandsons will be able to walk back into the pure radiance of the past', he wrote at the end of his epic poem *Africa*.[6]

In order to accommodate his view of the development of human history, Petrarch devised a splendidly bold scheme for classifying its different periods: a first and golden era – that of Classical Civilization – to be followed by a median period of darkness – the Middle Ages – in turn to be followed by a new age of civilization reborn. Petrarch's tripartite division of all human history was much later adopted by Vasari, who applied this model – with all its imperfections – to the story of art in Italy. Unlike Vasari, Petrarch never used the word '*Rinascita*' in any of his writings. But he devised the intellectual framework without which the idea of a Renaissance could never have come into existence.

Yet when Petrarch died, in 1384, it was quite possible that his ideas about the classical past might die with him. He could have been remembered as little more than a discontented poet and intellectual, with interesting but somewhat idiosyncratic ideas, had it not been for the keenness with which those ideas were seized upon in Florence. It was in Florence that Petrarch's dream of a revival took deepest root. It was in Florence that his prophecy was given shape not in words alone but in the very stones of a city.

## THE CHANCELLOR

Leonardo Bruni, humanist, historian and former chancellor of the Florentine Republic, died on 9 March 1444, aged seventy. At his funeral he was crowned with a wreath of laurel and the sculptor Bernardo Rossellino was subsequently charged with his immortalization. The costly yet austere funerary monument [25] which Rossellino created for Bruni in the Florentine church of Santa Croce is an eloquent memorial to an eloquent man. Within a niche framed by a crisply carved arch, Rossellino's effigy of Bruni, classically draped and wearing a laurel wreath, lies sleeping on a bier supported by fierce Roman eagles. His face is turned towards the viewer. Modelled with gentle but close attention to physiognomic detail, probably from Bruni's death mask, it is the face of a very real and tired old man with slightly sagging jowls.

Bruni's memorial is impressive but also ambiguous. It seems unsure about what kind of immortality would be appropriate to confer upon him. In a little roundel set into the arch at the top of the tomb, a stone Virgin and Child form a heavenly welcome party. But the carved figure of Bruni below makes of him a Roman hero and the bier on which he rests has been placed, itself, upon a sarcophagus containing a Latin inscription:

> POSTQVAM LEONARDVS EVITA MIGRAVIT
> HISTORIA LVSET ELOQVENTIA MVTA EST
> FERTVRQUE MVSAS TVM GRAECAS TVM
> LATINAS LACRIMAS TENERE NO POTVISSE.

'Since Leonardo departed from life, history is in mourning, eloquence is dumb and the Greek and Latin muses cannot hold back their tears.' This might seem, to modern eyes, something of a paradox. With the blessing of Christ and the Virgin Mary a man enters the classical pantheon of fame, joining the heroes of the pagan classical world on the slopes of Mount Parnassus. There are hints here of tensions to come – the gulf separating such different views of the afterlife would not, in future, always be so easily bridged – but in the Bruni monument itself Christian faith and an idealized view of antiquity seem quite at peace with one another. Two dreams are enshrined together: a dream of eternal life among the blessed; and Petrarch's dream of a rebirth, of walking back into the 'radiance of the past' and living among the ancients.

The carved figure of Bruni clasps a book to his chest. It may be his *Panegyric to the City of Florence*, which he composed in 1403–4 and which remains the classic text of Florentine civic propaganda.[7] It was written in response to a political crisis. With the exception of Venice, Florence was then the only republic in Italy to have resisted rule by a single despotic individual or family, and the Florentines were painfully conscious of their singularity in this respect. For all its mercantile and commercial success, Florence was politically vulnerable during the early fifteenth century. Throughout Bruni's youth the Milanese, under the despotic rule of the Visconti family, had their eyes on the rich pickings to be had by conquering the city – a feat which they almost managed, on more than one occasion. Coluccio

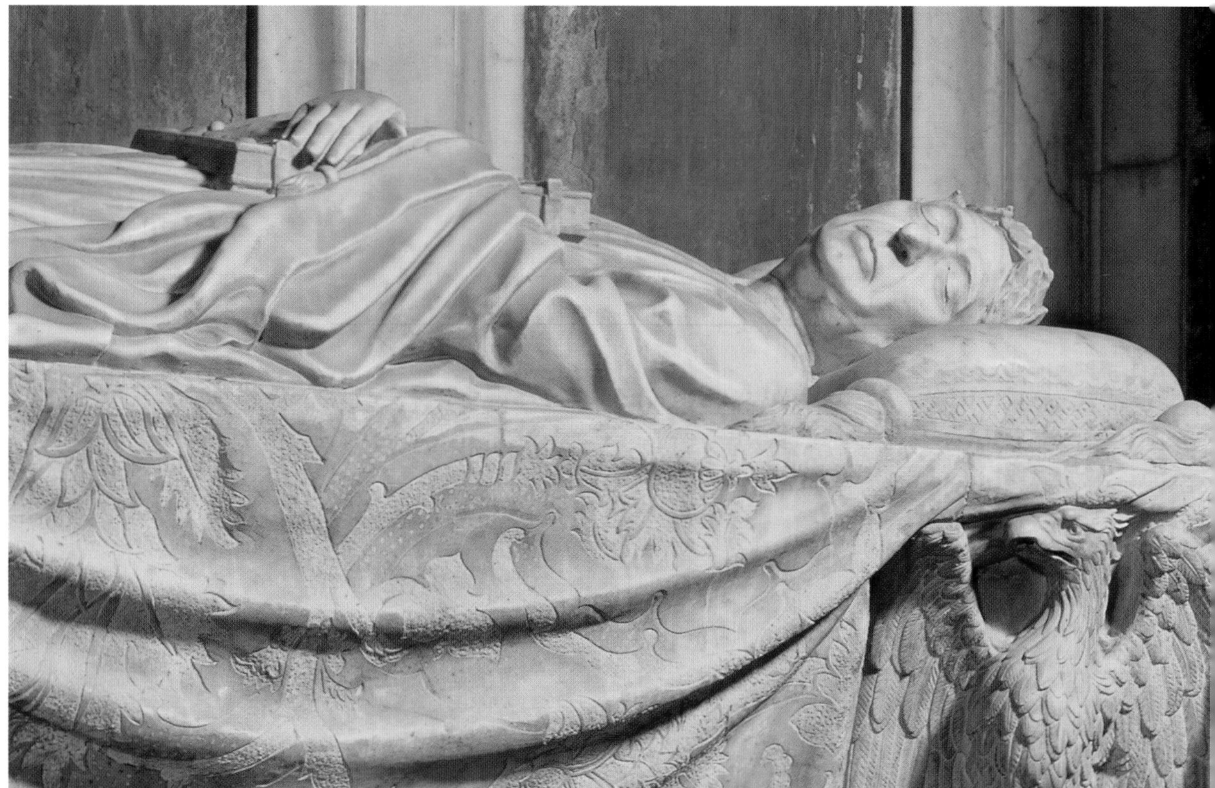

25 BERNARDO ROSSELLINO Tomb of Leonardo Bruni *c.* 1444–6

Salutati, Bruni's teacher, and the chancellor of Florence during these difficult years, had worked hard to formulate a series of propagandistic counterblasts to the Milanese threat. Salutati had drawn heavily on the conveniently republican rhetoric of Petrarch's hero, Cicero, to create an ideology of Florentine 'liberty' coloured heavily by the classical past. But it was Bruni who perfected that ideology. He strove to bolster Florence's defences against all future threats of invasion by employing the only weapons in the use of which he, as a humanist scholar, had been trained: words. He created a rousing image of Florence behind which the people were to rally.

The peroration in which he did so most fully, his *Panegyric*, was modelled on the *Panathenaicus*, a eulogy of Periclean Athens by the Greek author Isocrates. In the *Panegyric* Bruni envisaged Florence as a material and spiritual paragon of the ideal *polis*. The city, he said, was the very epitome of cultural enlightenment, political virtue and mercantile initiative. Florentine merchants, he boasted, had travelled to the very perimeters of the known world (as far afield even as that cold and obscure place known as Britain, 'an island situated almost on the edge of the world'). Florentine citizens enjoyed unparalleled rights. Florentine soldiers fought valiantly for the principle of Italian liberty, no matter how heavily the odds might be stacked against them.

Bruni's Florence, another Athens and a second Rome, was to stand firm for liberty against the despotism of tyrants. It was to stand for true civilization against what he and his generation had been taught by the writings of Petrarch to regard as the barbarism of the 'dark ages'. Thus had the ideals of humanism, and the dream of a rebirth, been yoked to the very real political exigencies of a particular time, and a particular place. Out of the ideology to which Leonardo Bruni gave such eloquent expression, a new art and a new architecture would arise.

## ORSANMICHELE

The generation of artists who came to maturity in Leonardo Bruni's Florence were manifestly affected by the ideas to which he gave such rousing expression. The ethos of the city which he set out to create – independent, implacably opposed to despotic rule, indebted to the moral and political example of ancient Rome – would be reflected in their art.

The modest stone cube known simply as Orsanmichele [26] stands on the Via dei Calzaiuoli – the Street of the Shoemakers, now lined with rather expensive boutiques. Nowhere else can the case be argued, quite so vividly, for the Florentine Renaissance of the early fifteenth century as a stark and sudden reorientation of human sensibilities. The Via dei Calzaiuoli is one of the city's main thoroughfares, connecting the ancient religious heart of the city, the Piazza del Duomo, to its civic centre, the Piazza della Signoria. Orsanmichele thus stood at the mid-point of the city, fulfilling an unusual combination of sacred and secular roles. Built in the fourteenth century to house an image of the Virgin believed to have magical powers – an image to which the people of Florence prayed in droves during the many political crises which beset their town – it was the official church of the city's trade guilds. In times of war or famine its upper floors were used as the town's emergency grain store.

During the first quarter of the fifteenth century a small group of sculptors, working in stone and bronze, gradually filled the niches on the exterior of Orsanmichele. They created a stern, determined band of saints and martyrs, at once Christian and classical in spirit, to stand guard over the precious contents of the

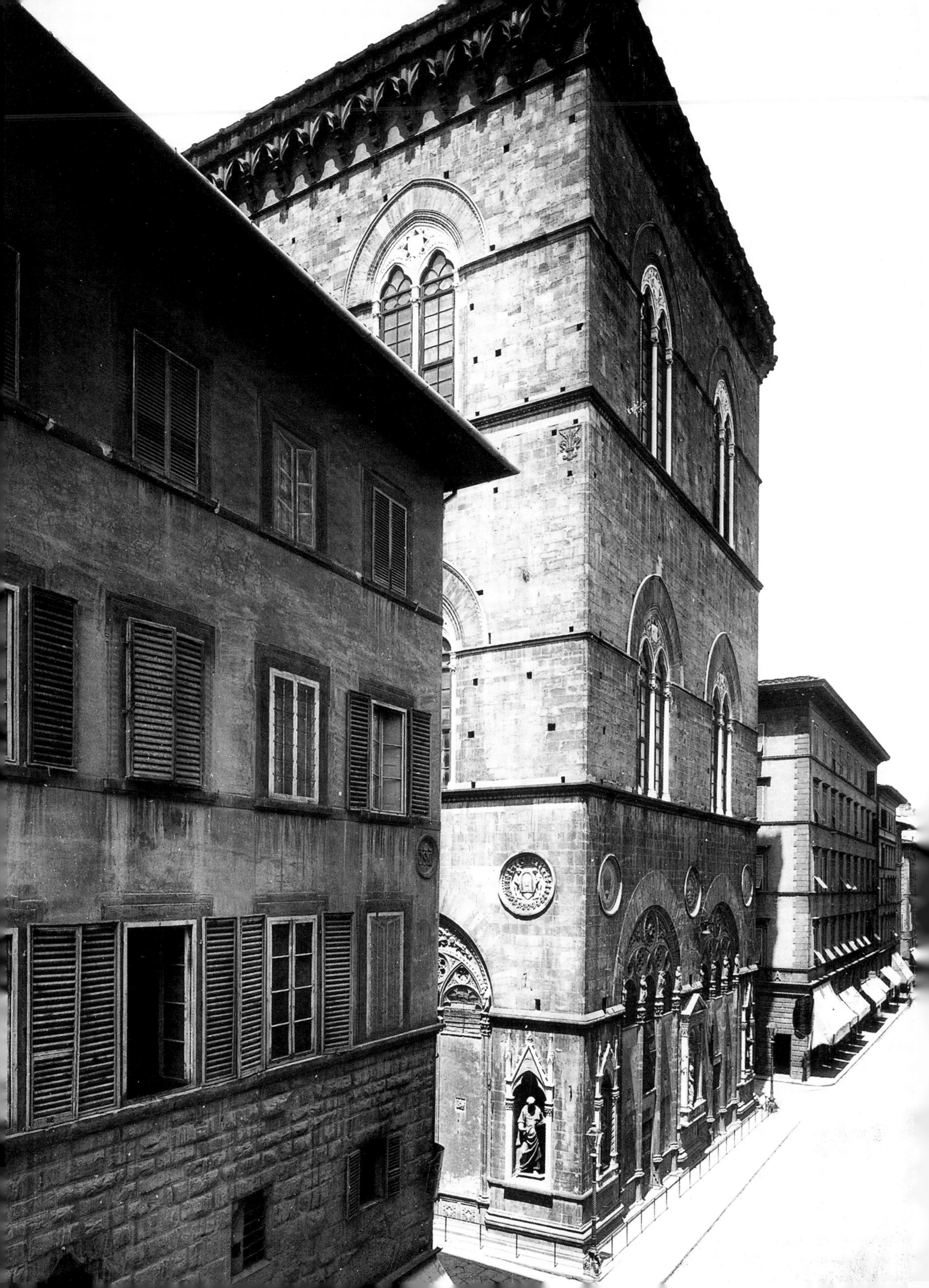

building. These works announced a new relationship between art and the people. Standing in niches set only just above head height, they seemed almost to speak to the man and woman in the street. The new public sculpture was, like Bruni's *Panegyric*, conceived in a spirit of defiance and civic celebration. Rhetorically persuasive, senatorially dignified, the tribe of heroes created by these sculptors embodies Bruni's dream of an ideal Florence.

The most incontrovertibly classical and Brunian of all the sculptures on the exterior is Nanni di Banco's masterpiece, *Four Crowned Martyrs* [27], created for the Florentine guild of stoneworkers and carvers. The martyrs in question were the patron saints of that guild: Castorius, Claudius, Symphorianus and Nicostratus, a group of early Christian sculptors who, according to legend, refused to carve a statue of the god Aesculapius for the Roman emperor Diocletian and were executed for their disobedience. Nanni made these Christian offenders of imperial Rome into the very image of republican fortitude. Indeed, the bold implication of his sculpture is that these men were more truly Roman, in their nobility of spirit, than those who martyred them. This seems to be a direct reflection of Bruni's ideas.

The author of the *Panegyric* had been very precise about which particular period of Roman history modern, fifteenth-century Florentines should seek to emulate. The Rome *not* to imitate, he said, was imperial Rome, that of Diocletian, Nero and Tiberius, with his 'lovers and gigolos, who were given to such unspeakable types of sexual behaviour'; of 'Caligula and other monsters and vile tyrants who were innocent of no vice and redeemed by no virtue'. The Rome which Bruni held up before his countrymen as theirs to resurrect was, instead, the Rome of the Republic, ruled by those 'many fine and outstanding leaders and heads of the Senate ... the families of the Publicoli, Fabricii, Corruncani, Dentati' in that period before the coming of the Caesars and the stopping up of the sacred springs of freedom. Nanni di Banco's conscientious objectors, men in togas standing up to an evil emperor, embody the communal solidarity which Bruni set out to promote in the city. Four heroes making their vows of obdurate resistance, standing firm against despotism, they form a semicircle of human resolve.

Nanni borrowed heavily from classical art in arriving at his final composition. The individual figures closely resemble draped figures in antique sculpture; and the uncommon motif of the cloth hung on the wall of the niche behind the four martyrs is found before the fifteenth century only in classical reliefs. The sculptures on Orsanmichele announce the advent not just of a new style, in Florentine art, but of a new ambition on the part of artists – a self-conscious desire to imitate and, if possible, surpass the statuary of the antiquity.

26 Orsanmichele, Florence 1337–80

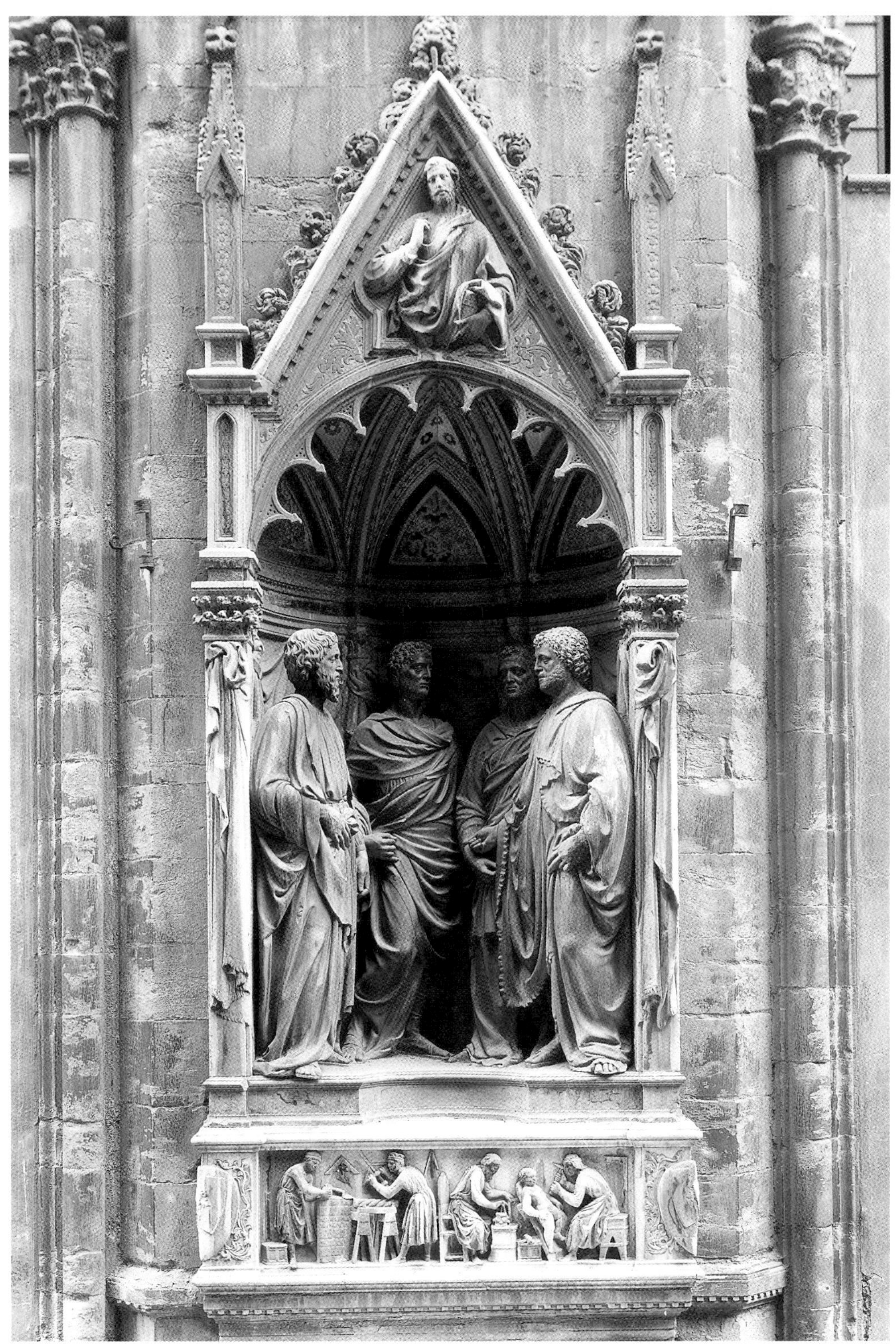

27 NANNI DI BANCO *Four Crowned Martyrs*, Orsanmichele, Florence (and 28, 29 opposite) *c.* 1412–15

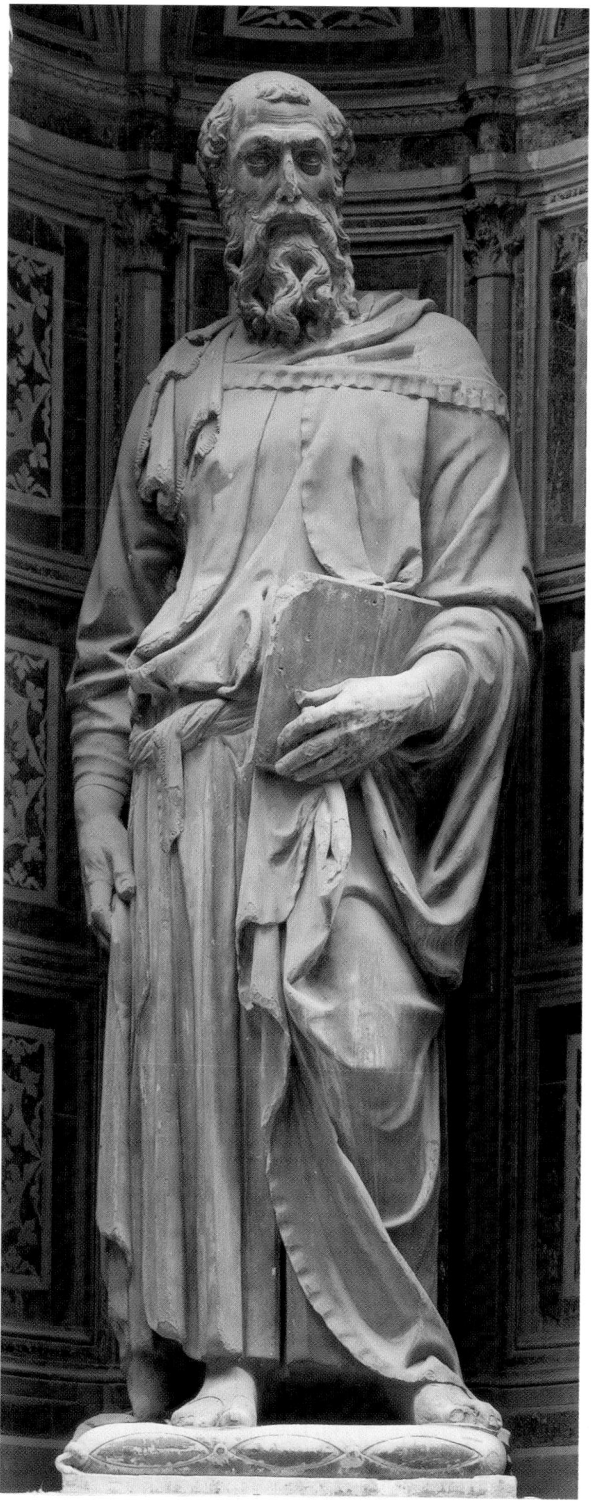

28 DONATELLO *St Mark* 1411–13

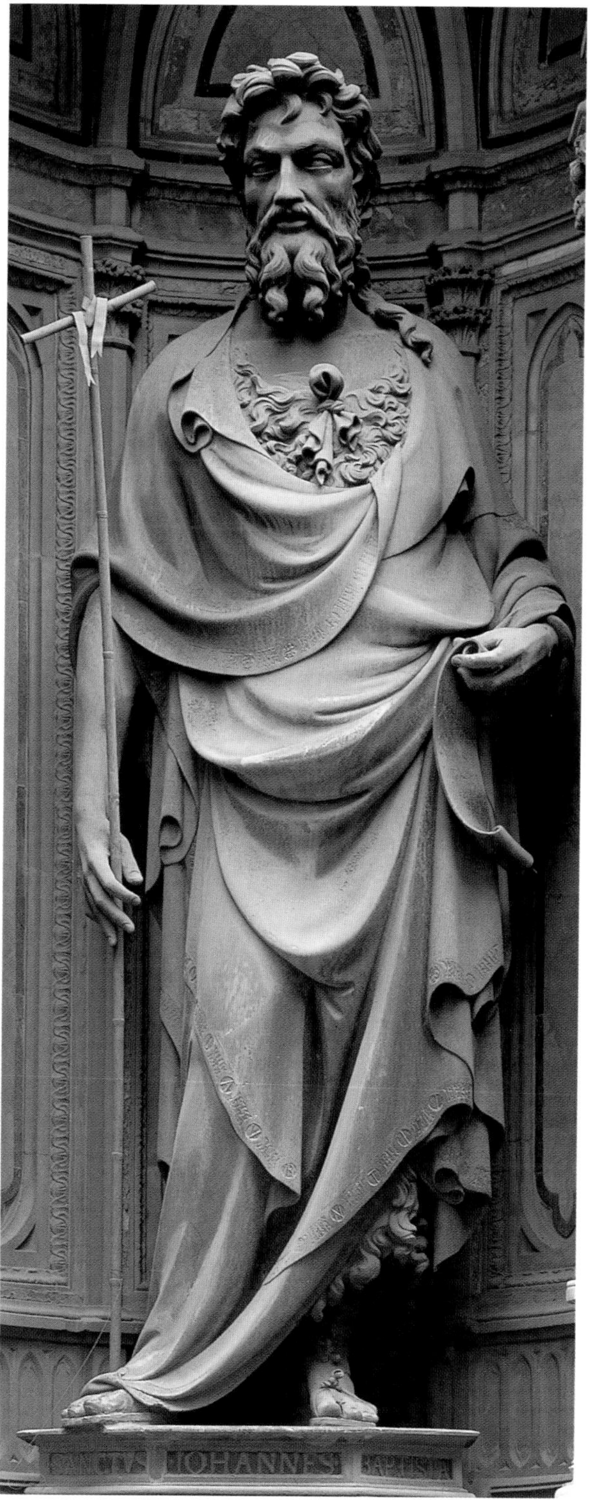

29 LORENZO GHIBERTI *St John the Baptist* c. 1412–16

One of the earliest of the Orsanmichele sculptures is Donatello's life-size marble figure of *St Mark* [28], created around 1411-13. It is the likeness of a real man in the real world. Before Donatello's time the saints and prophets carved for the façades of European cathedrals had conventionally been depicted as heavenly courtiers wearing rich and splendid clothes. But Donatello reinvented the genre by taking a great leap of the imagination, projecting himself back across the centuries and asking himself what the first prophets must really have been like.

The carved saint is not the occupant of some higher zone, not an icon, but God's spokesman on earth. Heaven is present in the sculpture, but it has been displaced to the psychology of the saint, awe of God's magnificence and terror implied by the profound and mystical nature of his gaze – at once abstracted yet focused, absolutely, on the higher truths related in the gospel which he carries under his arm.

While he consciously abandoned the mechanisms of mystification employed by many religious artists to have worked before him, Donatello was clearly influenced by those earlier Italian masters of naturalistic carving, Nicola and Giovanni Pisano. In many ways his work is best seen not as a sudden departure from medieval art – as it is often described – but as an intensification of its physical and psychological realism. That is not to say that Donatello was not an extremely innovatory artist. What he brought to art in his time was a new, more organic form of naturalism than that practised by his Italian predecessors. Whereas an artist such as Giovanni Pisano had drawn on the legacy of classical sculpture to give his figures an intense physical immediacy – to create a muscled back, or an agonized ribcage – those figures remain dramatic *images* of humanity rather than human individuals rendered in stone. It is difficult to imagine a Pisano figure in movement; but Donatello's *St Mark* looks as though he could step off his plinth at any moment.

Donatello's greatest innovation, in terms of the practice of sculpture in his time, was to make an absolute distinction in his own mind between the body and its clothes. There is evidence that the artist's preparatory procedures included the creation of a clay model of the figure, naked, which he then dressed in real clothes, basing his final carving on the result. This partly accounts for the physical plausibility and dynamism of the carved saint, the way in which his seems a body motivated from within, weight momentarily balanced on his right foot, but capable of further movement. More mysterious, and less accessible to technical explanation, is the strong sense of character with which Donatello endowed his creation. The pensive *St Mark* radiates an intense aura of mental singularity. A large part of the miracle of Donatello's work, to those who came after him, was that he seemed to have carved thought itself.

Orsanmichele was also a monument to the spirit of competition that was such a marked part of Florentine city life. The different Florentine guilds vied with one another to commission the most impressive public statues for the niches on the building's exterior. Donatello's *St Mark* was commissioned by the Arte dei Linaiuoli, the guild of linenmakers and upholsterers – hence the carved cushion on which the saint stands. Lorenzo Ghiberti's larger-than-life bronze statue of *St John the Baptist* [29] was commissioned by the Arte di Calimala, the guild of cloth-merchants.

Ghiberti's *St John* lacks the naturalistic coherence of Donatello's *St Mark* but is in its own way just as impressive a work of art. One of the largest sculptures to have been cast in bronze since antiquity, the work would have been regarded by Ghiberti's contemporaries as a tremendous feat of technological innovation. A towering figure in a hair shirt, with his vivid, living eyes, the *St John* is a severe and forbidding presence, an appropriately daunting image of the city's patron saint.

There is a fierceness about many of the figures carved for Orsanmichele, and that is an important part of their meaning too. Their defensive posture – most of them look tense or primed at least for action – seems to speak of the Florentine Republic's own sense of its political vulnerability at this period in its history. This mood of apprehension is most clearly expressed in the most renowned of all of the Orsanmichele sculptures, Donatello's *St George* [30]. Half man, half boy, this adolescent knight in armour, waiting for a dragon to vanquish, is rather too short to occupy his niche with absolute authority. This is a clever piece of psychological manipulation on Donatello's part – his way of making us feel the magnitude of the unseen horror his hero must face by building a hint of it into the scale relationships of the work. The hero was originally fitted with a sword and steel helmet – the sculpture was commissioned by the guild of armourers, who used it show off their wares – but that can scarcely have lessened the effect.

The saint with the physiognomy of a Greek god has worries forever on his mind. His brow is furrowed. The ideal Florentine, eternally vigilant, is not immune to anxiety. Yet Donatello's *St George* seems more too than an image of Florence alone. The statue is also the epitome of the artist's own changeable genius. The stone man is full of energies which he himself may not fully comprehend. He is alert, but tense, on the brink of all that he does not know, and all that he is about to become.

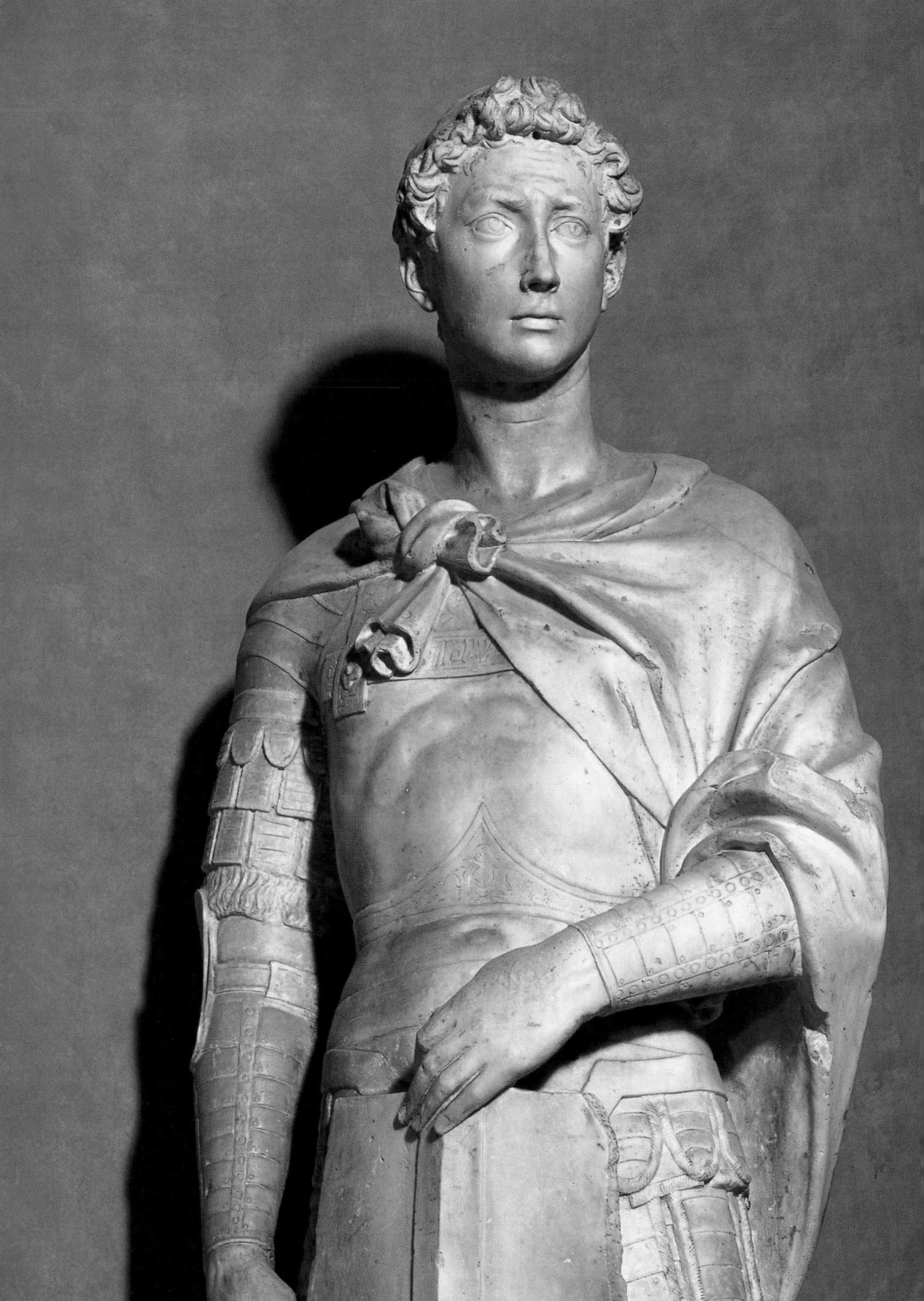

## IN THE SHADOW OF THE DOME

Orsanmichele was at the heart of a revolution in sculpture that swept across Florence during the early fifteenth century, and which spread across to the other buildings of the city. The primacy of sculpture in the early years of the Florentine *Rinascita* – the fact that it was unquestionably the art form which led the way in articulating the new Florentine sense of itself as a second, Christian Rome – can be difficult to appreciate. Many of the Orsanmichele sculptures have had to be brought indoors to preserve them against the effects of weather and traffic pollution. The solidarity which they once expressed has thus been dissolved and they have been turned into rather more solitary figures than their creators originally envisaged. They have become exhibits, no longer speaking to the people but muttering to themselves in museums. The same is true of most of the other works which completed the city's new tribe of heroic statuary: the multitude of equally extraordinary but yet more severely weathered sculptures carved by Donatello and his contemporaries, for the niches on the front of the cathedral and its belltower, the campanile. Taken altogether, thirty-four larger than life-size statues were carved for the public spaces of Florence: a great stone chorus proclaiming the indomitability of the republic.

Florence's political propaganda should, however, be taken with a pinch of salt. The city was never a republic in the modern sense, and although its leaders officially condemned despotism they were not always faithful friends of liberty themselves. Florence had a habit of annexing its neighbours and brought several previously independent cities including Volterra, Arezzo (Bruni's birthplace), Pisa and Cortona into submission.

What was perhaps most remarkable about the Florentines, during the years when their city was under threat, was their constant willingness to spend enormous sums of money on images – set up in all parts of the city, almost like totems, to ward off danger. It is as if they had more faith in art, with its propitiatory powers, than in armies. This was reflected in other spheres of activity too. The most impressive piece of architecture of the time was no military fortification but a huge and beautiful dome built to crown the city's cathedral [24].

The skeleton of the dome was constructed, under the direction of Filippo Brunelleschi, between 1420 and 1436. The humanist, architect and art theorist Leon Battista Alberti was in no doubt about the magnitude of this uniquely Florentine achievement. 'Who could be hard or envious enough to fail to praise Pippo [Filippo] the architect on seeing here such a large structure, rising above the

30 DONATELLO *St George* (detail) *c.* 1415–17

skies, ample to cover with its shadow all the Tuscan people', he wrote. 'Since this work seems impossible of execution in our time, if I judge rightly, it was probably unknown and unthought-of among the Ancients.'[8]

The new public statuary on Orsanmichele and the façade of the cathedral had addressed the citizenry at street level. Brunelleschi's great dome, its huge expanse covered with rust-red tiles – they catch the light, on sunny days, like the scales of some giant fish – was designed to be visible from every part of the city and at all times. Its address is not intimate but monumental. It is so huge and unavoidable a presence in the city that it is more like a fact of nature, a great rock or crag, than anything anyone actually made. Tourists ascending it today find themselves cheered, halfway up the climb, by a sign which tacitly acknowledges this: 'To the Summit', it announces.

Like the new bronze-cast sculptures of Ghiberti, Brunelleschi's dome was a technological marvel. The body of the cathedral had been substantially completed by the second half of the fourteenth century. The challenge, for the architect, was to figure out a way of building a dome above such a wide space without having to erect a forest of scaffolding. He devised a method of construction which made the dome self-supporting, thereby enabling the workforce to ascend, securely, within the structure as they built it. To keep the dome as light as possible, Brunelleschi designed a double shell built from bricks laid herringbone-fashion for maximum strength – a solution reached partly through ingenuity, and partly through the study of Roman and Islamic building methods.

Brunelleschi conceived the dome, to express the matter in humanist terms, as an architectural *imitatio* – a rivalrous homage to the antique, a Florentine version of the ancient dome of the Pantheon in Rome. But it is much larger than the Pantheon, being at the time of its construction the largest dome in the world (only to be superseded by that designed by Michelangelo for St Peter's a century and a half later); and although Brunelleschi visited Rome to measure and study classical buildings, in the end his dome owed precious little, aesthetically at least, to the architecture of antiquity. The dome is patently Gothic, not a Roman hemisphere but a lanterned vault arching skywards, its unclassical dynamism emphasized by the great white curving ribs of stone – they have also been likened to the spokes of an umbrella – which subdivide its exterior. The architect must have realized that a classical dome would have sat uneasily on top of Florence's great Gothic cathedral. In any event, the laws of physics decided the matter. A Roman, hemispherical dome of the size required by the existing medieval buttresses would have inevitably collapsed. The pointed dome was adopted by necessity and Brunelleschi was left to signal his intentions to rival antiquity – to indicate, so to speak, the moral and poetic sources for his own imagination – in the detail.

He did so in the tribunes surmounting the additional buttresses which he discovered he had to build to support the weight of the dome. Here, paired columns with Ionic capitals alternate with shell-headed niches, making each tribune a version of the centrally planned temples which Brunelleschi studied among the classical ruins of antiquity – small solid memories of Rome re-created, to somewhat surreal effect, high up in the air. Brunelleschi used the language of Roman architecture yet more playfully in the lantern which caps the dome. This, the crown of the whole design, was treated by the architect as a kind of stone bouquet where all kinds of classical architectural forms were to be picked out and rearranged at whim. A thing of lovely caprice, with its irregular arches and curving volutes sustaining a perfect cone on which sits a great gold ball and cross, it was finished by Michelozzo di Bartolommeo after Brunelleschi's death in 1446 and some part of its enjoyable eccentricity may perhaps be attributed to him. Whether that is the case or not the compromised, inventive, practical character of the dome as a whole speaks of the freedom with which Brunelleschi set out to rival antiquity.

## IDEAL ARCHITECTURE

Brunelleschi's dome was the largest symbol of the new in the new world of the Florentine *Rinascita*, but it was neither the first nor, in purely architectural terms, the most influential of his works. The earliest of his civic projects in Florence, begun in 1419, were his designs for the city's foundling hospital, the Ospedale degli Innocenti, and the square which it faces, the Piazza Santissima Annunziata. This was one of the first unified squares in the history of modern town planning, and in the process of instigating its design Brunelleschi broke decisively both with the existing vocabulary and the prevailing spirit of architecture in his time.

Simplicity is the key to his work, a hatred of elaboration so extreme that it became an article of faith. The beauty of the piazza is inseparable from Brunelleschi's love of the simple structural statement – repeated, in this case, in bold modular fashion until a space has been defined. The module here is an arch supported on two Corinthian columns, the diameter of the arch being a mathematically calculated multiple of the width of the columns. These arches enclose an arcade the depth of which repeats this same measure; each bay of the arcade is capped within not by cross-vaulting but by Brunelleschi's favourite symbol of perfection – a small dome.

Doing away with the *ad hoc* irregularity of planning in his time Brunelleschi sought to turn a piece of urban space into an image of perfect proportion and measure – a new kind of place in which men might move and speak more nobly, where they might perhaps find it easier to transform themselves into the senatorial beings whom the Orsanmichele sculptures told them they should aspire to emulate. The logic of this space was to be as instantly apprehensible, as impressively and incontrovertibly correct, as that of a well-turned mathematical proposition. Space has been shaped to model an ideal of clarity. Brunelleschi also drew on the legacy of Monastic architecture, however, and one could see the square as a species of urban cloister. Once again, the classical and the Christian were intertwined in early fifteenth-century Florence. The roundels set into the spandrels of Brunelleschi's arcade depict boys and girls, literally the foundlings for whom this architecture was built and figuratively the little children whom Christ would succour.

The grandest civic proposition behind the Piazza Santissima Annunziata was the idea that an entire city might be conceived as a work of art. The arcade's modular repetition carries the implication of infinite repeatability – as if the columns of the square could march to the same regular rhythm across the rest of the town, transforming that too into a vision of order. This was not an ambition that would ever be realized, either in Florence or anywhere else in Renaissance Italy.

The two great churches which Brunelleschi designed for Florence, San Lorenzo and Santo Spirito, are the most austere expressions of his architecture *all'antica*. Modelled on the Christian basilicas of early Roman architecture, as well as on Florentine Romanesque churches such as San Miniato al Monte, they are buildings in which structure is clearly meant to rule over ornamentation. The plainer of the two churches, Santo Spirito, is also the one which was more faithfully carried out to Brunelleschi's instruction, even though it was completed long after his death. The space of the crossing in Santo Spirito is a perfect square, a shape repeated exactly to form the choir and the transepts. The nave is four squares long. The aisle bays are the same length but exactly half the width. As in the arcades of the Innocenti scheme the result is an architecture which gives a powerful, sensuous immediacy to the mathematical clarity of its planning. Anyone standing anywhere in this precisely mapped-out grid of space instinctively knows that he is occupying an intellectual scheme. He feels his very being fixed within its co-ordinates.

Brunelleschi's approach to church design is still often described as the canonical 'rational' Renaissance refutation of the 'superstition' of the Middle Ages – a planned rebuttal of the medieval love of glimmering darkness and mysterious

31 FILIPPO BRUNELLESCHI Pazzi Chapel, Santa Croce, Florence, begun *c.* 1430–33

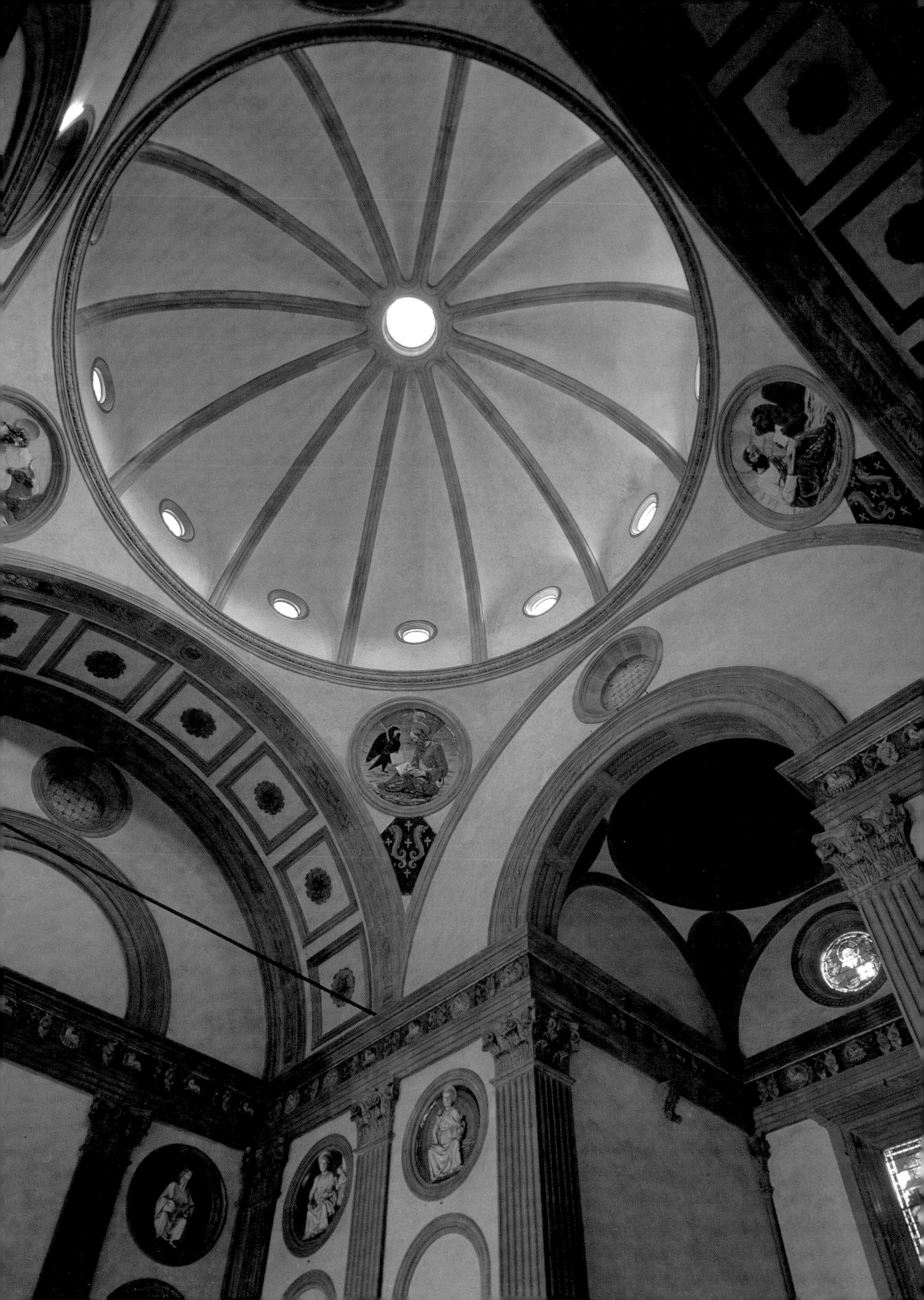

spatial ambiguity, exemplified by the great Gothic cathedrals. This is an idea which has its roots in the anti-clerical intellectual tradition of the nineteenth century – and which owes much to Burckhardt's ideas about Renaissance Florence as the workshop in which the modern, secular world was forged. But it is a misconception. To be sure, to walk into Santo Spirito is to come under the unwavering eye of the architect, to be defined within the logically determined perspective of his groundplan. But this is a vision of order shot through with religious meaning. The spatial clarity of the building should lead us to understand it as a microcosm. Brunelleschi's perfectly ordered architectural plan is an intimation, here on earth, of the Divine Architect's grand scheme.

The exhilarating paradox of Brunelleschi's work is that an architecture so keenly demonstrative of its own spatial limits should yet be able to conjure up such a powerful sense of the limitless. This is most apparent, aptly, in one of the smallest and most circumscribed of all his buildings, the Pazzi Chapel [31], where it is as if infinite space has been bound within a nutshell. Brunelleschi's contemporaries (and perhaps the Pazzi family itself, who commissioned it) may have been struck by the outrageous plainness of the building. It is in essence a simple domed cube, with walls of white stucco, containing only the plainest of stone altars. This bold emptiness is part of its meaning, an elevation of poverty to art which takes even Brunelleschi's standards of architectural restraint to a new extreme.

The underlying principle of all Brunelleschi's architecture, his ambition to express the numinous purely in terms of building structure, had always made the Brunelleschian style implicitly inhospitable to religious imagery – pictures of God being superfluous in buildings which picture the idea of God so absolutely in their form. In the Pazzi Chapel imagery was restricted to a few glazed terracotta roundels of the apostles by Luca della Robbia and Brunelleschi himself, sufficiently sweet and neutral not to interfere with the austerity of the plan. The intensity of the chapel's effect is achieved purely through the disposition of architectural elements, and the nature of that effect depends on the resolution of the contrast between the lower and upper parts of the space.

Below, Brunelleschi models a tense complex of shapes, an array of pilasters, capitals, rosettes, corbels, window frames, all carved from the softest *pietra serena* – that cool, grey Florentine stone which the architect used to such effect that it became almost his signature. They are sensual forms which appeal almost as much to the hand as to the eye, seductively tactile – they could almost be cut from soap rather than stone – and also somehow toylike. The implication is that they are not here for merely functional purposes – several of the window frames openly declare this by enclosing blank expanses of wall – but, rather, to perform some symbolic role. They are a shadow or type of our mundane lives, these blind entrances and exits.

Above, Brunelleschi designs our release. Over the chapel floats an eight-ribbed dome with lights let into its sides and an oculus at its centre. A dome within a cube, a circle within a square, it is a geometrical figure of absolute harmony. Leonardo da Vinci, many years later, drew an ideal man whose outstretched arms and legs formed four equidistant points on the diameter of a perfect circle. Brunelleschi's dome is less explicit about the meaning of its geometry but it too offers the prospect of a transfiguration: an end to the ordinary and the imperfect in a vision of heavenly symmetry. It is the summary of the space, a frame for divine radiance.

## THE DOORS

Florentine genius would never have shown itself as it did without Florentine money. The intellectual leaders of the city recognized this. It is characteristic of the specifically Florentine tenor of Florentine humanist thought that Leonardo Bruni should have dared to disagree with the great Petrarch on the question of wealth. Petrarch had taken a Stoic and Franciscan line on the acquisition of money, arguing that it was invariably the enemy of virtue. The more worldly Bruni took a very different view. In 1419 he translated Aristotle's *Ethics* for the richest merchant prince in all Florence, Cosimo de' Medici, and wrote an accompanying commentary in which he placed great emphasis on Aristotle's doctrine of the moral value of wealth. Another member of Bruni's circle, Stefano Porcari, expressed the Florentine attitude in a ringing speech delivered to the people outside the cathedral one day in 1427:

> Whence are our houses and palaces procured? From riches! Whence come our clothes? Whence the meals for us and our children? From riches! These consecrated churches with their decorations, the walls, the towers, the defences, your palaces and dwellings, the most noble buildings, the bridges, the streets, with what have you built them, whence do you obtain the means of preserving them, if not from riches![9]

But if nothing could be done without money, perhaps it is also true that nothing truly great could be done in Florence without the desire to outshine others. The principle of competition was enshrined in the processes by which works of art

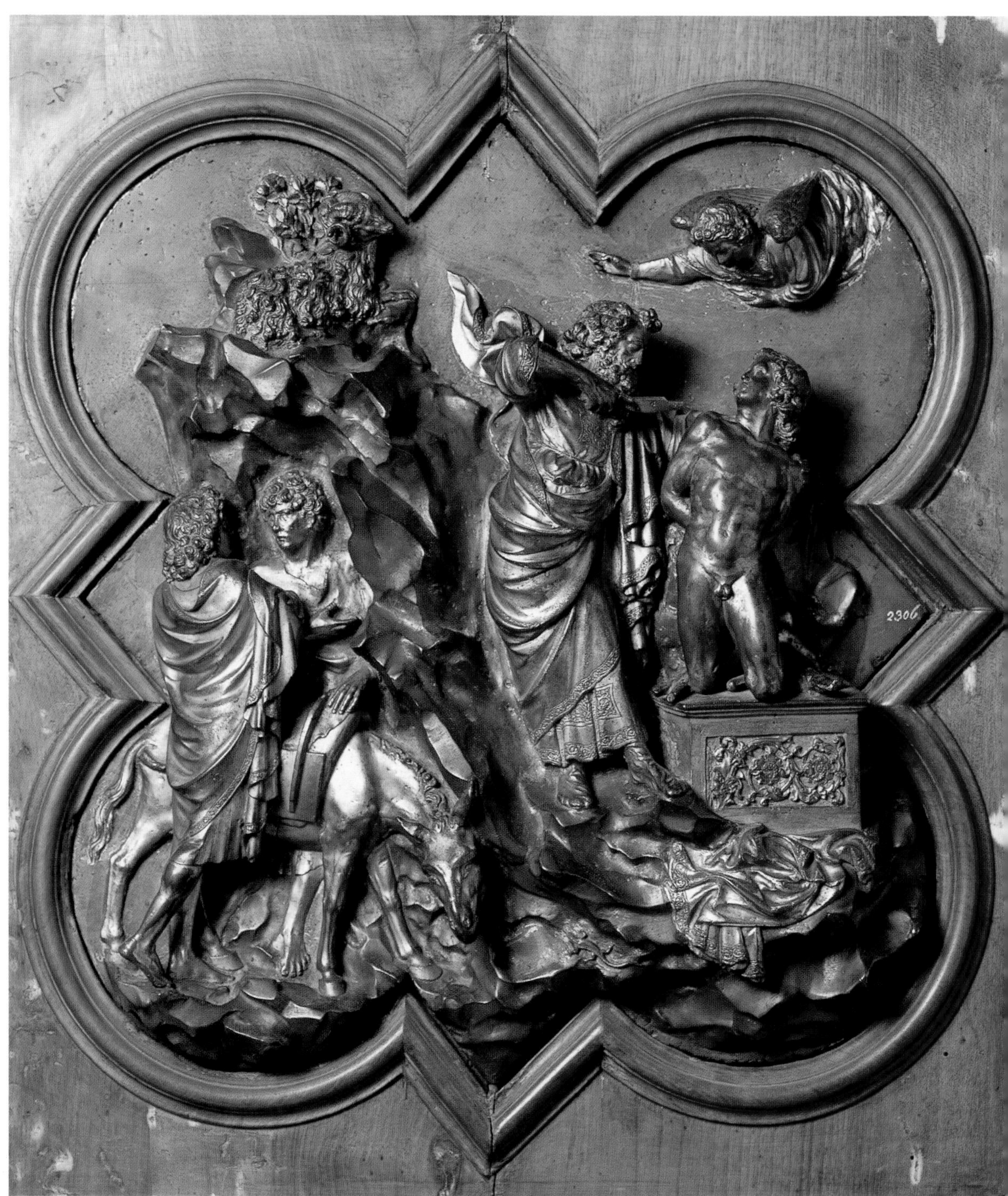


32 LORENZO GHIBERTI *The Sacrifice of Isaac* 1401–2

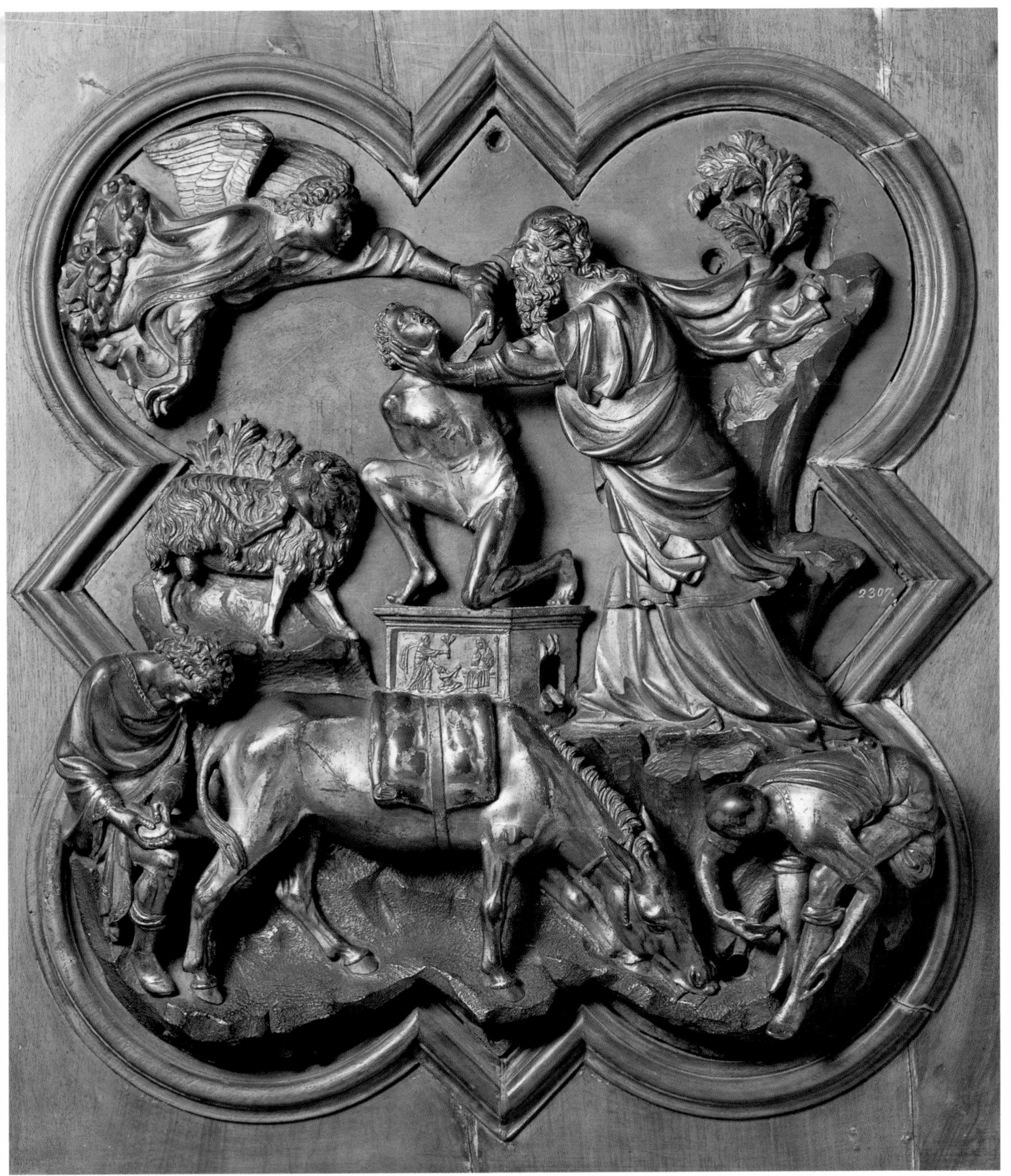


33 FILIPPO BRUNELLESCHI *The Sacrifice of Isaac* 1401–2

were commissioned, often through the guilds, making every artist a merchant of sorts too – a man selling his own talents, making a pitch to clinch a deal. Candidates would be invited to submit sketches or models or other demonstrations of their abilities and choice would then be made between them. For Giorgio Vasari, writing more than a hundred years later, the intensely critical, comparative spirit which animated the city and its artists was the chief explanation for Florentine pre-eminence in art. Vasari's description of Florence as a sink-or-swim city for artists has the ring of a truth learnt the hard way.

The most famous of the many competitions among artists resulted in one of the most multi-faceted works of fifteenth-century Florentine art. In 1402 Lorenzo Ghiberti, who had just turned twenty at the time, was awarded the commission to create an elaborately decorated pair of panelled bronze doors for the city's octagonal Baptistery. The competition had been especially fierce, involving seven artists altogether, including the brilliant Sienese sculptor Jacopo della Quercia, as well as Filippo Brunelleschi, who at that time was yet to specialize in architecture alone. Like the suitors in a fairy story, each artist was allowed exactly one year and a fixed amount of bronze, with the brief to create a single work of narrative relief sculpture on a given theme. In the end it came down to a straight match, a *combattimento*, between Ghiberti and Brunelleschi. Through a rare combination of circumstances the relief panels submitted by the two artists [32 and 33] have survived. They are now to be seen, side by side, in the Museo Nazionale del Bargello in Florence.

The subject which had been set by the commissioning guild of goldsmiths was *The Sacrifice of Isaac*, from Genesis 22: 1–19. Brunelleschi responded to the drama, the cruelty and violence of the Old Testament story with an almost peremptory, inspired brusqueness. Everything, in his version of the story, seems to happen at once. Isaac, eyes closed and mouth formed into a small round 'O' of terror, tries desperately to twist out of his father's grasp. But it is already a lost struggle, and Abraham grips Isaac's face with a great meaty paw of a hand while preparing to plunge the dagger into his small, neat body. He looks as though he is about to dismember his son, not merely kill him, and the intervening angel has to exert considerable force to stay his hand.

By contrast, Ghiberti's solution to the telling of the story was deliberately more elegant, arguably more sophisticated and certainly less troubling. His Isaac is a beautiful Greek nude, quite unlike Brunelleschi's skinny crouching boy, and he twists gracefully towards the knife held by his father. Ghiberti's Abraham is dressed in finer clothes than Brunelleschi's harsh prophet and appears to be less set on his task. He frowns and points the knife at his son but seems hesitant about actually using it, as if transfixed by the beauty of the boy. The angel hovering above does not need to intervene physically; a word will suffice.

Precisely why the members of the competition jury preferred Ghiberti's grace to Brunelleschi's vigour will never be known. They themselves might not have found it easy to articulate. The powerful awkwardness of Brunelleschi's interpretation of the story, the almost excessive psychological veracity which he forced into his image – the dangerous mania of Abraham, the witless fear of Isaac – may possibly have counted against him. On the other hand, Ghiberti's manifest technical skill must have weighed in his favour. Because he had developed a method of casting his entire relief in a single piece, his scene is more unified in conception and execution than Brunelleschi's. The latter was put together as a kind of metalwork collage, a method particularly apparent in the subordinate details, the donkey and the servants loitering below the main action, which have a distinctly added-on look. One of the corollaries of Ghiberti's contrasting ability to cast in a piece was the fact that he did not use up all the bronze allotted to him. That too may have counted with the patrons.

Ghiberti's reward was a lifetime's work. It took him two decades to complete the twenty-eight panels of the Baptistery doors. These pleased his patrons so much that in 1425 he won another commission, for a second pair of doors for the Baptistery – on which he then proceeded to work for another quarter of a century.

The subjects prescribed for the first set of doors were the four evangelists, the four doctors of the church and twenty scenes from the life of Christ. The intention was that Ghiberti's work should both complement and surpass the existing doors designed by Andrea Pisano, completed in 1336, for the east entrance to the Baptistery. Hence he was required to work to the same format as his predecessor, confining each of his reliefs – as he had done in the case of his competition panel – within the shape of a quatrefoil. He turned this circumscription to his advantage, especially in the scenes recounting the life of Christ, each of which is a *tour de force* of narrative compression.

The sequence begins with a powerfully abbreviated *Annunciation*, in which the Archangel Gabriel makes his important announcement to a sinuous, recoiling Virgin, while God the Father swoops down from heaven and the dove of the Holy Spirit, a bulletlike blur in the sky, makes a beeline for her womb. In its elimination of the extraneous, its close imaginative focus on the bare essentials of story, this panel set the standard for those to follow. There is an hallucinogenic clarity to the imagery of Ghiberti's first doors. *The Temptation* shows a statuesque Christ, fortified by a host of flying angels, resisting the blandishments of a tottering winged devil on a barren crag – an image of supernatural goings-on which needs no more specific a setting than this empty dreamscape. *The Storm on the Lake of Galilee* is comical rather than weird, contrasting the panic of the disciples, crammed into their storm-tossed boat, with the gently amused calm of Christ as he walks on water and bids the winds to subside. To stand before the doors is to be transfixed again and again by the flash of a sudden memorable image. It is like reading the Bible by lightning.

The spirit of competition was still strong in Ghiberti, even after he had started work on the doors. In creating them he was out to beat the sculptor of the previous pair, Andrea Pisano, and thus to outmatch the past. The more austere, restrained panels of Andrea's doors are liable to seem somewhat lacking in ingenuity by comparison with Ghiberti's scatter bombardment of biblical dramas. Ghiberti also set himself apart from Andrea by introducing elements of classical architecture here and there and giving the occasional figure the same graceful, Hellenistic, athletic character as that of Isaac in the competition relief. By the time of their final completion, in 1424, it seemed clear to Ghiberti's Florentine contemporaries that he had raised relief sculpture to a new level. In open acknowledgement of Ghiberti's genius, Andrea's doors were taken down from the main, east entrance to the Baptistery and moved to the less prestigious south side. Ghiberti's doors were put in their place.

Still, it seems, Ghiberti was not quite content with his own achievements. When he was commissioned to create his second pair of doors, he refused the easy option of a repeat performance. He set out to create an entirely new kind of relief sculpture, and the magnitude of the change which he wrought on his own style still seems remarkable. Setting up in competition, finally, with none other than himself, Ghiberti created his masterpiece, the 'Gates of Paradise', as Michelangelo called them.

Ghiberti's first decision was to reduce the number of individual panels from twenty-eight to just ten. In the process he did away with the device of the quatrefoil border so that the image in each of these new panels is evenly rectangular in shape, and much larger. Whereas in the first set of doors the figures stand proud of cursory backgrounds, here the eye is drawn past them, through space, into distinct fictive worlds. These works, on which Ghiberti laboured from middle age to old age, include some of the most ideal creations in all Italian art. Not quite sculpture, or quite painting, or craftsman's goldsmithery, they amount to a hybrid art form. Ghiberti was an eclectic artist who had learnt much from many different traditions

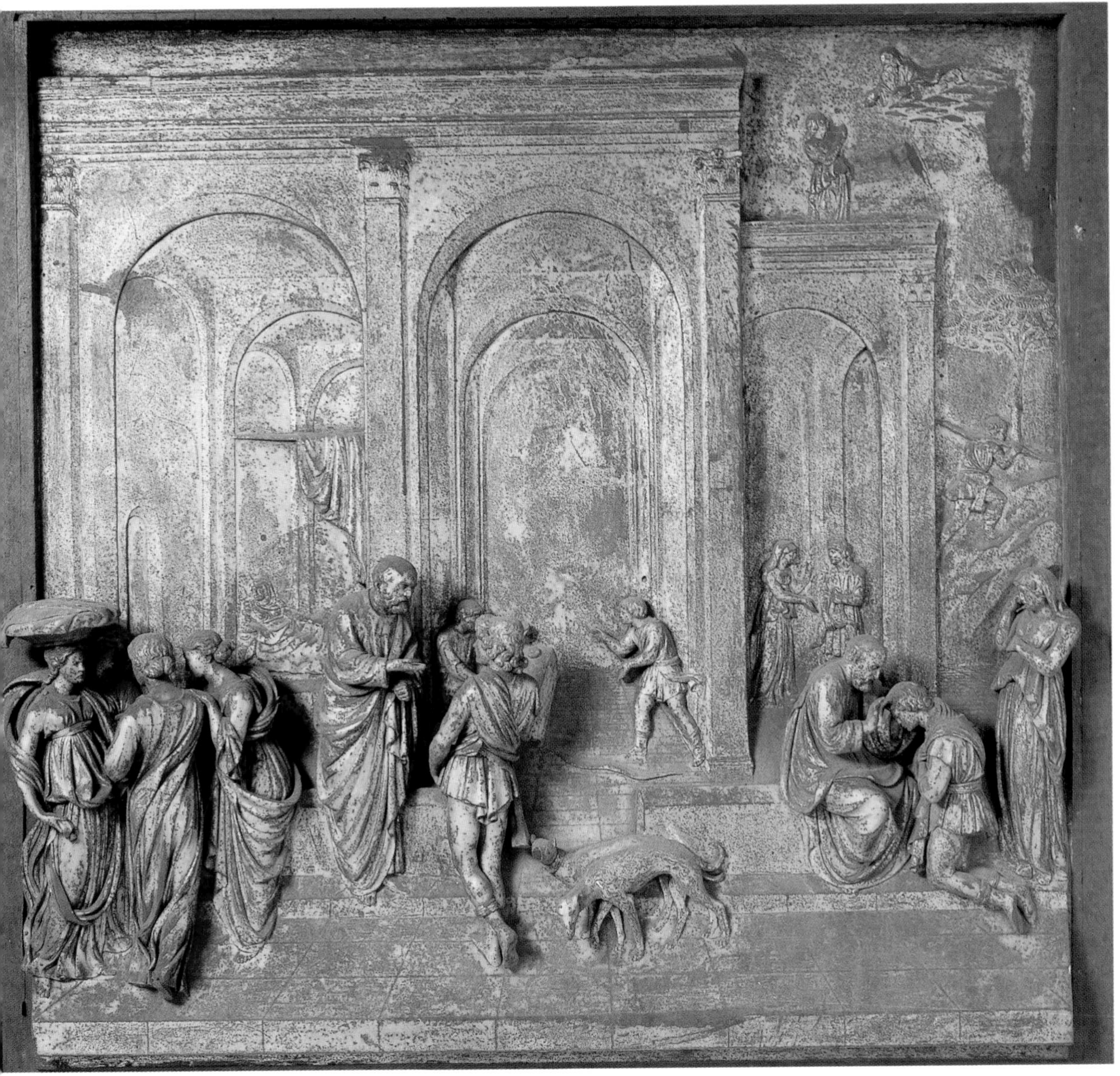

34 LORENZO GHIBERTI *Jacob and Esau*, panel from Baptistery doors, Florence *c.* 1435

of art. The ideal of female beauty which he brought to the three figures of Eve in the various parts of *The Creation and Fall of Man* owes something, perhaps, to the antique. It also owes something to the sinuous bodies of the saints and angels and Virgins in Sienese painting. The richness and intricacy of the work place it within a different tradition too, that of the court goldsmiths of Burgundy and Flanders. Doubtless other sources and echoes could be found besides. Yet the result is nothing other than a Ghiberti, a new invention and one that would itself become a source for countless artists of the future. Botticelli's *Venus* on her seashell and the nymphs on the grass in the *Primavera* are among the many daughters of this Eve.

In Ghiberti's panel of *Jacob and Esau* [34] a complex sequence of incidents has been choreographed into a vision of perfection. The biblical Jacob lived in the desert in tents but here he is in a classical city. Beneath a triple arcaded loggia, a group of dignified men and women solemnly go about the business of their lives. Machinations are afoot, since among the several incidents recorded in the panel are those in which the patriarch Jacob deprives his elder brother Esau of his birthright and tricks his father Isaac into giving him the blessing proper to the firstborn son; yet all undertones of conflict are submerged in the dreaminess and beauty of the scene. The figures in this world conduct themselves with inimitable orderliness, their every action as measured as the setting in which they find themselves.

The serenity and grace of the loggia, with its upright Corinthian columns supporting a clean, sharply incised entablature, with its flagged floor, measured with such geometrical precision that it appears to stretch back before our eyes, has been communicated to the men and women who inhabit it. They are higher beings, the noble old man who appears twice, sending one fine son out into the world and blessing the other; and, even nobler, the trio of young women in wind-blown gowns, for whom there is no narrative pretext, who stand and gossip, merely, before the gravid Rebecca, but who have been so idealized by Ghiberti that even at rest they look as though they are swaying to the unheard melodies of some distant golden music. They have been Midas-touched by the hand of the artist. Small wonder that when Ghiberti's patrons saw his new work, they repeated their earlier act of displacement – this time taking the artist's own first pair of doors off the east entrance, moving them to the north (where they remain) and replacing them with the latest and improved pair. Here was official proof that Ghiberti had, indeed, outshone himself.

The most extraordinary feature of Ghiberti's 'Gates of Paradise' is, in fact, the extent to which they depart from his previous set of doors. The huge gulf in style and ambition which separates the two sets suggests far more than changes in Ghiberti's sensibility. It demonstrates, with exemplary clarity, the coming to pass in fifteenth-century Florence of a large change in Western art itself.

The idea of progress has always been implicit in the very act of making art. Almost every sculptor, painter and architect believes that things can be done just a little better next time around. The idea of originality, too, has long been implicit. Those who argue that the gold-ground painter of the fourteenth century did not consider himself a unique individual with his own distinctive faults and excellences, his own style, do not give enough credit to the permanence of certain elements of the human character. But progress and originality in the sense in which those qualities were so insistently and acceleratedly sought by Ghiberti, in fifteenth-century Florence, a city itself possessed by dreams of change and transformation and improvement, gave a different impetus to the development of art. With the first pair of doors Ghiberti declared that conventions exist to be improved upon and refined; with the second pair he declared that conventions exist to be reinvented. In between those two statements there lay a new conception of the role of the artist as an agent of change.

## THE FLORENTINE RENAISSANCE IN PERSPECTIVE

The images on Ghiberti's doors were among the first to be created according to a new and sophisticated technique for achieving the illusion of depth on a flat surface. This was mathematically calculated perspective. Artists before Ghiberti's time had understood how to create a more or less convincing sense of spatial recession. But what he possessed, which they had never had, was an infallible method for deceiving the eye in this way. Its essential principle was mathematically regular diminution towards a fixed vanishing point, and the panels of the second set of doors are often almost like textbook illustrations of this. The flagstones on the floor of the panel of *Jacob and Esau* are drawn out like a graph-paper demonstration of the method.

The precise origins of mathematically calculated perspective are shrouded in mystery, but it is known for certain that they do lie in Florence during the first quarter of the fifteenth century. The consensus in the city itself was that the method was not actually devised by Ghiberti, but by his rival in the competition of 1402, Filippo Brunelleschi. This is plausible. In his work as an architect Brunelleschi showed himself to have been much preoccupied with spatial clarity, and it is logical that such a man might have experimented with new methods of depicting space. Images created according to the principle of mathematically calculated perspective seem to have carried trace memories of this Brunelleschian, architectural legacy into the later fifteenth century. In much Italian painting of that time, the world is seen in terms of an architect's elevations. As Michael Baxendall observes: 'There are many more right angles, many more straight lines and many more solids in Quattrocento paintings than there are in nature or had been in earlier painting.'[10]

The development of mathematically calculated perspective has been seen as a seismic shift in the life of the Western world. It has often been written about as if it were some epoch-making scientific breakthrough, on a par with Darwin's Theory of Evolution or Einstein's Theory of Relativity. Its significance is undeniable but should be kept in perspective.

For one thing it was not, strictly speaking, a scientific breakthrough. The optical science necessary for a mathematical understanding of how to create consistent perspective in art had been in existence for several centuries, in the work of the Arab mathematician al-Haitham, generally known as Alhazen (*c.* 965 - *c.* 1040). His works were known to Brunelleschi and Ghiberti: there is a copy of his work on optics, annotated by Ghiberti, in the Vatican Library. The chief innovation of the Florentines was to apply concepts such as those explained by Alhazen to painting. They did not invent the science. They used it.

It is probably no coincidence that a method for calculating the illusion of space so precisely should have been first applied in a city that was itself so taken up with measurement and calculation – a city of merchants and negotiators and bankers, where numeracy was not the exception, as it was in much of the rest of fifteenth-century Europe, but the rule. From Florence, mathematically calculated perspective spread and became the dominant convention, in later fifteenth-century Italy, for the visual representation of reality. One of its immediate effects on art was the editing out of much extraneous matter. Once painters felt bound by convention to make their images spatially coherent, they could no longer indulge in the proliferation of figures commonly jammed together in earlier art – which is one reason why there are fewer people visible in Italian fifteenth-century painting than in earlier painting.

But the commonly encountered notion that Brunelleschi's formulation of the laws of perspective provides dramatic visible evidence of a new, supposedly more 'rational' *Zeitgeist* in Florence, a turning away from the superstitions as well as the artistic styles of the Middle Ages, is highly suspect. This rationalist, positivist interpretation of Renaissance perspective is a legacy of rationalist, positivist nineteenth-century thought (a symmetry which is reason alone for distrust). The intellectual leap of faith on which it depends – the assumption, made by Jacob Burckhardt and others, that pictorial perspective can be equated with mental objectivity – receives no justification in the art of fifteenth-century Florence. The early pioneers of the new painting were more likely than not to use perspective as a means of enhancing the uncanny and mystical dimensions of their religious art. An example of this process is Masaccio's fresco of *The Trinity* [35], one of the earliest perspectivally

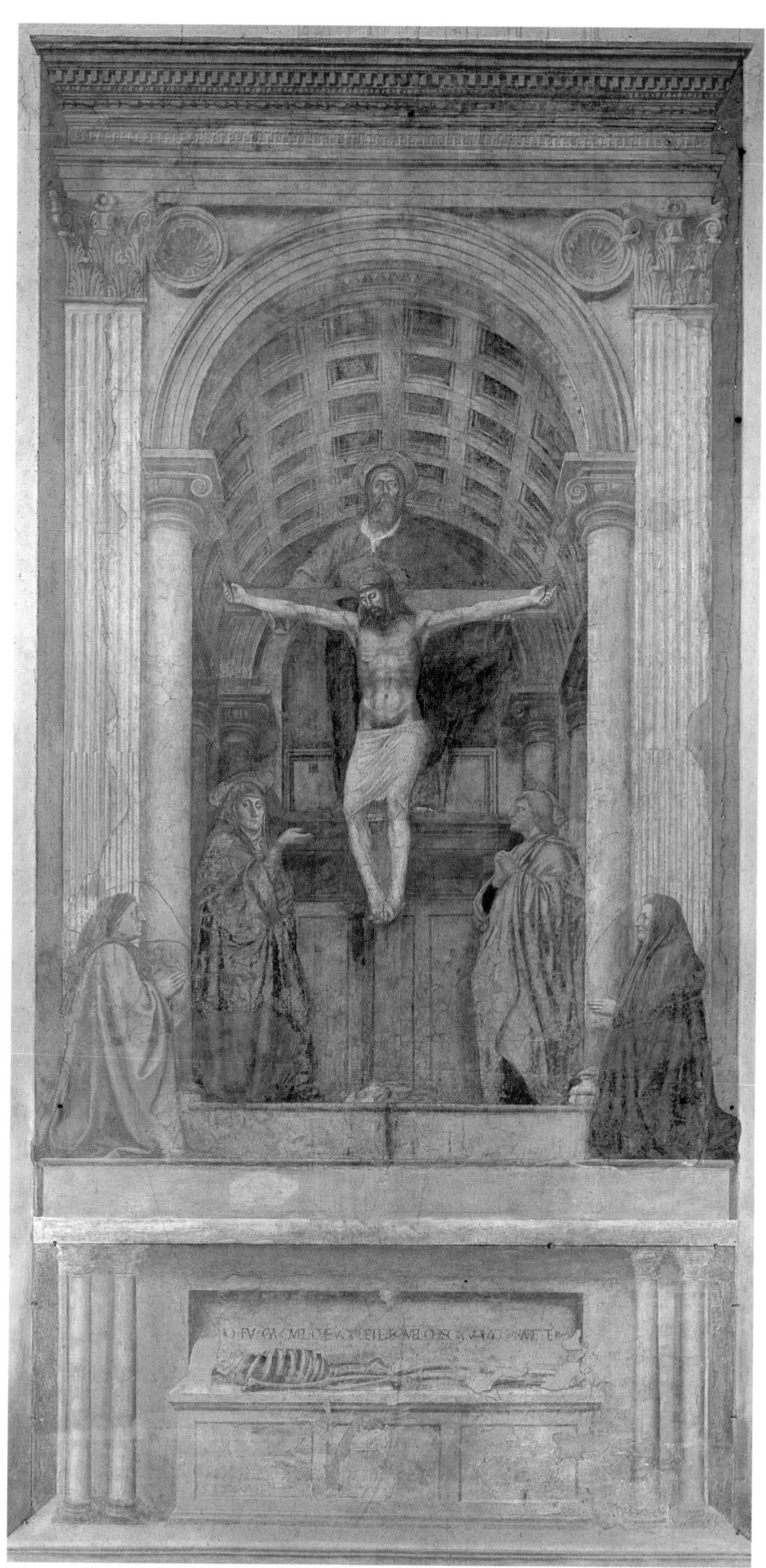

35 MASACCIO *The Trinity c.* 1425–7

'correct' Florentine paintings, created for the church of Santa Maria Novella some time between 1425 and 1427.

The theme of the painting is one of the mysteries of the Christian religion, the threefold identity of God as Father, Son and Holy Ghost. The Trinity had traditionally been depicted against a background suggesting limitless celestial space: pure gold or pure azure. But Masaccio placed his vision of the triune godhead within a classically inspired barrel vault like the apse of a Brunelleschi church. At the base of the painting lies a painted skeleton, a *memento mori* or reminder of mortality. The inscription above it makes a grim joke of this. 'What you are, I once was; what I am, you will become', it says, in Tuscan dialect. From here, the eye is led up, by degrees, past the large-scale figures of the donors who paid for the picture, towards the dignity of sainthood as embodied by Mary and John, and up and in again to the mystical heart of the picture. This is the crucified Christ, with the dove of the Holy Spirit hovering above him and, behind, the rugged face of God the Father, placed at the exact point in the scheme where all the lines of recession converge.

According to optical research, the viewer should place himself at a distance of 6.12 metres from the painting for a full appreciation of Masaccio's perspective scheme. It also helps to kneel. In the words of the fifteenth-century Florentine humanist Giannozzo Manetti: 'The truths of Christianity are as indisputable as the axioms of mathematics.'[11]

## BIG TOM

Masaccio was the shooting star in the Florentine firmament, gone almost as soon as his brilliance had been seen. The chief legacy of his short life is the fresco cycle which he undertook with his older collaborator, Masolino da Panicale, in the Brancacci Chapel in the Carmelite church of Santa Maria del Carmine.

The most panoramic and dramatically complicated of the frescos in the chapel, *The Tribute Money* [36], which he painted almost entirely without assistance, is the epitome of Masaccio's art. The picture tells an involved biblical story with admirable conciseness. Its theme is taken from the gospel of St Matthew (17: 24–7). Jesus and his disciples were at the gates of Capernaum by the Sea of Galilee when tax collectors came to Peter and requested a toll. Jesus told Peter to go fishing and look into the mouth of the first fish that he caught: 'Thou shalt find a piece of money, take that, and give it to them for me and thee.' Masaccio distilled three moments of time to a single frame. In the centre the tax collector confronts

Jesus and his disciples while Jesus points imperiously to the sea, his gesture repeated by an evidently somewhat bemused Peter – who knows it is a command he will have to carry out but who also seems to be debating, with some Doubting Thomas inside himself, whether it can possibly work. This central group is the fulcrum of the narrative, and everything else follows from it. Away to the left, Peter catches his fish and removes the coin from its jaws. To the right, Peter pays the tax collector his tribute, shoving the money into his hand with contempt.

A picture about an economic miracle has itself been constructed with a miraculous economy of means. The painter's evident hatred of elaboration extends from his spare, essentialist reduction of the biblical narrative to the simple landscape setting he devised for it. The place appointed is all it needs to be and no more: red earth, green sea, grey mountains, city walls. Painting has been made as simple as naming. Nothing in the picture seems to have been added for extraneous effect and even the trees are leafless, suggesting that the artist felt compelled to eschew foliage for fear – so wary was he of the merely ornamental – of the patterning to which it might tempt him.[12] Yet this is a real barren place, not an abstraction. It is a world in winter and a cold wind is blowing off the water.

Masaccio's style is grand but also earthy. Jesus and his followers are big-boned men wearing a timeless version of Roman dress, in distinction to the shifty, thick-set tax collector in his short pagan tunic – which is the painter's way of singling out this lone interloper in the bare groves of Christian virtue. The disciples are noble but not in any generic sense. The face of each is sharply individuated and together they constitute a crowd of solemn witnesses, each responding in his own way to the miracle unfolding before him. These men with craggy faces partake of the stoniness of the mountains in the background. The folds in their robes are echoed in the folds of the landscape behind them. Some form of geological simile may have been intended by the painter, to indicate the immensity, solidity and the permanence of the church. The standing of these men is emphasized literally too. Christ and his disciples have large, coarse feet and their toes are splayed out on the dark red earth.

Masaccio's style was self-consciously different from the styles of painting being practised elsewhere in Florence at the time. There is virtually no point of comparison between him and more traditional Florentine painters of gold-ground altarpieces, such as his prolific, moderately gifted contemporary Bicci di Lorenzo. Yet *The Tribute Money* does suggest that Masaccio took a close interest in the sculpture and architecture of his time. The central group of Jesus and his disciples looks almost as though hewn from stone, like a statuary group transposed into

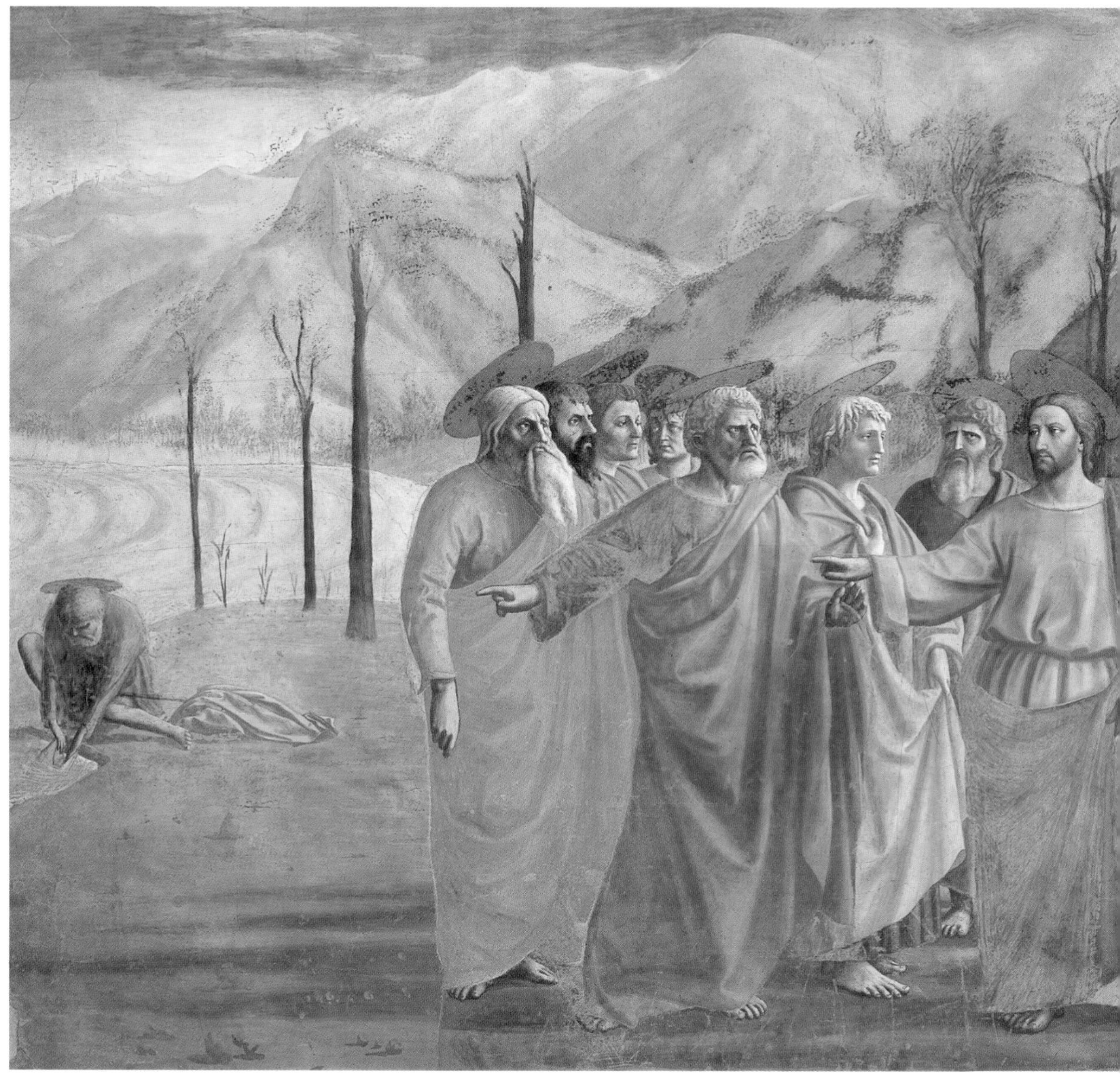

36 MASACCIO *The Tribute Money* (detail) *c.* 1427

fresco. They are strongly reminiscent of Nanni di Banco's *Four Crowned Martyrs* on the exterior of Orsanmichele [27].

Masaccio was capable of being influenced by other artists, but this does not seem to have dulled his responses to the world around him. In the Brancacci Chapel frescos he painted man as he is with tremendous sympathy. The scene of *St Peter Baptizing the Neophytes* has the biblical multitude of three thousand converts reduced to just nine men beside a river in another of his bleak and barren land-

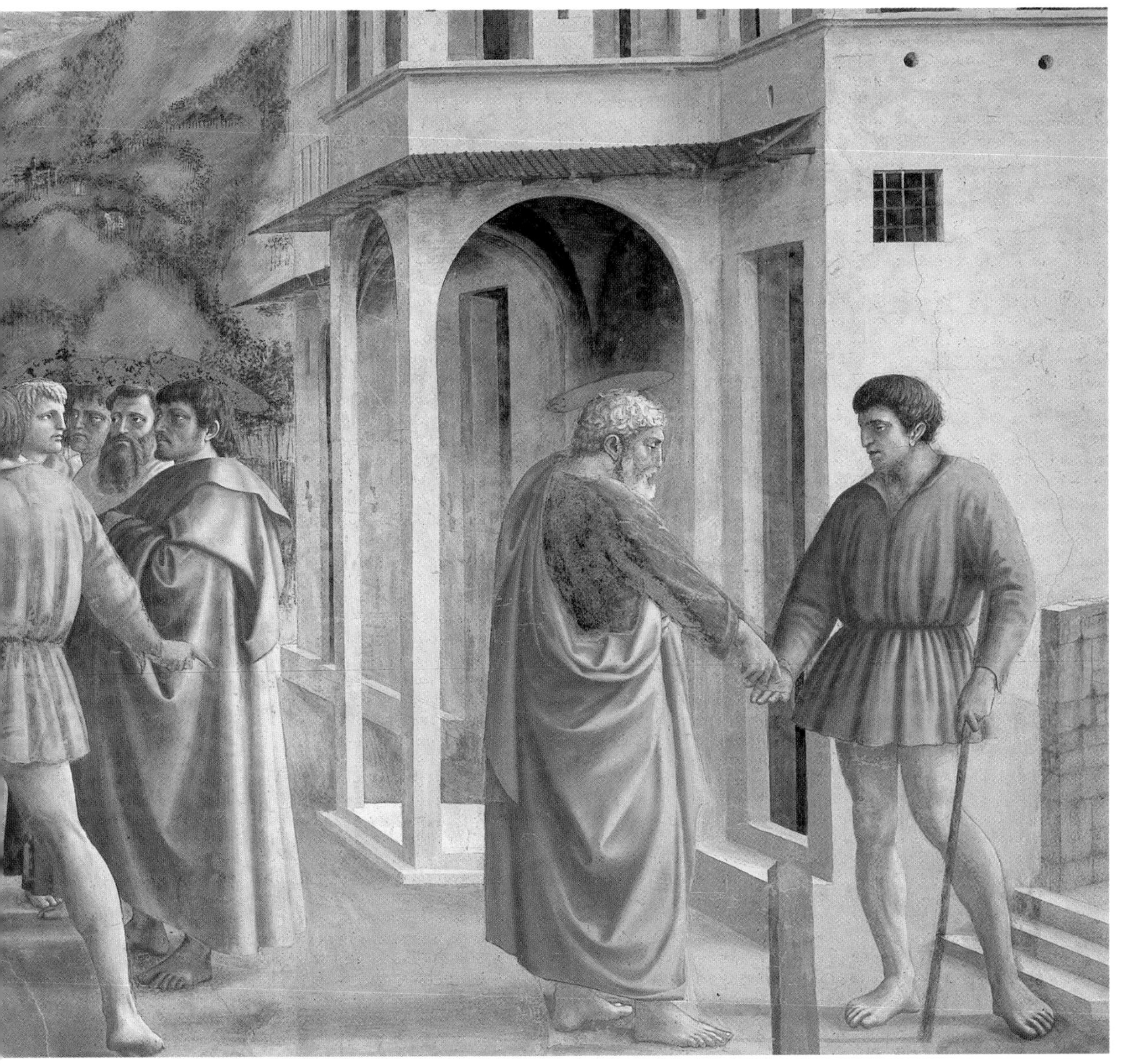

scapes. St Peter pours a bowl of evidently chilling water over one kneeling man's head, and as it flows over him it draws his hair down over his face in matted cords. The man next in line for baptism hugs himself against the cold and tries to still the chattering of his teeth. (This is probably the first painting of a shiver in Western art.) There is nothing academic about Masaccio's congregation of male nudes, no trace – as there might have been in the hands of later Renaissance painters – of the antique revival demonstration piece. The figures in the painting do not exist to be beautiful, or to prove the painter's erudition or to flaunt his compositional skills. They simply testify to the no-nonsense nature of his imagination. Outdoor baptism must have been like this.

Masaccio set another of the Brancacci frescos, *St Peter Healing with his Shadow*, in a street in contemporary Florence. The saint walks slowly towards us past a gathering of the hopeless and the crippled, and as he does so his shadow falls across a boy with withered legs sitting awkwardly on the ground and resting his elbows on an improvised wooden support. The boy's eyes are filled with a strange transfiguring light. The picture has an almost unnervingly documentary quality, the authenticity of a real scene remembered but then imaginatively redeemed – suddenly removed from the merely ordinary by the invention of a miracle.

Masaccio was not afraid or ashamed of allowing ugliness into his painting. That is part of his humanity. His realism, which does not flinch from the awkward or the grotesque, seems to anticipate that contempt for refinement which would animate the work of many of the toughest artists to come after him. He is a spiritual ancestor of painters as various as Bruegel and Rembrandt, neither of whom is likely to have known his work, as well as Degas, who almost certainly did.

Although Masaccio may justly be described as the first painter of the fifteenth-century classical revival, an artist who consciously strove to lend his figures the *gravitas* and nobility of antique statuary, there was also a powerful streak of asceticism in his sensibility. He had a deeply ingrained preference for the harsh, the immediate, the rugged and rough-hewn qualities associated with the works of the fourteenth-century Florentine painter Giotto. Giotto, in truth, was probably the single greatest influence on Masaccio, the ultimate source for his tremendous, heavy sculptural figures, momentous sense of drama, almost Franciscan respect for poverty and corresponding simplicity of his expressive means.

Masaccio's *Expulsion from Paradise* [1] in the Brancacci Chapel is the most extreme expression of his uncomfortably direct imagination. It is an awkward painting, because it makes a nonsense of clearcut distinctions between Gothic and Renaissance, being neither one nor the other but both at the same time. A man and a woman have been thrust from paradise. He covers his face in remorse. Hers is tilted up towards the cold light of day – the first postlapsarian day – but her eyes are closed and her mouth is half open in an ugly agonized wail. Her hands cover her breasts and her sex, making her a fifteenth-century equivalent to Roman representations of *Venus pudica*, the Venus of Modesty. But her misery has overwhelmed the classical source and we do not see her as a piece of art referring to another piece of art. We do not see her as a piece of art at all, but as a woman in anguish. A strong emotion has been made visible in a way that is unforgettable. There is no more wrenching image of human sorrow.

The painter's given name was Tommaso di Ser Giovanni di Mone. Masaccio was his nickname. It may be translated as 'big Tom', suggesting a large man. He certainly cast a long shadow over Florentine art. On Masaccio's death in 1428, at the age of twenty-seven, Brunelleschi, laconic in his grief, said: 'We have suffered a great loss.'

## DONATELLO

Legend has it that Masaccio included a portrait of Donatello in his fresco of *St Peter Healing with his Shadow*. He is said to be the bearded man standing on the end of the line of cured cripples, wearing a red *cappuccio* – a form of fifteenth-century Florentine headdress – and holding a suddenly redundant walking stick in his hands. Despite that, he seems more like a bystander than a participant in the miracle. His gaze is abstracted, his thoughts cloaked. If this is Donatello (and there are doubts), it seems an appropriately shadowy likeness of him.

The recorded facts about him are few but suggestive. His given name was Donato di Niccolò di Betto Bardi, and he was born in 1386 or 1387. His father, a manual worker in the Florentine wool trade, had an interest in contemporary politics and a capacity for violence. The record shows that he killed a political opponent in 1382 in murky circumstances – an incident which serves as a reminder that the men of Florence did not always resort to elegant Ciceronian debate when differences of opinion arose between them. Donatello himself may have inherited his father's temper. Archivists working in Pistoia have discovered the earliest known documentary reference to him. He was in that city in January 1401 when he got into a dispute with a man called Anichino di Pietro. Donatello hit him on the head with a stick and drew blood.

Donatello was probably trained, like Brunelleschi, as a metalworker. According to Florentine tradition (admittedly unverifiable), they were associates in their youth. Whether he went with Brunelleschi or not, it is likely that Donatello travelled to Rome early in life and that he studied the sculpture of antiquity. Returning to Florence, he spent a short period as an assistant in Ghiberti's workshop; but he must soon have felt that he was fitter to be the master than the apprentice in that particular relationship and in 1406 he was working in the marble workshop of Florence Cathedral. Within five years he had carved the *St Mark* for

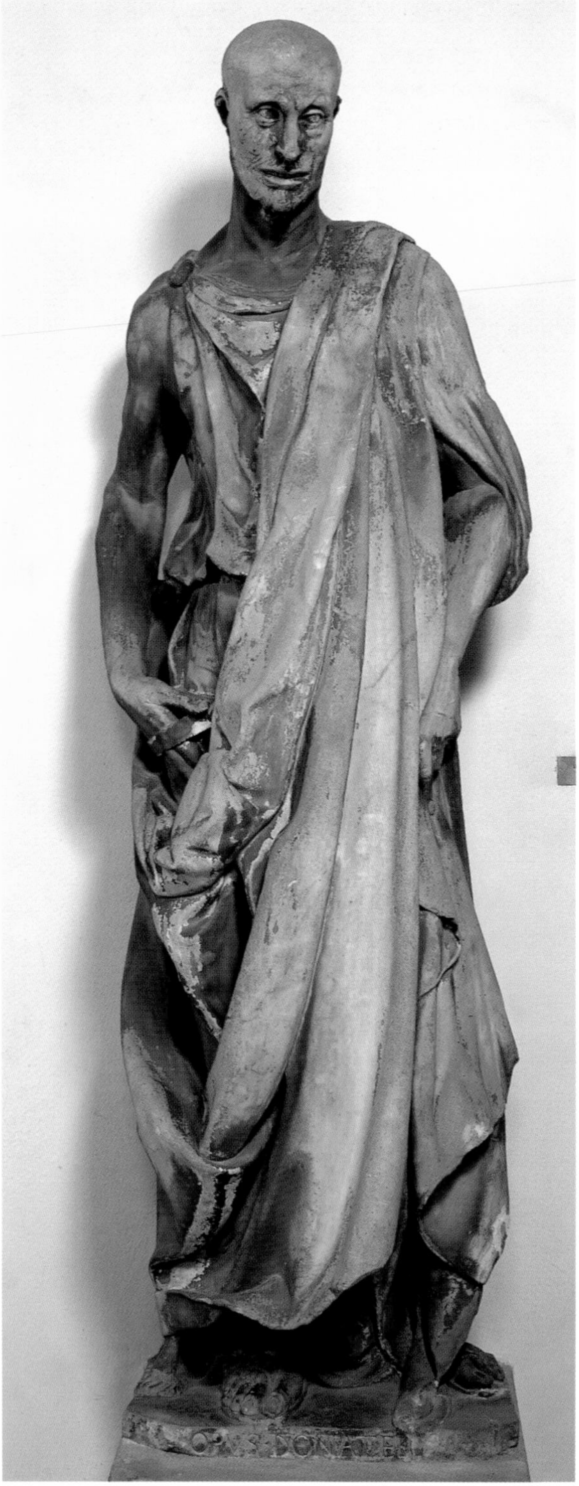

37 DONATELLO *Habbakuk (Zuccone) c.* 1415–35

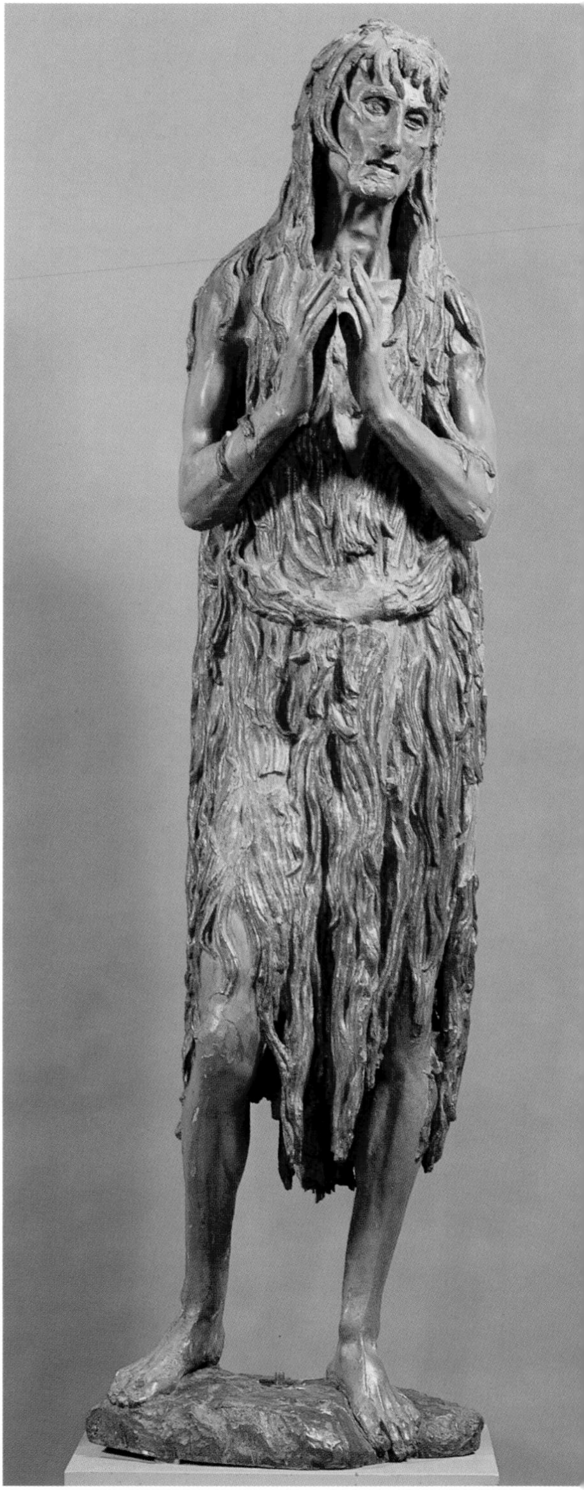

38 DONATELLO *Mary Magdalene c.* 1455

Orsanmichele [28], the most accomplished work of naturalistic sculpture created for more than a thousand years. He was in his mid-twenties.

There is a powerful strain of austerity running through the new styles of fifteenth-century Florentine art and architecture, visible in the work of both Brunelleschi and Masaccio and implicit in the sober aesthetic pronouncements of Alberti. But nowhere does it show more strongly than in the work of Donatello, where it is tinged by a more extreme emotion, a fervent asceticism. The first outburst of this feeling is to be seen in the series of prophets which the sculptor carved for the campanile of the cathedral between about 1415 and 1435.[13] Originally there were eight of them; only four survive, all now in the Museo dell'Opera del Duomo.

As in his work at Orsanmichele, Donatello turned his back on the convention of depicting the saints and prophets as heavenly courtiers. His four holy men are not fifteenth-century princes but religious fanatics, gaunt desert wanderers who have just stumbled barefoot out of the sands, their eyes wild with visions. Donatello's *Jeremiah* burns with the moral fire of the righteous, the appointed messenger of a stern Old Testament God: 'Cursed be the man that obeyeth not the words of the covenant' (Isaiah 53: 3). As he stands before us he seems to have the curse on his lips. The weathering which the statue has suffered positively enhances it. The rough-hewn prophet is beaten up but dauntless. He is the image of an indomitable, scary conviction.

The *Habbakuk* [37], or so-called *Zuccone* ('Pumpkin-head') is a less threatening and minatory figure than the *Jeremiah*, but a still more original creation. He is a prophet with a suspicion of the idiot about him, a holy fool with staring eyes and a half-open mouth. He looks noble but also cracked and in less ecclesiastical circumstances might be mistaken for a common madman – an irascible tramp mumbling to his inner demons. Vasari, who believed that the artist never created anything finer than this work, tells of him in his workshop before the figure, waving his chisel and challenging – almost imploring – the stone man to speak.[14] The story may be apocryphal but it communicates the intense concentration which Donatello brought to the task of imagining what a man might be or do. He was a shaman as well as an artist. He took the Renaissance project of revival, of plunging back towards some imagined origin, to its far extreme. Like another Pygmalion, he tried to bring inert matter to life.

Donatello's art often seems almost appallingly raw, as if the faculty of sympathy, in him, was somehow flayed. He had the ability to project himself so thoroughly into the lives and predicaments of others – those whose stories he was

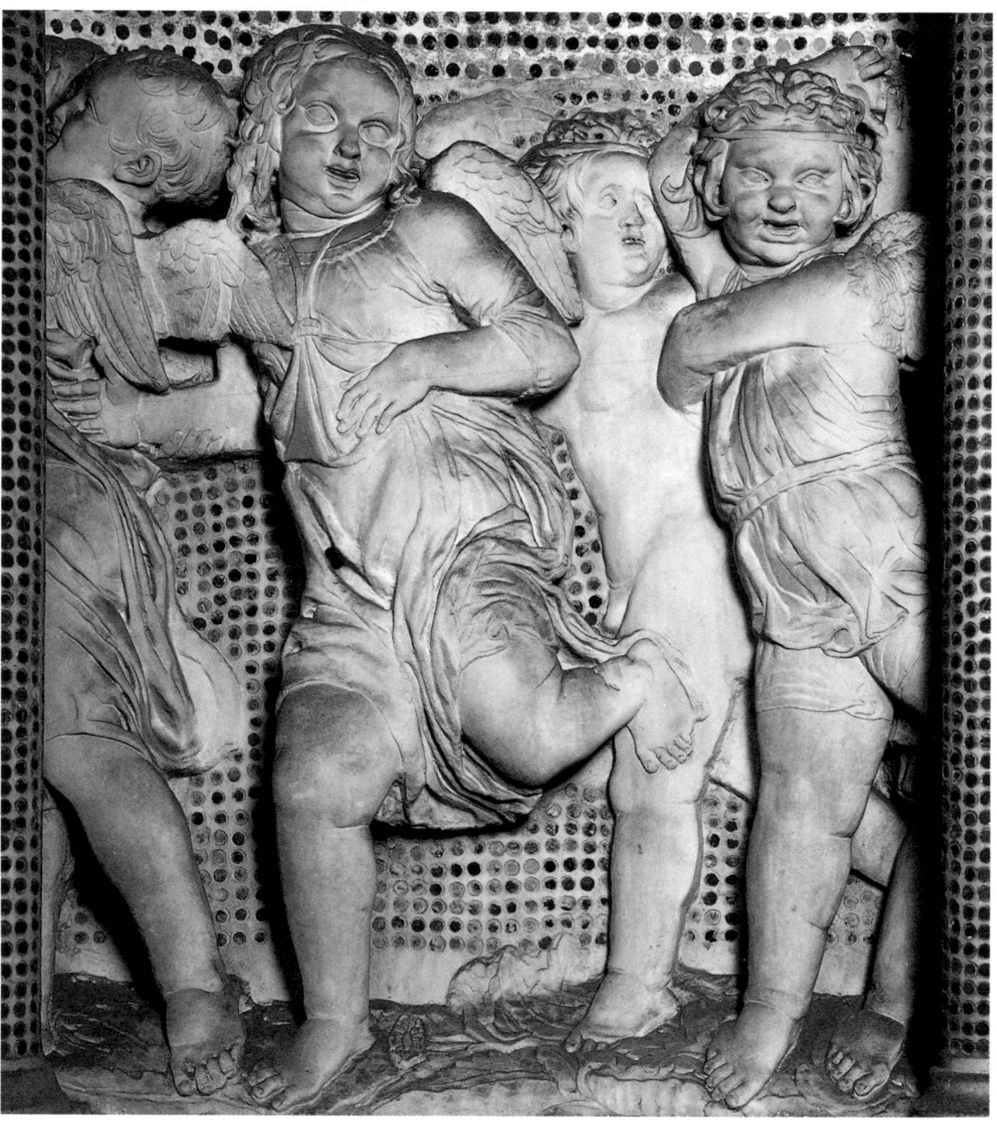

39 DONATELLO Singing gallery (detail) 1433–9

commissioned to embody – that the results frequently come as a shock. *Mary Magdalene* [38], created when the artist was in his seventies, is another fervent maniac, an emaciated and smelly old woman, cloaked in her own matted hair like a savage wearing an animal skin, her hands raised in prayer. The elegant gilding applied to her long and filthy locks enhances the paradox which she embodies. She is a sanctified hobo. She stands on a piece of rock which represents the wilderness in which she dwells. Her acquired disgust for the things of the flesh has animated Donatello's hand, which – one of the many technical marvels of his art –

40 DONATELLO *Gattemelata* 1447–53

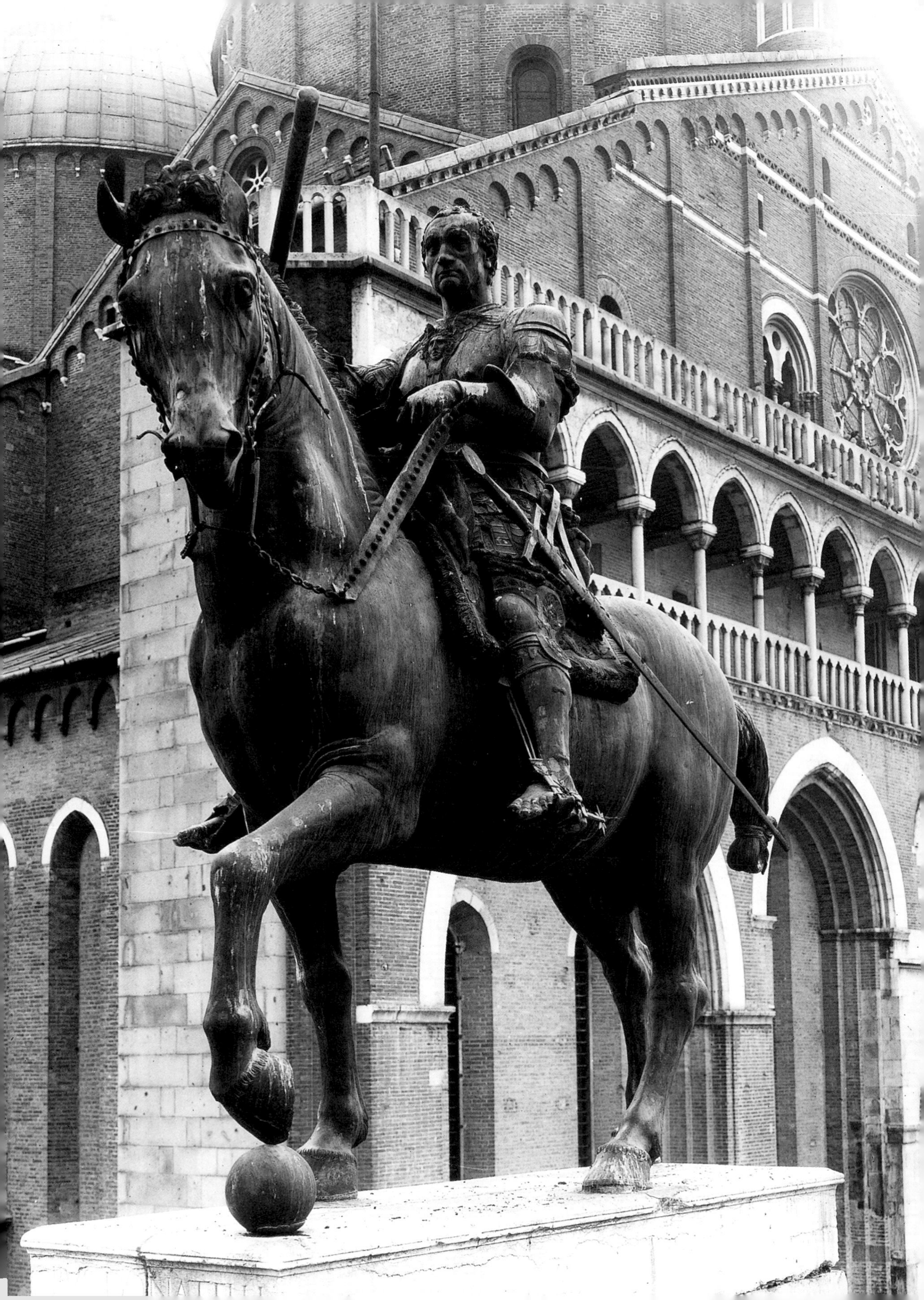

somehow brings the qualities of modelling to carved sculpture. Her shrivelled body seems already in decay. The skin on her face looks molten, like that of a burns victim. The strangeness of it is that she remains noble in spite of the artist's intentionally vile realism.

Donatello did not reserve his imaginative sympathies exclusively for those in the throes of an extreme, possessing piety. The same man who produced *Mary Magdalene* and the startling prophets on the campanile could also conjure up, as he did in his miraculously delicate *schiacciato* reliefs of the *Virgin and Child*, the hushed and intimate world of a mother and baby, alone and utterly absorbed in each other. To a certain extent Donatello's variety must have reflected the varying preferences of his patrons. His early works for Orsanmichele, notably the *St Mark* and the *St George,* were adapted to the dignified, classical tenor of Florentine humanist civic ideology, whereas the late *St John the Baptist* was a Franciscan commission, a fact which would not have discouraged the artist from his emotive depiction of the prophet. Yet the very fact that Donatello could meet the widely differing requirements of so many different forms of commission is part of his distinctive character as a sculptor. It is hard to think of another artist who has quite his blend of passion and impartiality, his ability to move between so many different forms of life and feeling, yet always with sympathy. It is a form of emotional ventriloquism.

Donatello had evidently been strongly affected by the sculpture of ancient Rome. The naturalism he learnt from antique sculpture was developed initially by the artist to psychological ends. The *St Mark* and *St George* were carved with unprecedented vitality, a vitality developed still further in his Santa Croce *Annunciation.* Within a beautifully decorated and fantastically ornate classical tabernacle, like a miniature proscenium arch theatre, he staged one of the most momentous events of the Christian story as if it were a classical play. An almost vestal Virgin moves away from the annunciate angel involuntarily as she hears his news. At the same time she turns her face towards the kneeling Gabriel and their eyes meet. Donatello thus, and with great gentleness, suggests a mixture of feelings on her part, surprise and reluctance becoming acceptance and humility. She might be about to collapse, or to kneel. Her stiff demeanour makes her a perfect vehicle for the drama of the story, a classical maiden who has been bent out of true, stunned by the import of what she has learnt about her destiny.

It is not possible to talk responsibly of Donatello's classical manner because he had more than one. Observation had taught him that the classical world was no one thing but a compound of many unfamiliars. He lived in Padua for several years

41 DONATELLO *David c.* 1430–45

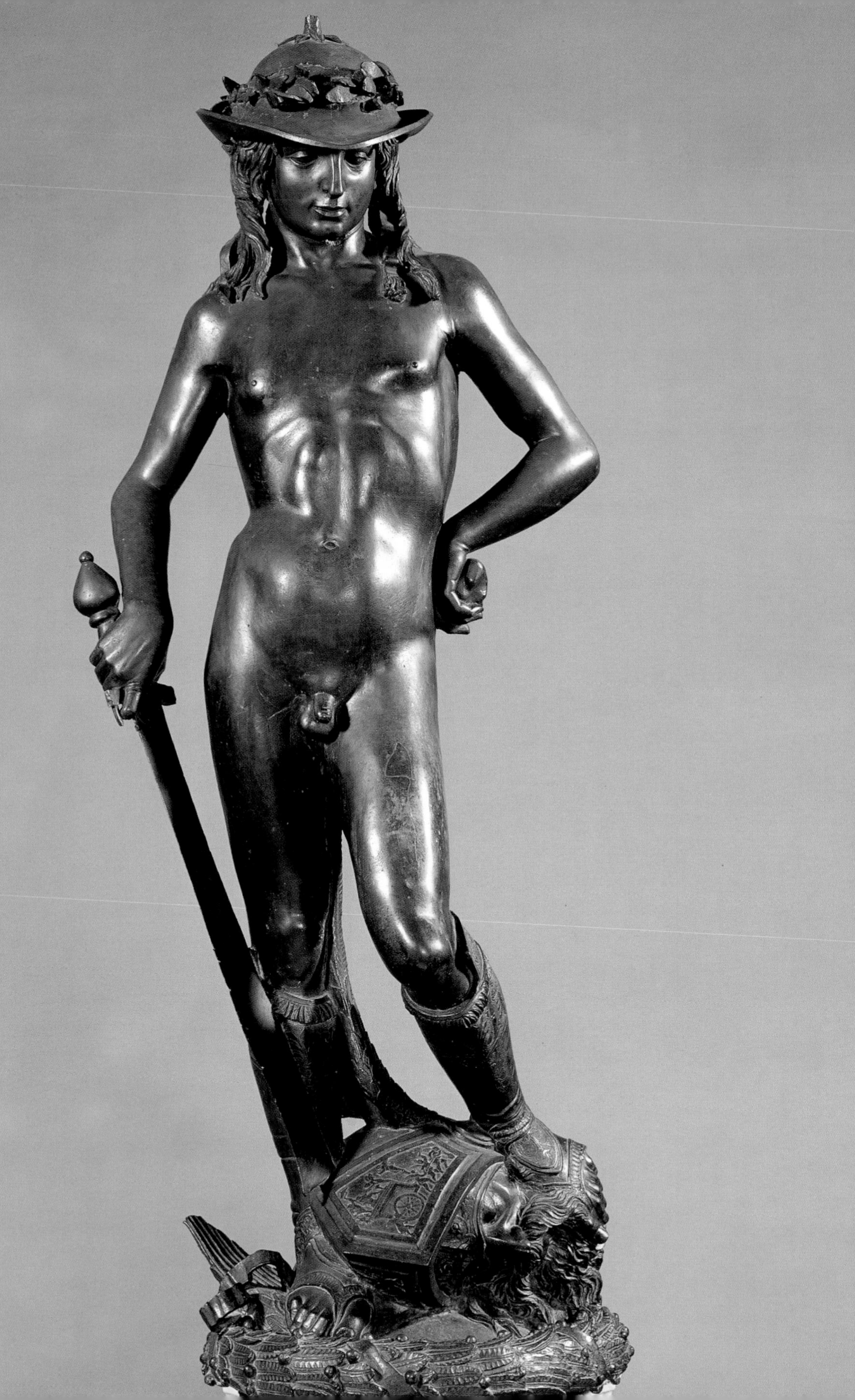

during the 1440s, creating among other works the first large-scale equestrian monument of the Renaissance, the so-called *Gattemelata* [40]. Commissioned in honour of Erasmo da Narni, one of the most powerful *condottieri* of the day, and inspired by the ancient Roman equestrian statue of *Marcus Aurelius*, this is the most instantly impressive of Donatello's purely secular works. It is a memorial so steeped in a dream of Roman military glory that it offers not the slightest hint of Christian redemption. A hired mercenary became, in Donatello's hands, a bronze precursor of Shakespeare's ruthless Roman general, Coriolanus. He is savage, martial Rome embodied: an unstoppable epic hero on a huge horse, advancing implacably to war.

The richness of invention, the strangeness, the alien quality that Donatello sensed pulsing through the statuary of antiquity worked on him like a drug. His imagination was opened up like Pandora's box and he himself may sometimes have been surprised by what flew out. The singing gallery which he sculpted for Florence Cathedral in the 1430s [39] is a headlong plunge into a yet more distant version of the antique past than that which would inspire the bronze horseman of Padua. It is perhaps the first religious work of the Florentine Renaissance where the relationship between an artist's classical style and his Christian subject matter seems positively uneasy.

The spirit of competition was as strong in Donatello as in all the other artists of fifteenth-century Florence. Although his singing gallery was commissioned to form a pair with the existing gallery in the cathedral, designed by Luca della Robbia just a few years before, in 1431, it is actually a riposte to it. Luca had conceived his work in lucidly classical terms, dividing its length into discrete reliefs of discreetly robed music-making angels, separated by paired Ionic pilasters and corbels decorated with acanthus leaves. It is his most considerable work, and a beautiful, graceful thing; but compared with the Donatello it looks pedestrian. Donatello conceived his work as a Dionysian refutation of Luca's calm Apollonian proposition, creating a continuous frieze of deranged dancing children with wings. Too maddened and disconcerting to be cherubs, they surge across a background of glittering mosaic which throws their weirdness into relief. Some of their faces were carved with such considered swiftness that they seem only half-formed, which makes them appear slightly out of focus, as if they might still be moving, stumbling and lurching drunkenly. This is a profoundly unstill work, and although it was carved for Florence Cathedral it delves into pre-Christian superstitions. These chubby, intoxicated, childish gods are pagan sprites, ancient incomprehensible deities of field and flower whose mood could easily turn. They seem on the edge of a dangerous mania, as if their festival might be the prelude to a dark rite.

A similar, veiled, mysterious, self-conscious erotic energy characterizes the famous bronze *David* [41], now in the Bargello, commissioned by the Medici family and one of the first free-standing naked figures to have been created since antiquity. David the giant-killer was a symbol of giant-killing Florence: small yet perfectly formed, defying imperial foes against all odds. There used to be an inscription on the base of the statue proclaiming that it was a symbol of Florentine liberty, but the truth is probably a little more complicated. This cold but sexy boy, with his strangely feminine figure, is no straightforward emblem of republican resolve. The true nature of his victory is not, perhaps, military but erotic. He is evidently too limp-wristed to kill anybody, let alone cut off a head as massive as the one on which he rests his left foot. The figure's kinky state of undress – he wears only a helmet and a pair of very fine boots of sensual floppy leather – makes his nakedness more alluring than would be the case were he simply nude. There is a biblical precedent for it but its effect is to make him seem entirely lacking in innocence. The erotic decorations on the dead Goliath's helmet, which show a Triumph of Cupid, contribute to the sexual suggestiveness of the work. So too does the plume of bird's feathers on the helmet, which strokes the boy's calf and inner thigh and reaches up to his crotch. This surrogate, feathery caress – it is probably not a coincidence, as Frederick Hartt observed, that *uccello* or 'bird' was fifteenth-century Florentine slang for phallus[15] – emphasizes the boy's desirability but also states his unavailability. The dead man cannot of course possess him, although the expression on the grizzled features of the decapitated head suggests that he might be dreaming just such a sensual dream; and neither can the viewer. *David* is a tantalus, a work of art not a real boy, an eternal self-absorbed flirt who knows that he will always arouse but never be violated. The statue represents another side of the Florentine classical revival. Men loved men in ancient Greece and Rome, after all.

Donatello's other essay on a patriotic Florentine theme, the intensely violent *Judith and Holofernes*, is another of the artist's imaginative excesses – a work of art too distracted to deliver the clean sharp blow of a propaganda message. Judith, slaughterer of the proud tyrant Holofernes, was Florence's other biblical *alter ego*, a suitably underdog heroine and therefore a sister in spirit to David the underdog hero. The inscription on the base of this statue remarks with glib assurance that 'Kingdoms fall through luxury, cities rise through virtue; / See the proud neck cut by the humble hand'. The statue itself, however, does rather more than exemplify the triumph of Christian Humilitas over pagan Superbia. It is an unpleasantly practical-minded image of a brutal death. Donatello's meditation on the biblical

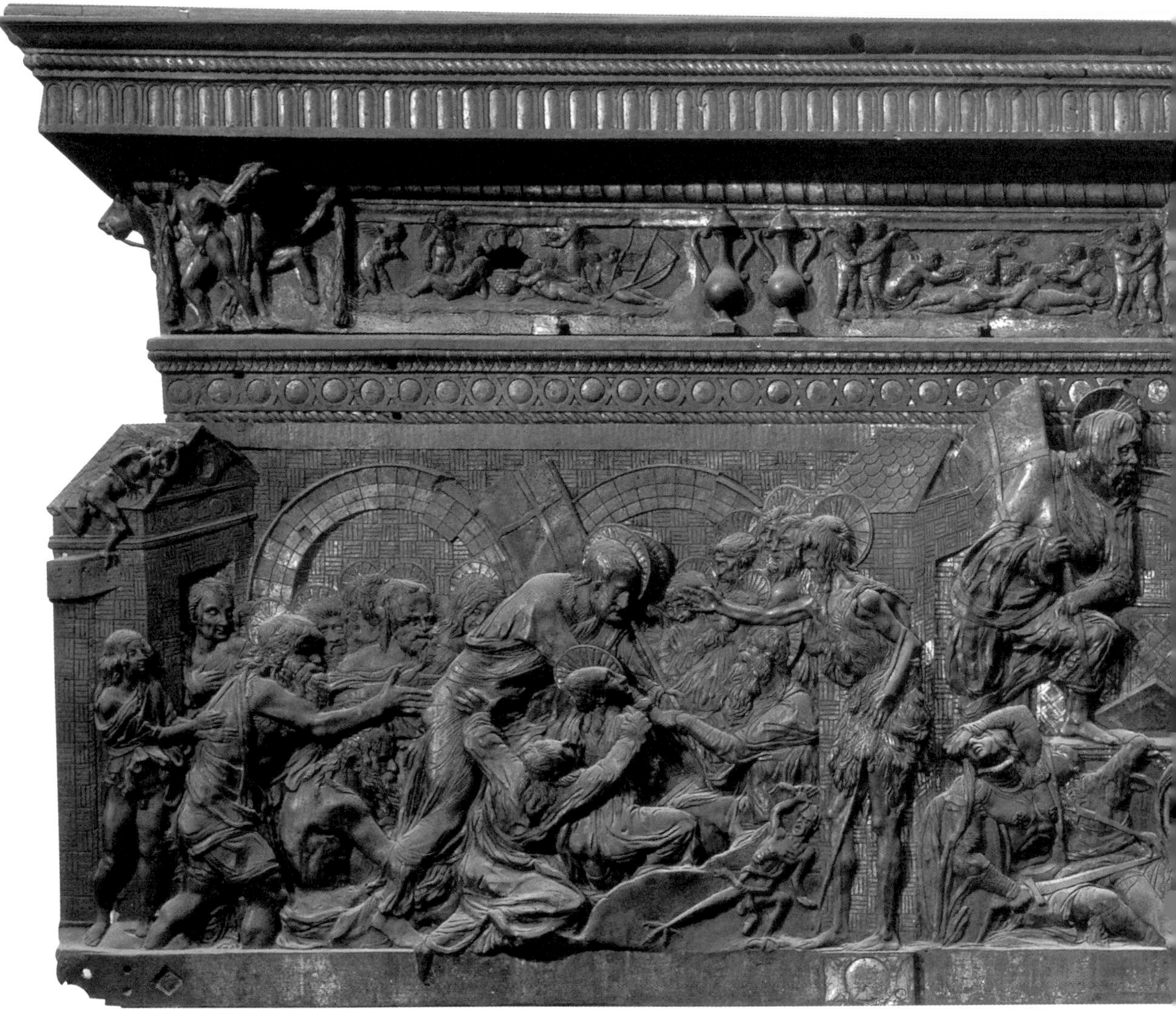

42 DONATELLO Ascension pulpit, San Lorenzo, Florence 1460–66

story evidently left him thinking a rather straightforward thought: how much effort it must take for a woman to decapitate a man. Judith has her foot in the fallen Holofernes' groin and she is in the middle of trying to cut his head off. The job is only half done, the neck semi-severed as gore wells out of a deep gash at his throat. She pauses over the gurgling mess. Who would have thought the young man had so much blood in him? She is about to have another go. She yanks Holofernes upright by the hair and raises her scimitar above her head.

The Florentines who first had to live with the sculpture were themselves occasionally troubled by Donatello's personification of their city as a blank-eyed

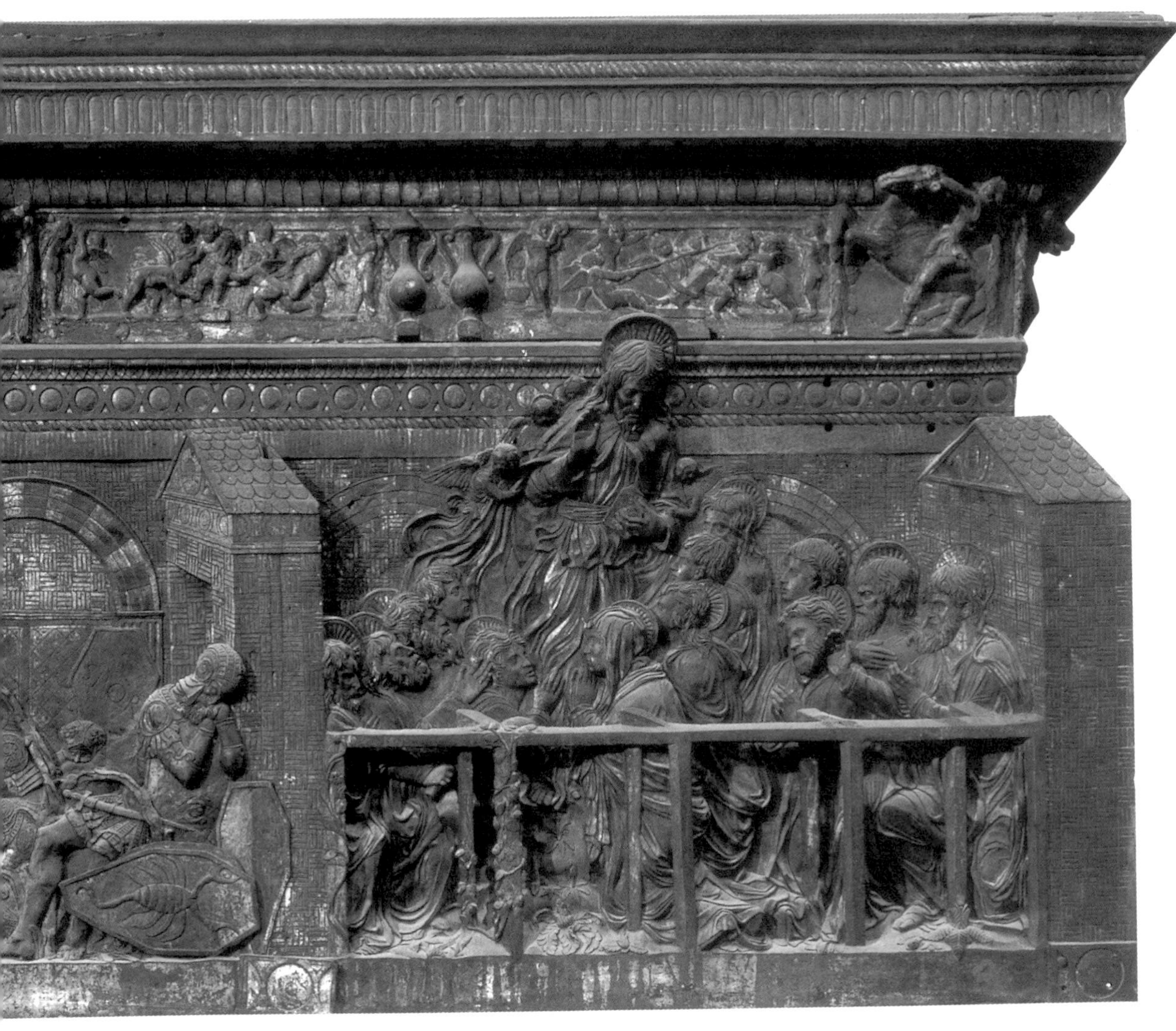

impassive murderess. The statue once stood immediately in front of the Palazzo della Signoria, Florence's town hall, but in the early sixteenth century it was moved away from this prime civic site to the Loggia dei Lanzi, just across the way, at the promptings of a minor civil servant called Messer Francesco. The sculpture was an ill omen, he argued; and besides it was not right that a woman should kill a man. Michelangelo's huge marble *David*, which needed a home, was put in its place.

Donatello lived for a long time, a very long time indeed by the standards of the fifteenth century. He undertook the last works of his life in the early 1460s, as he approached his eightieth year. His bronze reliefs on the two pulpits of

Brunelleschi's grand basilical church of San Lorenzo are intimate but pessimistic creations which he never quite finished. Parts were cast as he left them, out of respect, by his assistants; other parts were finished for him after his death. But their incomplete and fragmentary nature is part of their poignancy, an inchoate quality which speaks of the unmaking of the man who worked upon them.

The finest panel on the so-called Passion pulpit, to the left as visitors enter the church, is that which depicts *The Lamentation over the Dead Christ.* It has the finality of an old man's vision of death, a reality so close to him that he barely has to try to imagine it. The mourners all look like each other, an effect unusual in Donatello, who is otherwise so precise in his imagining of people, but which makes them in this case seem expressively archetypal – a Greek chorus assembled around the dead at the final scene of the Christian tragedy. In fine relief in the background, a group of horsemen have gathered. They seem unfinished but perhaps this unusual effect is also deliberate. It makes them look mistily distant, present but irrelevant because they are on their way somewhere else – perhaps they were meant to embody the indifference of the world. In the foreground, stretched out on his mother's knees here at Golgotha, the dead Christ's body is appallingly heavy. Every part of him – head, trunk, thighs, calves – requires support from one or other of the many lamenting figures. They seem frightened that if they let go the body might sink away from them into the very ground.

On the Ascension pulpit, on the other side of the church aisle, three complete scenes make a frieze: *The Harrowing of Hell*, *The Resurrection* and *The Ascension* [42]. Those who come to these images expecting glorious redemption after the tragedy of Christ's Passion and his death will be disappointed. Donatello's risen Christ is a sad and all too human figure. He seems like an impostor in the sacred story. In *The Harrowing of Hell* he is a stoop-shouldered depressive clawed at by Old Testament prophets craving a salvation that seems entirely out of his gift. He barely leaves the ground in *The Ascension*: a tense figure stiffly gesturing in benediction, he topples forwards on to the huddled mass of his disciples. This lack of upward momentum represents a significant departure from convention. But the most troubling image of all is that of *The Resurrection*, at the centre of the pulpit. Here we see the resurrected Christ emerging from the tomb not as a resplendent, reinvigorated, eternally beautiful youth, but as an exhausted old man, wrapped in his grave clothes, leaning on the banner of the Resurrection as if it were a crutch.

At the last, Donatello's imagination had failed him. All he could see was his own mortality staring him in the face. He died on 13 December 1466, having outlived all of his friends and rivals.

## HALF RIGHT

Because of the volatile nature of its politics; because Petrarch's revolutionary ideas about the classical world and the need to revive it took root in Florence as nowhere else; because of the genius of its artists, inspired both by the new Petrarchan ideal of rebirth and by the continuing Franciscan imperative to make sacred story seem real; because of the wealth (and perhaps, also, the usurer's guilt) of the mercantile patron class; because of the competitive spirit with which life in Florence was permeated – for all these reasons, and doubtless others besides, the city witnessed an extraordinary and sudden evolution in the way men thought and saw and created. There are times and places when mankind has – through some unforeseeable mixture of genius and circumstance – made a great leap in consciousness. Florence, during the first half of the fifteenth century, was one of those places at one of those times. Quite where that leap took mankind is another question, and one that remains open to debate.

Burckhardt's big ideas about a new 'objectivity' and a new spirit of 'individualism' are still extremely influential – even if they are not totally convincing. Considering the wholly religious uses to which Florentine artists put their chief pictorial refinement, mathematically calculated perspective, Burckhardt's notions about the decline of religion require some qualification. The end result of the Renaissance may well have been a certain weakening of the bonds of religious faith, in some places, and among some people. But as the general devoutness of Florentine religious art reminds us, that process was by no means as straightforward as Burckhardt's account made out.

The other side of Burckhardt's proposition – the idea that people became more psychologically self-aware during the Renaissance – stands up better to close scrutiny. Like many bold thinkers, Burckhardt overstated his case. The assumption that people living in pre-Renaissance times did not think of themselves as individuals – that they somehow lacked an interior mental life – is evidently somewhat inhumane, and it is contradicted both by common sense and by all historical evidence. But when one looks at the body of Florentine art, in all its life and vigour, it is plain enough that Burckhardt was on to something when he wrote of Renaissance man as 'a spiritual individual', who 'recognized himself as such'.

Looking back to antiquity, perhaps what the great Florentine artists of the fifteenth century really discovered was themselves. Their legacy to the future was a heightened curiosity about character, identity and motive: an immensely richer sense of what it might mean to be a human being.

CHAPTER THREE

# THE JOURNEY OF THE MAGUS

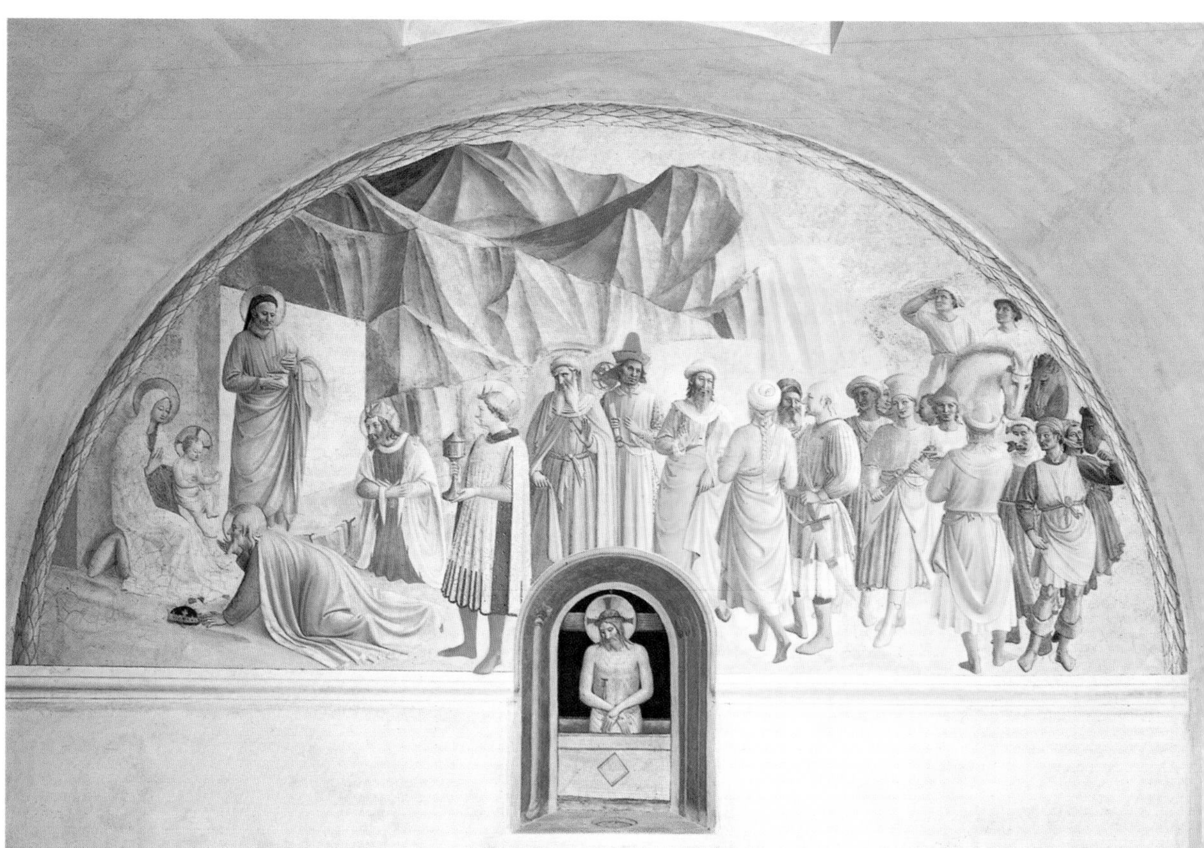

43 BENOZZO GOZZOLI *The Adoration of the Magi,* San Marco, Florence 1442

The painter is lord of all types of people and all things.
If the painter wishes to see beauties that charm him it lies in
his power to create them, and if he wishes to see monstrosities
that are frightful, buffoonish or ridiculous, or pitiable, he can be
lord and god thereof; if he wants to produce inhabited regions or
deserts or dark and shady retreats from the heat, or warm places
in cold weather, he can do so. If he wants valleys, if he wants
from high mountaintops to unfold a great plain extending
down to the sea's horizon, he is lord to do so; and likewise
if from low plains he wishes to see high mountains...
In fact whatever exists in the universe, in essence,
in appearance, in the imagination, the painter has first
in his mind and then in his hand.

LEONARDO DA VINCI, notebook entry

## THE COURT AND THE ARTIST

The courts of fifteenth-century Italy were artificial worlds built on foundations of hard political reality. Their purpose was to proclaim and preserve the power of Renaissance rulers: the Sforza in Milan, the Gonzaga in Mantua, the Este in Ferrara, the dynasty of Federigo da Montefeltro in Urbino. Many of the superb buildings erected to perpetuate the fame of those families still survive and most have been thrown open to a public which they once excluded. Inside their high-ceilinged halls and painted chambers, intricate with allegory, the Renaissance might seem very remote from modern life.

But it was in these opulent surroundings that the modern artist, with all his pains and privileges, first evolved. The princely patrons of Renaissance Italy competed with one another to commission works of art which would raise them to the firmament of immortality. As they did so, the painters, sculptors and architects from whom they came to expect so much – not only in terms of manual skill, but also intellectual attainment – became stars in that firmament too. In many ways this process liberated artists. But their new freedoms were to be accompanied, also, by a new set of problems.

## THE MEDICI AS MAGI

By the 1430s the Florentine Republic, while surviving in name, had effectively become a principality ruled by an élite of wealthy merchants. This oligarchy found a multitude of new uses for art and architecture. The pattern was to be repeated elsewhere in Renaissance Italy. Its end result was to be the transvaluation of art itself. The early stages of that process can be traced in some commissions by the Medici, the most powerful Florentine banking family of the fifteenth century.

In 1436 the head of that family, Cosimo de' Medici, began to pay for the reconstruction and fitting out of a Dominican friary in San Marco in Florence. It had long been expected of wealthy individuals that they should endow churches and build chapels, simultaneously strengthening the fabric of the Christian religion and (so it was believed) buying themselves a reduced attendance in purgatory. But for one man to donate an entire monastery, containing the most extensive library in Florence as well as forty-two individual monastic cells, was unprecedented. Until then, it had been the custom for such large-scale architectural commissions to be administered by the city's trade guilds and paid for out of public funds.

Each cell was decorated with an image to aid religious meditation. These frescos, by the Dominican Fra Angelico and his workshop, marry extreme clarity with stylistic restraint. Christ appears in most, often in scenes of the Crucifixion [44]. He appears like a vision, as if materialized from thin air. The paintings seem to hover like images projected on to a screen. Now that San Marco is a Fra Angelico museum the visitor may walk at will from cell to cell. But this denatures the works of the painter, making them into a sequence – an exhibition of Angelicos – which is not how they were intended to be seen. They were pictures to be locked away with, one to one, for hours on end. They have the character of hallucinations. That is, possibly, what they were intended to stimulate. Long, hungry contemplation of the image might bring it to life.

The Dominicans themselves may have been somewhat uneasy about the amount of private money lavished on their new surroundings. Fra Angelico's fresco *The Madonna of the Shadows*, painted in a prominent position on the upper floor of the friary, contains a figure of St Dominic who stares out at the viewer with great intensity while pointing to an open page in the book which he holds in his hands. The Latin text to which he wants to call attention contains a warning: 'Have charity, preserve humility, possess voluntary poverty. I invoke God's curse and mine on the introduction of possessions into this order.' This was not quite, perhaps, a question of biting the Medici hand that feeds, but the fresco was a lively reminder of the order's pauperist origins.

The pair of adjoining cells reserved for the use of Cosimo de' Medici himself is slightly different from the rest. Cosimo's matter for contemplation there was a painting of *The Adoration of the Magi* [43] by Fra Angelico's assistant, Benozzo Gozzoli. The space is as solemn and devotional as any of the other cells, as if to acknowledge that the rich man's desire for penance might be just as deep – if not even deeper – than that of the novice. But the meaning of Gozzoli's painting was not purely religious and his work may be seen as a harbinger of change. The theme of the three kings of Orient, the wise men who brought gifts to the infant Christ, was a pointedly appropriate one to set before a Medici. The painter was paying tribute to his patron's wealth and wisdom, even though his style remained simple and direct, purged of any trace of excess or luxury, in keeping with the austerity of the monastic ideal.

When the same artist was commissioned to depict more or less the same subject in a chapel in the Medici's private palace, however, piety took second place. The result was a very different work, in which devotion has been transferred from Christ to the pageant of wealth. Here Gozzoli was emboldened to expand on

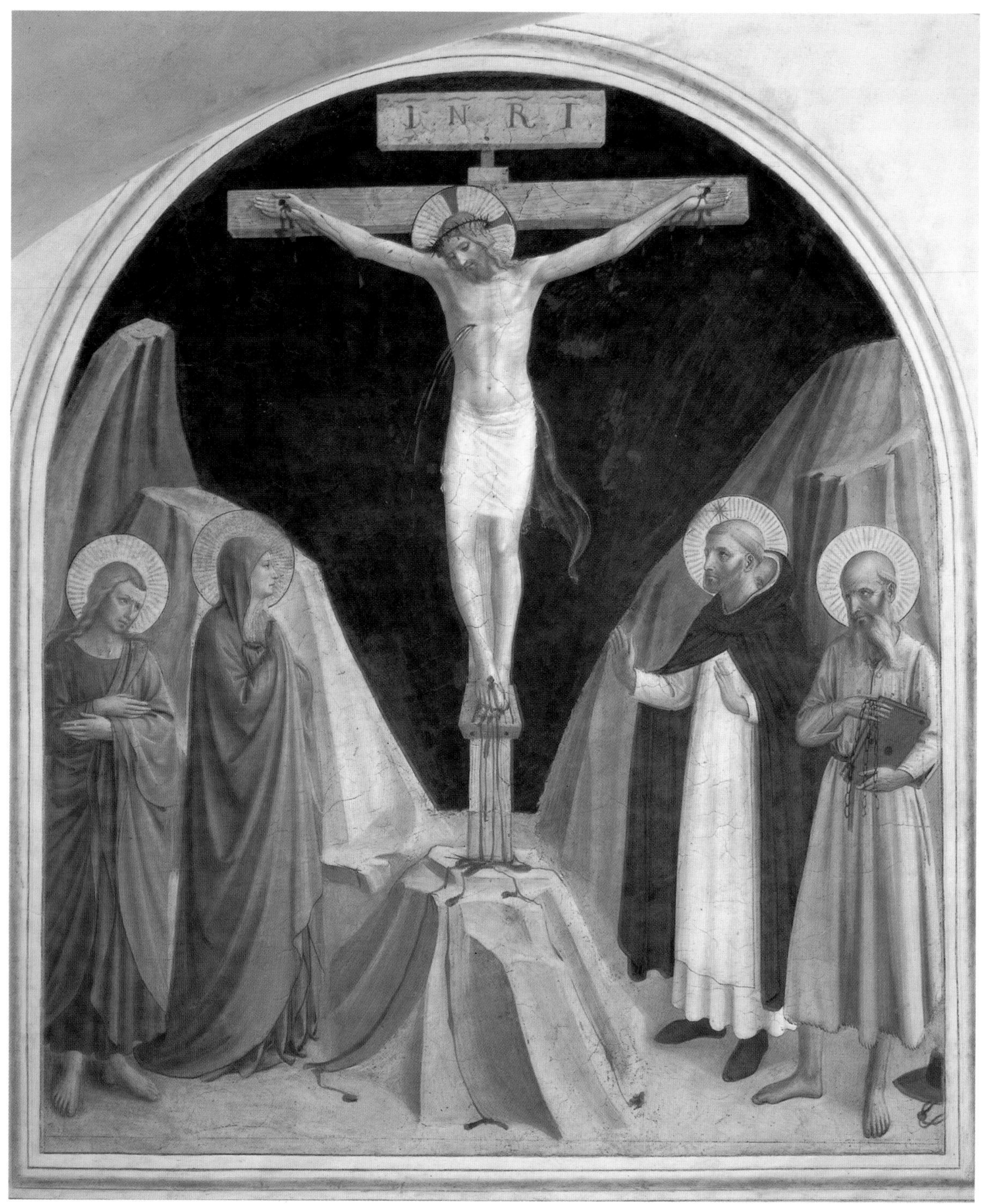


44 FRA ANGELICO *The Crucifixion,* San Marco, Florence *c.* 1440–45

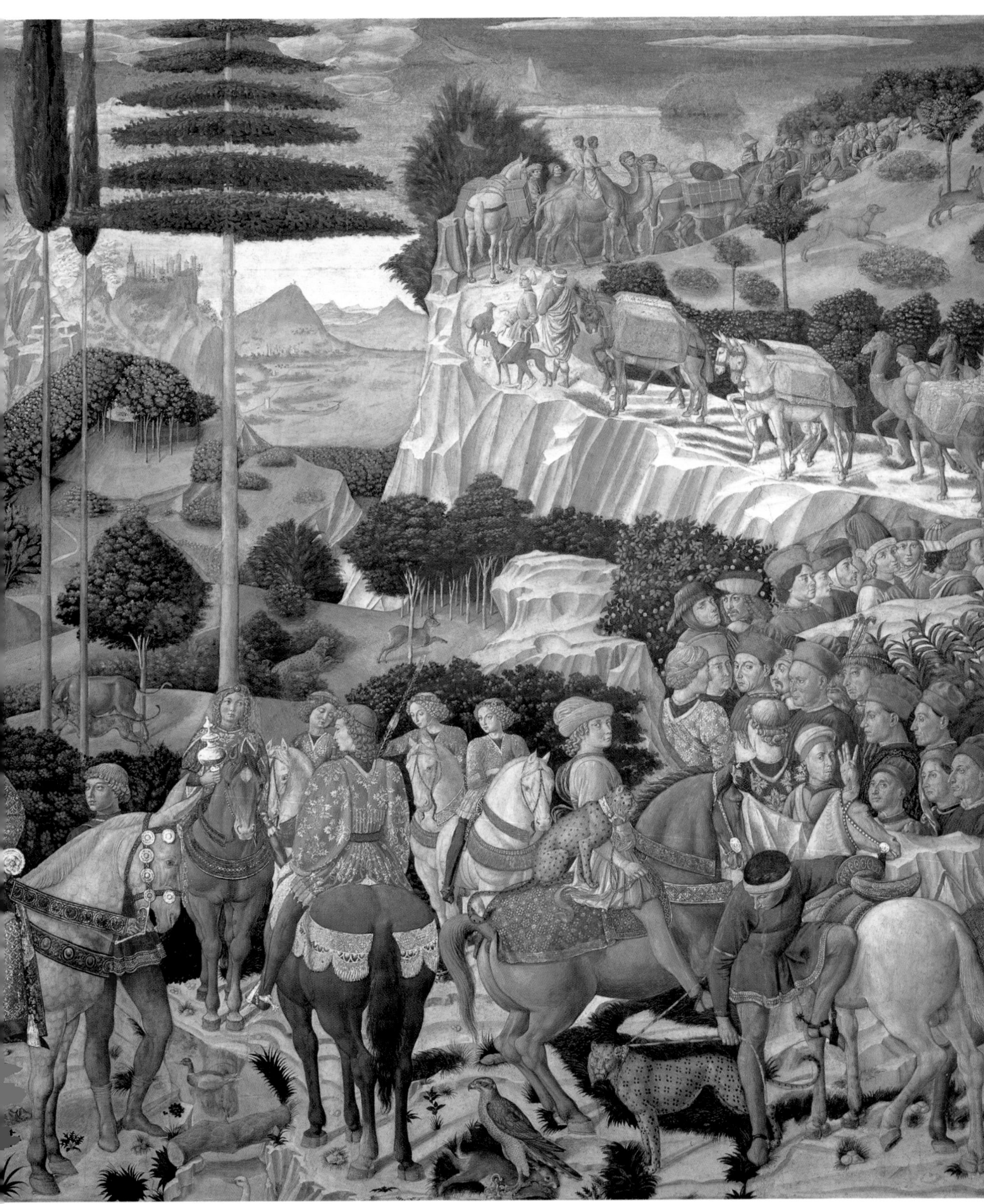

45 BENOZZO GOZZOLI *The Journey of the Magi* (detail) 1459–61

his San Marco *Adoration*, turning it into a continuous band of fresco running around the four walls of his patrons' private chapel [45]. Through a verdant, hilly landscape, where the trees seem to have grown quite of their own accord into fantastic topiary forms, a richly garbed cavalcade wends its unhurried way. Faery castles may be glimpsed on the hilltops and the spirit of these frescos as a whole is romantically profuse. According to a well-established but unverifiable tradition the first of the three magi is a portrait of Cosimo, while the third is a portrait of his young grandson Lorenzo. There are many other portraits besides. The artist proudly included himself in the illustrious company. His name is written around the circumference of his hat.

The Medici were closely identified with the magi, both in their own eyes and in the eyes of the city. The family belonged to an influential religious confraternity known as the Company of the Magi, a quasi-masonic group whose members played an even more active role in the ruling of Florence than the city's official governing body, the Signoria. The confraternity was also responsible for staging the *Festa dei magi*, a lavish annual pageant in celebration of its holy patrons, the three kings. This took the form of a large and splendid procession every year on the Feast of the Epiphany. Florence's normally strict sumptuary laws were relaxed for the day as the most prominent members of the confraternity dressed up as the Magi and their retinue to process, on horses caparisoned in silk, from the Baptistery to San Marco – which stood for Bethlehem and was thus the focus of their festival. The ritual was ambiguous. Elect members of the Medici family were celebrating the magi; but they were also being celebrated, themselves, *as* magi. The mesmerizing splendour of the *Festa*, with its interplay between representation and reality, is reflected in Gozzoli's rich and panoramic pageant of frescos.

By painting his patrons thus, as the shining heroes of their own cult, it is as if the artist has sanctified the condition of being wealthy itself. The richness which is spread across almost the entire painted surface, overflowing with detail, dense with saturated colours, highlighted in gold, exists, as the picture makes plain, to be contemplated as a form of blessedness. This effect is heightened by the beatific expressions on the faces of the participants. They are the very embodiment of worldliness yet they have the aspect of angels. The procession has been delineated with such insistent minuteness that it feels as though these people and their *possessions* – the harnesses of gold, the rings, the brocade – are the true objects of worship.

Yet precisely because Gozzoli's paintings are such vivid documents of Renaissance materialism they have often been regarded with condescension, as though their devotion to the things of this world means that they must be essentially trivial. But this is to miss the hypnotizing seriousness of the work, which gives the lie to the common assumption that materialism is always antithetical to spirituality. The love of riches expressed in the Medici Chapel draws its very power and appeal from the fervent displaced spirituality with which the pictures are saturated. Karl Marx believed one of the formative stages in the creation of a capitalist society was the development of what he called 'the fetishistic character of commodities' – a process in which covetable objects of human manufacture and trade became invested with a whole new range of associations, many of them drawn from 'the nebulous world of religion'.[1] In Gozzoli's paintings, created for a man whose family virtually invented international banking, that process of investiture can be seen taking place. The world of luxury goods, blessed realm of the wealthy, has been made to gleam with an unfamiliar radiance.

Occupying a prominent and extensive site on the Via Larga, the Medici Palace was in its time the largest and most splendid private dwelling in Florence. It is a massive, three-storey, fortress-like block with thick rusticated walls, which was designed, like the friary of San Marco, by the architect Michelozzo. Besides Gozzoli's frescos, one other Medici commission for the interior of this building has survived, albeit in a somewhat battered form. It consists of three battle scenes, painted on panel by Paolo Uccello, which once hung in a bedroom on the first floor.

The separate panels are now owned by three separate museums: the Uffizi in Florence, the Louvre in Paris and the National Gallery in London. But *The Battle of San Romano*, as the ensemble is known, is still, even in its dispersed condition, an impressively odd creation. It is a composite picture of impetuous battle joined between toy-like men and horses. The ground of the battlefield, thronged with armed men seated somewhat precariously on their rearing carousel steeds, is strewn with bric-à-brac – mostly broken shards of lance, all miraculously aligned to converge on the vanishing point of the picture. Uccello forced his pictorial world to run along the gridlines of a perspective scheme as surely as a train along a railway line, but his exaggeratedly correct construction of space is *so* correct that it runs counter to the effect of illusionism intended. In the London panel [46] a pole-axed foreshortened soldier lies prone but none the less obedient to the same perspectival parallelism as the shattered weaponry about him, as if all are responding to the pull of some hidden but tremendously powerful magnet. Things and people are not simply placed in space but seem as if they are being drawn into it, sucked in as if by a vortex.

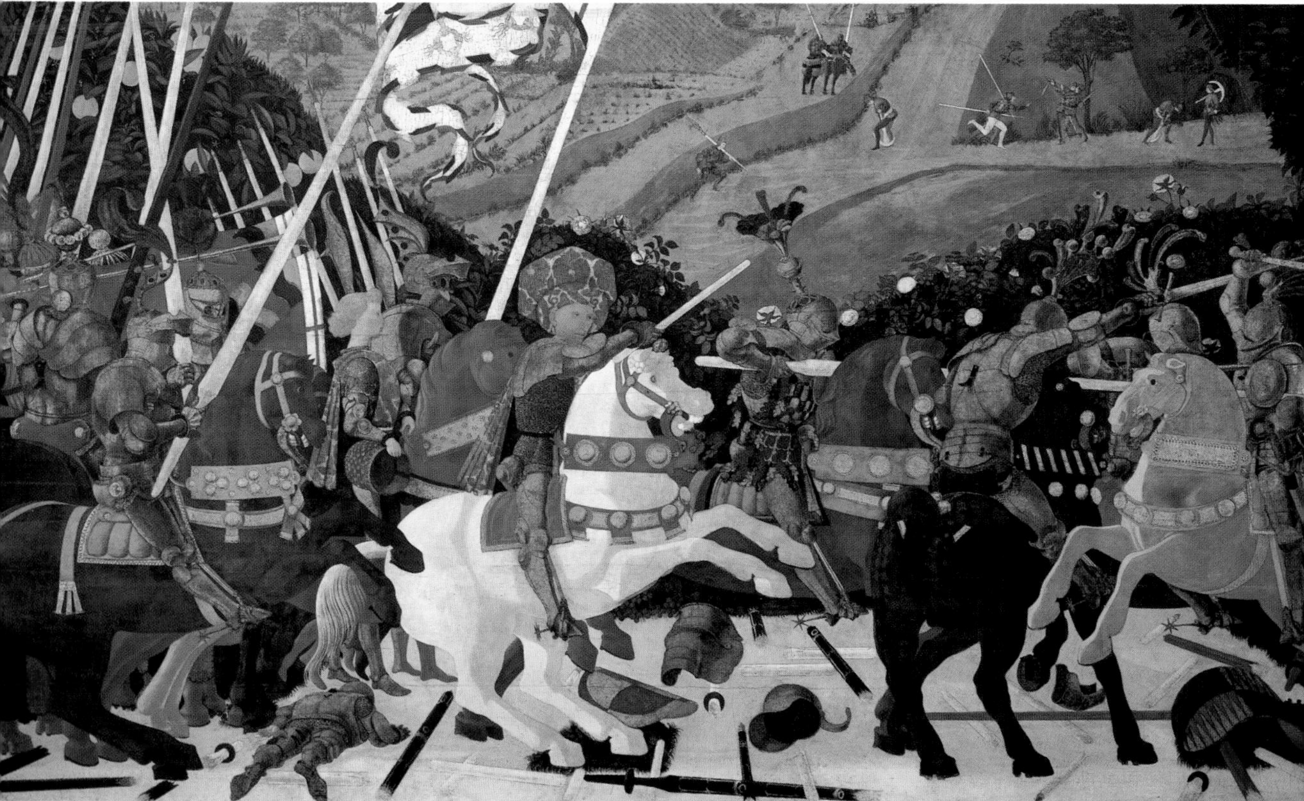

46 PAOLO UCCELLO *The Battle of San Romano* (detail) *c.* 1455

When *The Battle of San Romano* hung intact in the Medici Palace, the boldest of its meanings would have been rather clearer than it is now. Its subject was a victory for Florence over Siena, and its theme, therefore, the triumph of the Florentine state. The very presence of such a work in a private family dwelling carried subtle but unmistakable implications about that family's true place in the political hierarchy. Cosimo had become the effective head of the Florentine state. He was its prince in all but title. The fact that he should have deemed it important to enshrine that political message in a large and innovatory group of paintings is another sign of changes taking place in the fabric of society. Cosimo and his peers had begun to see a broader range of possibilities in art.

Medici patronage was undertaken, however, in a spirit of caution. One of the legacies of the city's long republican history was a strain of resistance to personal ostentation. 'Envy is a weed that should not be watered', Cosimo once remarked. But the rulers of smaller Italian principalities felt no such compunctions. They gave freer rein to their fantasies, and yet more status and independence to the artists and architects charged with realizing them.

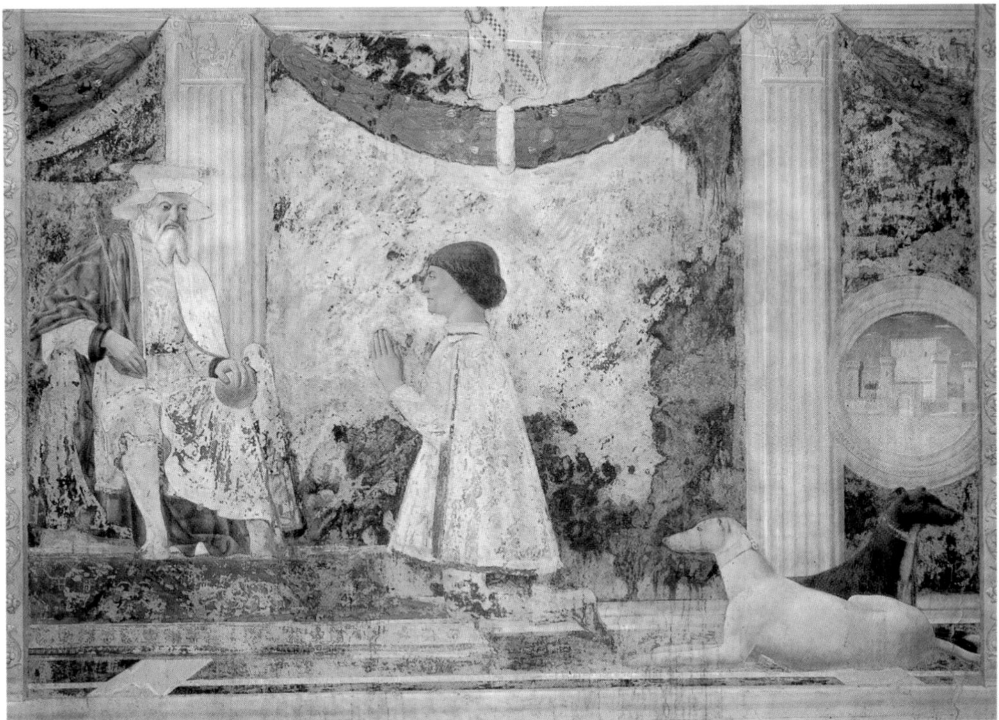

47 PIERO DELLA FRANCESCA *Sigismondo Malatesta before St Sigismund* 1451

## DEATH IN RIMINI

Sigismondo Malatesta, lord of Rimini, had a taste for self-aggrandizing spectacle which was matched only by the volatility of his temperament. Piero della Francesca, who was briefly a court painter to Sigismondo, saw this with his customary clear-sightedness. He painted a portrait of his employer [47], kneeling in profile before his name saint, St Sigismund, for one of the side chapels in the Riminese church of San Francesco. Sporting a splendid cloak, depicted in richly patterned paint now somewhat abraded by time, Sigismondo wears his hair in an elegant bob. His hunting dogs are beside him, an unusual inclusion in an ostensibly pious portrait of this kind. Above his head floats a coat of arms. The whole painting seems conceived in the spirit of heraldry. Sigismondo's hounds, one black, one white, are arranged with perfect symmetry, forming a device of dogs. Their master has high cheekbones, thin lips and cruel, indifferent eyes.

A considerably less flattering but even more memorable picture of him was painted by his contemporary, Pope Pius II, not in pigment but in words:

> Sigismondo Malatesta was an illegitimate member of the noble family of the Malatestas, and had a great spirit and a powerful body. He was an eloquent and skilful captain. He had studied history and had more than an amateur's knowledge of philosophy. He seemed born to do whatever he put his hand to. But he was so ruled by his passions, and abandoned himself to such uncontrollable greed for money, that he became a plunderer and a thief to boot. He was so dissolute that he raped his daughters and sons-in-law. When a boy, he often acted the female partner in shameful loves, and later forced men to act as women ... His cruelty was greater than any barbarian's, and he inflicted fearful tortures on guilty and innocent alike with his own bloody hands ... This was Sigismondo, a restless, sensual man and a tireless warmonger, one of the worst men that have ever lived or will live, the shame of Italy and the disgrace of our generation.[2]

The author of this well-turned piece of character assassination had good reasons for disliking Sigismondo, who had defied the pope's attempts to call a general peace on the Italian peninsula in 1459 and remained a thorn in the side of the papacy for several years afterwards. Although Pius exaggerated his sinfulness, the lord of Rimini was certainly an irascible man and a dangerous enemy. A professional soldier by trade, he had been enriched during the 1430s and 1440s by the constant warring over territory which was so much a part of the texture of Italian fifteenth-century life. He fought on the winning side in numerous small engagements and was well rewarded by his chief client, Alfonso I, King of Naples. A big fish in a rather small pond, Sigismondo spent his money in a spirit of *largesse* which makes even the most notable private commissions undertaken in fifteenth-century Florence seem cautious by comparison.

Like many Renaissance rulers, he had received a humanist education and his classical learning was reflected in his taste. But unlike his Florentine contemporaries he felt no need to negotiate the sensibilities of his fellow citizens. Nor did he feel any attraction to the implicitly republican styles of classical art which had been recently revived in Florence during the years of Leonardo Bruni's chancellorship. Being a despot and a soldier, Sigismondo wanted the artists working for him to evoke imperial Rome in all its triumphal grandeur.

Architecture was his favoured medium of self-aggrandizement. Leon Battista Alberti, himself a humanist scholar as well as an architect of growing repute, was the man whom he chose to advise him on the scheme closest to his heart. This was the transformation of the church of San Francesco into a mausoleum for Sigismondo and his court. It was to be a new kind of memorial, a Christian-cum-classical Malatesta hall of fame, resounding no longer to the glory of God alone, but also to that of a worldly ruler. The church of San Francesco was to become the Tempio Malatestiano – the Malatesta Temple [48].

Alberti clad the existing Franciscan edifice in marble, thus turning what had once been a large but functional, brick-built place of worship into a great white classical temple. Arcades of columns were added to both exterior sides of the church, supported by a stone wall into which was incised a pattern of letters, an intertwined S and I. Once believed, romantically, to stand for Sigismondo and Isotta, the mistress whom he married late in life, this is in fact an abbreviation of Sigismondo's name alone to 'Si'. This boldly affirmative self-proclamation alternates with a design of elephants, symbol of the Roman general Scipio, Hannibal's nemesis – and for that reason another of the *imprese* or personal emblems favoured by Sigismondo, who liked to see himself as a second Scipio.

Alberti devoted his utmost ingenuity to classicizing the western façade of the church. This was by no means an easy task given that the shape produced by a normal Christian church, with its high central nave, bears so little resemblance to that of any of the conventional forms of classical architecture. His solution to the problem was to model his new façade partly on classical temple fronts and partly on Roman triumphal arches, an idea which may have been suggested to him by the presence, in Rimini, of a considerable Arch of Augustus which has since been made the hub of the city's largest roundabout. Alberti thus made the whole church, by implication, the scene of Sigismondo's final triumphal march into death and eternity. The façade was never quite finished, because Sigismondo, whose fortunes waned in later life, eventually ran out of money and time. Neither was the huge dome which, rising above the façade, would have made the Tempio Malatestiano's naked ambition yet more visible than it is today.

Sigismondo may have been a feudal warlord from a provincial backwater of Italy, a *condottiere* of a kind to have prospered in Italy for centuries, but his education had given him different and larger ideas than those of his forebears. The new cult of the antique propagated by the teachings of the humanists seemed to offer a man such as him the passport to a higher status. In fiction, if not in fact, he could fight on the same battlefield as the Roman soldiers of the past. In fiction, if not in fact, he could carve his name into the adamantine marble of eternity.

The main changes to the interior of the original church involved the destruction of fourteenth-century frescos by Giotto and his school in order to make way

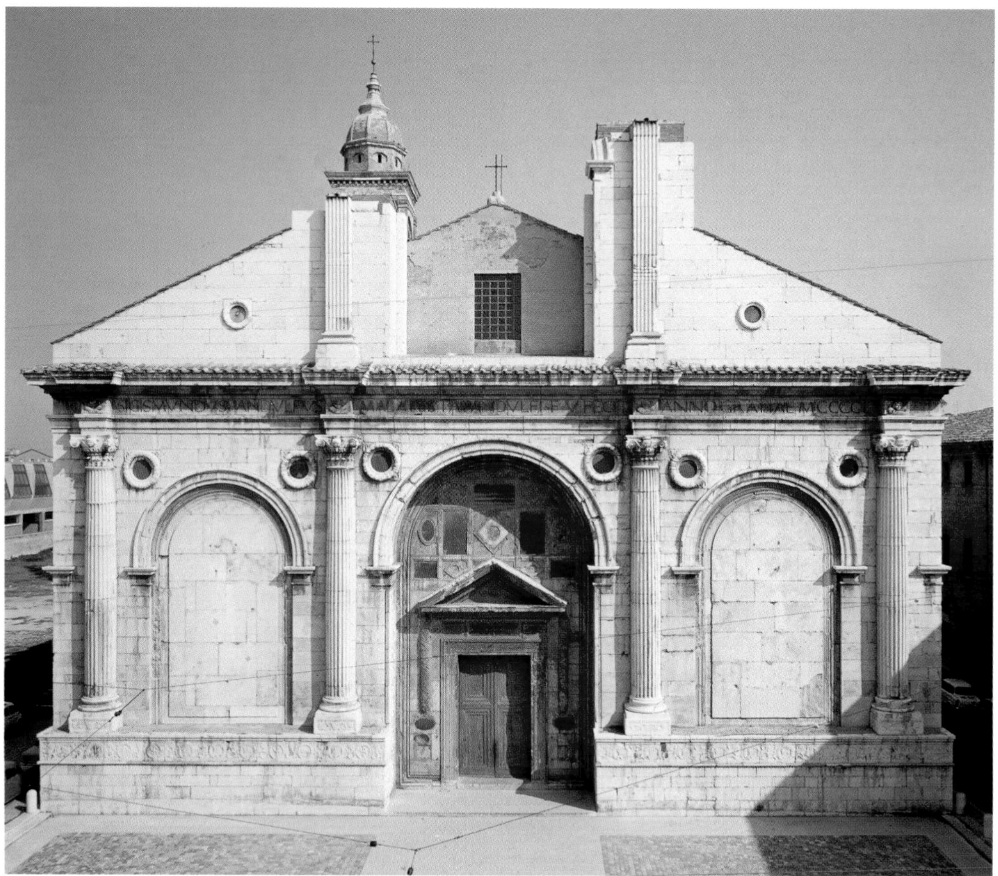

48 LEON BATTISTA ALBERTI Tempio Malatestiano, San Francesco, Rimini, begun 1453

for a series of chapels dedicated to St Sigismund, as well as to the Liberal Arts, the Planets and other unconventional subjects. Their decoration was undertaken by Agostino di Duccio, in the form of relief and free-standing sculpture, working to the instruction of Sigismondo and his humanist courtiers. The Chapel of St Sigismund is notable for its cornucopia of triumphal imagery. The Chapel of the Planets is decorated with the signs of the zodiac and other images alluding to the Egyptian theology of sun-worship. The walls of the Chapel of the Liberal Arts are embellished with images from Greek myth, including the Muses. The style of Agostino's reliefs is romantic and copious. A naked oarsman rows through monster-infested seas dotted with islands where castles tower and lions prowl. A figure of Luna holds her crescent moon like a child with a broken hoop, casting a worried glance up at the sky [49].

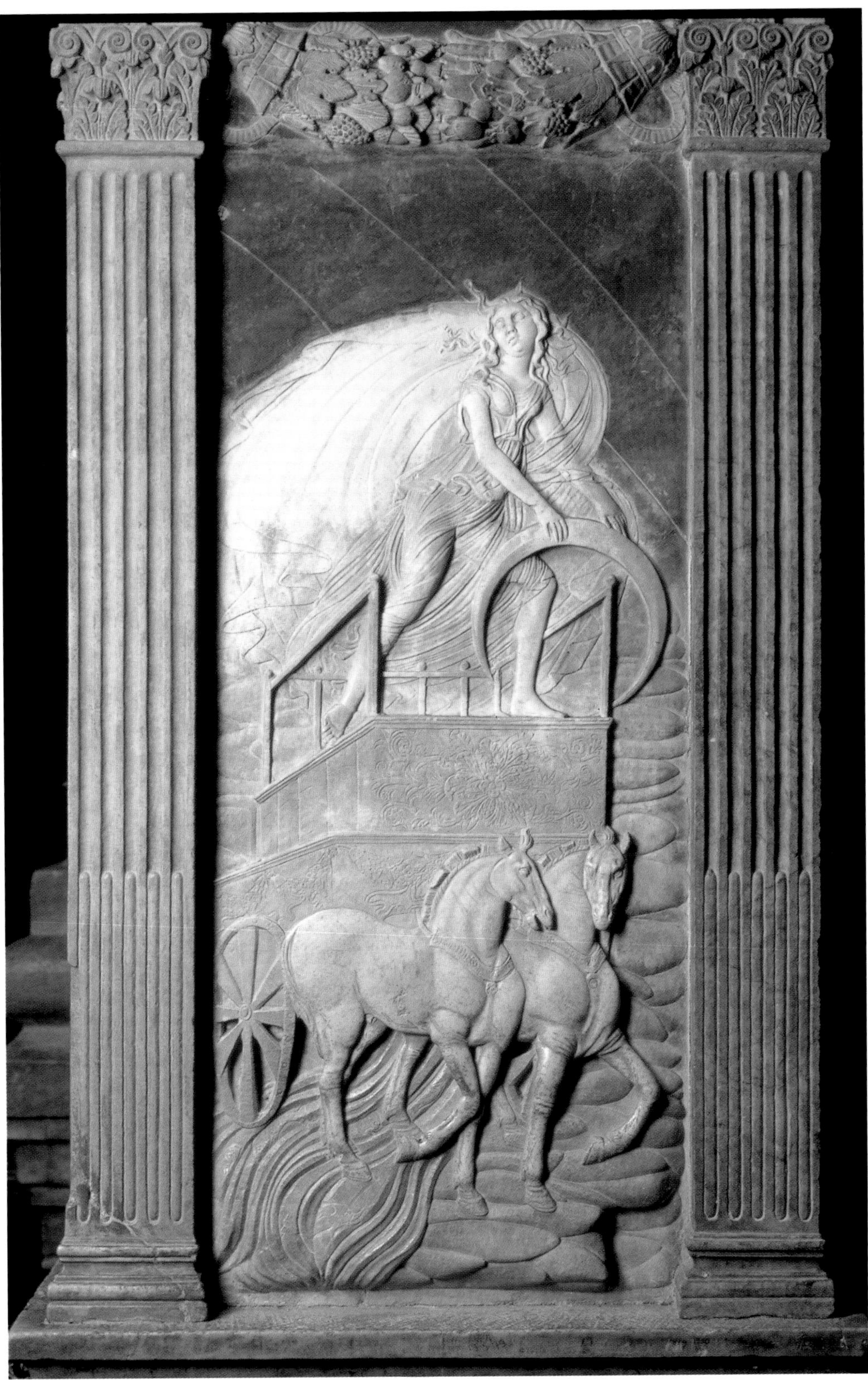

49 AGOSTINO DI DUCCIO *Luna*, Chapel of the Planets, Tempio Malatestiano *c.* 1451–3

This multitude of references to other religions and mythologies, in what remained a Christian church, gave Pius II an opportunity to be scandalized once more by the activities of his enemy – he accused Sigismondo of promoting devil-worship – but it should not necessarily be taken as a sign of impiety. The interior of the Tempio Malatestiano is bright and light-filled, the predominant colour scheme of its decorations white and a light blue like that of Wedgwood china. It is not the dark temple of evil rites depicted by Pius but, rather, a building which reflects the growing conviction, in humanist circles such as that gathered around Sigismondo, that *all* faiths, no matter how apparently distant from Christianity, were coded versions of the one true faith.

One of Sigismondo's courtiers, the military expert Roberto Valturio, praised the Tempio Malatestiano precisely on account of the arcane, recherché, sophisticated allusions of its imagery:

> These representations – not only because of the knowledge of the appearance of the figures, whose characteristics you, the most intelligent and unquestionably the most distinguished ruler of our time, have taken from the secret depths of philosophy – are especially able to attract learned viewers, who are almost entirely different from the common run of people.[3]

The Tempio Malatestiano does not mark a transition from piety to paganism. But it does measure the gap between older, popular evangelical forms of Christianity and that more intellectualized, courtly conception of the Christian religion which began to be developed in élite Renaissance society. There is pathos in the fact that the building should have been created from an existing Franciscan church. A place of worship initially designed to spread the faith to 'the common run of people' had been turned into one which, intellectually if not physically, was intended to exclude them.

## NEW TERMS

It would be a mistake to think of the Tempio Malatestiano as a work 'by' Leon Battista Alberti, for he was by no means in sole charge of its construction. He did not live in Rimini and his designs were received and for the most part discussed by correspondence. The precise nature of his contribution is therefore difficult to establish, but this is often the case when it comes to his works.

Alberti was one of the most influential Renaissance thinkers of the second half of the fifteenth century. But he remains difficult to categorize, because he was so versatile. He helped to persuade princes and patrons to build on a scale not seen since the days of ancient Rome. He singled out the leading artists of his time, and campaigned on their behalf, with a prescience that has been confirmed by the assent of posterity to nearly all of his judgements. Now best known for his writings on architectural theory, he was also active as a painter, sculptor, mathematician, architect, agent, impresario and critic. There is no single word to do justice to him, and he was in any case more than the sum of his parts.

Alberti left his mark on many important Renaissance centres in Italy, but a number of the buildings which he designed were never completed and survive only in fragmentary form. Works attributed to him in part, but only in part – a bit of an arch here, a belltower there – seem to abound. The rubric 'based on an idea by Leon Battista Alberti' hovers invisibly over a remarkable quantity of important Renaissance buildings. This tantalizing and imponderable ubiquity is perhaps a clue to his true importance. Taking advantage of the freedom afforded to him by his job in the papal civil service, he became an intellectual missionary who ensured that new ways of thinking about art and architecture were disseminated throughout the peninsula.

Alberti, born in 1404, was the illegitimate son of a nobleman, so it is perhaps logical that self-betterment should have become the theme of his life. He believed that a man of any birth or circumstances could raise himself up through force of will and intellect. His career as an intellectual catalyst had begun when he was thirty and relatively new to the papal curia. On visiting Florence, in 1434, as part of the retinue of Pope Eugenius IV, he recognized instantly that he had walked into a scene of artistic ferment. A year later he published his treatise *On Painting*, the first extended theoretical discussion of visual art ever written, in which he identified Brunelleschi, Masaccio, Ghiberti and Donatello as the founders of a new golden age. Alberti helped to make their work both famous and fashionable, the model for aspiring artists all over Italy. He made the Florentine *Rinascita* official, by writing about it. On the basis of what he had seen, and his own considerable learning, he also elaborated a new ideal of what art and artists should be.

The painter, Alberti said, must be educated in geometry and mathematics, so that he will understand how to create the illusion of space through perspective. He must be intellectually accomplished as well as manually skilful (there was a Platonic cast to Alberti's thought and he seems always to have felt a certain disdain for those who work with their hands alone). He must have a sufficiently broad literary education in order to be able to associate easily with the orators and poets who will advise him on his choice of morally elevated subjects. Yet when Alberti wrote *On Painting*, few if any such intellectually rounded painters actually existed. His book was a provocation and it helped to sow the seeds for a reassessment of the artist's place in society.

The spread of Alberti's ideas, coupled with the growing expectations of Renaissance patrons, brought about many changes. The more intellectually vigorous and up-to-date artists of the time became increasingly aware of the market for their talents. Thus Piero della Francesca, realizing, perhaps, that Sigismondo's fortunes were on the wane, left his employ and went to work for a different prince. By selling themselves to the highest bidder, painters were able to operate much more freely than they could have done within the traditional structure of the craftsmen's guilds. Yet they also had to adapt to the new world in which they hoped to thrive. In order to impress their learned and demanding employers at court it was no longer enough for them to be, merely, bearers of manual skill. They had to be able to demonstrate their own learning and sophistication. Thus the artist became a sort of travelling intellectual. The networks that linked one Renaissance court to another – traversed by painters as well as by poets, philosophers, mathematicians and a host of other men with nothing but their genius to declare – became an information highway.

At the centre of each of those networks there was always the patron. Ambitious patrons became, if not artists themselves, then impresarios, channelling the energies of those in their employ into the creation of that composite work of art which was the princely palace. Perhaps the most impressive monument to the Italian Renaissance patron's dedication to art, not just as a means of self-aggrandizement, but as a means of self-expression, is to be found in the town of Urbino.

## THE ONE-EYED MERCENARY

Piero della Francesca's preferred patron, Federigo da Montefeltro, Duke of Urbino [50], was richer than Sigismondo; he was a better soldier, having beaten Sigismondo in a decisive battle; and he was also considerably uglier, having lost the bridge of his nose and his right eye as a result of a jousting accident when he was young.[4] In official portraits, of which many survive, we see him invariably in profile. This was done to hide his disfigurement, but Federigo would probably have insisted on it anyway, because that was how the emperors of ancient Rome had always been portrayed on coins and medals.

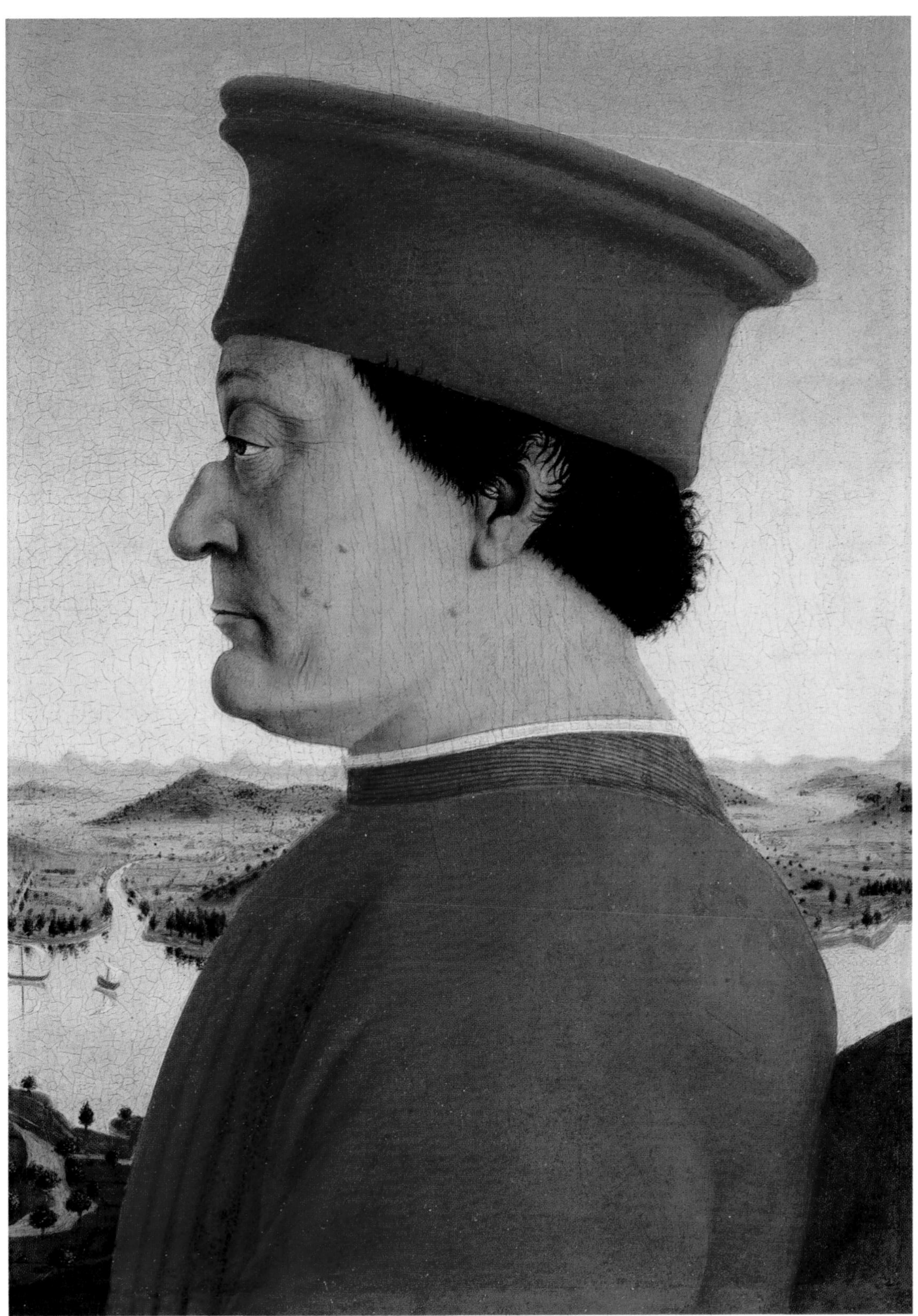

50 PIERO DELLA FRANCESCA *Federigo da Montefeltro* (detail of diptych) *c.* 1472

During his own lifetime (1422–82), Federigo was generally agreed to be the shrewdest military commander in Italy. He attributed much of his success to his education. When he was a child, he had spent two years in Mantua as a hostage of war, where he was taught at the famous humanist school of Vittorino da Feltre, as were the children of the Gonzaga family. Vittorino had introduced his new charge to the humanist curriculum, teaching him Latin, grammar, rhetoric, poetry, history and moral philosophy. This would stand Federigo in good stead, for it was as a cunning negotiator and diplomat – as a man of verbal as well as military persuasion – that he was to excel.

He made much of his fortune by taking his troops into battle and subsequently accepting large sums of money to refrain from engaging in military action. As coalitions formed and collapsed, Federigo played the field with skill. Wherever possible, he tried to make sure that his army was the potentially decisive force, thus enabling him to sell his services to the highest bidder. An opportunistic ally, he occasionally even served both sides, one after another, in a given conflict. But he was unusual among mercenaries in that he always honoured each agreement that he made. Federigo's many military successes enabled him to expand his own fiefdom of Urbino, and under his rule the city became the centre of what was in effect a territorial state.

From the late 1460s onwards he spent more money on the patronage of art than any other prince in the Italian peninsula. At the centre of his plans for Urbino lay his own palace. He set about incorporating the old castle of the counts of Urbino, together with several adjoining houses, into a new Ducal Palace that would be unparalleled in size and magnificence. The building, remodelled principally by the architect Luciano Laurana, was given a completely civilian façade, copiously decorated with Federigo's emblems. Conspicuous among these are his monogram 'Fe', alongside the sign of an exploding shell, to indicate his military prowess, and a pair of crossed keys standing for his role as commander in chief of the papal armies.

In Urbino, the ruler was the theme of his own palace. A carved inscription proclaiming the virtues of Federigo runs around the elegant arcaded courtyard which was once the centre of palace life. At the top of the staircase of honour, the main suite of rooms on the first floor, or *piano nobile*, is approached through an imposing pair of wooden doors set within a marble door-frame carved with Roman trophies of war. The doors themselves are inlaid with intarsia scenes in which putti gather garlands of fruit and figures of the Muses stand on top of pedestals. Out of martial valour has come plenty and beauty.

Despite Federigo's liking for classical styles of architecture – Alberti planned to dedicate his treatise on architecture to the duke – his taste was eclectic. He employed Venetians as well as Tuscans and the most intimate image of him has been attributed to a Northern artist whom he had tempted into his employ, Justus of Ghent. Federigo is depicted standing at a lectern, wearing a silver coat of armour and an ermine-trimmed red damask robe, and reading to his son Guidobaldo. The man of arms has become the man of letters. He has put off his helmet to read from a large book, which he clutches in meaty, paw-like hands. His face is bristly with stubble and he gazes somewhat bleary-eyed at his text.

The library from which that book came contained more or less the entire corpus of known Latin and Greek texts as well as many modern works (all manuscripts, since Federigo regarded the printed book as a vulgar novelty). It has subsequently been dispersed, but the duke's attachment to scholarship is still preserved in the most remarkable of the palace's many rooms and chambers, his study, or Studiolo [51]. Panelled with intricate intarsia decorations, and hung with portraits of a carefully selected group of famous men, the Studiolo is a composite work of art which was almost certainly designed in large measure by Federigo himself. Its dominant theme – like that of Justus's portrait of Federigo reading – is the perfect balance, in the ideal ruler, between the *vita activa* and the *vita contemplativa*, the active and contemplative lives. The leader of men, the Studiolo implies, must pursue learning with the same single-mindedness with which he pursues honour or gold or his enemies.

Federigo commissioned Justus to furnish the room with twenty-eight portraits of learned men, half of which remain *in situ*, the others having found their way to the Louvre. The pictures hang in two frieze-like bands just below the ceiling of the room. The upper level is dedicated to intellectual heroes, most of them drawn from the world of classical antiquity. They include Plato, Aristotle, Homer and Euclid, and collectively embody almost every category of intellectual activity recognized in Federigo's time: Logic, Astronomy, Music, Arithmetic, Moral Philosophy, Rhetoric, Poetry, Geometry, Law, Medicine. The lower level celebrates religious heroes, past and present. Here the selection seems to have been less intellectually programmatic, probably because Federigo felt obliged to include illustrious contemporaries and personal patrons such as Pope Sixtus IV, Pope Pius II and Cardinal Bessarion. But there is a strong overall emphasis on learning. Popular but unscholarly saints such as St Sebastian or St Francis of Assisi are excluded in favour of theologians such as St Augustine and St Thomas Aquinas – whose writings, declared Federigo, represented 'the purest and clearest doctrine'.

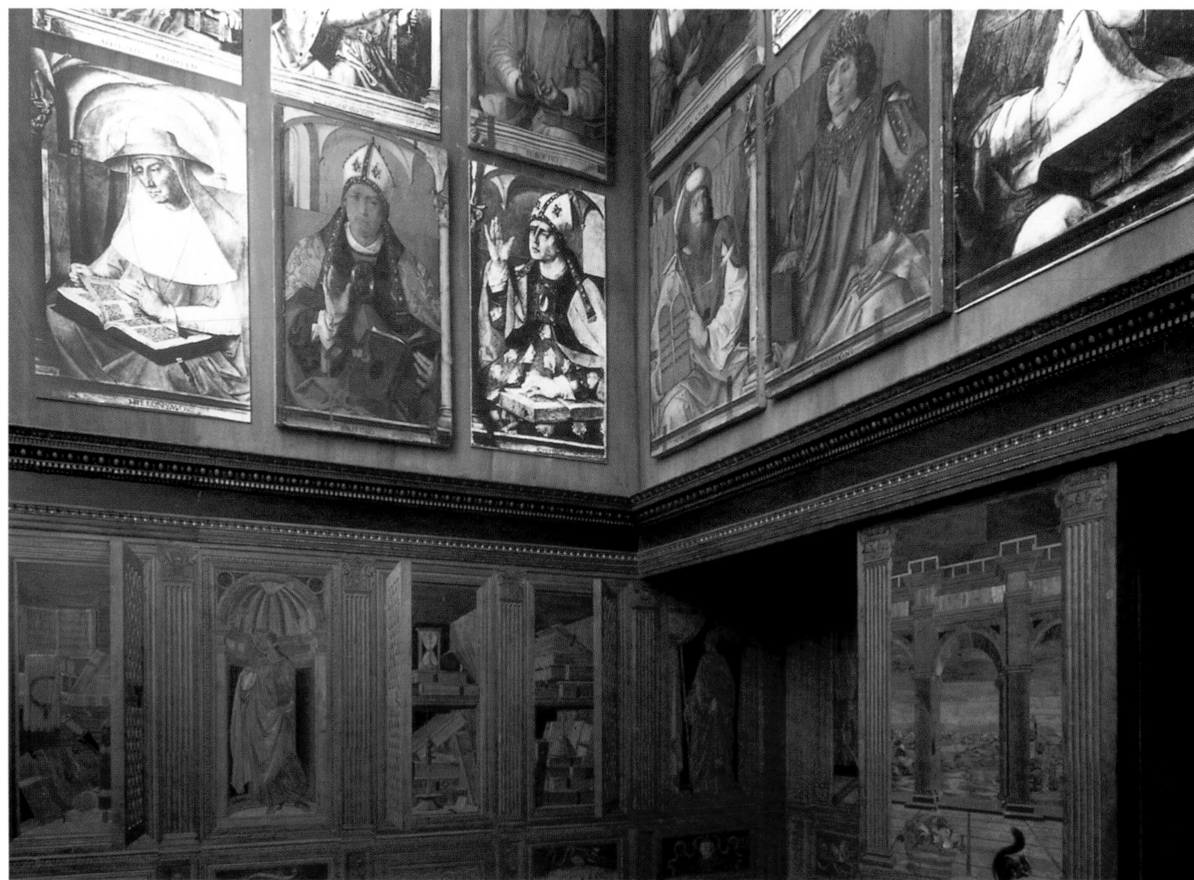

51 Studiolo, Ducal Palace, Urbino *c.* 1472–6

The doctors of the church appealed to the mind of an educated prince such as Federigo because they exemplified the role of learning in the sphere of religion, and because they had sought out patterns of Christian meaning in the texts of antiquity, such as the writings of Plato, centuries before the advent of humanist ideas about the classical world. Augustine and Aquinas and other scholastic theologians were greatly admired by later fifteenth-century Italian humanists, who saw them as pioneering forefathers of their own hermetic interpretations of Christianity. The Duke of Urbino is known to have been sympathetic to such views. He was the dedicatee of a Latin translation of Plato's *Republic* by the Florentine Neoplatonist Marsilio Ficino, for whom the ancient philosophies of Egypt, ancient Hebrew wisdom and the arcane works of Pythagoras were all prefigurations of Christian revelation. The frieze of famous men is an affirmation

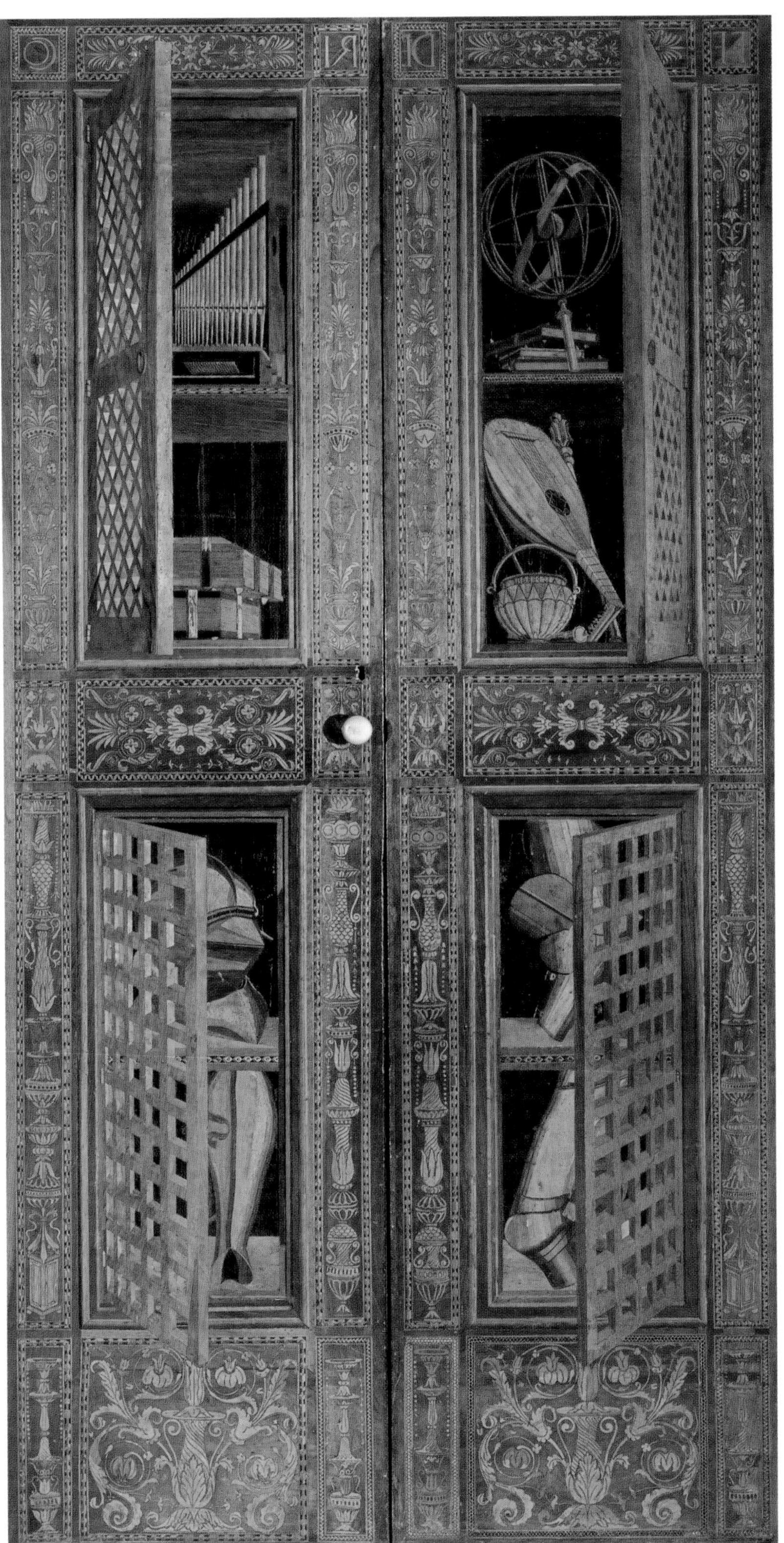

52 ARTIST UNKNOWN Intarsia doors, Studiolo, Ducal Palace, Urbino *c.* 1472–6

of the idea – shared by Federigo's well-educated enemy, Sigismondo Malatesta – that the classical and the Christian are complementary rather than antithetical.

But the Studiolo is most impressive, perhaps, in what it implies about the sheer intellectual range proper to the ruler. Nothing less than omnicompetence will do. He is to be on familiar terms with mathematicians and geometricians, moral philosophers and lawyers, poets and theologians alike. He is, ideally – and it is the idealism of the room that is its most enduring and admirable quality – to know everything. The aspiration to be a universal man is embedded in Federigo's Studiolo.

The decorations of inlaid wood with which the doors [52] and lower part of the room are panelled are among the most delicate and masterly examples of intarsia. An art form which, hitherto, had been most commonly applied to the decoration of choir stalls, has here been given a princely application. The profusion of motifs and the complexity of their juxtapositions make precise decoding of their hidden meaning difficult. Everything means something, but what it means – as in the case of crossword puzzle clues or acrostics – is not always clear at first view. Some of the objects represented, such as books, musical manuscripts and instruments, may be taken as further emblems of Federigo's intellectual achievements. Others, including a brilliant *trompe l'oeil* panel of an entire suit of armour hanging as if in a cupboard, evidently allude to his skill as a soldier. Placed between these panels, military and scholarly in their implication, is a seemingly innocent scene of nature: a squirrel with a spectacularly bushy tail, next to a basket of fruit, before an open landscape of field and flower. This image has been interpreted by Luciano Cheles, the most industrious investigator of the Studiolo's iconograpy: the prudent ruler (squirrel) enriched by the experience and humanity derived from his active-contemplative pursuits (symmetrical niches containing armour and books), provides for the well-being (basket of fruit) of his state (landscape).[5]

The Studiolo has little in common with a study, in the modern sense, or with later *Wunderkammern* or cabinets of curiosities (although such intellectual retreats would grow partly out of the attitudes which shaped it). It is more practical, and more engaged with life than rooms of that kind. There is something superbly aggressive about the way in which the intarsia decoration proclaims soldiery and learning to be two sides of the same coin. The spiked club and the grenade have been placed, literally, next to the inkwell and the lectern. The pen is not mightier than the sword, or vice versa. They are both part of the ruler's armoury. Federigo da Montefeltro led from the front on the battlefield and he also spearheaded the advance of learning; he was part of an intellectual advance guard – an avant-garde, even. The Studiolo was the room where he could draw on all the knowledge that he had stockpiled in his great library. There is nothing foppish or dilettanteish about the room. It is no ivory tower, but an intellectual arsenal.

Piero della Francesca's portrait diptych of the duke [50] and his wife, Battista Sforza (now in the Uffizi, Florence), shows them bust-length in profile, facing one another. They are in a high place and behind them an extensive landscape unfolds. Metaphorically, but not actually – for Piero in fact substituted a landscape very like that of his own childhood, around Borgo San Sepolcro – it is the landscape of their domain, seen from the bird's-eye view beloved of fifteenth-century Italian princes. The ornate original frame of the picture is decorated with eagles, another of Federigo's personal emblems. The *condottiere* and his wife have been painted with an eagle-eyed, quasi-Flemish attention to detail, although the duke is more vividly present to us than his spouse. Possibly because she had died before the portrait was painted (its precise date is uncertain), Piero depicted her as a pale ghost. Facing her, wrinkled Federigo bursts with life. He has four prominent warts on his tanned face. He has dark curly hair and wears a startlingly red pillbox hat to match his startlingly red tunic. The landscape behind Battista is in shade, which may suggest the shadow cast over Urbino by her death. The same landscape continues behind Federigo, but now it is bathed in bright sunshine, its colours bleached to tans and olive greens, passing away to the misty blue of distant mountains seen through heat haze. This idyllic painted world, where two boats float on a lake as still as the surface of a mirror, perhaps insinuates a meaning. Federigo is grieving with due solemnity before the memory of his wife but, despite her sad death, all is well in the state of Urbino.

The reverse side of each portrait is also decorated, with images of Federigo and Battista seated on Roman triumphal carriages on a rocky promontory high above the same landscape, painted this time in a harder light which models contours more sharply still than in the portraits. Battista's carriage is drawn by a pair of unicorns, symbols of chastity, and she is accompanied by a nun and figures symbolizing the three Theological Virtues, Faith, Hope and Charity. Federigo's carriage is drawn by white horses and he has the Four Cardinal Virtues as attendants, while a winged figure of Victory holds a ducal coronet above his head. Below him a fine *trompe l'oeil* inscription proclaims the legitimacy of his rule.

It is not difficult to understand why Federigo should have valued Piero's art. The painter elevated his patron to the status of a mythological character. Reality is recognized – Piero did, after all, paint Federigo warts and all – but only, ultimately, to be overcome. The state of Urbino is transformed, through the atmospheric alchemy of Piero's vision, into a paradise of stasis. No wind stirs on the plains below Federigo. The view from the palace window has been perfected. The world seen from on high has been turned into a place from which change has been banished along with all evil. Piero's style – the stillness and solemnity of his world, its timelessness and its momentousness – effects a translation of his sitter to a higher realm.

Ascending to the very top of his palace, up the spiral staircase constructed for him by his architect, and emerging on to the balcony encircling the summit of its tallest tower, Federigo could literally count himself lord of all he surveyed, could imagine that he had indeed mastered his world, intellectually as well as territorially, and had perhaps risen to some ideal, Platonic level of existence. In the long run, however, it would not be the rulers of Renaissance Italy who soared to the very highest peaks, but the people whom they employed: artists.

## ARTIST LAUREATE

In September 1464 the painter Andrea Mantegna and three friends went boating on Lake Garda. They wore classical fancy dress and read Latin poetry to one another as they rowed to a little island in the middle of the lake, where they visited some Roman remains. On their return they gave a prayer of thanks to the Virgin and her Son for having granted them 'the wisdom and the will to seek out such delightful places and such venerable monuments'.[6]

No fifteenth-century artist meditated longer or more profoundly on the world of antiquity than Andrea Mantegna; and no artist was more exercised by the moral and spiritual ambiguity that lies in wait for the Christian believer who falls too deeply and unreservedly in love with ancient Rome.

Mantegna had passed his youth in Padua, one of the main Italian university towns (the university was founded in 1222, the town having been an important centre of learning since antiquity). He must have walked, often, in the shadow of Donatello's modern-day Marcus Aurelius, the *Gattemelata* [40]. As a member of a leading circle of Paduan intellectuals during the 1450s, Mantegna became as deeply immersed in the study of ancient Roman civilization as any humanist man of letters. In 1459 he took up the post of court painter to the ruling Gonzaga family in Mantua. His life there, as he rose from the rank of craftsman to that of a fully fledged courtier, with his own palace and numerous servants, was a parable of the self-betterment of artists in fifteenth-century Italy. Mantegna showed that painters could be regarded as gentlemen – could even themselves become famous men like

53 ANDREA MANTEGNA Camera Picta (detail from north wall), Ducal Palace, Mantua *c.* 1465–74

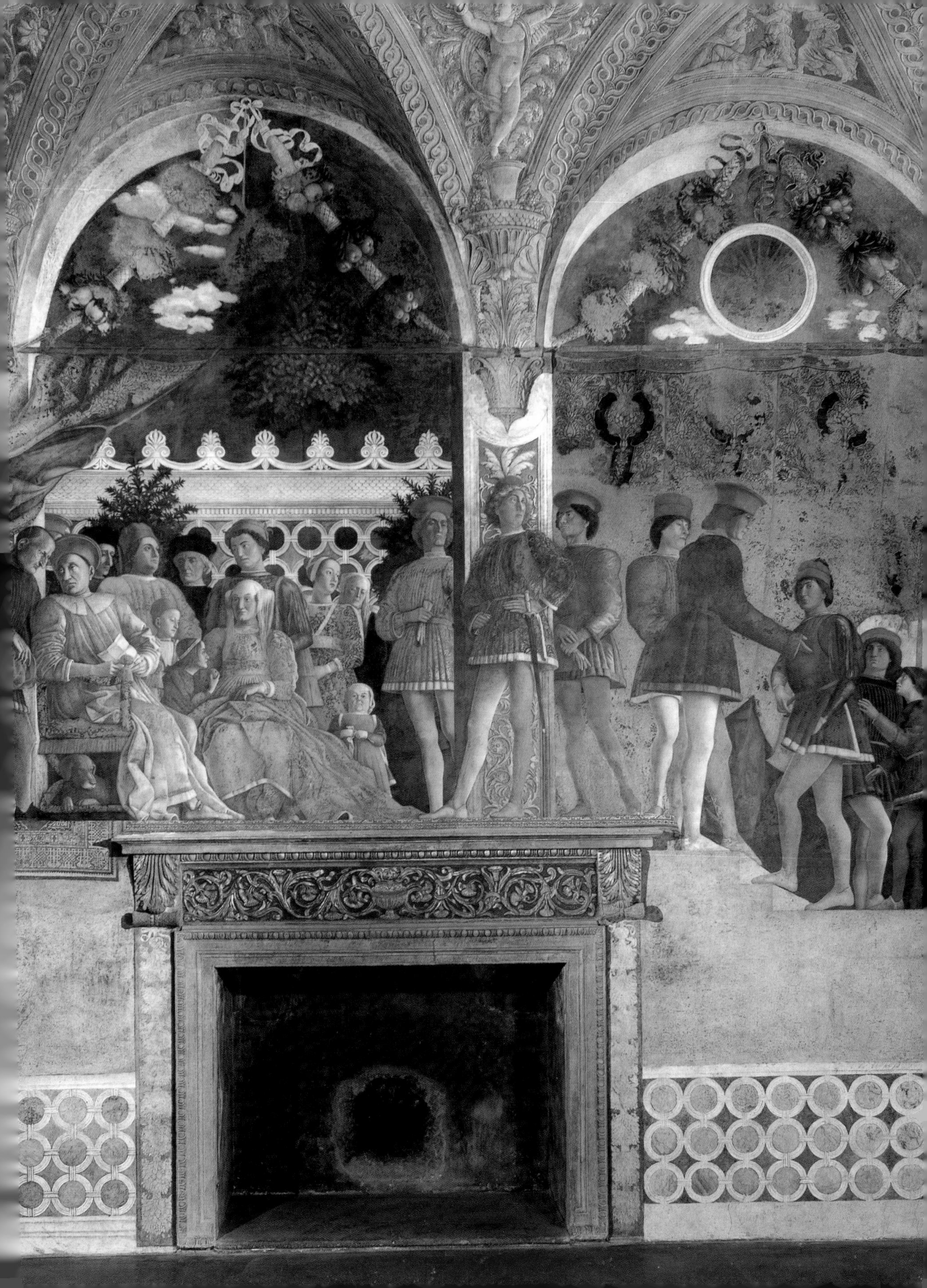

the heroes lauded in the frieze of Federigo da Montefeltro's Studiolo. This would not be lost on his contemporaries.

Almost the sole surviving trace of Mantegna's presence in the Ducal Palace at Mantua is the Camera Picta, a brilliant composite portrait of the court of the Gonzaga, painted around 1465–74, which runs around the walls of one of the main reception rooms on the *piano nobile* of the palace. The effect is somewhat reminiscent of Benozzo Gozzoli's chapel for the Medici, purged of the trappings of magnificent oriental fantasy and done in modern clothing. The prince no longer has to wear fancy dress to become his own cult. The paintings are like mirrors in which the rulers of the city could see themselves gloriously reflected.

Two different scenes are depicted. On the north wall Ludovico Gonzaga, seated on a throne beside his marchioness, Barbara of Brandenburg, and surrounded by members of his court including secretaries and advisers and an imperious female dwarf, is seen receiving a letter of considerable import [53]. The picture is said to illustrate a critical moment in the fortunes of Mantua, when Ludovico was called upon, in his capacity as *condottiere* and leader of a considerable mass of troops, to help the Milanese ruling family, the Sforza, consolidate its power. On the west wall the subject depicted is the so-called Meeting Scene. Here leading members of the Gonzaga, along with their dogs, horses, servants and children, stand and converse before a landscape. Also present are Christian I, King of Denmark, and Frederick III, Holy Roman Emperor. The picture is among other things a celebration of Gonzaga power and influence, placing the family at the very heart of fifteenth-century European politics. In the distance behind them may be seen an idealized town, perhaps meant to be Mantua itself. All this peace and harmony is sustained by the force of law, the picture declares in a detail so small it might easily be overlooked: a hanged man suspended from a gibbet at the distant city gate.

The light, spacious naturalism of the Camera Picta is the mask for a complicated play of *Realpolitik*. Each pose, each gesture, each glance, each and every suggestion of a relationship between the various figures, is charged with significance. Not all of its meanings are discoverable, but few other works offer a greater illusion of proximity to the life of a Renaissance court. Mantegna has painted the courtiers' magnificence but also their nerves. There is a powerful sense of reserve, caution and perhaps even, in just one or two of these faces, fear. The painter captured the cloak-and-dagger character of élite Italian society. Like Benozzo Gozzoli, Mantegna included a portrait of himself in his own work. But he only let himself intrude in a minor role, as a decorative gargoyle staring unsmilingly out

54 Courtyard, Andrea Mantegna's house, Mantua 1483

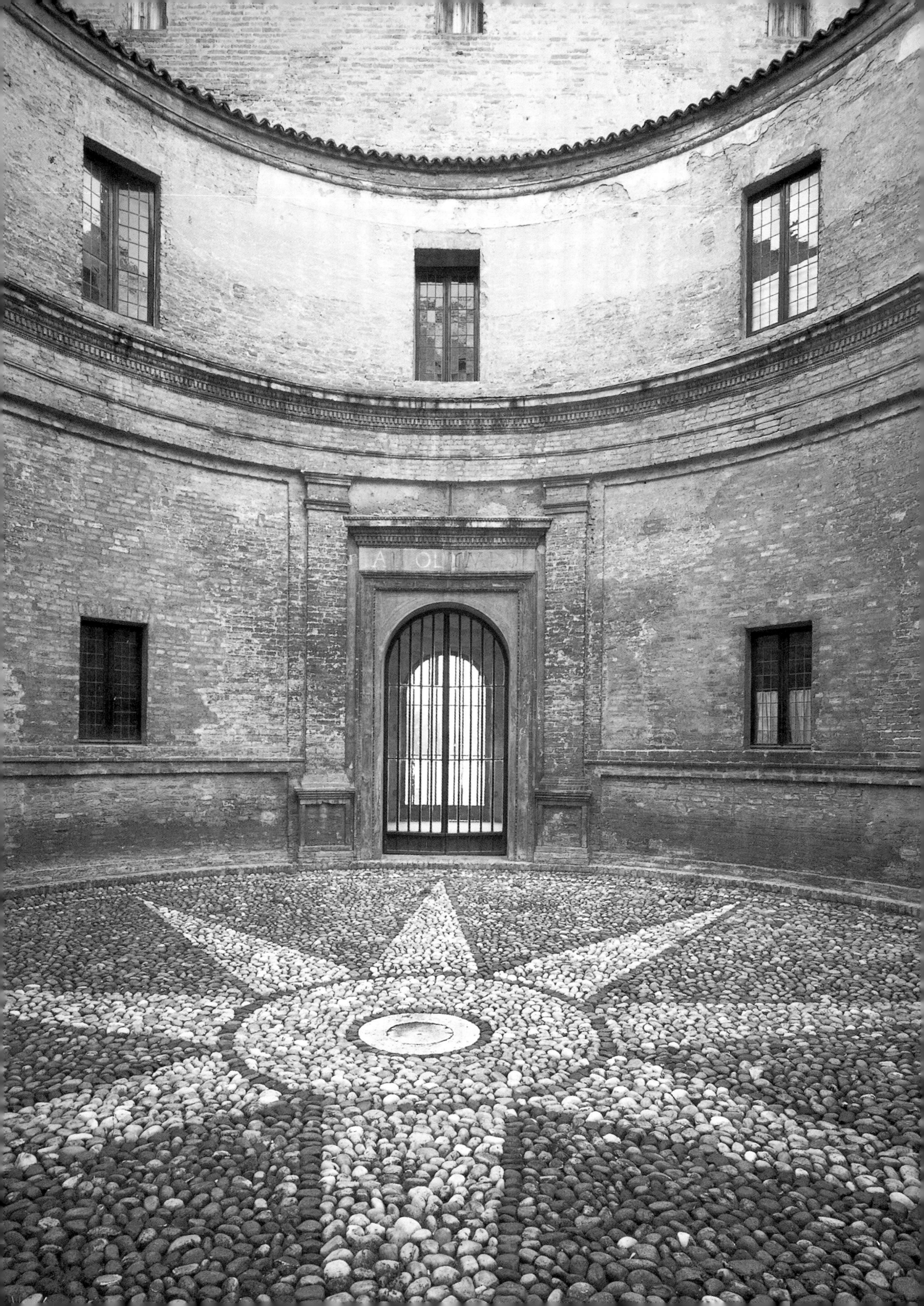

from a decorative painted border. In truth he was much more of a fixture in the lives of his patrons than Gozzoli – who left the employ of the Medici to become a journeyman painter of altarpieces – had ever been. Perhaps Mantegna did not need the illusion of belonging to the Mantuan court precisely because he was so integral a part of it.

The Gonzaga realized that they could prevent an artist with his talents from defecting to a rival court only by rewarding him with money and honours. Mantegna's house, which he designed and built in Mantua late in life (he died in 1506), is a monument to this shift in the balance of power between patron and painter. Made from brick, like Roman dwellings, it takes the form of a Spartan cube three storeys in height, enclosing a circular courtyard which was cobbled in two colours of stone to make the pattern of a many-pointed sun, a Gonzaga emblem which Mantegna was permitted to use. There is a church opposite the house, designed by the elusively omnipresent Alberti, who was an aquaintance of the painter. Alberti's ideas about the ennoblement of architecture through geometry may be assumed to have played some part in the shaping of Palazzo Mantegna, just as Alberti's ideas about the nobility of painting shaped Mantegna's art. The building exhibits a relish in geometrical form – it is a circle punched through a square – which is so extreme as to seem almost proto-modernist in character. In the central courtyard [54], circumscribed by a great curved wall, striking in its formal simplicity, Mantegna's sense of his own self-worth is still palpable. The star-shaped pattern traced in its cobblestones is an image, perhaps, of his stellar rise. The house as a whole proclaims that an artist working for princes has himself become a prince of sorts.

Mantegna was respected at court for his classical erudition while he was feared for the fieriness of his temper and the variability of his moods. His investigations into the world of antiquity went so deep that they took him to places which were dangerously incompatible with the shared assumptions about antiquity that coloured late fifteenth-century court culture. The process had begun before he even went to Mantua. His earliest classicizing pictures, a series of frescos of *The Life of St James*, which he painted for the church of the Eremitani in Padua in the first half of the 1450s, were largely destroyed by an Allied Bomb which scored a direct hit on the church during the Second World War. The pair of frescos which survive, together with old photographs of the rest, suggest that the young Mantegna had mixed feelings about imperial Rome. He seems to have been simultaneously thrilled and repulsed by it. In one of the pictures, under a Roman arch which seems to epitomize the brutality of the Roman military state, St James

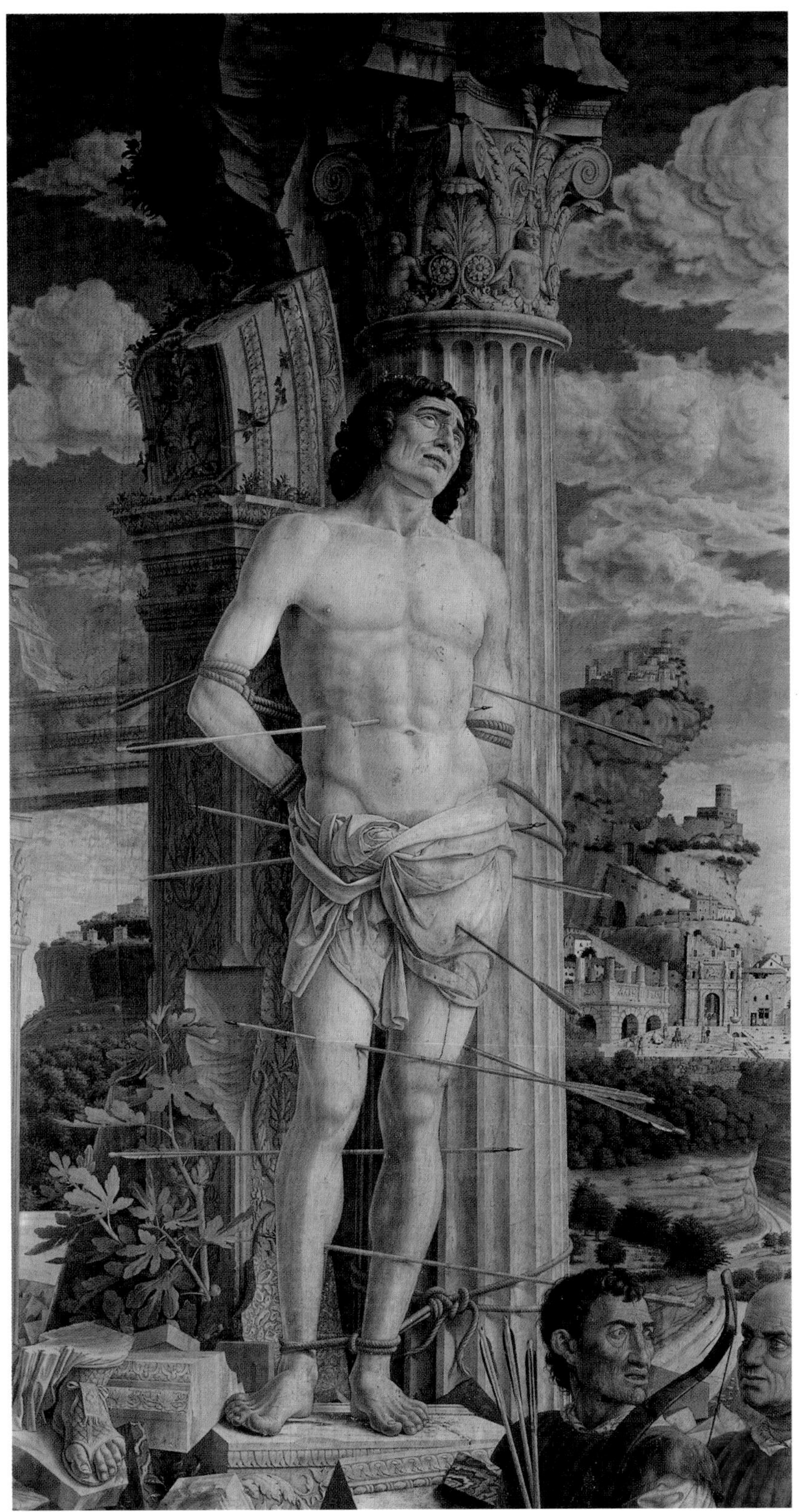

55 ANDREA MANTEGNA *St Sebastian c.* 1480

blesses a penitent even as he is being led to his death by a gang of efficiently indifferent, stony-faced legionnaires.

Mantegna was fascinated by imperial Rome, but he was under no illusions about its capacity for violence. The same, uncomfortably, seems true of his view of the Christian church. When the artist painted the languid *St Sebastian* [55], pierced with arrows amid the debris of classical civilization, it was unclear whether he felt more sorrow for the tortured body of the saint or the mutilated ruins of the past. Sebastian may have been martyred at the hands of pagans, but beautiful pagan Rome has been martyred too, the painting shows, at the hands of Christians. The painter's attitude to his theme looks like a form of stoical despondency – a harsh but phlegmatic observation of the workings of the world.

The awe-inspiring masonry of antiquity worked its way into Mantegna's imagination to such an extent that it seems, sometimes, as though his paint itself has turned to stone. No artist painted a harder world, and even when his devotional images eschew classical settings they are still lapidary in effect. His landscapes are punctuated by outlandish outcrops of sharp rock that make the people in them – saints and martyrs, the Virgin and Child – seem as vulnerable to evil as flesh is to stone.

Mantegna's most celebrated paintings on an overtly classical theme are his nine canvases presenting a composite re-creation of one of Julius Caesar's triumphal processions through Rome. The appeal of *The Triumphs of Caesar* [56] to his Gonzaga patrons[7] seems to have been twofold. Like many other Renaissance nobles, the Gonzaga liked to think of themselves as modern Caesars, and Mantegna's paintings made the association explicit. The patron's second and more compelling reason for wanting the pictures from Mantegna was the illusion that they might give him of being able to move among the figures of a past which he revered – to have Caesar and his cohorts with him, as though actually present, at his court. In 1492, while the pictures were still works in progress, the Marquis of Mantua wrote with excited pride to a friend of 'the Triumph of Julius Caesar which [Mantegna] is painting for us in images that are almost alive and breathing, so that the subject seems not to be represented, but actually to exist'.[8]

Once regarded as the greatest treasures of the Gonzaga collection, *The Triumphs of Caesar* are now in Hampton Court Palace, having been bought in 1629 by Charles I from a dissolute member of the family who preferred parrots and hermaphroditic dwarfs to paintings. The pictures were badly damaged in transit, probably by clumsy shore porters unloading them in England, but even in their abraded and much restored condition they make a powerful impression. Their scale is an important part of their meaning. They are life-size, like the figures in the Camera Picta, in order to heighten their actuality. Yet the impression they give is not one of unmitigated grandeur. Men on foot and on horseback file past in a seemingly endless procession, bearing along with them a cornucopia of plundered loot – statues, busts, military equipment, armour, vases, huge candelabra, coins, plate, banners.

Mantegna's painting is an unholy monument to worldliness, its theme being man's insatiable appetite for and fixation on *things*. He does not treat this unequivocally as cause for celebration. The figure of Julius Caesar, bringing up the rear of the accumulation of loot, is a remote and impassive figure. He could almost be dreaming up all that goes before him, as if the true subject of the work were a fantasy of conquest. Caesar's aura of still and solemn contemplation may have been designed to give pause for thought. Mantegna has constructed his untriumphal triumphs as if possessed of the melancholy conviction that every civilization – but perhaps above all Rome, which shaped itself so extensively from what it plundered elsewhere – is founded on a crime.

The implications of flirting with the Roman ideology of power and conquest would be made more explicit, not long after Mantegna's death, by the Florentine author Niccolò Machiavelli in his political writings. Machiavelli made the point that the Romans achieved what they did, until the reign of Constantine, precisely because they were *not* hampered by Christian sensitivities. For a prince to be ruthlessly effective, Machiavelli argued, he should divorce his pursuit and handling of power from his morality as a Christian. This alienation of the pragmatic self from the moral self – and the shocking, divided sense of identity which follows, logically from it – was not, as is often mistakenly believed, recommended by Machiavelli. His scandalizing works were intended as observations and *The Prince* (1523) is in part a work of devil's advocacy, calculated to reveal the ethical shortcomings of a purely politically motivated man. Machiavelli saw the moral fissure that was implicit in an unqualified worship of Rome, just as Mantegna had painted it.

At the end of his life, Mantegna had risen so high in the social hierarchy of Mantua that he was permitted to take over one of the chapels in the city's largest and most impressive church – Sant'Andrea, designed by Alberti on the model of a Roman basilica – and turn it into his own funerary chapel. It is a place where you can feel the painter's awareness that his life, in the sense of what he had achieved for himself and for artists, was almost as much of a masterpiece as anything in his oeuvre. Here he is buried, among several paintings and frescos by himself and studio followers. The walls are decorated with emblems, the *imprese* of the

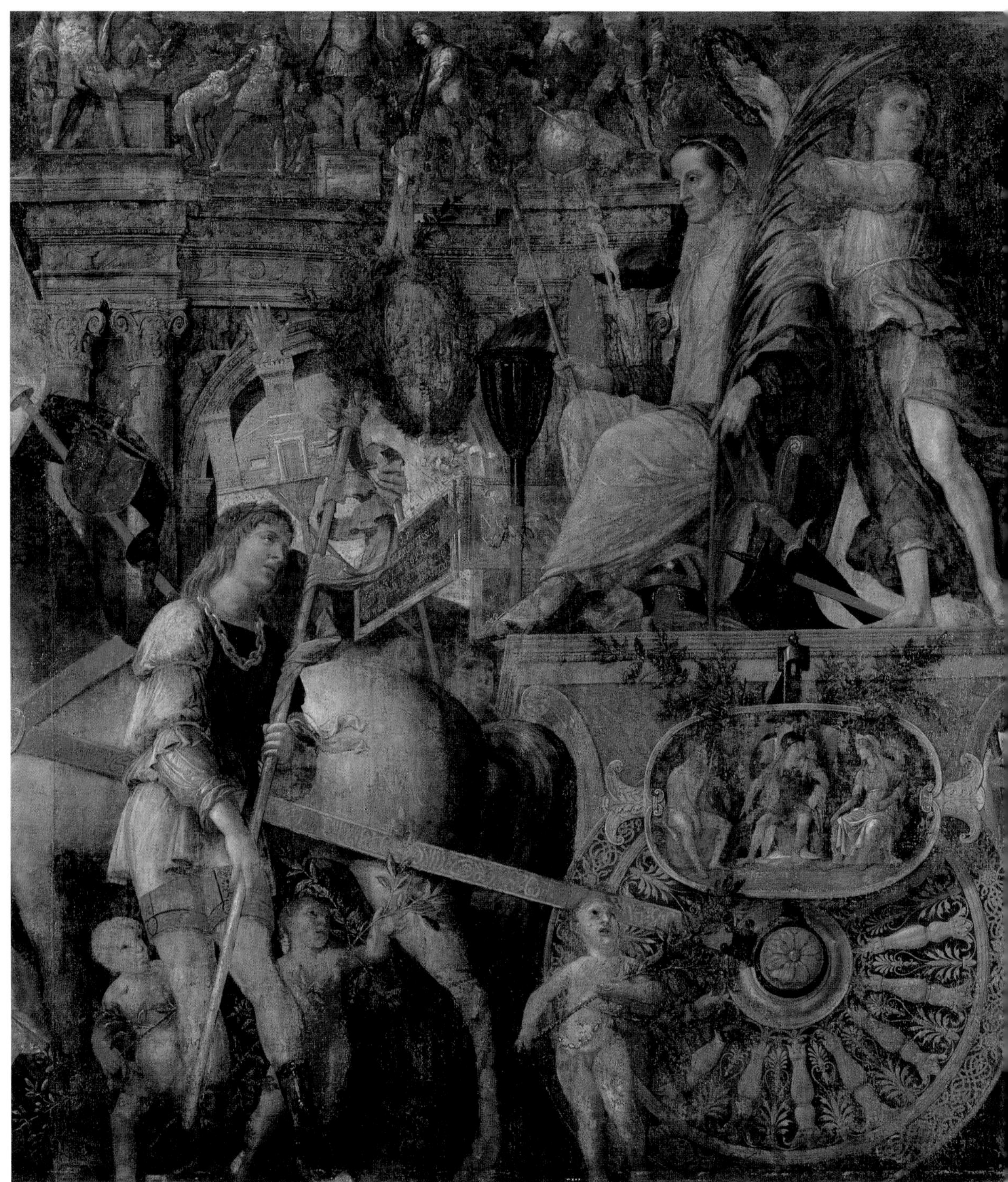

56 ANDREA MANTEGNA *The Triumphs of Caesar* (detail) *c.* 1484 - late 1490s

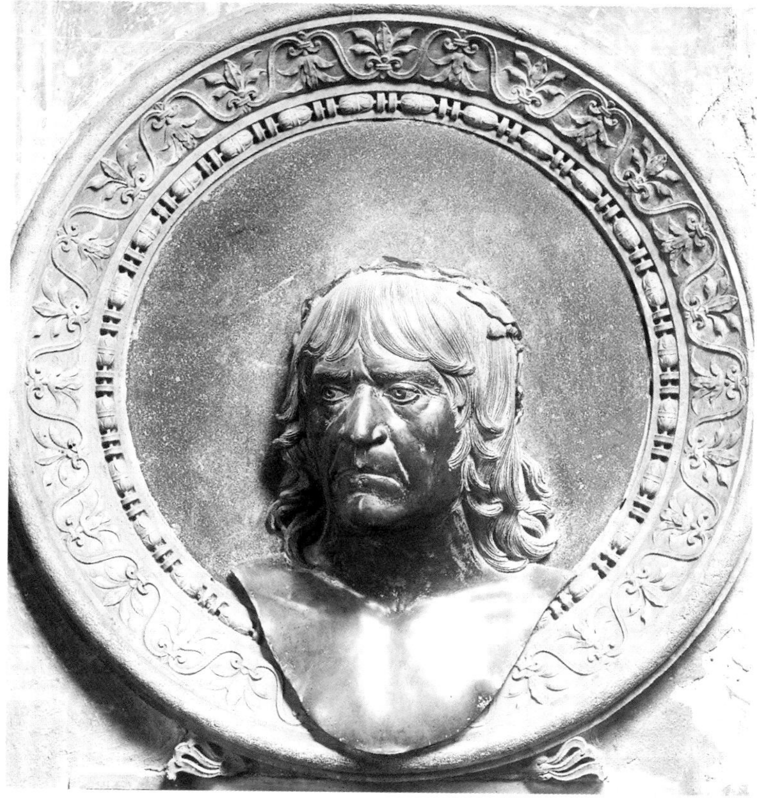

57 ANDREA MANTEGNA Self-portrait bust, Sant'Andrea, Mantua *c.* 1480

painter-prince. The artist also modelled the bronze self-portrait bust [57] which stands on a plinth just inside the entrance to the chapel. Wreathed in laurel, he confronts the viewer in the guise of an ancient Roman. Mantegna, unlike his patrons, did not see himself as an emperor, but as a Stoic. His gaze is impassive and inscrutable. His mouth is turned down at the corners.

## ART FOR ART'S SAKE

Portraiture of one kind or another was the secular art form which came to enjoy the most sudden ascendancy in fifteenth-century Italy. Even Mantegna's *Triumphs of Caesar* are portraits of a kind, in that they are works which represent the prince through a subject with which he identified. But there is clearly a world of difference between those canvases and a more literal triumphal portrait like Piero della Francesca's of Federigo da Montefeltro on his chariot. A new kind of imaginative latitude had been allowed to Mantegna. *The Triumphs* may be said to have marked a yet further widening of painters' horizons. The chief triumph, in the end, was that of the painter himself, who had won a freedom traditionally reserved for poets – to entertain or divert the courtly mind by conjuring up images of triumph, or love, or the gods of mythology.

In his treatise *On Painting*, in so many respects the prophetic book of Renaissance secular art, Alberti had encouraged artists to paint such themes before there was any serious demand for them. But in the later years of the fifteenth century a thriving market for poetical painting quickly developed. In Mantua the most enthusiastic sponsor of this new strain of fantasy in art was not Francesco Gonzaga himself but his wife, Isabella d'Este, who commissioned a multitude of paintings on classical themes and became known as the most enthusiastic art collector of her time.

Isabella had been brought up at the court of Ferrara, which under the patronage of her father Ercole d'Este had become a city noted for its extreme hospitality to learned men, especially mathematicians, astronomers and astrologers. While Ferrara was a centre of humanistic thought and letters, it was also one of the main conduits through which Arab learning and ideas reached Renaissance Italy. The heterogeneity of Ferrarese culture was expressed in its literature and its art. The Ferrarese poet Matteo Maria Boiardo combined elements from the tradition of courtly love poetry, from Virgilian epic and from chivalric romance, in his long and fantastical poem *Orlando inammorato* (1487). A similarly profuse and eclectic mixture of styles and traditions is to be found in the no less fantastical paintings created by Francesco del Cossa and others for the Sala dei Mese, or Room of the Months [58], in one of several Ferrarese Este palaces, the Schifanoia Palace ('Schifanoia' means, literally, 'escape nuisance'). The fresco cycle is divided into three different registers. At the bottom there are scenes simultaneously depicting the labours of the months and showing members of the Este court outside in their domain, represented as an ideal world; in the middle are the signs of the zodiac; at the top is a pageant of classical gods and goddesses.

Such was the milieu which had helped to shape Isabella d'Este's taste and intellect when, in 1490, at the age of sixteen, she left her home town to marry Franceso Gonzaga. She quickly established herself as a lady who was unusually eager, by the standards of the time, to acquire knowledge. There was a tradition of learned Este princesses, but even so Isabella was exceptional. She spent many years struggling to master Greek and Latin and even had a tutor in Hebrew so that she could read the Old Testament in its original language. Her intellectual curiosity was outdone, however, by her insatiable desire for art. She was, in her own words, *appetitosa* for painting and sculpture. But whereas noblewomen had traditionally commissioned religious works, Isabella wanted pictures on themes of her own choosing. To house them she constructed her own wood-panelled Studiolo, in the Ducal Palace of Mantua.

Five paintings commissioned by Isabella for her Studiolo are now in the Louvre. Lorenzo Costa furnished her with an allegory of her court as well as a scene of pastoral bliss known as *The Reign of Comus*; Pietro Perugino provided a work known as *The Combat of Love and Chastity*, thronged with nudes; while Mantegna contributed the so-called *Parnassus* [59] and *Pallas Expelling the Vices from the Garden of Virtue*. These works functioned collectively as an image of Isabella herself, or at least as an allegorical-mythical montage of the qualities to which Isabella aspired. The heroines are all disguised versions of her and cumulatively they paint the picture of a rather complicated – not to say divided – woman. She is Virtue; she is Chastity; she is Wisdom. But atop Mount Parnassus, as depicted by Mantegna, she may be identified with Venus bewitching Mars while her husband, Vulcan, languishes alone in a nearby cave. Isabella is presented to us as a virgin, but also as a *femme fatale*.[9]

It was important to her that the pictures in her Studiolo be painted by the very finest artists of her time. To that end, she dispatched her agents to every corner of Italy, to hector and importune the best *maestri* to paint for her. Leonardo da Vinci was one of those who refused her, but not for want of trying on her part. The playfulness of the pictures which she did obtain – Mantegna's two paintings for her Studiolo are almost the only light-hearted works in his oeuvre – seems to reflect her taste for the mildly erotic and the faintly grotesque. Art for Isabella seems almost to have been a way of playing with her identity, of savouring the different aspects of her personality – and therefore licensing her own variability. A new idea of the art collection, as a *divertissement*, was implicit in Isabella's Studiolo. The invention of painters was to be enjoyed, and enjoyed in an almost irresponsible manner. Pictures had become portable, movable objects which might be treated not only as tokens of the self but also as tokens for exchange. The notion of art for art's sake was not far away.

Prefigurations of this development had been seen in Florence. During the 1460s Antonio del Pollaiuolo had painted a series of large mythological pictures for the Medici on the theme of the labours of Hercules (they survive in the form of two miniature replicas, also by Antonio, now in the Uffizi). The landscapes in which the action takes place are placid idealizations of the Tuscan countryside. But

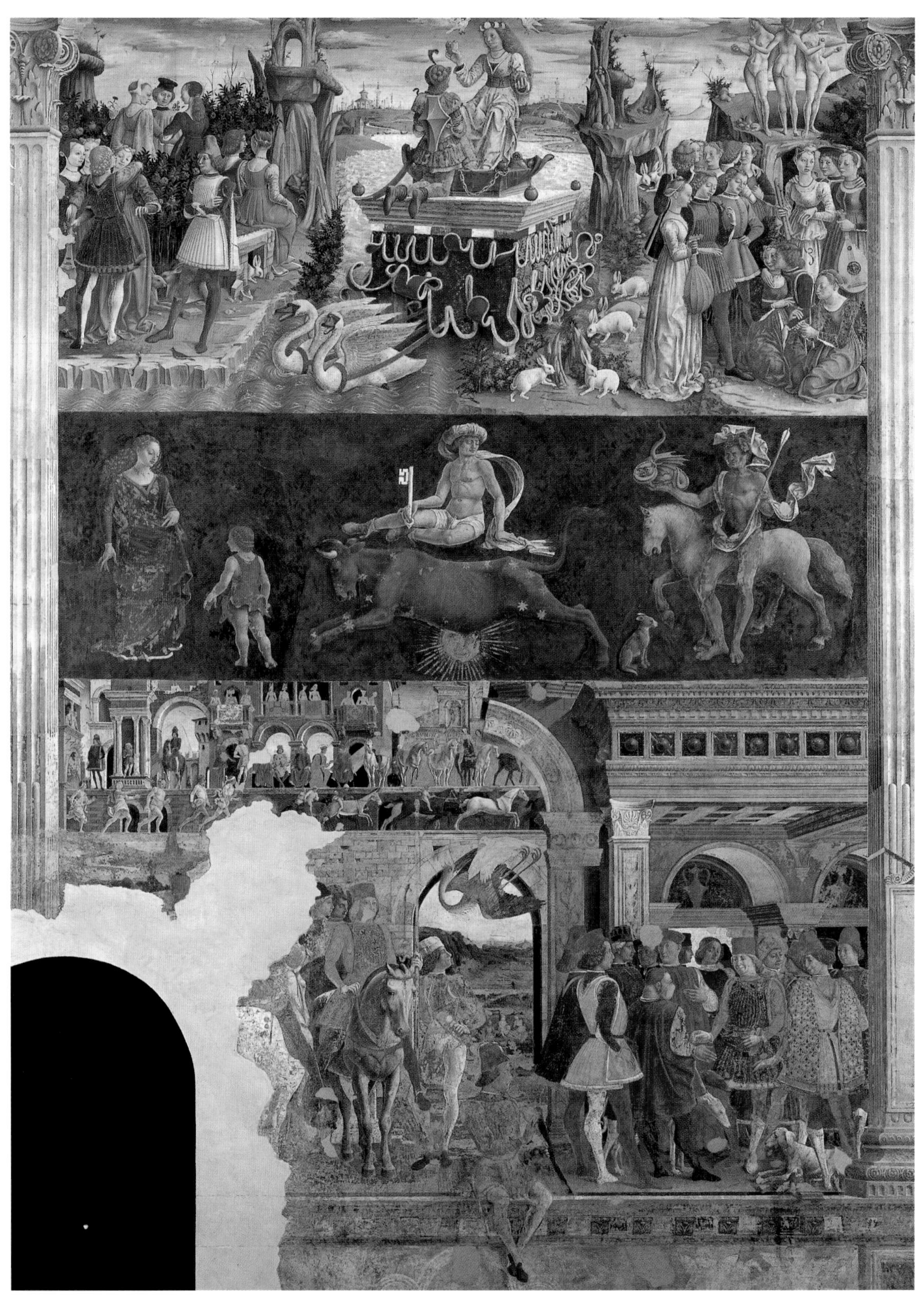

58 FRANCESCO DEL COSSA *The Month of April*, Sala dei Mese, Schifanoia Palace, Ferrara *c.* 1470

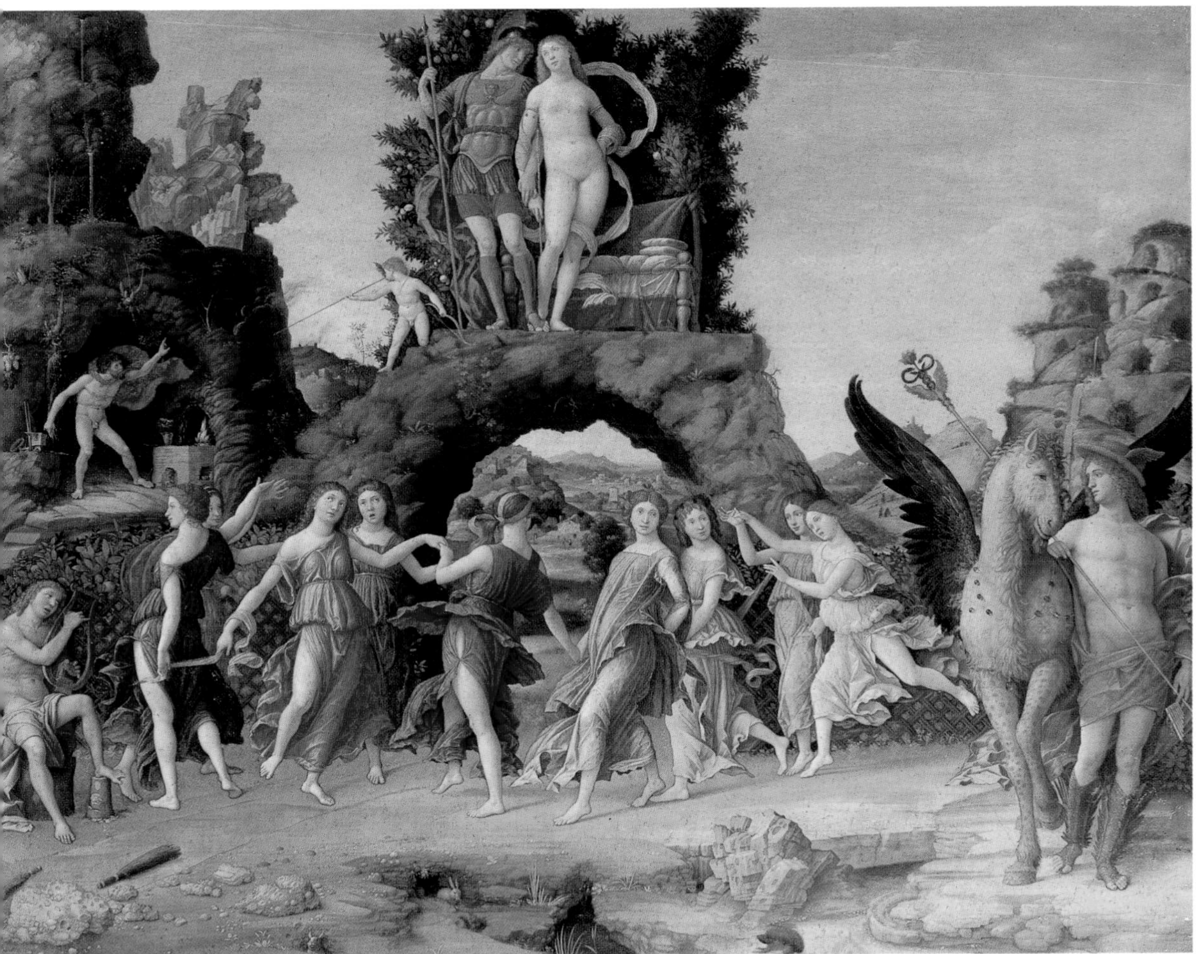

9 ANDREA MANTEGNA *Parnassus* c. 1495

within this idyll, instead of Christ or the Virgin Mary, we see a half-naked sinewy man engaged in muscular feats of heroism – slaying the Hydra in one panel, and squeezing the life out of Antaeus in the other. A kind of paroxysmal violence had been imported into Florentine painting. Fighting, writhing bodies had been made to seem fascinating in themselves. Athleticism alone – hands and thighs and torsos, twisting and under strain – was the object of the artist's (and patron's) admiration.

Bodies of this kind appear at their freest and most exuberant in the same artist's damaged but still beautiful frescos of the 1470s in the little-known Villa La Gallina – a merchant's country retreat, built near the church of San Miniato above

Florence. The mood here is much lighter and the figures are dancing rather than fighting. Ancient Greece exerted less influence on the Italian Renaissance visual imagination than ancient Rome, which had remained part of the very fabric of Italy. But Pollaiuolo's frescos for La Gallina are an exception to the rule. His Dionysian revellers are reminiscent of the figures who dance around Grecian urns.

The largest and most exhaustively discussed secular mythologies to survive from fifteenth-century Florence are two beautiful paintings of Venus done by Sandro Botticelli in the 1480s. The picture known as *Primavera* ('Spring') [2] has been dated the earlier of the two. It was almost certainly commissioned to celebrate a marriage in the Medici household where it originally hung. Its theme is love and fruitfulness and it may as a whole be taken as an image of the blessed condition of wedlock. Venus, the goddess of love, presides over a garden where it is eternally springtime, where golden fruit and every kind of wild flower under the sun grow in profusion, and from which bad weather is studiously excluded. A boyish Mercury with dark curly hair and pale translucent skin stands at the far left of the picture. With one hand on his hip, he has with the other hooked an encroaching raincloud on the caduceus which is his identifying prop. To Venus's immediate right stand the Three Graces, diaphanously draped and dancing in a circle, as they had been described by the Latin author Seneca, in a passage much admired by Botticelli's humanist contemporaries. Contemporary Florentine philosophy saw in these figures symbols of the three phases of love: beauty arousing desire leading to consummation. Above Venus's head the blindfolded Cupid aims a dart at one of the Graces – possibly a portrait of the Medici bride whom the painting was intended to compliment.

There was a long-standing tradition of marriage paintings on classical themes, in Italy, but such works were generally painted on to the side of wooden wedding chests (*cassoni*). Botticelli's picture was unprecedented both in its size, and in the complexity of its references to ancient myth and literature. The head of the Medici family at the time, Lorenzo il Magnifico, had gathered about him the Florentine equivalent of a humanist court, which included the poet Angelo Poliziano, the philosopher Pico della Mirandola and the leading proponent of late fifteenth-century Neoplatonism, Marsilio Ficino. The poetical inclinations of this intellectual élite may have been echoed in Botticelli's graceful and richly allusive painting.

Like many courtly paintings of the late fifteenth century, the *Primavera* reads like a frieze. To Venus's left a scene from Ovid's poetical calendar of the Roman year has been translated into paint. The west wind, Zephyr, seizes the nymph

Chloris, who blows the roses of spring from her mouth and seems almost fearfully to stumble into her own future. Beside her stands her own smiling later self. This figure personifies Chloris transformed, as a result of marriage to Zephyr, into the fulfilled goddess Flora. With full belly and wearing flowered fabric, she strews blossoms before her. Botticelli's painting may be arcane in many of its references, but the emotion in it is as clear as the lucid atmosphere in which the painter's finely drawn figures move. It is a painting about courtship, about pursuit and trepidation, about love and fulfilment.

The circumstances which led to the creation of Botticelli's yet more famous work, *The Birth of Venus* [60], are not known, but it is unquestionably another picture painted in anticipation or celebration of a wedding. Its title is misleading, because what the artist has depicted is the moment immediately after the birth of Venus. Having already been born, at sea, the goddess is about to step on to dry land. The wind, Zephyr, appears once more, again twined around his consort Chloris, this time blowing Venus to shore. An attendant, one of the three Hours, or Horae, is about to throw a cloak over the goddess's nudity. Botticelli painted the sea in an almost cursory manner, rendering it – like seas painted by children – as a pattern of wavy lines on a barely inflected ground. Venus standing in her shell, her long golden hair clasped to her in a gesture of modesty, is the image of fugitive, fragile innocence at the moment of its ending. She is a poetic representation of every bride to be. There is a lapidary quality to Botticelli's treatment of her, which is appropriate, since in stepping into the real world – into the world of love and marriage – she is about to step off her pedestal. He has made her a statue on the verge of becoming flesh.

The picture is about the crossing of a threshold. It is a poetic commemoration of the moment when a virgin becomes a wife and thus enters the world of procreation and reproduction. Botticelli finds cause, in this theme, for a certain wistful regret as well as for wholehearted joy in female fecundity. The Hora who is about to robe Venus's nakedness holds the mantle – the cloak of womanhood, metaphorically – between the fingers and thumb of her right hand. She does so in an arrestingly deliberate manner. The loop of red cloth thus formed, with such pointed care, takes the unmistakable shape of a woman's sex. A leaf, symbol of new growth, is folded within. Venus's golden tresses flicker out towards this charged detail like golden streaks of lightning. Lower down the picture, Botticelli arranged the strands of her hair, which Venus clasps to her in modesty, to form another, equally explicit image of a pudenda. These details are not so much a case of visual suggestion as of visual insistence. *The Birth of Venus* is about marriage – it is

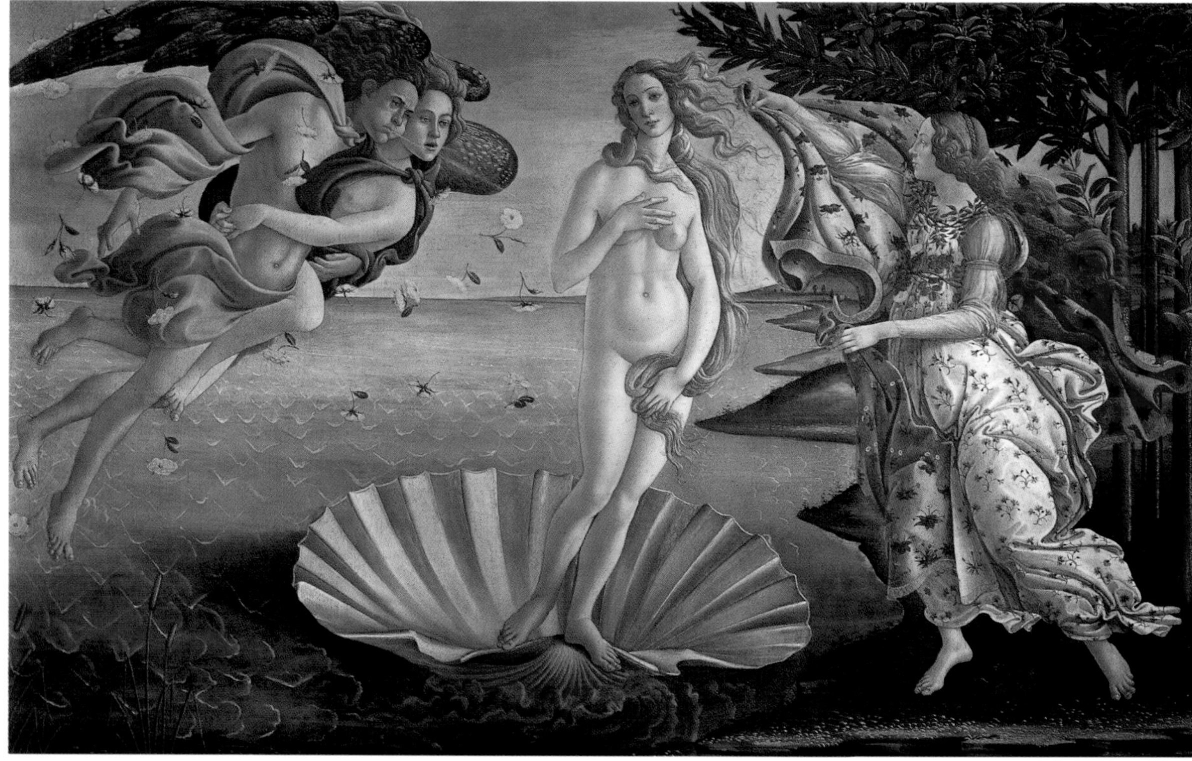

60 SANDRO BOTTICELLI *The Birth of Venus c.* 1485 (detail, opposite)

difficult to think of a picture which takes marriage more seriously – and sex is part of that. Its poetry is robust.

The most beautiful part of the picture is the face of Venus herself. Shaded by sadness, her expression recalls that of the Virgin Mary in much devotional art, lost in solemn contemplation of the fate which she knows will befall her son. Botticelli's Venus reflects a different kind of sadness, however. Her regret is for the loss of virginity. The translation to another stage of life carries with it a sadness for the life that was before.

In Botticelli and Mantegna, Alberti's ideal of what a painter could become – a man who, armed with a new seriousness and a new intellectual ambition, would take art to a new level of sophistication – had finally come to pass. This was not merely prescience, on Alberti's part, but persuasion. Mantegna knew Alberti; if Botticelli did not, he had certainly read him. In some respects the *Primavera* could almost have been painted brush in one hand and copy of the treatise in the other, so close does it come to fulfilling the desiderata that Alberti laid down in

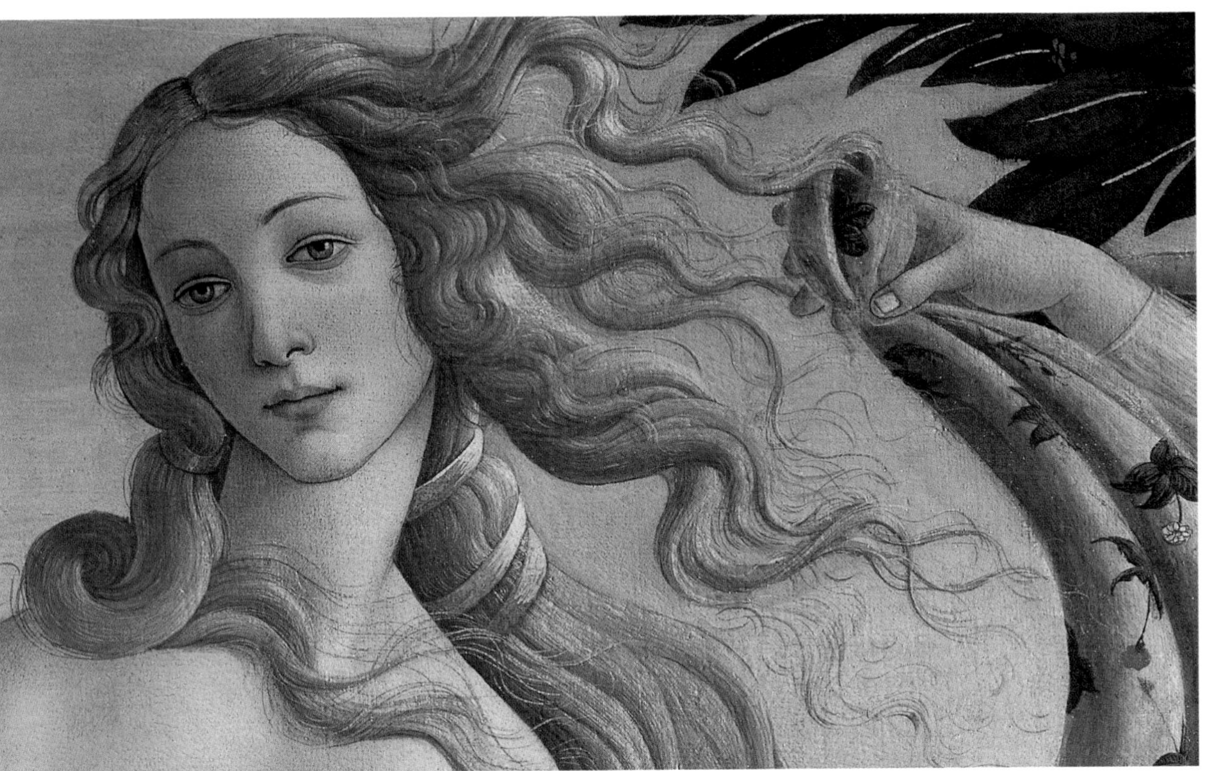

*On Painting* for the *istoria*, or narrative painting. Yet Botticelli did not slavishly follow the text. Alberti had proscribed the use of gold, in intellectually advanced painting, seeing it as a vulgar device to dazzle the eyes of unsophisticated men. It seems that Botticelli had too much respect for the masters of gold-ground painting to agree. His paintings are full of delicate touches of gold leaf – the highlights that play on Venus's shell, the golden grass beneath the feet of her attendant, to name just two instances. His work indicates his independence as well as his awareness of the art theory of his time.

Along with the new freedom of the artist had come a new sense of his own value, accompanied in some cases by a certain truculence. By the early years of the sixteenth century (Botticelli died in 1510 and Mantegna in 1506), it had become commonplace for patrons to make special allowances for an artist with exceptional talent. Towards the end of his life, for example, Mantegna was occasionally allowed by his Mantuan patrons to paint more or less what he liked. Yet this change also brought with it unfamiliar anxieties and problems.

The chief end of art remained, for most artists, the same as it had been for centuries: to communicate Christian stories, as clearly and as expressively as possible, to the general mass of people. But this had ceased to be the chief, or at least the sole, aspiration of the most ambitious artists of the Italian Renaissance. They had developed a new aim: to live up to the expectations of a social and intellectual élite, and to play an active part in the life of that élite. Their work became, inevitably, more remote from the lives of most people. It was thanks to their learning and sophistication that such artists who thrived during this period were able to achieve a higher social rank than their predecessors. But it was thanks, too, to their learning and sophistication that they lost the central position in society which had been enjoyed by their predecessors almost by right. No matter how fascinating and original their work might be, it no longer spoke unambiguously to everyone. The rise of the artist can also be seen as a form of marginalization.

Picasso remarked, on the condition of being a modern artist, that

> Painters no longer live within a tradition and so each one of us must re-create an entire language. Every painter of our times is fully authorised to re-create that language from A to Z ... In a sense that's a liberation but at the same time it's an enormous limitation, because when the individuality of the artist begins to express itself, what the artist gains in liberty he loses in the way of order.[10]

This comment could have applied equally in the Italian Renaissance. During the second half of the fifteenth century, a fundamental change in attitudes had taken place. The archetype of the creative genius had come into being. The figure whose life and work seems to mark this sea-change most definitively is Leonardo da Vinci.

## UNIVERSAL MAN

Leonardo da Vinci has become the most famous of all Renaissance artists. Yet he spent much of his life as an intellectual itinerant, preoccupied by his own, recondite concerns – a solitary frontiersman of artistic and scientific investigation, working at the fringes of society. Born in 1452, the illegitimate son of a Florentine notary, he spent much of his life attempting to prove the intellectual legitimacy of art. No one set out more determinedly than he did to shatter the preconceived idea that painting was merely a craft like any other, a form of low manual labour which, by definition, could not possibly require the exercise of the higher mental faculties.

'He who despises painting loves neither philosophy nor nature', wrote the artist in one of his voluminous notebooks. He continued:

> If you despise painting, which is the sole imitator of all the visible works of nature, you will certainly be despising a subtle invention which brings philosophy and subtle speculation to bear on the nature of all forms – sea and land, plants and animals, grasses and flowers, which are enveloped in light and shade.[11]

To Leonardo, painting was one of the highest vocations to which a man could be called. His notion of the artist's role in life was far grander than any previously conceived – grander by far, even, than that envisaged by Alberti in the pages of *On Painting*. For Leonardo, it was no longer enough for the artist merely to paint the magi. His life was itself to be a voyage into wisdom, the journey of a magus.

One of the artist's earliest independent works was in fact a depiction of *The Adoration of the Magi* [61]. The picture is an early instance of his famed inability or reluctance to complete many of the works which were commissioned from him. It remains no more than a sketch yet, unfinished though it is, it is also a work which signals Leonardo's immense ambition for each and every one of his pictures. Like other Florentine painters before him, the artist expanded the cast of three magi to a throng. Wise men, young men and angels gather around a serene if barely sketched-in Virgin and the imperious Child on her knee, forming a semicircle of adoration. The heterogeneity of this group, and the variety of pose and gesture contained within it, suggests that Leonardo may have intended it as some kind of panorama of humanity (a theme implicit in the subject, since the three magi were traditionally identified with the three known continents of the world). In the background of the picture, behind the crowd that is meant to stand for everyone, we see a place meant to stand for everywhere. The result is an unsettling landscape full of ruins – these broken buildings are probably symbolic of the Old Testament, superseded by the advent of the Son of God – in which ghostly men on horseback battle one another against an equally ghostly backdrop of towering mountains.

The fact that Leonardo later wrote with polemical exaggeration about the superiority of painting to sculpture has done much to obscure his indebtedness to the Florentine sculptural tradition. He had passed his youth and apprenticeship in Florence, in the studio of Andrea del Verrocchio. Verrocchio was first and foremost

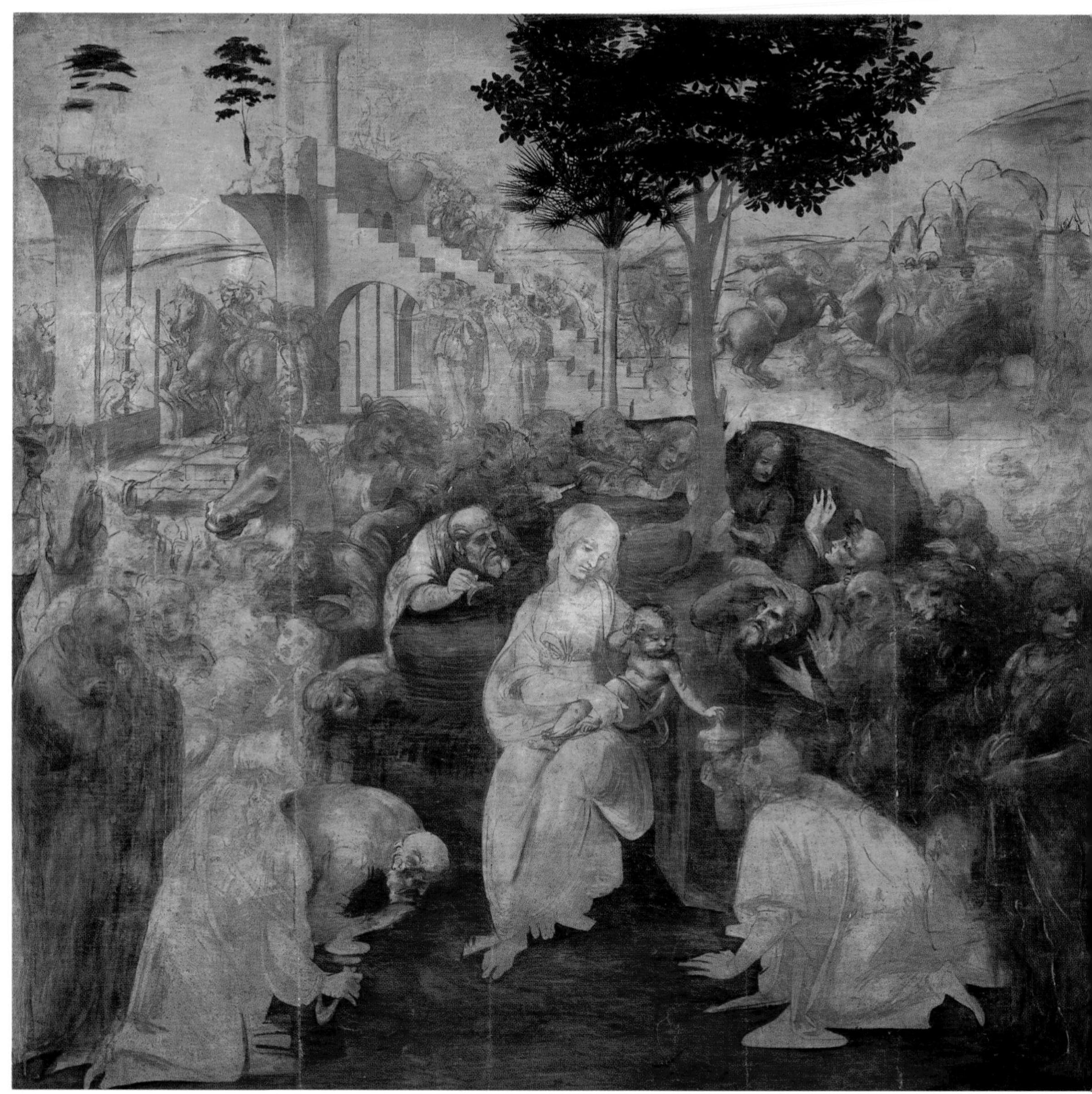

61 LEONARDO DA VINCI *The Adoration of the Magi* c. 1481–2

a sculptor, and *The Adoration* has more antecedents in Florentine relief sculpture than painting. It is full of reminiscences of the relief sculpture of Donatello, full enough to be seen, in part, as a homage. The frieze-like disposition of the heads; the expressive blurriness of the depiction; the way in which certain details of face and form seem to emerge with disturbing clarity from circumambient darkness; the restless, dynamic energy of the figures in the background – many of the most apparently original elements of Leonardo's work are transpositions of Donatello's effects into painting.

Florentine sculpture affected not only Leonardo's style but also, arguably, his outlook. Sculpture was among the most technologically challenging of Renaissance art forms. Many of the most striking bronzes created during the course of the fifteenth century – from Ghiberti's *St John the Baptist* [29] to Verrocchio's own *tour de force*, the *Doubting Thomas*, both for the exterior of Orsanmichele – seem to have been admired almost as much for their technological ingenuity as for their artistic quality. Leonardo's lifelong habit of attempting to dream up solutions to technological challenges, which resulted in many of his best-known 'inventions', including his sketches for various types of flying machine, may partly have stemmed from his grounding in the Florentine sculptural tradition.

Leonardo's desire to take on new intellectual challenges and the evident heterogeneity of his ambitions may have been behind his departure from Florence for Milan shortly after having completed *The Adoration of the Magi*. According to Vasari, Leonardo was sent at Lorenzo de' Medici's behest, taking as a gift a lute that he had made himself. Whatever the reason, once in Milan under the patronage of the ruling Sforza dynasty, he hoped to be able to demonstrate the full, many-sided nature of his talents. The Codex Atlanticus, one of the largest collections of the artist's unsorted and miscellaneous writings, contains the draft of a letter of self-recommendation which Leonardo appears to have written to Ludovico Sforza, Duke of Milan, at approximately this date. He offered his services primarily as a military engineer and inventor, but he also indicated his willingness to undertake architectural projects of various kinds, proclaimed his talent in painting and, finally, suggested that he be given the commission to create a long-planned but still unrealized monumental equestrian sculpture dedicated 'to the eternal honour of the prince your father, and the illustrious house of Sforza'.

With only one or two breaks, Leonardo was to spend nearly twenty years in Milan, from the age of thirty to the age of fifty. The nature of the life he led there has been coloured by Leonardo's own literary descriptions of the leisurely, sophisticated, courtly life of the sought-after painter:

> He sits in front of his work at perfect ease. He is well dressed and moves a light brush dipped in delicate colour. He adorns himself with the clothes he fancies; his home is clean and filled with delightful pictures and he is often accompanied by the reading of various beautiful works.[12]

But there is reason to believe that the image of Leonardo in Milan, as a multi-faceted genius employed by an admiring Sforza court to exercise the full range of his talents, from art to engineering – an image pursued by Kenneth Clark in his well-known biography of the artist – is more myth than reality.[13]

It seems unlikely that Leonardo was quite the cool aristocrat of intellectual speculation depicted in many accounts of his life. During the two decades that he spent in Milan, he never won any of the engineering or architectural commissions of which he dreamed. He was never given a salaried position at the Sforza court as a painter or sculptor, for the simple reason that the Sforza, unlike the rulers of Italy's smaller courts, such as Ferrara or Mantua or Urbino, did not employ court artists. Instead, they tended to commission each work of art to order, drawing on the large number of artists present in Milan, which was, with the possible exceptions of Florence and Venice, the largest city on the Italian peninsula. Furthermore, the signs are that Leonardo did not enjoy particularly high esteem among the Sforza. He received only two significant secular commissions to create lasting works of art, neither of which can be counted an unequivocal compliment to his talents.

One of these, for an enormous bronze equestrian monument to Ludovico's father, might have established Leonardo as a worthy successor to the Florentine sculptors before him. The bronze Sforza horse was a work intended to rival Donatello's *Gattemelata* in Padua [40], and to outmatch the equestrian monument to one of the Sforzas' greatest enemies, Bartolommeo Colleoni [93], which had recently been undertaken in Venice by Leonardo's master Verrocchio. Leonardo's plans for the Sforza monument [62] were extremely ambitious – his horse was to have been considerably larger than either Donatello's or Verrocchio's – but his very ambition may have been what undid him in the eyes of his patrons. A recently discovered letter written by the Florentine ambassador to Milan in the 1480s contains one bald but damning aside on the subject of Leonardo's plans for the casting of such an enormous work: 'I think,' wrote the ambassador, 'that Lodovico is not very confident that Leonardo knows how to carry it out.'[14] In 1493 the copper that had been set aside for the monument was given to the Sforzas' chief military engineer, Ercole d'Este, to turn into a cannon.

Leonardo's other main secular Sforza commission, besides his ephemeral activities as a designer of court entertainments, was the decoration of a room in the Ducal Palace known as the Sala delle Asse. But this was granted to him only when it turned out that Pietro Perugino was unavailable to do the work. The very nature of the commission tends to reinforce the impression that the Sforza were

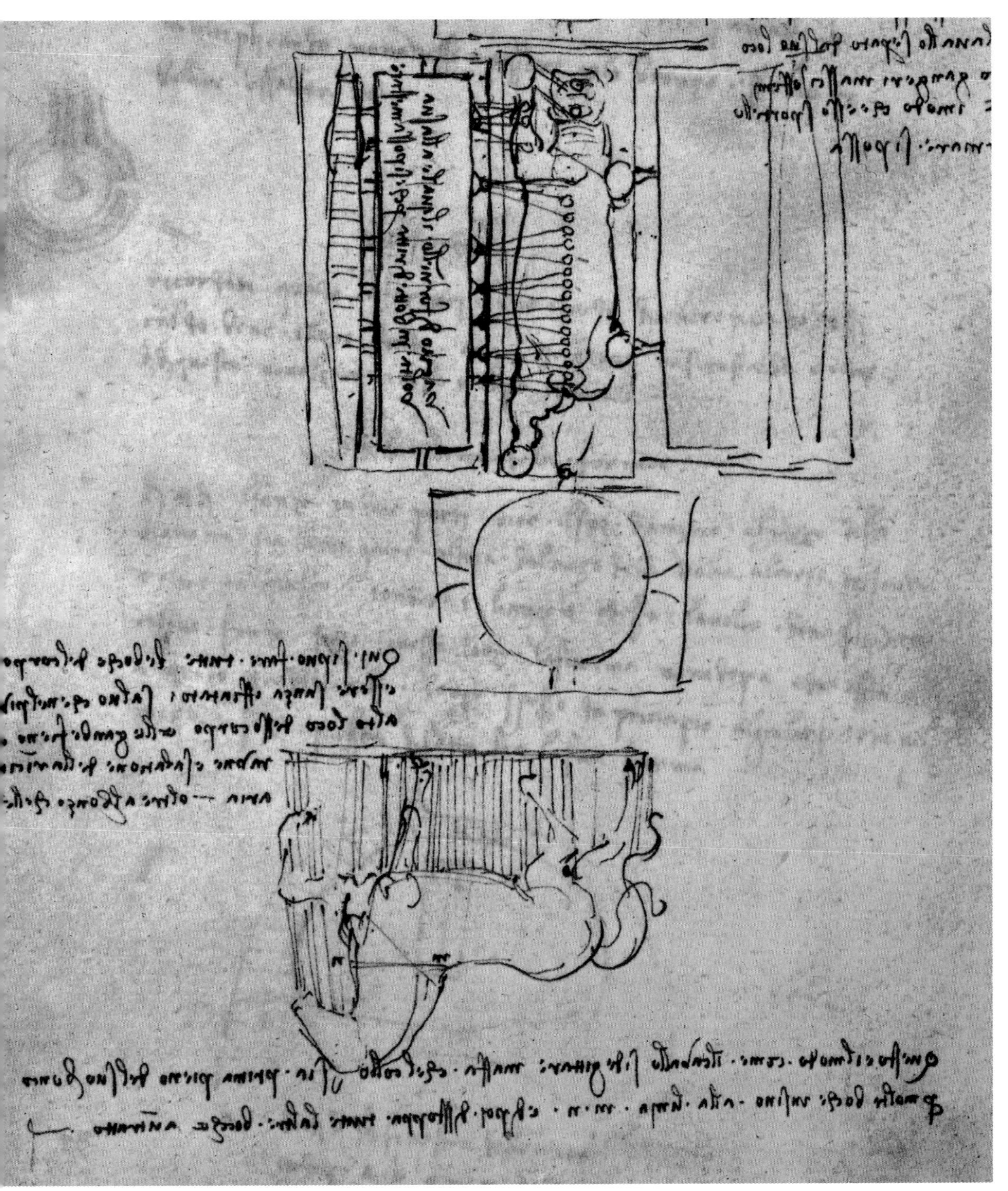

62 LEONARDO DA VINCI Design for the casting mould of the planned Sforza monument *c.* 1493

either unaware or unappreciative of Leonardo's special talents. His task was to fresco the room into the appearance of a leafy bower – a job carried out with a degree of enthusiasm which is difficult to discern today, owing to the overpainting of an early twentieth-century restorer. Enough remains of Leonardo's own work to suggest that he tried, however belatedly, to make his mark on a commission that was grounded in traditions of fine but banal courtly decoration. On the walls of the room he traced, with typically Leonardesque, fanatical accuracy, the root structures of the trees which bower the room. This touch of observation is a small gesture of independence. Instead of providing his patrons, simply, with a painted imitation of *millefleurs* tapestry work, Leonardo intruded, albeit at the margins of the commission, his own lofty conception of art as the visual expression of a painfully acquired and botanically researched knowledge.

The possibility that Leonardo's years in Milan may have been, for the most part, a time of frustration and failure lends an unfamiliar poignancy to his various intellectual enterprises. It was in Milan, after all, that he first elaborated his daring notion of the artist as a 'universal man', learned in all aspects of knowledge. It was in Milan that, in accordance with that notion, he first began to delve into the many branches of scientific enquiry that would preoccupy him for much of the rest of his life, keeping a notebook with him day and night in order to record his every perception, observation and discovery. Perhaps Leonardo's restless energy and curiosity were not signs of his confidence but of his insecurity. Perhaps his God-like notion of what an artist might be was a form of compensation for actual failure, called forth by an awareness of his patrons' indifference to him.

'He is not universal', said Leonardo, 'who does not love equally all that is in painting.'[15] The ideal painter, through his skill and knowledge, was to reveal the beauty and intricacy of the world as God had made it. With a mixture of Promethean hubris and Christian humility, Leonardo dared to envisage a painting not simply as an image but as a microcosm of the creation itself. This idea – with its concomitant implication that a picture might be charged with the highest significance, regardless of its subject matter – had far-reaching implications for art.

If the painter were to depict the world created by God with absolute fidelity he had to aspire, himself, to a God-like understanding of the world in all its aspects. Before he could paint human beings, the artist must study and master both anatomy and the way in which the motions of the mind are expressed in those of the face and the body. Before he could paint landscape, he must study and master geology. Before he could paint flowers and grasses, he must study and master botany. The sheer quantity of Leonardo's notes on almost every conceivable subject

– the notebooks he left at his death run to approximately 20,000 pages – might seem extraordinary. Yet it is the natural consequence of his views about what an artist should be. Leonardo actually tried to live out the ideal of the universal man – one who would encompass all human knowledge about every aspect of the world – enshrined in Federigo da Montefeltro's Studiolo. The attempt was doomed, inevitably, to failure, a failure that seems in retrospect heroic and pathetic by turns.

Leonardo's notebooks reflect the pattern, or lack of it, of his daily life. The Codex Atlanticus contains a short but revealing series of memoranda written by the painter to himself which gives a particularly clear picture of his scatterfire intellectual enquiries:

> Ask maestro Antonio how mortars are positioned on bastions by day or night; ask Benedetto Portinari by what means they go on ice in Flanders; get the master of mathematics to show you how to square a triangle; find a master of hydraulics and get him to tell you how to repair, and the costs of repair, of a lock, canal and mill in the Lombard manner.[16]

Leonardo doubtless embarked on some of these enquiries in the hope that he might, indeed, secure the military or engineering commissions he had originally hoped to get from the Sforza. As it turned out, the most elaborate mechanical devices which he was required to design appear to have been for stage machinery for court pageants, and for a pulley designed to raise a curtain concealing the ducal jewellery collection. Yet even when the commissions he had coveted fell through, Leonardo continued his researches into every subject under the sun – including, incidentally, the sun itself, which, he concluded in an assertively capitalized note to a sheet of studies, 'DOES NOT MOVE'.

Leonardo was not a painter who also became interested in science. He was a man who invented an ideal of what the painter should be in a sense that forced him to embrace every aspect of scientific investigation. Although Leonardo's concerns by no means matched those of the humanists – his primary interest lay less in understanding antiquity than in understanding nature – he did, none the less, share certain habits of thought with them. Humanist expertise in the science of philology, the study of words and grammar, had created an attitude of productive scepticism towards every manuscript. Leonardo took a similarly sceptical approach to the text of the natural world. One of the fundamental principles reiterated in his writings is that 'all sciences are vain and full of errors that are not born of experience, mother of all certainty, and that are not tested by experience'.[17]

Guided by this tenet and by an idiosyncratic mixture of limitless curiosity and cussed perseverance, he studied nature in all its aspects.

Yet Leonardo da Vinci was not a man ahead of his time, but a man *of* his time. It would be anachronistic to depict him as a modern scientist, inexplicably born into the wrong century and fighting to expand the superstitious, medieval world picture of those around him. (Although this is precisely how he is often presented.) As Martin Kemp, Stephen Jay Gould and other modern historians of science have shown, much of Leonardo's most intense research was undertaken precisely in order to bolster what might be termed the medieval world picture. He was fascinated by the correspondences he saw between different phenomena – he made drawings, for example, comparing the wave motions of water and of human hair – and seems to have felt, like many of his contemporaries and predecessors, that in such parallels the secrets of the world might be inscribed. His thought was rooted in the traditional philosophy of his time, with its belief in a correspondence between 'the body of man' and 'the body of the world'.

But although he did not by any means destroy the picture of the world which he had inherited, it is true to say that he did begin – albeit, in many instances, somewhat reluctantly – to see around its edges. By the time of his death in 1519, Leonardo had questioned, if not shattered, the Ptolemaic view of the universe. He had proved to his satisfaction that the Deluge [63] described in the Bible could not have been universal. His multitude of observations of a mass of natural phenomena may be said to constitute the beginnings of that questioning attitude to the physical universe which led to the scientific revolution of the seventeenth century. But for all that, his direct influence on subsequent thought must be counted negligible. Now that many of his notebooks have been published in facsimile, it is possible to follow him on his zigzagging, eccentric intellectual odysseys. Yet in his own lifetime he never organized any of the material in his notebooks. He never published any of his discoveries. His intense curiosity was mirrored by an equally intense privacy, which may partly have been inspired by the belief that the only man fit to judge Leonardo was Leonardo. The only public issue of his mind's revolutions was his work as a painter – and there was very little of that.

The Swiss-born artist Henry Fuseli (1741–1825) damned Leonardo as an intellectual libertine who wasted life, insatiate, in experiment – an unfair judgement but one which contains an element of truth. Leonardo was nearly seventy when he died, but fewer than twenty securely attributed, completed paintings survive. Discounting the decoration of the Sala delle Asse, the time he spent in

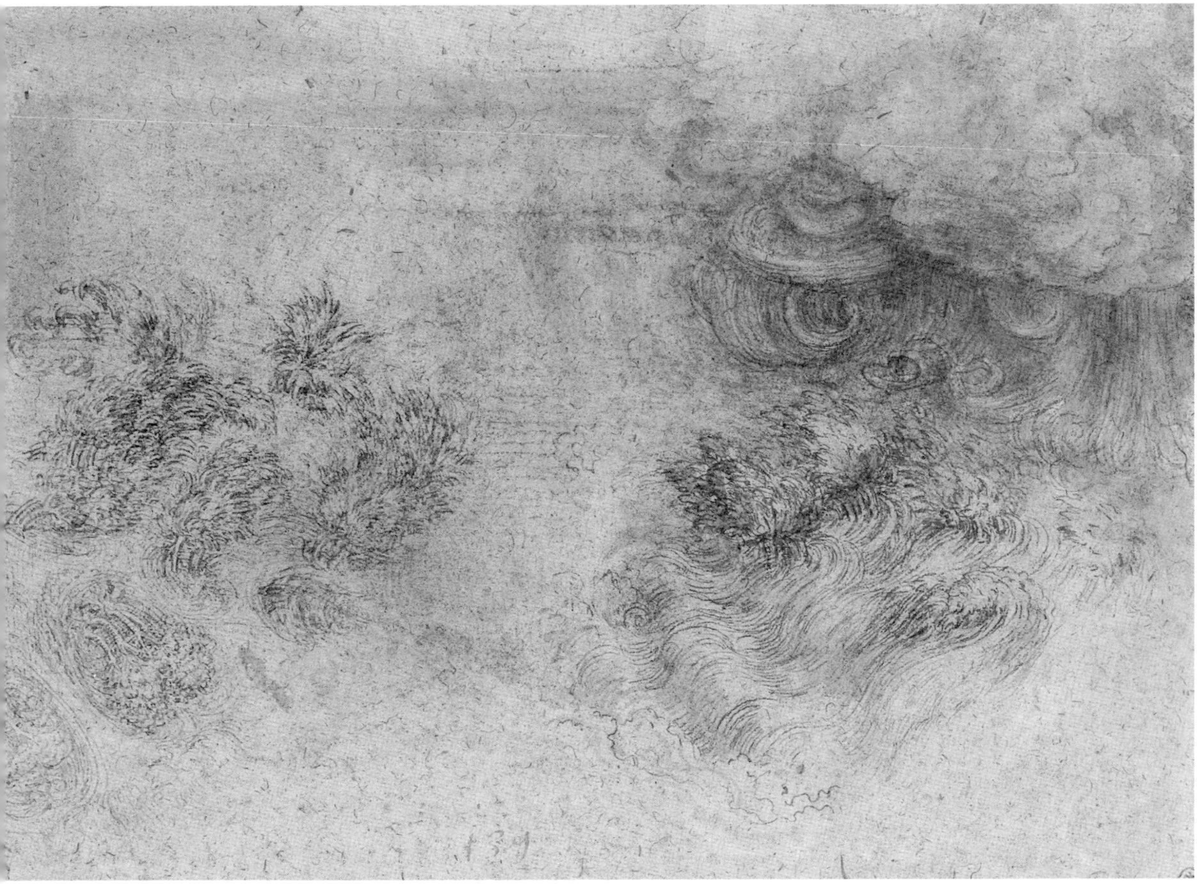

3 LEONARDO DA VINCI *The Beginning of the Deluge c.* 1514

Milan yielded just two or three known autograph paintings. Each of them has been deemed to be a turning-point in the course of Western art.

The significance of the first, *The Virgin of the Rocks* [64], now in the Louvre, is easier to assess than that of the second, *The Last Supper* [65], painted for the refectory of Santa Maria delle Grazie in Milan, because it is in considerably better condition, although such is the premium still placed on Leonardo's personal touch, the magic of his hand, that the authorities of the Louvre have not dared to clean the work for fear of what might disappear if they did. So although it is one of the best preserved autograph Leonardos in the world it is still very hard to see (a typical Leonardo paradox). It remains, notwithstanding that, a breathtaking creation.

Against a misty backdrop of rocks and mountains the Virgin presides over a meeting between the infants Christ and St John the Baptist. St John, emblem here of needy humanity, shelters in the folds of the Virgin's cloak and prays to Christ, who blesses him in return. The composition is unusual, but the originality of the picture lies less in its iconography than its technique, which in the context of the art of Leonardo's time may be said to constitute a new language of painting.

The chief innovations of the picture are Leonardo's handling of light and shade, his modelling of form, and his suggestion of distance through the depiction of atmosphere. The painting's position in the Louvre, opposite the pictures commissioned by Isabella d'Este for her Studiolo in Mantua, makes it possible to measure the distance between the sharp, artificially bright world of late fifteenth-century Italian painting and Leonardo's new, more subtly shaded vision of the universe.

The figure of the infant Christ is continuously modelled by light and shade with unprecedented skill. Leonardo learnt to paint like this through trial and error, during long hours spent studying light and its fall, and the effects of its interruption – a process that can still be traced in his scientifically precise notebook studies of the action of light falling on a sphere. The head of the Virgin, caressed by shadow painted as shadow had not been painted before, is a direct transcription into painting of one of Leonardo's most direct observations:

> Very great charm of shadow and light is to be found in the faces of those who sit in the doors of dark houses. The eye of the spectator sees that part of the face which is in shadow lost in the darkness of the house, and that part of the face which is lit draws its brilliancy from the splendour of the sky. From this intensification of light and shade the face gains greatly in relief ... and in beauty.[18]

That girl sitting in the doorway became the Virgin among the rocks. There are few better illustrations, in Leonardo's art, of the painter's reliance on observation – of the way in which his pure openness to his own senses, 'mother of all certainty', led him to bring elements of previously overlooked experience into art.

The technique of modelling form almost exclusively through tonal values brought a new term into the language of painting: *chiaroscuro*, Italian for light and shade. Leonardo's sensitivity to the optical qualities of the atmosphere is also manifest in his handling of so-called 'aerial' perspective, the gradual bluing of tones towards the horizon. This was a technique first developed by Northern European painters, but it was developed by Leonardo in *The Virgin of the Rocks* to the point where even in the foreground of the picture the viewer is aware of the density of the atmosphere. He painted the physical substance of the world with immense acuity – but he also painted the medium through which we apprehend it, and in doing so he brought the spaces between things into play as a subject for art.

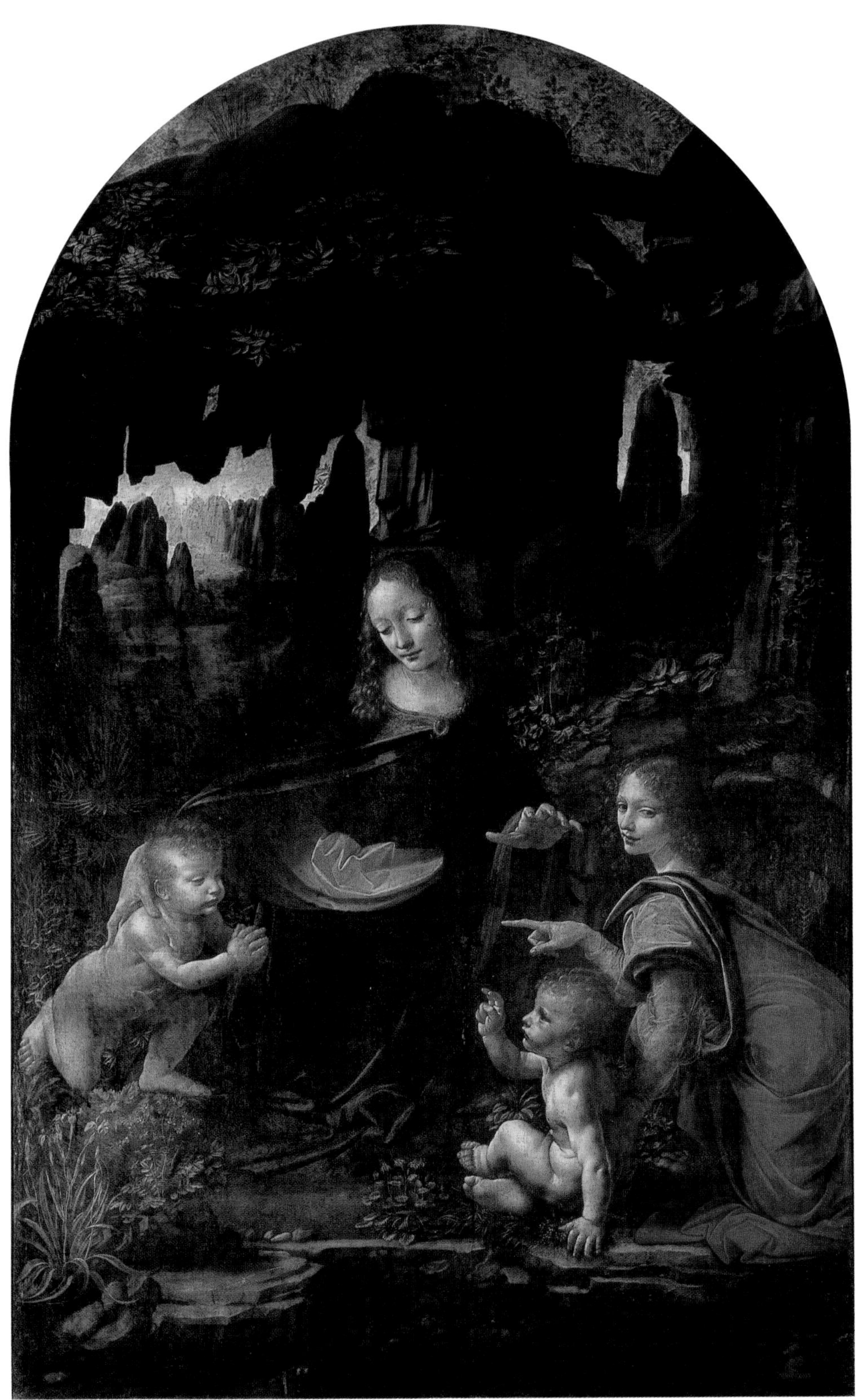

64 LEONARDO DA VINCI *The Virgin of the Rocks c.* 1483

In his notebook observations, the artist even made the vagaries of human perception itself a subject for depiction, noting for instance that 'if you move a lighted brand its whole course will seem a circle of flame ... because the organ of perception acts more rapidly than the judgement'[19] – an observation which would not find expression in painting until Titian and Rembrandt. The result was a quite new aesthetic, an aesthetic of indeterminacy or, so to speak, precise indistinctness.

Yet Leonardo's art was often liable to buckle under the strain of his own expectations for it. The second of his Milanese commissions, *The Last Supper* [65], is a work that was ruined by the artist's perfectionism. It was meant to be carried out in fresco, a medium which, because it requires completion of each section in a single session – the time in which plaster dries – was uncongenial to Leonardo, who clearly preferred to work more slowly than it allows. In a vain attempt to give fresco the malleability of oils, he experimented with a new mixed medium of his own devising, but even within his own lifetime the surface of the picture had begun to deteriorate and it is now the least well preserved of his works. Although the painting is difficult to decipher, its original effect still survives somehow in the ghost of its outlines. The apostles respond to Christ's revelation that one of them is about to betray him with a panorama of emotional response. It is another of Leonardo's attempts at universal comprehensiveness, a work that was meant to suggest the full gamut of human emotions.

In his most famous painting, the *Mona Lisa* [66], the artist attempted to transform the language of portraiture devised by Netherlandish artists such as Jan van Eyck and Rogier van der Weyden and naturalized, in Italy, by Piero della Francesca and others. Leonardo wrought a huge transformation on that tradition, and the chief innovation of this picture lies perhaps in its conception of time. Other painters had given life and expression to the faces of those whom they had painted but none had taken expression – defined by Alberti as the highest goal of the painter – to quite this extreme. What Leonardo did, never before achieved with this degree of subtlety, was to paint a face that seems to be in the middle of changing expression. This is an essential ingredient in the fame of the *Mona Lisa*, for it is this which has made so many people wonder about her. If hers is a face caught on the move, the landscape that stretches behind her is similarly mobile and alive. It is a place of water and mountains, which bears the marks of its own geological history and implies the ways in which it will change yet. Several of Leonardo's mountains teeter as though already on the point of collapse. While the mysterious woman embodies human time, the nanosecond in which a laugh can fade to a smile, her landscape suggests the infinitely longer time-span of natural history – on which Leonardo had begun to meditate while studying fossil deposits in the mountain ranges above Milan.

The painting is technically a portrait, although there is something of the demonstration piece about it. It may have been intended less as the likeness of a real woman than as an illustration of Leonardo's ideas about the equivalence between human beings and the world, as microcosm and macrocosm. 'In that man is composed of water, earth, air and fire', wrote the painter, 'his body is an analogue for the world: just as man has in himself bones, the supports and armature of his flesh, the world has the rocks; just as man has in himself the lake of the blood, so the body of the earth has its oceanic seas.'[20] His words could almost be a gloss on his painting.

But that is not to say that the *Mona Lisa* is an arid intellectual exercise. On the contrary, it is charged with feeling, although quite what that emotion might be is not easy to determine. Ever since Walter Pater wrote his purple prose poem in homage to Leonardo, in his book *Studies in the History of the Renaissance* (1873),[21] it has been fashionable to find something sinister in the painter's works – a sense that however carefully and objectively they may have been constructed they are somehow touched by evil. This is perhaps a reflection of the extent to which Leonardo has become identified, in the modern imagination, with the figures of Prometheus and Faust; but it may also be a response to something which he deliberately planted in his own work. The face of the *Mona Lisa* draws the viewer to the heart of this most twilit part of Leonardo's imagination. She looks out at us with a serene, disturbing, otherworldly expression on her face. The modelling of her face is the ultimate demonstration of Leonardo's mastery of *chiaroscuro* – almost every cell of painted skin seems to palpitate with life – yet there is also an undeniable challenge in her mysterious expression. The half-smile that plays across her face is a characteristic Leonardo touch. It makes of her a sphinx, and of the painting itself a riddle. Perhaps this depth of expression and mystery was Leonardo's way of attempting to show the immense amount of time and study and knowledge that went into this creation – his way of indicating that this is not just a picture, but the fruit of a lifetime's work.

As he grew older, Leonardo dreamed of pictures which would contain more and more information, writing long prose descriptions of subjects for future paintings which were quite evidently unpaintable. His 'Description of a Deluge and the Representation of it in Painting' is perhaps the most tragi-comically unattainable of such visions. Selective quotation is necessary, for the original runs to several thousand words:

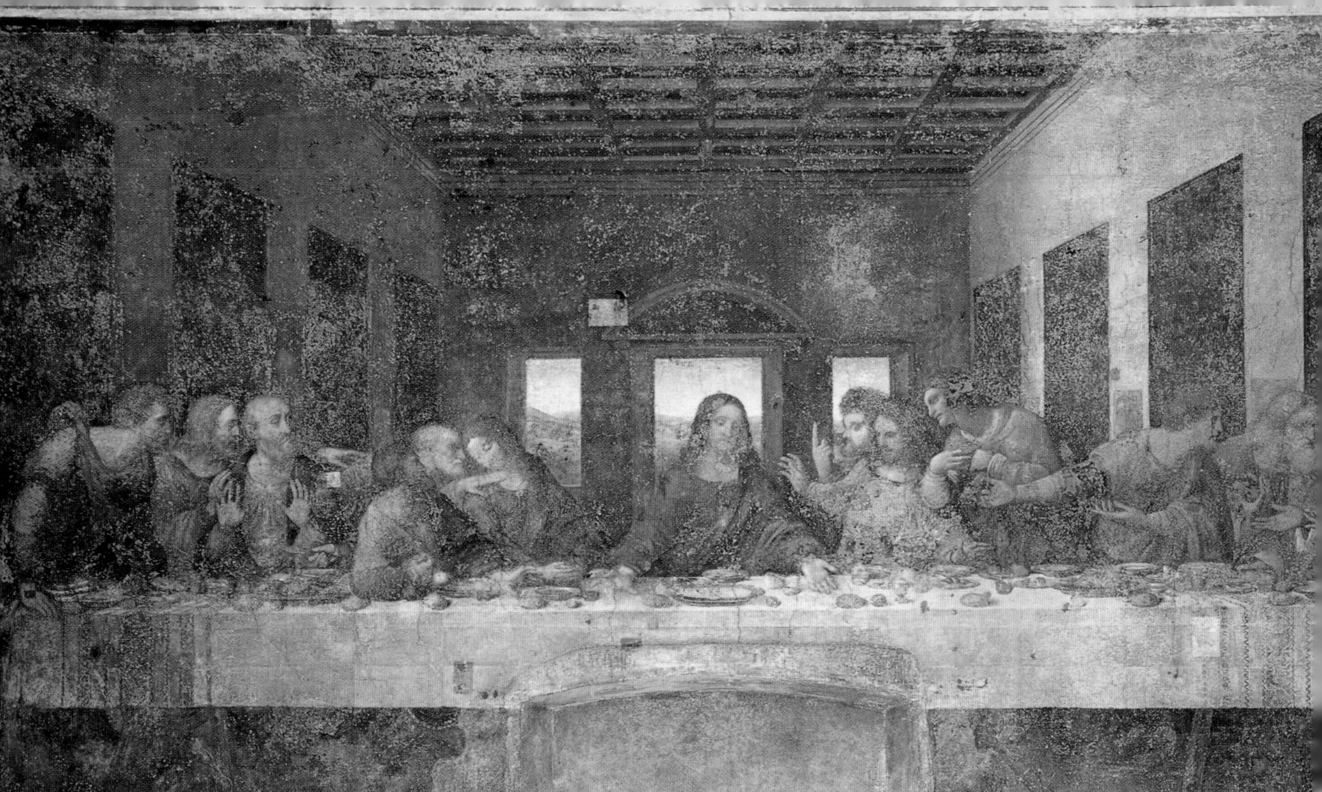

65 LEONARDO DA VINCI *The Last Supper* (detail) *c.* 1495–8

> Let the dark and gloomy air be seen buffeted by the rush of opposing winds and dense from the continued rain mingled with hail and bearing hither and thither an infinite number of branches torn from the trees mixed together with numberless leaves. All around let there be seen ancient trees uprooted and stripped by the fury of the winds; let there be seen fragments of the mountains which have already been scoured bare by their torrents fall into these very torrents and choke up the valleys; until the swollen rivers overflow and submerge the wide lands with their inhabitants. Again you might see on many of the mountain tops many different kinds of animals huddled together, terrified and subdued to tameness in company with men and women who had fled there with their children. And the waters which cover the fields are in great part strewn with tables, bedsteads, boats, and various other contrivances ... You might see groups of men with weapons in their hands defending the small spots that remained to them from the lions, wolves and beasts of prey.[22]

In such undepictable visions of universal apocalypse we can see Leonardo's dream of universal painting, also, coming to an end. Small wonder that, undone by the depth and complexity of his own ambitions for art, he should have become that peculiar paradox: the painter who could not bring himself to paint, in the sad

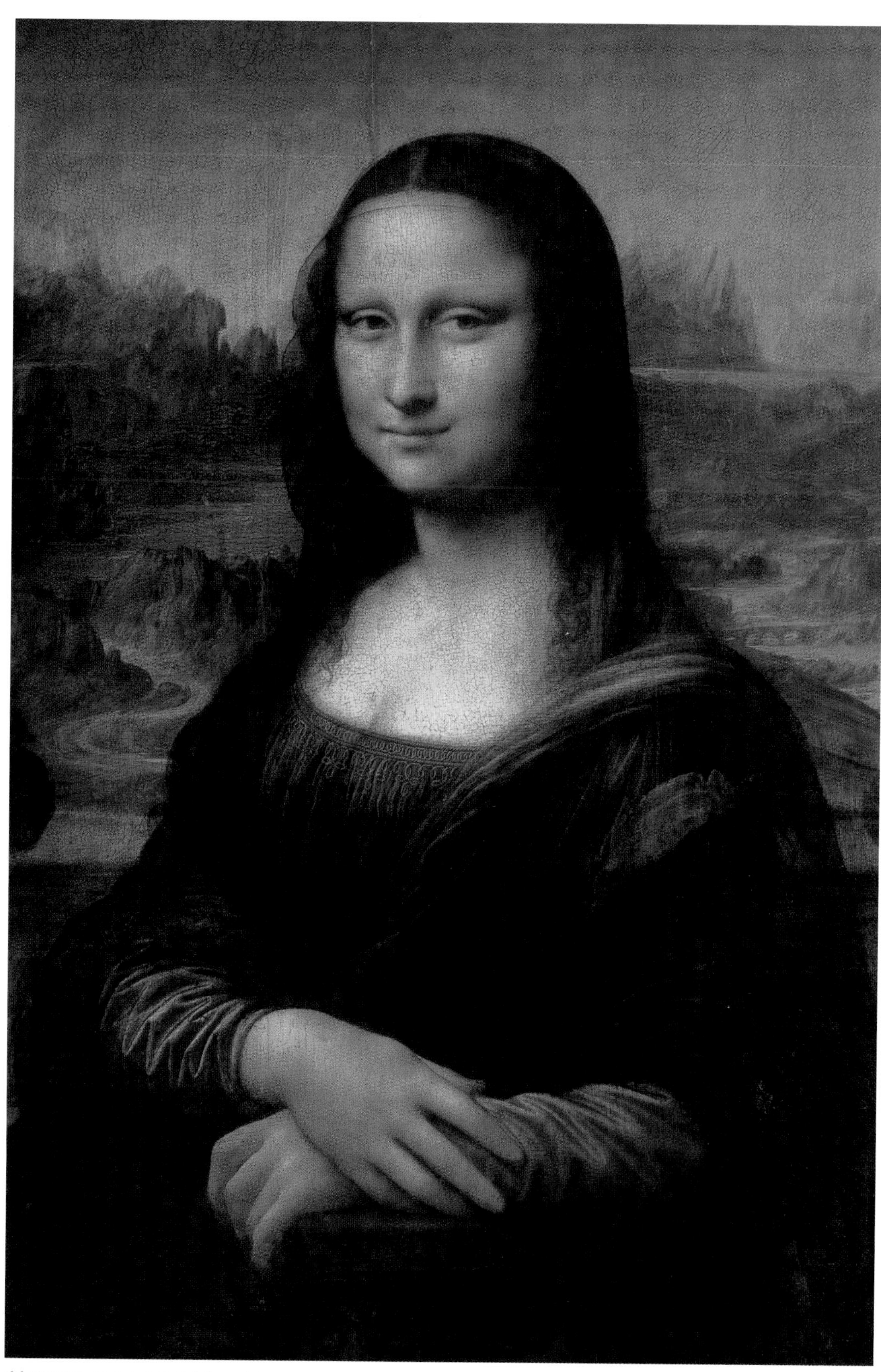

66 LEONARDO DA VINCI *Mona Lisa c.* 1503

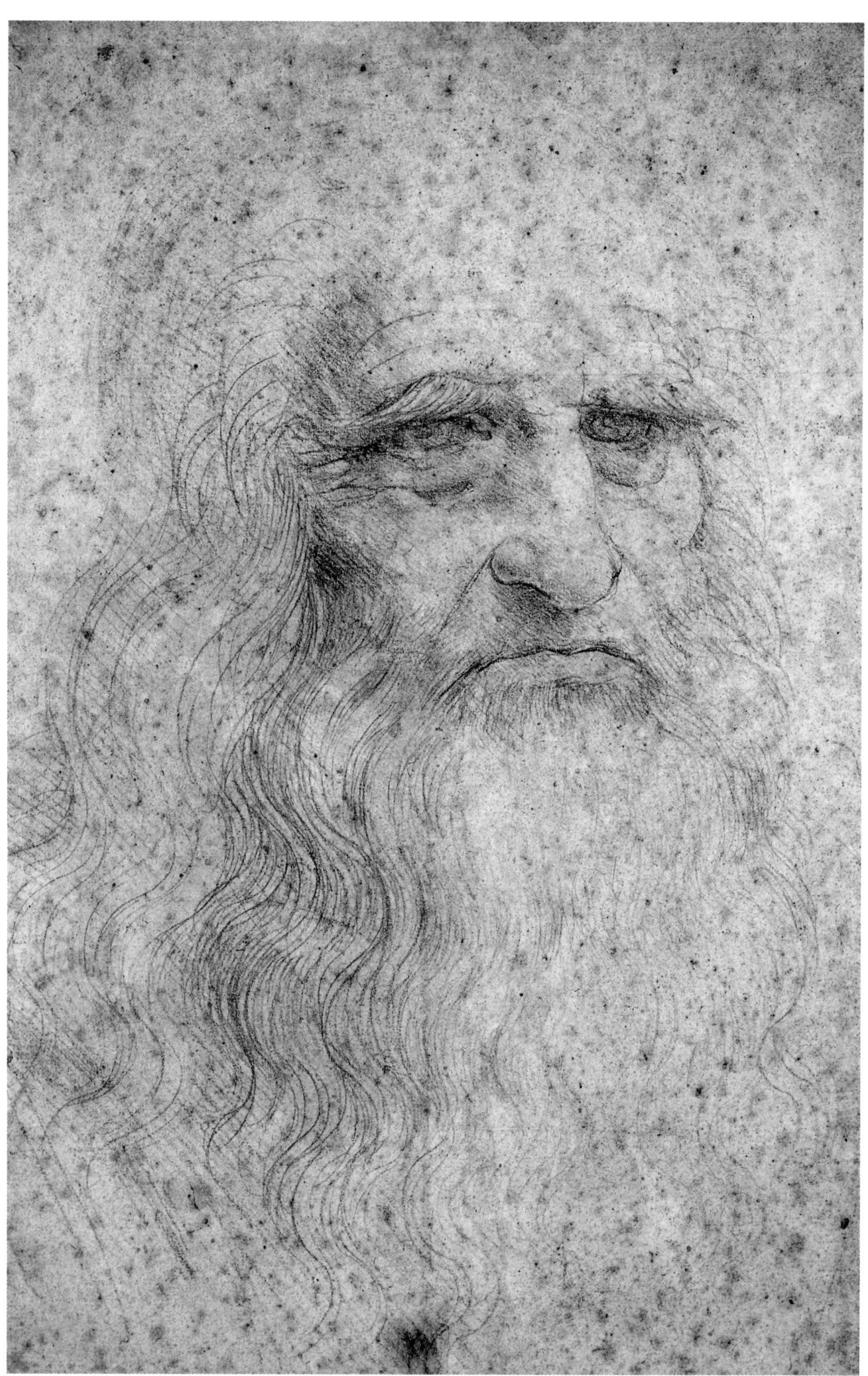

67 LEONARDO DA VINCI *Self-portrait c.* 1513

knowledge that whatever he *did* paint could not possibly live up to his encyclopedic expectations for painting.

Another reason, besides, may lie behind the chronic, unproductive procrastination of his later years. This is the sense he may have had that any painting he might create would be likely to expose the gaps in his would-be universal knowledge. To attempt to paint the figure of a man might remind Leonardo that he had not yet got around to perfecting his knowledge of the way the tendons in the arm control the movement of the wrist; to attempt to paint a stretch of water in a landscape might remind him that he had not yet quite got to the bottom of the dynamic principles governing the motion of whirlpools. Thus was art displaced to a life of endless study. The paradox of his position was that he had elevated painting to such a position of epistemological eminence, so far above mere craft, that he almost could not bear to practise it for fear of failing to live up to his own ideal.

After the years that Leonardo spent in Milan, he would return to Florence, move to Rome and eventually leave Italy altogether, in somewhat mysterious circumstances, for France. There he spent the last few years of his life. It has traditionally been said that the King of France, Francis I, revered him as a sage, and enticed him abroad to enjoy the pleasures of his conversation. The king's true feelings for Leonardo are difficult to establish with certainty. According to Benvenuto Cellini, Francis valued Leonardo's company more than that of any other man in the world.[23] Vasari even had Leonardo dying in the French king's arms (a subject popular with French artists of the Romantic period, especially Jean-Auguste-Dominique Ingres).[24] But Cellini and Vasari, socially ambitious Italian artists both, had a vested interest in promoting the image of the Italian artist as a fit companion for kings. All that is known for sure is that when Leonardo died, at Amboise, on 2 May 1519, Francis I was many miles away in another part of his kingdom.

In a self-portrait [67] drawn in his old age, we see Leonardo with a long flowing beard which makes him look like the magus he had always dreamed of becoming. He even looks a little like traditional representations of God the Father. But his brow is creased and he looks infinitely sad. At the last, his ambitions for painting finally set aside, Leonardo perhaps knew enough to know that there were an infinity of things that he did not know, and could never know, about the universe in which he lived. He knew he that could not be a second God, in the end, nor even a universal man. He could only be a man. The final fruit of all his aspirations appears to have been an unshakeable melancholy.

CHAPTER FOUR

# APOCALYPSE

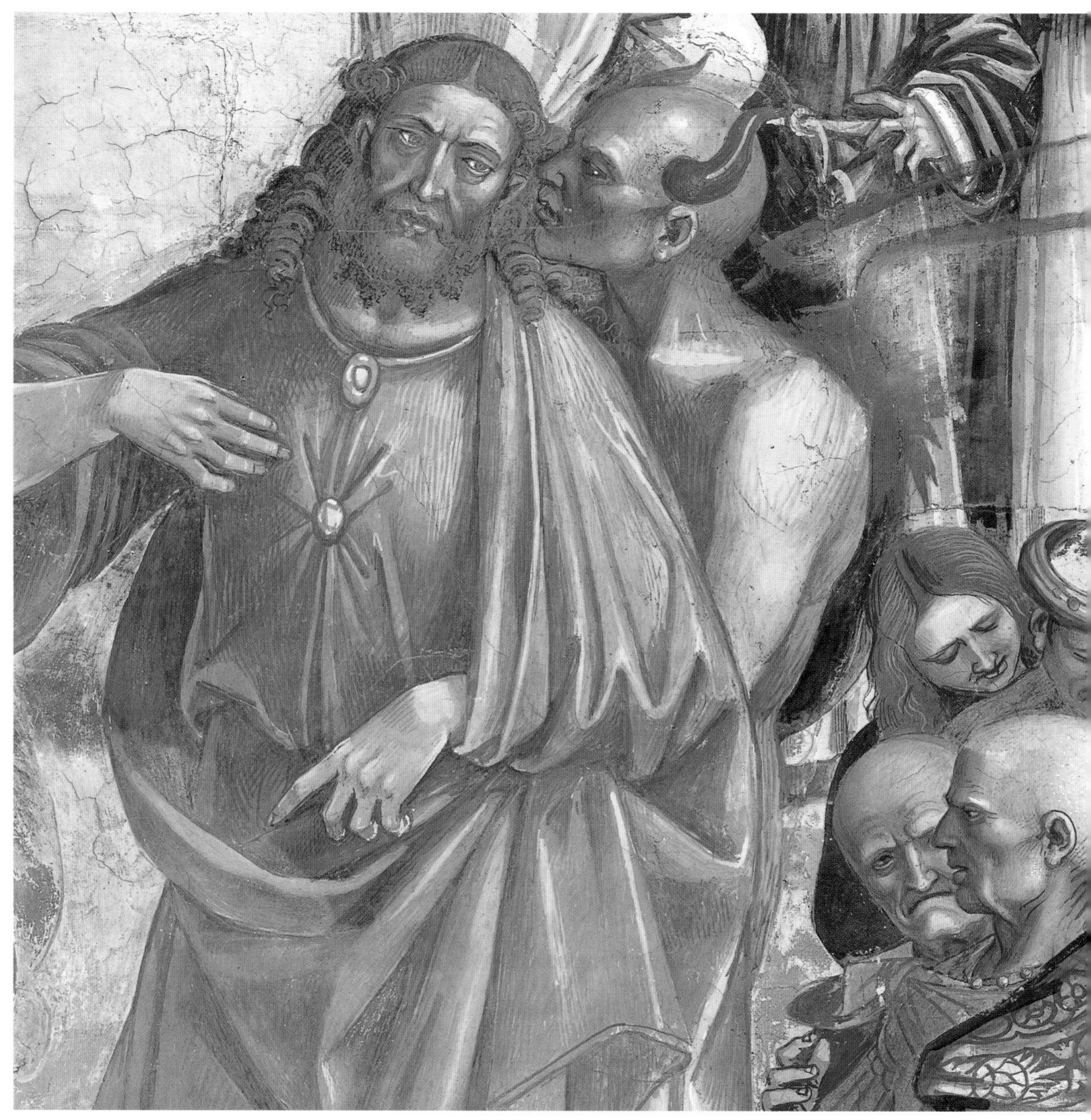

68 LUCA SIGNORELLI *The Stories of the Antichrist* (detail) 1499–1502

And behold, a pale horse; and he that sat upon him,
his name was Death. And hell followed him;
and power was given to him over the four parts of the earth,
to kill with sword, with famine and with death
and the beasts of the earth...

And, behold, there was a great earthquake,
and the sun became black as sackcloth of hair;
and the whole moon became as blood...

And the heaven departed as a book folded up;
and every mountain, and the islands,
were moved out of their places.

The Apocalypse of St John the Apostle, Chapter 6
*The Holy Bible* in the Douay Version, London 1956

## THE HIGH RENAISSANCE AND ITS ENEMIES

It has become customary to regard the first quarter of the sixteenth century as the climax of the Italian Renaissance and, by extension, the climax of the Renaissance itself. The art historical label which has been affixed to this period, the so-called High Renaissance, suggests a new level of attainment. The term is in some respects an appropriate one. Between approximately 1500 and 1525 the papal court in Rome sponsored the creation of a multitude of spectacular works of art and architecture. These included the buildings of Bramante, the sculptures and paintings of Michelangelo and all of the mature works of Raphael.

But this apparent golden age, made to seem all the more golden, in retrospect, by the brevity of its lifespan, had another side. The intellectual energies that had been unleashed by the Italian humanist preoccupation with the texts and texture of the classical world did not prove to be easily controllable. The art of High Renaissance Rome was only one expression of those energies. Even as it was being created another, equally influential branch of humanist endeavour was producing very different results in Germany and the Low Countries. There a powerful group of critical, sceptical humanists and priests, inspired by the Dutch scholar Desiderius Erasmus (*c.* 1466–1536), were preparing a challenge to the spiritual authority of Rome.

The literature, sculpture, architecture and painting of the time bear vivid witness to a fascinating chapter in the history of modern Europe. The disjunction that developed between Rome and much of the Christian world over which it claimed jurisdiction was mirrored in the continuous but uneasy play of artistic and intellectual influence between the Italian South and the Germanic North. Developing tensions were further exacerbated by a widespread fear of impending apocalypse – a millennial anxiety which seems to have permeated Europe in the early sixteenth century. To many men and women, it seemed that the end of the world was nigh. In a sense, it was.

### REVELATIONS

The most urgent preoccupation of late fifteenth- and early sixteenth-century society – if, that is, the peoples of European Christendom are counted *en masse* – was not the advancement of learning, humanist or otherwise. It was the Last Judgement, and the events leading up to it at the end of the world. This was the final reality against which Christian man's daily life was played out, the moment when time shall stop and eternity begin, when the elect shall ascend to eternal bliss and the damned descend to 'everlasting fire, prepared for the devil and his angels' (Matthew 25: 41).

Ends of centuries have always called forth prophets of doom, but the perennial *fin-de-siècle* fear of the end of the world reached epidemic proportions during the 1490s and after. In Northern Europe, where the Last Judgement had been a particularly popular theme with preachers and painters alike, depictions of the subject took on an intensity epitomized by the swarming, microscopically detailed paintings of Hieronymus Bosch (born Hieronymus van Aken, *c.* 1450). In the central panel of his *Last Judgement* [69] a bizarrely tiny Christ sits in judgement over a world gone to wrack and ruin. Bosch forsook the traditional arrangement of a Last Judgement, with the damned to Christ's left and the blessed to his right. A tiny group of the elect cluster around the Saviour in prayer, occupying with him a light-blue bubble of exemption from the fiery chaos that has engulfed the world. Everybody else in the painting may be considered damned for ever, and the bulk of the picture is given over to imagining, with a gleeful, torturer's ingenuity, the pains that they will suffer.

There is a disconcerting sense, in Bosch, of something small being viewed in microscopic close-up. Malevolence is made incarnate in these minutiae. Much space is given over to an unholy banquet hosted by assorted demons and monsters. People are sliced and steamed. They are fed into curious machines to be liquidized. They are barbecued and hung up to be smoked. They are consumed. The unconventional composition of Bosch's triptych extends to its iconography, to the extent that its precise subject is not entirely clear. The painter seems to have been influenced in certain details by the last, most obscure and terrifying book of the New Testament, the Revelation of John, also known as the Apocalypse.

The Italian peninsula was by no means immune to the doomy imaginings of apocalyptic prophecy. The conventional view of Italian Renaissance society around 1500, driven by a humanist élite contemptuous of religious superstition, and increasingly bent on classical revival and scientific discovery, is a distortion of the truth. Eschatological anxiety was just as pronounced in Italy at the end of the 1490s as it was elsewhere in Europe. In some ways it was yet more pronounced. The fifty years of relative peace which had followed the conclusion of the Treaty of Lodi in 1443 had been brought to an end by the French invasion of 1494. This event marked the beginning of the end of independence for all of the Italian city states, with the exception of Venice. Europe was to be dominated, increasingly, by a few superpowers. There was a widespread suspicion, on the Italian peninsula, that

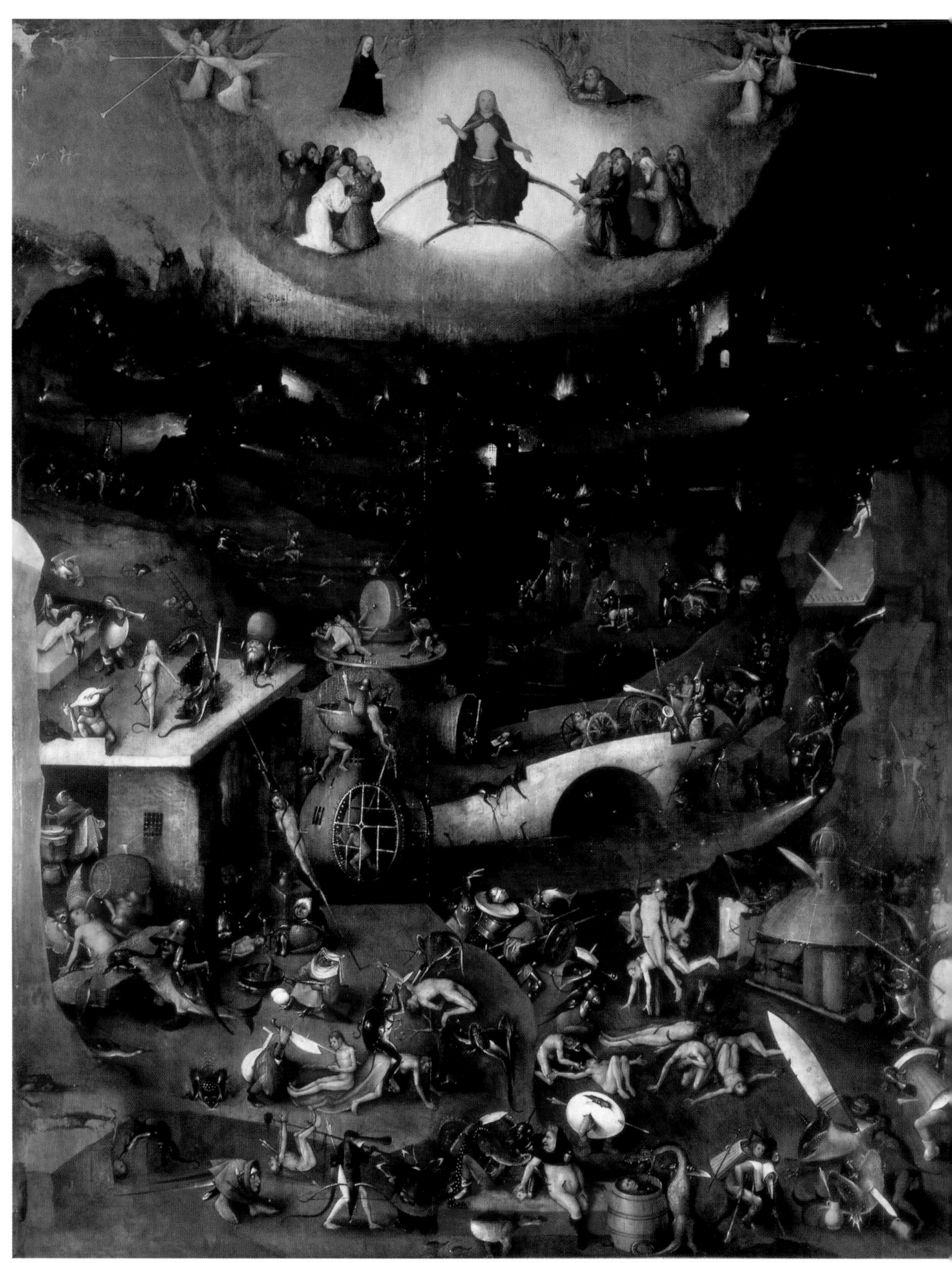

69 HIERONYMUS BOSCH *The Last Judgement c.* 1500

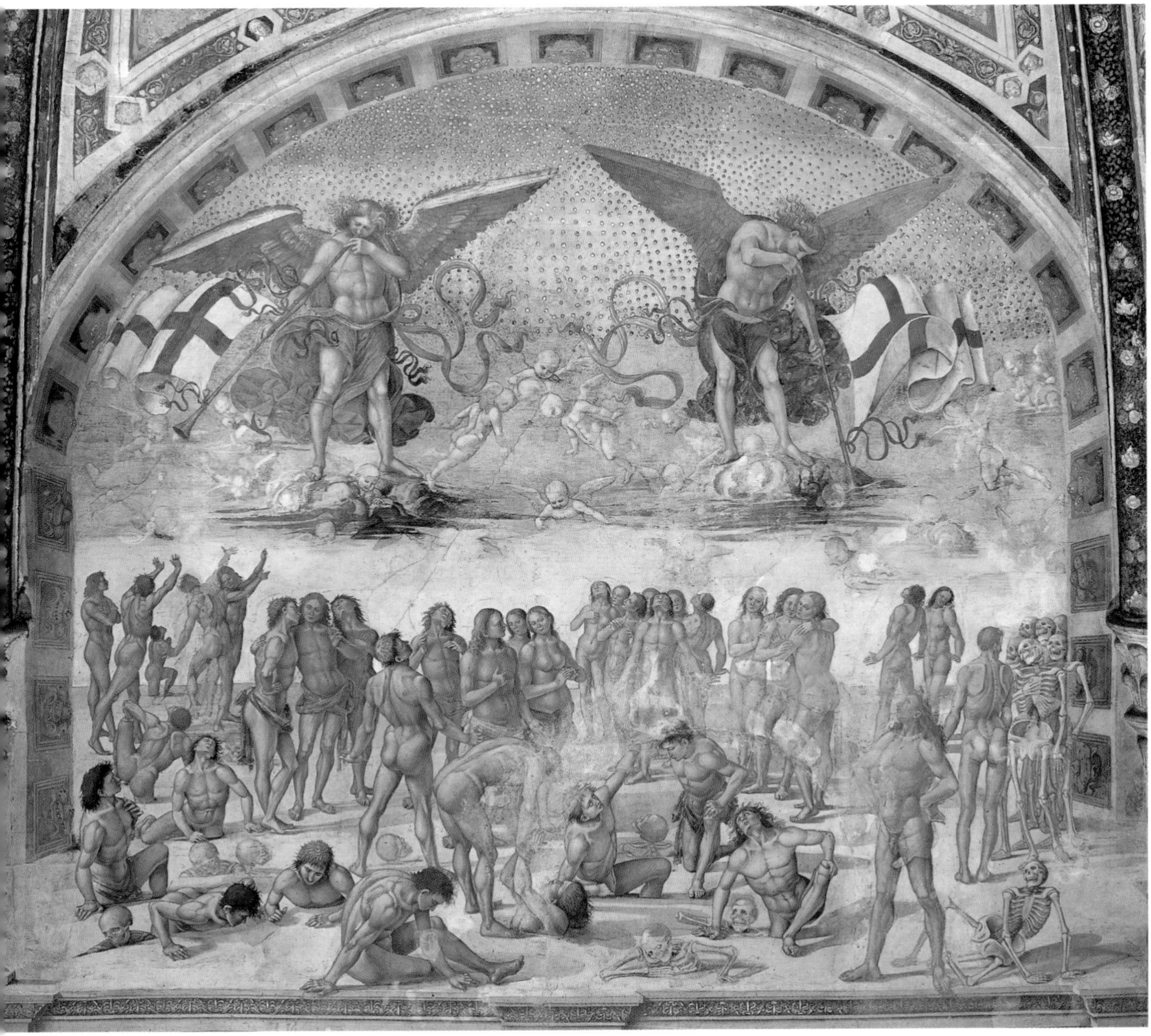

70 LUCA SIGNORELLI *Resurrection of the Dead* 1499–1502

men's destinies no longer lay in their own hands. Their world was to be fought over and divided by others. This sense of foreboding added fuel to their apocalyptic fears and longings.

Following the French invasion of Italy, the Medici were temporarily expelled from Florence and the city was all but taken over by the charismatic Dominican friar Girolamo Savonarola (1452–98). Savonarola systematically terrorized the people at large with descriptions of the end of the world, inflaming the popular imagination yet further by staging so-called 'bonfires of the vanities' – demonstrations of anti-materialist spiritual fervour during which people piled their luxuries into pyres and then watched as they were torched. His dictatorial stance within the Florentine Republic soon brought him into conflict with Pope Alexander VI, who excommunicated him in 1497. The following year Savonarola was expediently hanged and burnt at the stake. But his memory was an abiding example of the popular energies and the civil unrest that could be stirred up by prophets of the end.

In 1499 the painter Luca Signorelli (*c.* 1450–1523) began work on a series of frescos based on the Apocalypse, in the cathedral of the Umbrian town of Orvieto. The cycle includes a scene of *The Stories of the Antichrist*, one of the very few depictions of this subject in the history of art. Standing on a pedestal surrounded by the congregation whom he has beguiled, the Antichrist is preaching the words that the devil beside him is whispering into his ear [68]. The false Saviour is Christ-like in his dress, hair and physiognomy, but his eyes are clouded by dark intent. All the characters wear contemporary dress, which must originally have enhanced the sense that these events were close at hand. In the far background, a classical church – symbol of *the* church – is being looted for its plate and gold, some pieces of which have already accumulated around the Antichrist's pedestal. In the middle distance, the Antichrist performs a false miracle, raising a man from the dead. In the foreground at left, his followers are busy killing Christians. Signorelli included himself beside a particularly unpleasant scene of garrotting.

Orvieto was a key town in the papal states, and these frescos were almost certainly intended to carry a message of support for the papacy. The figure of the Antichrist may have been meant as a symbolic representation of Savonarola (or any other preacher with the temerity to set his authority against that of Rome). Signorelli's message, to his first audience, was as straightforward and to the point as his style. Defend Rome and the papacy and do not be taken in by false prophets.

The painter's *Resurrection of the Dead* [70] translates the moment when the last trumpet blows into a scene of high artifice. Awoken by a pair of admirably muscular angels with unusually long trumpets, the dead rise from the earth to form a congregation of nudes posed like models in a life-class. Signorelli's eagerness to demonstrate his knowledge of the structure of the human form may also explain his decision to include several risen souls as skeletons still waiting for the restoration of their flesh. They chat in friendly fashion with their more complete companions. Signorelli's *Heaven* is a Christian Parnassus reserved for the graceful, a place inhabited by languorous nudes with a Botticelli air about them. But he saved his most graphic imaginings for the scene of *Hell*. The damned (as usual) are uglier and considerably more animated than the blessed, torment being a greater stimulus to energetic movement than ineffable beatitude. Signorelli depicted the worst of all places as a tangled mass of humanity and multi-coloured devils with leathery, bat-like wings – a kind of sarcophagus frieze of atrocity, in which the act of garrotting, once again, is given prominence.

The vividly singular character of Signorelli's works has sometimes contributed to a perception of them as freakish and therefore marginal to the development of Italian Renaissance painting. Yet the ambition with which the artist has attempted to rephrase the lessons of Christianity using the pictorial language of antiquity should not be underestimated, even if that ambition was to be yet more fully realized, during the decades to follow, in Rome.

## ROME REBUILT

In 1503 Cardinal Giuliano della Rovere was elected Pope Julius II. Humanist poets hoping to flatter their way into his affections instantly apostrophized him as a second Julius Caesar, spiritual emperor of the Christian world. On at least one of the commemorative medals struck to celebrate his papacy he is described, in inscription, as 'Pope Julius Caesar'.

Caesar had conquered Gaul and Pope Julius, for his part, vowed to expel the French from the Italian peninsula. He did, in fact, succeed in driving them temporarily out of several of their Italian strongholds and in the process greatly enlarged the papal territories. During a prolonged military campaign in 1506–7 he gained control of Perugia and Bologna, and on his return to Rome he confirmed his image as a self-styled Caesar by re-creating an ancient imperial Triumph in which he was drawn through the streets of the city in a chariot drawn by four white horses. One of the arches through which he processed in such imperial style was inscribed with Caesar's famous words, 'I came, I saw, I conquered'. A warlike and politically ambitious man, Julius was dissatisfied with mere spiritual leadership of the Western world.

He was also dissatisfied with the condition of Rome. On his election, despite the best efforts of earlier popes, the spiritual capital of Christendom was a tumble-down place, more shantytown than metropolis. The city resembled little more than a series of linked villages clustered around the river Tiber.

The most dynamic of Julius II's predecessors, Pope Nicholas V, had been influenced by the ideas of Leon Battista Alberti and had dreamed of a Roman Renaissance. Nicholas had spelt out his vision for the future in a speech made to his cardinals as he lay on his deathbed, in 1455. He had argued that if the Roman papacy were to prosper, then Rome itself must be made to seem as majestic, as flawless and as permanent as the Christian faith itself:

> ... to create solid and stable convictions in the minds of the uncultured masses, there must be something that appeals to the eye: a popular faith, sustained only on doctrines, will never be anything but feeble and vacillating. But if the authority of the Holy See were visibly displayed in majestic buildings, imperishable memorials and witnesses seemingly planted by the hand of God himself, belief would grow and strengthen like a tradition from one generation to another, and all the world would revere it.[1]

Julius II was the pope who set out most determinedly to realize this vision of Rome, as both the greatest Renaissance city and the most magnificent Renaissance court of all. He had the advantage of great wealth, his revenues having been swelled by taxes levied in the expanding papal states, as well as by income derived from an alum mine which had first been discovered in Tolfa, on papal territory, in the early 1460s. Alum was an indispensable chemical used in the dyeing of textiles, still the chief manufacturing industry on the Italian peninsula during the early sixteenth century. It was also hard to come by, most supplies being imported from the western provinces of Muslim Turkey. As virtually the sole Christian supplier, Julius found himself sitting on the sixteenth-century equivalent of an oil-field.

His money enabled him to set about rebuilding Rome with the same urgency which he brought to his military campaigns. His chief architect and town planner was Donato Bramante (*c.* 1444–1514), whom Julius called to Rome at the very outset of his papacy. Like the Pope himself Bramante was an elderly man at the time, being in his sixtieth year on Julius's accession. But the pope's self-confidence, and his evident confidence in Bramante, seems to have provoked a last burst of energy in him. Under Julius's patronage, the architect began a process of urban renewal which would convulse Rome for more than a century and a half.

Neither Julius nor his architect were entirely sentimental about the ghosts of the classical past, and they set about their self-appointed tasks with a vigour which might have dismayed the modern heritage lobby. The creation of the new Rome of the popes necessarily involved considerable further destruction of the old Rome of the Caesars, and Julius was happy to treat the ruins in the Roman Forum as a stone quarry for his own buildings. The most devastating and the boldest of the demolitions that he authorized involved the complete destruction of the most venerable religious building in Rome, the ancient basilica of St Peter's, originally constructed by the first Christian emperor Constantine. Julius ordered old St Peter's to be pulled down in 1506, on the dubious grounds that the church was already collapsing. Despite widespread fears that St Peter himself, buried beneath the basilica, might be disturbed by such an act, Bramante went ahead in his role as supervisor of the demolition, thus earning himself the nickname 'Bramante *ruinante*' – Bramante the wrecker.

Julius may well have been emboldened to take on the reconstruction of St Peter's by the millennarian belief that time was running out before the end of the world. Giles of Viterbo, Prior General of the Augustinian order of monks and a strong influence on the papal court during the early sixteenth century, gave eloquent expression to this sense of impending doom in a sermon given in the pope's presence in 1507. 'After more than 250 popes, after 1500 years, after so many Christians and emperors and kings, you and you alone ... will build the roof of the Most Holy Temple so that it reaches Heaven!'[2] He was alluding to the moment when, in fulfilment of the visions of the Apocalypse, the faithful would enter the New Jerusalem. But 'the Most Holy Temple' might also have been understood as a reference to St Peter's, the foundation stone for which had been laid just a year earlier.

Bramante's original groundplan for the new basilica survives, while a bronze medal struck to commemorate the laying of the foundation stone gives a fairly clear picture of what he wanted it to look like in elevation. The medal shows a huge, centrally planned temple, pillared and pedimented, capped by a vast hemispherical dome. Like Brunelleschi before him, Bramante was influenced by the ancient domed temple of the Pantheon in the centre of Rome, which had been converted to Christian use in the seventh century, as well as by antique and Christian ideas about the sacred significance of certain geometrical forms.

The foundations for the piers that were to support the domed crossing of Bramante's St Peter's – thus forming, in groundplan, a circle within a square – were completed just three years after work had begun. But little more progress was made before Bramante's death in 1514. The building would eventually occupy twelve architects and twenty-two popes and take more than a century and a half to complete. Bramante's St Peter's is buried inside the basilica which took its place. Possibly the truest and certainly the most palpable impression of what it might have been is provided by the one centrally planned church in the Roman High

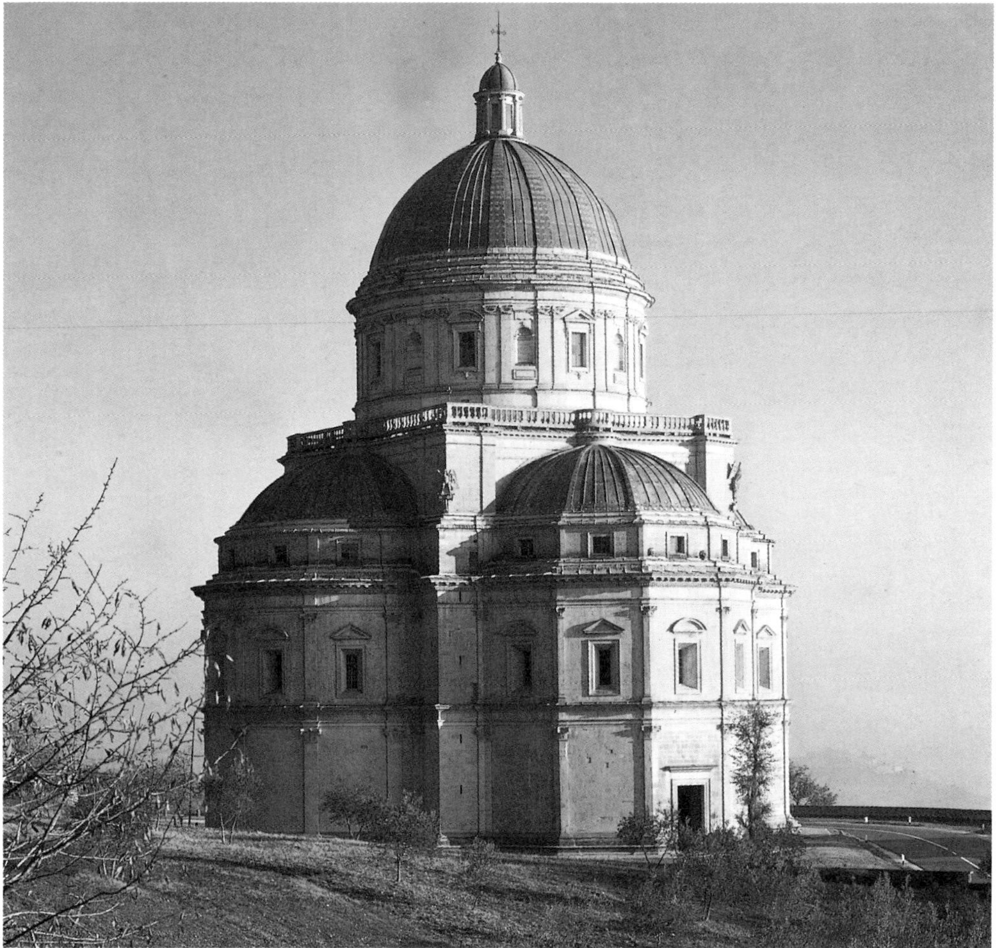

71 DONATO BRAMANTE/COLA DA CAPRAROLA Santa Maria della Consolazione, Todi, begun 1508

Renaissance manner which actually did get built on something approaching the scale envisaged by Bramante – albeit not in Rome itself.

The pilgrimage church of Santa Maria della Consolazione [71] stands in lofty isolation on a plateau just beneath the hilltop town of Todi, in Umbria. It was begun in 1508, to Bramante's design, and built under the supervision of Cola da Caprarola. In many ways the incongruously rustic location of the church only serves to enhance its grandeur. Four polygonal apses, each one roofed by a semi-dome, grow outwards from a central square core above which a dome rises. Inside, the building remains stark and undecorated, making it – as Bramante seems to have wished St Peter's to be – a purely architectural expression of the ideas of holiness and awe-inspiring perfection. Inside, there are no windows at eye level, a circumstance which forces the gaze upwards, to the contemplation of the circular dome, flooded with light by a stunning geometrical arrangement of multiple oculi, intended to symbolize divinity in all its perfection and majesty. Here pattern and light alone – patterns *of* light, kaleidoscopic in their complex symmetry – convey the sense of God.

Conventional Christian churches, with their naves and transepts and choirs, literally imitated the shape of the cross on which Jesus's body was stretched. But Santa Maria della Consolazione, being centrally planned, does not do that. Instead, it symbolizes an idea of God's perfection. So while it is undeniably impressive, it must also be said that it enshrines a somewhat remote and intellectual theology.

## AN IDEAL WORLD

For Julius, as for most princely patrons of the Renaissance, architecture was the leading art form. But other arts also had a place in his programme for the revitalization of the city. Bramante suggested that a fellow countryman and distant relative of his, a young painter called Raffaello Sanzio and known as Raphael, from Urbino, might also be worth employing. So it proved. He began work for Julius in 1508, when he was in his mid-twenties, and so outshone all his rivals that he was soon put in sole charge of painting the large rooms in the suite of papal apartments on the second floor of the Vatican.

The so-called Stanza della Segnatura – named thus because the most important papal documents were signed and sealed there – was originally a library. Its walls are decorated with frescos showing an assembly of great men, past and present, engaged in spirited debate. Piles of books feature prominently in each painting. The scheme as a whole is, simultaneously, a kind of dramatized catalogue of an ideal library, in which authors past and present move and speak to one another in idealized settings, and a painted disquisition on the proper uses of learning. The idea of a pantheon of great men, gathered in a space intended to celebrate learning, derived partly from the decoration of existing studies such as the Studiolo of Federigo da Montefeltro [51]. But Raphael's innovation was to activate such a scheme. He brought poets, philosophers, sages and theologians to life.

The most celebrated fresco in the room is *The School of Athens* [72]. The artist has placed the philosophers of antiquity and other masters of natural science in an imaginary architectural setting possibly based on the remains of the Basilica of Constantine in the Roman Forum. At the centre of the group Plato points

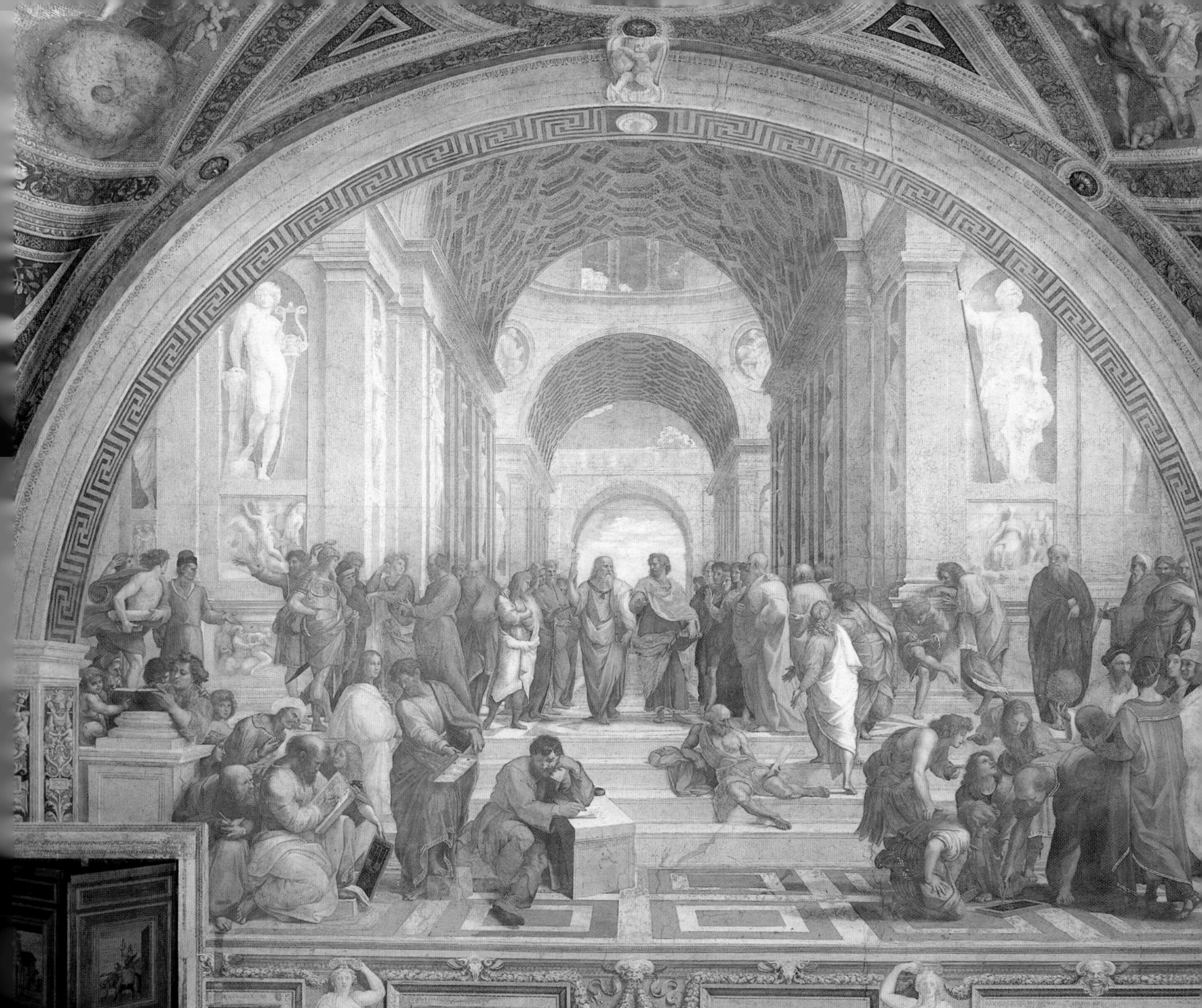

72 RAPHAEL *The School of Athens*, Stanza della Segnatura, Vatican Palace, Rome 1510–11

upwards towards heaven and the seat of higher truth. Beside him, Aristotle points downwards, possibly indicating that for him the seat of true knowledge is the world. On all sides other figures muse and debate with one another. Several contemporary portraits have been incorporated into the picture. Plato, for example, has been given the features of Leonardo da Vinci.

Knowledge in Raphael's painting is envisaged as a dynamic continuum, epitomized by the group of figures just to Plato's left. Here Socrates, in green, holds forth to an attentive group of listeners of different ages and uncertain identity, including an attentive old man, a rapt young soldier and a rather absent-minded boy. As the philosopher counts off points on the fingers of his left hand, one of his audience calls urgently for pen and paper, and a young man laden with parchment – the embodiment of the amanuensis, his windblown orange cloak cunningly furled by the artist so that his very clothing resembles a rolled document – rushes in from the left to transcribe the words of the sage. Literature has been dramatized as a scramble to preserve thought before it dies on the air.

Raphael's subject is the way in which, through books, men discover what other men have thought, and go on themselves, in turn, to develop new ideas. This process is not entirely idealized. The advance of learning is seen as a sociable, yet at the same time a paradoxically solitary activity. Some of the thinkers present seem lost in thought or in the books which they are reading and writing. Others, like Heraclitus, head propped on one elbow (a portrait of Michelangelo), seem plunged in melancholy. The vitality of Raphael's work derives in no small measure from his inclusion of these hints of dissatisfaction and difficulty. Research, reading and writing are often lonely activities.

Raphael's idealism is touched throughout by humanity, and he makes room for touches of humour here too. Pythagoras, in the bottom left-hand corner of the picture, is so wrapped up in his theorems that he does not notice the plagiarist who has insinuated himself at his elbow, stealing his ideas even as they are formulated. The pantheon of the learned includes exam cheats.

Opposite *The School of Athens*, as a Christian complement to the gathering of classical sages, is the fresco known as the *Disputa*. Assembled before a white marble altar in an ideal landscape, popes, bishops, saints and theologians, past and present, discuss Christ's sacrifice and the nature of the sacrament. Before them, at the dead centre of the picture's perspective, stands a gold monstrance, delicately incised with the monogram of Julius II, containing the consecrated Host. Above them hovers the Trinity, accompanied by the Virgin and saints. All theological learning, Raphael's picture thus indicates, exists to confirm the truth of the doctrine of the Eucharist.

In fact, such idealism was contradicted by the realities of Europe in his time. The vigorous but essentially harmonious intellectual and religious concord envisaged in Raphael's scheme of paintings was anything but a reflection of the truth. Julius II had not encouraged debate. He had suppressed church councils and theological debate, taking an autocratic line on matters of church doctrine. The gap between the Roman church's lofty theology and that developing elsewhere in Europe was growing wider. While the papacy liked to claim dominion over all of Christendom, in reality it paid little attention to the changing needs and beliefs of many Christians. In the absence of true spiritual leadership from Rome, much of Northern Europe had been evolving its own, distinct religious culture – a world apart from that of the papal court but also on collision course with it.

## NORTHERN EUROPE AND ITS DISCONTENTS

The ground was prepared for popular rebellion against the authority of the Roman church by the persistence, in Northern Europe, of strong traditions of popular ascetic piety. This played a part in fostering a widely shared suspicion of the pomp and majesty of the Roman church.

A particularly extreme artistic expression of early sixteenth-century Northern European religious asceticism is the Isenheim Altarpiece of Mathis Nithardt-Gothardt, known as Matthias Grünewald (*c.* 1475/80–1528). This work, created around 1515 for the high altar of the chapel of the leprosy hospital in the monastery of St Anthony of Isenheim, in Alsace, was originally a 'transforming altar' – its two sets of wings could be unfolded to present three different images. Now on display in the Musée d'Unterlinden, Colmar, France, it has been dismantled so that all the panels can be seen at the same time.

When the altarpiece was closed (most of the time) Grünewald's thoroughly non-Italianate and aggressively ugly *Crucifixion* [73] would have been the only visible image. Set in a dark and barren landscape, against a lowering sky, Christ's gigantic and agonized body, pricked with thorns and covered with suppurating sores, is extended on the cross. His flesh is a sickly and gangrenous green, against which the red of his blood, oozing from his hands and feet and side, is all the more prominent. There is a morbid vibrancy in this use of complementary colours. The work seems well calculated to impress its captive audience of hospital inmates, many of them lepers. Painful illness and sickness unto death were seen as redeeming experiences, the human equivalent of Christ's own suffering during his Passion. By painting Christ as though he were infected with a horrible skin disease, Grünewald made this connection yet more explicit in the minds of his congregation. His art may have helped them to see their own suffering as a way of getting closer to God.

While Grünewald's style has little in common with that of leading Italian masters of the time, this seems to have been a deliberate choice on his part rather than a sign of provincial ignorance. In the panel devoted to *St Anthony*, the artist seems almost to have been flaunting his familiarity with those Italian Renaissance innovations – manifest both in the saint's heroic anatomy and the delicate, Leonardesque blending of light and shade in the background landscape – which the rest of the Isenheim Altarpiece so starkly repudiates.

On some of the inner panels of the altarpiece, Grünewald's morbidity gives way to visionary imagination. In the panel of *The Resurrection* [74] a radiant Christ rises heavenwards in an unfurling column of drapery, a great disc of light behind him. Soldiers around the tomb cower before the vision as though struck by lightning. It is possible that this image was reserved for the view of the canons whose work it was to tend the sick and the dying. It may have been intended to remind them that there was light at the end of the tunnel of human suffering. A message of hope is embodied in the figure of the risen Christ, his body healed, spotless and unblemished. But the abiding impression left by the altarpiece is not one of optimism. In the panel depicting *The Visions of St Anthony* – a work which makes even the nightmare imaginings of Bosch seem, by comparison, almost mild – the world has run mad, teeming with monsters. It is tempting to imagine that Grünewald may have meant this work to be interpreted as some form of commentary on his age.

The idea that the world was in deep spiritual peril acquired particular force in Northern Europe during the early decades of the sixteenth century. The driving intellectual force behind this was Erasmus. His satires, polemics and religious writings polarized theological opinion and sowed the seeds for religious upheaval. He gave a decisive twist to the development of humanism in Northern Europe, which under his influence bred a generation of discontented, idealistic thinkers and clerics preoccupied with reforming the established church, and with making Rome see the error of its ways.

Like all humanist scholars, Erasmus was an intellectual heir of Petrarch. But he recast Petrarch's thought. He called not for a Renaissance of classical learning but for a *spiritual* Renaissance. While Petrarch had called for the rebirth of ancient Greece and Rome, Erasmus demanded the rebirth of the church.

Erasmus's call for spiritual renewal had its genesis in the deceptive quiet of the library. As a young scholar, he was one of the first men to grasp the broader implications of the relatively new discipline of philology. The scientific study of language and its history had been rapidly developed by humanists during the course of the fifteenth century, as a tool for distinguishing between earlier and later manuscripts of the works of classical authors. The primary motive behind the advance of philological science was the dawning awareness that languages, like societies, alter through time. Armed with a knowledge of the ways in which Latin usage had changed over the centuries, a humanist scholar would be able to distinguish between (for example) an original manuscript of Cicero and later copies or paraphrases. But in the hands of Erasmus and his followers, another and more contentious use was found for this science of grammatical and vocabular minutiae. Applied to the Latin texts of the New Testament, philology became the most

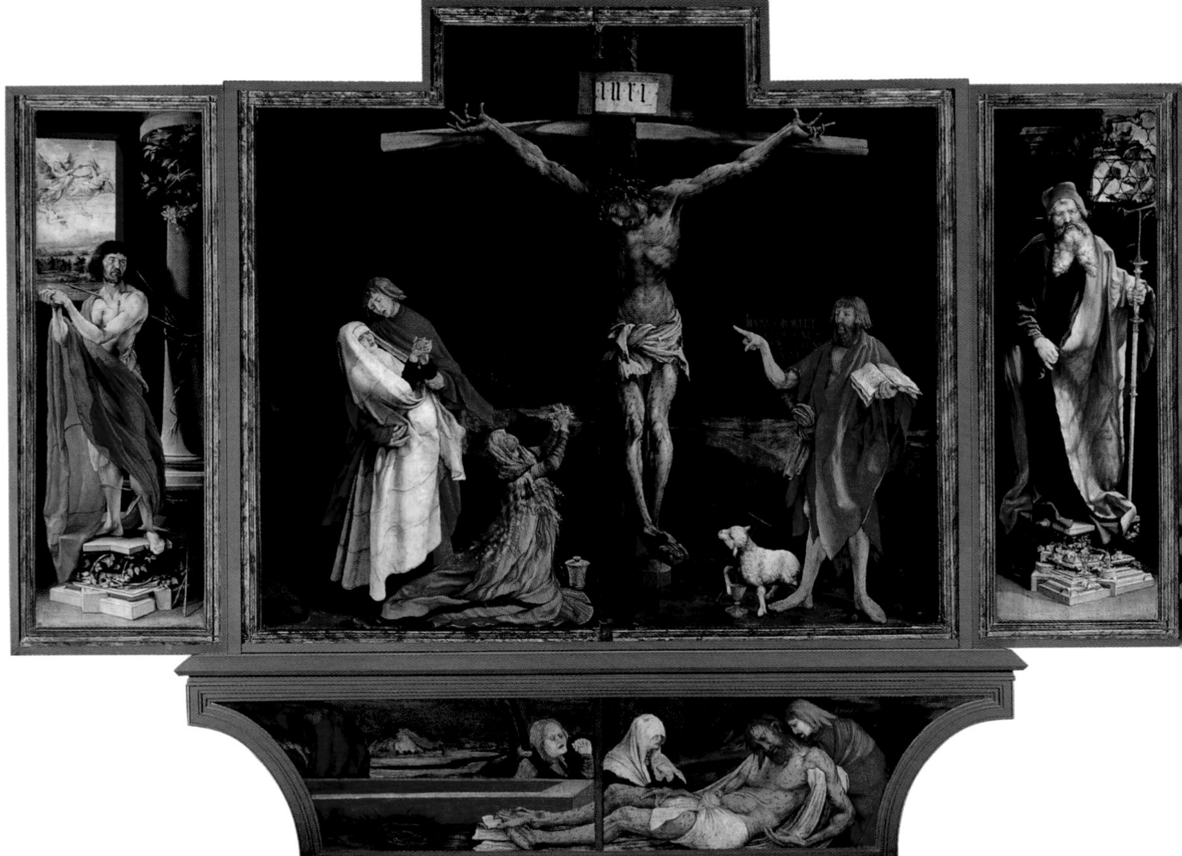

73 MATTHIAS GRÜNEWALD Isenheim Altarpiece (closed position) *c.* 1515

potent weapon in the armoury of those who would dare question the doctrinal status quo.

Erasmus comprehensively applied this new empirical science of words to the Word itself. He devoted much of his life to a philological analysis of biblical texts. The ambition that drove him to this arduous enterprise was, in essence, a simple one. He wanted to take Scripture away from the theologians and to purify the sacred text of all the accretions with which they had barnacled it. He wanted to recover God's message in its purity. Side-effects of his work included a greater availability of holy writ to ordinary people, and a more widespread questioning of the right of the established church to mediate and interpret the Bible.

Erasmus's ideas spread quickly across the map of early sixteenth-century Northern Europe. Part of the appeal of his intellectual position lay in its extremism,

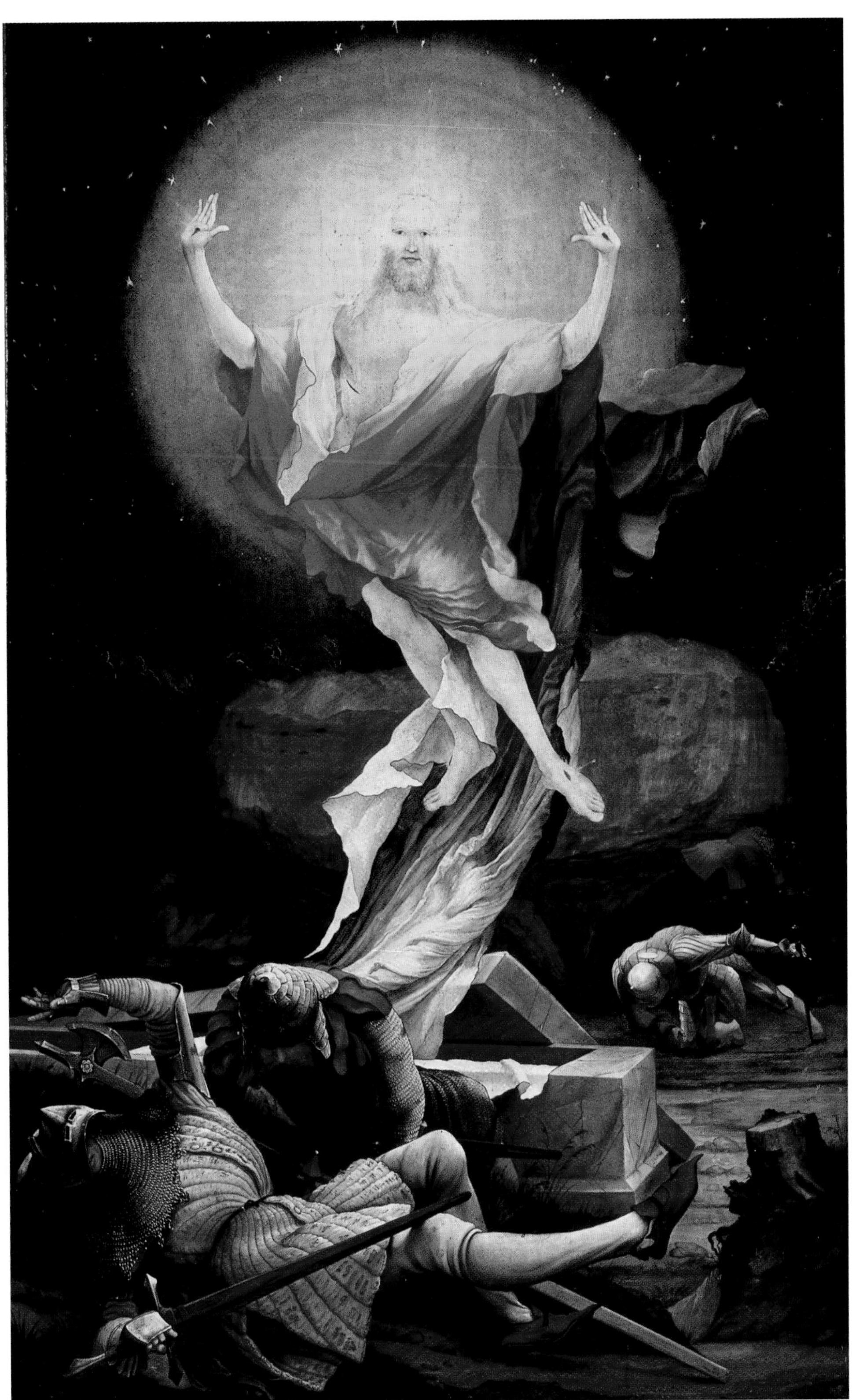

74 MATTHIAS GRÜNEWALD *The Resurrection* (wing detail), Isenheim Altarpiece *c.* 1515

which suited the apocalyptic mood of the times. People were in search of extreme spiritual solutions. Another reason for the popularity of Erasmus's ideas lay in their consistent anti-materialist, anti-élitist tenor. A dislike of Rome's lofty disengagement from the concerns of the people at large, and a suspicion of its excessive emphasis on ceremony, were among the corollaries of his call to spiritual regeneration through the unmediated Word of God. The wit, eloquence and passion with which Erasmus argued his position also helped to make him an intellectual hero of his time. But his work was popularized above all by the new technology of the printing press, which made new and powerful ideas almost impossible to censor.

Printing with movable pieces of type was invented in Germany in the 1420s, and by the 1450s, in the hands of Johannes Gutenberg of Mainz, it had been turned into a genuine medium of mass communication. But it was Erasmus who first demonstrated the power of the printed word to change society by inflaming public opinion. Supported by Johann Froben, his printer in Basel, he used the publishing house to establish a new kind of political domain.

His most impassioned supporters were to be found in what is now Germany. In the early sixteenth century, this was not a nation state but a mass of independent principalities loosely incorporated within the Holy Roman Empire. Towns such as Augsburg, Strasbourg and Nuremberg, which were dominated by an oligarchy of wealthy merchants and bankers, were gradually penetrated by humanist ideas. Groups of scholars teaching in Northern European grammar schools and universities formed Erasmus's first intellectual constituency; and it was partly through their agency that his ideas spread and gained in popularity. As a result Northern humanism was coloured from the outset, as its equivalent in Italy had never been, with a spirit of religious reformism.

The artist Albrecht Dürer (1471–1528), also born in Nuremberg, was in many respects a kindred spirit to Erasmus. A learned and well-travelled man, he visited Italy in his youth and took inspiration from Italian thought and art. He exchanged works of art with Raphael and noticed with some envy, while in Italy, how much higher the status of artists was there than in his homeland. During his travels he remarked that 'here I am a gentleman, at home a parasite'.[3] But, like Erasmus, although Dürer absorbed many Italianate ideas, he remained very much his own man.

Dürer's lofty sense of his vocation is reflected in several self-portraits. One of the most striking of these works, painted in 1500, shows the artist full-face, with flowing hair, staring hypnotically out at the viewer [75]. He has depicted himself as a magus, a wise man, a German Leonardo da Vinci. But however Italianate the work might seem, it is shot through with a deep and distinctively Northern European piety. The visage could be that of Christ – a resemblance enhanced by the unusual, full-face pose, normally reserved for depictions of God. Yet rather than being purely self-glorifying or arrogant, this gives the painting a broader spiritual dimension. Dürer's self-portrait (no less than Grünewald's Isenheim Altarpiece) is a reminder of man's duty to think and meditate on Christ's example. It implies that the essence of Christianity lies not in ceremony or ritual, but in the duty of the individual to forge his own direct relationship with God.

Like Erasmus, Dürer was also a master of the new printing technology. The popularity of prints, and the relative ease with which they could be mass produced and sold, gave him the freedom to choose his own subject matter. The fact that his work was marketed to a relatively broad cross-section of the public also meant that Dürer – unlike many of his Italian contemporaries, working in the more rarefied atmosphere of aristocratic or papal courts – had to ensure that his art kept faith with the needs and feelings of a broad section of the population.

Early in his career, Dürer responded to the wave of apocalyptic feeling which swept through Europe during his lifetime with a series of large woodcuts illustrating scenes from the Revelation of St John. These works enjoyed enormous popularity from the time of their first issue in 1498. Among the many visions described in Revelation is that of four figures on horseback who shall descend upon the earth trampling all before them. Dürer's *Four Horsemen of the Apocalypse* sets it down in black and white. Urged on by an avenging angel in the sky, the pitiless advancing horsemen have been caught, almost as in a snapshot, as they crush a variety of stricken human beings beneath them. The images follow the biblical source closely. Each of the horsemen – from the first, the so-called 'Conqueror', with his bow and crown, to the last, Death, on a pale and skeletal horse – is equipped as in the text. On the ground, one of the figures standing for fallen humanity is a king, his crowned head already half swallowed up by the maw of hell – which Dürer depicted as a kind of dragon-cum-dog. The politically subversive implications of the Apocalypse contributed to its mass popularity. It was a subject well calculated to appeal to the disenfranchised and the poor, for at the end of the world distinctions of rank and class count for little.

There was a strong intellectual and contemplative side to Dürer's sensibility. He did not only terrify his audience. He also furnished his contemporaries with a memorably heroic image of the type of scholarship that was changing their world. The artist's engraving of *St Jerome in His Study* (1514) is one of the most enduring, intimate images of learning. Accompanied only by his traditional lion, which snoozes on the floor before him, the saint is absorbed in his books. The room in which he sits is flooded with light, which streams in through windows glazed with circular panes like the bottoms of beer bottles, and which makes rich patterns of refraction on the rough walls of the room. Jerome's own balding pate, bent over his text, emits light. He is a scholar and, literally, *illuminatus*.

Dürer's *St Jerome* captures the moral and spiritual seriousness which animated Northern humanists and scholars. Jerome is seen working on his translation of the Bible, just as Erasmus and other Northern humanists were doing in Dürer's time. The artist may well have meant that connection to be made. The picture can be seen as a kind of displaced portrait of the Erasmian scholar, toiling away at his philological analyses of the Bible. It is a distinctively Northern European counterpoint to Raphael's slightly earlier depiction of the progress of learning in *The School of Athens*. While Raphael's cultural ideal is a brightly coloured exchange of ideas, albeit tempered by hints of duress and loneliness, Dürer's vision of learning is utterly solitary: an isolated scholar sits huddled over his book, intent on discovering truth through the word. Dürer seems to announce his own sympathy with the subject by filling the print with evidence of his own hard labour. The multiplicity of optical effects and deceptions, within the medium of a steel engraving, shows superlative, beguiling skill.

The most highly prized religious art form in Northern Europe at the time was neither painting nor printmaking, however, but wooden sculpture. In this genre too it is perhaps possible to sense the early stirrings of a Reformation sensibility. One of the masters of limewood carving in Renaissance Germany – he was certainly the most successful in worldly terms, eventually gaining election as mayor of Würzburg – was Tilman Riemenschneider (*c.* 1460–1531). Among Riemenschneider's finest works is the large retable which he carved for the municipal corporation of Rothenburg ober der Tauber, an abidingly picturesque town not far from his base in Würzburg, between 1499 and 1505.

The elaborate carved shrine which Riemenschneider made was to house a relic purporting to be a drop of Christ's blood. The artist created a towering construction of intricately worked wood, surmounted by a figure of Christ as the Man of Sorrows, designed to frame a dramatic carving on the appropriately Eucharistic theme of *The Last Supper* [76]. The work illustrates the moment when Christ announces that 'one of you shall betray me ... It is he to whom I shall give this morsel when I have dipped it' (John 13: 21, 26). Its composition is unusual. Usually, Christ at the Last Supper is seen seated in the middle of his disciples but here he is

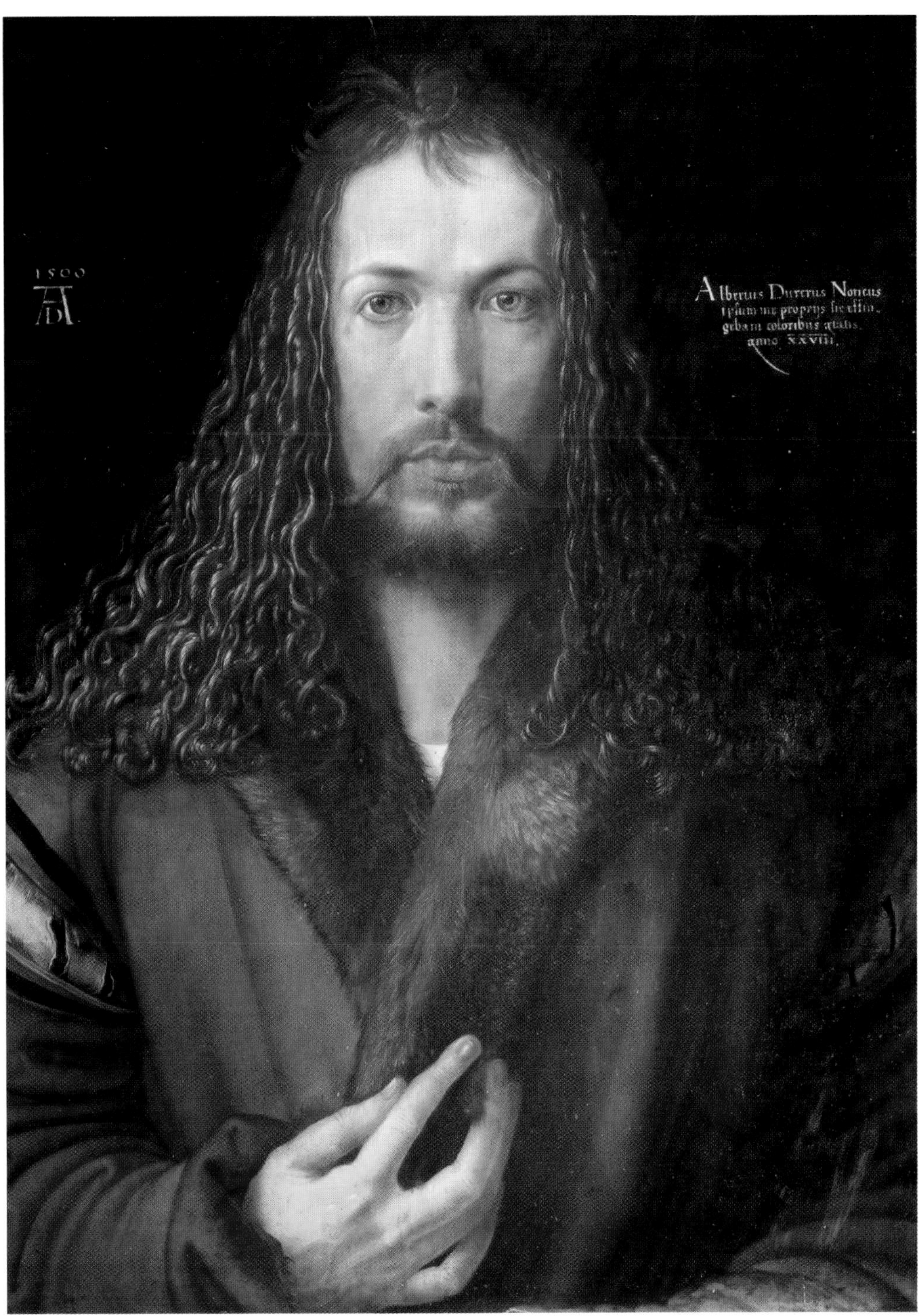


75 ALBRECHT DÜRER *Self-portrait* 1500

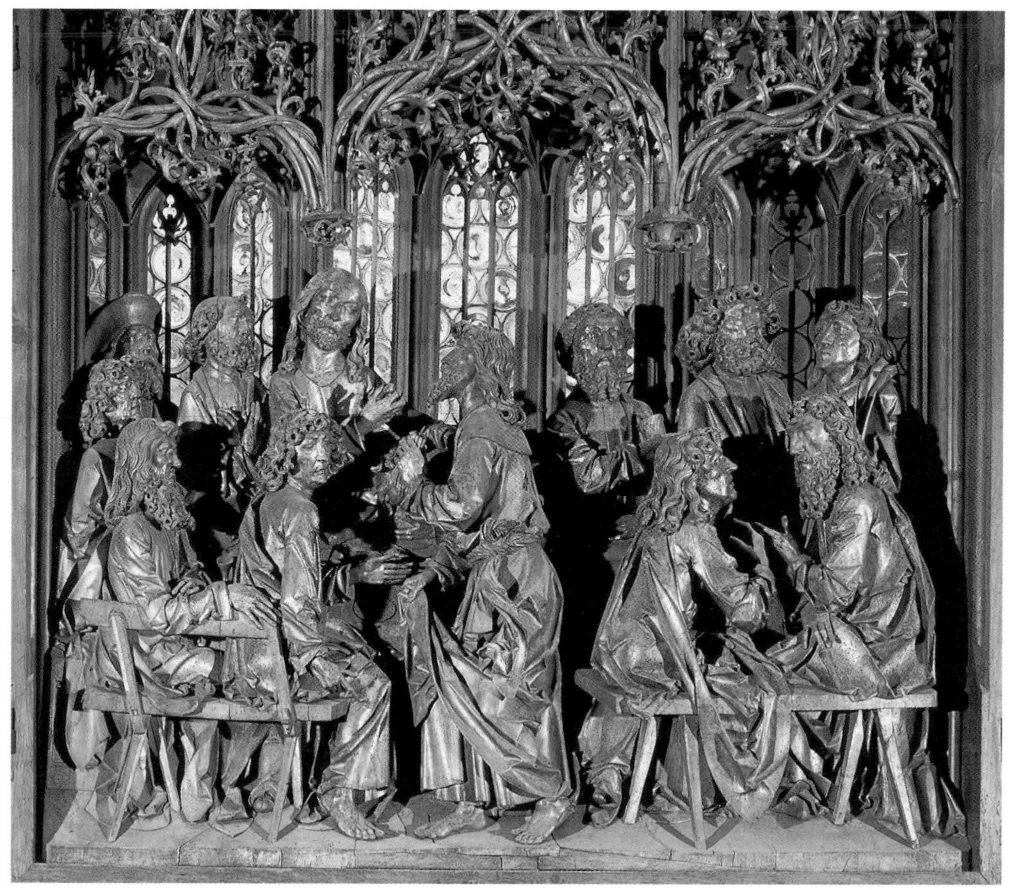

76 TILMAN RIEMENSCHNEIDER *The Last Supper* (detail), Church of St Jacob, Rothenburg *c.* 1499–1505

standing behind the table at the left of the group of apostles gesturing towards Judas. It is Judas who, moneybag in hand, seated on the near side of the table, occupies the central position in Riemenschneider's composition. The carving, which still occupies its original position in the chapel for which it was created, might almost have been designed to be lit theatrically by the sun as it moves through the sky. As the day wears on, Judas becomes progressively isolated and for a few moments he is actually spotlit, alone in his guilt.

Riemenschneider's work is, despite the fineness of its carving, sober and restrained. The faces of Christ and his apostles, framed by looping spirals of hair – a wonder of virtuoso carving and Riemenschneider's hallmark as an artist – are gaunt and sunken-cheeked. Unlike many Northern European sculptures of the period, Riemenschneider's masterpiece remained ungilded and unpainted, as if to complement the plainness of the Eucharistic meal which it commemorates. Flickering in its shadows, a pauperist aesthetic is at play.

## THE DIVINE MICHELANGELO

The very notion of a pauperist aesthetic might have struck Julius II as an oxymoron. While Riemenschneider was finishing his altarpiece, the pope was planning a huge and complicated monument to himself. He had in mind a tomb the size of a temple, supported by a multitude of statues of naked young men. The man whom he chose to undertake this grand scheme was a young sculptor from Florence.

Michelangelo Buonarroti (1475–1564) had called himself to the pope's attention – had made himself, indeed, the only possible choice of sculptor for a man with Julius's monumental ambition – by creating the largest and most widely admired sculpture of the male nude in the history of post-classical art. This was the tremendous figure of *David* [77], armed with a sling and stone, which the sculptor began in 1501 and finished in 1504.

Michelangelo's statue is over 4 metres high and was carved from a single huge block of marble which had defeated the efforts of several Florentine sculptors before him. The *David* is a direct descendant of the life-size saints and prophets with which Donatello and his contemporaries had changed the public face of Florence in the early years of the fifteenth century. The resolve expressed by Donatello's marble *St George* [30], carved for the façade of Orsanmichele, is restated in the frowning, preoccupied features of Michelangelo's hero. This white stone giant, Christian in iconography, classical in form, was patently intended as another reincarnation of the old myth of Florence the indomitable republic.

But despite his impressive musculature and stern expression, there is a dreaminess and sensuality about the *David*, a fundamental lack of urgency in the lassitude of his pose and the limpness of his wrist. The statue seems not to embody republican virtue but a distant and elevated beauty. It is an evocation of divinity, should one choose to see it in Neoplatonic terms, in the shape of a perfectly proportioned and flawlessly beautiful male figure.

Michelangelo, who came from a once prosperous Florentine family fallen on hard times, had been given much encouragement by the Medici family in his adolescence. As one of a number of promising individuals accepted into the Medici household, he seems to have been familiar with Marsilio Ficino's poetic Neoplatonism, the influence of which may be felt not only in his art, but in his poetry and prose. He may also have known the two exceptionally beautiful classical *poesie* painted for members of the family by Botticelli during this period. Extreme sensuality combined with a tantalizing idealism, quite possibly of a Neoplatonic cast, characterizes both the *Primavera* [1] and *The Birth of Venus* [60]. It characterizes the *David* too. The family resemblance is explicit in the pose and gesture of Michelangelo's nude, which is so much the male mirror-image of Botticelli's Venus that it could almost be a pendant to it, realized in monumental sculpture.

Less than a year after he had finished the *David,* Michelangelo was summoned by Pope Julius II. The memorial to the pope which brought Michelangelo to Rome was to have been a huge free-standing structure occupying pride of place in the new St Peter's. Had it ever been completed, it would have been over 15 metres high and have occupied an area of approximately 200 square metres. It was to have been a modern counterpart to the long-vanished Mausoleum at Halikarnassos in Ionia, one of the Seven Wonders of the Ancient World.

The largeness of spirit with which some of Julius's projects were invested doomed them necessarily to incompletion. The tomb proved to be a frustrating commission which would occupy the artist, on and off, for some forty years. But the few figures that Michelangelo eventually made for it are among his most beautiful and original creations. The majority of them, a series of sculptures in varying states of finish, now divided between the Accademia in Florence and the Louvre in Paris, are statues of captives. The least finished seem as though still trying to struggle into existence from the stone that confines them. The artist insisted, in his writings on art, that sculpture was primarily an intellectual activity. His half-realized captives are creations that suggest the strong pull this fantasy had over him. Their lack of finish makes them still semi-conceptual, like thoughts that have only begun to take form. Forever suspended between idea and execution, they seem to declare Michelangelo's reservations about the realization of *any* idea – to complete a work being inevitably to spoil the purity of the original conception, to mire it in the real world.

*The Dying Slave* is the most finished of the captives. A drowsy, narcissistic figure, he seems almost to enjoy the restraining effect of his flimsy bonds, touching himself and the cords that bind him with a languid, caressing gesture. Like all of the other captives, this statue was intended to occupy one of the niches on the lower level of the tomb, although its precise allegorical meaning within the overall scheme remains open to debate. *The Dying Slave* may have been meant to symbolize, as captives had classically done, the territories conquered by that modern Caesar, Pope Julius. It may have been meant to symbolize the captivity into which arts and letters would fall following the death of the great pope. It is also possible that the sculpture may have been intended to signify the everlasting soul, shuffling off this mortal coil, awakening from the sleep of mortal life into eternal blessedness.

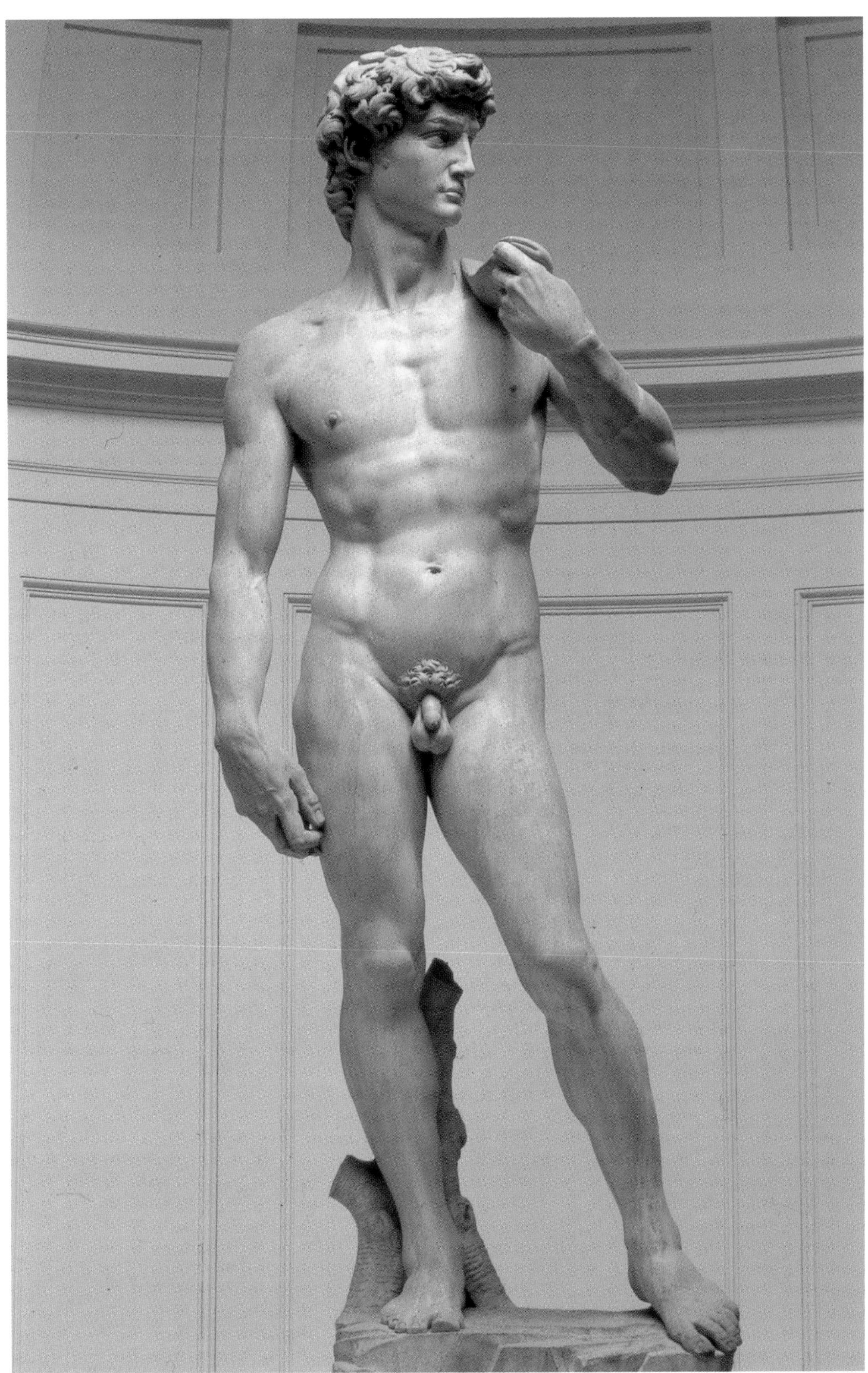

77 MICHELANGELO *David* 1501–4

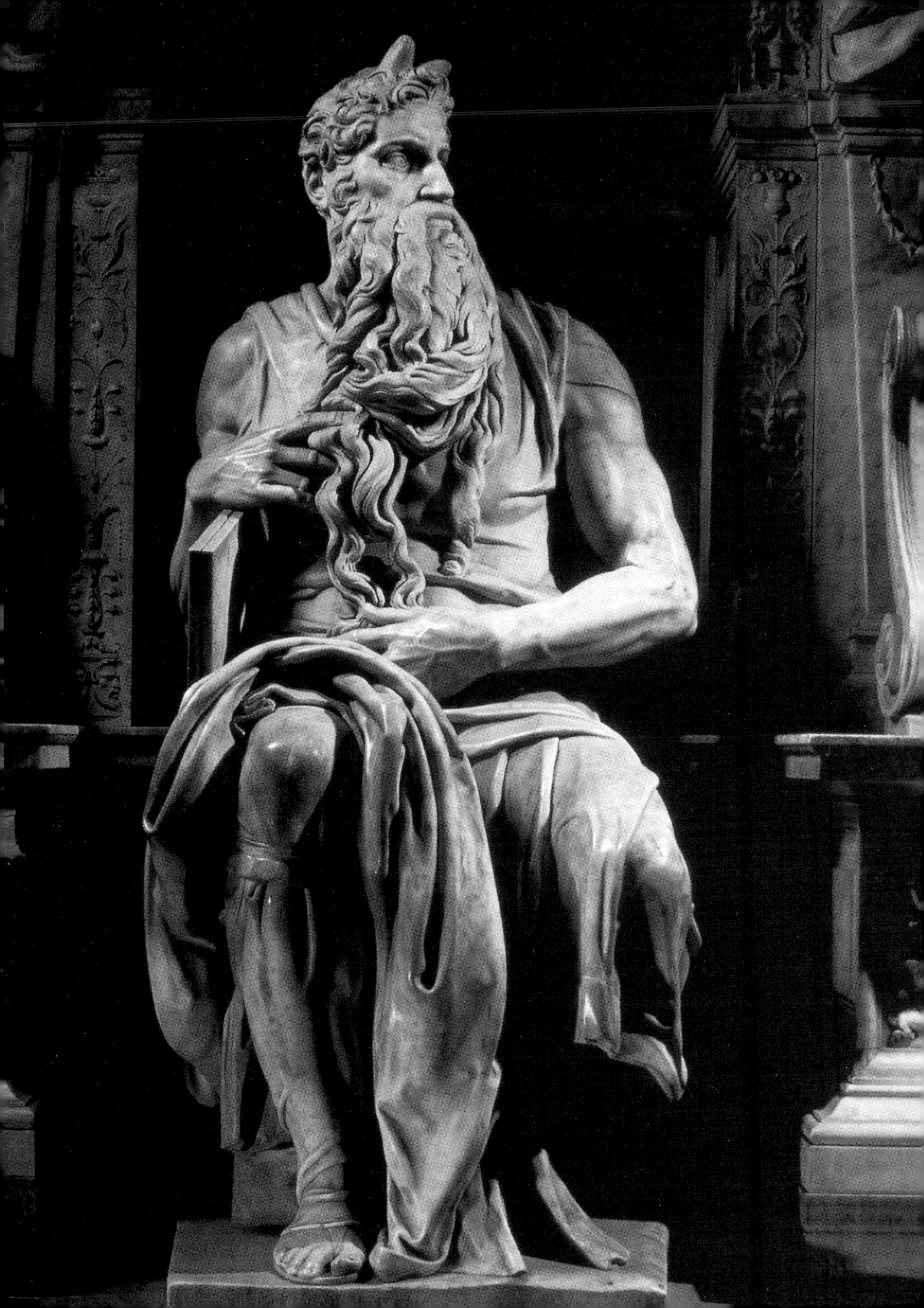

Because the tomb was never finished, the individual works which Michelangelo made for it have floated free of whatever precise meanings were originally intended for them. In the case of this particular sculpture, all such meanings have in any case been submerged in the voluptuousness of its form. The effect made by forty such figures, supporting the structure of a pope's tomb in St Peter's, would have been unprecedented. The papal sepulchre, had it ever been created, would have been a gallery of naked figures.

Yet sensuality below was to have been tempered by thunderous piety above. Of the four over life-size sculptures of prophets that were originally to have surmounted the tomb, the only one that Michelangelo executed is the *Moses* [78], which dominates the much reduced memorial to Julius eventually erected in the church of San Pietro in Vincoli, Rome. Frowning and majestic, the stone prophet seems to incriminate the unimpressive monument of which he forms part (not exclusively the work of Michelangelo) for representing such a sad climbdown from Julius's original grand plan. The figure of *Moses* is superhuman, a seated prophet reminiscent of Donatello's prophets carved for Florence a century earlier but, by comparison with them, hugely exaggerated and removed from reality. The introspection of Donatello's holy men has metamorphosed, in the lofty outward gaze of Michelangelo's prophet, into an equally fierce but more theatrical form of musing. There is something almost monstrous about the horned prophet with his yard of flowing beard and his massive, prominently veined arms, furiously knotted with muscle. Michelangelo's contemporaries used the word *terribilità* to describe the air of severe, forbidding religious sublimity emanated by such a figure as *Moses*; this quality became associated by extension with Michelangelo himself.

When the artist first heard, in the spring of 1506, that the tomb for Julius had sunk in the list of the pope's priorities – funds having been diverted to the continuing construction of St Peter's – he immediately left Rome in a fit of temper. Julius succeeded in enticing him back with considerable difficulty, having cast around for a commission suitably grand and sufficiently demanding for Michelangelo's talents. He had found it in the form of the ceiling of the largest chapel in the Vatican, the Sistine Chapel, named after Pope Sixtus IV, who had ordered its construction. The artist agreed, reluctantly, to paint it for him.

It took Michelangelo nearly four years, between 1508 and 1512, to complete the decoration of the ceiling [79]. His frequently stated belief that painting is an inferior art form to sculpture is to some extent reflected in the work that resulted, a fresco cycle that aspires to the condition of sculpture. Michelangelo turned the vault of the chapel into a huge, *trompe l'oeil* architectural structure, decorated with

78 MICHELANGELO *Moses*, San Pietro in Vincoli, Rome *c.* 1513–15

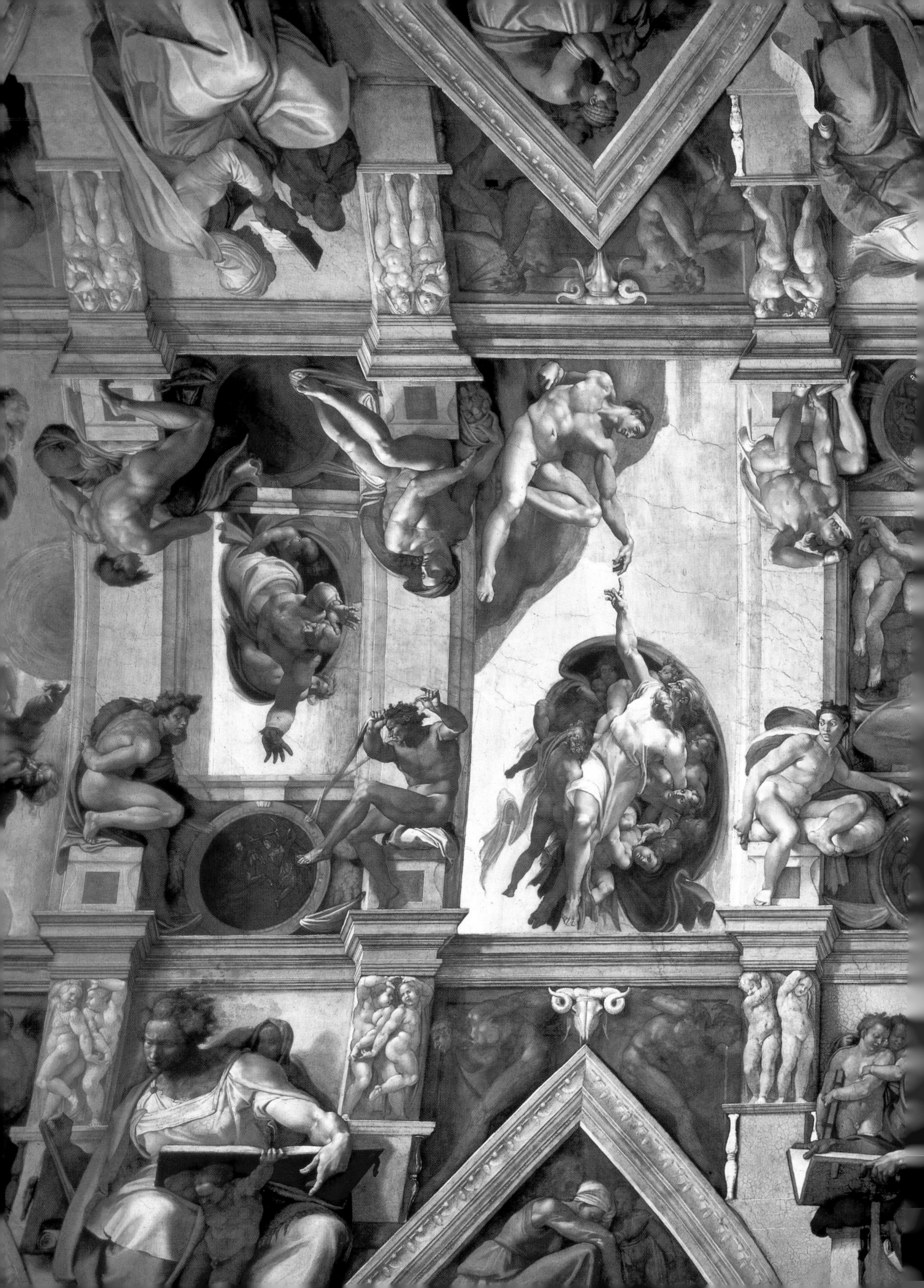

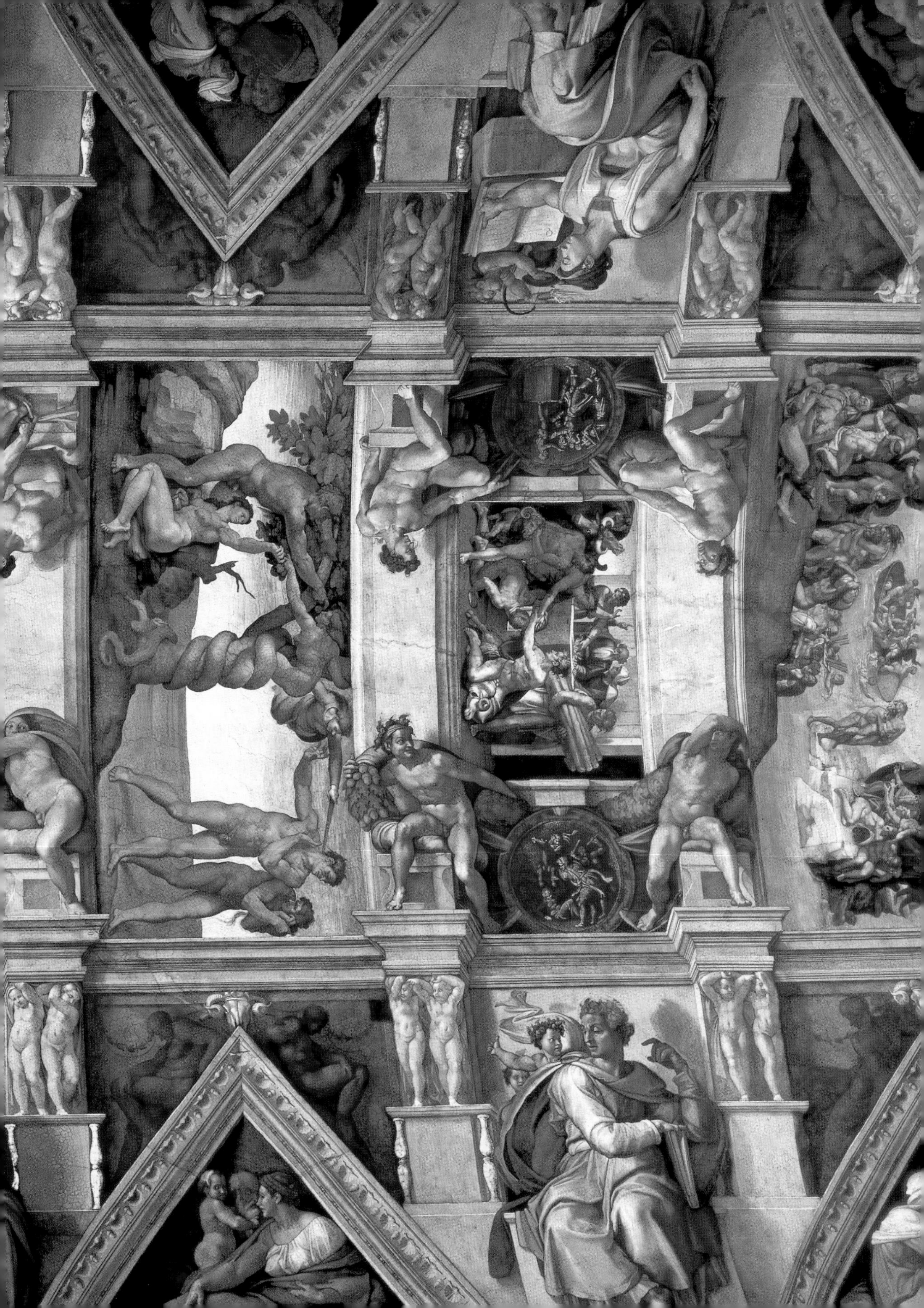

a multitude of figures, many of which resemble painted pieces of statuary. In scale and ambition the Sistine ceiling is the Julius tomb finally realized, not in stone but in paint.

Michelangelo depicted scenes from the Book of Genesis. He did so in nine narrative paintings which, framed by the imaginary architecture of the fresco cycle, run from the east to the west end of the chapel. The earliest scenes (which he actually painted last) are *The Separation of Light from Darkness, The Creation of the Sun, Moon and Planets* and *The Separation of Land from Water.* These episodes of primal creation, rarely attempted in previous Christian art, roused Michelangelo himself to the creation of a new form of visual majesty. He re-imagined the Christian God as a cloaked and musclebound patriarch, a stern heroic athlete who soars imperiously through abstract heavens, who reaches up into chaos to part dark from light, who forms planets with a gesture even as he wheels through space to perform yet other mighty acts. In the most famous image of the entire ceiling, the grey-haired God surges across empty space in a billowing cape full of weird excited angels, reaches out towards the reclining figure of Adam, and imparts, across the few inches of air that separate their outstretched fingers, the spark of life that makes man move and breathe.

Michelangelo's God is creative energy incarnate, the embodiment of a higher reality putting all the works of man – to which the later and somehow shrunken scenes of storytelling allude – into perspective. He has much in common with the mighty stone *Moses* of the Julius tomb. He may also have embodied Michelangelo's sense of his own capabilities. He is God as artist, creating form from void and darkness; and it takes only the slightest shift in mental perspective to see in him, as well, the image of the artist as God. Michelangelo took the idea of the artist as a magus, a second creator – even, as Leonardo da Vinci had expressed it, another God – to new extremes. But the vaulting sublimity of the artist's imagination should not be seen as mere Promethean hubris, even if there was an element of that in his character. As the scene of *God Creating Adam* makes explicit, all that lies within man was itself planted there by divinity. In unleashing his own energies Michelangelo was paying tribute to God, not stealing fire from the heavens.

*The Temptation and Expulsion* is the only one of the narrative paintings on the vault created in the same monumental vein as the Creation scenes. The fall of man is shown as a decline from beauty into distortion. Prelapsarian Adam and Eve are anatomically ideal beings with perfectly coiffured hair. The same creatures in their postlapsarian condition, seen across the dividing line of the Tree of Knowledge,

79 (PREVIOUS PAGES) MICHELANGELO Ceiling of the Sistine Chapel, Vatican Palace, Rome 1508–12

twined round with a wily feminine serpent, have become grimacing caricatures of their former selves, still impressive but mean and graceless in face and form. It is characteristic of Michelangelo that he should express their tragedy primarily in terms of anatomy and physique. His resort to melodrama in the faces of his fallen Adam and Eve – which are masks next to the faces of Masaccio's Adam and Eve in the Brancacci Chapel [1] – reveals the artist's relative lack of interest in human character at this point in his life. Only the body and the soul interest him; rarely the psyche. He elevates all that he paints out of reality and into myth.

The ceiling is so full of allusions to classical sculpture that it sometimes seems almost like a painted version of a Roman art collection. The figure of Adam is based in part on a fragment of antique art known as the Belvedere Torso, while his pose is derived from that of antique river gods. Many of the other figures on the ceiling contain reminiscences of the Roman marble group of *Laocoön and his Sons*, which Michelangelo helped to unearth after its discovery in a vineyard on the Esquiline Hill in 1506. This was clearly an inspiration behind one of the most disorientating images on the ceiling, *The Brazen Serpent*, in which worshippers of the false idol writhe in the coils of serpents.

The Sistine Chapel ceiling was controversial in Michelangelo's own lifetime. Less than ten years after it was completed Pope Hadrian VI condemned it as 'a bathroom of nudes', a crude judgement but one which conveys how startling Michelangelo's work could seem to his contemporaries. The artist had included many elements, both aesthetic and erotic, which seemed to have almost no theological justification.

On each of the twenty pedestals of the imaginary architecture which frames the nine scenes from Genesis, Michelangelo perched a single naked male figure, mysterious in significance and beautiful in form. These, presumably, were Hadrian's nudes in the bathroom. Twisting and turning, sometimes gesturing, sometimes lost in contemplation, they epitomize the artist's boldness and originality. But how these nudes or *ignudi* were meant to relate to the rest of the cycle is not known. Their overall meaning is as ambiguous as that of the captives carved for the Julius tomb, which they so closely resemble – and to which they are, surely, closely connected. Some of them seem simply pagan-decorative. Others seem charged with intent. Were they meant as the *animae rationali* – emblems of the rational spirit – of the huge and daunting Prophets and Sibyls who occupy the lunettes directly beneath them? Were they intended as symbols of divine perfection, images of the spotless soul turning to God?

Many of them, especially the *ignudi* surrounding the Creation scenes, which were painted last, appear too troubled and restless for that to be the case. It may be plausible to view them as mediators between this world and the next, images of the struggle of the human spirit. Michelangelo's poetry contains passages on this theme. He was a principal Renaissance sonneteer of Christian-Platonic aspiration, who wrote of the soul's necessary struggle to free itself of the bonds of the flesh. Whatever their meaning, the *ignudi* amount to an extraordinary invention. The scale relationships of Michelangelo's ceiling, which mean that these figures are actually bigger than many of the protagonists of the narrative paintings which they border, makes their presence seem all the more emphasized. Their energies shiver across the ceiling, setting up a perpetual tremor of disturbance. They are a chorus of turmoil and aspiration.

Together with Giotto's paintings on the walls of the Arena Chapel, Michelangelo's paintings for the ceiling of the Sistine Chapel are the most celebrated frescos of the Christian painting tradition. Yet they mark a very different moment. A great gulf separates Michelangelo from Giotto. The Sistine Chapel is grander than the Arena Chapel, but it touches the heart less directly. Pathos has been replaced by aesthetic beauty. Intimacy has been replaced by sublimity.

## JULIUS TRIUMPHANS

As Julius's papacy entered its later years, the artistic riches of Rome accumulated at an ever swifter rate. Shortly after Michelangelo completed his frescos for the ceiling of the Sistine Chapel, and while work continued on Bramante's St Peter's, Raphael started on the second and last of the Vatican decorations that he was to paint for Julius.

His theme, this time, was not learning but power. In the Stanza d'Eliodoro Raphael extolled the might of Julius and his army, celebrated the pope's triumphs and affirmed God's protection over the papacy. In tune with the martial, aggressive nature of his new subject matter, the artist also abandoned the pictorial language of equipoise and harmony that he had developed in *The School of Athens* for a more dynamic mode. The energy with which Michelangelo invested the human form passed into Raphael's figures. The painting after which the room was named, the large fresco of *The Expulsion of Heliodorus*, depicts an infrequently represented incident from the Apocrypha (II Maccabees 3). The general Heliodorus, attempting to carry off the treasure of the Temple of Jerusalem, is struck blind and expelled from the holy place by a heavenly horseman and two young men of great strength and

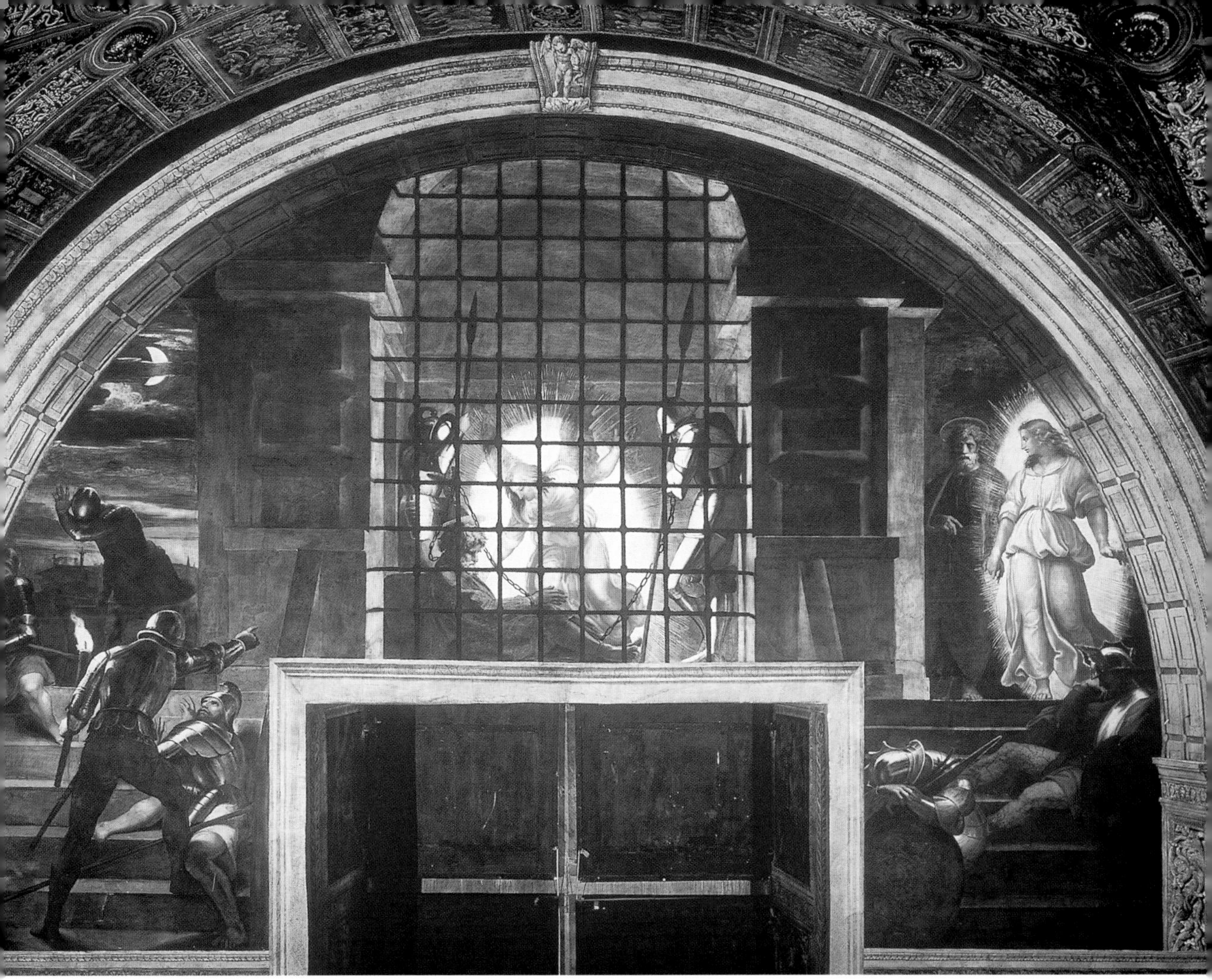

◌ RAPHAEL *The Liberation of St Peter from His Chains*, Stanza d'Eliodoro, Vatican Palace, Rome 1511–14

perfect beauty. The two youths have the physiques of Michelangelo's *ignudi* and the momentum of his airborne God on the Sistine ceiling; Heliodorus and his accomplices reel before this triple attack like the confused masses in Michelangelo's *The Brazen Serpent*. On the opposite side of the painting, set in a golden classical domed temple which must surely have been inspired by Bramante's St Peter's, Pope Julius and his entourage contemplate this scene with satisfaction.

The fresco was to be understood as an allegory of Julius's own defence of the papacy, and Italy, against the invading French. So too was the fresco that faces it, which depicts the legendary *Repulse of Attila from Rome*, a miracle in which the unarmed Pope Leo III routed Attila and his heathen hordes. The pope, seated on a white horse, has only to raise his finger for Attila and his supporters to fall into confusion and start wheeling round in retreat. Perhaps because the subject was so similar to *The Expulsion of Heliodorus*, Raphael subsided, here, into a kind of parody of his own previous work (although the intervention of assistants may also be partly to blame). There is a kind of wooden absurdity to the picture, an overemphatic straining for effect, crystallized in the total contrast between the calm and static pope and his convulsed foes. In its peculiar lack of conviction the fresco can be seen as a High Renaissance prefiguration of Soviet Socialist Realist art.

The Stanza d'Eliodoro also includes what turned out to be Raphael's valediction to his patron, a brilliant nocturnal drama entitled *The Liberation of St Peter from His Chains* [80], a subject drawn from the Acts of the Apostles (12: 1–11). Raphael shows a bearded St Peter being freed from prison while his guards slumber. The saint faintly resembles Julius, who regarded St Peter in chains as his own alter ego.[4] Light-singed, ragged clouds drift across a crescent moon, its beams caught and reflected in the burnished armour of Peter's guards. The grizzled apostle slumbering behind his grid of iron bars is released by an angel of fire, who draws him by the hand towards the prison stairs. On the threshold of freedom, he stands half in shadow, half in light. There is an expression of solemnity, mingled with trepidation, on his face. The pope died on 21 February 1513, while Raphael was perhaps still at work on the painting. It became his epitaph, the image of Julius's final release from the prison of mortal existence into the light of God.

## JULIUS EXCLUSUS

After Julius II's death, Erasmus wrote an imaginary account of the pope meeting St Peter at heaven's gate, entitled *Julius exclusus*. The first German edition was published to an enthusiastic reception in 1523. Its frontispiece is a small, scurrilous woodcut in which a swarthy and disconcertingly Teutonic Julius, dressed in armour, followed by his troop of Swiss guards and accompanied by his evil genius, swaggers up to the door of paradise. The letters PM, stamped on to his breastplate, stand for 'Pontifex Maximus'; but in the ensuing conversation Erasmus has St Peter suggest that in Julius's case they should be short for 'Pestilential Maximum':

> PETER: Immortal God, what a sewer I smell here! Who are you?
> JULIUS: So you know what sort of a prince you're insulting, listen a bit … The Venetians, previously not conquered by anyone, I crushed in battle … I drove the French, who were then the terror of the whole world, completely out of Italy … when I died I left five million ducats…

> PETER: Madman! All I hear about is a leader not of the church but of this world, more wicked than the pagans …
> JULIUS: You would say otherwise if you had witnessed even one of my triumphs … the horses, the parades of armed soldiers … the lavishness of the displays, the triumphs, the booty … myself carried aloft like some divine thing … So you won't open?
> PETER: To any, sooner than to such a pestilence; you yourself are a great builder: build yourself a new paradise.[5]

Erasmus, the most penetrating and inflammatory critic of Julius's Rome, disliked not only the pomp and worldliness of the papacy but also what he considered to be its fatal, insular, lofty indifference to the spiritual well-being of Christendom. He objected to the pope's neglect of his spiritual duties, but above all he singled out Rome's spendthrift culture of personal self-aggrandizement, epitomized not only by Julius's own commissions but also by those of his courtiers, such as the Sienese banker Agostino Chigi, who spent a fortune on his splendid palace (now the Villa Farnesina) decorated by Raphael and assistants.[6]

It was not just the way in which the papal court spent its wealth which inflamed its Northern critics, however, but the way in which that wealth had been acquired. In order to raise the large amounts of money needed to pay for its numerous architectural and artistic works (for even Julius's great wealth proved insufficient to fund his projects) the papacy had adopted a cynical policy of selling redemption for hard cash. This was done through the sale of Indulgences, which were printed pieces of paper granting the purchaser an officially sanctioned papal pardon for his sins.

Instant remedies for guilty souls, these were sold all over Christendom by the agents of Rome, who hawked them like itinerant peddlers trading in quack nostrums. A particularly brisk trade in Indulgences was pursued in Germany, where some of the more unscrupulous papal agents would even sell pardons to people for sins which they intended to commit. This conveniently enabled a sinner to spend the night in a brothel, to commit a robbery, or act out whatever other sin might take his fancy, confident in the knowledge that he had already bought God's forgiveness for the crime.

The works which the popes of High Renaissance Rome hoped would build their church up almost to the heavens were, in part at least, responsible for precipitating one of the greatest crises in the history of the papacy. Julius II's successor, the Medici Pope Leo X, lacked his warrior-like energy but shared his

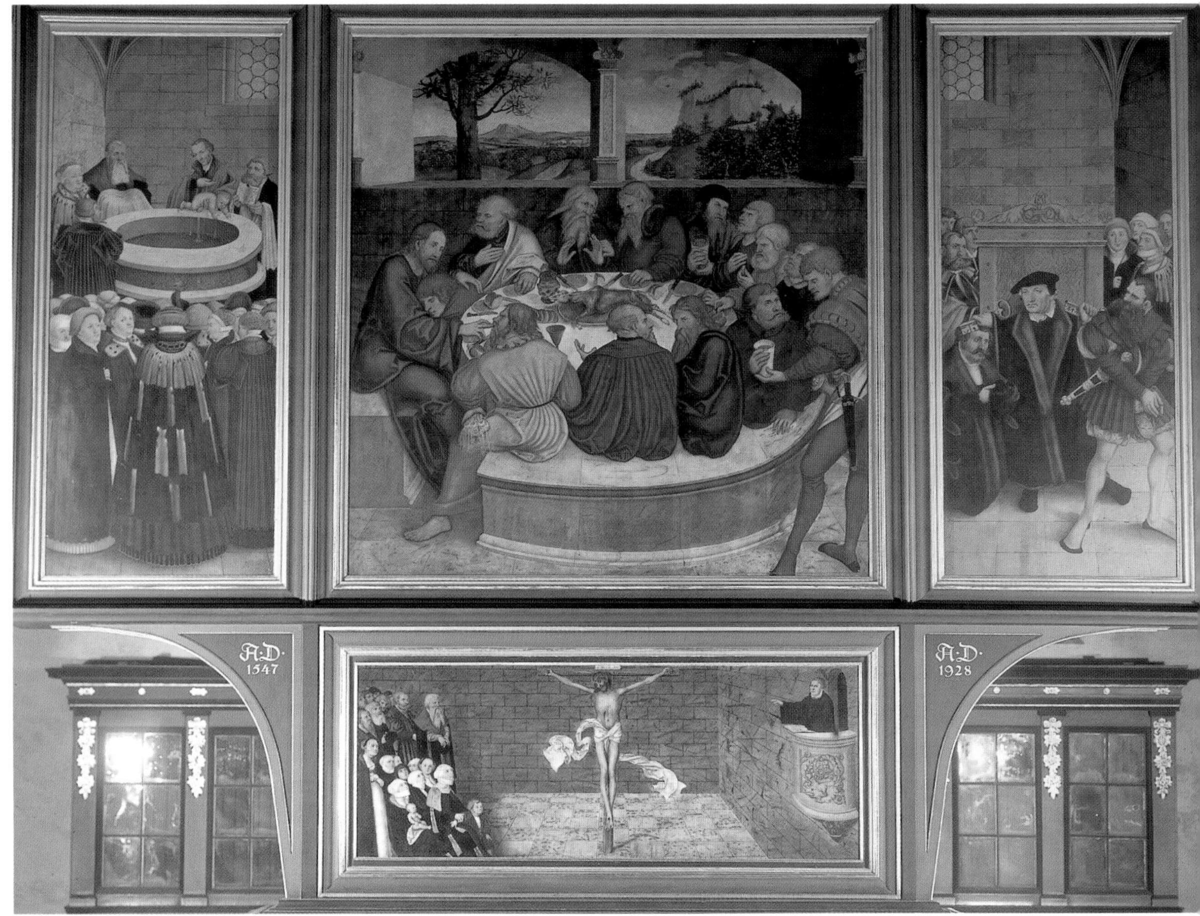


81 LUCAS CRANACH THE ELDER *The Last Supper*, Church of St Mary's, Wittenberg *c.* 1539

determination to make Rome the grandest city in the world, pursuing the policy of raising capital through the sale of Indulgences with shameless aggression. In 1514 plans had been laid to raise an unprecedented sum of money by preaching the St Peter's Indulgence, intended to fund the building of St Peter's. In 1517 the pope's German commissioner, one Johann Tetzel, went about marketing these promises of deliverance from evil to the population at large. One eyewitness who saw Tetzel selling Leo's Indulgences to workers at the St Annaberg mines in Bavaria remarked that:

> It is remarkable what this ignorant and impudent friar gave out. He said that if a Christian had slept with his mother, and placed the sum of money in the Pope's indulgence chest, the Pope had power in heaven

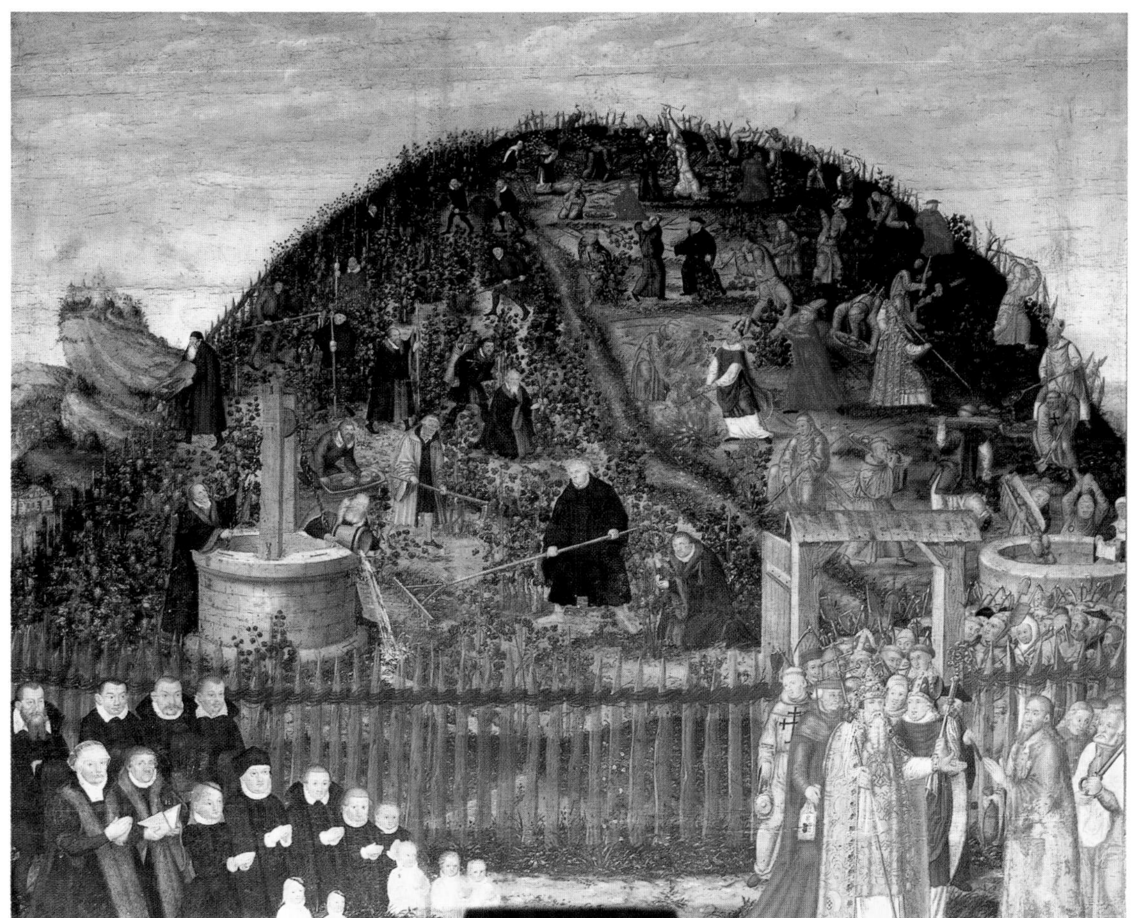

82 LUCAS CRANACH THE YOUNGER *The Lord's Vineyard* c. 1569

> and earth to forgive the sin, and if he forgave it, God must do so also... Item, so soon as the coin rang in the chest, the soul for whom the money was paid would go straightaway to heaven.[7]

No one was more outraged by Tetzel's activities on Leo's behalf than the priest and protester Martin Luther (1483–1546). Luther wrote ninety-five theses objecting to the sale of Indulgences, and on 31 October 1517 nailed them to the door of the castle church at Wittenberg. His objections, taken up by local publishers, printed and distributed all over Europe, caused widespread controversy and placed Luther in an extremely powerful position. His call for the reform of the Roman church became the most urgent issue of the day.

Unlike Erasmus, Luther was not a humanist, but he belonged to a generation whose outlook had been powerfully affected by the rise of humanist education in Germany, and which had found a rallying cry in Erasmus's call for spiritual renewal. During the 1520s Luther devised a new approach to Christian theology which made even Erasmus seem conservative by comparison. Whereas Erasmus sought to get back to the primary, original text of the Bible, Luther attempted to act on the Word of God thus revealed and purified, and to use it to reform the church itself. Thus did he, as a contemporary saying had it, 'hatch the egg which Erasmus laid'.

One of Luther's primary criticisms of the church was that it placed too much ritual between believers and God – that it acted the part of mediator where mediation was often distracting and unnecessary. In Luther's reformed church, the importance of a specialized priesthood was greatly reduced, because he thought all men should regard themselves as priests; and the number of sacraments was reduced from seven to two. Whereas Erasmus had been content to criticize the church in the hope of persuading it to change its ways, Luther was determined to take direct action against it. He did not believe that the Church of Rome was capable of reforming itself. Luther's ideas about the importance of a simple, direct faith spread and were taken up eagerly in many parts of Northern Europe. What had been a single albeit uneasily unified Christendom began to divide with startling rapidity.

Lucas Cranach the elder (1472–1553), who was Luther's lifelong friend, became in effect the official artist of the Lutheran Reformation. His altarpiece in the church of St Mary's in Wittenberg [81], Luther's home town, is a visual manifesto for the reformed faith. Only two sacraments are represented, Baptism in the right-hand panel, and the Eucharist, in the form of a *Last Supper*, in the centre, thus reflecting Luther's sacramental minimalism. The democratic tenor of Lutheran teaching, his emphasis on all mankind as a universal priesthood, is conveyed by Cranach's choice of a round table around which Jesus sits with his disciples – depicted as portraits of Luther and his circle, including one of Cranach's sons and Hans Lufft, a printer and publisher who produced and distributed many reforming texts. A German landscape may be glimpsed out of the window.

One of the side panels is a painted attack on false ritual, showing a man confessing insincerely while remaining unrepentant in his heart; on the other side, one of Luther's right-hand men, Philip Melancthon, baptizes a baby, thus demonstrating the moral right of an unordained but God-fearing scholar to perform a duty hitherto reserved for the clergy. In the predella panel, Luther faces his congregation from a pulpit and simply points with outstretched hand to the figure of Christ on the Cross. Thus was the new simplicity of Lutheran faith made manifest. The altarpiece is a prosaic and rather dull work of art, but then Luther possibly valued probity rather more than what he might have seen as the inappropriate vaulting grandeur embodied by the religious art of High Renaissance Rome.

Lucas Cranach the younger (1515–86) was to carry on the good work of defining the post-Reformation world. At the back of the same church in Wittenberg hangs his tidy-minded allegory of religious division in Europe, *The Lord's Vineyard* [82], a topical updating of Christ's parable about the good and bad vineyard labourers (Mark 12: 1–12 and Luke 20: 9–19). Europe is depicted as a vineyard which looks like a vegetable garden or plot of allotments. On the right-hand side of the path that runs through the middle, Catholics are making a hash of their part of the garden. The pope is digging up plants with his mitre while his cardinals and priests, too lazy to draw water, pour stones down the well and find a multitude of other ways of further poisoning their already barren allotment. To the left, Luther and his colleagues in black are diligently hoeing and weeding and watering their predictably fertile, verdant patch of land.

In reality Europe had rapidly become a rather more complicated place than this neat little garden of opposing theologies might imply. Just as Erasmus could not control what he had started, and had to look on powerless as Luther drew his own, more radical conclusions to problems he had first identified, so Luther, too, soon found himself unable to shape the religious revolution he had unleashed. During the 1520s his ideas spread and mutated. Christendom was not merely riven in two, but split into many.

## ROME SACKED

During the years of the Lutheran Reformation, the terrors predicted in Revelation became steadily more entangled, in many people's minds, with the actual events of their troubled time. The opposition between Protestant and Catholic could easily be made to seem like a realization of St John's violent and powerfully ambiguous prophecies. Large numbers of Christian believers became convinced that the final conflict was about to be played out. This was certainly the message embodied in much contemporary satire. The Apocalypse became an even more popular subject with artists than it had been at the start of the century, but now it was treated in a more pointed way. The evil monsters that swarm through St John's vision, such as the Antichrist or the Scarlet Whore of Babylon, were given

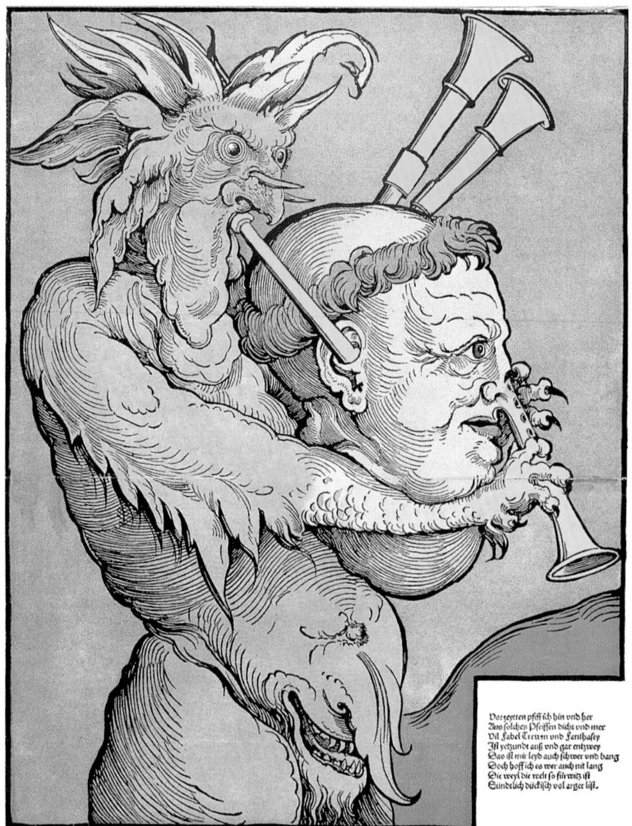


83 ERHARD SCHÖN *Devil Playing the Bagpipes c.* 1530

pope's mitres. Catholic priests were depicted as instruments of the devil. German satires were thronged with topical details, which were included in order to single out the enemy. Catholic priests were cast as instruments of the Devil, and one of Dürer's most prolific followers in Nuremberg, Erhard Schön, created a wonderfully literal variation on this theme in his print of *c.*1530, *Devil Playing the Bagpipes* [83] – the bagpipes in question being a corpulent caricature of a priest's face.

Artists in Northern Europe seem to have been much more alive to the polemical effectiveness of print technology than their counterparts in Rome. Papal propaganda still tended to be produced in the form of large frescos, to impress envoys or diplomatic visitors to the city – images which were, inevitably, far less widely disseminated than those being produced in such quantities north of the Alps. Rome was losing the propaganda war, and perhaps in reflection of this it

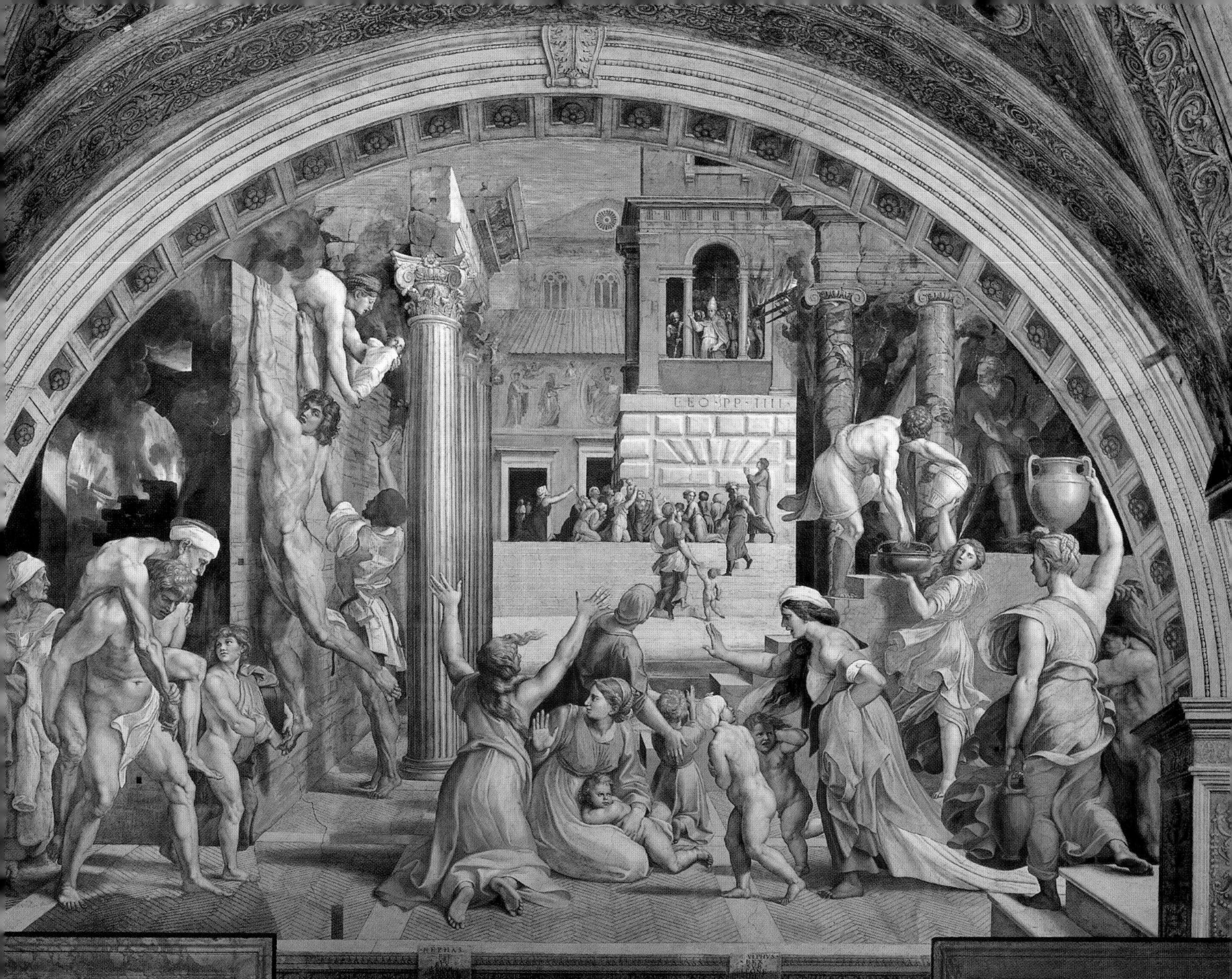

RAPHAEL *Fire in the Borgo*, Stanza dell'Incendio, Vatican Palace, Rome *c.* 1514–17

seems possible to discern a lessening of conviction behind such propaganda as was being created in the city.

The chief work of painting created for Pope Leo X by Raphael during the years of Lutheran controversy was a cycle of frescos in the Stanza dell'Incendio, or Stanza of the Fire in the Borgo [84]. Pride of place in this, the penultimate of Raphael's Vatican decorations, before his premature death in 1520, was given to the depiction of a miracle performed by Leo X's namesake, Leo IV, in 847. The picture was meant to emphasize papal authority but instead it has a panic-stricken air. According to legend, a fire had broken out in the Borgo, an area near the papal apartments, which the pope miraculously extinguished with a benediction from his balcony. Raphael chose to depict the moment just before the conflagration ceased, when public panic was at its height. To the right, a group of graceful young women in flowing classical robes pass pitchers and bowls of water to a wiry grey-haired man desperately trying to douse the flames raging in a classical portico. To their left, a group of men, women and children in various states of undress are fleeing from the conflagration. In the centre, the pope stands on his balcony above a beseeching crowd and calls for divine intervention with a gesture of his hand. The painting is unconvincing, partly because of its scale relationships. Raphael was evidently more interested in the foreground panic than in the papal miracle being enacted in the middle distance. The pope, miniaturized by the perspective scheme of the picture, seems a small and unconvincing figure. He has a weak chin and bad posture. It is difficult to believe that the fire will, indeed, go out.

Raphael's inability or reluctance to sing the praises of Leo with quite the verve he had devoted to singing the praises of Julius seems, with hindsight, like a form of perceptiveness. Leo's election was a disaster for Rome. 'God has given us the papacy,' he famously remarked, 'now let us enjoy it.'[8] His spendthrift tendencies weakened the church financially, and as one contemporary satire expressed it: 'Leo has eaten up three pontificates: the treasury of Julius II, the revenues of his own pontificate, and those of his successor.'[9] His inability to stem the tide of Erasmian and, latterly, Lutheran discontent with the Roman church proved even more damaging to the papacy. The full consequences of his inaction were not apparent at the time of his death, and others reaped what he had sown.

The Reformation was finally and viciously brought home to the population of Rome during the papacy of Clement VII. In May 1527 many thousands of Charles V's imperial troops, who had been based in Northern Italy, but who had been unpaid for months, moved south to Rome. They captured the city, looting and pillaging, raping and murdering as they went. On the first day alone, 8000 of its inhabitants were indiscriminately slaughtered. Eventually, 23,000 out of a total population of 55,000 were to die. Many of them were tortured. The atrocities committed were, in part at least, fuelled by a spirit of religious sectarianism. The most bloodthirsty looters and pillagers were radical Lutherans. They were determined to humiliate Rome, to visit upon it a punishment of veritably biblical proportions. Priests were stripped naked and forced to take part in obscene parodies of the Mass, before being butchered. Nuns were raped and killed. Such acts can only have been encouraged by the belief that if the pope was really Anti-Christ, as Luther's supporters had argued in words and shown in art, then his allies must be the human embodiment of the forces of evil.

At the height of the Sack, Luther's name was scratched into Raphael's fresco of the *Disputa* in the Vatican apartments. Despite subsequent repair and restoration, this significant graffito is still legible when the fresco is lit by a raking light.

A picture intended to block out the unwelcome reality of dispute within Christendom – a painting which masked real disagreement with a show of debate, subsumed within universal theological agreement – had been scarred by the very dissenters whose existence it ignored. The moment when the forces of Reformation finally punctured the skin of High Renaissance Rome is thus captured for ever. The knife that cut Luther's name into the fresco may have been put to bloodier uses besides.

## MICHELANGELO'S RECANTATION

The Sack brought home the depth of the divide separating Lutherans and Catholics and the extent to which it had transformed the landscape of Christendom. Lutheran ideas had a profound effect on men and women everywhere, regardless of whether they chose to call themselves Protestants or remained loyal to the Roman church. Luther's anti-materialism and his belief in the importance of man's direct, unmediated relationship with God provoked a pan-European reassessment of the very foundations of the Christian faith. All Christians, not just Northern European Christians, underwent a kind of reformation during the 1530s and 1540s.

In Rome there was, it is said, a deathly hush after the Sack. It was as if the Apocalypse had indeed come to pass, and the vanity and aspirations of the popes had brought their own reward. The Catholic church finally began to reform itself, although it was by now too late for the breach between Protestant and Catholic to be healed. The artist whose work most fully reflected this shift in priorities was Michelangelo. His last two frescos, in the Pauline Chapel, which adjoins the Sistine Chapel, depict *The Conversion of Saul* [85] and *The Crucifixion of St Peter* [86]. Commissioned by Pope Paul III in 1542, they are awkward and in many ways ugly pictures, brusque, blatant and almost savage in their piety.

The first to be completed represents *The Conversion of Saul*. Michelangelo treated the subject in a thoroughly personal way, showing a disdain for harmonies of composition or any other merely aesthetic grace. Above, Christ descends from the heavens like an avenging angel and casts a thunderbolt with his right hand. Beneath, on the ground, Saul lies dazed and temporarily blinded while his bolting horse rears and his attendants scatter. The initial impression is one of great busyness, of a momentous event taking place amid obscuring crowds of ancillary figures. The sky is thick with Christ's heavenly host and the earth is congested by Saul's fleeing followers. But Michelangelo is patently uninterested in the majority

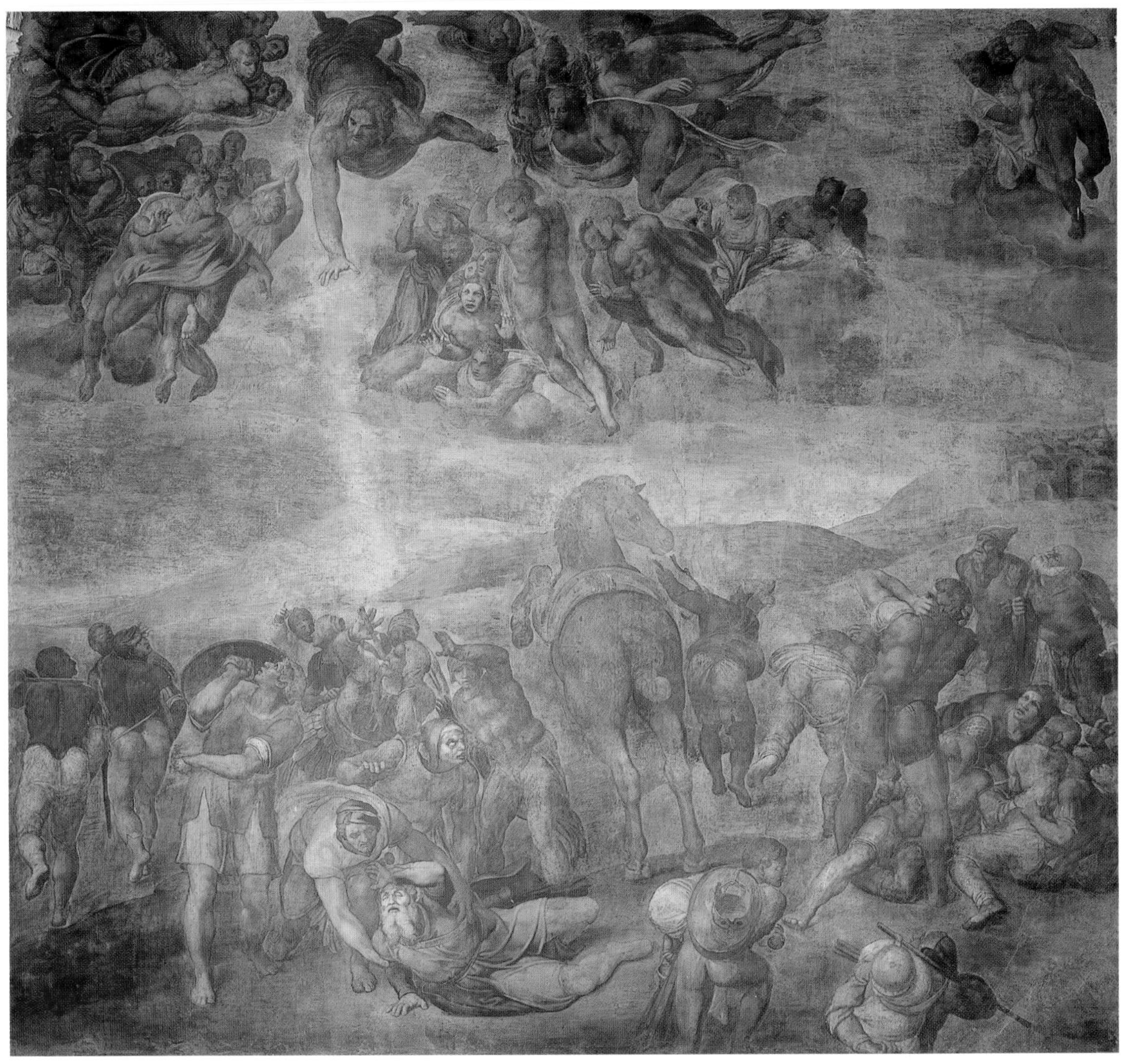

85 MICHELANGELO *The Conversion of Saul* 1542–5

of the figures with which he has staffed the scene. His attention is so exclusively focused on the relationship between the all-powerful Saviour and the stunned Saul that the rest seem to fly off like chaff in the wind. Christ above is the middle of a centrifuge, a still point of authority from which his attendant angels seem to spin away – an effect enhanced by the curious disjointed groupings which Michelangelo devised for this heavenly host, which makes them look like the broken pieces of a jigsaw puzzle – while Saul's stocky but inelegant followers are almost all running away, as if trying their best to get out of a picture which has no place for them.

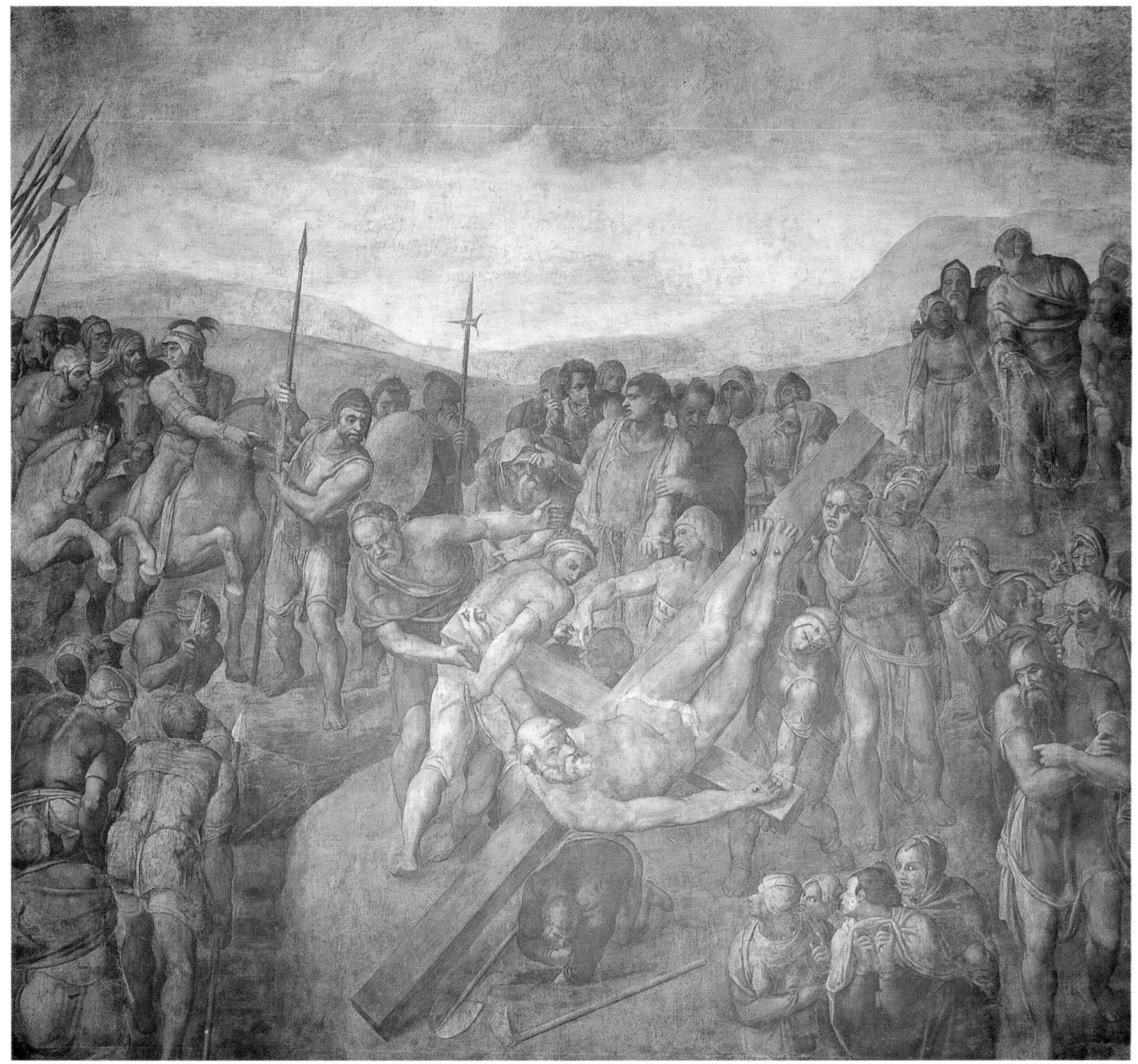

86 MICHELANGELO *The Crucifixion of St Peter c.* 1545–9

The painting is not a success, exactly, but it is powerfully expressive of the artist's changed priorities in the last decades of his life. Here Michelangelo is no longer a Renaissance man, in the sense that the desire to compete with the art of ancient Greece and Rome has ceased to motivate him. Beauty holds no appeal. All that matters, Michelangelo now declares, is blind faith, and the only parts of the painting to have been handled with true conviction are the two figures who communicate the spiritual heart of its message: Christ above and Saul down below, whose eyes are closed and whose pained but rapt expression speaks of private communion with God. Michelangelo painted Saul not as a young man, as he is in the Bible, but old and grey. It is possible that the artist intended the figure as a kind of self-portrait.

Vasari, who knew Michelangelo well, left a memorable description of the artist in his old age, ascetic and evidently somewhat indifferent to appearances:

> Michelangelo's constitution was very sound, for he was lean and sinewy and … he could always endure any fatigue and had no infirmity, save that in his old age he suffered from dysuria and gravel … As he grew old he took to wearing buskins of dogskin on his legs, next to the skin; he went for months at a time without taking them off, then when he removed the buskins often his skin came off as well… His face was round, the brow square and lofty, furrowed by seven straight lines, and the temples projected considerably beyond the ears, which were rather large and prominent. His body was in proportion to the face, or perhaps rather large; his nose was somewhat squashed, having been broken…; his eyes can best be described as being small, the colour of horn, flecked with bluish and yellowish sparks. His eyebrows were sparse, his lips thin (the lower lip being thicker and projecting a little), the chin well formed and well proportioned with the rest, his hair black, but streaked with many white hairs and worn fairly short, as was his beard, which was forked and not very thick.[10]

Late in 1549 the old man in the dirty buskins completed *The Crucifixion of St Peter*, yet more intimidating and impressive than *The Conversion of Saul*. A solemn, baleful painting, it sticks in the memory like a fishbone in the throat. On a barren hillside a crowd has gathered to witness the martyrdom of Peter, who has been nailed to a cross which is being lifted into position by a gang of burly Roman soldiers. According to the biblical Apocrypha, Peter insisted on being crucified upside down, and that is how we see him – except that he is the one looking at us. He has raised himself up and wheels round awkwardly on the instrument of his torture to stare us in the eye. His torturers seem not actively malicious but passive, hypnotized, like sleepwalkers acting out a compulsion (it is possible that Michelangelo was influenced by Calvinism and its severe doctrine of predestination). All is terror and stunned silence. The grim face of Peter is overpoweringly urgent, nailing you to the spot as surely as the saint's feet are nailed to the heavy cross of blond wood. It is difficult to think of any other picture, anywhere in the world, in which the protagonist looks you in the face and will not let go, quite like this. All the other figures are ghosts, the soldiers arriving in an irrelevant clamour in the upper left-hand corner epitomizing the irrelevance of human history itself – a busy but pointless march of mundane events across the field of the world – to Michelangelo's vision of things at this moment in his life.

Peter, the Rock on whom Christ built his church, symbolized the papacy, but Michelangelo's picture goes beyond papal propaganda. It looks more like a reminder to the popes of their duty to live, not for worldly glory, but by the memory of the very first pope's life and sacrifice – placed at the heart of the Vatican by a man who had worked for the papacy, and had seen the foibles and frailties of living popes at first hand, for more than forty years. Many years earlier, Pope Leo X had confided to the painter Sebastiano del Piombo: 'Michelangelo is terrible; one cannot deal with him.' St Peter, like Saul in the fresco opposite, is possibly an idealized self-portrait. Walking into the chapel and finding this apparition feels like suddenly coming face to face with old, devout, fiery Michelangelo himself.

The pope who had commissioned *The Crucifixion of St Peter* died in 1549, before the work was finished. Michelangelo recognized that his own time was running out. Shortly afterwards he wrote a sonnet in which he announces the end of his life and renounces art. The artist dedicated it to Giorgio Vasari, who printed it in his Life of Michelangelo. The best English translation is perhaps that by Elizabeth Jennings:

> Already now my life has run its course,
> And, like a fragile boat on a rough sea,
> I reach the place which everyone must cross
> And give account of life's activity.
> Now I know well it was a fantasy
> That made me think art could be made into
> An idol or king. Though all men do
> This, they do it half-unwillingly.
> The loving thoughts, so happy and so vain,
> Are finished now. A double death comes near –
> The one is sure, the other is a threat.
> Painting and sculpture cannot any more
> Quieten the soul that turns to God again
> To God, who, on the cross, for us was set.[11]

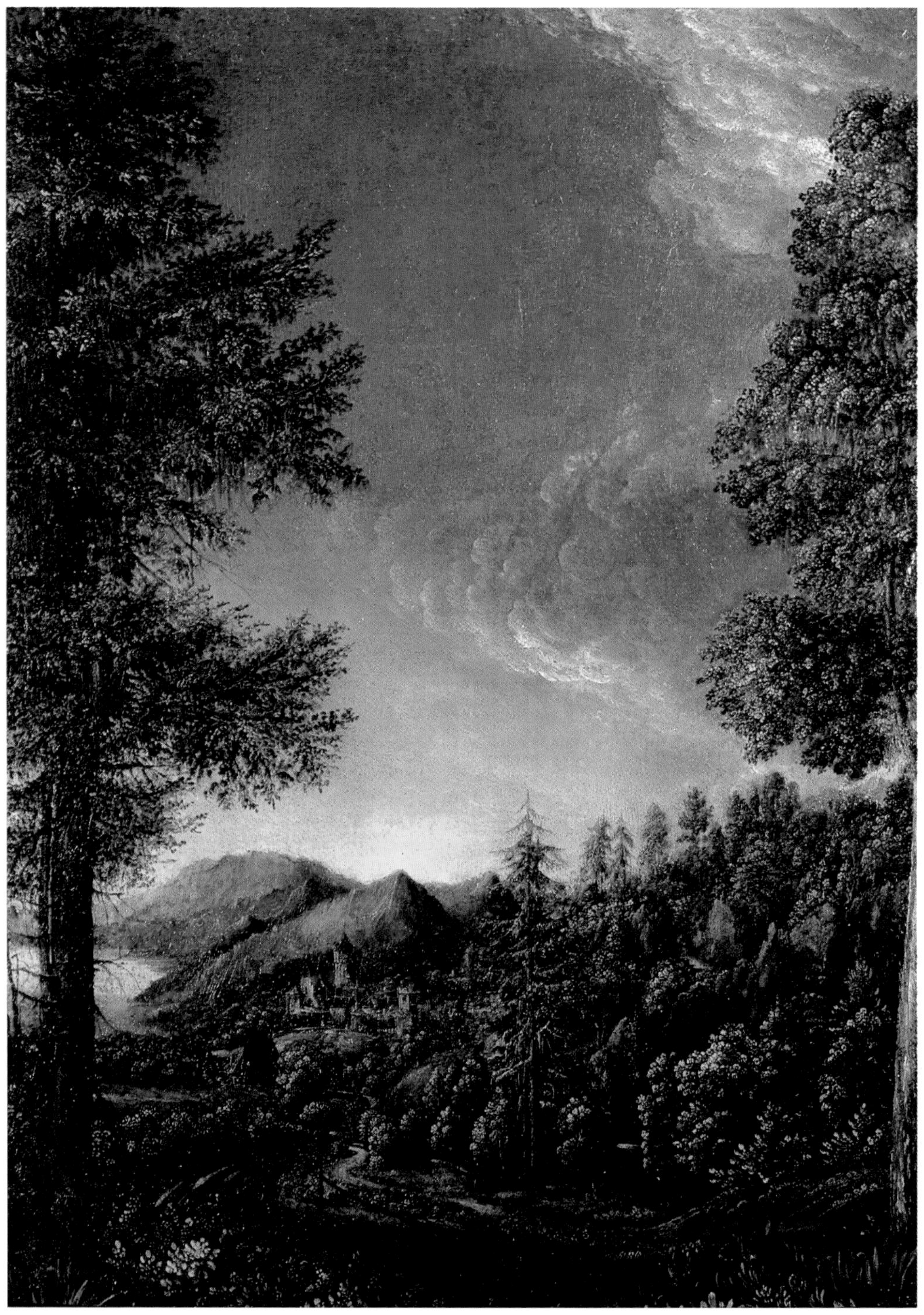

87 ALBRECHT ALTDORFER *Landscape with Castle c.* 1520–32

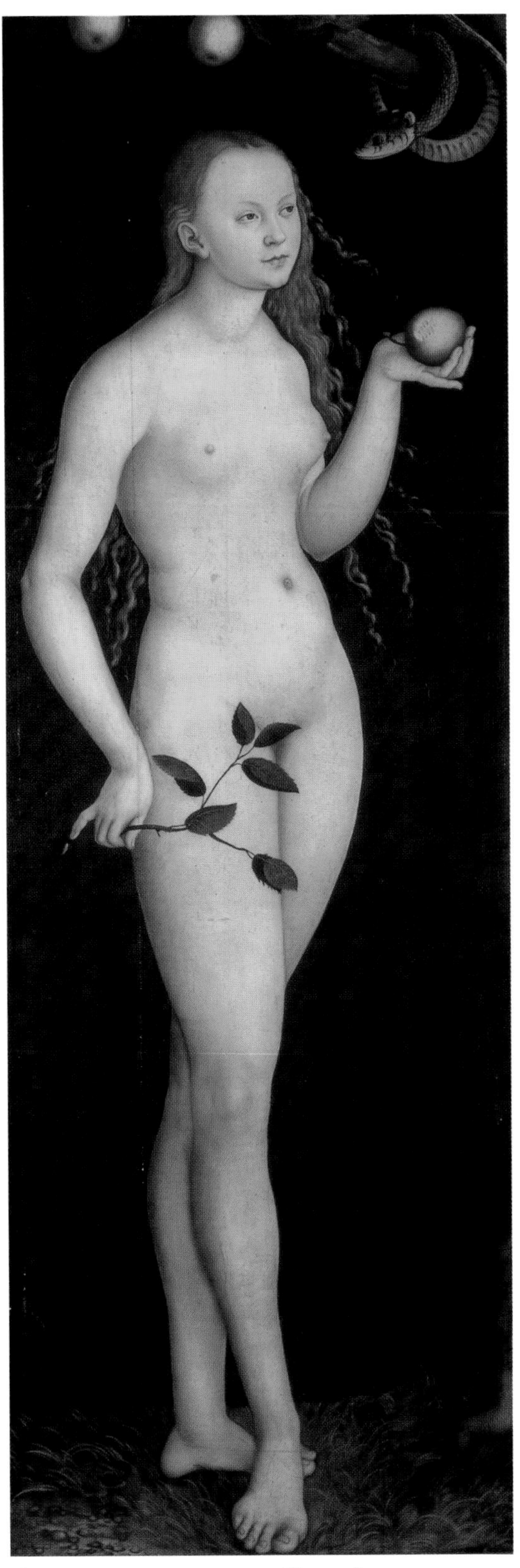

88 LUCAS CRANACH THE ELDER *Eve* 1528

When Michelangelo painted his last pictures he was in the middle of his own, personal Reformation, rejecting the sophistication and grace of his earlier works, turning his back on the passion and love which he had once brought to the depiction of the male nude, creating an art which spoke of its own creator's disillusionment with art itself, and his readiness for the beyond. In the Pauline Chapel, he snapped his wand.

## A WAVERING DANCE

In Northern Europe artists did not have to turn on their own work. It was done for them. One strain of Protestant thought came to hold that religious images got in the way of man's relationship with God, and huge quantities of religious art were burnt and smashed. In Britain, where the radical leaders of the Churches of England and Scotland developed a particularly virulent and extreme version of Luther's ideas, more or less all pre-Reformation religious art was destroyed.

The Northern Reformation's impact on art was by no means entirely negative, however, and one of the most striking developments of the post-Reformation period would be the migration of religious energies into secular forms of painting. The rise of Northern European landscape painting can be partly attributed to this vein of displaced spiritual expression. The mystical landscapes of the Bavarian Albrecht Altdorfer (*c.* 1480–1538), a contemporary of Dürer and Cranach the elder, are characterized by clouds tracing patterns of sublime beauty above woodland so thick that the whole seems to embody some vitalist principle of Creation itself [87]. The advent of Protestantism was also a catalyst for the development of new, secular forms of painting such as the portrait, Protestants being by definition prone to introspection. Mythological and genre painting flourished too in Northern Europe, so to say that Protestant art was only and always sober would be a distortion of the truth. For example, Lucas Cranach the elder gave visual expression to Luther's belief that sexual arousal is good for the soul in a large number of allegorical erotic paintings. The Cranach nude, a long-necked temptress with small, apple-shaped breasts and a mischievous expression in her eyes [88], is a reminder that Northern post-Reformation art could take many unpredictable forms.

The philosophical consequences of Reformation and its aftermath were just as devastating – more devastating, ultimately – than its theological consequences, or its consequences for art and artists. At the start of the sixteenth century it was still possible to believe in the possibility of absolute truth. By the middle of the century that belief had been irrevocably eroded.

The Italian humanists had dreamed of bringing all belief systems, the totality of human knowledge, no less, into a grand unifying synthesis of natural and revealed truth. Raphael had painted this dream on to the walls of the Stanza della Segnatura, Julius II's ideal library. But it was a dream that failed. Erasmus and, following him, Luther and the early Protestants had dreamed of purifying the text of the Bible and thereby recovering the Word of God. This too was a dream of universal concord, although a very different one. It also failed, because its chief result was not unanimous agreement about God's purposes, but further disagreement on what those purposes might be. The Word of God is not easily fathomable and the reformers rediscovered its imponderability.

Across the divide separating Catholic and Protestant there was a recognition among many of the leading minds of the period that the very fabric of Europe had changed. 'The only thing that is certain is that nothing is certain,' was the stoical maxim adopted by a spokesmen of this new culture ruled by doubt and uncertainty, the French essayist Michel de Montaigne (1533–92). Montaigne was a learned bibliophile and humanist. Yet he considered his huge library as conclusive proof that philosophy invariably leads to disagreement and conflict – a truth borne out by his personal experience, as a man living through wars of religion in France during the second half of the sixteenth century.

In his essay 'On Books'[12] Montaigne defined his pleasure in reading. He reads, he says, not in order to attain a state of enlightenment, certainly not in hope of finding out the truth. He reads in order to discover and enjoy the multiplicity of human consciousnesses which have preceded his own – and to savour each in the full glory of its idiosyncrasy. Montaigne's library is neither Raphael's assembly of learned concord nor Erasmus's workshop of truth. It has room only for humanity. It is a place thronged with competing subjectivities, each to be cultivated – sceptically but sympathetically – in its unrepeatable difference. Books, wrote Montaigne, testify to man's multifariousness, and to 'the diversity of his dogmas and fantasies'. To be civilized, for him, is not to strive for ultimate enlightenment, but to strive for reconciliation to its unattainability.

Montaigne was a dry writer with a light touch and few pretensions. Yet he summed up, in his glancing way, a great turn in the mind of man. Henceforth, the process of civilization itself would be perceived differently: not as one of consensual advance towards *the* truth, but as an almost random accumulation of individual truths and self-expressions. For Montaigne, uncertainty is the very rule of human existence: 'Constancy itself is nothing but a languishing and wavering dance.'[13]

CHAPTER FIVE

# LIGHT AND LIBERTY

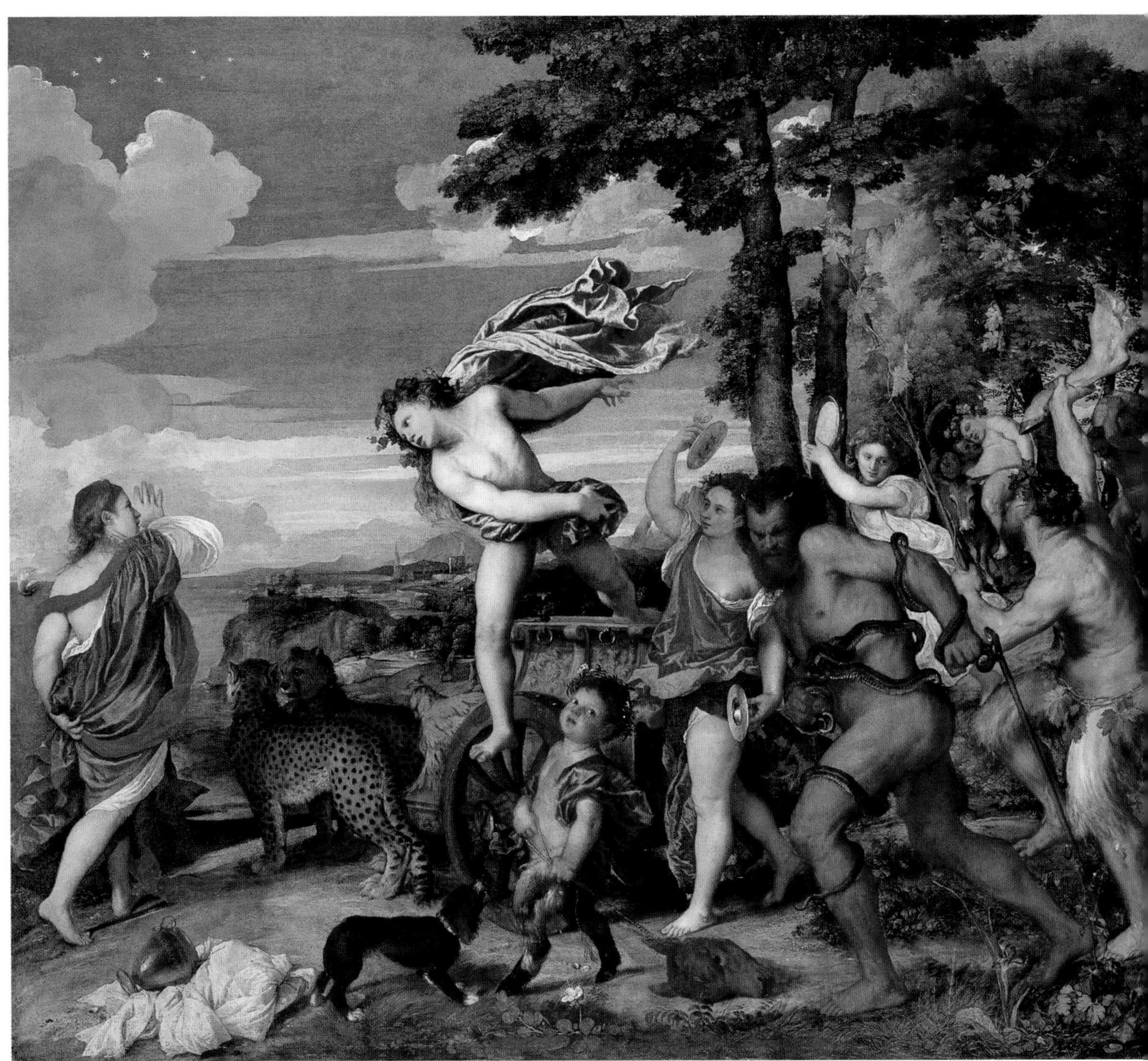

89 TITIAN *Bacchus and Ariadne* 1522–3

Venice is the best exemplar of human wit and ingenuity.
Despair of man and go to Venice: you will cease to despair.
If human beings can build a city like this,
their souls deserve to be saved.

ANTHONY BURGESS, foreword to *Venice: An Illustrated Anthology*, 1988

When first upon the traveller's sight opened the long ranges of columned palaces – each with its black boat moored at the portal – each with its image cast down, beneath its feet, upon that green pavement which every breeze broke into new fantasies of tessellation … when first … the gondolier's cry, 'Ah! Stali,' struck sharp upon the ear, and the prow turned aside under the mighty cornices that half met over the narrow canal … and when at last that boat darted forth upon the breadth of silver sea, across which the front of the Ducal palace, flushed with its sanguine veins, looks to the snowy dome of Our Lady of Salvation, it was no marvel that the mind should be so deeply entranced by the visionary charm of a scene so beautiful and so strange, as to forget the darker truths of its history and its being.

JOHN RUSKIN, *The Stones of Venice*, 1853

## LOVE AT FIRST SIGHT

Ariadne has been abandoned by her lover, Theseus. Suddenly awake, clothes in disarray, she waves desperately towards the sea, where his ship is no more than a disappearing speck on the blue horizon. But even as one lover departs another miraculously materializes, announced by a clash of cymbals. As she turns to look she sees the wine god, Bacchus, leaping towards her from a golden chariot drawn by leopards. Wreathed in vine leaves, a windblown crescent of pink-purple silk billowing about his shoulders, he is frozen for ever in mid-air with a love-smitten expression on his face. Arrested in the midst of his revels, accompanied by a retinue of nymphs and satyrs who form a now forgotten bacchanal, he seems stunned by emotion. Bacchus stares at Ariadne. Ariadne answers his gaze. The energy crossing the void between them is almost palpable. The stretch of sky that separates their staring, desiring faces seems itself shot through with feeling – a dawn sky, blue modulated with traces of yellow, appropriate to the theme of dawning love.

Titian (or Tiziano Vecellio, *c.* 1485–1576) painted *Bacchus and Ariadne* [89] in Venice at the start of the 1520s. Now, like so many great Venetian pictures, it is no longer in the city itself but in the National Gallery in London. The painter's true theme, despite appearances, is not the encounter of Bacchus and the abandoned Ariadne on the isle of Naxos. Titian has taken mythology as a pretext to dwell on an aspect of life. *Bacchus and Ariadne* is an unforgettable painting of love at first sight. The artist has depicted the way in which the world seems to come to a stop at the moment when people fall for each other.

Titian's work takes us to the heart of the Venetian contribution to Renaissance civilization as a whole. If the Renaissance is regarded as a process through which man opened his mind to unexplored aspects of the world, and of his own humanity, then Venice, just as much as Florence, has to be seen as one of its capital cities. Florence and Venice represent, in many respects, the polar opposites of Italian Renaissance civilization – the point has often been made, but it is no less true for that – and if the genius of Florence showed itself, above all, in sculpture, Venice showed its true colours in the field of painting. Venetian painters looked at the overlooked. They painted sexual desire. They found new ways of depicting death. They painted the human face with unparalleled sensitivity. They painted landscape, and the fall of light. In painting all of those things, they changed the way in which people thought about painting itself.

*Bacchus and Ariadne* was done on a piece of canvas 175 cm high and 191 cm broad. It was made from very little: some cloth, covered with pigments made from ground up stone, plant extracts, coloured earth. Yet it is, none the less, an entire world, vibrant and vital, full of life and passion. Why should it have been the Venetians who made so much of this humble art form, painting? Perhaps the answer is to be found in their city, which was itself a world erected on mud and silt – a place conjured up, like a picture, from almost nothing at all.

## BUILT ON MUD

According to one legend Venice was founded by a band of noble Trojans, not long after the fall of Troy. The truth is slightly different, although Venice was indeed born out of destruction and pillage, and founded by refugees.

A cluster of mud flats and small islands off the Adriatic coast of the Italian mainland was settled in Roman times by groups of fishermen. These settlements lay at the watery fringe of the Roman province of Venetia which, following the break-up of the Roman Empire, became part of the Eastern, or Byzantine Empire, ruled from Constantinople. But following the Lombard invasions of the late sixth century, the province was overrun and many of its citizens took refuge in the lagoons, taking with them as much of their wealth and property as they could.

Scattered fishermen's enclaves, for centuries the only human habitation on the lagoon, were colonized by ever-growing numbers of refugees. A city sprang up, its shape determined by the patterns of silt deposited by tidal waters as they ebbed and flowed through the lagoon. Venetia squeezed itself into Venice. Protected by the sea, the Venetians retained their independence from the Lombard kingdom. After the fall of Ravenna in 751, they came to consider themselves the last unconquered part of the old empire in all of Italy. Although Venice eventually became independent of Byzantium – Venetian crusaders even sacked Constantinople in 1204 – the city's art and institutions would reflect Byzantine influence for centuries.

The island of Torcello still gives a vivid impression of the first lagoon settlements. Lying about 11 km to the north-east of Venice, it was settled very early on in the troubled history of the Venetian lagoons, and by the fourteenth century had a population of some 20,000. Now, thanks to the gradual decay of the Venetian maritime empire and the incursions of malaria, much of the island has reverted to its natural state and few people live there. Served only once each hour by the local water-bus service, the place often has a melancholy air.

One of the first things that strikes the visitor to this marooned, lonely island town is the sheer pragmatism of the first Venetians. The amount of work involved

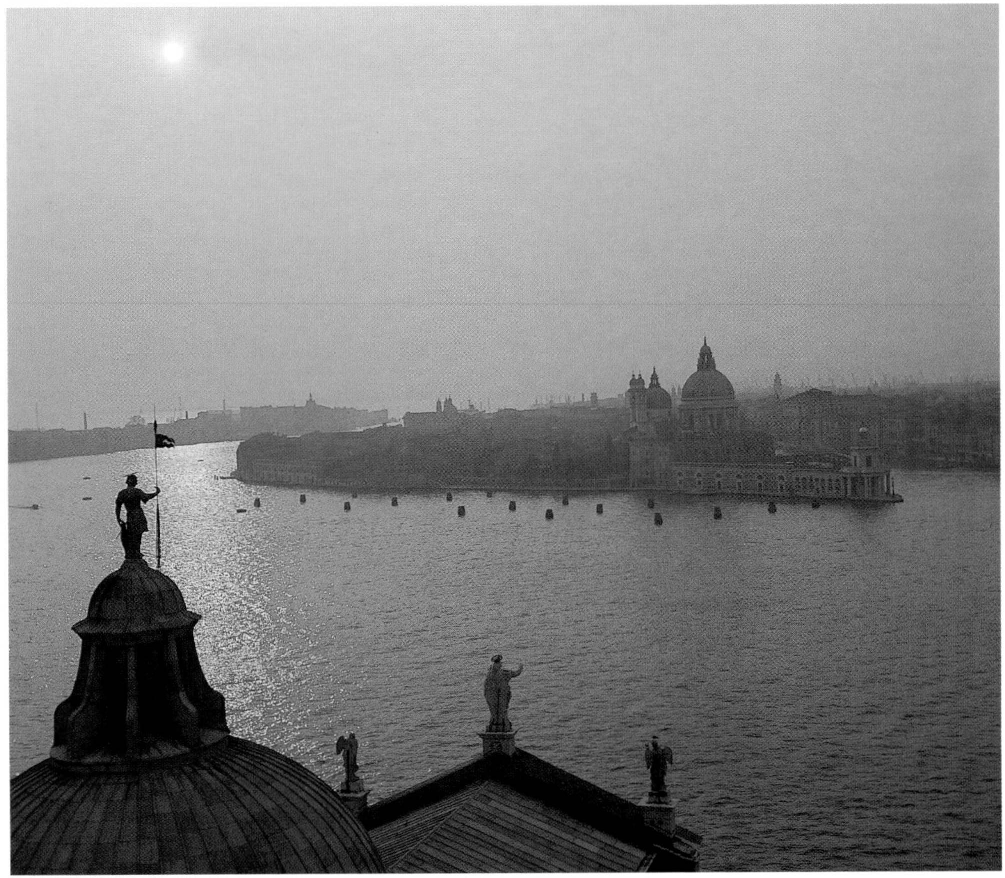

90 Venice from the island San Giorgio Maggiore

in raising a town in such a place as this – transporting stone, digging foundations, shoring up fortifications – must have been immense. The notion that Venice is a fundamentally romantic place is exposed, in Torcello, as a romantic folly. The Venetians were the most practical of people, their whole lives built on a strategy for survival, every building raised a testimony to their ingenuity.

The Bishop of Altino transferred his seat to Torcello in 638 when forced to flee from the mainland. Santa Maria dell'Assunta, which dates from that time, is Venice's first cathedral. Its interior was richly decorated with mosaics and Byzantine-style relief carvings, in a long and intermittent campaign of work stretching from the seventh to the twelfth century. It enshrines the Christian as opposed to the classical foundation myth of the Venetians. According to this version of events their city did not spring from the ashes of pagan Troy, but came

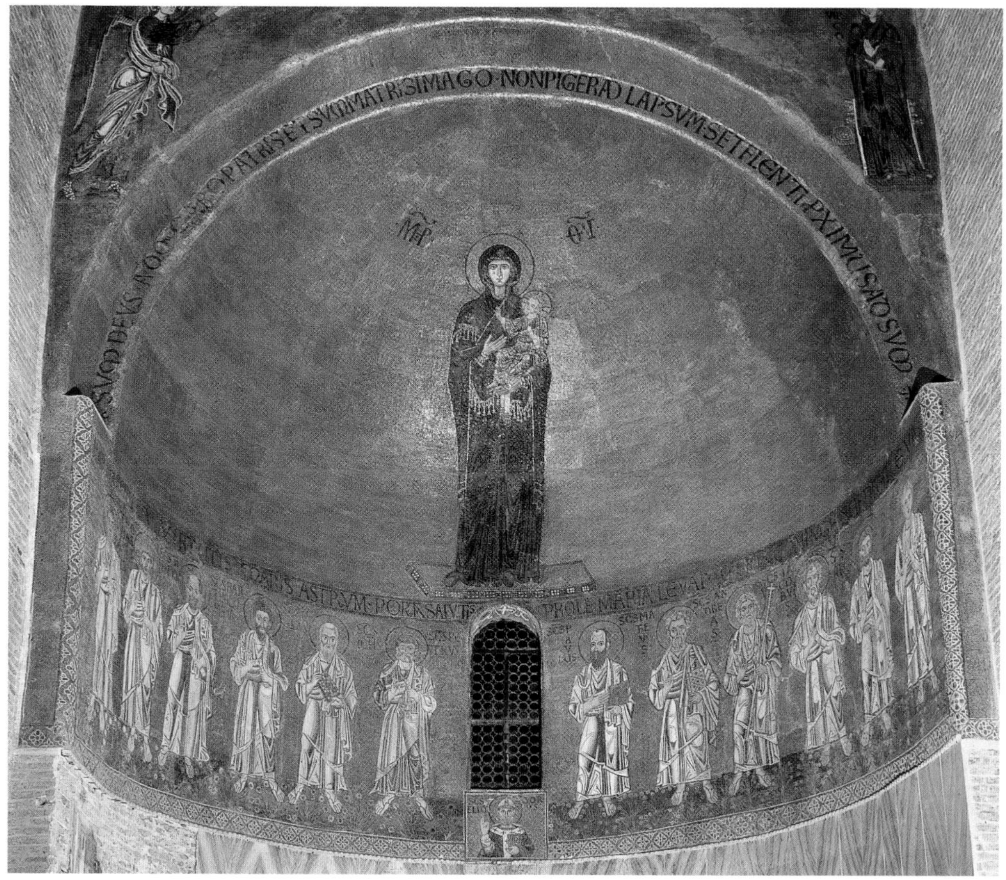

91 *Virgin and Child*, apse, Santa Maria dell'Assunta, Torcello, late 12th century

into being under the blessing and protection of the Virgin Mary on the feast day of the Annunciation (the Venetians had little difficulty in combining Christian and classical myths of themselves). In the glittering semi-dome above the high altar and forming the focal point of adoration and worship, there is a mosaic image of the Virgin with the Christ child in her arms [91]. Standing in a glittering field of golden tesserae which represents the infinite beatitude of heaven, she is a beacon of hope and divine love. She towers over the congregation like a lighthouse over a sea of gold.

The cathedral at Torcello inspired John Ruskin to a passage of prose as highly coloured as any Venetian painting. In *The Stones of Venice* he compared the building's shape to that of a great boat, and advised anyone who would truly understand the spirit of the Venetians themselves to 'repeople its veined deck with the shadows of its dead mariners, and strive to feel in himself the strength of heart that was kindled within them, when … the pillars of it had settled in the sand, and the roof of it had been closed against the angry sky that was still reddened by the fires of their homesteads.'[1] There is a kernel of truth within his Gothick Victorian fantasy about dead mariners and their strong feelings. The special qualities of Venetian thought and art are inseparable from the Venetian sense of having been persecuted and having survived.

## LOOKING OUTWARDS

Venice, according to the boast of one of its medieval chroniclers, was the freest of Italy's many free cities. It had no city walls because the lagoon was its moat; it had no palace guard except workers from its chief shipyard; it had no parade ground for military drill and display except the sea. The Venetians were unique not merely by virtue of where they lived, but where they were forced to look for the means to subsist. Like a city in a desert, Venice at the start of her history had precious little farmland to feed her inhabitants, while the lagoon yielded only fish and salt. Venetian merchant-sailors gradually developed an unparalleled network of long-distance trade routes. To maximize profits the Venetians dealt in goods such as oriental silks and spices, which were precious but not bulky. By the fourteenth century, Venice was one of the most thriving metropolitan centres in Western Europe, with a population of some 120,000. Venetian ships sailed to Alexandria and Beirut in the Eastern Mediterranean, to Constantinople and into the Black Sea, through the straits of Gibraltar to north-western Europe and around the southern tip of Italy to Sicily and North Africa.

Carvings of Moors' heads and camels are still to be found all over the city, together with bits and pieces from Roman antiquity and quantities of loot gathered on escapades here, there and everywhere. The famous horses of San Marco, taken from Constantinople, are the most conspicuous of such accumulated treasures. The bones of St Mark himself, the patron saint of the city, which were appropriated from his tomb in Alexandria in the ninth century, are the most holy. The pair of enterprising Venetian merchants responsible for this *sacra furta*, or holy theft, hid the relics in a basket of pork to put prying Muslim customs officials off the scent. It sometimes feels as though Venice itself was not so much a city built as one begged, borrowed and stolen.

The multi-racial, market-oriented, outward-looking nature of Venetian Renaissance society – together with its fondness for the textures and colours of the bazaar – is reflected in the surfaces of its art. When Vittore Carpaccio (*c.* 1460–1525/6) was commissioned in 1488 to paint a number of pictures telling the story of St Ursula's life he reinvented hagiography as maritime adventure. The saint's life unfolds in successive panoramas which seem to invoke the amplitude of Venetian horizons. Almost every episode is a scene of departure or arrival, of richly dressed delegations meeting to greet one another, to exchange views and to do a little business. Ambassadors arrive, ambassadors return, ambassadors depart, in successive scenes of the painter's now obscure narrative, while behind them, always, there are ships, pennants aflutter, sails swelled by the wind. If it is difficult to concentrate on the religious storytelling that is, perhaps, because the painter himself found such concentration difficult. He has distilled the energies that animated Venice itself: its wanderlust, its love of fine stuffs and fabrics, its sense that diplomacy, the act of getting along with others, is what makes the world – *its* world, certainly – go round.

## THE CULT OF IMPERSONALITY

At the centre of Renaissance Venice, its unmoved mover, the key to its power and prosperity, stood the figure of the doge. It is impossible to begin to understand the city without understanding the significance which he and his office held. In about 1501 Giovanni Bellini painted the portrait of *Doge Leonardo Loredan* [92]. It is fascinating, not because of what it shows but because of all it conceals. We see a man, bust-length on a field of blue, splendidly garbed in a damascened silk tunic and matching *corno*, the Venetian equivalent of a royal crown. But look into his eyes and there is not a flicker of legible emotion, and hardly a hint of character. Bellini's doge is poker-faced, impassive. This is the image of a man who has been subsumed into his office, of a person who has suppressed his personality to become the figurehead of the state.

Renaissance Venice, like Renaissance Florence, was a republic. But the Venetians' distrust of individual pride and power was even more pronounced than that of the Florentines. The office of the doge was the pre-eminent expression of this. He was elected from a restricted group of patrician families – not, importantly, a single family – through a complicated system of nominations. He was often old and although he played a vital symbolic part in the life of the city he was discouraged from holding active power. Like the kings and queens of the rest of Europe, he was invested with a divine right to rule, for according to Venetian belief he was St Mark's representative on earth. But true power rested with a

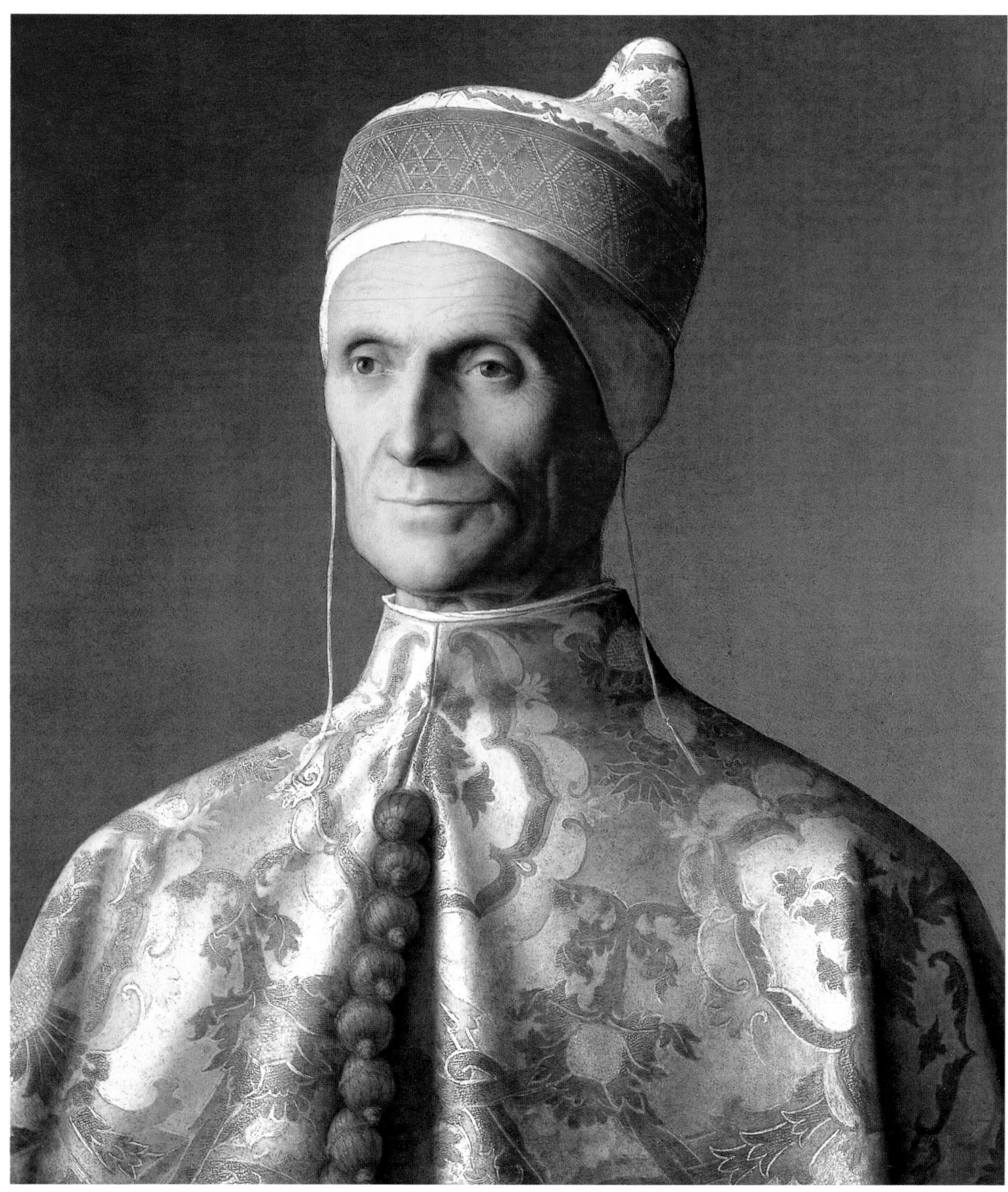

92 GIOVANNI BELLINI *Doge Leonardo Loredan* (detail) *c.* 1501

republican Council of Ten, elected, like the doge, from a restricted pool of aristocrats. The doge was controlled in other ways too. As a general rule it was only on his death, when it was rather too late to go to his head, that he might be glorified as an individual. So the great tombs and chapels of the doges, while undeniably superb – few more so than the multi-storey marvel of funerary sculpture that is the tomb of Pietro Mocenigo, constructed in 1476–81 by Pietro Lombardo in the church of Santi Giovanni e Paolo – are also somewhat deceptive. The keynotes of the city's politics were control, and self-control. The system of highly selective but rigidly enforced democracy worked well. The Florentine Republic was dead by the mid-sixteenth century; the Venetian Republic lasted more than 200 years longer, until it was subdued by Napoleon.

There is little reason to suppose that wealthy, powerful and successful Venetians were unattracted by the magnificence, even immortality, which the Renaissance artist might confer upon them. They were probably no more innately modest than any of the other princes, nobles and *condottieri* of their time. But like the doge, they too were prevented from setting themselves up on a pedestal. The point is illustrated by the greatest exception to the rule of Venetian reserve: the bronze equestrian monument of *Bartolommeo Colleoni* [93], set on a Carrara marble plinth in Venice in 1496.

Colleoni was a *condottiere* from the town of Bergamo, a Venetian dependency, who had spent much of his distinguished military career serving the Venetian Republic. At his death in 1475, he had requested that the Venetian senate execute his will, which it had agreed to do in exchange for a large sum of cash. A problem emerged, however, in the form of Colleoni's demand that an equestrian monument be erected posthumously, in his honour, before the basilica of San Marco. It was not that a *condottiere* in the service of Venice had never been similarly honoured. The Paduan captain Erasmo da Narni, nicknamed Gattamelata, had been memorialized by Donatello as a modern Marcus Aurelius in the square outside his home town's most prominent church, the Franciscan basilica of Sant'Antonio [40]. What scandalized the Venetians was the notion that such a monument might be erected within their city itself, at the very heart of the republic.

The Florentine Andrea del Verrochio was employed and he responded with an incarnation of harsh, lockjawed might. Colleoni's steed paws the earth imperiously while his master, commander's baton in his clenched fist, surveys the scene around him with lofty disdain. But for all its swagger and panache, the Venetians never loved the work. Designed by an artist from Florence, an alien city, it enshrined what was, to them, an alien and dangerous ideal. It is the image of the hero, the proud and powerful individual set on high, which Venetians had always distrusted. As if to signal their independence from the notion which Colleoni had foisted upon them, the members of the senate diluted the effect of their accession to his wishes by departing from them in one crucial respect. They refused, as the *condottiere* had wished, to set his image up before San Marco. Instead, late in the day, they decided to place the statue in the northern quarter of the city, in the relative obscurity of the Campo Santi Giovanni e Paolo. The figure of the epic hero had entered the city, only to be morally excluded.

The Venetians favoured corporate rather than personal display. Shows of public solidarity such as that depicted in Gentile Bellini's *Procession in the Piazza San Marco* [94], now in the Accademia in Venice, played a vital part in civic life. Members of the different guilds, corporations and foreign communities who made up the city would march together in unison – each individual body thus submitting to incorporation, symbolic and actual, within the body politic of the state. Bellini's picture is difficult to scan, at first, because the artist's attention seems so even, his attitude to all the different groups and individuals so impartial, that the eye does not know where to focus. The picture is almost deliberately boring, being a panorama in which everyone looks the same – many of the figures, dressed in identical uniforms, seem almost like clones of each other – and in which no one seems more important or significant than anyone else. But that is its point. It is an image of what the Venetian Republic aspired to be: a seamless society, entirely without tension.

## VICTOR CARPATIUS FINGEBAT

A powerfully corporatist ethos was all the more essential in Venice because of the extreme diversity of the peoples within the city. The skill with which the Venetian state made room for each of the different groupings within it was epitomized by the institution of the *scuola*. The *scuole* were devotional confraternities, each centred on a particular building in the city, where a specific group of lay people could gather to worship. There were many such institutions in Venice during the second half of the fifteenth century: six larger ones, the so-called Scuole Grandi, and more than 200 smaller ones, the Scuole Piccoli. They accepted both rich and poor into their ranks, one of their primary functions being the redistribution of wealth. Poorer members could earn alms by taking part in the funeral processions of their wealthier counterparts. As a forum for debate the *scuola* allowed ordinary citizens to participate in the political life of the Venetian Republic.

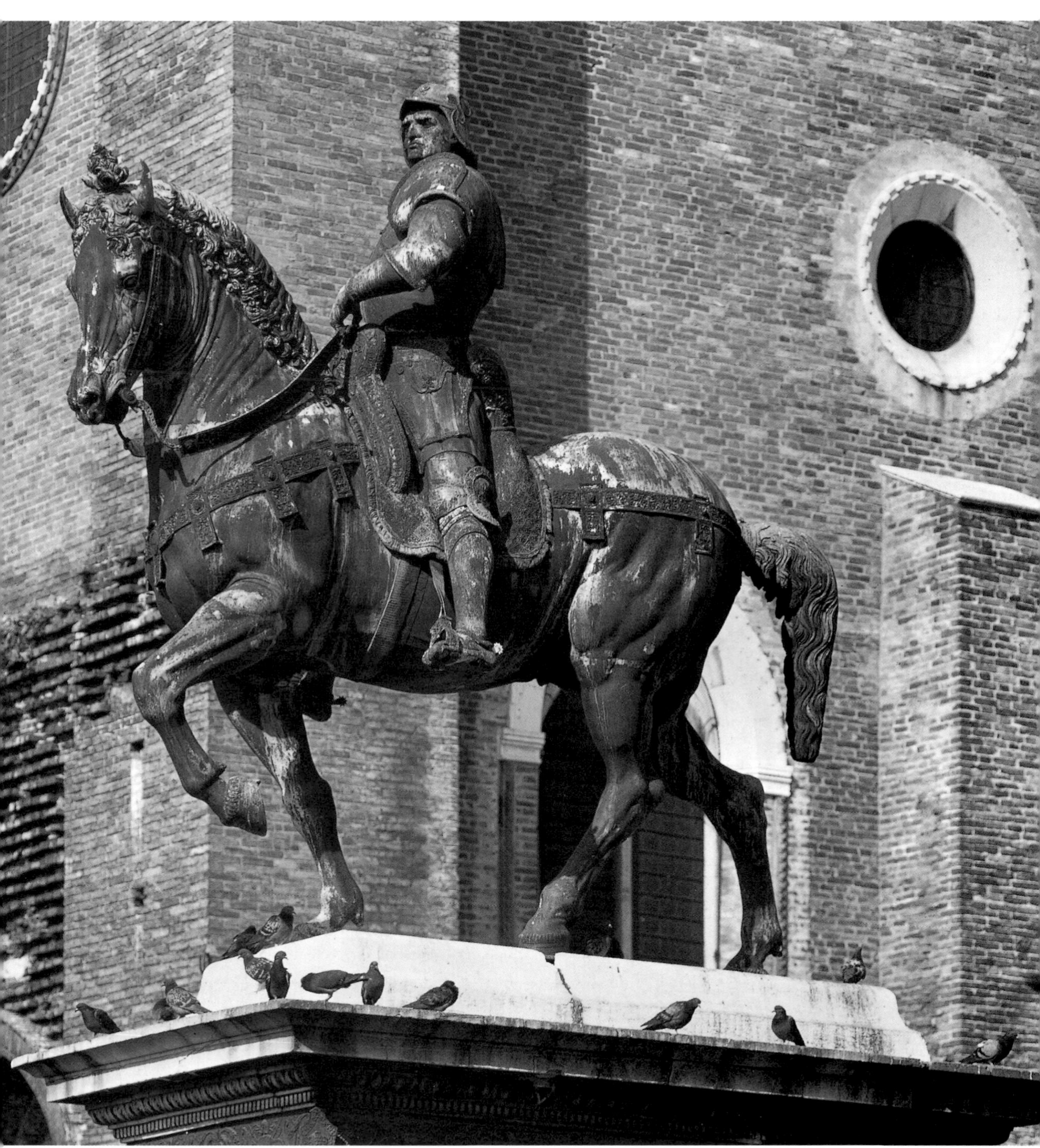

3 ANDREA DEL VERROCHIO *Bartolommeo Colleoni* 1480–88/96

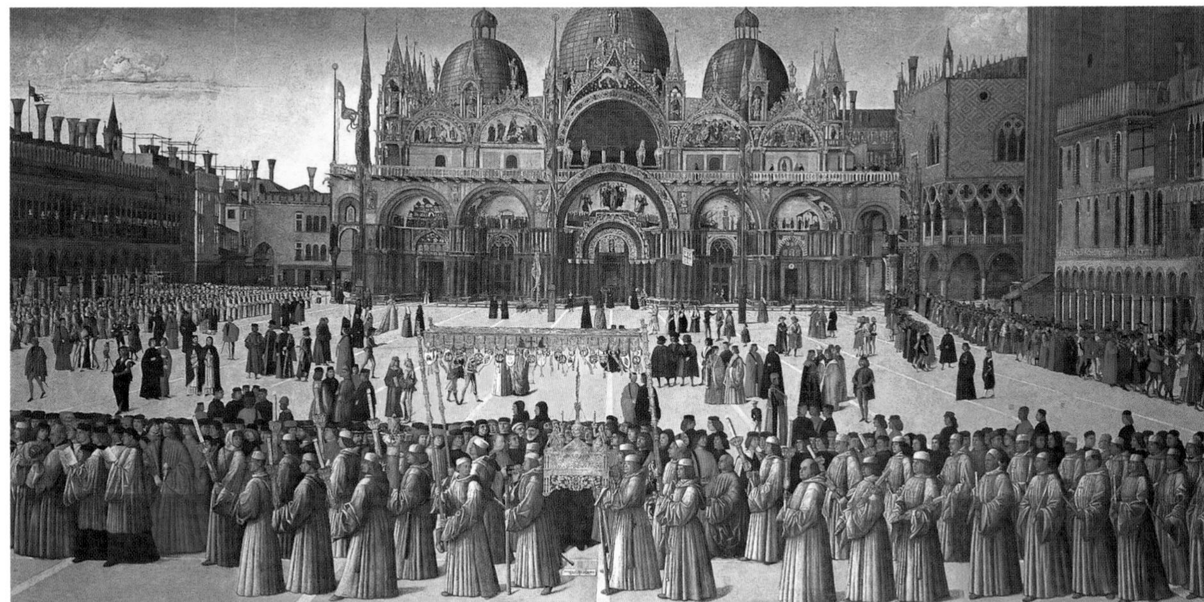

94 GENTILE BELLINI *Procession in the Piazza San Marco* 1496

Certain *scuole* represented the different foreign communities in Venice. Only one such survives, almost intact, together with the paintings by Carpaccio originally commissioned for its main meeting room. The Scuola di San Giorgio degli Schiavoni was founded by the colony of Dalmatians in Venice in 1451. Dalmatia, now part of Croatia, was at the time under Venetian control. Dalmatians living in Venice gathered at their *scuola* under the patronage of Saints George, Tryphon and Jerome (who had himself been born in Dalmatia). Carpaccio was commissioned to depict stories from their lives and in concentrating on Jerome, the scholar saint, and George, the soldier, he placed complementary Christian models of the active and contemplative life before the eyes of the confraternity.

The earlier scenes emphasize St Jerome's miraculous gifts and intense piety. Accompanied by the lion which, according to legend, he tamed, he enters the precincts of his monastery, in the process terrifying several monks who fly in all directions before him [95]. Next we see his emaciated dead body, laid out to rest in a dry and desert setting, while his lay brothers kneel before the example of his piety and join in recalling his words and deeds. The sobriety and measure of Jerome's worldly existence are expressed in the structure of Carpaccio's pictures, formed now from buildings, sky and red earth composed into blocks and planes with a geometrical minimalism.

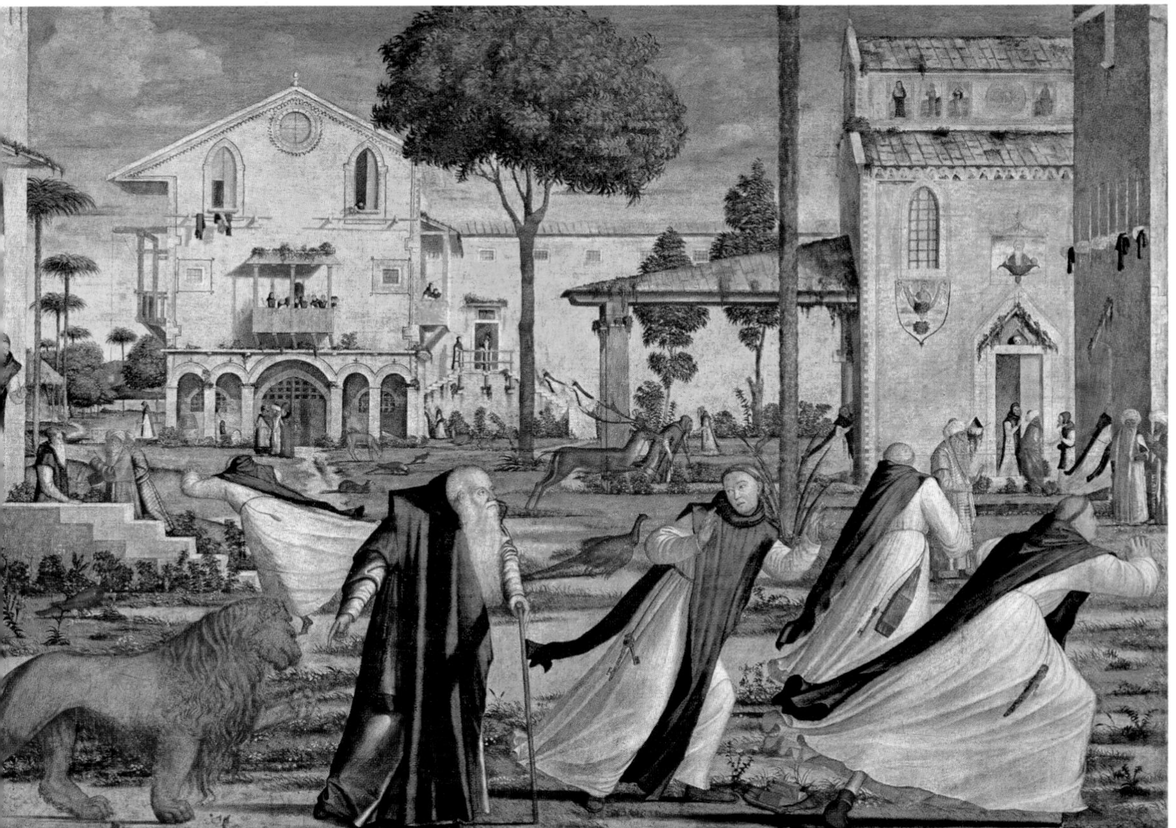

'ITTORE CARPACCIO *St Jerome Leading the Lion into the Monastery* c. 1502

The arid tonality of these scenes changes in the third and last painting in the Jerome cycle, *The Vision of St Augustine* [96], which illustrates a text in which St Jerome is said to have appeared to St Augustine as a beam of light. The miraculous, here, has been transplanted to the world of everyday life – early sixteenth-century everyday life, to be precise. St Augustine, fifth-century Bishop of Hippo, has been turned into a Venetian Christian humanist in his study. Books are all around him, stacked on every surface of the room. Objects from the classical world, statuettes and bronzes, are ranged along a shelf. This is a man who has studied the sciences, such as astronomy – an armillary sphere hangs above his desk – but who also believes in the mystical correspondence between the well-ordered heavens and the harmony of song. Two scores are open at his feet, proffered almost as footnotes to this theme of harmony or correspondence between man's music and the music of the spheres.

Light enters the room from the right, binding all these disparate objects together and spellbinding both the saint at his desk and his little white dog on the floor beside him. This illumination is at once physical and metaphysical, both the light of the everyday world and the light of God. Yet because Carpaccio treated the light purely naturalistically, resisting the temptation to place some phantasm of St Jerome standing in the sun, the gentle glow which bathes the saint's face symbolizes all that we cannot see but can only sense. This light seems to irradiate Augustine from within as well as illuminate him from without, transfiguring him even as it models his features with such objective clarity. Carpaccio signed the picture in Latin, suggesting his own humanistic learning: 'VICTOR CARPATIVS FINGEBAT'. '*Fingebat*' not '*pingebat*' – created, not painted – as if the artist wanted to hint at his own belief that in making it he had, Leonardo-like, created something magical and even god-like.

Carpaccio's other works in the *scuola*, depicting episodes from the life of St George in the Holy Land, are at once more active and fantastical, opening up worlds not of contemplation and mystical rapture but of chivalric valour and oriental exoticism. St George slays a dragon in a grisly landscape full of body parts, including a half-chewed damsel long past distress. He then proceeds to convert a host of disbelievers. As they lay aside their turbans to be baptized, so are the ranks of Christendom swelled. The theme of conversion, of people conspicuously foreign being absorbed into the Christian community, may have had special significance in a Venetian *scuola* representing foreigners, an institution which itself symbolized social incorporation. Also, like St George, the Dalmatians had fought valiantly against the unconverted infidel – in their case, in the perennial Venetian wars against the Turks. It was largely in recognition of that fact that they were allowed to create such a splendid *scuola*. The building was affirmation of their place and their standing in the republic.

## GHETTO

Some citizens within the republic (as within all republics) were more equal than others. But Venice was unusual in that it found room for more or less everybody, and found ways to ensure their peaceful coexistence. Those ways were not always particularly pleasant, but they were predictably pragmatic. The most conspicuous symbol of the Venetian determination to include the foreign and the other was not any of the city's *scuole*, but an entire area, the Jewish Ghetto – the first ghetto to be called such – which was founded in 1516 in order to accommodate the influx of

German and Italian Jewish refugees flooding into the city to escape the wars of the League of Cambrai.

'Ghetto' was a Venetian word for foundry, and the Nuovo Ghetto, or New Foundry, where the Jews were to live, under Venetian protection but also under strict Venetian control, was an island on which they were locked up every day at nightfall. By thus accommodating them within their city, the Venetians allowed Jews a relatively privileged status which they found nowhere else in Italy at that time – allowing them to set up loan banks and to trade with the East, while protecting them from the persecutions and pogroms that befell them elsewhere. But the ghetto was no model of ethnic co-operation and understanding. The Venetian used the Jew, excluding him from the Venetian state even as he included him, and the money he brought in, within the Venetian economy. Jews were not allowed to own land, and were each required to wear a yellow (later red) hat to indicate their separateness from the Christian republic which tolerated their existence.

In Shakespeare's *The Merchant of Venice*, written at the very end of the Renaissance, we hear them answering back to the institutionalized injustice to which they were subjected – tolerated for their money, reviled for their beliefs – in Shylock's angry words:

> Hath not a Jew eyes? Hath not a Jew hands, organs, dimensions, senses, affections, passions? Fed with the same food, hurt with the same weapons, subject to the same diseases, healed by the same means, warmed and cooled by the same winter and summer, as a Christian is? If you prick us, do we not bleed?[2]

Shylock, the usurer, loses out to Antonio, the merchant of Venice, and ends as a victim of the Venetian state. Tricked out of the bloody revenge that prejudice and oppression have driven him to seek, he exits the play with the strangled, haunting words 'I am not well'. It was ever thus in Venice, one suspects, in reality as well as fiction.

## THE TURK

Gentile Bellini, who stayed at the Ottoman court in Constantinople during the 1470s, left a small but charged record of the society that he encountered there, in the shape of his portrait of *Sultan Mehmet II* [97]. We see a hook-nosed man in a turban gazing off to the left. The sultan is a Persian miniature framed by an Italian

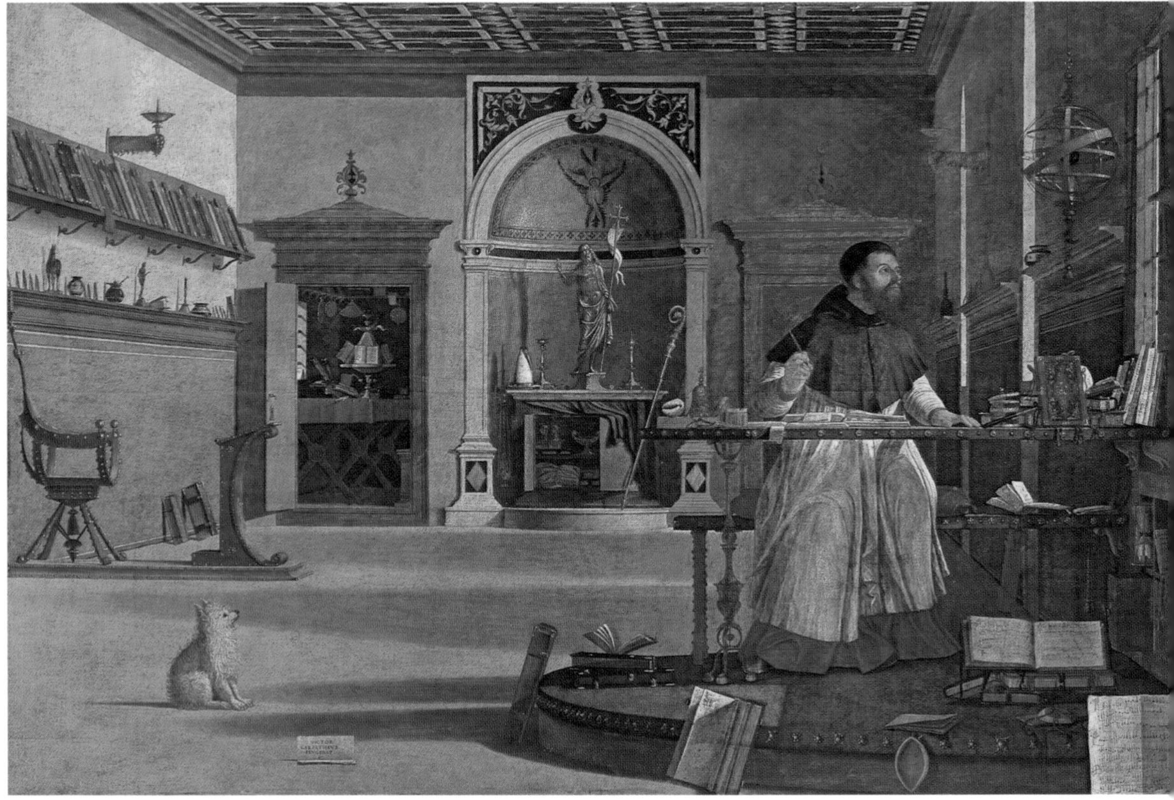

96 VITTORE CARPACCIO *The Vision of St Augustine c.* 1502

Renaissance window. It is a composite image and one which, perhaps diplomatically, conceals the painter's thoughts about the world in which he found himself. The stories which Bellini told about his stay, on his return, fill in the picture somewhat. Among the most sensational is his account of how, one day, he showed Mehmet II a depiction of John the Baptist's severed head. The sultan took issue with the painter, saying that the representation was insufficiently realistic and clinched the argument by having one of his slaves beheaded on the spot. 'There, that's what a decapitated head really looks like!'[3] The tale, whether apocryphal or not, encapsulates an attitude to the Turk in which admiration and alarm are mixed in equal measure.

The Ottoman Empire was the enemy with which the Venetians alternately warred and negotiated – Gentile Bellini's services had been loaned to the sultan, whose portrait he painted as a diplomatic gift – but as time wore on they also found themselves facing new challenges to their maritime supremacy from the

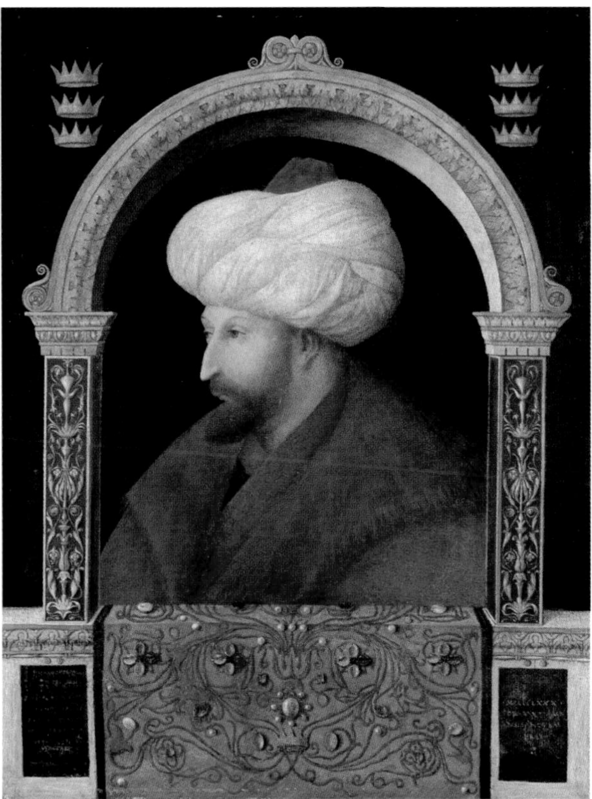

97 GENTILE BELLINI *Sultan Mehmet II* 1479

fleets of Spain and other countries. In order to establish its thriving trade in the Eastern Mediterranean, Venice had had to establish its own sort of empire, one bent not primarily on territorial conquest but on the acquisition of trading rights. The Venetians had taken over ports down the Dalmatian coast and throughout the Greek islands, but throughout the fifteenth and sixteenth centuries this loosely strung chain of territorial possessions was increasingly under challenge and threat.

The most important building in Renaissance Venice, if not the most beautiful, was the Arsenale [98] (the word 'arsenal' is derived from the Arabic *darsina'a*, a house of industry). It was more shipyard than arms factory, although munitions as well as boats were produced there. Built in the twelfth century and much expanded over the intervening period, by the late fifteenth century a new galley was being produced there, by Venice's army of shipyard workers, every 100 days. The Arsenale was the engine room of the city, the source of her might. Without naval power, Venice was nothing. This is the message so thunderously declaimed by

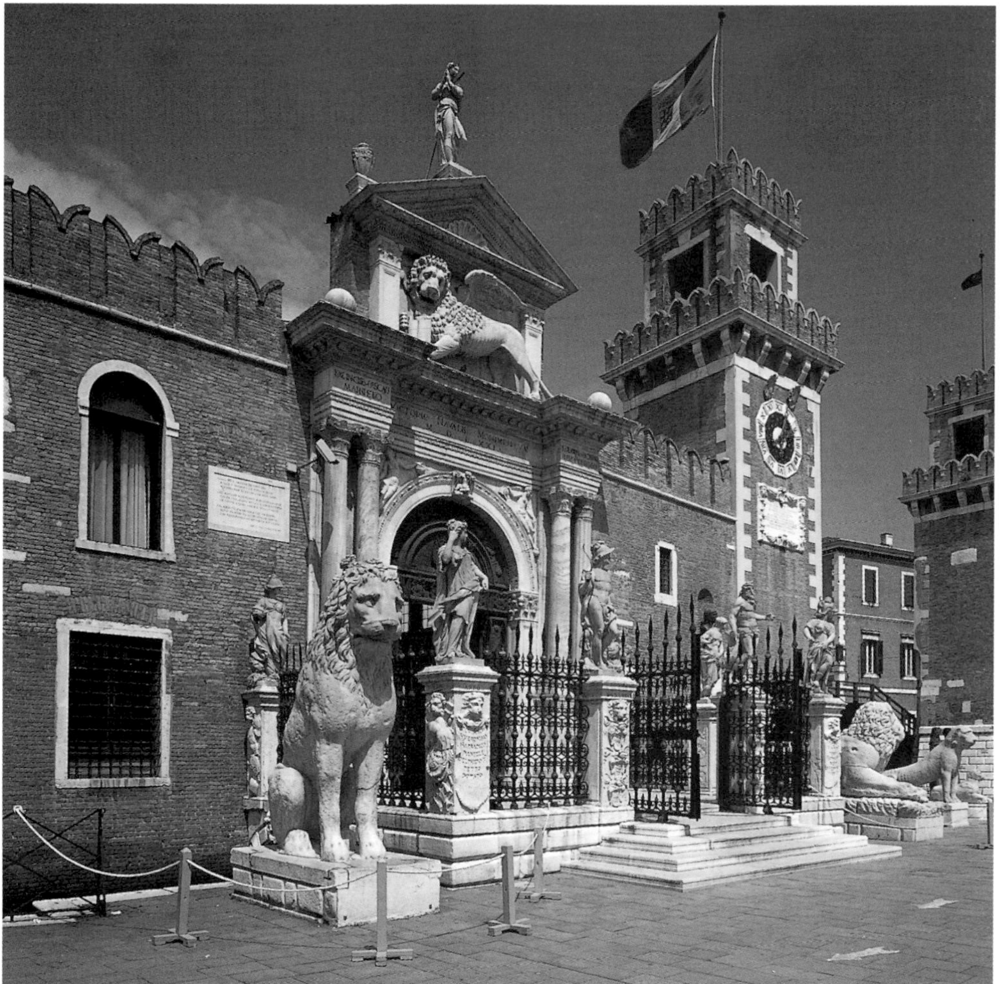

98 Entrance to the Arsenale, Venice 1460s

its gateway, constructed in the 1460s. Richly embellished with figures allegorizing the might of the Venetian Republic, it was the first piece of classical Renaissance architecture to be erected in the city. The winged lion of St Mark, framed by the pediment of the arch, prowls his ledge like a caged beast. His teeth are bared in a snarl.

The bite of Venetian military force which that lion symbolized cannot be sensed with any great vividness in modern Venice. The Arsenale is empty now, only to be colonized briefly once every two years by the Venice Biennale, which makes of this former tunnel of enterprise a string of galleries of modern art. The transformation is bathetic but in its way appropriate. The stockpile on which Venice's military advance guard once drew is now filled with the ephemera of the would-be *avant-garde*, just as Venice itself has metamorphosed from a warlike republic into a bit of a museum.

To understand what Venetian mastery at sea could mean, to the peoples who experienced it at first hand, it is useful to visit a former Venetian possession such as Crete. The island, which occupies a key position along the shipping lanes from the Adriatic to Asia Minor, was taken over by the Venetians in the early thirteenth century and kept under their control until 1669, when the Turks finally prised it from their grasp. Venetian rule in Crete was not particularly kind or benevolent. The local, Orthodox religion was suppressed, members of the native aristocracy were killed and their lands appropriated, the island was given a new name, Candia, and a Venetian duke was installed. The walled cities and fortifications built on Crete by the invaders from the Serene Republic and stamped in so many places with St Mark's lion are a reminder that Venetian architecture – contrary to the impression given by the architecture of Venice itself – was not all grace and light. The star-shaped fortifications of Candia are 3 km long. Crete's multitude of Venetian fortresses protected its rulers against revolt from within and from the Turks without. Venetian Crete with its fortifications shows us, so to speak, another view of the graceful Venetian swan – paddling like mad to keep afloat in a dangerous world.

## ADD NOT SUBTRACT

One of the paradoxes of Venice is that while it was an exemplary Renaissance city, in its drive and its openness to new ideas, it was also the one most thoroughly opposed to the notion of a Renaissance in the starkest sense of that word. The Venetians subscribed to the belief that ancient Rome and Greece held out much for the modern world to emulate and study – so that, for example, the Venetians brought back Cretan scribes well versed in ancient Greek, to enhance their own classical learning. But the idea that the more recent past must in the process be thrown over or abandoned, rejected as old-fashioned or barbaric, was always anathema to them.

Venice was founded on accretion rather than rejection, addition rather than subtraction, with synthesis as its guiding principle. The principle was applied vertically as well as horizontally, so just as the Venetians took things and ideas from many places – Constantinople, Alexandria, Crete – so too did they take from many eras. Embracing the classical past never meant, to the Venetian mind, rejecting the legacy of Byzantium, or that of the Middle Ages. Anything the Venetians loved, they kept. This was how they made their world. There is something insecure about it, as a method. It suggests a compulsion to grab hold of things and hoard them, never to let them go. A heightened consciousness of transience and a heightened desire to resist it come naturally, perhaps, to a people living in a city that looks, any minute, as if it might float away.

This aspect of the Venetian sensibility is epitomized by the central building of Venetian civic life. Ruskin went so far as to call it 'the central building of the world'.[4] The Doges' Palace [99] is certainly a building which could only have been constructed in a city guarded by the sea. It is not a fortress, like equivalent examples of civic architecture in Italy, but an open structure, almost lace-like in its delicacy. Begun in 1340, added to and remodelled throughout the Renaissance, it was for centuries a living symbol of the openness of Venetian civilization. The building is a compendium of Arabic and Islamic motifs, its sources of inspiration ranging wide, from North African Mamluk architecture to that of ancient Syria, including Seljuk decoration familiar to Venetians from their travels in Iran and eastern Turkey. Lit up by the light of the morning sun, its façade as pink as a prawn, it was a perpetual reminder to Venetians of all that Greco-Roman civilization, alone, could not offer them.

The Islamic is married to the Gothic, in the Doges' Palace, and Gothic art too had a long afterlife in Venice. The Gothic style was not merely allowed to persist there. It flourished, long after Renaissance men from other parts of Italy had pronounced it uncivilized and retrograde. The Venetian nobleman's palace is a good example of this conservatism, which was both aesthetic and practical. Constructed according to a tried and trusted formula, it was a place of trade as well as a family residence and its essential features remained unchanged over centuries. At the bottom, there was to be a waterfront portico for loading and unloading merchandise, for boats and for storage; on the *piano nobile*, or main living quarters, there were projecting balconies, to enable the inhabitants to take the air; while the upper storey, or attic, consisted of servants' quarters. Towards the end of the fifteenth century, elements of a classical architectural vocabulary were integrated into this unique and highly specialized building type. But the Gothic and Byzantine styles were never entirely rejected.

The enduring Venetian affection for Gothic had its effect too on artists' workshops. Mid-fifteenth-century Venetian patrons and artists were well aware of the vogue for the classical style that was sweeping across the Italian peninsula. This

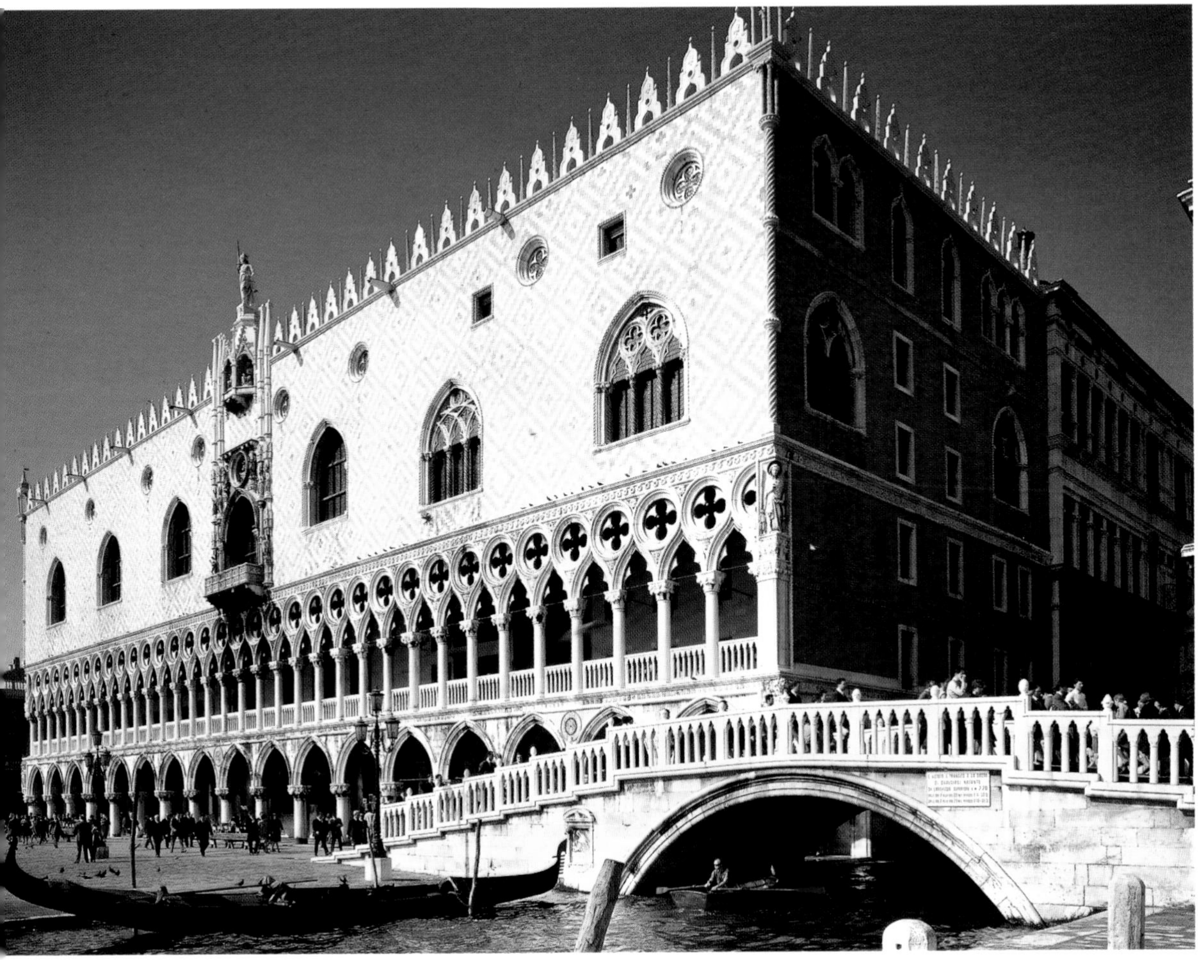

9 The Doges' Palace, Venice, begun *c.* 1340

was in part a phenomenon driven by Venetian artists, such as Jacopo Bellini (*c.* 1400–70), whose antiquarian interests were shared by his son-in-law Mantegna. But in Venice itself, Renaissance classical style stole up quietly and gradually. There was no Florentine revolution, no Gang of Four in the mould of Brunelleschi, Donatello, Masaccio and Ghiberti, and no corresponding sense that the Gothic was destined to become a discontinued line.

So when the nuns of the well-endowed Benedictine convent of San Zaccaria set out to create an appropriate setting for the precious holy relics in their possession – a typically Venetian miscellany including a fragment of the True Cross, a bit of Christ's crown of thorns, pieces of the Virgin Mary's clothing and the entire body of St Tarasio, another *sacra furta* from Constantinople – they commissioned an elaborate work in the Gothic style. The altarpiece in question, commissioned in 1443 from the frame-maker Lodovico da Forlì, unites Gothic paintings and sculptures already in the possession of his patrons, with some newly created gold-ground panels from the workshop of Antonio Vivarini. It has a coherence which belies the multifarious origins of its constituent parts. Architectural in its effect, the towering polyptych has the grandeur of the west front of Canterbury or Exeter Cathedral, but realized in bright painted and gilded wood.[5] Many of the nuns of San Zaccaria were drawn from the upper echelons of society, and as daughters of rich merchants they can be assumed to have shared the general aristocratic Venetian taste for gold and glitter and the beauty of finely wrought things. In its way, Vivarini's golden evocation of the heavenly city of Jerusalem, with the saints and angels and the Virgin and Child enthroned, at its centre, is a matchless creation. Its otherworldly splendour has been enhanced by the gradual flooding of the church crypt, which makes of it a typically Venetian achievement in another way too: a vision of heaven raised above the water.

## FATHER AND SON

Artistic production in Venice, like so much else in the life of the city, was founded on a sense of communal enterprise. This led to a distinctive sense of tradition and continuity, reflected in the fact that many of the leading Venetian Renaissance artists founded family workshops. Here too Venice was different from Florence, where, although a similar workshop system operated, there was a more nakedly competitive ethos, which fostered a more aggressive sense of artistic identity. In Florence, the artist may have admired previous achievement but his essential task was to vanquish and surpass it. In Venice, the artist sought not to kill the father but to learn from him, and to build on his achievements.

Venetian art developed through innovations, discoveries and ideas that were passed down from father to son – literally and visibly so, in the case of the books of drawings that Jacopo Bellini created and then passed on to his sons Gentile (*c.* 1429–1507) and Giovanni (1431/6–1516). Partly because so few of his finished paintings survive, Jacopo Bellini remains in many respects the unsung genius of the Venetian art tradition, his work being familiar to art historians but little known to a more general public. One of his notebooks is in London, in the British Museum, while the other is in the Louvre [100]. Done on parchment and paper, his drawings were the building blocks of the Venetian painting tradition.

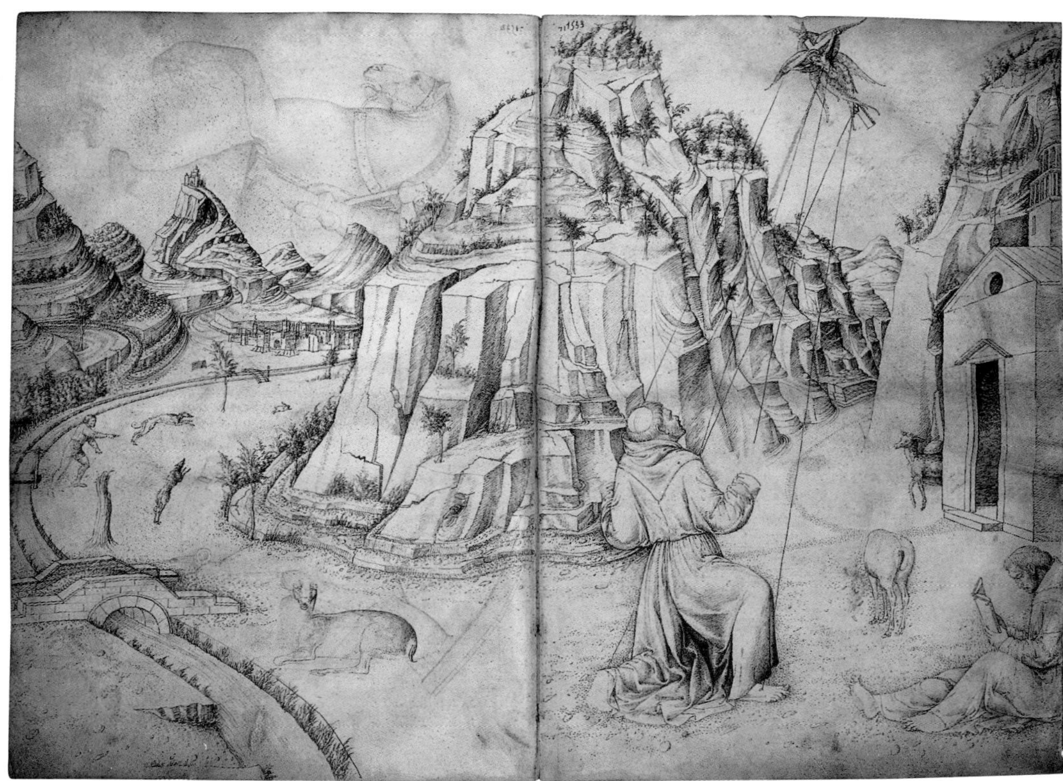

100 JACOPO BELLINI *St Francis Receiving the Stigmata c.* 1450–55

Jacopo's precious albums – precious materially as well as artistically: fifty goatskins were used in the creation of the Paris drawings – show him to have been a pioneer. He mastered the mathematics of Florentine linear perspective. He plunged himself into the study of the antique past. He was the first Venetian artist to bring classical mythology graphically to life. He was one of the first to depict the world around him, its labourers and workers as well as its aristocrats, with documentary objectivity. His sketchbooks laid out the future of Venetian art itself: its strains of mythological fantasy; its realism; its preoccupation with the depiction of landscape and atmospheric effects; its portrayals of human consciousness and feeling.

Gentile Bellini acquired his father's eye for documentary detail and put it to use in his own eyewitness paintings such as *The Procession in the Piazza San Marco* [94]. But Giovanni was the more gifted of the two brothers. In adapting his father's ideas, he transformed them. His altarpiece of *The Baptism of Christ* [101], painted

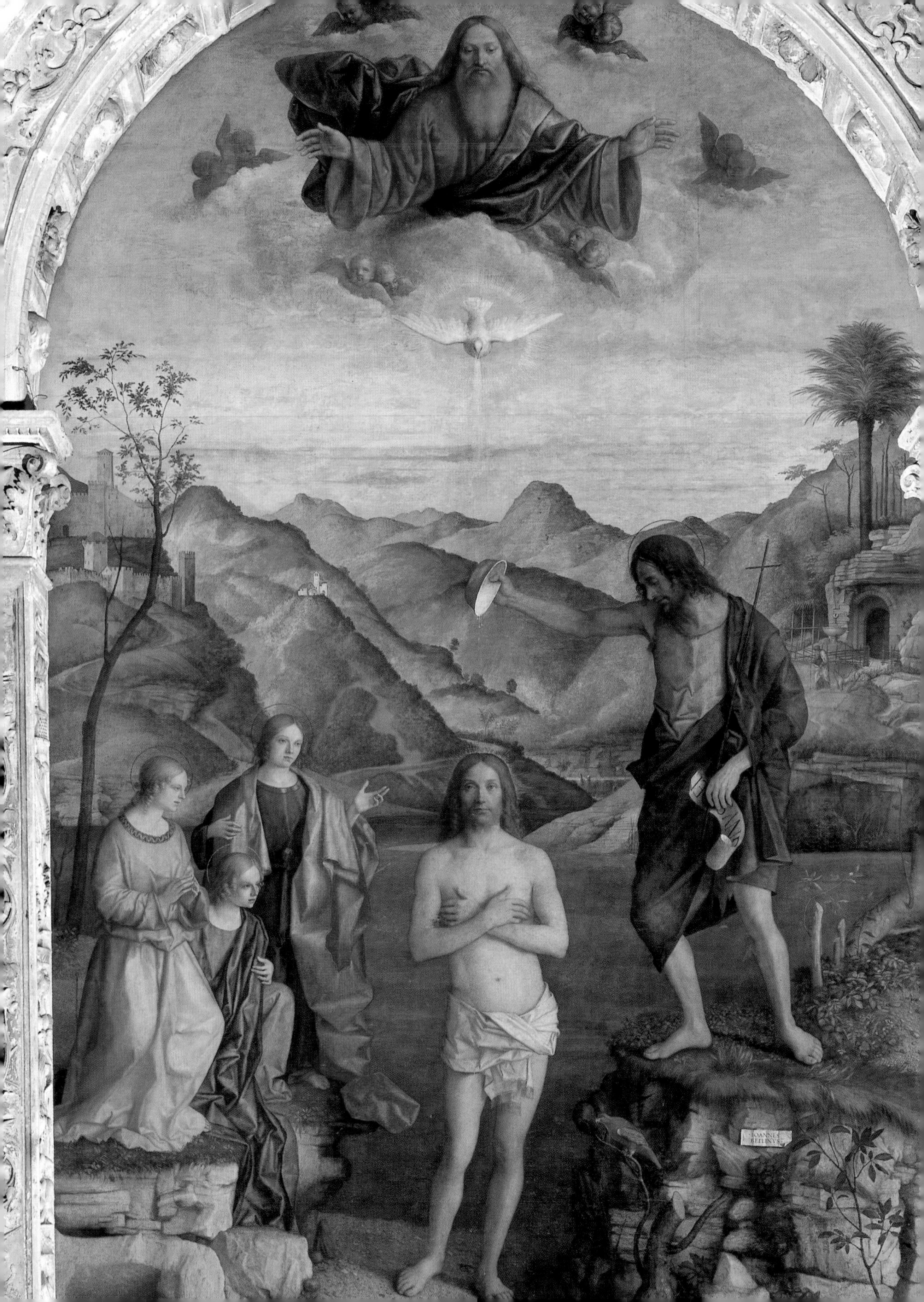
IOANNES
BELLINVS

around 1500 and still in its original frame in the church of Santa Corona in Vicenza, is reminiscent of two different drawings of the same theme by Jacopo. But Giovanni formed from those hints and suggestions a whole that seems as immutable and certain as the figure of Christ who stands so firm and sure before us, gazing into our eyes.

A single straight line of divinity bisects the picture, running from the face of God the Father, through the beak of the dove of the Holy Spirit, through the drops of limpid water dripping from the bowl held by the Baptist, down on to Jesus's head. The deep landscape which unfolds in the background, makes the whole visible world seem to have been baptized in a message of hope, saturated with the blessings of God. A painter's genius has made all, in this place, appear touched with holiness. Bellini's landscape is like the emotions of hope and joy fashioned into a place: a winding fertile valley that recedes in carefully plotted geometrical perspective, through perfectly judged shadings of aerial perspective, back through greened and blued mists to mountains on a horizon irradiated with the golden tints of a new day.

Such effects recall the work of Leonardo da Vinci, who visited Venice in 1500 at around the time when Bellini painted his altarpiece, and whose work had a strong influence on Venetian painting. But Bellini's achievement was very different from that of Leonardo. Leonardo's landscapes are the flaunts of his science, repositories of the artist's knowledge about the world. The distinctiveness of Bellini's landscape lies more in the realms of poetry than science, for however compellingly believable the landscape in the Santa Corona *Baptism*, it is evident that the picture is not driven by empiricism but by the force of religious emotion.

## IN ARCADIA

In an almost unnaturally green landscape, under a stormy sky lit up by a snake of yellowish lightning, a half-naked woman sits on a tussock breastfeeding a child. On the opposite side of the stream running away beside her, past a pair of broken columns and a ruined Roman aqueduct to a bridge in the middle distance, stands a handsome young man dressed as a soldier. He looks at her. She looks at us. There is a slight air of challenge in her expression.

Much ink has been spilled on the subject of the *Tempesta* [102], a small painting by the short-lived but influential Venetian painter known as Giorgione. It is one of less than half a dozen securely attributed works by his hand. Some interpreters have seen the picture as a representation of the four elements. Others have seen it

101 GIOVANNI BELLINI *The Baptism of Christ c.* 1500

as an allegory of the human senses, others again (perhaps least plausibly of all) as an opaque political commentary on the state of Venice in the early sixteenth century.

The *Tempesta*, painted *c.* 1505, was a novelty: a non-religious subject, placed within a landscape setting. Not only was its subject new but so was the response which it demanded from the viewer. It is a picture which exists to provoke what the English poet Andrew Marvell would apostrophize around 1652 as 'a green thought in a green shade'.[6] It is a painting which aspires to the condition of poetry – indeed to the condition of a very specific type of poetry, namely that of pastoral.

During the second half of the fifteenth century in Italy there had been a renewed interest in the classical literary genre of the pastoral. During the late 1480s the Neapolitan poet Jacopo Sannazaro had completed his chief poetical work, a pastoral romance called *L'Arcadia*, which drew both on a rich classical tradition of bucolic poetry and set the pattern for the pastoral as one of the most popular genres of European literature for the next 200 years and more. With Sannazaro's work was reborn the ancient notion of landscape as a place of reverie, to which urban man might retire to indulge in frequently melancholic musings on the nature of love, the passage of time and the hubris of human endeavour. Landscape might also hold out the promise of redemption through nature. The retreat to pastoral was linked, in the classical and Renaissance mind alike, with the dream of recovering a lost golden world of untroubled rustic simplicity – a landscape of the mind peopled by serene and wise shepherds and shepherdesses, a secular paradise known as Arcadia.

Landscape had always had a particular, charged meaning for Venetians. The land was what they had lost touch with, the Eden from which they had been expelled when they were forced to build their city in the sea, right at the start of their history. This may begin to explain why they made so much of pastoral, playing with its meanings and elevating its status. In the classical tradition, pastoral is the prelude to epic. Virgil educates himself by writing the *Georgics* and learns wisdom in rustic meditation, in order that he may go on to write the forceful epic that is the *Aeneid*. But the Venetian art tradition reverses this classical order of priorities, shunning the epic hero and his glorification and elevating the pastoral, and other contemplative or hedonistic modes of art, to the highest pinnacle.

The most original work of Italian Renaissance pastoral literature associated with Venice is the *Hypnerotomachia Poliphili*, a romance written around 1470 by the Dominican friar Francesco Colonna and printed by the Venetian Aldus Manutius in 1499. An outstandingly beautiful book, including some 165 woodcuts, it enjoyed great popularity in patrician and educated circles. The book's title may be translated as 'the love struggle of Poliphilo told in a dream', and it is a work which continues to elude precise categorization. Part romance, part pastoral, part architectural fantasy, it is a literary-cum-pictorial creation in which an almost bewildering variety of motifs and motives are combined. It has been described as the first stream-of-consciousness novel. Its plot (if it may be called that) defies responsible summary, consisting of a complex sequence of dreams and dreams-within-dreams in which the book's hero, Poliphilo, in search of his true love, Polia, roves through darkened woods and gardens and groves. In the process he explores a multitude of curious buildings, including a pyramid of 1410 steps erected in honour of the sun, as well as a fallen colossus inside whose bronze body he finds a metal heart inscribed with epigrams and aphorisms on the subject of love. The poem and its illustrations are unified by a fetishistic intensity. All the chief objects of Poliphilo's obsession – not only Polia herself, who is described as the embodiment of antiquity, but the various monuments among which he wanders – seem to inflame his imagination to the point of sexual arousal. At the end of the poem he awakens, frustrated, and yearns to dream again.

The *Hypnerotomachia*'s dream world, pastoral-erotic-antique, may take us closer than any other literary source to the meanings embedded in Giorgione's enigmatic *Tempesta*. Giorgione is known to have been influenced by the woodcuts in the *Hypnerotomachia*. It is possible that the *Tempesta* was itself intended as a freely worked illustration of the poem. The supposition is strengthened by the broken columns in the middle distance of the painting, which may allude to the poet's name ('*colonna*' being Italian for column), as well as by the fact that in one of the poem's scenes Poliphilo encounters the goddess Venus, suckling Cupid. Whether the influence was direct or not, Giorgione's hero, like Colonna's, seems held for ever on the edge of a world that he cannot enter. A stream separates him from the girl, while the metaphorical river of time separates him from the classical past, which lies in ruins about him. The storm in the background marks the passing of more time – and the violence of time and nature – with its lightning flash. The picture is, perhaps, a meditation on the transience of love and all the things of this world.

Giorgione's work signalled the advent of a new kind of landscape art in Italy, untethered from pure – or even primary – religious meanings. But in secularizing the religious landscape of Bellini in this way, Giorgione did not only free painting to explore new territory, he opened up a new possibility, depicting a world from which God has abruptly absented himself, leaving man and woman alone. There are portents in Giorgione's lightning flash. Look at his storm long enough and you may even hear the distant thunder of romanticism.

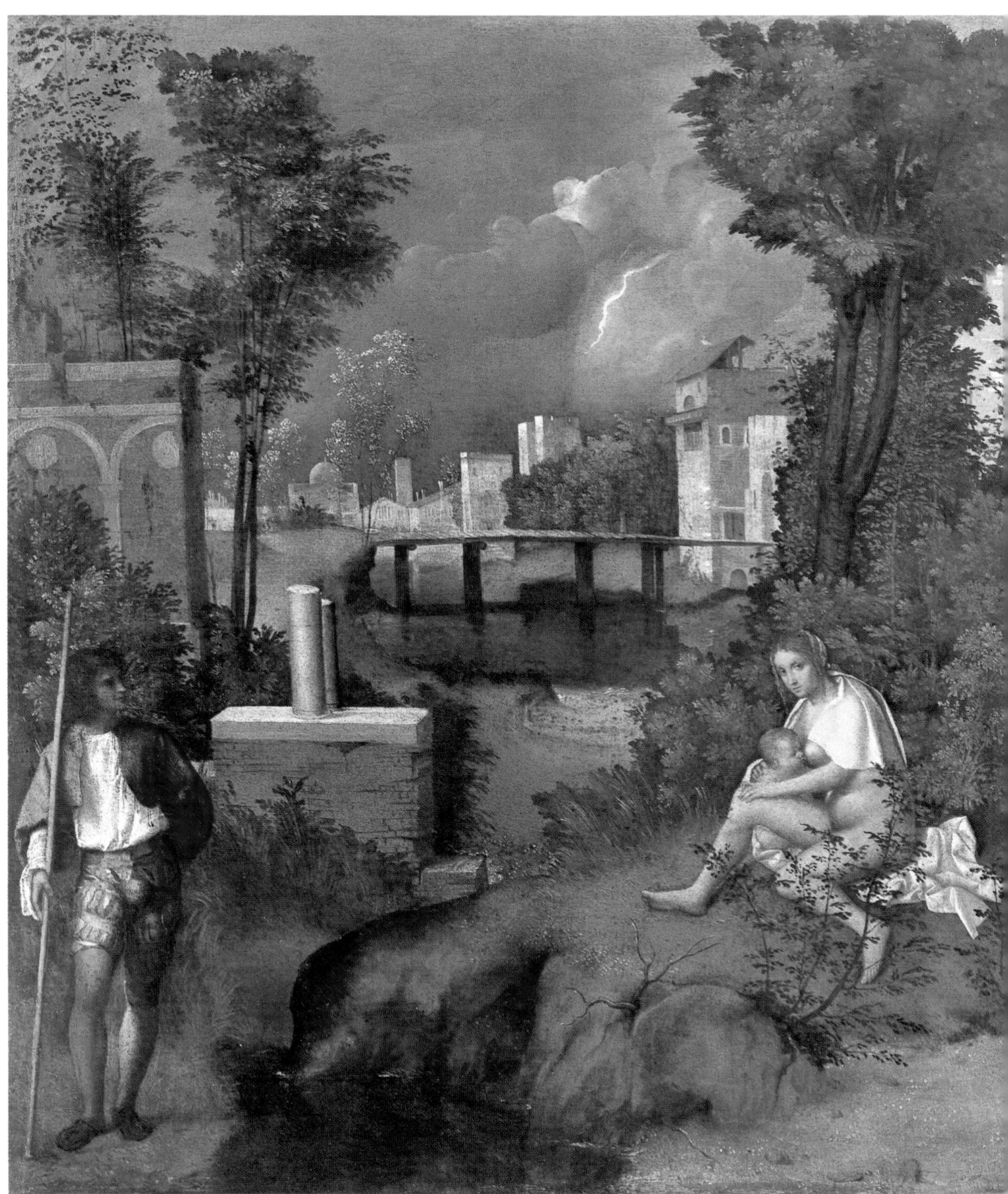

102 GIORGIONE *La Tempesta c.* 1505

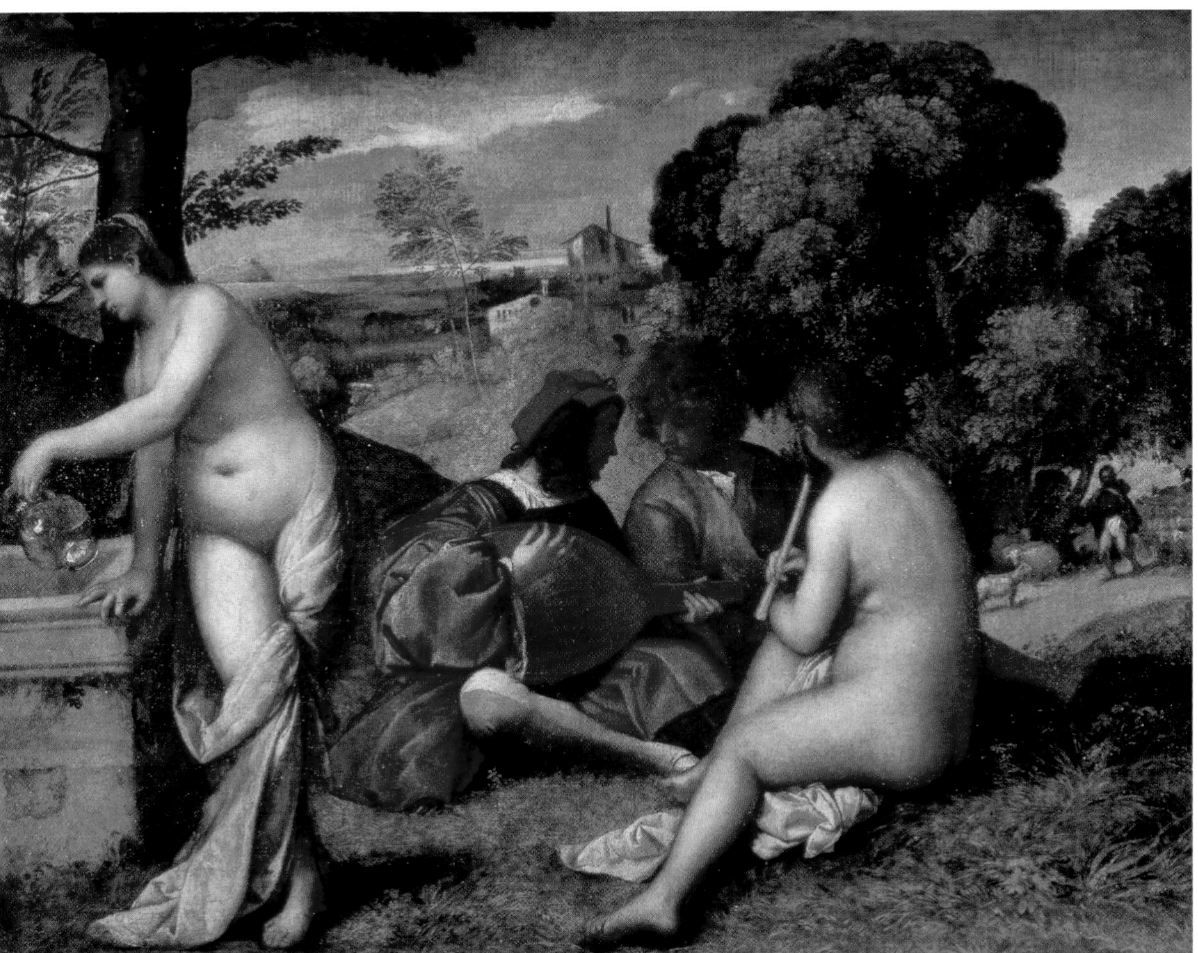

103 GIORGIONE/TITIAN *Concert Champêtre* c. 1510

## THE DECISIVE MOMENT

A painting now in the Louvre, called the *Concert Champêtre* [103], has been attributed both to Giorgione and to Titian. It may even have been completed by Titian after Giorgione's untimely death in 1510, which would make it the epitome of the almost metempsychotic relationship that seems to have existed between the two artists. The attribution remains contested, but the beauty of the picture does not. In an idealized wooded landscape a finely dressed lutenist converses with the shadowy figure of a shepherd. Beside them are two naked women, the Muses of this idyll, one of whom is filling a jug with pure water from a well, the other pausing momentarily from playing the wooden flute which she holds in her hands. The precise meaning of the picture is as difficult to establish as that of the *Tempesta*, but its broader implications are clear enough. A man of the city, in his gorgeous clothes of silk, has come to the countryside to retune the strings of his soul, to find beauty and inspiration and perhaps, too, to be reminded of one or two home truths. It is a quintessentially Venetian picture, in that it is a painting which inherently encourages a passive, contemplative response on the part of the viewer – surrender to a mood.

Venetian secular painting offers itself up to be contemplated and to be enjoyed. Its appeal is to the mind but also to the senses. It does not exist to provoke action, but to stimulate thought and produce pleasure. In Venice, painting became more collectable and more covetable than ever before. If Giorgione started the process, Titian carried it through. The difference between them is encapsulated in the contrast between Giorgione's *Sleeping Venus* [104] and Titian's *Venus of Urbino* [105]. Giorgione's Venus, asleep in a landscape which seems to echo the contours of her own body, is still touched with the mystery and the aura of a goddess. She seems to represent, not quite a real woman, but the divine principle of fertility. In Titian's *Venus of Urbino*, the goddess has been woken up. She has been brought indoors too, and the ideal world depicted by Giorgione has become a boudoir. Titian's Venus looks the viewer full in the eyes, as if to greet her lover. She has the air of a courtesan (of which there were many in Renaissance Venice), and perhaps Manet was telling a truth about her, as well as making a name for himself, when he refashioned her as a truculent disillusioned Parisian whore, four centuries later, in his *Olympia* (Musée d'Orsay, Paris). The sexual promise held out in the eyes of Titian's Venus is untainted by Olympia's world-weariness; but her gaze is equally direct.

Titian made art more erotic and more independent of prescribed meanings and conventions than ever before. In becoming blatant objects of desire, his paintings also became blatant objects of exchange: things to be loved and treasured, bought and sold. This was not an entirely new development, nor an entirely Venetian one – the beginnings of the modern art market may be traced back to the previous century – but Titian's part in it was, none the less, paramount.

The Italian scholar and humanist Francesco Priscianese described a summer visit to Titian's house in a letter to a friend:

> On 1 August I was invited to celebrate the kind of bacchanal which, I know not why, is called *ferrare agosto*, so that for most of the evening

> I argued about it in a delightful garden belonging to Missier Titiano Vecellio, the excellent Venetian painter (as everyone knows), a person truly suited to spice every worthy feast with his pleasantries. There were gathered together with the said Missier Titiano (because birds of a feather flock together) some of the most rare intellects that are found today in this city, and from our set principally Missier Pietro Aretino, the new miracle of nature ... Here, before the tables were set out, because the sun despite the shade was still making his heat much felt, we spent the time looking at the lifelike figures in the excellent pictures which fill the house and in discussing the real beauty and charm of the garden, which everyone marvelled at with singular pleasure. The house is situated on the far end of Venice by the edge of the sea, and from it one sees the pretty little island of Murano and other lovely places. As soon as the sun set, this part of the sea teemed with gondolas adorned with beautiful women and resounded with the varied harmony of voice and musical instruments which accompanied our delightful supper until midnight.[7]

It is not difficult to understand the intoxicating effect which Titian's art, presented in such circumstances, may have had on those visiting his house. There is something very modern-sounding about Priscianese's description. He might be describing a gallery opening at the Venice Biennale today, where dealers still take advantage of the Venetian setting to make the art they are trying to sell seem blessed with some kind of magic. Titian has been given insufficient credit as an entrepreneur.

There is no portrait of Priscianese himself, but a vivid impression of the milieu of collectors to whom Titian and his work appealed may be had from the brilliant portrait of *Andrea Odoni* (Royal Collection, Hampton Court) by Lorenzo Lotto, painted in 1527. Odoni was a wealthy merchant of Milanese origin – an immigrant, like many Venetians – with an exceptionally fine art collection. He made money from customs duties on wine and is said to have had paintings of Bacchus on the façade of his house. He followed the common Venetian habit of displaying a reclining Venus in his bedroom, and owned paintings by Titian and Giorgione as well as the antique marbles and bronzes with which Lotto depicted him. While revelling in the world of pagan antiquity, Odoni holds fast to his Christian faith, symbolized by the cross which he holds in his left hand in the portrait. Uncovered in a recent restoration, the cross seems to have been painted out earlier this century, perhaps to make Odoni conform more closely to a secular

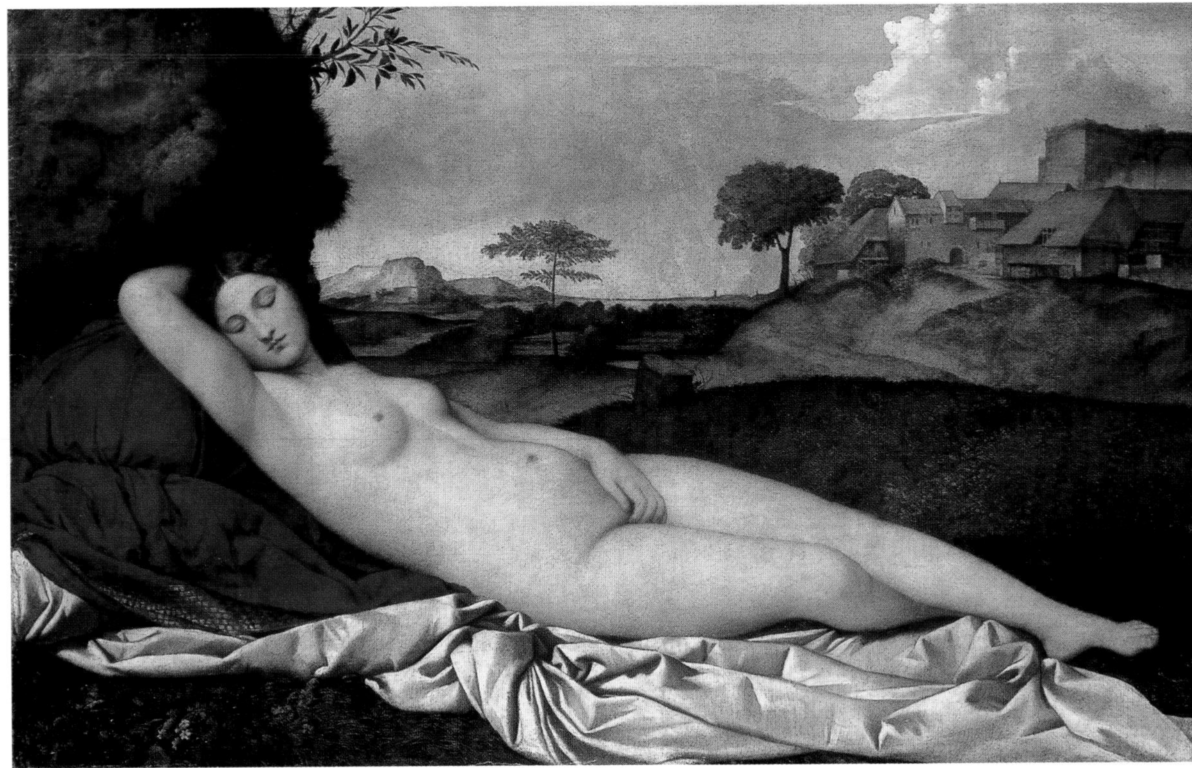

104 GIORGIONE *Sleeping Venus c.* 1510

age's notions of Renaissance man, as a being entirely free of religious superstition. In fact it is an interesting detail, giving depth to the somewhat uneasy expression on the sitter's face. It is as if he were aware of the potential spiritual anomalies implicit in his idolatrous worship of the pagan past. The same moral unease, accompanied by an exhilarating sense that they were dabbling in something risqué, even a little dangerous, may have been felt by such men when they gazed upon the naked Venuses and scenes of bacchic revelry painted for them by Titian.

Titian fascinated his contemporaries with the unpredictability and variety of his work. He reinvented every area of art that he touched, transforming not only the nude and the mythology – or *poesia*, as such work was called – but also portraiture and religious narrative painting. He did so in part by applying the same sense of drama that we find in his *Bacchus and Ariadne* [89] to those other genres. Like some gaslight impresario, he had the characteristically original idea of treating *The Martyrdom of St Lawrence* as a night scene. The painting, in the Church of the Gesuiti, Venice, is a drama of light and of fire, which carries too a meaning of redemption. The brazier on which the saint's body writhes glows with evil intensity, calling to devout minds, perhaps, the idea of the fires of hell. The

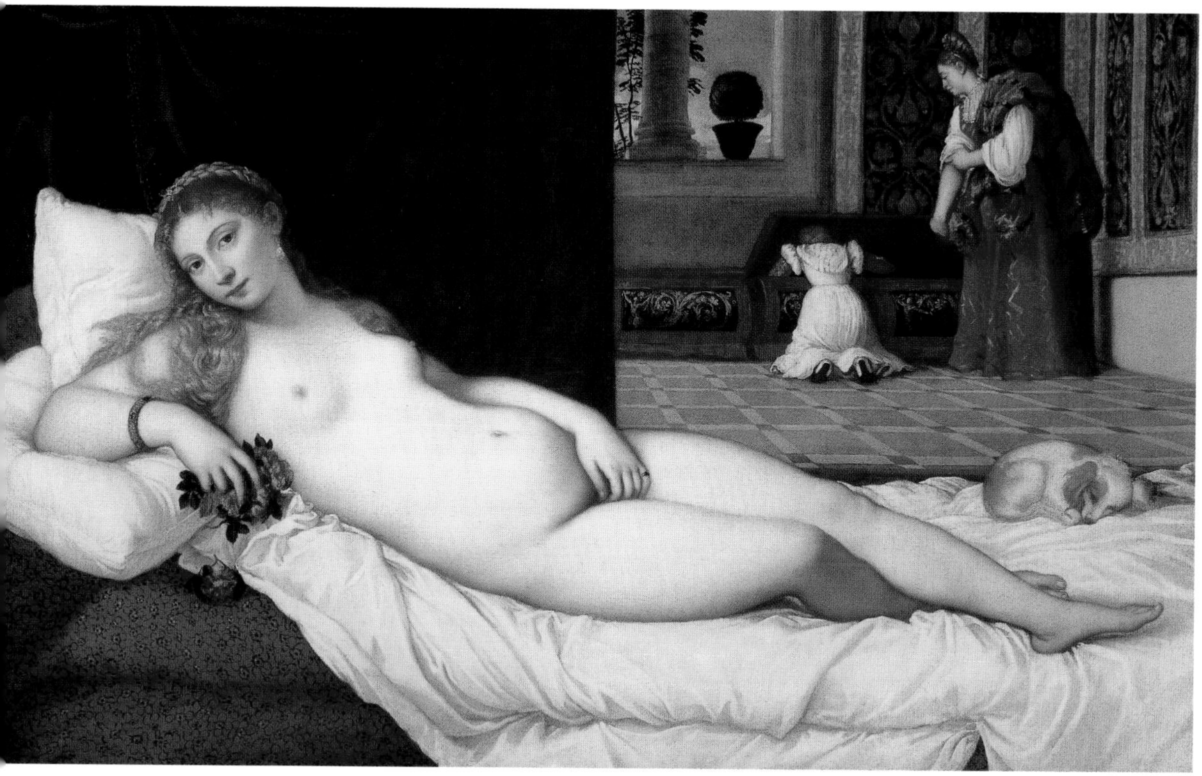

105 TITIAN *Venus of Urbino* (detail) 1538

flickering torches close by, which dimly illuminate a classical building, suggest the upward motion of the saint's soul as he dies. There is another, supernatural light above – the light of heaven, which seems to rend a hole in the sky through which Lawrence's spirit may aspire at this, the moment of his death.

The picture demonstrates Titian's masterful sense of what seventeenth-century art criticism would term 'the decisive moment' – the moment when all the meaning, all the poignancy, all the drama of a story seems compressed into a pregnant split second. He dramatized the portrait too, creating not just a likeness of those whom he painted but animating them, making them seem as though caught at some ominous or vital moment of their lives. The unknown young man with a glove, in the so-called *Portrait of an Englishman* [106], now in the Pitti Palace in Florence, seems more alive than any painted representation has a right to be. He has been caught for ever on the point of momentous utterance. A light gleams in his eye. He is handsome but above all he is urgent, seeming to embody the same sense of uneasy inner consciousness that Shakespeare wrote into the part of Hamlet, soliloquizing on the nature of his own being. So too did Titian manage to make one of the ugliest men in the known world, the Holy Roman

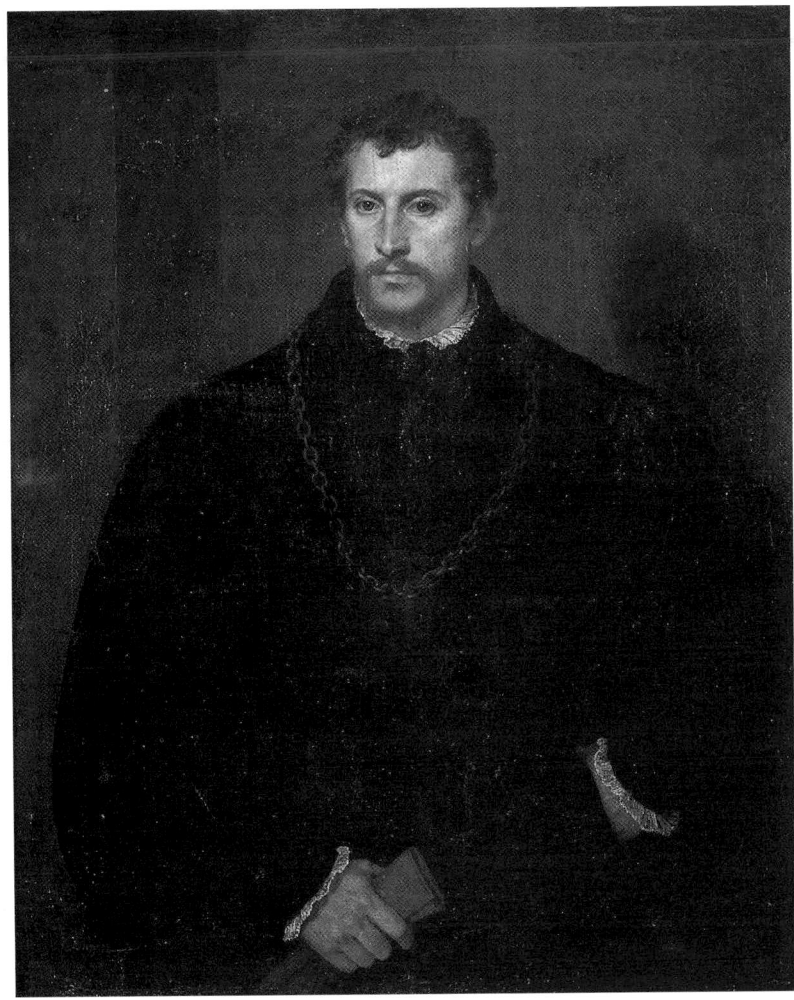

106 TITIAN *Portrait of an Englishman c.* 1540–45

Emperor Charles V, with his jutting Habsburg jaw, seem the very embodiment of imperial might, mounting him on a noble charger and having him advance through a green and wooded landscape, with implacable intent, towards the unseen Protestant foe.

Titian was not only one of the greatest painters of the Renaissance, he was the first painter truly to master the conditions of a new age and its art market. As the pre-eminent ambassador for Venetian painting, he understood that it was vital to place his works of art with the right people, to distribute the evidence of his talent in the right places. Titian himself stayed in one place, his house, with its beautiful garden and all the paintings on its walls, while the world came to him petitioning for favours. Even more than Mantegna, in his Mantuan palace at the start of the sixteenth century, Titian embodied the painter-as-prince. His work was owned and admired by the most powerful men of the sixteenth century – by kings and popes as well as by the mighty rulers of Spain. In this way Titian's painting entered the very bloodstream of European civilization. More than any other Renaissance artist, he shaped the future of painting. Rubens, Poussin, Rembrandt, Velázquez, Watteau, Chardin, Delacroix, Constable, Monet, Degas – all learned to paint in the school of Titian. His painting became the raw material of painting itself.

## THE RETURN TO THE LAND

While Spanish power played its part in spreading the Venetian word – or image – it was simultaneously curtailing Venetian military and political ambition. From the mid-fifteenth century onwards Venice's maritime and trading empire, challenged by Spain and by the continuing advance of the Ottomans, began to contract. These were the first stages in a long but inexorable process. The Venetians, who had already established a significant territorial state on the Italian peninsula, looked increasingly to expand their inland empire, strengthening their hold on subject cities such as Vicenza and Padua. Land had become the best available investment open to them, by the second half of the sixteenth century, and the reclamation of marginal land one of the most profitable forms of industry. Driven back to the terra firma by necessity, they turned again to the landscape – this time envisaged not as an Arcadia but as a source of profit and of a guaranteed food supply.

In making their move from trade to agriculture, the Venetians awoke from pastoral reverie and unearthed a different and more practical aspect of the classical past. Ancient Roman authors such as Varro and Cato had extolled agriculture as an occupation worthy of gentlemen. The Venetian aristocrat on his estate in the Veneto came to see himself as a modern equivalent of the Roman noble in his *villa rustica*. This was expressed in architecture. A new form of building, both practical and idealized – a cross between farmhouse and Roman temple – came into being. It was developed most extensively by Andrea Palladio (1508–80) in the villas which he designed for his patrons in the territories of the Veneto.

In Palladio's architecture, a notion which had gathered momentum during the Renaissance – namely that a building might itself be as perfectly formed and as covetable as a work of art – was taken to its logical conclusion. Playing variations on his chosen theme, the temple-like dwelling in rural surroundings, the architect created villas monumental and villas playful, villas dominant and villas retiring.

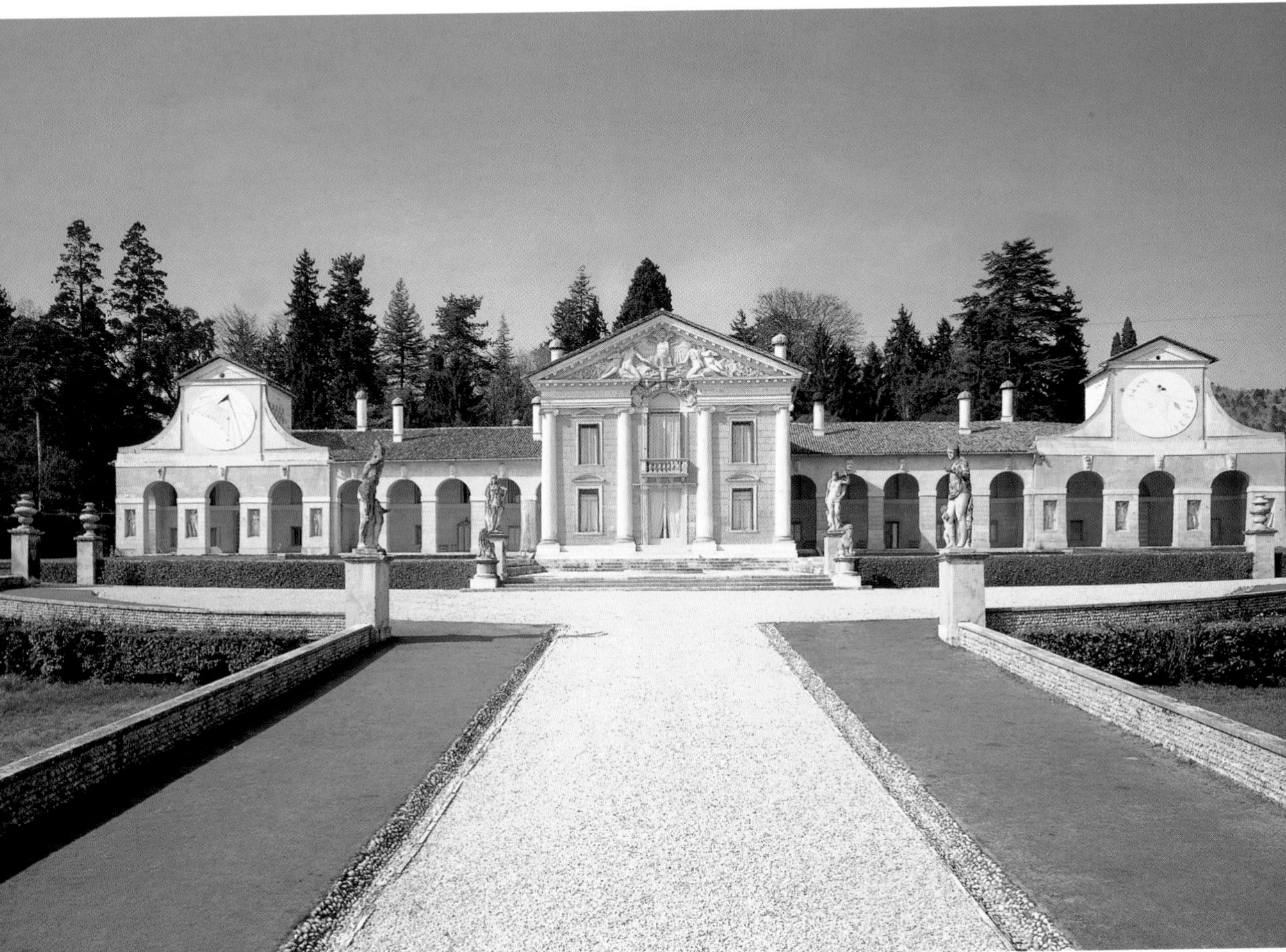

107 ANDREA PALLADIO Villa Barbaro, Maser, late 1550s

Much of the pleasure that Palladio's work offers lies in the study of the sometimes minute but always interesting changes he made to his central idea each time he designed a new building. Like a modern artist who has deliberately chosen to restrict his means, Palladio constructed an oeuvre out of improvisation: small moves made within a field of artifice.

The Villa Barbaro (now Volpi) at Maser [107 and 108], created for the brothers Daniele and Marcantonio Barbaro in the late 1550s, is one of the most perfectly preserved of Palladio's works. Forming a long and relatively low-lying line of buildings, it is confident rather than imposing. The temple-like central block of the main front is flanked by roomy arcades for storage of grain and other materials,

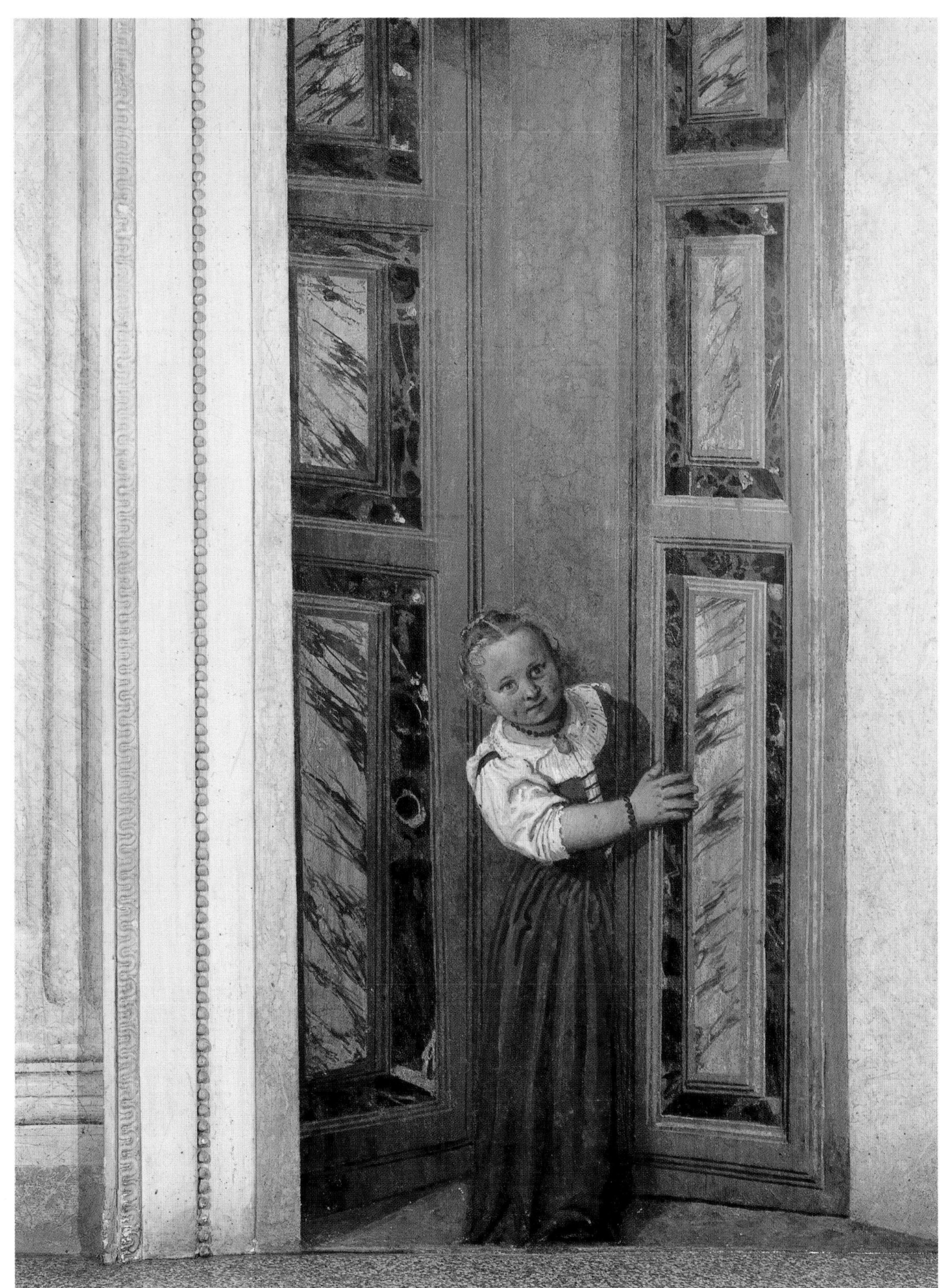

108 PAOLO VERONESE *Trompe l'oeil*, interior, Villa Barbaro, Maser *c.* 1561

beauty and usefulness cheek by jowl. Daniele Barbaro was one of the leading members of the Venetian patriciate in the second half of the sixteenth century as well as a humanist scholar of distinction. The author of a commentary on Vitruvius and a treatise on perspective, he is likely to have had a say in the design of the villa. He certainly helped to plan its decorations.

Daniele Barbaro was particularly interested in the lost traditions of Roman scenographic painting, and he was fond of quoting ancient descriptions of the wall decorations Romans had in their villas – *trompe l'oeil* images of landscape, mountains, forests, buildings, people and animals. Palladio's contemporary Paolo Veronese (*c.* 1528–88) was commissioned to re-create such scenes on the interior of the Villa Barbaro and the result was a sudden and wonderful enhancement of the illusionistic tradition founded by masters such as Gozzoli and Mantegna during the previous century. Veronese made blank walls into landscapes, opened up ceilings into skies and peopled the house with the figures of those who once lived there so that visiting, now, one is constantly surprised by ghosts: a little girl opening a door [108], a huntsman coming in from outdoors, accompanied by a couple of mischievous and hungry-looking dogs.

Veronese's pictorial *coups de théâtre* are the perfect complement to the staged spectacle which Palladio had made of a building.[8] Coming to the countryside, the Venetians had discovered not another version of pastoral but a new and exuberant form of theatricality.

## THE USES OF SPECTACLE

As real Venetian power diminished, Venetian art and architecture became ever more self-assertive. It is as if grand spectacle served increasingly as a compensation for political disappointments. Nowhere is this more magnificently exemplified than in Palladio's church of San Giorgio Maggiore, a gleaming white vision of the heavenly city materialized on the lagoon. Splendid artifice such as this could make Venice seem indeed blessed by God and destiny, even if reality suggested otherwise.

San Giorgio Maggiore is a Roman High Renaissance building in Venice. It has been aptly described as St Peter's on the sea. The Venetian Republic had begun to take the imperial grandeur of ancient Rome to heart in the 1530s, when Jacopo Sansovino had been commissioned to renovate and classicize the Piazza San Marco, at the very centre of the city. Sansovino's most celebrated Venetian building, his long arcaded Library of St Mark's, with its richly decorated façade supported by two orders of columns, Doric and Ionic, led Pietro Aretino to hail him as 'the modern Vitruvius'.[9] But the Venetian embrace of classical grandeur was never to be quite complete, and certainly never exclusive.

The city was given the opportunity to present a more unified and less bewilderingly multi-faceted aspect to the world by two great fires of 1574 and 1577, which destroyed a large part of the Doges' Palace. Palladio, who had by then succeeded Sansovino as the city's classical architect of choice, proposed that it be rebuilt to his own *all'antica* designs. This was a typical gesture, epitomizing both Palladio's radicalism and his disdain for local tradition – characteristics implicit even in his Latin name, which he adopted because he preferred its Roman associations to those of the traditional Venetian name with which he had been born, della Gondola. But the offer was rejected, and Venice continued to flaunt the plurality of its culture.

The increased scale and the more blatant theatricality of Venetian architecture in the time of Palladio found its counterpart too in painting. Veronese was one significant figure in this development. Another was Jacopo Robusti (1519–94), nicknamed Tintoretto because his father was a dyer. He employed similarly enveloping effects of scale and perspective, but combined them with the mobile and broken type of paint surface which Titian had introduced to Venetian painting in his later works. The masterpiece of Tintoretto's life was the cycle of approximately fifty paintings with which he turned one of the most splendid of Venice's larger *scuole* into an all-absorbing theatre of religious contemplation.

The Scuola Grande di San Rocco was founded in honour of the remains of St Roch, the patron saint of plague victims. According to legend, his body was brought to Venice from France in the hope that it might protect the city from outbursts of bubonic plague. Venice was always vulnerable to pestilence and infection because so many boats and people constantly flowed through it.

Responding to the urgency of his commission, Tintoretto created a range of penumbral light effects, so that each holy event in his painting seems to unfold in a world crackling with spiritual electricity. In *St Mary of Egypt in Meditation* he reinvented a characteristically Venetian species of picture, the night scene. The landscape in which the penitent whore sits has been painted as if in coppery grisaille so that her face, haloed with a smudged circle of yellow paint, seems like a sun in a darkened world. All around her, light playing on wind-blown leaves and water has been applied in thick trails of impasted white – the most immaterial substance rendered in the most materially insistent way. There are similarly luministic impastoed loops and dabs of white paint in the landscapes of John Constable (he called such touches of white his 'snow'), whose art was, like Tintoretto's,

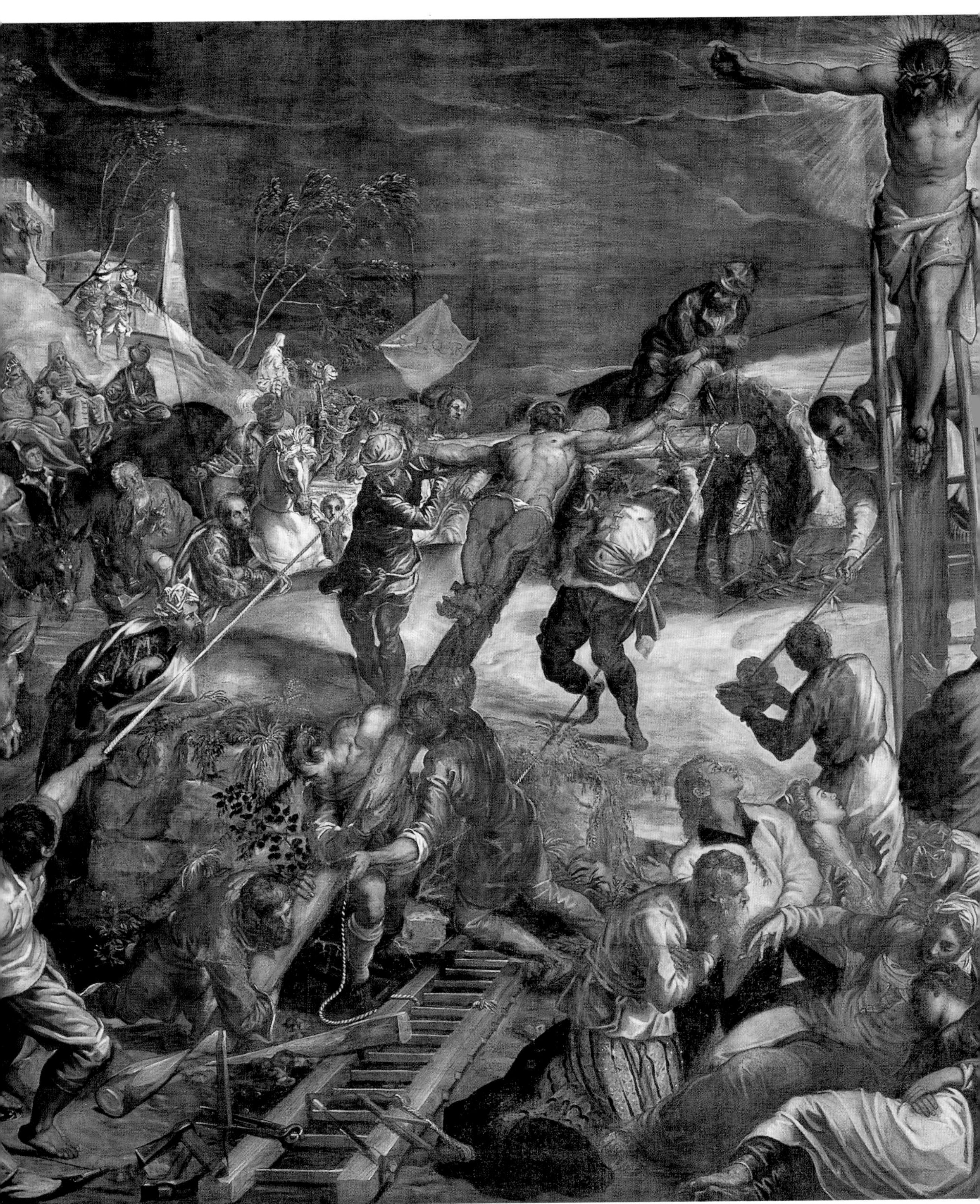

109 TINTORETTO *The Crucifixion* (detail) 1565

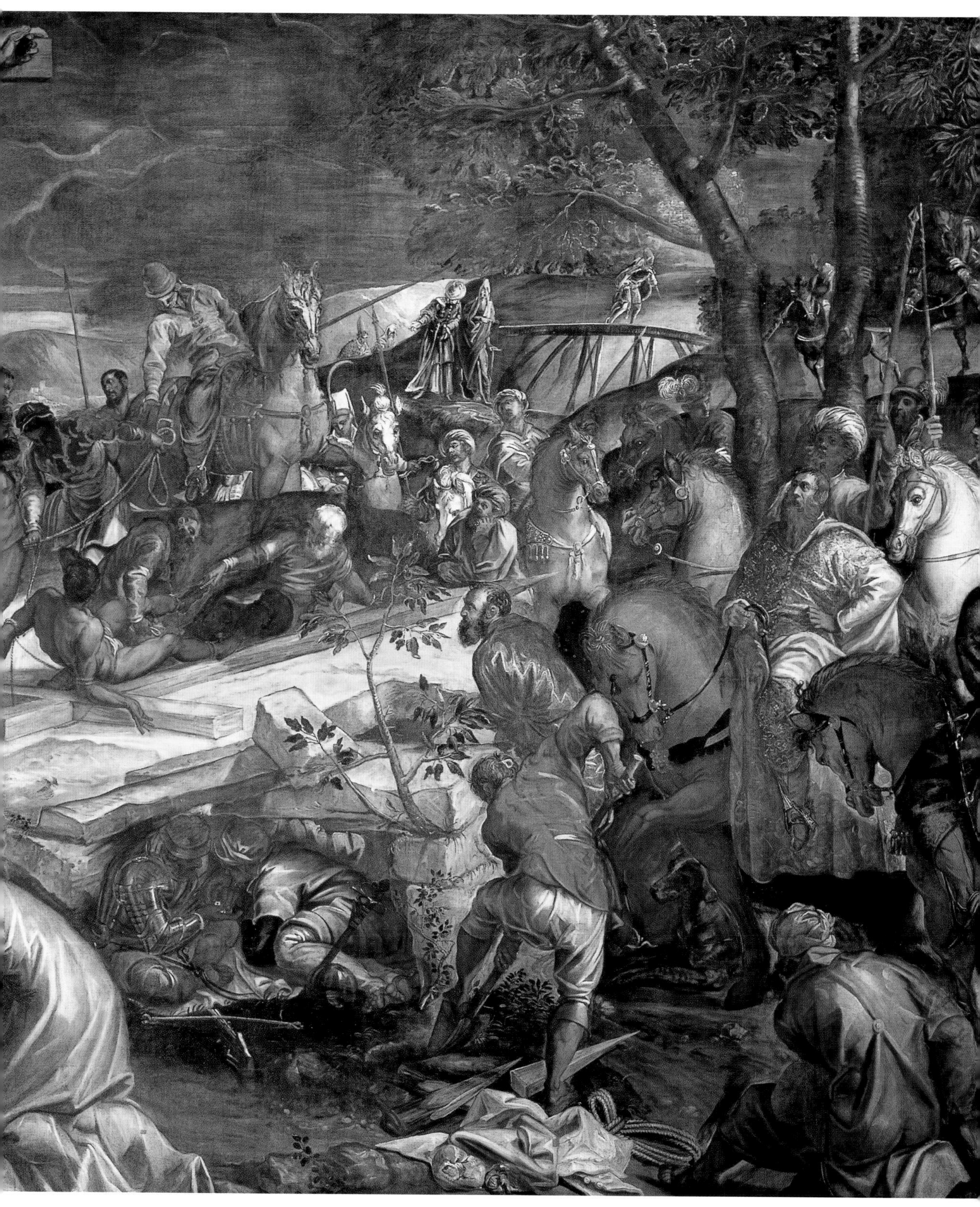

nourished in a landscape of canals (albeit more than two centuries later and in Dedham Vale not Venice). The Venetian milieu, in which light can seem like flakes or drops, reflected in the water dripping off an oar, must surely have played a part in Tintoretto's work. His light effects may recall, too, Samuel Taylor Coleridge's descriptions of watersnakes, in *The Ancient Mariner*: 'They moved in tracks of shining white, / And when they reared, the elfish light / Fell off in hoary flakes ... They coiled and swam; and every track / Was a flash of golden fire.'[10]

The climactic work in Tintoretto's San Rocco cycle, and the principal painting in its *albergo*, or chief council chamber, is an enormous depiction of *The Crucifixion,* over 12 metres wide [109]. The artist possibly took as his text: 'And I, if I be lifted up from the earth, will draw all men to me. This he said, signifying what death he should die' (John 12: 32–3). Tintoretto painted Golgotha as a panorama to which, as if magnetized, the whole world seems to have been drawn. A mass of people, some on horseback, some on foot, have gathered to witness the most momentous event in Christian history. The penitent thief's cross is being raised, while the impenitent thief continues faintheartedly to resist the attentions of those tying him to his cross. All the lines of force and perspective in the painting – lines made by ropes and ladders and slabs of rock, as well as lines implied by pointing hands and pointed looks – converge on the figure of Christ. His shadowed head emits lines of radiance, a halo that makes of him a second sun as well as the Son of God, the very centre of all the busy world that surrounds him, and the still point that gives a meaning to all its bustle. Behind him, as storm clouds gather, the real sun sets in colours of dried blood. The heir to Bellini as well as to Titian, Tintoretto set this solemn Christian drama in a landscape that echoes Christ's own Passion. You could remove all the figures and the painting would still communicate the emotion of tragic loss.

The most engulfing of all Tintoretto's works is the vast billowing vision of *Paradise* [110] which he and assistants created on the far wall of the Sala del Maggior Consiglio in the Doges' Palace between 1588 and 1592. It is a cauldron of saints, divinities, angels and the blessed. A painting so large that it cannot be taken in at a single glance, a picture which exceeds the range of the human optic, can seem to whirl us into its very structure. This was a truth on which the greatest artists of the Baroque and Rococo would build. But Tintoretto's painting also seems to look forward further in time, to anticipate the panoramic scale of so much modern painting. Jackson Pollock's 'allover' canvases of the 1940s and 1950s – pictures infused perhaps not with a dream of paradise, but with inchoate pantheist yearning – are variations on a Tintoretto theme.

## VENICE AS IDEA

Tintoretto's work epitomizes the perennially unpredictable, experimental character of Venetian art during the sixteenth century as a whole. During his lifetime, even as the Venetian empire was dissolving, the example of Venetian painting was beginning to infiltrate Western art, eventually permeating it to such an extent that it came to assume the condition more of a moral example than that of a merely local art tradition.

One of the first painters to encounter Venice as idea and example, and to use Venice as a means of discovering his own originality, was an icon painter from the island of Crete called Domenikos Theotokopoulos (1541–1614), known as El Greco, 'the Greek'. The art of Venice, where he studied for a brief but vital formative period in the 1560s, taught him much in terms of technique. His art, with its flickering light effects and aspiring elongated figures, was partly shaped by Tintoretto's style. But what El Greco acquired in Venice above all – it was what helped him in turn to become one of the most original artists of his age – was his sense of what a painter could be.

The rapturous and disorientating quality of El Greco's art, particularly that produced in Toledo, where he eventually made his home, has been traditionally attributed to his presumed Spanish mysticism. Recent research, however, has shown El Greco to have been a rather cooler and more critically intelligent artist than was once commonly believed, and the influence of the Venetian tradition on his development is widely acknowledged. He owned Daniele Barbaro's 1556 edition of Vitruvius's *Ten Books of Architecture* and the 1568 edition of Vasari's *Lives of the Artists*. El Greco's marginalia to those works show the extent to which he had absorbed certain Venetian ideas about painting. He challenged the idea that mathematical proportion is the measure of beauty, criticized excessive idealization in art, attacked Michelangelo for his inability to paint portraits and remarked that Raphael was far too dependent on antiquity – a fair summary of the undoctrinaire ethos, tinged by anti-Roman and anti-Florentine sentiment, which governed Venetian painting as a whole. In Venice, El Greco learnt to trust his own originality; and he learnt that it was not necessary for a modern, 'Renaissance' artist to throw off his past altogether and rush headlong into the arms of the antique.

El Greco spent his maturity in Spain but was always, essentially, a painter formed by Venice. He was the first artist of his kind – a moral rather than geographical Venetian, so to speak – but he was only the first of many. Rubens was to be a Venetian living in Antwerp. Delacroix was to be a Venetian living in Paris.

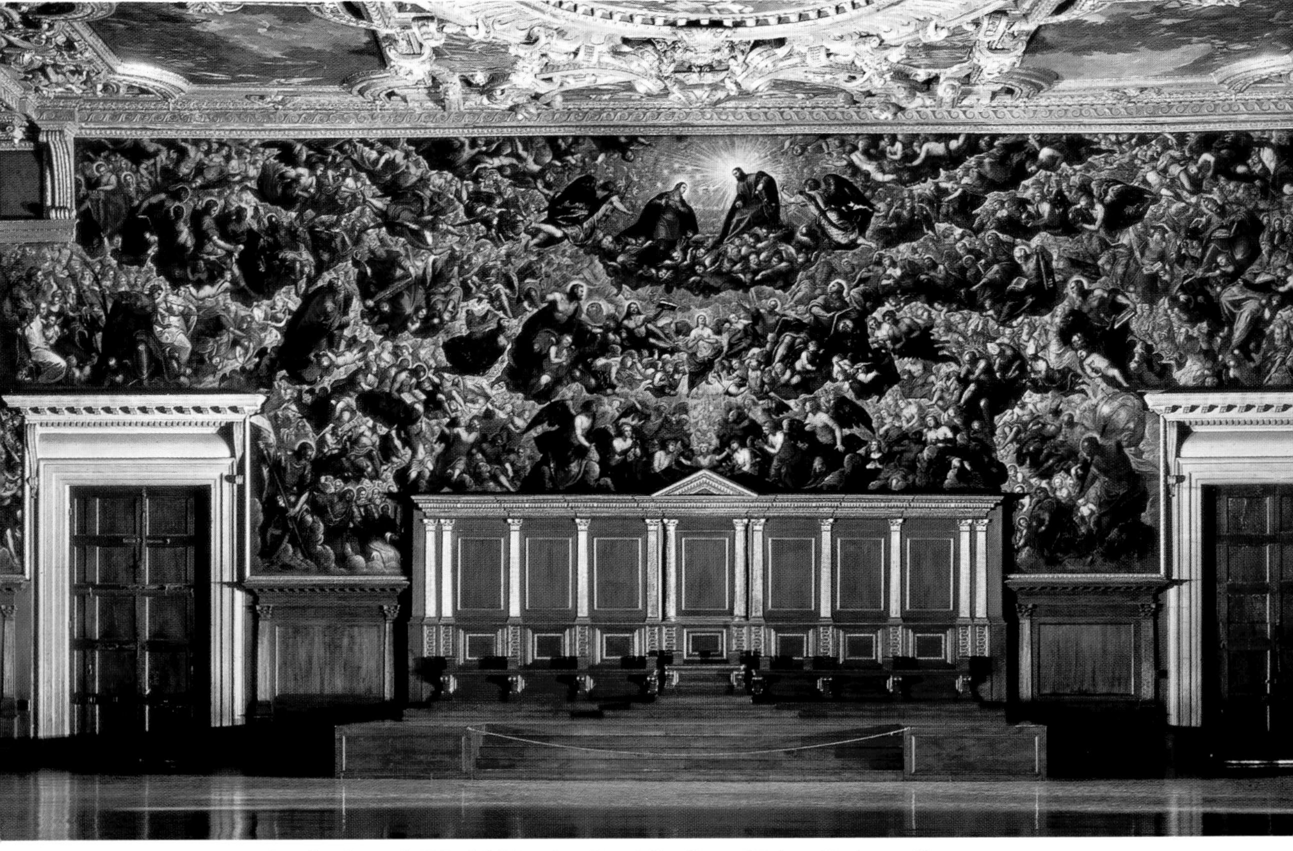

110 TINTORETTO *Paradise,* far wall, Sala del Maggior Consiglio, Doges' Palace, Venice 1588–92

Turner was to be a Venetian living in London. By the end of the sixteenth century, and perhaps for ever afterwards, Venice was no longer a place. It had become an attitude: a state of mind.

## PIETÀ

At the end of his life Titian painted a *Pietà* [112], an image of the dead Christ with mourners, which the artist intended to place over his tomb in the church of the Frari. He died, of the plague, before he could finish it, in 1576, and the last touches were respectfully applied by Palma Giovane. It is a work which speaks with morbid eloquence of the unmaking of a man. At the last, Titian wrought a kind of violence on his own technique. What was once brightly coloured has gone grey. Flesh that was once almost palpitatingly alive has died. The mosaic in the apse above the limp body of Christ gleams, but with such a dull light that it is almost impossible to make out the image of the pelican pecking its breast, traditional

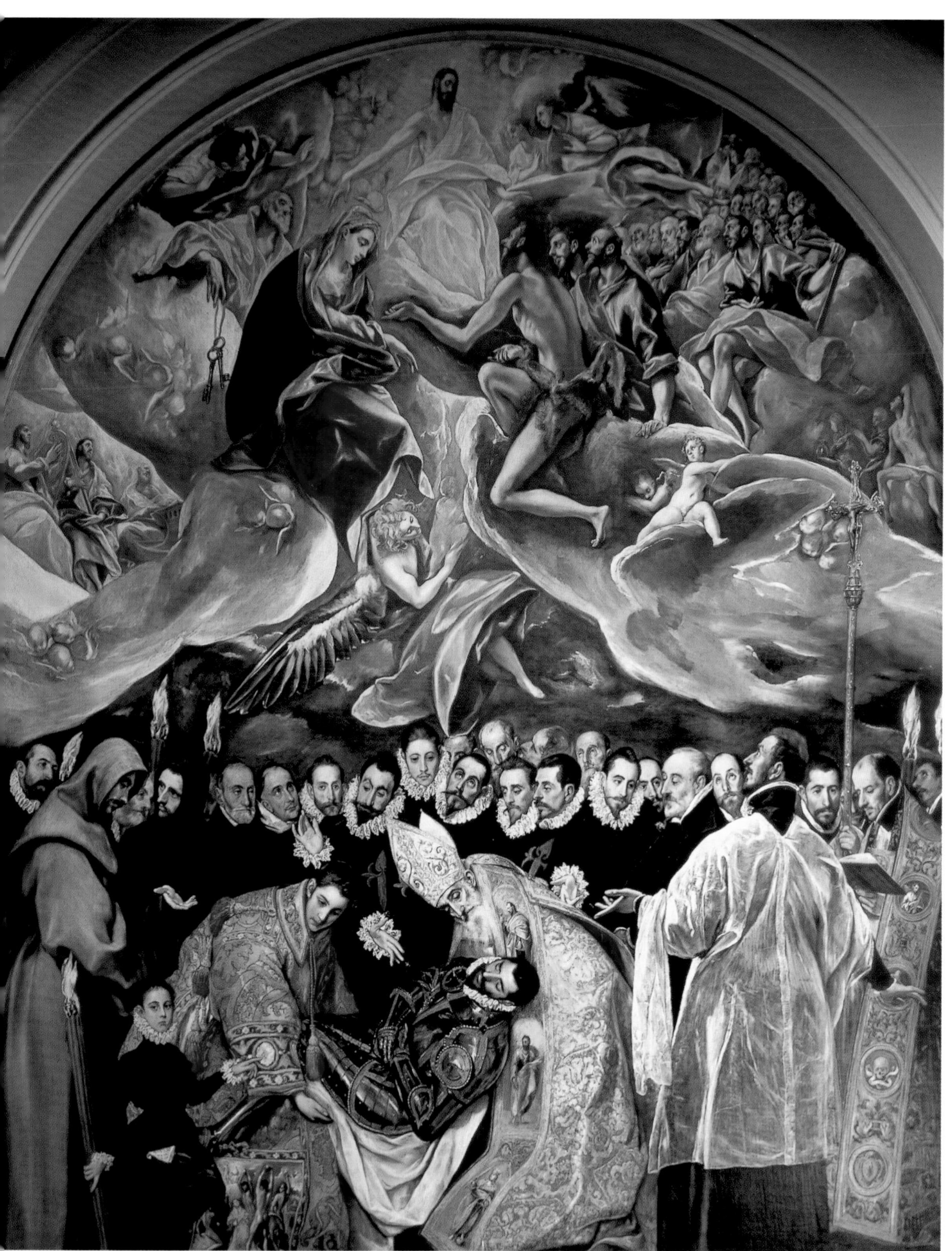

11 EL GRECO *The Burial of Count Orgaz* 1586–8

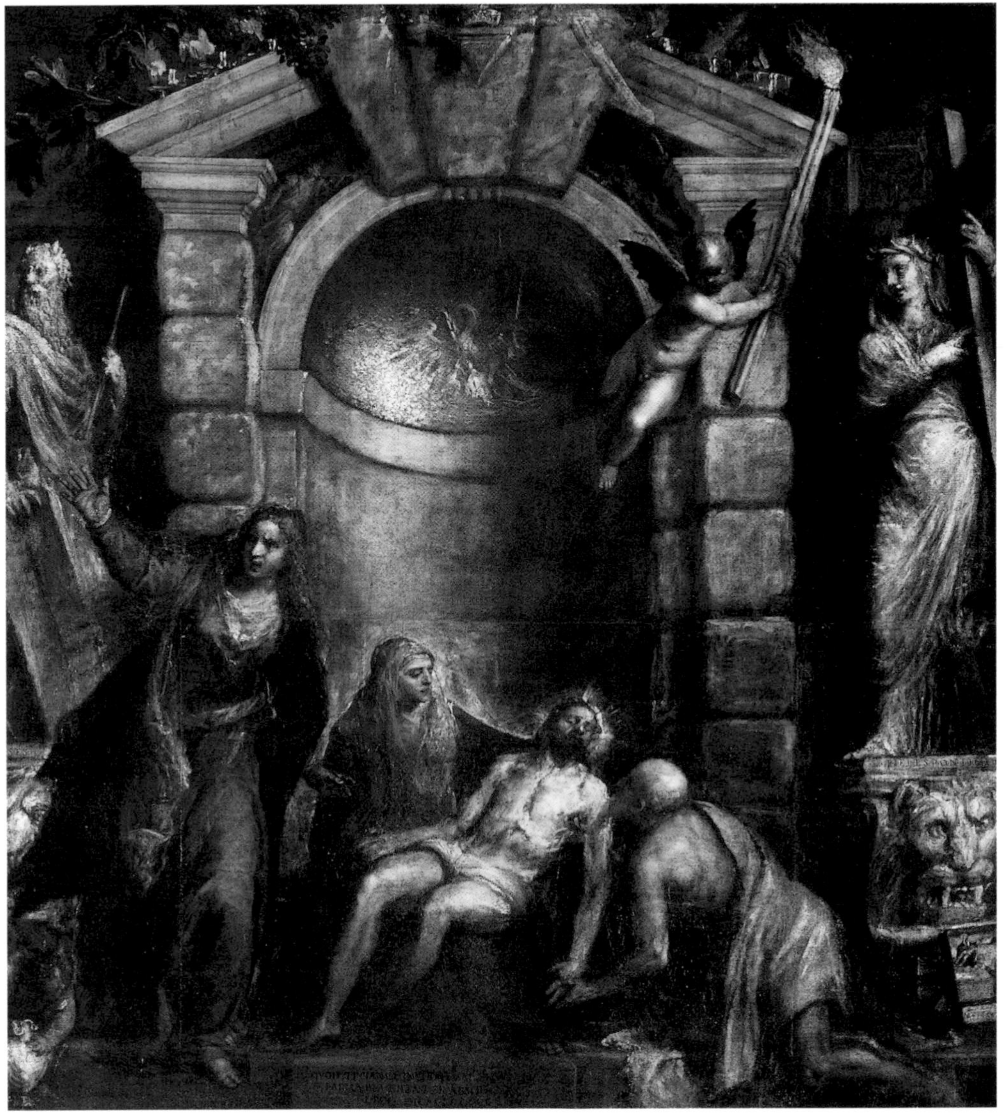

112 TITIAN *Pietà c.* 1576

symbol of Christ's sacrifice, so sketchily figured by these tesserae. The torch held aloft by a melancholy putto (the putto was painted by Palma) gutters like a dying candle. The statues standing to either side of the scene of mourning seem themselves on the point of disintegration. In this world where everything is coming apart, paint itself seems on the point of its own dissolution.

Christ's dead body is a blur, a failed representation – a botch, it might almost seem – which is, perhaps, the profoundest touch of all. As the shadows eat into this too frail flesh, as the dead body seems to fade and unfocus before the eye of the beholder, it becomes clear that what Titian has painted is not a thing, a body, but the process of death itself. As we look we see something that we know we will never, truly, be able to fix our eyes upon – that is the true meaning of this indistinct yet infinitely pathetic head with its distant, strange, averted half-grimace of disappeared consciousness – because it lies beyond and away from us. Death is another country, which we will not know until we are there, and perhaps not even then. Titian included himself in the figure of St Jerome, clasping Christ's pasty hand and staring into his shadowed eyes, as if contemplating his own mystery.

Titian's *Pietà* is a reproof to all those who have seen in Venetian art enchantment and seduction but a fundamental lack of seriousness. The classic accusation levelled at Venice – both to the art of Venice, and Venice as the embodiment of a certain set of ideas about art – is that of intellectual insufficiency. The objection, which is as old as the Renaissance itself, was stated in its classic form by Giorgio Vasari, who complimented Venetian artists on their colour, or *colore*, but complained that they lacked probity in the art of drawing, or *disegno*.[11] Venetians could enchant but their expression of ideas was found wanting, the Neoplatonic assumption behind Vasari's distinction being that drawing was the immediate expression of a mental idea and therefore superior to colour, which exists merely to decorate the idea. Drawing equals intellect. Colour – and paint, with all its mess – equals matter. Therefore draughtsmen like Michelangelo are greater than colourists or painters such as Titian.

This is, of course, nonsense. Titian showed that painting and drawing are one and the same thing – that the act of making any mark, even marks as apparently messy and muddy and inchoate and smudged as those from which his *Pietà* are formed – can be an expression of the highest order of intelligence and humanity. The artists and theorists of the Florentine and Roman Renaissance tradition sought to raise their status by arguing that art was truly an intellectual activity, only coincidentally done by men who worked with their hands. But the Venetian tradition proposed a yet more radical transfiguration of the artist, because it showed us again and again that certain types of artistic meaning can only be expressed through matter, and the manipulation of matter. The power and the depth of painting comes from the fact that it is, indeed, made by man using his hands.

CHAPTER SIX

# THE END OF THE RENAISSANCE?

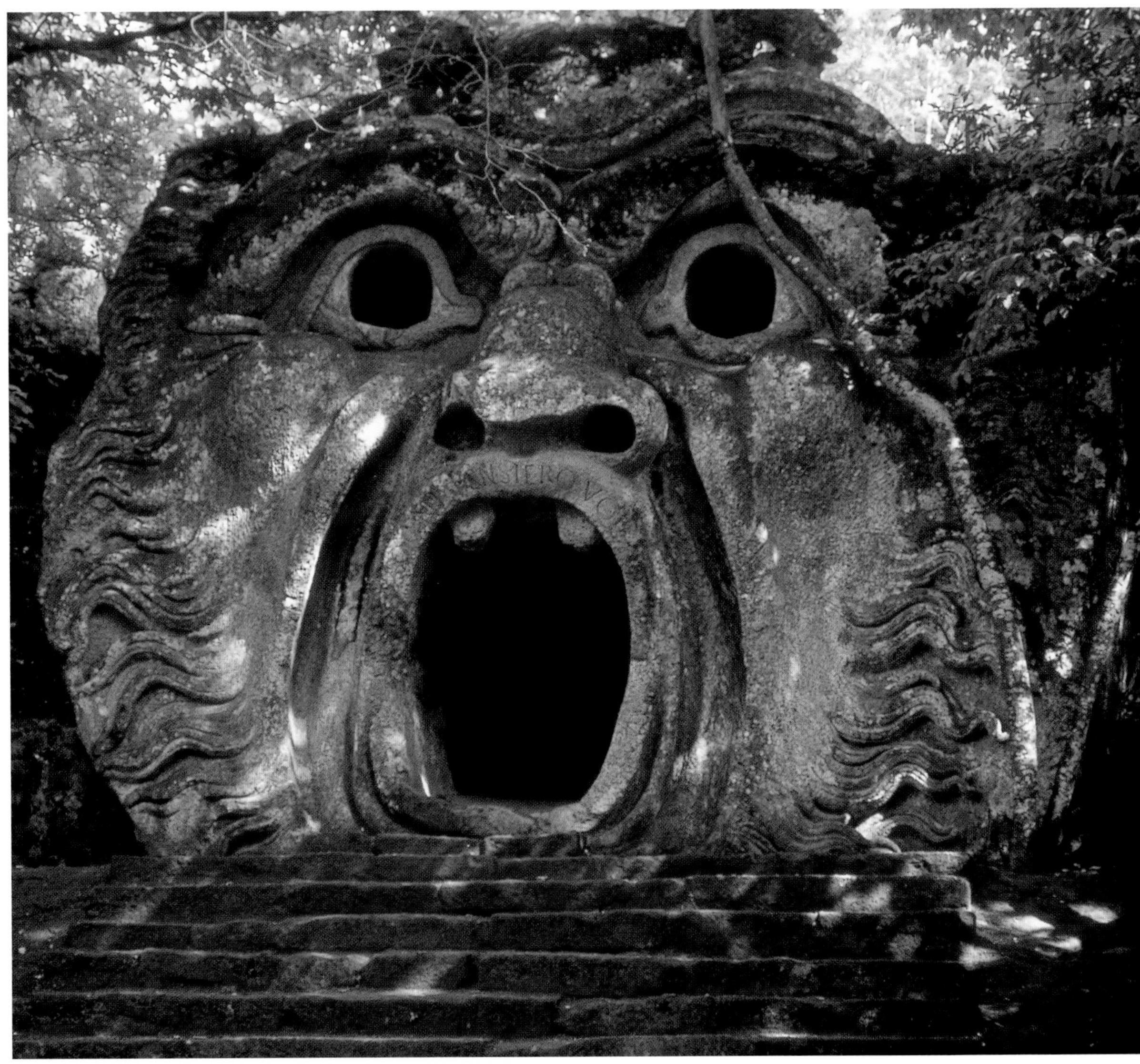

113 *Mouth of Hell*, Villa Orsini, Bomarzo *c.* 1560s–80s

It is the most serious difficulty of the history of civilization
that a great intellectual process must be broken up into single,
and often into what seem to be arbitrary categories,
in order to be in any way intelligible.

JACOB BURCKHARDT, *The Civilization of the Renaissance in Italy*, 1860

Periods of crisis are generally described as periods of transition.
All historical periods, however, are periods of transition,
for change is characteristic of them all. None has fixed boundaries,
the legacy of the past is never absent, and there are always
anticipations and promises of the future, including promises
that remain unfulfilled.

ARNOLD HAUSER, *Mannerism*, 1965

## COUNT ORSINI'S GARDEN

Count Pier Francesco Orsini was a man much given to melancholy. The premature death of his wife, Giulia Farnese, and other troubles contributing to the decay of the once proud Orsini dynasty, darkened his outlook on life. Like the world-hating Jacques in Shakespeare's *As You Like It*, he seems to have come to regard the world around him with a somewhat self-advertising disgust. Orsini retreated noisily from the world of human affairs into nature, albeit a nature much improved by art.

The count spent much of the last three decades of his life, until his death in 1584, creating an elaborate garden filled with fantastical carvings and architectural follies. Laid out on a steep hillside at the back of the Orsini palace in Bomarzo, between Rome and Orvieto, it fell into neglect until it was rediscovered in 1949, by the Surrealist painter Salvador Dali and the author Mario Praz. They believed that it expressed a profoundly 'modern' sensibility – a misinterpretation symptomatic of the gulf of misunderstanding which seems still to separate us from the late Renaissance world and its artefacts.

Although Bomarzo is in many ways an eccentric place, it is no mere freak or folly. Its apparent weirdness is precisely what makes it poignant. To visit it is to see the world of the Renaissance receding further into the past, along with the garden's own monuments, such as the carved nymph whose precise meaning has been forgotten and who now lies on her back, stone dead, in a patch of shrubbery, overgrown and greened by lichen. Many other sculptures loom up like apparitions: a huge tortoise with a castle jutting up from its shell; a screaming face of stone; a monster devouring itself. They are puzzling, like the conceits of a poem which we no longer quite know how to read. Yet this very sense of distance opens some meanings of Bomarzo to us, even as it closes others. The cruel passage of time, the replacement of one world by another, and another – these are not merely morals to be drawn, by the romantically disposed visitor, from the decay of the place. They are among the presiding themes of the garden, placed there by its morbidly intellectual creator, Orsini himself. Bomarzo is a grove shot through with reflections on death and the frailty of all human hopes – broadening from expressions of personal regret and loss into a meditation on human civilizations, their coming and their passing. There is, perhaps, no better place than this to begin to try to understand what happened to the Renaissance during the course of the sixteenth century, as it changed and developed and took on a multitude of new forms.

The garden's monuments also include two sphinxes, a huge stone elephant with the figure of a soldier writhing in the coil of its trunk and a pair of seductively smiling harpies doing the splits. Elsewhere there is a fighting stone dragon, evidently influenced by Indonesian sculpture (Orsini was widely read in the travel literature of his time and his garden reflects the larger world opening up before the eyes of sixteenth-century voyagers and explorers), as well as a startling carving of a giant rending a man limb from limb. The setting devised for would-be picnickers is the garden's best-known folly and has become its emblem. It is certainly exemplary in its strangeness, being a stone pavilion in the form of a gaping head [113] reminiscent of the traditional entries to hell depicted by painters of *The Last Judgement*. Entering through its maw, the visitor is invited by the architecture to set out his food on the carving's tongue, which serves as a table. As a metaphor for the encroachments of time on the human body – even as we eat, we are being devoured – this can hardly be bettered.

The sculptures and follies are carved out of the living rock, a technique said to have been borrowed by Orsini from the gardens of India. He clearly relished the creation of his conceits and in his pleasure we can see, writ large, the enjoyment which the men and women of the late Renaissance took in artifice for its own sake. Yet pleasure is tempered throughout by philosophical reflections. The garden contains a ruined Roman nymphaeum and a pair of enormous ruined classical fragments – two fallen spandrels – all of which seem at first sight to be genuine relics of the distant past but which soon disclose themselves as Renaissance fakes. Despite their cleverness, these fabricated architectural ruins are parables of human impotence in the face of nature and time. The world is formed, they intimate, from layerings and obliterations such as these.

Orsini made his garden, he said, to '*sfogar il core*', to relieve his aching heart. He borrowed the phrase from Petrarch, although his principal literary inspiration is more likely to have been the work of another Italian writer. The structure of the garden is designed as a slow upward ascent through grotesquerie, monstrosity and temptation to the Temple of Virtue, a mausoleum built to the memory of Orsini's deceased wife. This imitates the narrative patterns of Italian romance literature, specifically Ludovico Ariosto's long chivalric poem *Orlando furioso*, from which several of the inscriptions carved on to the monuments in the garden are derived. Walking up towards the Temple of Virtue, the visitor encounters a series of temptations and undergoes a series of adventures which correspond with varying degrees of closeness to the erotic traps and monsters – demons within and without – that beset Ariosto's hero Orlando during his long travels. This makes of Bomarzo a stoic's arcadia, a rambling but predominantly acerbic pastoral world filled with a collection of symbols of life's pitfalls.

The unusual tilt of Orsini's sensibility is epitomized by the so-called Leaning House. This is a building pitched at the same angle as that to which the Leaning Tower of Pisa has declined, with the difference that it was designed to lean. Since it carries the Orsini arms it seems to have been meant as an emblem of the personal and dynastic reverses suffered by the House of Orsini, thus satirically inverting the self-proclamation and auto-puffery that was the norm of secular aristocratic Renaissance art. From within the house itself, only two views are to be had: the world seen at an angle, on the tilt, as if to suggest that all mortal existence is thus precarious; and the sky, a heavenwards perspective implying escape through ascent, or at least through setting the mind on higher things. The Leaning House is an apt emblem of late Italian Renaissance civilization itself – in love with its own fertile ingenuity, confident in its wit, intelligence and learning, but also increasingly aware of the possibility of its own passing. The overriding moral of Count Orsini's garden is that enunciated by the nineteenth-century French author Joseph-Arthur de Gobineau, in a different context: 'All human societies – all, without exception – have their decline and fall.'[1]

## GIORGIO VASARI'S HOUSE

If the follies of Bomarzo embody the unquiet id of late Renaissance Italy, its complacent ego is encapsulated in the decidedly uncrooked house which the painter and theorist Giorgio Vasari made for himself in his native town of Arezzo during the 1540s and 1550s. But even this apparently untroubled monument to the confidence of mid-sixteenth-century Renaissance man is not without traces of anxiety. Vasari, the chief interpreter if not the only begetter of the Italian Renaissance – he was the first man to use the term '*Rinascita*', or Renaissance, to describe a rebirth of art and letters – was not immune to morbid premonitions.

He bought his house in Arezzo when he was in prosperous middle age. The son of a mere ornamental potter – his name is derived from the Italian for vase-maker (*vasoio*) – he had done well for himself. In Florence, where he had another residence and a studio, he was considered one of the most prominent artists of the day. The Casa Vasari was to be a monument to success, an allegory both of the progress of the Renaissance in Italy and of the rise of the artist – the rise of Giorgio Vasari in particular.

On the ceiling of his chief reception room [114] he painted a female personification of Virtue holding Fortune by the forelock while Envy squirms at her feet. The walls are embellished with figures symbolizing the good qualities which Vasari

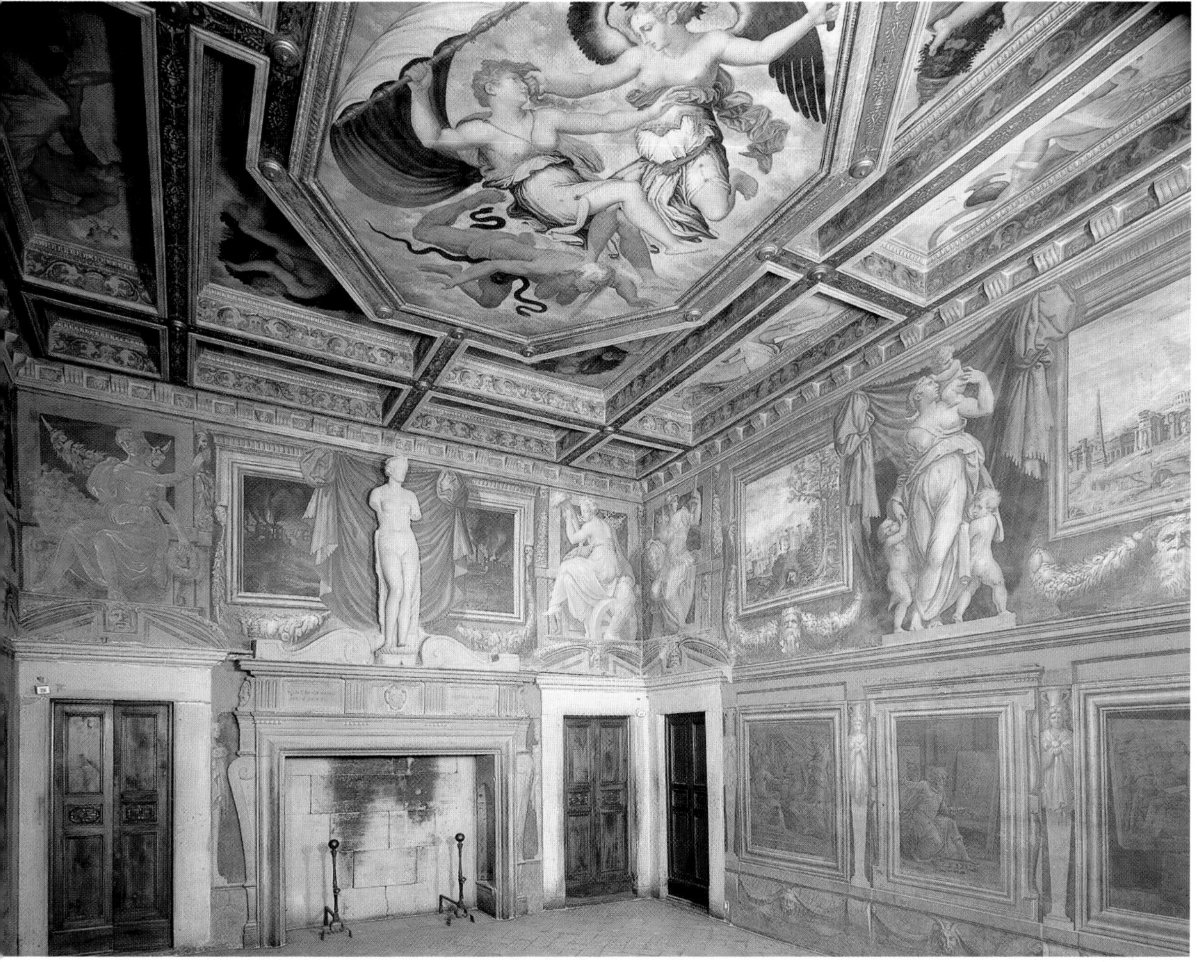

4 GIORGIO VASARI *Virtue, Fortune and Envy* (ceiling), Casa Vasari, Arezzo 1548

felt had helped him to his pre-eminent situation, including Labour, Justice, Honour, Concord, Wisdom, Charity, Liberality and Prudence. Elsewhere there is a figure with his back to the visitor, a painted book and eyeglass resting beside him on a *trompe l'oeil* windowsill, possibly a self-portrait. It all amounts to a splendidly naked piece of self-congratulation, which recalls Vasari's memorably smug response to the sneering 'How do you do?' of a ne'er-do-well painter Jacone and his drunken friends:

> I am well, my dear Jacone. I was once poor like all of you and now I have three thousand *scudi* or more; you thought me foolish, but the monks and priests consider me to be a worthy man; I once served you and now I have this servant to wait upon me and take care of this horse;

> I once wore those rags that are worn by painters who are poor, and now I am clothed in velvet; I once went on foot and now I ride a horse: so, my dear Jacone, everything is going quite well; God be with you.[2]

Vasari also decorated his house with episodes from the lives of ancient painters, depicted as though in bronze relief. By furnishing his home with these works – illustrations, for the most part, of episodes described by the Pliny the elder in his *Natural History* – the artist was suggesting his own moral if not actual descent from the masters of antiquity. Yet Vasari, like his contemporary Count Orsini, seems to have had a well-developed sense of the vulnerability of all human civilizations, and this too is one of the themes of the decorations of his house, which include a lively depiction of the burning of Troy, the act of destruction which was prelude to the building of Rome, as well as several panoramic depictions of Rome itself in ruins. Vasari envisaged history as a cycle of destruction and revival, every rise followed inevitably by a fall.

During the years when Vasari was decorating his house in Arezzo he was also busy preparing the first edition of his *magnum opus*, the first monumental work of Renaissance art history, *The Lives of the Artists*. Despite its triumphant celebration of the fact that art and artists had gained such widespread respect in Vasari's time, the book is predicated on an inherently morbid conception of the processes of history. Near the end of his introduction to the second edition, drawing a pointedly fatalistic moral from his own view of the processes of history, Vasari described how he had wished to be of service to the artists of his day 'by showing them how a small beginning leads to the highest elevation, and how from so noble a situation it is possible to fall to utterest ruin, and consequently, how these arts resemble nature as shown in our human bodies, and have their birth, growth, age and death'.[3] Elsewhere he expressed a similarly tempered exuberance at being part of the highest phase of the Italian Renaissance, 'of which I may safely say that art has done everything that is permitted to an imitator of Nature, that it has risen so high that its decline must now be feared rather than any further progress expected'.[4] It is as if the very structure of his thought betrayed an anxiety, however reluctantly expressed, that his own lifetime coincided with the end of all that he had chronicled.

This is understandable. Even as he was writing his account of the revival of the arts in modern Italy, religiously motivated iconoclasts were cutting a swathe through the churches and monasteries of Northern Europe. In Italy the deliberations of the Council of Trent, which began sitting in 1546, were also to have an extreme if less physically destructive influence on the course of art. There may have been another reason besides for Vasari's anxiety. Once it is possible to describe something, as he had described the Italian Renaissance, once a phenomenon has taken on sufficient form to have been recognized as such, perhaps its energies have indeed begun to diffuse. If a tone of belatedness occasionally sounds in Vasari's *Lives*, that too is unsurprising. Given the achievements of Raphael, and of Titian and Michelangelo, who both remained active into the 1550s and beyond, it must have been difficult for any artist of that time not to feel, to some degree, that he was living in the shadow of giants.

## MICHELANGELO'S EXAMPLE

The man whom Vasari had placed at the pinnacle of his age was Michelangelo, the only living artist of note included in the first edition of *The Lives*. Yet Michelangelo, precisely through being the innovator that Vasari praised, had helped to sow the seeds of the destruction of Renaissance art. Pursued in one direction, his spirit of invention would lead to the discrediting of artistic virtuosity itself in Italy. Pursued in another, it would lead to a world characterized by such diversity that the word 'Renaissance' would simply cease to adhere to it.

Florence, the city in which Vasari would rise to prominence, was also where Michelangelo created two of the most remarkable works of the second half of his career. Conceived in the 1520s, although their execution would stretch into subsequent decades, both are attached to Brunelleschi's church of San Lorenzo. One is a piece of architecture, being the vestibule to a library; the other is a mortuary chapel, conceived as an architectural ensemble containing tombs and sculptures. Yet each, while performing its necessary function, exemplifies an impressively absolute dissatisfaction with the merely functional.

The Laurentian Library vestibule [115], designed by Michelangelo and carried out largely by Bartolomeo Ammanati, is one of the supreme examples of Renaissance artistic licence. It seems almost perverse to describe it as a work of architecture because it is really something else altogether, for which there is no precise name. It is a kind of abstract sculpture formed from the elements of classical architectural style yet in a spirit of such wanton disregard for their conventional uses that they are utterly transformed by the process. Thus we find an interior on to which has been grafted a multitude of massive, monumental forms usually found on the exteriors of buildings – heavy, window-like tabernacles alternating with paired classical columns of grey *pietra serena*. It is as if the grand

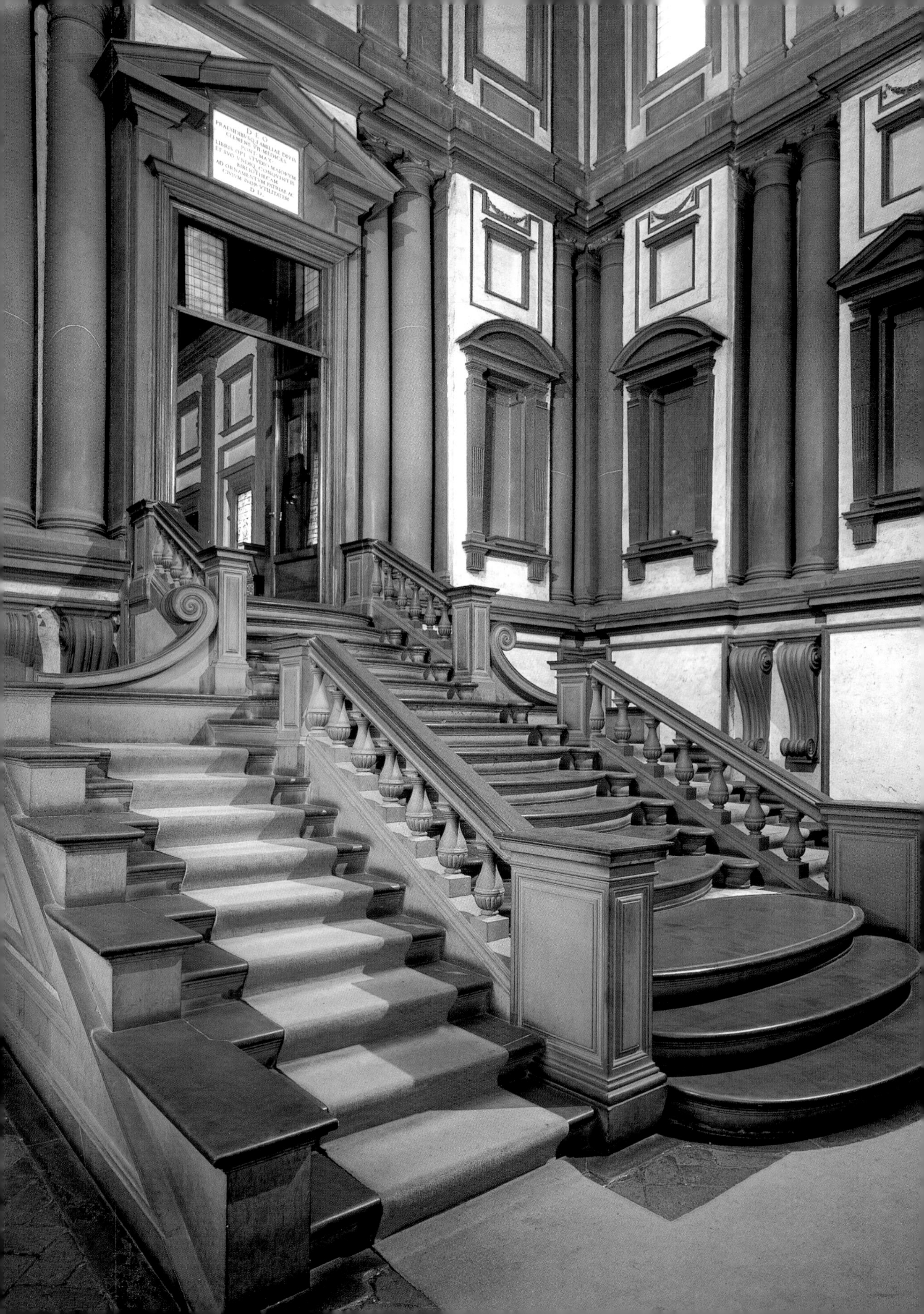
D E O
PRAESIDIBVSQ FAMILIAE DIVIS
CLEMENS VII MEDICES
PONT MAX
LIBRIS OPT STVDIO MAIORVM
ET SVO VNDIQ CONQVISITIS
BIBLIOTHECAM
AD ORNAMENTVM PATRIAE AC
CIVIVM SVOR VTILITATEM
D D

façade of some Renaissance palace has been folded in on itself, as if the four walls of an inside have been created, origami-like, from an exterior.[5] The perversity of this effect enhances the squeezed and mildly claustrophobic space thus enclosed and decorated with superabundant superfluity. All the architectural members in the vestibule flaunt their inutility: the windows are blind; the pillars have simply been attached to a wall which they play no part in supporting; and pairs of enormous voluted brackets, instead of holding anything up, as brackets normally do, simply hang suspended from a moulding. The only part of the scheme which is truly functional is the staircase which, with its sensually curved central flight of steps, seems almost to flow into the vestibule like lava.

Attempts have been made to find evidence of Michelangelo's psychological alienation in such consciously irrational details. Vasari had a rather more straightforward explanation. The artist, he said, disliked 'poverty' in any part of any of his works. The praise of variety in works of art as an antidote to tedium was a commonplace of sixteenth-century Italian aesthetics, so Vasari's view of the matter is more plausible than that of those moderns who would credit the artist anachronistically with angst. Equally, however, the Laurentian Library vestibule seems to express more than Renaissance *horror vacui* alone. Dumb stone has been conjured into speech. The artist created a cramped house of confusion from which his staircase, leading to a long reading room beyond, offers the welcome prospect of release. It is significant that the stairway in question should lead to a library, seat of knowledge. Just as Count Orsini's garden proposes a journey upwards to Virtue out of confusion, so does Michelangelo's library vestibule evoke the ascent of the intellect.

Michelangelo's other creation in Florence during this period was a mortuary chapel dedicated to members of the Medici family [116]. In the New Sacristy of San Lorenzo blind tabernacles alternate with classical columns, the same framework as in the Laurentian Library, but here put to the service of a double-edged vision of worldly glory. Attached to two facing walls of the interior, it shapes a pair of triumphal arches housing heroic, idealized, larger than life-size statues of the dead men to be memorialized. Loftily enthroned as Roman generals, noble of physique and solemn of visage, they preside in majesty over a room which marks – with a morbid and deflating bathos – the passing of all that they represent.

The cold and forbidding atrium in which the artist chose to set the apotheosis of Giuliano de' Medici and his cousin Lorenzo, Duke of Urbino (not to be confused with the earlier and more famous Lorenzo de' Medici, il Magnifico), might be the antechamber of Death itself. One of the deceased, Lorenzo, had been

115 MICHELANGELO Vestibule, Laurentian Library, San Lorenzo, Florence, begun 1524

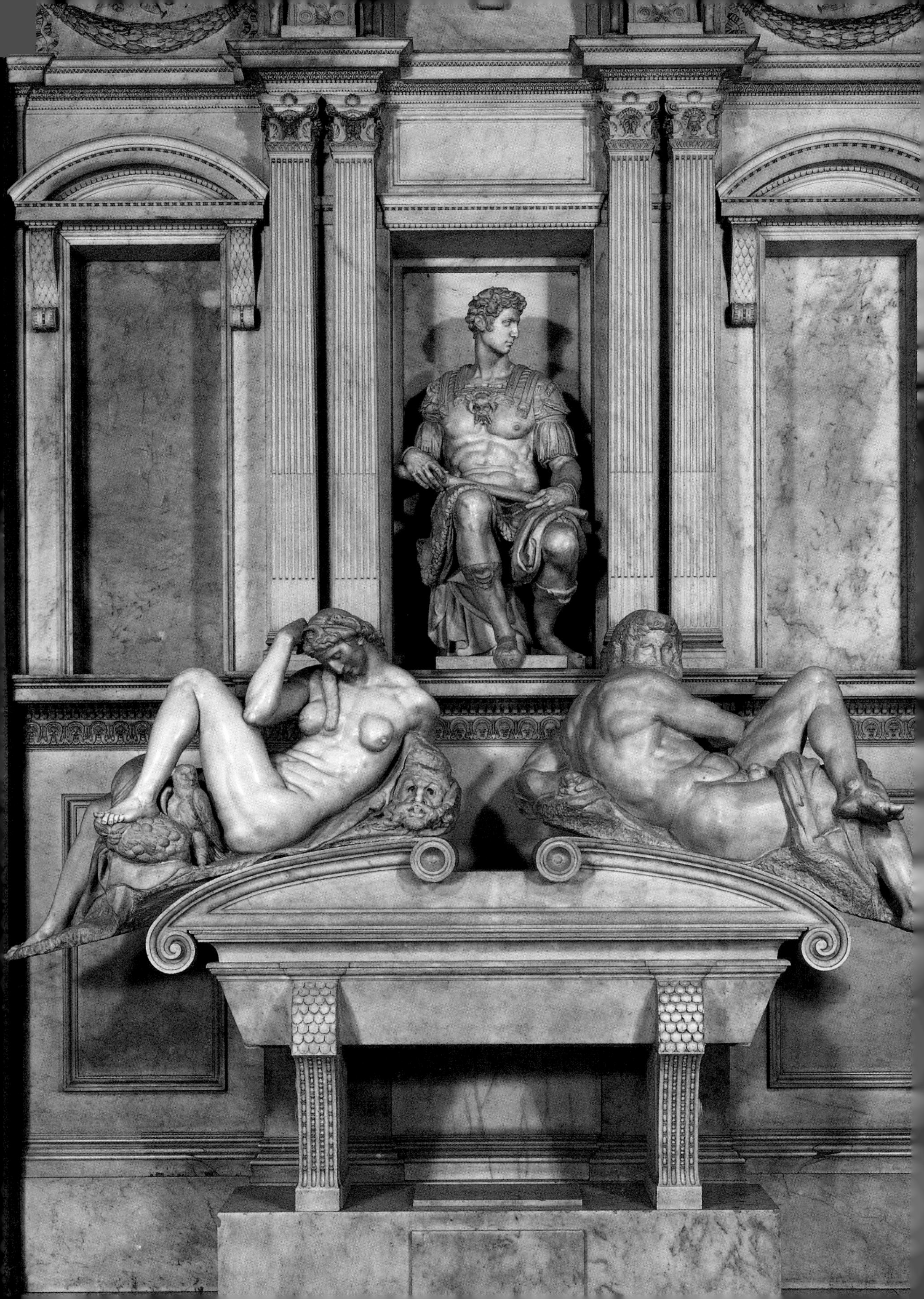

the dedicatee of Machiavelli's *The Prince*; Michelangelo represented him as a cloaked and armoured soldier deep in thought, but in a place where musing or calculation can do no one – not even a man versed in the ruthless ways of Machiavelli's prince – the slightest good. The capitals of the columns forming the triumphal arches of the chapel's architecture are worked with grotesque faces which seem to mock, while mounted on sarcophagi placed before the heroes on high there are paired figures of *Night and Day* and *Morning and Evening*. These uneasily reclining nudes, infinitely weary descendants of ancient Roman river gods – and thus distant relations of Michelangelo's *Adam* on the Sistine Chapel ceiling – symbolize the passing of time. They are imperfectly finished, but this only strengthens their effect. The blur of unfinish is accidentally eloquent. All is always in flux, moving and changing inexorably. The melancholic force with which the figures embody this conventional message thus contributes to the New Sacristy's power as an ensemble. The meanings which it enshrines are forbiddingly straightforward. *Tempus fugit. Sic transit gloria mundi.* The prince, along with all his worldly concerns and stratagems, is rendered an irrelevance by the very memorial which seems to commemorate him.

Michelangelo's moral example was enormous. But his influence might be said to have operated in two not always complementary ways. By reinventing his style with each new work that he created, he introduced a kind of fertile insecurity into the very fabric of art and helped to create a climate in which every sculptor or painter had to have his own distinctive manner, or *maniera*. Michelangelo's work also insisted, in its every sinew, that art express the higher aspirations of spirit and intellect. This aspect of his monumental achievement was less perfectly understood by his contemporaries and followers than his formal originality.

## PONTORMO'S INTROSPECTION

No artist built on Michelangelo's achievements with fiercer originality than the painter Jacopo Pontormo (1494–1556). Vasari – who knew him but possibly exaggerated his strangeness for effect – depicted him as an eccentric, melancholic, misanthropic figure. Pontormo's reputation went into sharp decline after his death. Although it was revived in the early twentieth century, when people became sensitive once more to the excruciating beauties of his art, much of his work had already by then been lost or badly damaged. But the works which survive, almost intact, in the Capponi Chapel in the church of Santa Felicita, Florence, are enough to confirm him as one of the greatest Renaissance painters.

116 MICHELANGELO Tomb of Giuliano de' Medici, New Sacristy, San Lorenzo, Florence 1524–34

Pontormo began work in the Capponi Chapel in 1525 and finished in 1528, in the aftermath of the Sack of Rome. This was a moment when Florence, too, was in one of its periodic political convulsions, the Medici having been temporarily expelled and republican rule briefly reinstated. Pontormo's creation has the extreme and even mildly hysterical qualities of a work of art produced in a state of emergency. At the heart of it we find an image of desperate loss and severance – a depiction of the dead Christ being separated from his mother, after the Crucifixion, and carried away to the tomb by a pair of transfixingly anxious bearers [117].

The most immediately striking feature of the chapel's decoration is its concatenation of sharp and acid colours: metallic blues, lime greens, lemon yellows. These lend the scenes depicted – an *Annunciation* and the more prominent *Entombment* – an eerie and unreal quality, making them seem less like representations of the real than of visions. The influence of Michelangelo's Sistine Chapel may be felt in Pontormo's choice of colour, albeit tuned to a yet higher pitch; but Pontormo's treatment of his main theme, the *The Entombment*, suggests that he was meditating on the most original of Michelangelo's early religious sculptures, the *Pietà* in St Peter's, Rome. In his painting Pontormo enacted a kind of violence on Michelangelo's vision of the young and beautiful mother cradling an Adonis-like Christ in her lap. He has, so to speak, imagined the parting of Michelangelo's fused mother and son – the moment just after he has been lifted off her knees.

At the heart of the picture – 'its widowed centre', in Leo Steinberg's memorable phrase[6] – is the Virgin's empty lap, the physical root of her wrenching sorrow. In this part of the picture, the void in its middle from which all else seems to emanate, the hand of the Magdalene, lit as if by a spotlight, clutches a fold of drapery. It is a detail in which seems compressed – grasped – the ruling emotion of the painting as a whole: the passionate desire to hold on to that which is loved, even as it slips away. The Virgin's own hand, reaching out towards her son in a gesture of longing and farewell, is empty. The drama of hands is also a drama of eyes, so that to look the figures in the face is to see one restless, troubled gaze multiplied, although all the figures look pointedly in different directions. The monumental unity of the image – the main figure group is like a relief sculpture carved from a single piece of wood or stone – finds a restless counterpoint in this complicated play of starings. This has the effect of pulling the image apart or at least hinting at the imminent dissolution of energies and parting of bodies which is presaged in the moment when Christ's body is transported to the sepulchre.

Pontormo invested his subject with an intensity of feeling which may owe as much to Northern European as to Italian influences. It is known that he admired

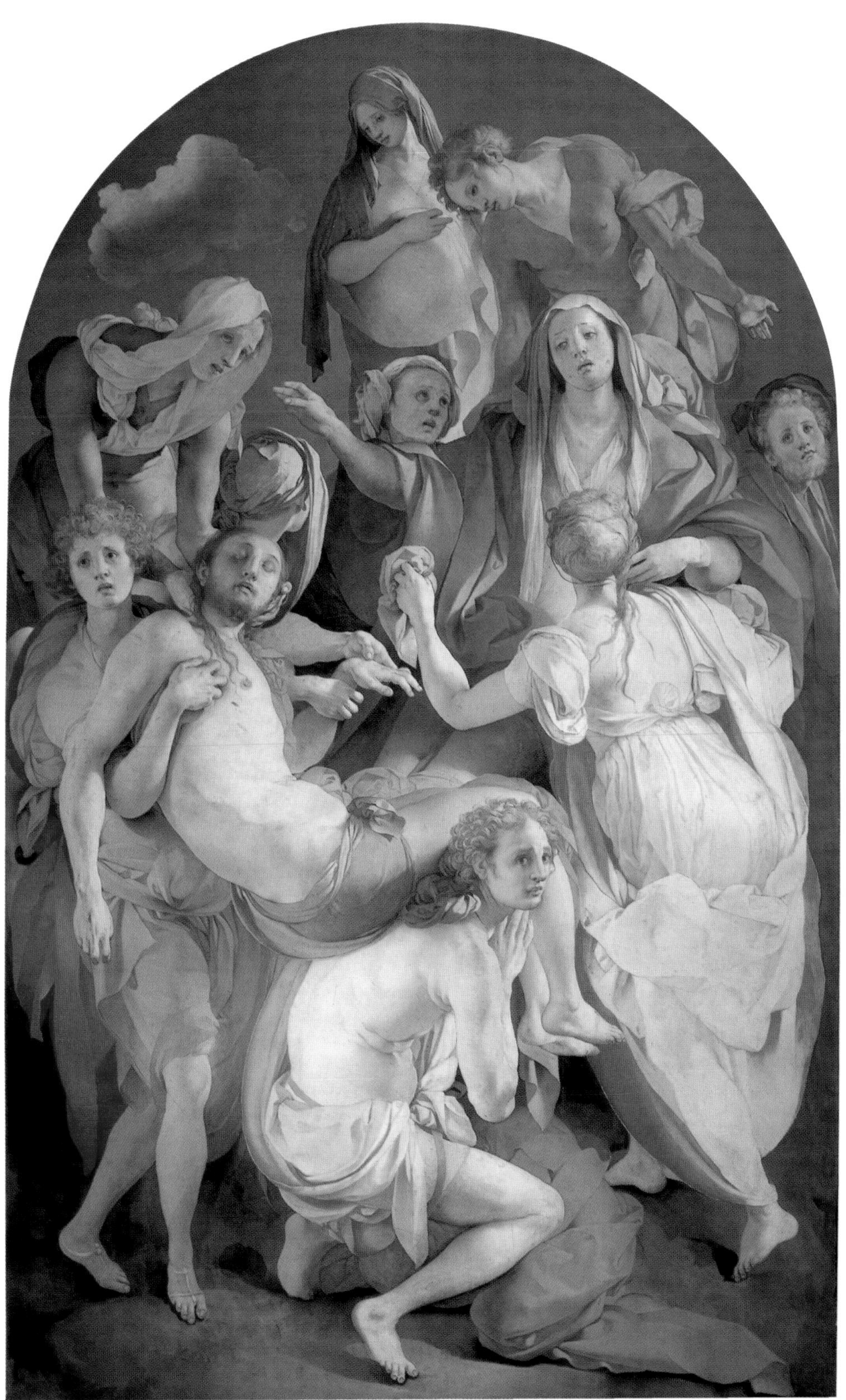

117 JACOPO PONTORMO *The Entombment c.* 1527–8

the work of Dürer; and the awkward passions and unrelieved longings which surge through his painting like waves communicate a paroxysmic piety more familiar from German or Flemish art of the period. The result is a new style, entirely and unmistakably Pontormo's own. He took the conventions established by generations of Florentine painters and simply tore them up – so it is as if the Florentine Renaissance itself is being unmade, being dissolved before our very eyes. Mathematically calculated perspective has been done away with. There is no space in this painting, certainly no space that the eye and mind can measure. The figures are larger than the solitary, luridly lit cloud which hovers over them, and indeed all the laws of nature would seem to have been temporarily suspended. The dead body of Christ has no weight, while his mother levitates as she grieves. It is as if flesh, propelled upwards by spiritual desire, has metamorphosed into some more fluid substance. The Virgin and those around her rise up into the thin, clear air of Pontormo's painting like a jet of water issuing from a Renaissance fountain.

## CORREGGIO'S THEATRE

The 1520s and 1530s were an extremely fertile period in the history of Italian religious art, a fact often overlooked by those inspecting the period too eagerly for signs of artistic senility or decadence. It would be unrealistic to explain the phenomenon by a single cause, but the influence of the Reformation, which had made man's relationship with God the single most pressing concern of sixteenth-century Christendom, should not be underestimated. In Florence the gathering clouds of religious ferment seemed particularly dark, and that may have played a part in encouraging artists to seek out new ways of reinforcing Christian belief. Other Italian cities too were incubating mutations in religious art. In Venice, Titian was at the height of his powers as a religious artist; while, in Parma, an equally brilliant if currently less fashionable painter, Correggio (*c.* 1489–1534), was refashioning the conventional pieties of that city's relatively pedestrian painting tradition.

*The Martyrdom of Four Saints* [118], in the Galleria Nazionale of Parma, is one of the most startling pictures of the first half of the sixteenth century. On a patch of ground, beside a rock, beneath the trunk of a tree, a kneeling man and woman – they have been identified as St Placidus and St Flavia – are in the process of being murdered. He wears a monk's habit, while she is more splendidly garbed in fluttering robes of blue and gold. He is having his head cut off by an elegantly twisting executioner, depicted in *contrapposto*. She is being stabbed through the heart by an equally handsome killer in a swirling, windblown red cloak which billows above his head like a splash of blood. Beside them lie the remains of their two co-martyrs – a modest litter of corpses and severed heads economically strewn by Correggio so as not to distract from his leading man and leading lady. Given centre stage and starring roles, each greets death like a long-awaited lover. While the blue-green landscape beyond him seems to flicker with responsive energy and excitement, light glancing on rivulets of water, St Placidus, whose bared neck has already been gashed, awaits the blow which will finally despatch him with upturned eyes and an expression of swooning rapture. St Flavia, for her part, looks heavenwards in delight as the sword pierces her side and she expires, lips parted in a last gasp of pleasure, making martyrdom look as enticing and releasing as an orgasm.

Correggio was a more theatrical artist than Pontormo. Whereas Pontormo created an art of agonized introspection, Correggio set out to paint the human face and body in the throes of mystical religious experience. He wanted to convey, not the vision itself – which remains opaque, hidden for ever *behind* the clouded dying eyes of his hero and heroine – but the experience of having it. His method was to make that experience seem like a form of displaced sexual rapture. Virtuous death had never been depicted in this way before.

Correggio's originality in the treatment of religious themes may have been sparked by another aspect of his practice, namely his work in the genre of risqué, erotic mythological painting with which the courtly patrons of the time liked to decorate their walls. In *The Martyrdom of Four Saints* Correggio had given religious art a transfusion of erotic appeal from the body of secular, mythological Renaissance painting: the saints are depicted as if enjoying the sensual raptures of libidinous classical gods and goddesses.

Having received commissions for several mythological works from patrons in Mantua during the 1520s, towards the end of his life Correggio painted a series of bold and inventive illustrations of *The Loves of Jupiter* for the Holy Roman Emperor Charles V. Here Correggio's mastery of the secular genre of erotic mythological painting found its fullest expression. His large canvas of *Jupiter and Io*, now in the Kunsthistorisches Museum in Vienna, makes even Titian's erotic mythological paintings seem almost blatant and vulgar by comparison. The king of the gods comes down to earth wreathed in smoke to ravish the object of his desires. Correggio's enraptured Io is enfolded in a thick grey cloud which seems to alter shape where it touches her most intimately, transforming itself into wispy suggestions of a man's hands and lips. She swoons with pleasure, surrendering to her shapeshifting lover and parting her lips to accept the vaporous kiss.

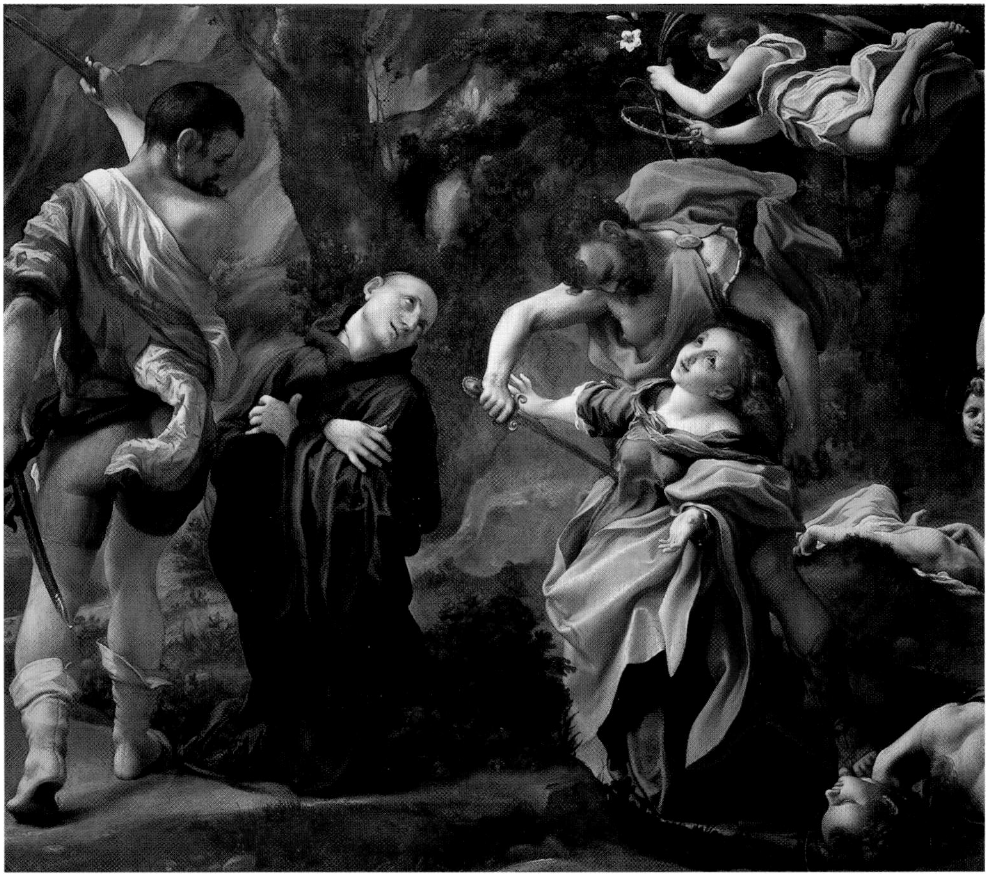

118 CORREGGIO *The Martyrdom of Four Saints c.* 1522

In Correggio's work, as in sixteenth-century Italy as a whole, the sacred and the profane were constantly being shaped by one another: orgiastic mythology could suggest orgasmic martyrdom which could, in turn, become mythological ecstasy. His *Ganymede and the Eagle* (Kunsthistorisches Museum, Vienna), also from Ovid and for Charles V, is patently adapted from the angel supporting a cloud in one of the squinches that Correggio decorated in the dome of Parma Cathedral. In yet another metamorphosis within this chain of transformations, Correggio's vortex-like depiction of coiled ascending clouds and angels sweeping the Virgin heavenwards in the centre of that same dome itself owes a debt to Mantegna's perspective games on the ceiling of the Camera degli Sposi, in the Ducal Palace of Mantua. As the century progressed it came to seem increasingly as if the barriers separating Italian religious and secular art had almost ceased to exist.

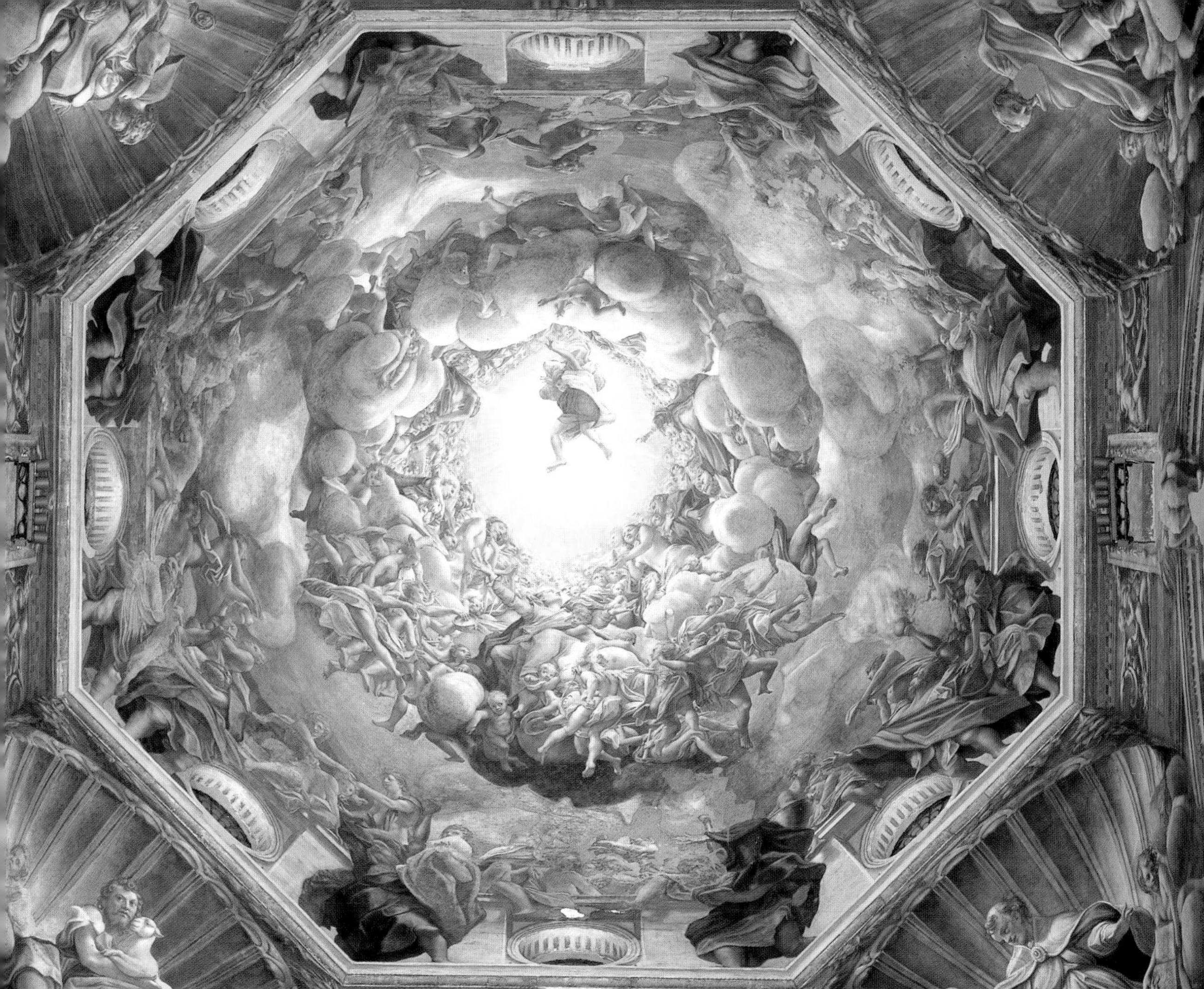

119 CORREGGIO *The Assumption of the Virgin*, Dome, Parma Cathedral *c.* 1530

The theme of Correggio's fresco in the dome of Parma Cathedral [119] is joy unbound. Whereas Pontormo's paintings in the Capponi Chapel project the viewer into the inner space of contemplation, this is a work that whirls the viewer upwards as if to join the Virgin herself in her ascent to the vault of heaven. Its perspective is a tornado – a twister. The extreme originality of the dome disconcerted some people when they first saw it. According to legend one of the canons of the cathedral compared the fresco to 'a stew of frogs' legs'.[7] Titian came to Correggio's defence when he saw the work a few years after its completion. The Venetian artist, possibly admiring the extent to which Correggio had transformed and reinvigorated the example of his own *Assumption of the Virgin* (in the church of the Frari, Venice), remarked that the artist's reward for creating such a masterpiece should have been enough gold coins to fill the dome itself.

## ABSOLUTE ARTFULNESS

The instability and restlessness which characterized so much Italian religious art from the 1520s onwards also found expression in Renaissance courts. There too the rules of art were bent and broken. The Palazzo Te, in Mantua, is one of the chief monuments to the aristocratic world of the Renaissance during this time. A palace dedicated to pure pleasure, its every nook and cranny seems designed to stave off boredom with the frisson of spectacle. It was built and decorated for Federigo Gonzaga, between 1527 and 1534, by the painter and architect Giulio Romano, aided by teams of assistants. The effect of Giulio's ensemble has been diminished by the fact that the palace is no longer, as it once was, an island. Nowadays it is a traffic island, surrounded by roads where formerly there was water. Yet its structure, a low-lying network of buildings linked by courtyards, still vividly communicates the love of what Vasari was to describe as 'pleasing variety'.

Since Mantua and its surrounding landscape are unrelievedly flat, the architect was unable to exploit changes of level to create different views of the palace. Instead, he designed a complex of buildings which change like different scenes in a play as the viewer walks through and past them. The entrance, set into a rusticated façade, leads to an elegant classical courtyard, which leads into a tall loggia, which in turn leads, via a bridge across an ornamental stretch of water, into a wide open space. By offering a multitude of different vistas of itself, the palace holds out the promise of an architecture that will never run out of surprises.

Every façade is different and each is enlivened by some witty conceit or novelty. The pediments over some of the windows are formed from stones that fail to meet, making a shape like the broken apex of a triangle and thus suggesting that they have been forced out of shape by pressure from below. Some elements in the friezes which run along the top of Giulio's façades have been designed to look as if they have slipped out of place, like imperfectly aligned building blocks in a child's game. Giulio took Michelangelo's licentiousness but played it as comedy. This is a building confident enough to pretend its own disintegration.

The keynote of the Palazzo Te is not refinement but another aesthetic desideratum of the time, *copia*, or copiousness. The interior is almost pathologically dedicated to variety, consisting of suite after suite of rooms decorated by Giulio and his workshop on themes calculated to amuse the patron and satisfy his vanity. There is a room dedicated to Ovid's *Metamorphoses*. There is a room which simulates a stable, with frescoed tethered thoroughbreds standing patiently on all sides.

There is a room dedicated to *Cupid and Psyche* which contains a multitude of erotic scenes painted in deliberately bawdy style. Camels and elephants and a gaggle of delectable nudes lounge and debauch in the scene of *A Noble Banquet*, a picture which looks like the prelude to an orgy. The adventures of the gods are painted in a mock-heroic burlesque style which represents a self-consciously irreverent opening up of earlier Renaissance cults of antiquity, a domestication of mythology which turns it into a mirror for pleasure-seekers rather than idealists. Elsewhere there are jokes that play on the spectator's point of view. The indecorous potential of illusionistic ceiling painting – the way in which it invites the viewer to look up the skirts of its protagonists – is exposed in a deliberately unflattering picture of a charioteer. Anyone who has ever wondered what ancient Romans wore under their togas will find an answer here.

There is a kind of fairground ribaldry at work in the palace's most celebrated room, which brings Giulio's accumulation of shows and spectacles to its thunderingly bathetic climax. This is the Sala dei Giganti, or Room of the Giants, all four walls of which have been painted to simulate a circular temple in an advanced state of collapse. Various monstrous ogres writhe and struggle in the rubble. Looking up at the ceiling of the room, the spectator finds a tour de force of illusionism. Giulio's depiction of Jupiter and the assembly of the gods, whirled round in a vortex of clouds [120], is so closely based on Correggio's dome in Parma Cathedral [119] as to amount to a kind of in-joke. The tawdry theatre can be enjoyed precisely because it wears its tawdriness on its sleeve. It is an overblown jape which seeks forgiveness through self-mockery. Giulio's work in the Sala dei Giganti doubtless had specific meanings and associations – it may have been an explicit allegory of the fate that befalls those who challenge authority – but at its most straightforward it was, simply, an advertisement of its creator's wit and skill. It worked and his fame spread. Giulio is the only Renaissance artist to be mentioned by Shakespeare.[8]

At the slightly later Villa d'Este in Tivoli, the pleasure palace of Cardinal Ippolito d'Este and his descendants, the patron's infatuation with artifice overflowed the bounds of the house. Here it seems that the world itself has turned into a work of art. This is a place where every rock has a human (or animal) face and where even caves turn out to be man-made creations, dripping grottoes still encrusted with the often inscrutable remains of Renaissance fancy. Like the interior of the Palazzo Te, the garden of the Villa d'Este is a monument to the uncontainable passion for spectacle which characterized the sixteenth-century Italian nobility – as well as a Renaissance harbinger of modern civilization,

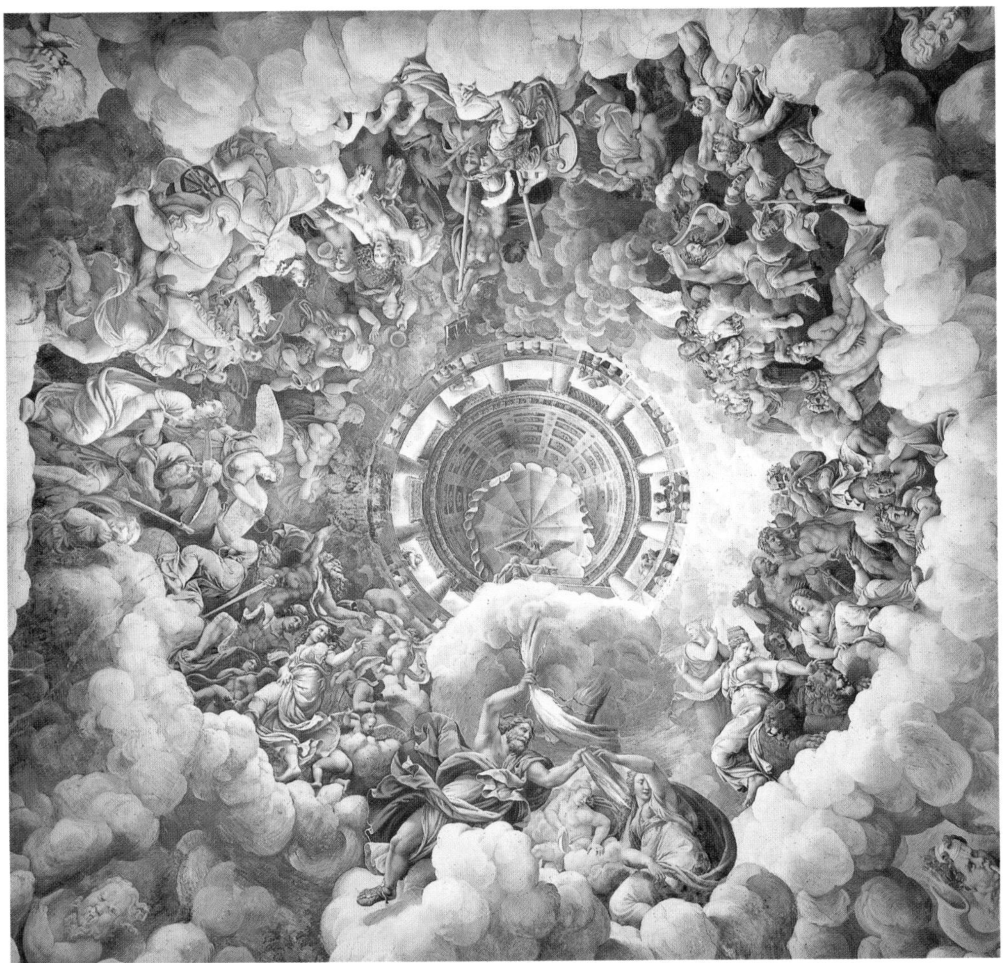

120 GIULIO ROMANO Ceiling, Room of the Giants, Palazzo Te, Mantua 1530–32

intolerant of boredom, channel-hopping, saturated with imagery designed to amuse and advertise.

Much has changed at the Villa d'Este on account of later additions and alterations, but one thing has remained constant: the garden's spectacularly abundant use of water, the supply of which required Ippolito to build an aqueduct that called forth comparisons with the heroic water engineering of the ancient Romans. Everywhere there are fountains, providing a constant and importunate watery show. Some were designed specifically to soak the visitor. Such elements of surprise theatrics and audience participation (however unwilling) turn the garden, with all its contrivance, into a kind of wet pantomime. Many of the water sculptures echo the elaborate *intermezzi* or theatrical entertainments of the time. The fountain in which a ship floats, on the garden's upper terrace, may reflect the sixteenth-century

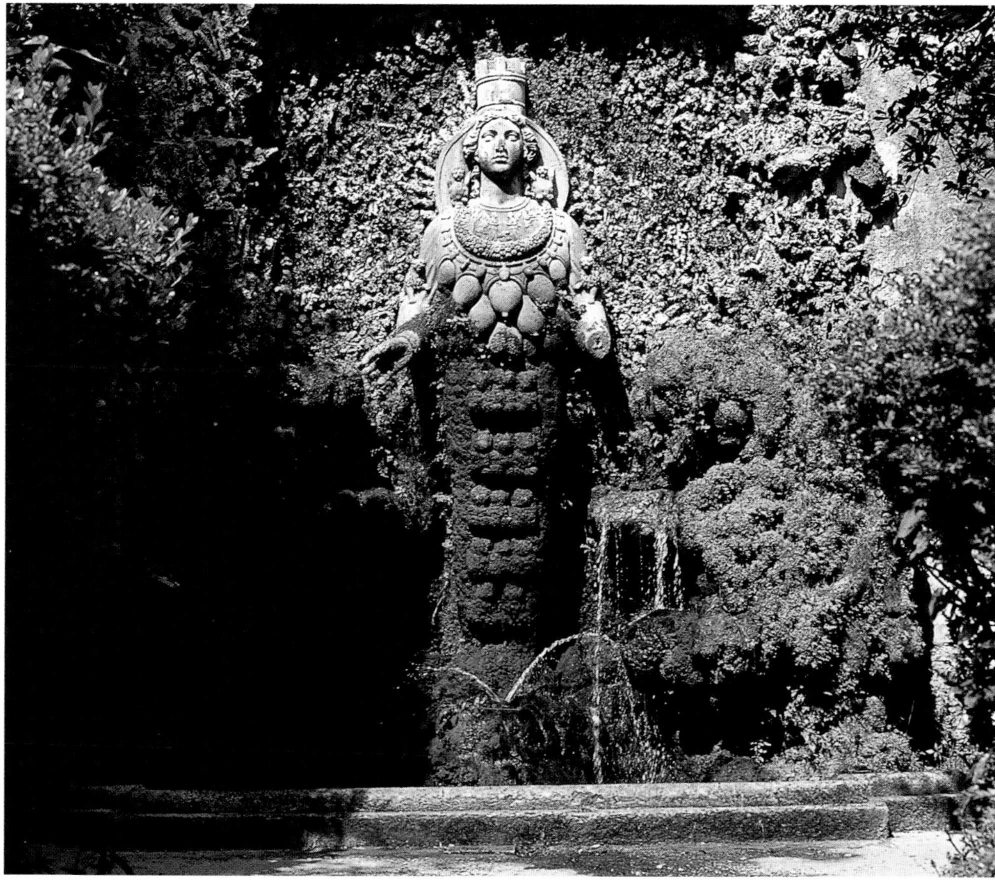

121 *Fountain of Diana of Ephesus*, Villa d'Este, Tivoli, late 16th century

interest in staging *naumachie* or sea battles, one of which was performed in the flooded courtyard of the Pitti Palace in Florence under the Medici.

The love of variety, in itself a perennial human impulse, has rarely been as pronounced as it became in the upper echelons of sixteenth-century Italian society. Literary theorists spent much ink debating to whom should be awarded the palm of most pleasingly varied classical author. Some favoured Homer, whose elaborate description of the ornate shield of Achilles, in *The Iliad*, became an aesthetic prototype for writers, artists, goldsmiths, furniture-makers and other purveyors of prolific ingenuity. But Ovid was the presiding genius of this phase of the Italian Renaissance. His fables, concerning transformation and metamorphosis, are the nonpareil allegories of art's own miracle, which is to enact a metamorphosis on matter.

The fountain is a symbol of inexhaustible creativity, a source that never runs dry. The work which most fully expresses the superabundant spirit of the garden at Tivoli is to be found not at its centre but at its edge. The figure of *Diana of Ephesus* [121] stands at the bottom of the garden, back to the wall. Water spouts from her many lactating breasts. An ancient nature goddess, worshipped in classical and early Christian times, her influence had helped to shape the mother-cult of the Virgin Mary. Here, transformed into a fountain, she seems an apt symbol of the uncontrollable fertility of later Renaissance art.

## ARTFUL ABSOLUTISM

Villas were a refuge from the city, but what about the art of the city itself? Florence, once the very capital of Italian Renaissance civilization, was a measure of just how much had changed by the mid-sixteenth century. Here the flourish of high artifice was harnessed to the ambitions of the Medici dynasty and resulted in the creation of a new civic environment. From his accession to the Dukedom of Tuscany in 1537 until his death in 1574, Cosimo de' Medici presided over a transformation in which politics and aesthetics were intertwined. The imperfect, intermittent but tenacious republicanism which had characterized Florence for centuries finally gave up the ghost during his reign, and the city at last accepted autocratic rule – a transition which was accompanied and possibly eased by Cosimo's devotion to grand public spectacle.

Cosimo was determined to perpetuate his own memory and stamp Florence with his image. Art was his political instrument, just as it had been Leonardo Bruni's political instrument a century earlier. But man's conception of art and politics had undergone much change during those hundred years, and even works consciously commissioned by Cosimo to complement the achievements of the early Renaissance only emphasize the chasm separating his world and that of his less openly hubristic predecessors. Despite the unprecedented scale of the public works undertaken for Cosimo, his vision of the city has proved somewhat unpopular with posterity, as unloved as Giambologna's impressive equestrian statue of the duke himself, which stands in a prominent place in the Piazza della Signoria attracting the regular attention of pigeons but little more than the occasional incurious glance from the mass of tourists generally to be found in the square.

The Florentine career of Giorgio Vasari flourished under Cosimo's rule. Vasari, who dedicated both editions of *The Lives of the Artists* to 'the most illustrious duke', was charged with architectural works as well as paintings. One of his most impressive creations was a large office building to house the growing bureaucracy of sixteenth-century Florence. The Uffizi, as it came to be known – *uffici* being Italian for offices – later became the city's first art gallery. It has been only rarely appreciated, itself, as a work of art. Vasari's chief architectural commission shows the clear influence of Michelangelo's style, but somewhat systematized, perhaps to express a bureaucratic fondness for regularity. Two monumental and extremely long colonnaded façades, punctured by pedimented windows arranged in repeating units of three, face each other across a courtyard, like mirror images of one another. Out of this monotony Vasari has conjured a *coup de théâtre*. To stand between the two façades looking towards the picturesque arch that leads from the courtyard to the Arno is to experience the parallel lines of Vasari's *uffizi* as if they were some kind of theatrical illusion – not a real building at all, but a massive piece of scenography and a dizzying demonstration of vanishing-point perspective.

The most demanding task which Duke Cosimo I required Vasari to carry out was the decoration of the Palazzo della Signoria, the palace which had, for centuries, housed the government of the Florentine Republic but which Cosimo I converted into his personal residence. The artist eventually spent the best part of seventeen years working on what became the single most extensive programme of palace decoration undertaken during the sixteenth century. It was a scheme which was to set the pattern for the art of absolute rulers, all over Europe, for a century and more. Here, more clearly than anywhere else in Cosimo's Florence, did the transformation of the city involve the erasure and rewriting of its past. One of Vasari's first acts was to destroy two legendary, albeit incomplete, works of art of the earlier Renaissance: a pair of full-size works in progress for monumental paintings commemorating Florentine military victories, created by Leonardo da Vinci and Michelangelo, but never finished due to the former's faulty fresco technique and the latter's departure for Rome in 1506. Having whitewashed the walls of the Salone dei Cinquecento, where those works were still to be seen in the 1560s, Vasari and his assistants replaced them with two enormous triptych-shaped battle paintings.

On the wall opposite what is now the main entrance to the room are depicted three victories over the Sienese, traditional enemies of Florence, while on the entrance wall itself an answering triptych shows Pisa and Venice reeling before Florentine might. Vasari, like generations of Renaissance artists before him, was competing with the past. As well as seeking to outdo the works of Leonardo and Michelangelo, he also looked further back to the most complete Florentine

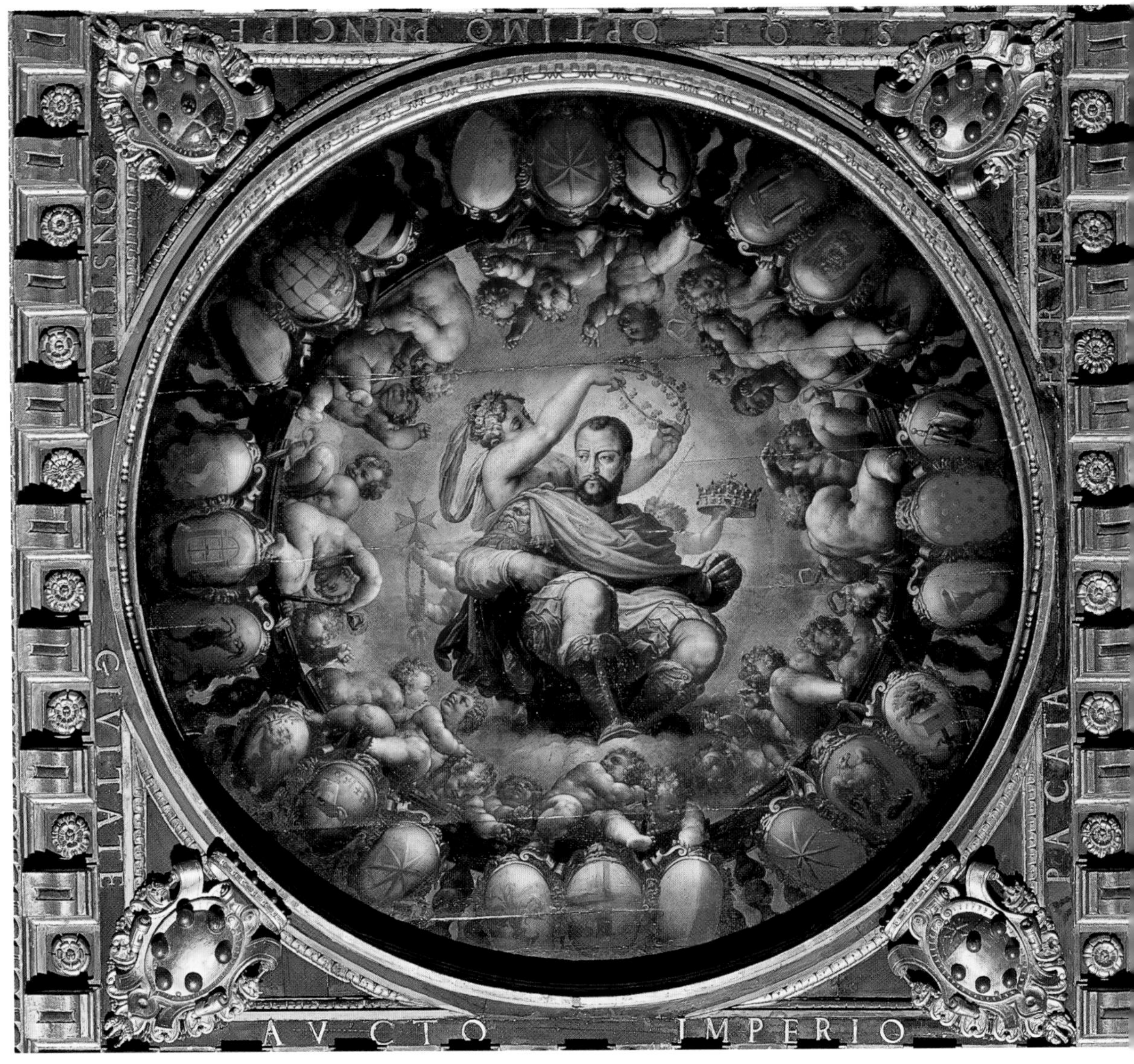


122 GIORGIO VASARI *Cosimo I* 1565

precedent for his battle paintings, which was Paolo Uccello's *The Battle of San Romano* [46]. This had been created for relatively secluded contemplation in the Medici Palace on the Via Larga, at a time when the Medici still believed that envy was a weed which should not be watered. Vasari adopted the busy frieze-like composition of Uccello's work, but its diverting experiments in perspective clearly held no appeal for him, and neither did its relative modesty. The immediate effect of Vasari's work is one of thunderous jingoism. The enormous scale of his paintings is matched by their inflated triumphalism; in the Salone dei Cinquecento it is as if

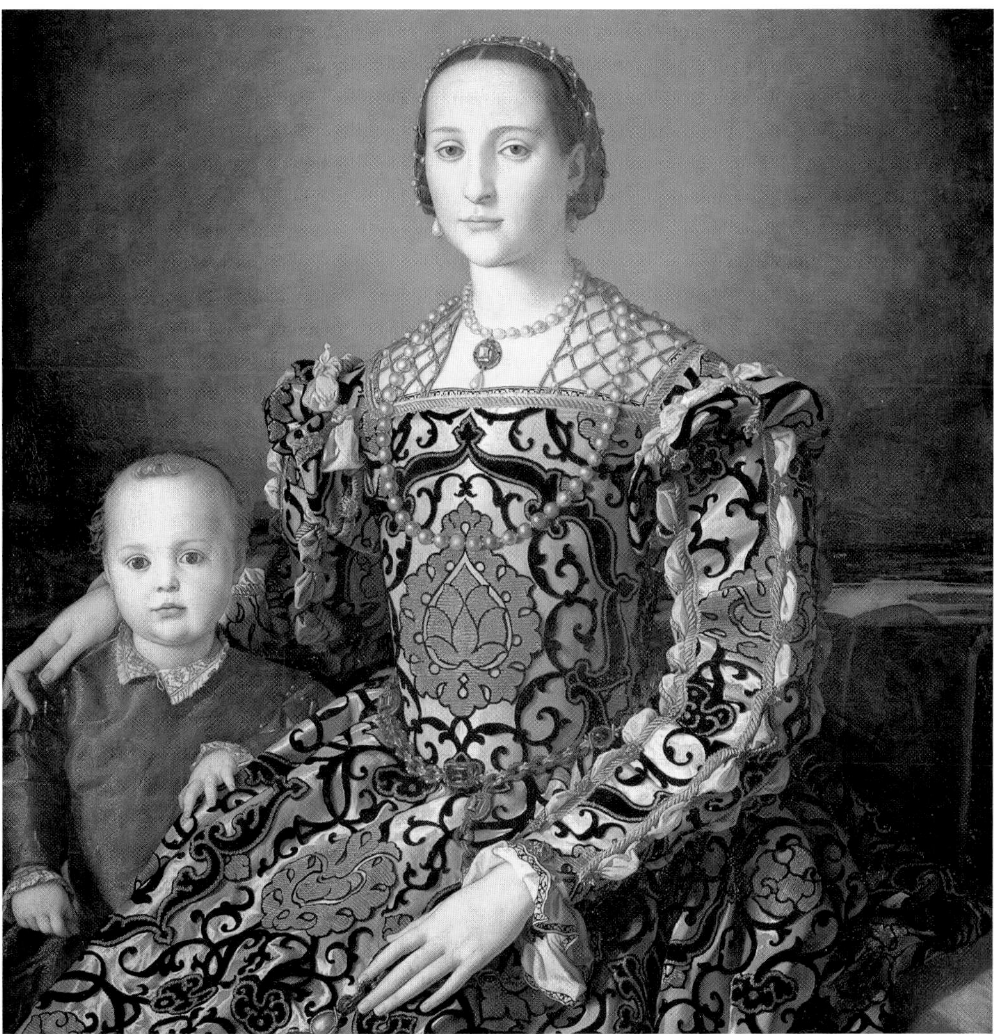

123 AGNOLO BRONZINO *Eleonora of Toledo with Her Son Giovanni de' Medici* (detail) *c.* 1546

Medici pride, having been leashed in for so long, has suddenly been released. Vasari crowned his scheme with several paintings on the ceiling, on the theme of Florentine history since 70 BC. At the centre, as its sun, its unmoved mover, presiding over the multitudinous massacres and military parades which seethe around and beneath him, Vasari placed his patron, borne aloft by angels [122]. Thus was Cosimo I apotheosized as the culmination of all known history.

Vasari was extremely proud of his works in the Palazzo della Signoria. In *The Lives of the Artists*, he was unstinting in their praise:

> I venture to assert that I had occasion to paint everything that the human mind and imagination can envisage: a multitude of bodies, faces, costumes, dresses, helmets, cuirasses, head-dresses, horses, armour, breast-plates, artillery of every kind; combats, battles, ships, storms, rain, snow and so on.[9]

A different assessment of his genius as a creator of large scale was made by Michelangelo who, when told by the breathless artist that he had carried out one particularly ambitious and extensive series of paintings in just 100 days, instantly shot back: 'It looks like it.' But that is too curmudgeonly a view of Vasari's achievement as a history painter, and his lively, highly violent works are considerably more interesting than their reputation might suggest. Their shortcomings may, in part, be attributed to the sheer number of assistants whom the artist had to employ in order to cover the acres of wall which he was required to decorate.

The cult of more – more invention, more art, more variety, Vasari's 'multitude' of cuirasses and head-dresses and horses – also produced in some respects a culture of less – less skill, less care, less focus. Yet this was not simply a case of Renaissance art declining. Another way of looking at it might be to say that artists had discovered, in one of the many consequences of their new-found status and success, a new difficulty to overcome. How might studio assistants be trained to produce a more even standard of work? How might the efforts of different individuals be better harmonized? These were questions which Vasari began to ask – one of his answers being the foundation of a Florentine art academy, a function of which was to raise levels of skill – but they would be addressed more effectively in the seventeenth century, when Rubens and Bernini each in very different ways managed the large-scale workshop production of art.

By no means all the works commissioned for the Palazzo della Signoria in Cosimo's time were trumpet fanfares or military marches. The most delicate paintings were carried out by Pontormo's adopted son, Agnolo Bronzino, working in one of its smallest rooms. Just as Vasari's battle paintings seem almost like a reprise of Uccello's *Battle of San Romano*, so Bronzino's chapel for Cosimo's wife, Eleonora of Toledo, may be seen as a sixteenth-century remake of Benozzo Gozzoli's chapel in the Medici-Riccardi Palace. In Bronzino's decorations, religious subject matter has been made a pretext not for a display of wealth, as it was in Gozzoli's work, but for a display of stylishness and grace. The paintings illustrate episodes from the life of Moses, which may have been intended to allude flatteringly to Cosimo as the leader of his people, but the eye is drawn to figures at random and purely by their beauty: a man drowning gracefully in a curiously still and literally red Red Sea; a water-carrier with rippling muscles, his body turned in an elegant *contrapposto*.

Bronzino's style, spiritually, morally and emotionally anaesthetized though it was, seems to have suited his patrons well. Cosimo's rule was effective but he was incommunicative, and he and his consort cultivated an aristocratic *hauteur* and a distance from their subjects. Bronzino put a beautiful face on such coldness and the portraits which he painted of his almost solipsistically aloof patrons are among the most immutably wrought works of their century, object lessons in how to make every composition seem an inevitability. Bronzino's portrait of Eleonora with one of her young sons [123], now in the Uffizi, is a counter to all those historians who have argued for too mechanistic a connection between the rise of the Renaissance portrait and a growing interest in the contents of human consciousness. The face of Bronzino's Eleonora is a mask. She has nothing to declare but her visible perfection. The work can be seen to epitomize *maniera*, a word increasingly used during the sixteenth century to denote a style not necessarily stamped with the artist's individuality, but essentially 'stylish', armoured in its own virtuosity.

The most visible public art commissioned by Cosimo was also characterized by a kind of virtuoso superficiality. Style replaced content. The Piazza della Signoria, the city's largest public square, became a kind of sculpture park – no longer a school of stern morals but, instead, an arena in which artists competed with one another to create beautiful demonstrations of their own skill. A daringly bravura instance of this public 'art for art's sake' is Giambologna's celebrated *Rape of the Sabine Woman* [124], completed almost a decade after Cosimo's death but unimaginable without the changes which his commissioning policy had wrought on the civic climate of Florence. The sculpture is a naked exercise in exhibitionism. What is being exhibited? First and foremost, the body of a beautiful woman, borne aloft by the man who has captured her, despite the objections of a second man, on whose defeated, crouching body the victor kneels. Secondly, it is the skill of Giambologna himself that is on show, his ability to create a work of art as unified and yet as mobile as a flickering flame from three separate but intertwined bodies. The woman's captor seems himself captured by her beauty, and he holds her up as if she were a prize, or as if they were dancing together rather than struggling. She twists more artfully than hysterically, thus ensuring that almost every part of her body, carved in stone that seems even to yield to the touch like flesh, is held up for display.

Giambologna began his work with no particular subject in mind, only choosing *The Rape of the Sabine Woman* – a legend about the founding of Rome – when he learnt that an entirely subjectless work of sculpture was unacceptable even to his open-minded Medici patrons. The work remains all but subjectless. The spiralling rhythms of the sculpture invite – even demand – the spectator to walk all around it, thus paying just as much attention to the figures' beautifully proportioned bodies as to their faces. Giambologna set out not to educate the man in the street but to seduce him, and turn him into a connoisseur.

Cosimo I, the man who did not give audiences to the people, certainly made sure that they were given a lot of art: art to stun them and to entertain them; art to manipulate their feelings and to influence their ideas; most of all, art to remind them who was in charge. But Cosimo did *not* give them art which spoke to the people, which addressed them as an orator in the street might address his audience. Florentine Renaissance art, even in the time of Michelangelo, whose Neoplatonism had already marked a turn away from the intimacy of the past, had lived through dialogue. Now the dialogue was over and the monologue of the absolutist had begun.

The work which sums up this altered state is the statue of *Perseus* commissioned by Cosimo in 1545 from one the most garrulous, glamorous and immodest artists of the Renaissance, Benvenuto Cellini. A triumphant feat of the metalworker's art as well as of the sculptor's imagination, it is a creation in which the aestheticism and absolutism of Cosimo's Florence seem perfectly fused. Cellini's *Perseus* [125] makes decapitation look ominously easy. He has cut off the Medusa's head at a single stroke – which he proves by holding it aloft as the first blood of death still spurts from it in spiralling rivulets of bronze (a virtuoso touch). The artist signed the torso of the *Perseus* by decorating it with a thin strap of fabric on which his name can be found. It is tempting to think of the work as an instance of Cellini's exuberant role-playing, as if there were a level at which this is an unofficial self-portrait as well as an official emblem of Cosimo, Cellini's prince and patron. Might this effortless and glamourized slayer of monsters be a yet more idealized realization, in art, of the fantasy alter egos Cellini created for himself in his *Autobiography*, where he cuts a dashing and rather romantic figure, sword always at the ready?

The statue negates such speculation because its true, unpleasant genius lies in the extent to which Cellini managed to exclude personality from it. His *Perseus* is a baleful creature, purged altogether of sentiment. He has no interior complexities to worry him – or to reassure those who stand before him. This quality of lofty,

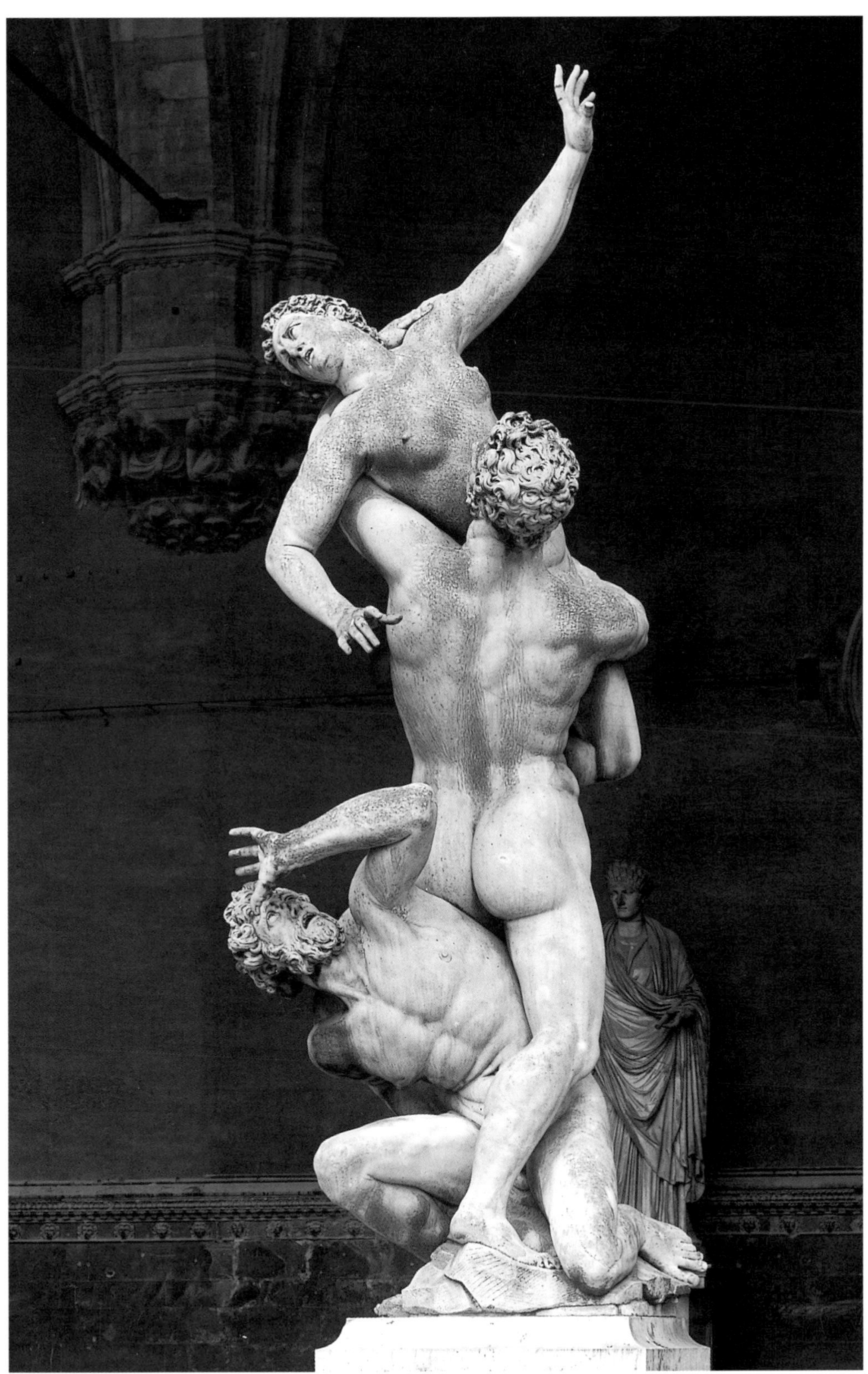

124 GIAMBOLOGNA *Rape of the Sabine Woman* 1582–3

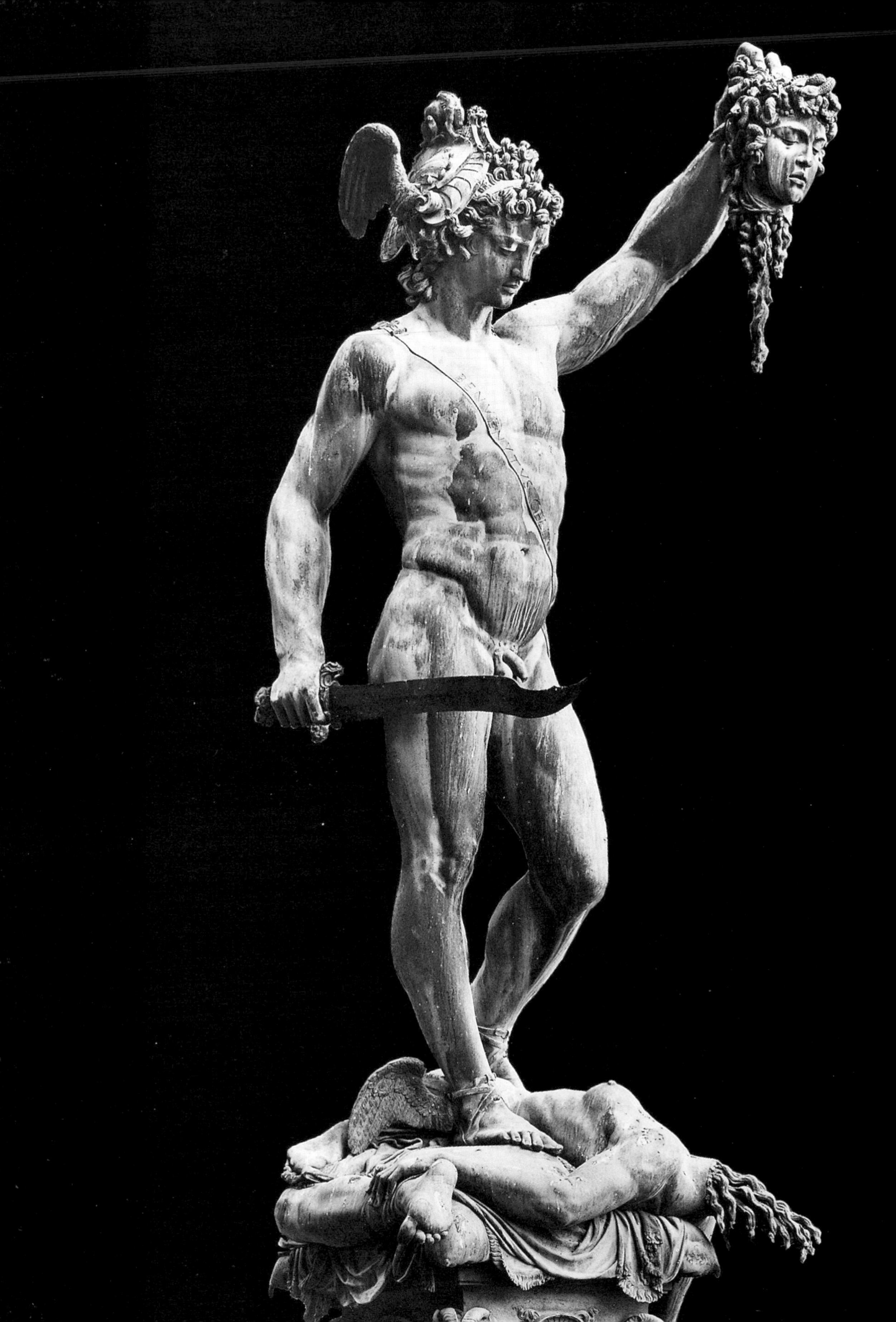
BENVENVTVS

inscrutable reserve is part of what makes the work seem, still, so alien and removed. Its chilling classicism – the alienating way in which it seems to reach back to extreme antiquity, genuinely reincarnating not just the flawless beauty but also the ruthlessness of a Greek epic hero – may have been one of the keys to Cosimo's known satisfaction with it. It is not, as earlier Florentine sculptures of the hero (or heroine) had been, a role model to aspire to. It is the image of a leader, set above the people, exulting in his own beauty and power. Obey, or die.

## THE FRENCH RENAISSANCE (WITH A PINCH OF SALT)

It was in the sophisticated and self-consciously stylish form typified by the work of Cellini and his contemporaries that Italian Renaissance styles of art and architecture spread to the rest of Europe. Francis I, King of France, was at the forefront of the vogue for all things Italian among the crowned heads of the time; and Cellini himself played a leading role in the dissemination of Italian style at the French court. As Francis's goldsmith from 1537 to 1545, he created many intricate objects for his patron, all of which have since been lost or melted down save for the extraordinary solid gold, enamel and ebony salt cellar [126] now in the Kunsthistorisches Museum in Vienna.

Cellini's salt cellar is larger than most photographic reproductions, scaleless as they are, might suggest: approximately 25 cm high and a little more than 30 cm wide. It is more tabletop work of art than condiment-holder, and given the range of its references may be regarded almost as a portable history of Florentine sculpture. There are echoes of Ghiberti's golden doors here, as well as of Michelangelo's New Sacristy sculptures, copied in several of the figures that stud this most luxurious of luxury objects. On top of its elaborately inlaid base two principal figures, both naked, face one another. A solid gold Neptune is flanked by a gold-enamelled salt-boat, with a fierce face as its prow. Opposite him reclines the goddess of earth, holding a cornucopia and squeezing her breast, to signify abundance, a virtue further embodied in the form of a reclining figure on top of the miniature temple, complete with Ionic columns, designed by Cellini to hold the peppercorns. The fruits of the marriage of earth and sea were thus seen to furnish the king's table, just as Cellini had furnished it with a caprice, a dinnertime conversation piece for connoisseurs and cognoscenti.

Francis had acquired a taste for Italian art during the successful Italian campaigns pursued under his rule during the years immediately following his

125 BENVENUTO CELLINI *Perseus with the Head of Medusa* 1545–53

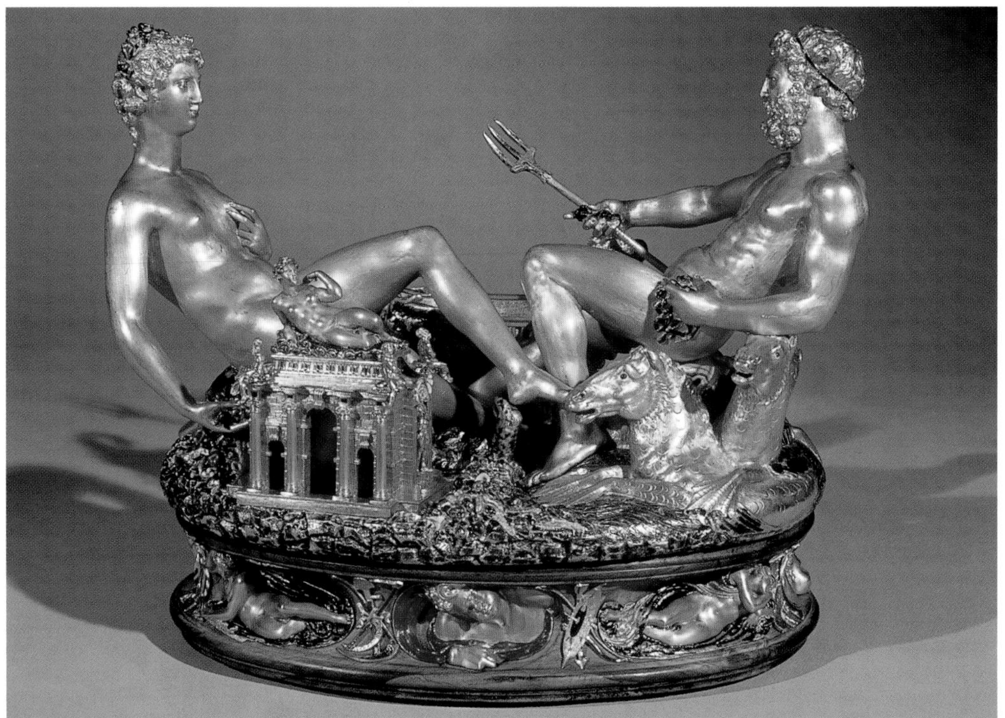

126 BENVENUTO CELLINI *Salt Cellar of Francis I* 1540–43

accession in 1515. During the late 1520s and after, when military defeat and subsequent imprisonment at the hands of Charles V had taken some of the edge off the king's political ambition, he conceived a prototypically French *grand projet*. He set out to create a court as magnificent as any in Italy, embellished by the work of the very finest Italian artists, but on his own soil.

The test tube in which Francis chose to conduct this experiment was the Chateau of Fontainebleau. For centuries it had been the hunting lodge of monarchs and princes, but under his rule it was converted into an Italianate palace, albeit one with many distinctively French architectural features. Inside, the Gallery of Francis I [127] is the first, most fully achieved and most intellectually impenetrable example of the French Renaissance envisaged by the king. Its decoration was carried out, largely to Francis's own programme, by the Florentine painter Rosso Fiorentino. He was aided by several assistants including woodcarvers and sculptors who created cartouches in between Rosso's pictures, as well as frames for them, which are themselves so elaborate that the whole is best seen as a composite work formed from a conjunction of several arts. The shape of the scheme was dictated

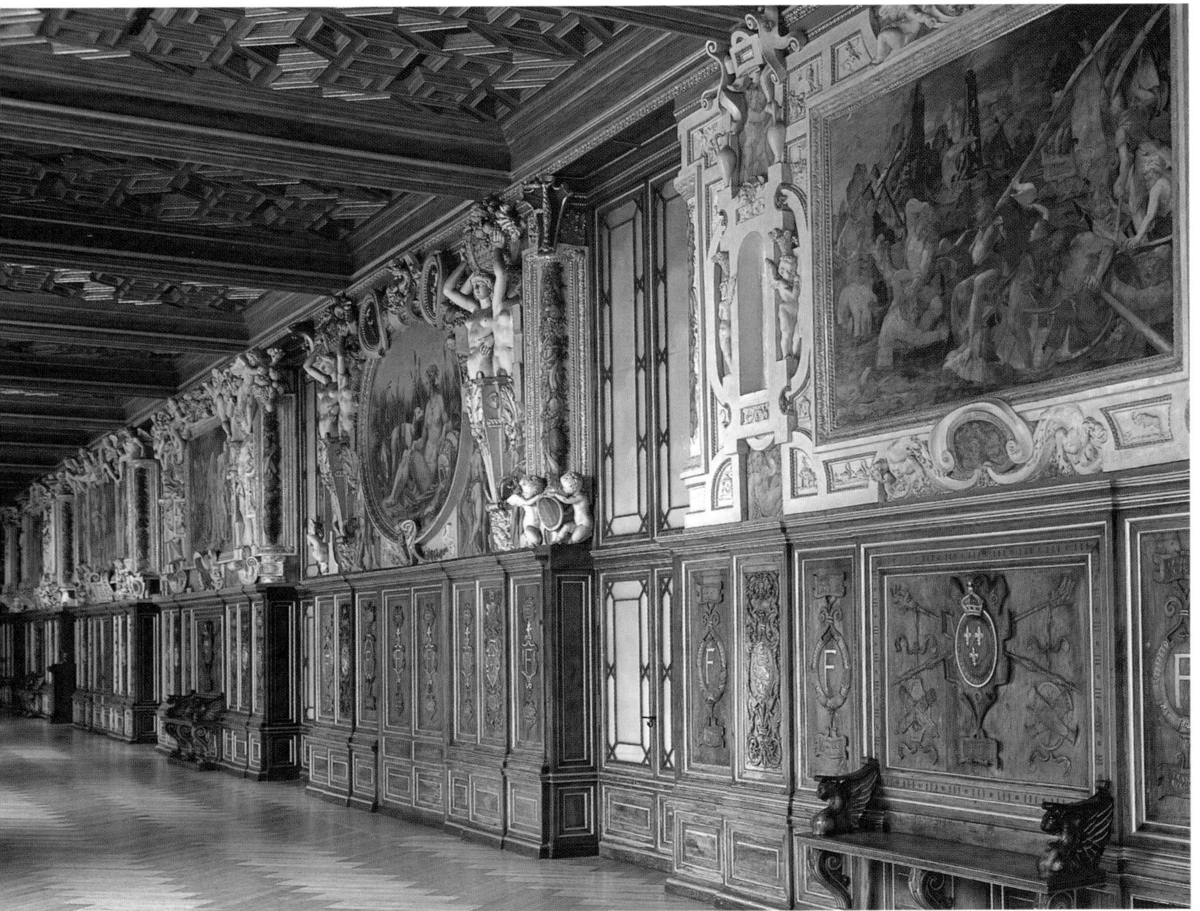

27 ROSSO FIORENTINO Gallery of Francis I, Chateau of Fontainebleau 1534–9

by the architectural design of an aristocratic Northern European gallery, long and relatively low-ceilinged, to which Rosso had to adapt his ideas. Thanks to the idiosyncrasies of French court architecture and the demands of his patron, the painter and his assistants produced something different from any work seen hitherto in Italy. The transmission of Italian artistic style also entailed its transformation.

The gallery is decorated with fourteen frescos, the majority illustrating themes which are either unprecedented or extremely rare in painting, for example *Cleobis and Biton* drawing the chariot of their mother, Eudippe, from the temple. The baffling clottedness of many of the narratives and allegories Rosso was required to illustrate appears to have bred a mixture of overelaboration and lassitude in his style. It is likely that the painter himself may not have fully appreciated (or even have been let in on) the significance which several of these subjects held for his patron. The figures in the paintings seem at once overcrowded and lacking in internal drive or motivation. This is partly explicable by the fact that many of them have been borrowed, in pose and anatomy, from works familiar to Rosso in Renaissance Rome. It is almost as if they are refugees who have sleepwalked in from another world, where they knew their purpose, but in arriving here have forgotten it. Their dreamy and disconnected air is enhanced further by the mist of deterioration through which such frescos as *The Fire at Catania* or *The Shipwreck of Nauplius* – with their clear paraphrases of, respectively, Raphael's *Fire in the Borgo* [84] and Michelangelo's *Deluge* – must nowadays be seen.

Taking visitors around the gallery appears to have become a sort of game for Francis I. Sphinx-like in his portraits by Jean Clouet, positively devious-seeming in the more psychological portrayal by Titian, he was a man who enjoyed armouring himself in enigma. According to the English ambassador at court, Henry Wallop-Calendar, Francis kept the only key to the room in his pocket. In the view of the king's learned sister, Marguerite d'Angoulême (who became Queen of Navarre), Francis *was* the only key to the room. 'Your buildings are like a dead body without you,' she wrote to him. 'Looking at a building without hearing your intentions for it is like reading in Hebrew.'[10] On some occasions, however, Francis's picture-puzzle is decipherable even to those unversed in the nearly rabbinical complexities of its allusions. The many-seeded pomegranate which the king holds in the fresco known as *The Unity of the State* symbolizes the French nation, its many components held in unity by Francis, dressed like a Roman to signify that he is a modern Caesar under whom all of Gaul has been united. The temple into which he strides in the allegory of *Ignorance Banished* – leaving behind, on its steps, a tangled knot of overweight, debauched figures wearing blindfolds who collectively embody stupidity and sin – signifies the realm of enlightenment into which he is leading the French with his cultural policies.

Despite the impression which it gives of an arcane, closed world, a freak of royal fancy, this room and the art within it were to have a considerable influence. Napoleon said that Fontainebleau was the true home of the kings of France. That may or may not be true, but there is a good case to be made for it as the primary sourcebook of French public art and architecture. This is literally so, in that the strapwork decoration, a novel and prominent part of Francis's gallery – stucco carved into shapes resembling folded and cut rolls of leather, interspersed with motifs such as festoons of garlands, putti and statues – was to be extensively copied and adapted. But the pervasiveness and significance of Fontainebleau's influence cannot be truly grasped at the level of such minute detail, because what was inaugurated there was not merely a style but a mentality: a boldly appropriationist French attitude to antiquity.

In few other countries would the nation-state come to be so boldly identified, by its rulers, with the grandeur of ancient Rome. Paris is the proof of this, a city of wide open vistas and grand (frequently grandiose) monuments, a composite of classicisms testifying to the mighty pretensions to ancient grandeur of many to have ruled there. The tradition has extended into modern times, so that Francis I's classical Louvre, much enlarged and developed by later French kings as well as by Napoleon, has now been barnacled with the addition of a huge glass pyramid, like a transparent version of the pyramid of Gaius Cestius in Rome, as a memorial to the presidency of François Mitterand (Mitterameses II, as the French press satirically dubbed him). The Arc de Triomphe, a nineteenth-century addition to the thumping assertions of antique pomp and majesty which run through the city on a straight Roman axis, has its late twentieth-century echo in the yet more huge Arche de la Défense – only a complex of apartments and shops, and more modernist-abstract in shape, but still thoroughly antique-grandiose in spirit. The French acquired a taste for Renaissance classical triumphalism late. But there is a sense in which the country's political leaders have never grown out of it.

## LITTLE ITALY

In Britain, the reception of Italian Renaissance artists and artistic styles was to have a more chequered history. Henry VIII, Francis I's contemporary, competed with him both politically and as a patron of magnificent art and architecture. Very little of Henry's palace architecture and decoration survives, but his first ambitious commission from an Italian artist is still to be found inside Westminster Abbey. The bronze tomb of Henry VIII's father and mother, Henry VII and Elizabeth of York [128], was created by Pietro Torrigiano, a sculptor who had tangled with Michelangelo while both were studying Masaccio's frescos in Florence. The two artists had a fist-fight on the steps of the church of the Carmine, during which Michelangelo's nose was badly broken – crushed like a biscuit, Torrigiano later boasted. This episode led to his flight from Michelangelo's Medici supporters in the city and thus, indirectly, to his work in London.

The tomb, which Torrigiano completed in 1518, is a treasure of Florentine Renaissance art locked up inside a casket of English Gothic architecture. It is, however, considerably more restrained than the Medici tombs created by the artist's victim and rival Michelangelo. Influenced in part by local English traditions of effigy sculpture, Torrigiano did not create a monument to himself and to artistic genius, but rather, he created a dynastic tomb for a dynastic setting. There are touches of foreign iconography, such as the putti at the tomb's corners, a feature which would have been an unfamiliar one in England at the time. However, the most powerful novelty of the work was the absolute anatomical realism with which the artist modelled the features of king and queen, who look as though peacefully sleeping.

Torrigiano's royal tomb, a little bit of Florence stranded in London, was an island of Italian Renaissance style on which little would be built. Torrigiano himself seems not to have enjoyed his sojourn in England – he pops up in Cellini's *Autobiography* ranting about 'those filthy beasts, the English'[11] and implying that the work he had done for them was a pearl cast among swine – but there were more deep-seated reasons for the failure of Italian artists to colonize the British Isles. The reception of Italian style was partly mitigated by the strength of existing local traditions. Gothic was still efflorescent in Britain in the early sixteenth century, as is richly demonstrated by the stone crockets and other intricate architectural decorations which surround the tomb. But it was the Reformation which decisively sundered whatever links were being forged between Italy and Britain during this time. The conversion of Britain to Protestantism meant that Italian, Catholic, artists were very unlikely to travel there.

None of which is intended to imply that Britain was in any way to be regarded as an outsider looking in on the world of the Renaissance. Indeed, the British played an active part, taking some elements and developing them in new ways, while rejecting others. The new learning, especially the ideas of Erasmus and other Northern humanists, found fertile ground in Britain, which produced its own humanist scholars such as Thomas More; and while Italian artistic styles were patchily transmitted and received, Northern artists readily found employment in Britain.

Henry VIII's chief court artist was one of the most gifted Northern oil painters ever to have lived. In 1533, shortly before he began working for the English king, Hans Holbein (1497/8–1543) created a picture which remains one of the most enduring monuments to this vital but uneasy moment in the history of Europe – a moment when, even as Renaissance civilization was expanding and taking on new forms in new places, it was also rapidly fragmenting. The picture in question was not in fact painted for Henry VIII himself, but for a Frenchman who had come to visit the king on diplomatic business.

128 PIETRO TORRIGIANO Tomb of Henry VII and Elizabeth of York, Westminster Abbey, London 1512–18

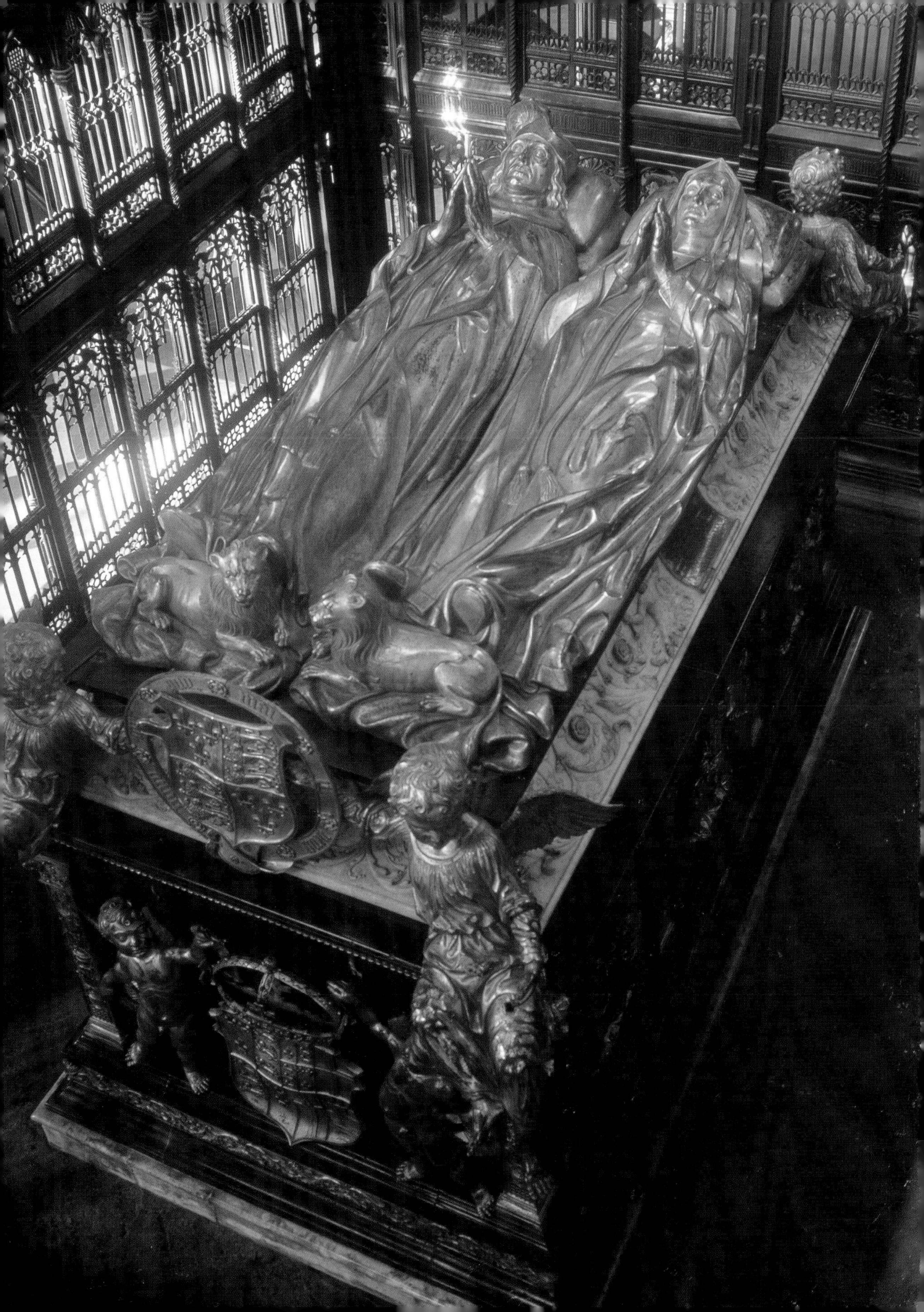

## 'LET DIVISION BE MADE'

The weather was freezing, his lodgings were damp and he was unable to shake off an apparently interminable cold. 'I am, and have been, very weary and wearisome,' he wrote to his family. 'I am the most melancholy, weary and wearisome ambassador in the world.'[12] The year 1533 was not a good one for Jean de Dinteville. But with the help of Hans Holbein, he managed to put a brave face on it.

Dinteville is the man on the left in Holbein's *The Ambassadors* [129], wearing the salmon-coloured satin shirt and the black silk gown lined with lynx fur. These were probably the same sumptuous clothes which he had bought to wear as France's representative at the coronation of Anne Boleyn, Henry VIII's new queen, in Westminster Abbey on 1 June that year. Did he, while he was there, inspect the tomb by Torrigiano? He certainly resented how much attendance at this inauspicious ceremony cost him. 'I shall have to go to great expense for this coronation,'[13] he complained in another of his gloomy letters home.

Holbein, who was himself something of a diplomat, portrayed de Dinteville with a countenance unclouded by such mundane concerns. Wary and self-possessed, the French ambassador stares out from the canvas as if daring the viewer to guess his thoughts. Those of his companion, Georges de Selve, Bishop of Lavaur, seem even more cloaked. He is the living image of inscrutability. Impassive and sombre, even his posture makes him look secretive. He holds his long damask robe about him almost defensively. He leans on a closed book, appropriately enough.

*The Ambassadors* was commissioned by Jean de Dinteville to hang in his family's chateau at Polisy. The painting is the pictorial equivalent of a Renaissance nobleman's cabinet, the most precious piece of furniture in the house, a repository of secrets and of special knowledge, reserved only to those who understand the trickery of its construction. The composition of the picture is literally reminiscent of a cabinet. The two men leaning on their elbows are like human doors that have swung open to reveal a mass of intriguing bric-à-brac stacked on the shelves between them. This has been the matter of their contemplation; now it has been opened to our gaze. Holbein's double portrait is a carefully constructed cipher devised to test the ingenuity of those who would decode it. Almost every detail is a tantalizing clue, hinting at hidden significance: the closed green curtains that form the backdrop to the scene; the often unnoticed crucifix which they almost conceal; the scientific instruments; the globes; the books; the lute with the broken string; the blur of a skull, painted in anamorphic perspective, hovering over the elaborate Cosmati-work tiled floor.

Thanks largely to the pioneering detective work of Mary Hervey, a tenacious historian who established the identities of Holbein's sitters in 1900,[14] the keys have been furnished to many if not all of the picture's secret compartments. It is known that Jean de Dinteville travelled to London in 1533 and met Georges de Selve on 23 May. He noted the meeting in a letter to his brother, also a diplomat, and told him to mention it to no one. Dinteville's mission to London took place at a time when the political map of Europe was being redrawn. The ambassador would have known that these were difficult years for his country. France had recently lost all of its northern Italian territories to Charles V, whose disaffected troops had also sacked Rome in 1527, polarizing religious differences. Meanwhile the uncontrollable popularity of new Lutheran ideas could unbalance the political status quo yet further. France was simultaneously threatened from within by Protestant dissenters and from without by the quickfire spread of Protestant ideas to other powerful states. The impending division of Europe, as much as the English weather, must have contributed to de Dinteville's melancholy.

Georges de Selve was greatly exercised by the religious divisions of the time. He had spent much of his career on religious-cum-diplomatic missions trying vainly to stem the tide of Lutheran reform. In May 1533 he may have been in London on similar business, meeting with clerics sympathetic to the reformers' cause, like Thomas Cranmer, and seeking to dampen the smouldering embers of the English Reformation. Dinteville himself had probably been sent to impress upon Henry VIII that the French would take a dim view of plans to establish a separate Church of England. But as soon as he got there, it was plain that Henry had already decided to do just that in order to grant himself a divorce from Catherine of Aragon and marry Anne Boleyn, thus alienating the papacy and opening the way to the conversion of the English to Protestantism. So it was that the two ambassadors found that they could merely witness events which they themselves were powerless to influence. Alone in their room, they are like Rosencrantz and Guildenstern, men who can only watch from the wings as extraordinary events take their course centre stage.

The objects heaped on to the shelves on which both men rest their elbows symbolize the disarray into which their world had fallen. The various astronomical instruments on the upper shelf of the table in the picture, which include a celestial globe as well as a number of different mechanisms for telling the time by the motions of the sun – a cylindrical shepherd's dial, two quadrants, a polyhedral sundial and a torquetum – are all misaligned for use in a northerly latitude. This is unlikely to have been an oversight on the artist's part, since one of his closest

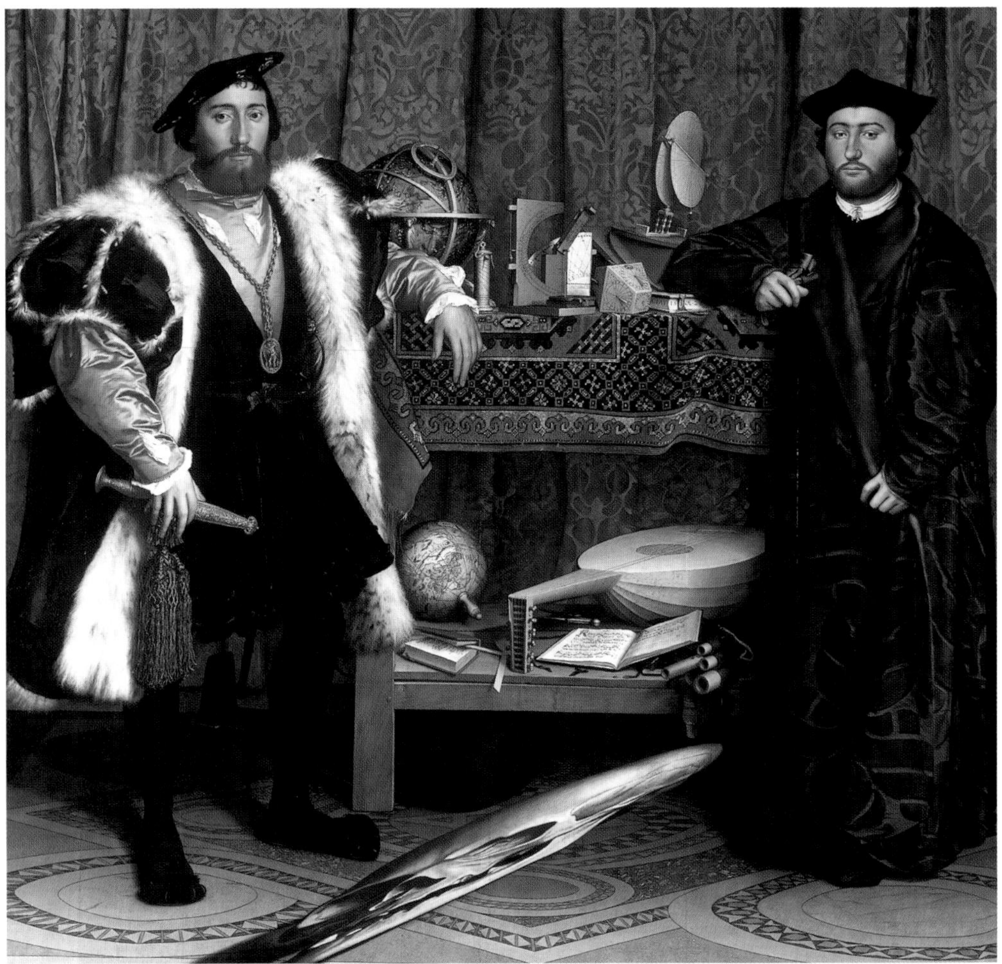

129 HANS HOLBEIN THE YOUNGER *The Ambassadors* 1533

friends in London was the astronomer Nikolaus Kratzer. The misaligned instruments are emblems of chaos, of the heavens out of joint – a disharmony to which the lute with a broken string, conventional symbol of discord, also alludes.

If the theme of the upper shelf is discord in the heavens, most of the objects on the lower shelf refer to anarchy down below, in the sublunary sphere of human affairs. The celestial globe has been replaced by a terrestrial globe on which may be made out the words 'Baris' and 'Pritannia' – spelling had not been standardized in the sixteenth century and these are thought to be Holbein's renderings of his own Germanic pronunciation of 'Paris' and 'Brittany'. The open book immediately below the globe (literally, its subtext) is an apparently innocent work of practical mathematics, Peter Apian's *New and Reliable Instruction Book of Calculation for Merchants*. But it is open at a most un-innocent page, which begins with the word

'*Dividirt*': 'Let division be made'. To those with sharp eyes and the ability to think laterally – or to those let in on the secret by the Dinteville clan in Polisy – this was a reference to the religious schism that was tearing Europe apart in the 1530s. Division was indeed being made.

The objects depicted may speak of the wreckage of the ambassadors' hopes and aspirations but the two men are not downcast because, as the painting also shows, there is another and yet larger scheme of things by which they are content to live their lives and be judged. At the very bottom of Holbein's picture, there is the most paradoxically blatant statement of its cryptic nature. The unclear object jutting up from the floor still seemed a complete mystery as recently as 1867, when the then director of the National Gallery, Ralph Wornum, described it as an inchoate shape like 'the bones of some fish'.[15] Thanks to subsequent research, the exact point at which the viewer must stand in order to read this detail correctly is now known: at a right angle 120 mm away from the wall surface, 1040 mm from the bottom of the picture and 790 mm to the right of it, the blur resolves itself into a grinning skull, symbol of inevitable death. At the very top of the painting the patient viewer will find the last piece in the puzzle, the detail that fixes all the other details in place. The crucifix in the top left-hand corner is the counter to the skull, standing for the Resurrection, for God's gift of eternal life to all those of true faith. It is from the smaller truth of a broken world, in the here and now, to this larger truth, under the gaze of God, that the ambassadors turn to stare us straight in the eye. They may have failed in their schemes and projects but, piously sure of their own redemption, they stand on the verge of eternity with admirable sang-froid. Holbein's painting contains, locked within its still surface, the wracks and tumults of a turbulent passage of history. It is an image not just of two men alone with their thoughts, but of the shifting consciousness of the times.

## 'TH' INTERTRAFFIQUE OF THE MIND'

The terrestrial globe on the lower shelf in *The Ambassadors*, segmented by longitude and latitude lines, places 'Europa' in the wider context of the world, charting some of the new commercial networks which were developing during Holbein's lifetime. A divided Europe, riven as it was by political and religious strife, was none the less united in its pursuit of gain. The trade winds carried ships further away than ever before. More of the world was opening up before men's eyes.

Traffic in goods was accompanied by what the Elizabethan alchemist, magus and philosopher John Dee (1527–1608) called 'th' intertraffique of the mind'.[16]

Ideas as well as commodities flowed from place to place with ever-increasing rapidity, penetrating every part of Europe. Many of those ideas were inevitably Italian in origin – a reflection of the peninsula's importance as the fountainhead of humanist scholarship and primary source of new approaches to the getting and using of knowledge. But there was more to the exchange of ideas at this time than the import-export of Italian civilization alone. Northern humanism, which had already taken its own, separate course, sowing the very divisions lamented by Holbein's ambassadors, continued to pursue other lives. The intellectual world of the Renaissance itself was being transformed, changing shape as it expanded.

One of the most vigorous commercial and financial centres in mid-sixteenth-century 'Europa' was the Northern city of Antwerp. Charles V had chosen to make it the principal port of his vast empire in the 1520s. During the decades to follow, as ships from all countries flowed in and out of its harbour, where the river Scheldt meets the North Sea, it became one of the wealthiest cities in the Western world. Its population doubled during the first half of the sixteenth century and by 1550 more than 100,000 people lived there. New public buildings arose to confirm the city fathers' new sense of civic pride. The culminating achievement of Antwerp's public works programme was Cornelis Floris's huge and florid town hall in the city centre. A traditional Flemish building type has been embroidered with a mass of classicizing details lifted from Sebastiano Serlio's manual on architecture. Amid all the columns there is the inscription SPQA. Yet another city had come to think of itself as a second Rome.

The true centre of sixteenth-century Antwerp is to be found elsewhere, however, in a less prominent but more remarkable building. The publishing house founded by Christophe Plantin (*c.* 1520–89), now the Museum Plantin-Moretus, contains the oldest intact printing presses in the world and is the only Renaissance printing establishment to have survived into the present. Behind the building's grand façade (a Louis XV addition) are many of the rooms in which Plantin originally lived and worked, grouped around a picturesque courtyard of brick buildings with stepped roofs.

From these modest premises, the French-born Plantin established himself as the leading printer of his time, taking advantage of Antwerp's trading links and favourable maritime position to disseminate books – containers of new knowledge and new ideas which possessed a magical potency – throughout Europe. The works published by Plantin included Vesalius's researches into human anatomy, the pioneering botanical studies of Rembert Dodonaeus and a body of publications by the cartographer Abraham Ortelius, including the *Theatrum Orbis Teatrum* or

*Theatre of the World*, the first modern atlas, which established Antwerp's international fame as the leading centre for scientific geography. Such was public demand that during the three decades of his career as a printer Plantin produced 2450 separate publications. Books published under his imprint, the sign of the golden compasses, were sold not only in Flanders, but in France, England, Spain, Italy and elsewhere.

Plantin's establishment was more than a printing house. It was a crucible of intellectual change. The walls of the library of the Museum Plantin-Moretus are completely lined with his books, like bricks, suggesting a house built from words. Books produced in such large numbers as this made ideas permanent by preserving them, but they also helped to undermine belief in the permanent validity of any one idea or set of ideas. The printed book set the pattern for developing human knowledge in Western society, through the exchange of views, through argument and counter-argument. In doing so it helped to create a world in which no single viewpoint was immune from the interrogation of the enquiring mind.

Surrounded by the works of Vesalius and Ortelius, Lipsius and Erasmus, one is struck by a sense that a critical mass of knowledge and awareness was being reached during this period. Although almost all of the writers published by Plantin had their intellectual roots in the world of earlier Renaissance humanism, many of them were reaching out to explore worlds of knowledge too multifarious to be corralled within the term 'Renaissance' itself. The late sixteenth century was marked not only by the diffusion of the classical languages of art and architecture and of classical learning but by their rapid dissolution in the broad stream of European civilization. What had once seemed like a new rediscovery of the ancient world became part of a common cultural flow.

Pieter Bruegel the elder (*c.* 1525/30–69), was another vigorous participant in this process. Largely because Karel van Mander's life of Bruegel of 1604 included the unreliable assertion that he came from peasant stock, the painter was long regarded as a kind of folk artist, raw and untutored.[17] This is a myth. 'Peasant Bruegel' had close links with many of the Antwerp humanists in Plantin's circle, including Ortelius. Bruegel's frequently rumbustious portrayals of peasant life, such as *A Country Wedding* (Kunsthistorisches Museum, Vienna), should not be viewed purely in the context of Netherlandish genre painting and popular prints, for while Bruegel was undoubtedly continuing a strong local tradition – with roots stretching back to at least the fifteenth century – the very fact that Ortelius was his friend and patron shows that the artist's work also appealed to the sensibilities of Northern European humanists. Ortelius even went so far as to write a Latin eulogy of Bruegel, comparing him with the masters of classical antiquity: he 'depicted many things that cannot be depicted, as Pliny says of Apelles. In all his works more is always implied than depicted. This was also said of Timanthes.'[18]

One of the hidden implications of Bruegel's art is that a painting can be classically inspired without necessarily containing a single figure in a toga or a single example of classical architecture. Inspecting *A Country Wedding*, a depiction of two peasants rushing headlong towards a village festival to squander their money, Bruegel's more learned contemporaries would probably have noted the numerous symbolic touches planted like evidence to indicate the painting's moral: the image of a disapproving Madonna tacked to a tree; the cross formed by two trampled bits of straw on the ground, signifying the drunken couple's heedlessness of Christian virtues. But as Christian humanists, the scholarly members of Bruegel's audience would also have had little difficulty in appreciating his debt to antiquity: the way in which he had reinvigorated the classical mode of satire to impart a Christian lesson.

The grandeur of Rome held little appeal for Bruegel. Instead he scratched at the scabrous underbelly of the ancient world, reviving the satirical-comical tradition embodied by classical grotesquerie and authors such as Horace and Martial. Juvenal is the Roman satirical author whose spirit Bruegel most truly revived, observing the world and its folly while revealing nothing of himself. 'Go madman, run all over the Alps, to become the schoolboys' favourite and a subject of declamation' – so runs Juvenal's scathing judgement of once-mighty Hannibal.[19] Bruegel's *Fall of Icarus*, now in the Musée des Beaux-Arts in Brussels, expresses a similar, phlegmatic contempt for vainglorious heroics, together with a satirist's relish in pointing to their failure. A farmer ploughs his furrow and a shepherd dozes over his flock while the tiny figure of Icarus plunges inelegantly into a corner of the sea. All we see of him is a pair of splayed legs in the middle of a splash. None of the people in the picture spots him. As W.H. Auden observed, the pathos lies not in the fact of Icarus's fall but in the fact that it goes unnoticed.

Bruegel is a comic artist of the most serious kind, who finds his truths not among heroes and headline-seekers but in the ordinary world. The quotidian life glimpsed in so much Renaissance art, whether it be that of Duccio or Van Eyck or Mantegna, was placed by Bruegel at the very centre of painting – made its sole subject. In the so-called 'Cycle of the Months' the artist expanded an earlier tradition of calendar illustrations and tapestries to create a new kind of composite work of art: a panorama of human existence. The cycle once consisted of twelve paintings, although only five have survived: three are in Vienna's Kunsthistorisches

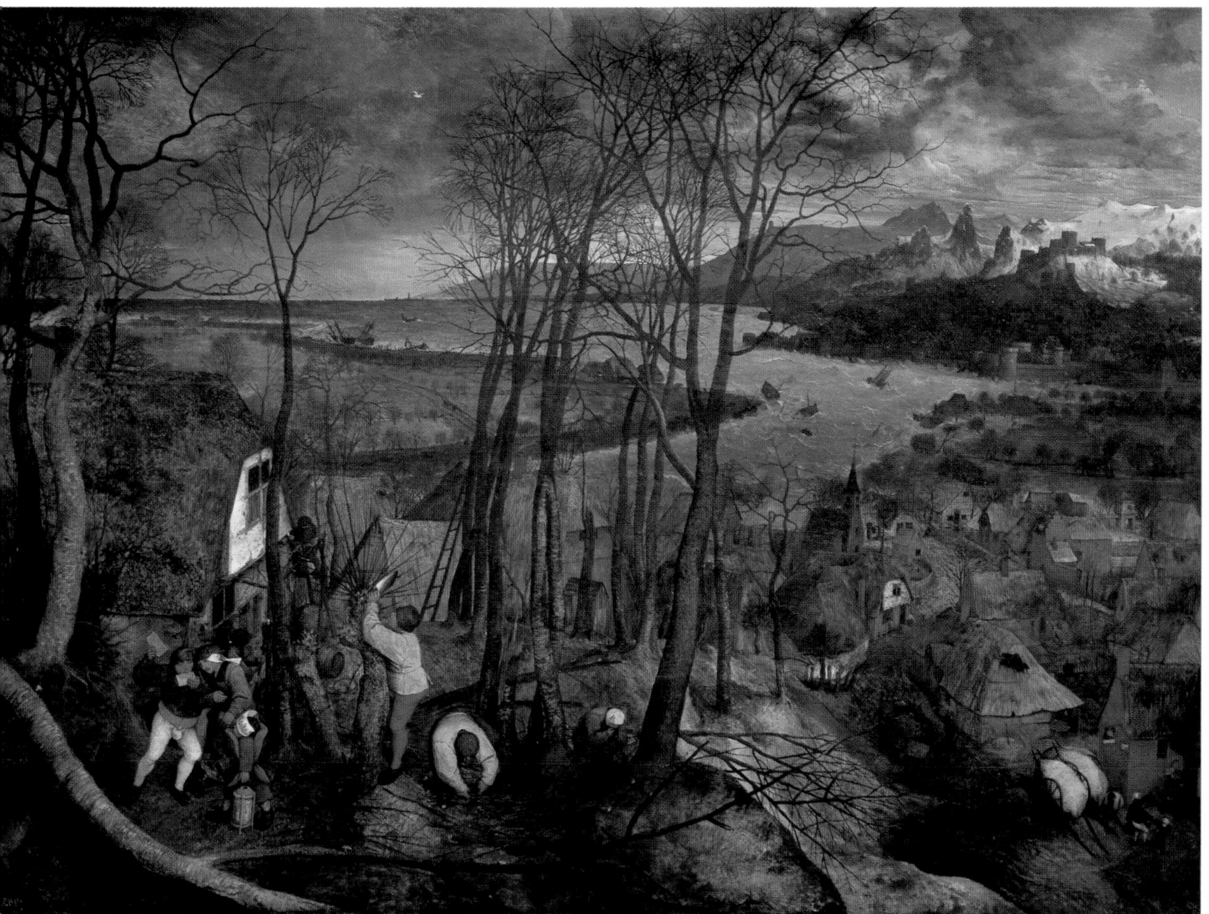

130 PIETER BRUEGEL THE ELDER *The Gloomy Day* 1565

Museum; one in the Metropolitan Museum in New York; and one in the National Gallery in Prague. All twelve were originally painted for the villa of Niclaes Jonghelinck, a banker and humanist scholar. A decade earlier Jonghelinck had commissioned twelve paintings depicting the labours of Hercules from Frans Floris (*c.* 1517–70), the leading mythological painter in Antwerp at that time. Bruegel's patron would have known Pliny the elder's description of Roman patrician villas, decorated with paintings of rural life as well as heroic deeds – so it is a fair assumption that Bruegel's twelve pictures were intended as a pastoral complement to the epic of Hercules' labours. Bruegel is likely to have drawn some inspiration from Virgil's reflections on man, landscape and agriculture in his *Georgics*.

Bruegel muses on man's diurnal relationship with the natural world, and his poetry, like Virgil's, finds much room for prosaic detail, furnishing the viewer with a compendious record of sixteenth-century farming techniques. He depicts haymakers and rakers and harvesters, along with the precise way in which trees are pollarded and twigs bound. That last detail is to be found in the scene representing February, *The Gloomy Day* [130], painted towards the end of his life. Two men are at work in the centre of the picture while, to the left, as a chill wind whips in from the sea, a slightly drunk man crams waffles into his mouth and a woman, who may be his wife, and a child, presumably hungry themselves, look on. At the bottom of the rise on which these characters stand there is a village, its houses thatched against the cold. Some roof repairs are being carried out on the nearest house. A man is dancing, and trying to get his child to join in, while a fiddler plays. Beside them another man pisses against the wall. Bruegel's attitude to the subjects which he painted remains unfathomable. But the picture makes space for more responses than amused superiority to the antics of the peasantry. The artist seems so absorbed in depicting the world that he has gone beyond judgement, into an observation of the way life is. He helps us not only to see, but almost to feel the nature of a peasant's life, to sense the bitter cold suffered by those scratching out a living on the land.

There is sympathy, perhaps, but no trace of sentimentality in Bruegel. Minor characters acquire a new prominence and in the process ordinary, inconsequential life is given a new value. The humanity that runs right through Renaissance art and literature seems to broaden yet further during the second half of the sixteenth century. This is true of Bruegel, and more so of Shakespeare, gifted with the broadest imagination of any author, prepared to explore the world of the gravedigger as well as the prince, the buffoon as well as the philosopher, the savage as well as the magus. There is no such thing as a life not worth noticing.

## COUNTER-REFORMATION

Italy too was changing rapidly during the second half of the sixteenth century. The Council of Trent, which sat from 1546 until 1562, formulated the Catholic church's response to the divided world which Holbein's ambassadors had dreamed, futilely, of healing. The Protestant Reformation provoked a Catholic Counter-Reformation. Censorship and control became the order of the day. Counter-Reformation theology stood firmly in opposition to the artistic and intellectual experimentation which had characterized the lives and works of so many

Renaissance men. In Italy, conflict between church and artist, church and intellectual, was inevitable.

Two years after the Council of Trent had ended so did the life of Michelangelo. The artist died, aged eighty-nine, in Rome, and doubtless he would have been buried there had not Cosimo de' Medici appropriated his body. Michelangelo's cadaver, concealed inside a hay bale, was smuggled out of Rome by Cosimo's agents and then taken to Florence, where the artist was to be buried with full pomp and ceremony in the church of San Lorenzo. Vasari, helped by members of the newly formed Florentine art academy, arranged the funeral, a solemn and splendid event described at length in the final pages of his biography of Michelangelo.[20] It was as if the Renaissance itself had died.

Bronzino marked this end of an era a year or two later by furnishing the same church of San Lorenzo with a large fresco of *The Martyrdom of St Lawrence* – a work which could almost be a textbook illustration of the religious improprieties of which an artist in thrall to *maniera* might be guilty. It is shocking precisely because it seems so much more graceful than it should be. The subject, after all, is a particularly gruesome martyrdom, involving hot coals and much charred flesh. But Bronzino's beautiful and muscular St Lawrence writhes on his griddle like an athlete doing stretching exercises, while his torturers prance about him striking self-consciously picturesque attitudes that Bronzino no doubt intended to epitomize the 'pleasing variety' required by the increasingly formulaic courtly aesthetics of the period. The result is a patent absurdity: a martyrdom enacted by ballet dancers. A secular aesthetic, of facility and elegance at all costs, has been misapplied to a subject which demands very different qualities. The source for many of the figures in the painting was the art of Michelangelo, which Bronzino – doing it much violence in the process – treated as an academy. Bronzino's paintings seem almost calculated to have made Michelangelo turn in his grave.

Work such as Bronzino's was, too, a red rag to the Counter-Reformation bull. According to the Council of Trent's decree on the subjects and motives of works of art, 'all lasciviousness must be avoided, so that images shall not be painted or adorned with a seductive charm'.[21] Bronzino had violated not merely the letter of Counter-Reformation law, but its spirit. Too much latitude had been taken by too many artists for too long. It was felt that there was an excess of nudity in modern religious painting, an excess of irrelevant detail, much of it drawn inappropriately from pagan myths and legends. There was an insufficient focus on the essentials of the faith. From now on, the Council determined, there was to be no more of that interplay between the pagan and the Christian which had characterized the work of such diverse artists as Correggio, Michelangelo and Bronzino. Radical action was taken.

Ironically, although it was Michelangelo's followers who had aroused the wrath of the Counter-Reformation by pursuing originality, ingenuity and artfulness to such extreme lengths, it was Michelangelo himself whose work was to bear almost the worst brunt of the Council of Trent's decisions. Bronzino's painting in San Lorenzo survived intact, thanks to the relatively relaxed atmosphere of Florence and the fact that he was one of Cosimo's preferred artists; but in the more critical climate of Counter-Reformation Rome, even a work as pious as Michelangelo's *Last Judgement* was severely criticized. In creating it, it was said that the artist had included too many indecorously nude figures, as well as the inappropriate figure of Charon ferrying the dead over the river Styx. Michelangelo's work was even physically altered. Daniele da Volterra, later nicknamed 'il Braghettone' (the Breeches Maker), was hired to paint strategically placed folds of drapery over the genitalia of the figures tumbling down the wall in the *Last Judgement*.[22]

The reformers of the 1560s dreamed of doing away with a large part of the Renaissance because they believed it had clouded the Christian picture. What they were attempting to do, in a sense, was to wind the clock back to the very *beginnings* of the Italian Renaissance. It is as if they were trying to go all the way back to what might be called the innocent Renaissance, the Renaissance of Giotto, Nicola Pisano and his son Giovanni – who had found, in Greco-Roman naturalism, a vocabulary with which to express a new and vivid piety, but who had not yet fully opened the Pandora's box of antiquity.

Gabriele Paleotti, one of the leading vigilantes of the Counter-Reformation, summed up its chief requirements of art with admirable clarity in his *Discorso intorno le immagini sacre* (1582):

> If we see the martyrdom of a saint rendered in lively colours without being shattered by it, if we see Christ being fastened to the cross with dreadful nails, we must be of marble or wood if we do not feel deeply moved, if our piety is not stimulated afresh and our inner being is not deeply affected by remorse and devotion.[23]

Vivid, simple and extremely literal art was what Paleotti called for. The one legacy of the Renaissance that the Counter-Reformers refused to abolish was the use of realistic images to move and persuade people.

A good place to see what this meant in practice is the Roman church of Santo Stefano Rotondo, where in 1563 a group of artists – not particularly talented but well instructed in Counter-Reformation piety – began to fresco the walls of this ancient circular church. The subjects prescribed were a particularly violent assortment of martyrdoms, which the artists depicted with great thoroughness. They painted martyrs crushed and bleeding, martyrs burned, martyrs skinned, martyrs boiled, martyrs mutilated in a variety of ways. These stern pictures of bloody suffering for God were meant as a school for evangelical Catholics. Thus was the ascetic creed of Paleotti embodied. But there is something oddly lifeless about this cyclorama of torture and pain. Despite their grimly insistent piety, the pictures themselves have a dulled, dutiful, by-rote quality. Dead pictures as well as pictures of dead people, they prove that it is not possible to turn back the clock. The attempt to go back to the very beginnings of the Renaissance in Italy really marked its end.

The lifeblood of Renaissance art had been the licence to invent and to innovate, and the role of the church in permitting that had been vital. But after the Council of Trent, the church saw its role differently. Its duty was to check and curb and redirect the imagination of artists, to ensure that the relationship between style and content should never again become as skewed as in the art of Bronzino (for the aesthetics of the Counter-Reformation were certainly a reaction to the notion that the pursuit of a 'stylish style', almost for its own sake, could ever be appropriate in a religious context). This marked a great change, and the new attitude of the church – combined with the spread of art academies such as that founded in Florence by Vasari, which also tended to promote the idea that there was a right and a wrong way of doing things – inaugurated a time when aesthetic rules came more and more to govern artistic practice.

Generalizations of this kind are inevitably fraught with danger, and the history of Italian art after the Council of Trent is hardly one of stasis and decline. The shadow-plays of Caravaggio, whose art is shot through with a new and enhanced form of morbid realism, were also produced in the climate of the Counter-Reformation – evidence enough that Tridentine theology had not stifled artistic originality. But it is perhaps fair to say that never again, after the Council of Trent, would art in Italy be quite as polymorphously diverse and experimental as it had been during the most vigorous years of the Renaissance. For all the energy and brilliance of the art that was to follow, there is a heightened degree of uniformity about it – especially in the religious sphere, where a common style prevailed as it had never done before.

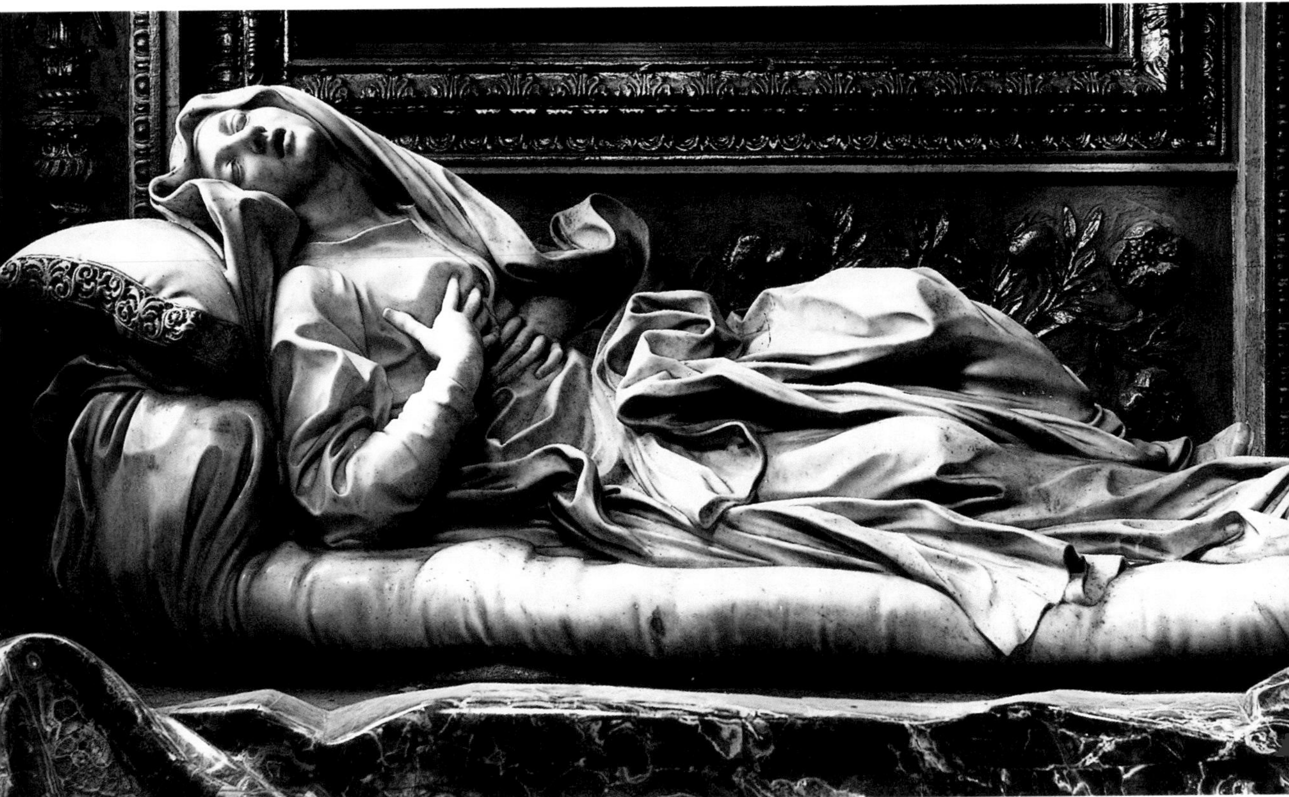

131 GIANLORENZO BERNINI *The Blessed Ludovica Albertoni*, San Francesco a Ripa, Trastevere, Rome 1672–4

'Baroque' is the name that has been given to the style of sculpture, painting and architecture that gradually emerged in Italy as the sixteenth century reached its end. With its faintly pejorative connotations of the bizarre, it is another of art history's misleading terms, applied long after the period itself. But it has at least the negative virtue of indicating that the word 'Renaissance', albeit itself never an entirely satisfactory tool of description, had outlived its usefulness by the start of the seventeenth century.

It would, of course, be wrong to give the impression that some historical portcullis simply descended and the Renaissance became, almost overnight, a thing of the past. Despite the fact that it seems inappropriate to talk of 'a Renaissance civilization' after 1600 or so, there is still a huge residue of Renaissance *in* civilization. A concrete (or rather marble) example of what is meant by this is to be found in the Chapel of the Blessed Ludovica Albertoni, in the Roman church of San Francesco a Ripa in Trastevere.

*The Blessed Ludovica Albertoni* [131], created in 1672-4 by Gianlorenzo Bernini (1598-1680), shows the enduring influence of the Counter-Reformation on Italian art. Bernini's monument vividly embodies the sense of priorities first announced in the decrees of the Council of Trent: the cool artifice of *maniera* has been completely rejected, in favour of an art that wrestles with the depiction of faith and the spiritual mysteries of Christianity in a much more emotive way. Bernini's Ludovica lies on her back, eyes closed, head flung backwards, on a mattress that may be meant to represent her deathbed – it is possible the artist meant to depict her death throes – but is certainly the bed in which she receives Christ into her heart like a lover. Her nun's habit has been whipped into a turmoil by the passion with which she has embraced God, in mystic communion. But for all its headily Baroque emotionalism, Bernini's art is full of echoes of the Renaissance. Bernini's virtuosity, the sheer delicacy with which he has carved stone into flesh and rippling cloth, is unthinkable without the example of Michelangelo (specifically Michelangelo's extremely proto-Baroque *Pietà* in St Peter's). Bernini's work owes most of all, both in its theatricality and in its intense, displaced eros, to Correggio. This melting stone Virgin in the throes of her pious orgasm is St Flavia in Correggio's *Martyrdom of Four Saints* [118], but realized in sculpture. *The Blessed Ludovica* might not be a Renaissance work of art but it is one that could never have come into existence had it not been for all the innovations made by the artists of the Renaissance. Even as the Renaissance was over, its afterlives had begun.

## EPILOGUE

'After the darkness is dispelled,' Petrarch had written, 'our grandsons shall walk into the pure radiance of the past.' But what exactly *was* that past, that unsullied antique origin to which so many, after Petrarch, dreamed of returning? Was it the Athens of Pericles, or the Rome of the Caesars? The men and women of the Renaissance themselves never reached a consensus on such questions. Indeed, the history of the Renaissance – and post-Renaissance – suggests that a large part of the appeal of Petrarch's vision of going back to an ideal classical past lay, precisely, in its openness to many interpretations.

Petrarch's invention was a metaphor of rebirth which, as those to follow him soon discovered, could be used to glorify or dignify almost any individual as a Caesar or Cicero, and which could be used to dress up almost any ideology in the pure white toga of virtue. During the course of centuries, this is indeed just how it has been used. France alone has experienced several Renaissances following the

Renaissance of Francis I, the most influential of which was, ideologically speaking, its exact opposite: the regicidal 'rebirth' of the French Revolution, when the calendar was turned back to Year Zero and Jacques-Louis David painted his contemporaries in Athenian fancy dress. Britain too has had its Renaissance, in the eighteenth century, when Members of Parliament almost believed the noble fiction that the House of Commons was the Roman Senate rebuilt, and when milords built themselves country houses as grand as temples. The ideal city of Zamoyski in Poland, a Renaissance utopia erected from nothing in the sixteenth century, testifies to the geographical spread of Petrarch's dream of rebuilding some ideal past in the present. Denmark's Renaissance came in the nineteenth century, when the sculptor Bertel Thorvaldsen was invited by Copenhagen to commemorate the foundation of the modern Danish state by furnishing the people with a huge museum filled with classical statues – a gallery of moral examples for a new republic which still, quaintly but idealistically, persists in the centre of the city.

The dream of classical rebirth polished to such a shine in the marmoreal surfaces of Thorvaldsen's sculpture may never again seem as untarnished as it did then. There are two chief reasons for this. One of the positive legacies of twentieth-century thought has been the development of intellectual pluralism, a side-effect of which has meant that few people now believe in the idea that the model for civilization can be said to lie in any one time or place. One of its negative legacies – the appropriation of the classical languages of art and architecture by the abominable regimes of Nazism and Fascism – has had a similar effect. Hitler rebuilt Berlin as a second Athens, equating the purity of Greece and Rome with the genetic purity of the Aryan race. Mussolini turned Rome into a stage-set for his own sinister theatre of classical fantasies. The huge statues of sporting heroes he had placed in his Stadio dei Marmi – musclebound homages to Michelangelo's *David* – are simultaneously the most chilling and absurd monuments to this dark period in modern European history. The guardians of Mussolini's tyrannical folly, they look down with unfading disapproval as modern joggers trundle round and old ladies walk their dogs on what was once a Fascist field of dreams. It was here that the Renaissance ideal of rebirth was forever sullied. It survives as a source for ideas, but a source which has been both diluted and poisoned.

Renaissance man dug as well as dreamed, and what he literally excavated from the past was something at once more palpable and more enduring than any fantasy of rebirth or revival. It was, simply, the image of man perpetuated in art. The ambition to transform pigment and stone into a representation of life is part of a wider anthropological impulse. It is behind many myths, ancient and more

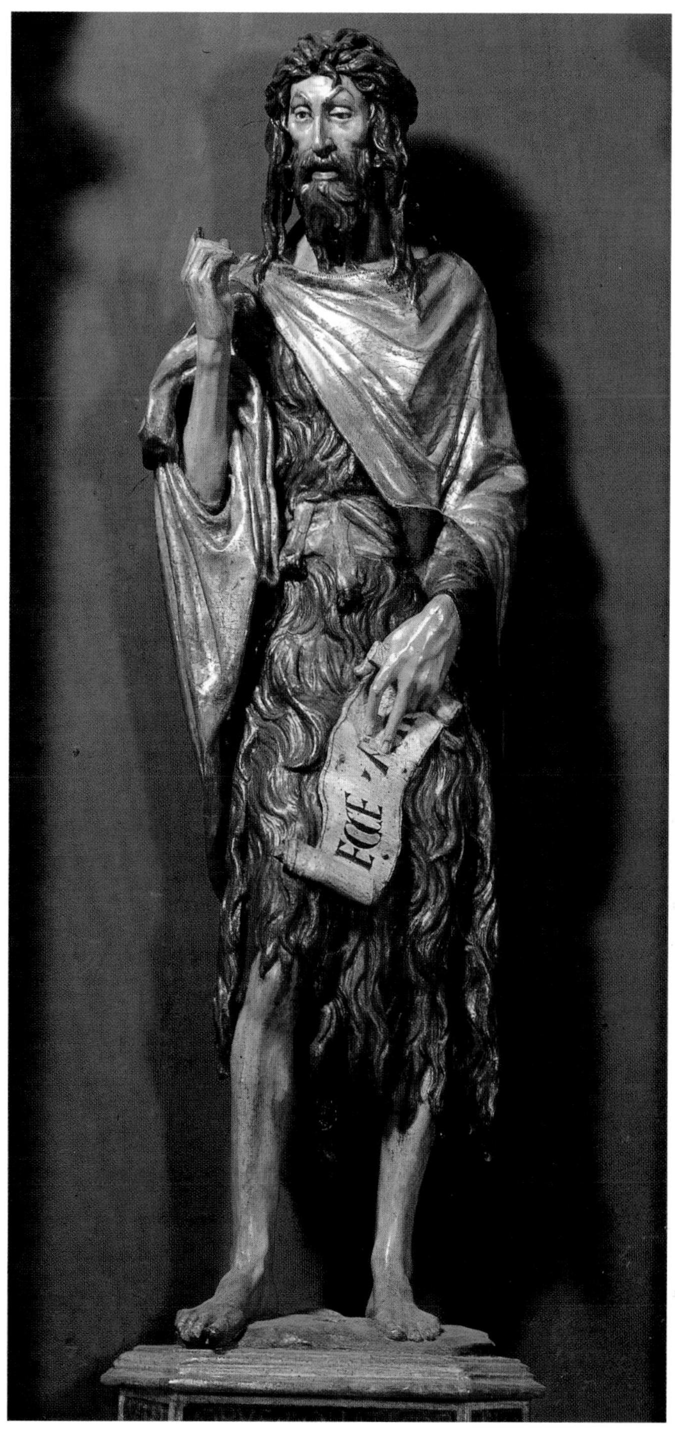


132 DONATELLO *St John the Baptist* 1438

modern – Pygmalion carving a statue that comes to life or Dr Frankenstein creating his monster – but it was from the Roman past that the Renaissance retrieved it. Until the rise of the mendicant orders and the revolution in piety with which this book began, the naturalism of the images created in antiquity – and pre-antiquity, even – had been largely lost from view. The importance of this revival cannot easily be overstated.

The vivid image of man, the image which seems to preserve the spark of life and even, perhaps the soul – this became the irreducible core of Western art during and after the Renaissance. There have been efforts to displace or replace it, notably by twentieth-century artists pursuing non-representational goals. But it has never been seriously challenged as the primary medium of visual communication – and latterly, the primary medium of all communication – in the Western world. The advent of nineteenth-century photographic technology, and the subsequent arrival of related media such as film and television, has guaranteed its centrality in modern life. But unless people had wanted such technology, unless the Renaissance had taught them to desire images of living reality so strongly, would they have invented it? The camera is literally a mechanized way of creating Renaissance perspectives – the 'Alberti box', as it has been called. And what is a film, but a fresco cycle at twenty-four frames per second? The imagery of living presence is all around us, in the cinema, on the street, in the home. It is everywhere we look, provoking us, inciting us to buy or to sell, to vote or to fall in love, arousing us on street corners or shouting at us from the side of a bus.

But perhaps the most enduring legacy of the Renaissance lies not in any form of revival – whether of classical ideas, or of realistic depiction – but in the new way in which it taught people to think about their own nature. It was not just the image of man, but an idea of man, that the Renaissance put at the centre of our world. Consciousness in a living organism, body and soul: that is how we think of human beings; and that is what all the great Renaissance artists, from Giovanni Pisano to Pieter Brueghel, albeit in their very different ways, depicted. When we look at a great work of Renaissance art, such as Donatello's statue of *St John the Baptist* [132], we can see this more clearly than if we simply ponder it as an abstraction. The miracle is not just the conjuring up of humanity, of the life force or living presence. The miracle lies in the delicacy and precision with which a moment of feeling has been caught – and in the magnitude of the revelation communicated by this capturing of something that seems so fugitive and, at once, so endlessly fascinating. The message forever trembling on the Baptist's lips is the message of the Renaissance itself. What is inside a man can be a whole world.

# NOTES ON SOURCES

**HAPTER ONE**
Vasari's *Lives of the Artists* was first published
ı Italian in 1550, followed by a second,
ıbstantially enlarged, edition in 1568. Unless
therwise stated, the translations in this book
re those of A.B. Hinds (London, 1970); this
uotation is from vol. 1, p. 6. Much the best
urrent edition is that edited by David
.kserdjian (London, 1997), which, unfortu-
ately, appeared after the chapters relating
ɔ Vasari had been substantially written.
The notable exception is the harrowingly
ealistic twelfth-century *Deposition* by
enedetto Antelami in Parma Cathedral.
This painting has been moved to the rather
rander church of Santa Chiara, within the
ity walls of Assisi, in recognition of the
nportant part it played in Francis's life.
St Bonaventure, quoted by Timothy Verdon
'St Francis of Assisi, Christmas at Greccio
ıd the Birth of Renaissance Art'. This
npublished lecture was given by Professor
ıow Monsignor) Verdon at the National
Gallery of Art in Washington in December
990, and the author was kind enough to let
ıe draw upon it.
Quoted by Verdon, op. cit.
Quoted by Elvio Lunghi, *The Basilica of
t Francis of Assisi* (London, 1996), p. 65.
Leonard von Matt and Walter Hauser, *St
rancis of Assisi: A Pictorial Biography* (London,
955), p. 67.
*Meditations on the Life of Christ*, ed.
Ragusa and R. Green (Princeton, 1961),
. 320.
'The entire design appears to grow on a
ngle stem, like some great, heavy-laden vine.'
ohn White, *Art and Architecture in Italy 1250–
400* (London, 1966; 2nd edn. 1987), p. 137.
**o** I am indebted to Frederick Hartt, who
oints out Michelangelo's borrowing in
is *Italian Renaissance Art* (London, 1987),
. 121.
**I** The main source for painters wishing to
lustrate the lives of the saints is *The Golden
egend*, a medieval manual of ecclesiastical
ɔre, primarily based on the Latin text of
ıcopus de Voragine (1230–98).
**2** Dante, *Inferno*, Canto III, 22–8; English
ans. by Ronald Bottrall, from *Dante's Inferno:
ith Translations Broadcast in the BBC Third
rogramme* (London, 1996).
**3** Antonio Panizzi, quoted in *Byzantium:
reasures of Byzantine Art and Culture from
ritish Collections*, ed. David Buckton
London, 1994), p. 11.
**4** Cecilia Janella, *Duccio di Buoninsegna*
Florence, 1991), p. 21.

**CHAPTER TWO**
**1** Orson Welles, interpolation in *The Third Man*, filmed 1949; script, Graham Greene and Carol Reed, 1969, p. 114.
**2** Jacob Burckhardt, *The Civilization of the Renaissance in Italy* (German original, 1860); trans. S.G.C. Middlemore (Vienna, 1878, rev. edn, 1945), p. 70.
**3** Ibid., p. 48.
**4** Michael Levey, *Florence* (London, 1996), p. 19.
**5** I have drawn substantially on G. Nauert's elegant synthesis in his *Humanism and the Culture of Renaissance Europe* (Cambridge, 1995).
**6** Petrarch, *Africa*, IX, 451–7, in *Francesco Petrarca Opere*, trans. Enrico Bianchi (Florence, 1975).
**7** Leonardo Bruni, *Panegyric to the City of Florence* (Latin original, 1403–4); trans. B. Kohl, in *The Earthly Republic*, ed. B. Kohl and R. Witt (Philadelphia, 1961), pp 158–62.
**8** Leon Battista Alberti, *On Painting* (Latin and Italian, 1435–6), trans. John R. Spencer (New Haven and London, 1956), p. 40.
**9** Quoted in Hans Baron, 'Franciscan Poverty and Civic Wealth as Factors in the Rise of Humanistic Thought', *Speculum*, vol. 13, no. 1 (1938), p. 22.
**10** Michael Baxendall, *Painting and Experience in Fifteenth-century Italy* (Oxford, 1972).
**11** Quoted in Eugenio Battisti, *Brunelleschi: The Complete Work* (London, 1981), p. 45.
**12** It has been suggested that the trees originally had leaves, painted *a secco* and since lost.
**13** The precise dates for these sculptures are disputed, but it seems almost certain that they were in the artist's workshop for a long time.
**14** Vasari, op. cit., 'The Life of Donatello'.
**15** Frederick Hartt, *Donatello, Prophet of Modern Vision* (London, 1974), p. 71.

**CHAPTER THREE**
**1** Quoted in *Fetishism: Visualising Power and Desire*, ed. Anthony Shelton (London, 1995).
**2** Quoted in Francesco Borsi, *Leon Battista Alberti: The Complete Works* (London, 1986), p. 92.
**3** Quoted in Alison Cole, *Art of the Italian Renaissance Courts* (London, 1995), p. 27.
**4** It has been pointed out to me, by a friend and art historian who is blind in one eye, that there is a school of thought which holds that Federigo merely lost an eye in the accident and had the bridge of his nose subsequently cut away, by his surgeons, in order to widen the angle of vision of his remaining, good eye. Given his ingenuity, and the importance of clear-sightedness to him, I find this an extremely plausible, albeit unusual, suggestion.
**5** Luciano Cheles, *The Studiolo of Urbino: An Iconographic Investigation* (Pennsylvania, 1986), p. 64.
**6** The excursion was recorded by Felice Feliciano, who was present. His account is reprinted in Paul Kristeller, *Andrea Mantegna* (Berlin and Leipzig, 1902), pp 523–4, doc. 34.
**7** Whether Francesco himself was Mantegna's chief patron when he painted *The Triumphs* remains open to dispute, but it was certainly a Gonzaga commission.
**8** Quoted in John Hale, *The Civilization of Europe in the Renaissance* (London, 1993), p. 203.
**9** There is evidence that Isabella herself was embarrassed by the risqué associations of some of these images. For an illuminating acccount of the complexities of her position at court, and her role as patron, see L. Jacobus, '"A lady more radiant than the sun": Isabella d'Este's creation of a personal iconography, Mantegna and fifteenth-century court culture', ed. Ames-Lewis and Anka Bednarek (Birkbeck College, London, 1993).
**10** Quoted in Françoise Gilot and Carlton Lake, *Life with Picasso* (London, 1990), pp 67–8.
**11** *Leonardo's Notebooks*, selected and edited by Irma Richter (Oxford, 1980 edn), p. 195.
**12** Leonardo da Vinci, *Trattato della pittura*, ed. Angelo Borzelli (Lanciano, 1914), para. 32.
**13** Kenneth Clark, *Leonardo da Vinci* (Cambridge, 1939; rev. edns 1959, 1988).
**14** Evelyn Welch, *Art and Authority in Renaissance Milan* (New Haven, 1995).
**15** *Leonardo's Notebooks*, op. cit., p. 170.
**16** Ibid., p. 304.
**17** Ibid., p. 5.
**18** *Trattato della pittura*, op. cit., para. 90.
**19** *Leonardo's Notebooks*, op. cit., p. 139.
**20** Ibid., p. 45.
**21** Walter Pater, *Studies in the History of the Renaissance* (London, 1873).
**22** *Leonardo's Notebooks*, op. cit., pp 187–93.
**23** Benvenuto Cellini, *Autobiography*, written 1558–66; *The Autobiography of Benvenuto Cellini*, trans. G. Bull (Harmondsworth, 1956).
**24** Vasari, op. cit, 'The Life of Leonardo da Vinci'.

**CHAPTER FOUR**
**1** Quoted in Eamon Duffy, *Saints and Sinners* (London and New Haven, 1997), p. 139.
**2** Quoted in George L. Hersey, *High Renaissance Art in St Peter's and the Vatican* (Chicago, 1993), p. 12.
**3** Letter of 1506 from Dürer to Willibald Pirckheimer, cited in Heinrich Wolfflin, *The Art of Albrecht Dürer* (German original, 1905); Eng. trans. (Oxford, 1971), p. 29.

**4** Julius had identified with St Peter in chains ever since he had been a cardinal, when his titular church in Rome was San Pietro in Vincoli – the church, literally, of 'St Peter in Chains', where his memorial by Michelangelo, in its much reduced form, was eventually to be sited.
**5** Erasmus, *Julius Exclusus* (Latin original, 1517); the extract printed here is from *The 'Julius Exclusus' of Erasmus*, trans. P. Pascal, introduction and critical notes by J.K. Sowards (Bloomington, 1968). My attention was first called to the work by Loren Partridge's book *The Renaissance in Rome 1400–1600* (London, 1996), pp 10–11.
**6** The villa is so named because Cardinal Alessandro Farnese (1520–89) was responsible for its completion.
**7** Quoted in A.G. Dickens, *Reformation and Society in Sixteenth Century Europe* (London, 1966), p. 61.
**8** Quoted in Hersey, op. cit, p. 18.
**9** Quoted in Partridge, op. cit., p. 128.
**10** Vasari, op. cit., 'The Life of Michelangelo'.
**11** Sonnet LXV, *The Sonnets of Michelangelo*, trans. Elizabeth Jennings (London, 1969), p. 86.
**12** Montaigne, 'Des Livres', (Paris, 1997), p. 27.
**13** Quoted in Charles Taylor, *Sources of the Self: The Origins of Modern Identity* (Oxford, 1986), p. 179.

**CHAPTER FIVE**
**1** John Ruskin, *The Stones of Venice*, 3 vols (1851–3), ed. J.G. Links (London, 1960), p. 139.
**2** William Shakespeare, *The Merchant of Venice*, Act III, sc. i.
**3** The story about Mehmet and the decapitated head is recounted by Hartt, op. cit., p. 398.
**4** Ruskin, op. cit., p. 19.
**5** I am indebted to the scholarship and generosity of Peter Humfrey, who very kindly furnished a brief explanation of the complexities of the altarpiece in question.
**6** Andrew Marvell, *The Garden and other poems* (London, 1993).
**7** Priscianese's letter, which dates some time before 1540, is given in Juergen Schulz, 'Houses of Titian, Aretino and Sansovino', in *Titian, His World and His Legacy*, ed. David Rosand (New York, 1982), p. 82 (in English translation) and pp 108–9 (original Italian).
**8** Palladio himself, however, seems to have felt differently. The architect remained pointedly silent about Veronese's pictorial interventions, and there is reason to suppose that he resented them.
**9** In a letter of July 1545 Aretino wrote to Sansovino: 'You are the man who knows how to be Vitruvius'; see Pietro Aretino, *Lettere sull'arte*, ed. E. Camesasca, 3 vols (Milan, 1957–60), vol. II, p. 78.
**10** Samuel Taylor Coleridge, 'The Rime of the Ancient Mariner', ed. Paul H. Fry (London, 1999).
**11** For example, in his opening paragraphs on Titian: Vasari, op. cit., 'The Life of Titian'.

**CHAPTER SIX**
**1** Quoted in Fernand Braudel, *Le Modèle Italien* (Paris, 1994), p. 10.
**2** Vasari, op.cit., 'The Life of Aristotile da Sangallo'. In this case I have adopted the translation published in the parallel text version of the *Lives* edited by Paola Barocchi and Rosanna Bettarini, as quoted by Patricia Rubin in her *Giorgio Vasari: Art and History* (New Haven, 1995).
**3** Vasari, op. cit., vol. I, p. 18.
**4** Ibid., vol. I, p. 203.
**5** I am indebted, in my observations about Michelangelo's architectural inside-outness, to John Shearman's brilliantly revealing account of the effect of Michelangelo's Laurentian Library staircase in *Mannerism* (Harmondsworth, 1967).
**6** Leo Steinberg, 'Pontormo's Capponi Chapel', *Art Bulletin*, vol. LVI (1974), pp 385–99.
**7** Quoted in David Ekserdjian, *Correggio* (New Haven and London, 1997), p. 254.
**8** 'That rare Italian master, Julio Romano', *The Winter's Tale*, Act V, sc. ii. Shakespeare, however, referred to the artist as if he were a sculptor.
**9** Vasari, op. cit.
**10** Quoted in Jean-Marie Perouse de Montclos, *Fontainebleau* (Paris, 1998), p. 73.
**11** Benvenuto Cellini, op. cit.
**12** Jean de Dinteville, quoted in Susan Foiste *Making and Meaning: Holbein's Ambassadors* (London, 1998).
**13** Ibid.
**14** Mary Hervey, *Holbein's Ambassadors: The Picture and the Men, a Historical Study* (London, 1900).
**15** Quoted in Foister, op. cit.
**16** Quoted in Hale, op. cit., p. 282.
**17** Karel van Mander, *Het Schilderboek* (Haarlem, 1604). In this compilation van Mander was making a conscious attempt to do for artists in the North what Vasari had done for artists on the Italian peninsula.
**18** Quoted by Walter S. Gibson, *Bruegel* (London, 1977), p. 12.
**19** Juvenal, *Satires*, X, 166; quoted in *The Oxford History of the Classical World*, ed. John Boardman, Jasper Griffin and Oswyn Murray (Oxford, 1986), p. 687.
**20** Vasari, op. cit., 'The Life of Michelangelo'
**21** Decree drafted at the last session of the Council on 3 and 4 December 1563. Quoted in Arnold Hauser, *Mannerism*, vol. 1, p. 76 (London, 1965).
**22** Michelangelo, whose own attitude to art during his later years had become ambivalen to say the least (see the sonnet quoted on p. 217), made no objection to Daniele's alterations and seems even to have approved of them.
**23** Quoted in Arnold Hauser, *Mannerism* (London, 1965), p. 76.

# NOTES ON WORKS

**CHAPTER ONE**
**Jacket** *The Dying Slave*, *c.* 1514 (for the Tomb of Julius II).
Michelangelo Buonarroti, 1475–1564.
Marble, height 229 cm.
Musée du Louvre, Paris, France.
**1** *Expulsion from Paradise*, mid-1420s
Masaccio, 1401–28.
Fresco, 208 x 88 cm.
Brancacci Chapel, Santa Maria del Carmine, Florence, Italy.
**2** *Primavera* (detail), *c.* 1482.
Sandro Botticelli, 1445–1510.
Tempera on wood, 203 x 314 cm.
Galleria degli Uffizi, Florence, Italy.
**3** *St Francis Receiving the Stigmata*, 1296–7.
Giotto di Bondone, 1266/7–1337.
Fresco.
Upper Church, Basilica of San Francesco, Assisi, Italy.
**4** Basilica of San Marco, Venice, Italy.
Begun *c.* 1063.
**5** *Translation of the Relics of St Mark* showing *Christ Pantocrator*, *c.* 1270.
Artist unknown.
Mosaic.
Porta di Sant'Alippo, main façade, Basilica of San Marco, Venice, Italy.
**6** Interior of Santa Croce, Florence, Italy.
Begun 1294.
Architect – various.
**7** *St Francis and Scenes from His Life*, 1235.
Bonaventura Berlinghieri, active 1228–74.

Altarpiece, tempera on panel, 152 x 116 cm.
San Francesco, Pescia, Italy.
8 *Christus Triumphans (Christ Triumphant upon the Cross),* late 12th century.
Artist unknown.
Basilica of Santa Chiara, Assisi, Italy.
9 *Christus Patiens (Christ Suffering on the Cross), c.* 1250–55.
Coppo di Marcovaldo, active 1260–76.
Tempera on panel, 293 x 247 cm.
Museo Civico, San Gimignano, Italy.
10 *Adoration of the Magi* (detail), 1259–60.
Nicola Pisano, *c.* 1220–before 1284.
Marble, height of pulpit, *c.* 460 cm.
Pulpit, Baptistery, Pisa, Italy.
11 *The Nativity* (detail), 1302–10.
Giovanni Pisano, *c.* 1245/50 – before end 1319.
Marble, height of pulpit, 461 cm.
Pulpit, Cathedral, Pisa, Italy.
12 *The Last Judgement* (detail), *c.* 1310–30.
Lorenzo Maitani, active 1290–1330.
Marble.
Pilaster, façade, Cathedral, Orvieto, Italy.
13 *The Betrayal of Christ* (detail), *c.* 1303–6.
Giotto di Bondone, 1266/7–1337
Fresco, 200 x 185 cm.
Arena (Scrovegni) Chapel, Padua, Italy.
14 *The Lamentation c.* 1303–6.
Giotto di Bondone, 1266/7–1337.
Fresco, 200 x 185 cm.
Arena (Scrovegni) Chapel, Padua, Italy.
15 *The Lamentation* (detail), *c.* 1164.
Artist unknown.
Fresco.
St Pantaleimon, Nerezi, Macedonia.
16 *St John the Baptist, c.* 1164.
Artist unknown.
Fresco.
St Pantaleimon, Nerezi, Macedonia.
17 *Christ Pantocrator* (detail – *Last Judgement*), *c.* 1225–1325.
Artist(s) unknown.
Mosaic.
Ceiling, Baptistery, Florence, Italy.
18 *The Virgin and Child Enthroned*, central front panel, *Maestà* (detail), 1308–11.
Duccio di Buoninsegna, active 1278–1319.
Tempera and gold leaf on panel, 213 x 396 cm.
Museo dell'Opera del Duomo, Siena, Italy.
19 *The Transfiguration, Maestà* (detail), 1308–11.
Duccio di Buoninsegna, active 1278–1319.
Tempera and gold leaf on panel, 48 x 50.5 cm.
Predella panel, National Gallery, London, UK.
20 *Corpus of Christ,* from the *Well of Moses* (Chartreuse of Champmol, near Dijon).
Begun *c.* 1396.
Claus Sluter, *c.* 1360 – before 1406.
Stone, height 64 cm.
Musée Archéologique, Dijon, France.
21 *Virgin and Child in an Interior, c.* 1435.
Jacques Daret (attributed), *c.* 1400/05–*c.* 1468 (workshop of Robert Campin).
Oil on panel, 18.7 x 11.6 cm.
National Gallery, London, UK.
22 *The Deposition, c.* 1435.
Rogier van der Weyden, *c.* 1399–1464.
Oil on panel, 220 x 262 cm.
Museo del Prado, Madrid, Spain.
23 *Madonna and Child with Saints* (San Zaccaria altarpiece), 1505.
Giovanni Bellini, 1431/6–1516.
Oil on wood, transferred to canvas, 500 x 240 cm.
San Zaccaria, Venice, Italy.

**CHAPTER TWO**

24 Dome, 1420–36.
Filippo Brunelleschi, 1377–1446.
Cathedral of Santa Maria del Fiore, Florence, Italy.
25 *Tomb of Leonardo Bruni,* 1444–6
Bernardo Rossellino, 1409–64.
Marble, height 715 cm.
Santa Croce, Florence, Italy.
26 Orsanmichele, 1337–80.
Architect uncertain.
Sandstone.
Exterior, Via dei Calzaiuoli, Florence, Italy.
27 *Four Crowned Martyrs, c.* 1412–15
Nanni di Banco, *c.* 1384–1421.
Marble, life-size.
Orsanmichele, Via dei Calzaiuoli, Florence, Italy.
28 *St Mark,* 1411–13.
Donatello (Donato di Niccolò di Betto Bardi), 1386/7–1466.
Marble, height 236 cm.
Orsanmichele, Florence, Italy.
29 *St John the Baptist, c.* 1412–16.
Lorenzo Ghiberti, 1378–1455.
Bronze, height, 255 cm.
Orsanmichele, Florence, Italy.
30 *St George* (detail), *c.* 1415–17.
Donatello, 1386/7–1466.
Marble, height 206 cm.
Museo Nazionale del Bargello, Florence, Italy.
31 Interior, Pazzi Chapel, begun *c.* 1430–33.
Filippo Brunelleschi, 1377–1446.
Glazed terracotta roundels – Luca della Robbia, *c.* 1399–1482.
Santa Croce, Florence, Italy.
32 *The Sacrifice of Isaac,* 1401–2.
Lorenzo Ghiberti, 1378–1455.
Bronze, 53.3 x 42 cm.
Museo Nazionale del Bargello, Florence, Italy.
33 *The Sacrifice of Isaac,* 1401–2.
Filippo Brunelleschi, 1377–1446.
Bronze, 53.3 x 42 cm.
Museo Nazionale del Bargello, Florence, Italy.
34 *Jacob and Esau, c.* 1435.
Lorenzo Ghiberti, 1378–1455.
Gilded bronze, 87 x 87 cm.
Panel from Baptistery doors, Florence, Italy.
35 *The Trinity, c.* 1425–7.
Masaccio, 1401–28.
Fresco, 667 x 317 cm.
Santa Maria Novella, Florence, Italy.
36 *The Tribute Money* (detail), *c.* 1427.
Masaccio, 1401–28.
Fresco, 255 x 580 cm.
Brancacci Chapel, Santa Maria del Carmine, Florence, Italy.
37 *Habbakuk (Zuccone), c.* 1415–35.
Donatello, 1386/7–1466.
Marble, height 206 cm.
Museo dell'Opera del Duomo, Florence, Italy.
38 *Mary Magdalene, c.* 1455.
Donatello, 1386/7–1466.
Painted wood, height 188 cm.
Museo dell'Opera del Duomo, Florence, Italy.
39 Singing gallery – '*Cantoria*' (detail), 1433–9.
Donatello, 1386/7–1466.
Marble and mosaic, overall 348 x 570 cm.
Museo dell'Opera del Duomo, Florence, Italy.
40 *Equestrian Monument to Erasmo Narni (Gattamelata),* 1447–53.
Donatello, 1386/7–1466.
Bronze on marble and stone base, height 340 cm.
Piazza del Santo, Padua, Italy.
41 *David, c.* 1430–45.
Donatello, 1386/7–1466.
Bronze, height 158 cm.
Museo Nazionale del Bargello, Florence, Italy.
42 *Ascension Pulpit* (south pulpit), *c.* 1460–66
Donatello, 1386/7–1466.
Bronze, 123 x 292 cm.
San Lorenzo, Florence, Italy.

**CHAPTER THREE**

43 *The Adoration of the Magi,* 1442
Benozzo Gozzoli, *c.* 1420–97.
Fresco, 175 x 357 cm.
Tabernacle, 86 x 60 cm.
Cell 39, San Marco, Florence, Italy.
44 *The Crucifixion with the Virgin, Saints John, Dominic and Jerome, c.* 1440–45.
Fra Angelico, *c.* 1395/1400–55.
Fresco, 178 x 150 cm.
Cell 4, San Marco, Florence, Italy.
45 *The Journey of the Magi* (detail – with Giuliano de' Medici and Joseph, Patriarch of Constantinople), 1459–61.
Benozzo Gozzoli, *c.* 1420–97.
Fresco, width *c.* 750 cm.
Chapel, Palazzo Medici-Riccardi, Florence, Italy.
46 *The Battle of San Romano, c.* 1455.
Paolo Uccello, 1397–1475.
Tempera on panel, 182 x 320 cm.
National Gallery, London, UK.
47 *Sigismondo Malatesta before St Sigismund,* 1451.
Piero della Francesca, *c.* 1420–92.
Detached fresco and tempera, 250 x 340 cm.
San Francesco, Rimini, Italy.

**48** Façade, Tempio Malatestiano, begun late 1453, left incomplete 1468.
Leon Battista Alberti, 1404-72.
Marble, porphyry and Istrian stone.
Tempio Malatestiano, San Francesco, Rimini, Italy.
**49** *Luna, c.* 1451-3.
Agostino di Duccio, 1418-81.
Marble relief.
Chapel of the Planets, Tempio Malatestiano, San Francesco, Rimini, Italy.
**50** *Diptych with Portraits of Federigo da Montefeltro* (detail) *and Battista Sforza, c.* 1472.
Piero della Francesca, *c.* 1420-92.
Oil on panel, each panel, 47 x 33 cm.
Galleria degli Uffizi, Florence, Italy.
**51** The Studiolo, Ducal Palace, Urbino, Italy, *c.* 1472-6.
Intarsia doors possibly designed by Sandro Botticelli, 1445-1510, and Francesco di Giorgio, 1439-1501.
*Series of Portraits of Famous Learned Men* by Justus of Ghent (and Pedro Berruguete?, *c.* 1450/55-*c.* 1504), Ducal Palace, Urbino, Italy and Musée du Louvre, Paris, France.
**52** Intarsia doors. See note above.
**53** *Camera Picta* (or *Camera degli Sposi*, detail), *c.* 1465-74.
Andrea Mantegna, 1430/31-1506.
Fresco, 600 x 807 cm.
Ducal Palace, Mantua, Italy.
**54** Courtyard, Andrea Mantegna's house, Mantua, Italy, 1483.
**55** *St Sebastian, c.* 1480.
Andrea Mantegna, 1430/31-1506.
Canvas, 255 x 140 cm.
Musée du Louvre, Paris, France.
**56** *The Triumphs of Caesar*, Canvas IX – *Caesar on His Chariot* (detail ), *c.* 1484-late 1490s.
Andrea Mantegna, 1430/31-1506.
Tempera on canvas, 266 x 278 cm.
Hampton Court, London, UK.
**57** Self-portrait bust, *c.* 1480.
Andrea Mantegna, 1430/31-1506.
Bronze bust set in roundel against porphyry background.
Sant'Andrea, Mantua, Italy.
**58** *The Month of April, c.* 1470.
Francesco del Cossa, 1436- *c.* 1477/8.
Fresco.
Sala dei Mesi, Schifanoia Palace, Ferrara, Italy.
**59** *Parnassus, c.* 1495.
Andrea Mantegna, 1430/31-1506.
Egg tempera on canvas, 150 x 192 cm.
Musée du Louvre, Paris, France.
**60** *The Birth of Venus* (and detail), *c.* 1485.
Sandro Botticelli, 1444-1510.
Tempera on canvas, 172.5 x 278.5 cm.
Galleria degli Uffizi, Florence, Italy.
**61** *The Adoration of the Magi, c.* 1481-2.
Leonardo da Vinci, 1452-1519.
Oil on panel, 240 x 246 cm.
Galleria degli Uffizi, Florence, Italy.
**62** Design for the casting mould of planned Sforza monument, *c.* 1493.
Leonardo da Vinci, 1452-1519.
Biblioteca Nacional, Madrid, Spain.
**63** *The Beginning of the Deluge, c.* 1514.
Leonardo da Vinci, 1452-1519.
Pen, ink and brown wash over black chalk on paper, 15.7 x 20.3 cm.
Royal Collection, Windsor, UK.
**64** *The Virgin of the Rocks, c.* 1483.
Leonardo da Vinci, 1452-1519.
Oil on panel, 200 x 122 cm.
Musée du Louvre, Paris, France.
**65** *The Last Supper* (detail), *c.* 1495-8.
Leonardo da Vinci, 1452-1519.
Tempera and oil over ground limestone, 460 x 880 cm.
Refectory, Santa Maria delle Grazie, Milan, Italy.
**66** *Mona Lisa, c.* 1503.
Leonardo da Vinci, 1452-1519.
Oil on panel, 978 x 533 cm.
Musée du Louvre, Paris, France.
**67** *Self-portrait, c.* 1513.
Leonardo da Vinci, 1452-1519.
Red chalk on paper, 33.3 x 21.4 cm.
Biblioteca Reale, Turin, Italy.

**CHAPTER FOUR**
**68** *The Stories of the Antichrist* (detail), 1499-1502.
Luca Signorelli, *c.* 1450-1523.
Fresco.
Chapel of San Brizio, Cathedral, Orvieto, Italy.
**69** *The Last Judgement, c.* 1500
Hieronymous Bosch, *c.* 1450-1516.
Oil on panel, 164 x 127 cm.
Akademie der bildenden Kunste, Vienna, Austria.
**70** *Resurrection of the Dead*, 1499-1502.
Luca Signorelli, *c.* 1450-1523.
Fresco.
Chapel of San Brizio, Cathedral, Orvieto, Italy.
**71** Santa Maria della Consolazione, Todi, Italy, begun 1508.
Cola da Caprarola, 1494-1518, to a design by Bramante, *c.* 1444-1514.
**72** *The School of Athens*, 1510-11.
Raphael (Raffaello Sanzio), 1483-1520.
Fresco, height 579 cm.
Stanza della Segnatura, Vatican Palace, Rome, Italy.
**73** Isenheim Altarpiece (closed position), *c.* 1515.
Matthias Grünewald (Mathis Nithardt-Gothardt), *c.* 1475/80-1528.
Panels 240 x 300 cm.
Musée d'Unterlinden, Colmar, France.
**74** *The Resurrection* (wing detail), Isenheim Altarpiece, *c.* 1515.
Matthias Grünewald, *c.* 1475/80-1528.
Panel, wings 269 x 142 cm.
Musée d'Unterlinden, Colmar, France.
**75** *Self-portrait*, 1500.
Albrecht Dürer, 1471-1528.
Limewood, 67 x 49 cm.
Alte Pinakothek, Munich, Germany.
**76** *The Last Supper* (detail), *Holy Blood Altarpiece, c.* 1499-1505.
Tilman Riemenschneider, *c.* 1460-1531.
Lindenwood, overall height 900 cm (approx)
Church of St Jacob, Rothenburg, Germany.
**77** *David,* 1501-4.
Michelangelo Buonarroti, 1475-1564.
Marble, height, 410 cm.
Galleria dell' Accademia, Florence, Italy.
**78** *Moses, c.* 1513-15.
Michelangelo Buonarroti, 1475-1564.
Marble, height, 235 cm.
San Pietro in Vincoli, Rome, Italy.
**79** Ceiling of the Sistine Chapel, Vatican Palace, Rome, Italy, 1508-12.
Michelangelo Buonarroti, 1475-1564.
Fresco.
**80** *Liberation of St Peter from His Chains,* 1511-14.
Raphael, 1483-1520.
Fresco.
Stanza d'Eliodoro, Vatican Palace, Rome, Italy.
**81** *The Last Supper c.* 1539.
Lucas Cranach the elder, 1472-1553.
Church of St Mary's, Wittenberg, Germany.
**82** *The Lord's Vineyard, c.* 1569.
Lucas Cranach the younger, 1515-86.
Oil on panel.
Church of St Mary's, Wittenberg, Germany.
**83** *Devil Playing the Bagpipes, c.* 1530.
Erhard Schön, *c.* 1491-1542.
Woodcut with hand colouring, 32 x 24 cm.
British Museum, London, UK.
**84** *Fire in the Borgo,* 1514-17.
Raphael, 1483-1520.
Fresco, base 673 cm.
Stanza dell'Incendio, Vatican Palace, Rome, Italy.
**85** *The Conversion of Saul,* 1542-5.
Michelangelo Buonarroti, 1475-1564.
Fresco, 620 x 666 cm.
The Pauline Chapel, Vatican Palace, Rome, Italy.
**86** *The Crucifixion of St Peter, c.* 1545-9.
Michelangelo Buonarroti, 1475-1564.
Fresco, 620 x 666 cm.
The Pauline Chapel, Vatican Palace, Rome, Italy.
**87** *Landscape with Castle, c.* 1520-32.
Albrecht Altdorfer, *c.* 1480-1538.
Oil on parchment attached to panel, 30.5 x 22.2 cm.
Alte Pinakothek, Munich, Germany.
**88** *Eve,* 1528.
Lucas Cranach the elder, 1472-1553.
Oil on panel, 172 x 63 cm
Galleria degli Uffizi, Florence, Italy.

**CHAPTER FIVE**
**89** *Bacchus and Ariadne*, 1522–3.
Titian (Tiziano Vecellio), *c.* 1485–1576.
Oil on canvas, 175 x 191 cm.
National Gallery, London, UK.
**90** Venice from the island of San Giorgio Maggiore, Venice, Italy.
**91** *Virgin and Child,* late 12th century.
Artist unknown.
Mosaic. Apse, Santa Maria dell'Assunta, Torcello, Lagoon, Venice, Italy.
**92** *Doge Leonardo Loredan*, *c.* 1501.
Giovanni Bellini, 1431/6?–1516.
Oil on panel, 62 x 45 cm.
National Gallery, London, UK.
**93** *Equestrian Monument to Bartolommeo Colleoni,* 1480–88/96.
Andrea Verrocchio, 1435–88 (completed by Alessandro Leopardi, active 1482–1552).
Bronze, height 400 cm.
Campo Santi Giovanni e Paolo, Venice, Italy.
**94** *Procession in the Piazza San Marco,* 1496.
Gentile Bellini, 1429?–1507.
Oil on canvas, 367 x 745 cm.
Galleria dell'Accademia, Venice, Italy.
**95** *St Jerome Leading the Lion into the Monastery*, *c.* 1502.
Vittore Carpaccio, *c.* 1460–1525/6.
Oil on canvas, 141 x 121 cm.
Scuola di San Giorgio degli Schiavoni, Venice, Italy.
**96** *The Vision of St Augustine*, *c.* 1502.
Vittore Carpaccio, *c.* 1460–1525/6.
Oil on canvas, 141 x 211 cm.
Scuola di San Giorgio degli Schiavoni, Venice, Italy.
**97** *Sultan Mehmet II,* 1479.
Gentile Bellini, 1429?–1507.
Oil on canvas, 70 x 52 cm.
National Gallery, London, UK.
**98** Entrance to the Arsenale, Venice, Italy, 1460s.
Antonio Gambello (attributed), active 1453–81.
**99** The Doges' Palace, main façade, Venice, Italy, begun *c.* 1340.
**100** *St Francis Receiving the Stigmata*, *c.* 1450–55.
Jacopo Bellini, *c.* 1400–70/1.
Ink and silverpoint on parchment.
Musée du Louvre, Paris, France.
**101** *The Baptism of Christ*, *c.* 1500.
Giovanni Bellini, 1431/6?–1516.
Oil on panel, 410 x 265 cm.
Garzadori Chapel of St John the Baptist, Santa Corona, Vicenza, Italy.
**102** *La Tempesta*, *c.* 1505.
Giorgione, 1477/8?–1510.
Oil on canvas, 82 x 73 cm.
Galleria dell'Accademia, Venice, Italy.
**103** *Concert Champêtre*, *c.* 1510.
Giorgione, 1477/8?–1510 or Titian, *c.* 1485–1576.
Oil on canvas, 110 x 138 cm.
Musée du Louvre, Paris, France.
**104** *Sleeping Venus*, *c.* 1510.
Giorgione, 1477/8?–1510.
Oil on canvas, 108 x 175 cm.
Gemaldegalerie, Dresden, Germany.
**105** *Venus of Urbino* (detail), 1538.
Titian, *c.* 1485–1576.
Oil on canvas, 119 x 165 cm.
Galleria degli Uffizi, Florence, Italy.
**106** *Portrait of an Englishman*, *c.* 1540–45.
Titian, *c.* 1485–1576.
Oil on canvas, 111 x 93 cm.
Galleria Palatina, Palazzo Pitti, Florence, Italy.
**107** Villa Barbaro, late 1550s.
Andrea Palladio, 1508–80.
Maser, near Treviso, Italy.
**108** *Trompe l'oeil* (girl in doorway), *c.* 1561.
Paolo Veronese, 1528–88.
Fresco.
Sala a Crociera, Villa Barbaro, Maser, near Treviso, Italy.
**109** *The Crucifixion* (detail), 1565.
Jacopo Tintoretto, 1519–94.
Oil on canvas, 536 x 1224 cm.
Sala dell'Albergo, Scuola Grande di San Rocco, Venice, Italy.
**110** *Paradise*, 1588–92.
Jacopo Tintoretto, 1519–94.
Oil on canvas, 700 x 2200 cm.
Sala del Maggior Consiglio, Doges' Palace, Venice, Italy.
**111** *The Burial of Count Orgaz*, 1586–8.
El Greco (Domenikos Theotokopoulos), *c.* 1541–1614.
Oil on canvas, 460 x 360 cm.
San Tome, Toledo, Spain.
**112** *Pietà*, *c.* 1576.
Titian, *c.* 1485–1576.
Oil on canvas, 351 x 389 cm.
Galleria dell'Accademia, Venice, Italy.

**CHAPTER SIX**
**113** *Mouth of Hell*, *c.* 1560–80s
Various (sculptures attributed to Simone Mosca Moschino, baptized 1553–1610).
Stone.
Villa Orsini, Bomarzo, Italy.
**114** *Virtue, Fortune and Envy* (ceiling), 1548.
Giorgio Vasari, 1562-1625.
Fresco.
Sala del Trionfo della Virtu, Casa Vasari, Arezzo, Italy.
**115** Vestibule, Laurentian Library, San Lorenzo, Florence, Italy. Begun 1524.
Michelangelo Buonarroti, 1475–1564.
**116** Tomb of Giuliano de' Medici, 1524–34.
Michelangelo Buonarroti, 1475–1564.
Marble.
New Sacristy, San Lorenzo, Florence, Italy.
**117** *The Entombment*, *c.* 1527–8.
Jacopo Pontormo, 1494–1556.
Oil on panel, 313 x 192 cm.
Capponi Chapel, Santa Felicita, Florence, Italy.
**118** *The Martyrdom of Four Saints,* *c.* 1522.
Correggio, 1489–1534.
Oil on canvas, 157 x 182 cm.
Galleria Nazionale, Parma, Italy.
**119** *The Assumption of the Virgin*, *c.* 1530.
Correggio, 1489–1534.
Fresco, 1093 x 1155 cm.
Cupola, Cathedral, Parma, Italy.
**120** Ceiling, Room of the Giants, 1530–32.
Giulio Romano, 1499?–1546.
Fresco.
Palazzo Te, Mantua, Italy.
**121** *Diana of Ephesus*, late 16th century.
Sculptor unknown (Giglio della Vellita?).
Stone.
Villa d'Este, Tivoli, Italy.
**122** *Apotheosis of Cosimo I,* 1565.
Giorgio Vasari, 1562–1625.
Oil on panel.
Ceiling, Salone dei Cinquecento, Palazzo Vecchio della Signoria, Florence, Italy.
**123** *Eleonora of Toledo with Her Son Giovanni de' Medici*, *c.* 1546.
Agnolo Bronzino, 1503–72.
Oil on panel, 115 x 96 cm.
Galleria degli Uffizi, Florence, Italy.
**124** *The Rape of the Sabine Woman,* 1582–3.
Giambologna, 1529–1608.
Marble, height *c.* 410 cm.
Loggia della Lanzi, Florence, Italy.
**125** *Perseus with the Head of Medusa*, 1545–53.
Benvenuto Cellini, 1500–71.
Bronze, height 550 cm.
Galleria degli Uffizi, Florence, Italy.
**126** *Salt Cellar of Francis I*, 1540–43.
Benvenuto Cellini, 1500–71.
Gold, enamel and ebony, 26 x 33 cm.
Kunsthistorisches Museum, Vienna, Austria.
**127** Gallery of Francis I, 1534–9.
Rosso Fiorentino, 1494–1540.
Chateau of Fontainebleau, France
**128** Tomb of Henry VII and Elizabeth of York, 1512–18.
Pietro Torrigiano, 1472–1528.
Gilt bronze, white marble, black touchstone.
Westminster Abbey, London, UK.
**129** *The Ambassadors* (Jean de Dinteville and Georges de Selve), 1533.
Hans Holbein the younger, *c.* 1497/8–1543.
Tempera on panel, 207 x 210 cm.
National Gallery, London, UK.
**130** *The Gloomy Day*, 1565.
Pieter Bruegel the elder, *c.* 1525/30–69.
Wood, 118 x 163 cm.
Kunsthistorisches Museum, Vienna, Austria.
**131** *The Blessed Ludovica Albertoni*, 1672–4.
Gianlorenzo Bernini, 1598–1680.
Marble, over life-size.
Altieri chapel, San Francesco a Ripa, Trastevere, Rome, Italy.
**132** *St John the Baptist*, 1438.
Donatello, 1386/7–1466.
Painted and gilded wood, 141 cm.
Santa Maria Gloriosa dei Frari, Venice, Italy.

# BIBLIOGRAPHY


ACKERMAN, J.S., *Palladio*, Harmondsworth, 1966.

ACKERMAN, J.S., *The Villa: Form and Ideology of Country Houses*, Princeton, 1990.

ALBERTI, L.B., *On Painting*, trans. Spencer, J.R., New Haven and London, 1956.

AMES-LEWIS, F. and BEDNAREK, A. (eds), *Mantegna and Fifteenth-century Court Culture*, London, 1993.

AMES-LEWIS, F. (ed.), *New Interpretations of Venetian Renaissance Painting*, London, 1994.

ANDERSON, J., *Giorgione, The Painter of Poetic Brevity*, Paris and New York, 1997.

ARETINO, P., *Lettere sull'arte di Pietro Aretino*, Camesasca, E. (ed.), 3 vols., Milan 1957-60.

ASTON, M., *Panorama of the Renaissance*, London, 1996.

AVERY, C., *Florentine Renaissance Sculpture*, London, 1970.

BALDASS, LUDWIG VON, *Hieronymus Bosch*, New York and London, 1960.

BARON, H., 'Franciscan Poverty and Civic Wealth as Factors in the Rise of Humanistic Thought', *Specula*, Journal of Medieval Studies, vol. 13, no. 1, Jan. 1938.

BARON, H., *The Crisis of the Early Italian Renaissance*, 1955, rev. edn., Princeton, 1966.

BARON, H., 'Burckhardt's "Civilisation of the Renaissance" a Century after Its Publication', *Renaissance News*, vol. 13, pp 207-22, 1960.

BATTISTI, E., *Brunelleschi: The Complete Works*, London, 1981.

BATTISTI, E., *Filippo Brunelleschi*, Milan, 1976, rev. 1983.

BAXANDALL, M., *Giotto and the Orators: Humanist Observers of Painting in Italy and the Discovery of Pictorial Composition, 1350-1450*, Oxford, 1971.

BAXANDALL, M., *Painting and Experience in Fifteenth-century Italy*, Oxford, 1972.

BAXANDALL, M., *The Limewood Sculptors of Renaissance Germany*, New Haven and London, 1980.

BEK, L., *Towards a Paradise on Earth: Modern Space Creation in Architecture, a Creation of Renaissance Humanism*, Odense, 1980.

BELTING, H., *The Image and Its Public in the Middle Ages: Form and Function of Early Paintings of the Passion*, trans. Bartusis, and Meyer, R., New Rochelle, 1990.

BEMBO, PIETRO, *Gli Asolani*, trans. Gottfried, R., Bloomington, 1954.

BENESCH, O., *The Art of the Renaissance in Northern Europe*, Cambridge MA, 1945.

BERENSON, B., *The Study and Criticism of Italian Art*, 3rd series, London, 1902-16.

BLACK, C., GREENGRASS, M., HOWARTH, D., LAWRANCE, J., MACKENNEY, R., RADY, M. and WELCH, E., *Atlas of the Renaissance*, London, 1993.

BLUNT, A., *Artistic Theory in Italy 1450-1600*, Oxford, 1946.

BLUNT, A., *Art and Architecture in France, 1500-1700*, The Pelican History of Art Series, London and Baltimore, 1953.

BOARDMAN, J., GRIFFIN, J. and MURRAY, O., *The Oxford History of the Classical World*, Oxford, 1986.

BOBER, P.P. and RUBINSTEIN, R.O., *Renaissance Artists and Antique Sculpture: A Handbook of Sources*, Oxford, 1986.

BONNET, J., *Lorenzo Lotto*, Paris, 1996.

BONSANTI, G., *Giotto*, Padua, 1988.

BORSI, F., *Leonbattista Alberti: The Complete Works*, Milan, 1973, London, 1989.

BOUCHER, B., *Andrea Palladio – The Architect in His Time*, New York, 1994.

BOUCHER, B., *Italian Baroque Sculpture*, London, 1998.

BOUWSMA, W.J., *A Usable Past – Essays in European Cultural History*, Berkeley, Los Angeles and Oxford, 1990.

BRAUDEL, F., *The Mediterranean and the Mediterranean World in the Age of Philip II*, 2 vols, London, 1972.

BRAUDEL, F., *Le Modèle Italien*, Paris, 1994.

BROWN, J., *The Golden Age of Painting in Spain*, New Haven and London, 1991.

BROWN, J., *The Renaissance*, series ed. Lockyer, R., London and New York, 1988.

BRUCKER, G., *Renaissance Florence* (various edns avail.), Berkeley, Los Angeles and London, 1983.

BUCKTON, D., *Byzantium: Treasures of Byzantine Art and Culture from British Collections*, exhibition catalogue, British Museum, London, 1994.

BUCHANAN, I., 'The Collection of Niclaes Jongelinck: II, The Months by Pieter Bruegel', *Burlington Magazine*, August 1990.

BURKE, P., *The Italian Renaissance, Culture and Society in Italy*, rev. edn., Cambridge, 1987.

BURKE, P., *The European Renaissance: Centres and Peripheries*, Oxford, 1988.

BURKE, P., *The Renaissance*, 2nd edn., Basingstoke, 1997.

BURKHARDT, J., *The Cicerone*, 1855, English trans., London, 1879.

BURKHARDT, J., *The Civilisation of the Renaissance in Italy*, first edn., 1860, trans. Middlemore, S.G.C., London, 1944.

BYRON, R., *The Birth of Western Painting: A History of Colour, Form and Iconography, Illustrated from the Paintings of Mistra and Mount Athos, of Giotto and Duccio and of El Greco*, New York, 1968.

BYRON, R., *The Byzantine Achievement: An Historical Perspective, AD 330-1453*, London, 1987.

BURKHARDT, J., *Renaissance Portraiture*, New Haven and London, 1990.

CAMPBELL, L., *The Fifteenth-century Netherlandish Schools*, National Gallery, London, 1998.

CAMPBELL, L., FOISTER, S. and ROY, A. (eds), 'Early Northern European Painting', *National Gallery Technical Bulletin*, vol. 18, London, 1997.

CASTIGLIONE, B., *The Book of the Courtier*, trans. Bull, G., London, 1967.

CELLINI, B., *The Autobiography of Benvenuto Cellini*, trans. Bull, G., Harmondsworth, 1956.

CHAMBERS, D. S., *The Imperial Age of Venice, 1380-1580*, London, 1970.

CHAMBERS, D. and MARTINEAU, J. (eds), *The Splendours of the Gonzaga*, exhibition catalogue, Victoria and Albert Museum, London, 1981.

CHAMBERS, D. and PULLAN, B. (eds), *Venice – A Documentary History, 1450-1630*, Oxford, 1992.

CHASTEL, A. (ed.), *L'Art de Fontainebleau – Proceedings from the International Colloquium on the Art of Fontainebleau*, Paris, 1975.

CHASTEL, A., *The Sack of Rome – 1527*, Princeton, 1983.

CHASTEL, A., *French Art, The Renaissance 1430-1620*, trans. from French by Dusinberre, D., Paris and New York, 1995.

CHASTEL, A. with KLEIN, R., *The Age of Humanism: Europe 1480-1530*, trans. Delavenay, K.M. and Gwyer, E.M., London, 1963.

CHELES, L., *The Studiolo of Urbino: An Iconographic Investigation*, Pennsylvania, 1986.

CLARK, K., *Leonardo da Vinci – An Account of His Development as an Artist*, Cambridge, 1939, rev. ed., Harmondsworth, 1967.

CLOUGH, C.C., 'Federigo da Montefeltro's Patronage of the Arts, 1468-82', *Journal of the Warburg and Courtauld Institutes*, vol. 36, 1973.

COLE, A., *Art of the Italian Renaissance Courts – Virtue and Magnificence*, London, 1995.

CORMACK, R., *Painting the Soul: Icons, Death Masks and Shrouds*, London, 1997.

CUTTLER, C.D., *Northern Painting, from Pucelle to Bruegel, Fourteenth, Fifteenth and Sixteenth Centuries*, Fort Worth and London, 1991.

DAVIES, N., *Europe – A History*, Oxford, 1996.

DEMUS, O., *Byzantine Art and the West*, London, 1970.

DERBES, A., *Picturing the Passion in Late Medieval Italy*, Cambridge, 1996.
DICKENS, A.G., *The Counter-Reformation*, London, 1968.
DICKENS, A.G., *Reformation and Society in Sixteenth-century Europe*, London, 1966.
DUFFY, E., *Saints and Sinners – A History of the Popes*, New Haven and London, 1997.
DUNKERTON, J., FOISTER, S., GORDON, D. and PENNY, N., *Giotto to Dürer, Early Renaissance Painting in the National Gallery*, New Haven and London, 1993.

EISLER, C., *The Genius of Jacopo Bellini, The Complete Paintings and Drawings*, New York, 1989.
EISENSTEIN, E.L., *The Printing Press as an Agent of Change: Communications and Cultural Transformations in Early-Modern Europe*, 2 vols., Cambridge, 1979.
EKSERDJIAN, D., *Correggio*, New Haven and London, 1997.
ELKINS, J., *The Poetics of Perspective*, Ithaca and London, 1994.
ELLIOTT, J.H., *Europe Divided – 1559–1598*, London, 1968, repr., 1990.
ELTON, G.R., *Reformation Europe – 1517–1559*, Fontana History of Europe Series, London, 1963.
ERASMUS, D., *Collected Works of Erasmus*, trans. and annotated Thompson, C. R., Toronto and London, 1997/8.
ERASMUS, D., *The 'Julius Exclusus' of Erasmus*, trans., Pascal, P., intro., Sowards, J.K., Bloomington, 1968.

FERGUSON, W.K., *The Renaissance in Historical Thought*, Cambridge, Mass., 1948.
FERGUSON, W.K., 'The Interpretation of Italian Humanism: The Contribution of Hans Baron', *Journal of the History of Ideas*, vol. XIX, 1958.
FIELD, J.V., *The Invention of Infinity – Mathematics and Art in the Renaissance*, Oxford, 1997.
FINDLEN, P., *Humanism, Politics and Pornograhpy in Renaissance Italy, The Invention of Pornography*, Hunt, L. (ed.), New York, 1993.
FOISTER, S., *Making and Meaning: Holbein's Ambassadors*, exhibition catalogue, National Gallery, London, 1998.
FORTINI-BROWN, P., *Venice & Antiquity*, New Haven and London, 1996.
FORTINI BROWN, P., *The Renaissance in Venice – A World Apart*, London, 1997.
FORTINI-BROWN, P., *Venetian Narrative Painting in the Age of Carpaccio*, New Haven and London, 1988.
FRANKLIN, D., *Rosso in Italy*, New Haven and London, 1994.
FRASER JENKINS, A.D., 'Cosimo de Medici's Patronage of Architecture and the Theory of Magnificence', *Journal of the Warburg and Courtauld Institutes*, vol. 33, 1970.
FREEDBERG, D., *The Power of Images: Studies in the History and Theory of Response*, Chicago, 1989.
FREEDBERG, S.J., *Painting in Italy 1500–1600*, 3rd edn., New Haven and London, 1993.
FRIEDLANDER, M., *Early Netherlandish Painting: from Van Eyck to Bruegel*, trans. from German, Kay, M., ed. with notes Grossmann, F., London, 1956.

GADOL, J., *Leon Battista Alberti, Universal Man of the Renaissance*, Chicago, 1969.
GIBSON, W., *Bruegel*, London, 1977.
GILOT, F. and LAKE, C., *Life with Picasso*, London, 1990.
GOFFEN, R., *Giovanni Bellini*, New Haven and London, 1989.
GOFFEN, R., *Piety and Patronage in Renaissance Venice: Bellini, Titian and the Franciscans*, New Haven and London, 1989.
GOFFEN, R., *Masaccio's Trinity*, Cambridge, 1998.
GOLDSCHEIDER, L., *Donatello: Complete Phaidon Edition*, London, 1941.
GOLDSCHEIDER, L., *Ghiberti*, London, 1949.
GOLDTHWAITE, R.A., *Wealth and the Demand for Art in Italy 1300–1600*, Baltimore, 1993.
GOMBRICH, E.H., *The Heritage of Apelles*, Oxford, 1976.
GOMBRICH, E.H., *Norm and Form: Studies in the Art of the Renaissance*, London, 1978.
GOMBRICH, E.H., *Symbolic Images*, London, 1972, 2nd edn., 1993.
GOODMAN and MACKAY (eds), *The Impact of Humanism on Western Europe*, London and New York, 1990.
GOULD, C., *Parmigianino*, New York, 1994.
GREENHALGH, M., *Donatello and His Sources*, London, 1982.
GRIFFITHS, G., HANKINS J., THOMPSON, D. and HAMPTON, B., (eds), *The Humanism of Leonardo Bruni*, New York, 1987.

HALL, P., *Cities in Civilization*, London, 1998.
HALE, J., *The Civilisation of Europe in the Renaissance*, London, 1993.
HALE, J.R., *Renaissance Europe: Individual and Society – 1480–1520*, Fontana History of Europe Series, London and New York, 1971.
HARTT, F., 'Art and Freedom in Quattrocento Florence', *Essays in Memory of Karl Lehmann*,. Sandler, L.F. (ed.), pp 1140-31, New York, 1964.
HARTT, F., *History of Italian Renaissance Art – Painting, Sculpture, Architecture*, London, 1970, rev. edn., 1987.
HARTT, F., and FINN, D., *Donatello: Prophet of Modern Vision*, New York, 1973, London, 1974.
HASKELL, F., *History and Its Images: Art and the Interpretation of the Past*, New Haven and London, 1993.
HATFIELD, R., 'The Compagnia de'magi', *Journal of the Warburg and Courtauld Institutes*, vol. 33, pp 107–44, 1970.
HAUSER, A., *Mannerism*, 2 vols, London, 1965.
HAY, D., *The Italian Renaissance in Its Historical Background*, 1961, 2nd edn., Cambridge, 1977.
HAYUM, A., *The Isenheim Altarpiece, God's Medicine and the Painter's Vision*, Princeton, 1989.
HERSEY, G., *High Renaissance Art in St Peter's and the Vatican*, Chicago, 1993.
HERVEY, M., *Holbein's Ambassadors: The Picture and the Men, a Historical Study*, London, 1900.
HEYDENREICH, L.H. and LOTZ, W., *Architecture in Italy 1400-1600*, Harmondsworth, 1969.
HIBBARD, H., *Michelangelo*, 2nd edn., Harmondsworth, 1985.
HILLS, P., *The Light of Early Italian Painting*, New Haven and London, 1987.
HOLBERTON, P., *Palladio's Villas – Life in the Renaissance Countryside*, London, 1990.
HOLMES, G., *The Florentine Enlightenment 1400–50*, Oxford, 1992.
HOLMES, G., *Renaissance*, London, 1996.
HONOR, H. and FLEMING, J., *A World History of Art*, 3rd edn., London, 1991.
HOOD, W., *Fra Angelico at San Marco*, New Haven and London, 1993.
HOPE, C., *Titian*, London, 1980.
HOPE, C., 'The Early History of the Tempio Malatestiano', *Journal of the Warburg and Courtauld Institutes*, vol. 55, 1992.
HOWARD, D., *Jacopo Sansovino, Architecture and Patronage in Renaissance Venice*, New Haven and London, 1975, 2nd edn., 1987.
HOWARD, D., *The Architectural History of Venice*, London, 1980.
HUIZINGA, J., *The Waning of the Middle Ages*, Leiden, 1919, English trans., London 1924.
HUMFREY, P., *The Altarpiece in Renaissance Venice*, New Haven and London, 1993.
HUMFREY, P., *Painting in Renaissance Venice*, New Haven and London, 1995.
HUMFREY, P., *Lorenzo Lotto*, New Haven and London, 1997.

JANELLA, C., *Duccio di Buoninsegna*, Florence, 1991.
JARDINE, L., *Worldly Goods, A New History of the Renaissance*, London, 1996.
JONES, R. and PENNY, N., *Raphael*, New Haven and London, 1983.

KAMEN, P., *Philip of Spain*, New Haven and London, 1997.
KEMP, M., *Leonardo da Vinci – The Marvellous Works of Nature and Man*, London, 1981.
KEMP, M., *The Science of Art: Optical Themes in Western Art from Brunelleschi to Seurat*, New Haven and London, 1990.
KEMP, M., *Behind the Picture: Art and Architecture in the Italian Renaissance*, New Haven and London, 1997.
KEMPERS, B., *Painting, Power and Patronage – The Rise of the Professional Artist in Renaissance Italy*, trans. from Dutch, Jackson, B., 1987, London, 1994.
KENT, F.W., SIMONS, P. and EADE, J.C. (eds), *Patronage, Art and Society in Renaissance Italy*, Oxford, 1987.
KITZINGER, E., 'The Byzantine Contribution to Western Art of the Twelfth and Thirteenth Centuries', *Dumbarton Oaks Papers*, vol. 20, 1966, pp 25-48.
KLEIN R. and ZERNER, H., *Italian Art, 1500–1600, Sources and Documents*, Evanston, 1989.
KOENIGSBERGER, H.G., MOSSE, G.L. and BOWLER, G.Q., *Europe in the Sixteenth Century*, London and New York, 1968, 2nd edn., 1989.
KRISTELLER, P.O., *Andrea Mantegna*, Berlin and Leipzig, 1902.
KRISTELLER, P.O., *Renaissance Thought, The Classic, Scholastic and Humanistic Strains*, London, 1961.

LANE, F.C., *Venice – A Maritime Republic*, Baltimore and London, 1973.
LAZZARO, C., *The Italian Renaissance Garden*, New Haven, 1990.
LEONARDO DA VINCI, *Trattato della Pittura*, Borzelli, A. (ed.), Lanciano, 1914.
LEONARDO DA VINCI, *The Notebooks of Leonardo da Vinci*, Richter, Irma (ed.), 1952, Oxford, 1980.
LEVEY, M., *Florence – A Portrait*, London, 1996.
LEVEY, M., *The Early Renaissance*, Harmondsworth, 1967.
LEVEY, M., 'Dürer and the Renaissance', from *Essays on Dürer*, Dodwell, C.R. (ed.), Manchester, 1973.
LEVEY, M., *The High Renaissance*, Harmondsworth, 1975.
LIEBERMAN, R., 'Real Architecture, Imaginary History: The Arsenale Gate as Venetian Mythology', *Journal of the Warburg and Courtauld Institutes*, vol. 54, 1991.
LIGHTBOWN, R., *Botticelli*, 2 vols, Berkeley, 1978.
LIGHTBOWN, R., *Mantegna, with a Complete Catalogue of the Paintings, Drawings and Prints*, Oxford, 1986.
LOGAN, O., *Culture and Society in Venice 1470–1790, The Renaissance and Its Heritage*, Studies in Cultural History, Hale, J.R. (series ed.), London, 1972.
LUNGHI, E., *The Basilica of St Francis of Assisi: The Frescoes by Giotto, His Precursors and Followers*, London, 1996.

MACHIAVELLI, N., *The Prince*, trans. Skinner, Q. and Price, R., Cambridge, 1988.
MALAND, D., *Europe in the Sixteenth Century*, 2nd edn., Basingstoke, 1982.
MANDER, KAREL VAN, *Het Schilderoek*, Harlem, 1604.
MANETTI, A., *The Life of Brunelleschi*, Saalman, H. (ed.), Pennsylvania, 1970.
MARTINEAU, J. and HOPE, C. (eds), *The Genius of Venice, 1500–1600*, exhibition catalogue, Royal Academy of Arts, London, 1983.
MARTINES, L., *Power and Imagination: City-States in Renaissance Italy*, New York, 1979.
MARVELL, A., *The Garden and Other Poems*, London, 1993.
MAT, L. VON, *St Francis of Assisi, A Pictorial Biography*, text by Hauser, W., trans. from German by Bullough, S., New York, 1956.
MEISS, M., *Painting in Florence and Siena after the Black Death*, Princeton, 1951.
MICHELANGELO, *The Sonnets of Michelangelo*, trans. Jennings, E., London, 1969.
MOHLO, A., 'The Brancacci Chapel: Studies in Its Iconography and History', *Journal of the Warburg and Courtauld Institutes*, vol. 40, 1977.
MOLHO, A. and TEDESCHI, J.A. (eds), *Renaissance Studies in Honour of Hans Baron*, Florence, 1971.
MONTCLOS, JEAN-MARIE PEROUSE DE, *Fontainebleau*, Paris, 1998.
McCARTHY, M., *The Stones of Florence and Venice Observed*, London, 1972.

NAUERT, C.G., *Humanism and the Culture of Renaissance Europe*, Cambridge, 1995.

ONIANS, J., *Bearers of Meaning, The Classical Orders in Antiquity, the Middle Ages and the Renaissance*, Princeton and Cambridge, 1988.

PANOFSKY, E., *Early Netherlandish Painting, Its Origins and Character*, 2 vols, Cambridge MA, 1953.
PANOFSKY, E., *The Life and Art of Albrecht Dürer*, Princeton, 1955.
PANOFSKY, E., *Renaissance and Renascences in Western Art*, New York, 1960.
PARKER, G., *Europe in Crisis – 1598–1648*, Fontana History of Europe Series, London, 1979, 1990.
PARTRIDGE, L., *The Renaissance in Rome*, London, 1996.
PATER, W., *The Renaissance*, New York, 1873, London, 1961.
PERNIS, M.G. and SCHNEIDER ADAMS, L., *Federigo da Montefeltro and Sigismondo Malatesta: The Eagle and the Elephant*, New York, 1996.
PETRARCH, F., *Selections from the Canzoniere and Other Works*, trans. with intro. and notes by Musa, M., Oxford, 1985.
POPE-HENNESSY, J., *Italian Renaissance Sculpture*, London, 1958, 3rd revision, New York, 1985.
POPE-HENNESSY, J., *Catalogue of Italian Sculpture in the Victoria and Albert Museum*, London, 1968.
POPE-HENNESSY, J., *Italian High Renaissance and Baroque Sculpture*, 3rd edn., Oxford, 1986.
POPE-HENNESSY, J., *Donatello, Sculptor*, New York, 1993.
POPE-HENNESSY, J., RAGIONERI, G. and PERUGI, L., *Donatello*, Florence, 1985.
PORTER, R. and TEICH, M. (eds), *The Renaissance in National Context*, Cambridge, 1992.

REARICK, W.R., *The Art of Veronese, 1528–1588*, Washington, 1988.
ROSAND, D. (ed.), *Titian, His World and His Legacy*, New York, 1982.
ROSAND, D., *Painting in Sixteenth-century Venice: Titian, Veronese, Tintoretto*, rev. edn., Cambridge, 1997.
RUBIN, P., *Giorgio Vasari – Art and History*, New Haven and London, 1995.
RUNCIMAN, S., *Byzantine Style and Civilization*, Harmondsworth, 1975.
RUSKIN, J., *The Stones of Venice*, 1851-3, reissued Links, J.G. (ed.), London, 1960.

SAALMAN, H., *Filippo Brunelleschi: The Buildings*, London, 1993.
SANNAZARO, J., *Arcadia and Piscatorial Eclogues*, trans. with intro. by Nash, R., Detroit, 1966.
SEIGEL, J.E., 'Civic Humanism or Ciceronian Rhetoric?', *Past and Present*, no. 34, July 1966.
SENNETT, R., *Flesh and Stone – The Body and the City in Western Civilization*, London, 1994.
SETTIS, S., *La Tempesta interpretata*, Turin, 1978; English trans. as *Giorgione's Tempest: Interpreting the Hidden Subject*, trans. Bianchini, E., Chicago, 1990.
SHAW, C., *Julius II, The Warrior Pope*, Oxford, 1993.
SHEARMAN, J., *Mannerism*, Harmondsworth, 1967.
SHEARMAN, J., *Raphael's Cartoons in the Collection of Her Majesty the Queen and the Tapestries for the Sistine Chapel*, London, 1972.

SHEARMAN, J., *Only Connect – Art and the Spectator in the Italian Renaissance*, Princeton, 1994.
SHELTON, A. (ed.), *Fetishism: Visualising Power and Desire*, London, 1995.
SKINNER, Q., *Foundations of Modern Political Thought*, 2 vols, Cambridge, 1978.
SMITH, J.C., *Nuremberg, A Renaissance City, 1500–1618*, Austin, 1983.
SPIKE, J.T., *Masaccio*, New York, 1995.
STEINBERG, L., 'Pontormo's Capponi Chapel', *Art Bulletin*, vol. LVI, 1974.
STRIEDER, P., *Dürer – Paintings, Prints, Drawings*, trans. Gordon, N.M. and Strauss, W.L., London, 1982.
STUBBLEBINE, J., 'Byzantine Influence in Thirteenth-century Italian Panel Painting', *Dumbarton Oaks Papers*, vol. 20, 1966, pp 85-102.
SULLIVAN, M., *Bruegel's Peasants: Art and Audience in the Northern Renaissance*, Cambridge, 1994.

TAYLOR, C., *Sources of the Self: The Origins of Modern Identity*, Oxford, 1986.
TOMLINSON, J., *Painting in Spain, El Greco to Goya, 1561–1828*, London, 1997.
TURNER, J. (ed.) *The Dictionary of Art*, 34 vols, London, 1996.
TURNER, R., *The Renaissance in Florence – The Birth of a New Art*, London, 1997.

VASARI, G., *The Lives of the Artists*, trans. Hinds, A.B. (ed.) with intro, Gaunt, W., London, 1963, 1970; and *Lives of the Artists*, Ekserdjian, D. (ed.), London, 1997.
VERDON, T. and HENDERSON, J. (eds), *Christianity and the Renaissance: Image and Religious Imagination in the Quattrocento*, New York, 1990.
VERDON, T., *St Francis of Assisi, Christmas at Greccio and the Birth of Renaissance Art*, (unpublished).
VORAGINE, JACOBUS DE *The Golden Legend, Reading on the Saints*, trans. Ryan Granger, W., 2 vols, Princeton, 1993.

WACKERNAGEL, M., *The World of the Florentine Renaissance Artist*, Leipzig, English trans., Princeton, 1981.
WARNKE, M., *The Court Artist*, Cambridge, 1993.
WELCH, E., *Art and Authority in Renaissance Milan*, New Haven and London, 1995.
WELCH, E., *Art and Society in Italy 1350–1500*, Oxford, 1997.
WETHEY, H., *The Paintings of Titian*, 3 vols, London, 1969-75.
WHITE, J., *The Birth and Rebirth of Pictorial Space*, 1957, 3rd edn., London, 1987.
WHITE, J., *Art and Architecture in Italy, 1250–1400*, 1966, 2nd. edn. 1987, 3rd edn., New Haven and London, 1993.
WIGHTMAN, W.P.D., *Science in a Renaissance Society*, London, 1972.
WIND, E., *Pagan Mysteries in the Renaissance*, London, 1958.
WITTKOWER, R., *Architectural Principles in the Age of Humanism*, 1949, 3rd edn., London, 1962.
WOLFFLIN, J., *The Art of Albrecht Dürer*, Munich 1905; ed. and annotated, Gerstenberg, K., London, 1971.

# PICTURE CREDITS

BBC Books would like to thank the following for providing photographs and for permission to reproduce copyright material. While every effort has been made to trace and acknowledge all copyright holders, we would like to apologize should there have been any errors or omissions. For Museum and other acknowledgements please refer to the Notes On Works page 326.

AKG London: pages 192 (Erich Lessing), 203, 207, 210, 218, 254, 302 (Erich Lessing) and 315 (Erich Lessing); Alinari: pages 68, 70, 101, 143, 299, 300 and 320; Ancient Art and Architecture Collection Ltd: pages 39, 226 and 240; The Bridgeman Art Library: pages 10, 55, 58, 106–7, 110, 114, 123, 130, 174, 195 198–9, 206, 219, 251, 266, 267, 270, 278, 283 and 307; ET Archive: pages 79, 186 AND 196; The National Gallery Picture Library, London: pages 46, 50, 118, 222, 230, 239 AND 310; RMN/Louvre, Paris: page 245; The Royal Collection © 1999 Her Majesty Queen Elizabeth II: pages 142 Rodney Todd-White and 161; SCALA: pages 3, 6–7, 14, 15, 18, 19, 22, 23, 26, 27, 29, 31, 34, 38, 42, 43, 49, 51, 66, 71 (both), 74, 82, 83, 87, 91, 94–5, 98 (both), 100, 103, 115, 119, 122, 127, 131, 135, 137, 139, 146, 147, 150, 151, 154, 157, 163, 166, 167, 168, 170, 175, 180, 182, 187, 191, 211, 214, 215, 227, 233, 234, 235, 238, 243, 246, 250, 255, 256, 258, 259, 262–3, 268, 275, 280, 286, 287, 290, 291, 294, 295, 303 and 323.

# INDEX

Page numbers in *italic* refer to the illustrations